ALSO BY JANE SHERRON DE HART

The Federal Theatre, 1935–1939: Plays, Relief, and Politics

Sex, Gender, and the Politics of the E.R.A.: A State and the Nation
(co-authored with Donald G. Mathews)

Women's America: Refocusing the Past
(founding editor with Linda K. Kerber)

RUTH BADER GINSBURG

RUTH BADER GINSBURG

A Life

Jane Sherron De Hart

ALFRED A. KNOPF New York 2018

THIS IS A BORZOI BOOK
PUBLISHED BY ALFRED A. KNOPF

Copyright © 2018 by Jane Sherron De Hart

All rights reserved. Published in the United States by Alfred A. Knopf, a division of Penguin Random House LLC, New York, and distributed in Canada by Random House of Canada, a division of Penguin Random House Canada Limited, Toronto.

www.aaknopf.com

Knopf, Borzoi Books, and the colophon are registered trademarks of Penguin Random House LLC.

Pages 721–723 constitute an extension of the copyright page.

Library of Congress Cataloging-in-Publication Data
Names: De Hart, Jane Sherron.
Title: Ruth Bader Ginsburg : a life / Jane Sherron De Hart.
Description: New York : Knopf, 2018. | Includes bibliographical references and index.
Identifiers: LCCN 2018004415 (print) | LCCN 2018005358 (ebook) |
ISBN 9781400040483 (hardcover) | ISBN 9780525521594 (ebook)
Subjects: LCSH: Ginsburg, Ruth Bader. | Women judges—United States—
    Biography. | Judges—United States—Biography. | United States. Supreme
    Court—Officials and employees. | BISAC: BIOGRAPHY & AUTOBIOGRAPHY /
    Lawyers & Judges. | LAW / Constitutional. | SOCIAL SCIENCE / Women's Studies.
Classification: LCC KF8745.G56 (ebook) | LCC KF8745.G56 D44 2018 (print) |
    DDC 347.73/2634 [B]—dc23
LC record available at https://lccn.loc.gov/2018004415

Front-of-jacket illustration by Katherine Ross;
spine image by Charles Dharapak / AP;
back-of-jacket image by Bettmann / Getty Images

Jacket design by Stephanie Ross

Manufactured in the United States of America
First Edition

For Jerry
for unwavering love and support

Contents

Preface

An American Icon

The year was 1993. The president of the United States strode toward the lectern in the White House Rose Garden, accompanied by a diminutive sixty-year-old woman in a cobalt-blue suit and dark sunglasses. Before a bipartisan sprinkling of the Senate Judiciary Committee, family members, friends, and the national press, Bill Clinton presented his replacement for the retiring justice Byron White—Judge Ruth Bader Ginsburg.

In the months and years ahead, he predicted, the nation would come to know much more about the woman at his side. "People will find, as I have," he pledged, that "this nominee is a person of immense character. Quite simply, what's in her record speaks volumes about what is in her heart." She has stood "for the individual, the person less well off, the outsider in society, and has given them greater hope by telling them that they have a place in our legal system." Indeed, Clinton continued, "many admirers of her work say she is to the women's movement what former Supreme Court Justice Thurgood Marshall was to the movement for African Americans."

Following the president to the lectern, the nominee responded graciously. Thanking him—and especially New York's senator Daniel Patrick Moynihan, who first brought her to Clinton's attention—she followed the introduction of her family with a statement that was at once personal and political. "The announcement the President made is significant, I believe, because it contributes to the end of the days when women, at least half the talent pool in our society, appear in high places only as one-at-a-time performers." Noting that Justice Sandra Day O'Connor was sitting on the Supreme Court and nearly twenty-five women served on the U.S. Court of Appeals, two as chief judges, she predicted that more would follow.

She then recalled her daughter's 1973 high school yearbook, where her firstborn, Jane, had listed under "ambition" her hope to see her mother nominated to the Supreme Court. The next line read, "'If necessary, Jane will appoint her.'" "Jane is so pleased, Mr. President, that you did it instead, and her brother, James, is, too."

Then Ginsburg turned to the many to whom she felt indebted: a revived women's movement and the civil rights movement of the 1960s, from which feminists in the United States had drawn inspiration, as well as colleagues and family. And with a deft touch, she mentioned that this was not the first time that a member of her family had stood next to Hillary Rodham Clinton, whom she herself had met just that day. "There is another I love dearly with whom the First Lady is already an old friend." Holding up a photograph of Mrs. Clinton surrounded by nursery school children singing "The Toothbrush Song," she pointed to "my wonderful granddaughter, Clara." She also thanked her husband, Marty, "my best friend and biggest booster," her mother-in-law, Evelyn, "the most supportive parent a person could have," and children with "tastes to appreciate that Daddy cooks ever so much better than Mommy and so phased me out of the kitchen at a relatively early age." She concluded with a tribute to her mother, Celia Amster Bader, "the bravest and strongest person I have ever known. . . . I pray that I may be all that she would have been had she lived in an age when women could aspire and achieve, and daughters are as much cherished as sons." Those final words left the president fighting back tears.

· · ·

AS I WATCHED the ceremony on the evening news, it never occurred to me that five years later I might actually meet the justice, much less write about her. My work as a historian had taken a new turn when I began exploring the "dual constitutional strategy" that had been devised by feminist lawyers in the late 1960s to secure gender equality in the law. One prong of that strategy sought ratification of an equal rights amendment (ERA) to the Constitution prohibiting gender-based discrimination. The other called for litigation efforts to persuade the Supreme Court to strike down laws that discriminated on the basis of gender.

Ginsburg, then a law professor at Rutgers and later at Columbia University, spearheaded the latter effort in the 1970s under the auspices of the Women's Rights Project of the American Civil Liberties Union (ACLU).

Having lately completed a fine-grained analysis of efforts in a key southern state that twice came two votes short of ratifying the amendment, I had turned to another project. Midway into that exercise, I began research for a chapter in which I hoped to make use of Ginsburg's women's rights litigation as an example of judicial policy making. Heading to the Seeley Mudd Library at Princeton University, where the archives for the ACLU are deposited, I wanted to understand how, in less than a decade, a law professor known primarily for her expertise in civil procedure and comparative law, someone who prior to 1973 had never argued a case before the Supreme Court, became the nation's foremost litigator for gender equality. Being in the right place at the right time—Ginsburg's characteristically modest explanation—tells part of the story. But it does not explain how she acquired the capacious vision of equality that she brought to her litigation, her strategic sensibility, or her passion for justice.

I found just one case file containing correspondence between the ACLU's legal director Melvin Wulf and "Kiki" Ginsburg, who had volunteered to write the brief for a test case known as *Reed v. Reed*. Her brief won the case, convincing the justices for the first time in the nation's history that gender-based discrimination violated the equal protection clause of the Fourteenth Amendment. Eager to see files for her cases following *Reed*, I asked for the records of the Women's Rights Project. They were not at the Seeley Mudd Library, I was told; they must still be in New York at the ACLU's national office. Regrettably, they were not. Indeed, nobody seemed to know where they were. When I finally appealed to Justice Ginsburg to help track down the records, she discovered that they had been lost in a move of the ACLU's headquarters. Offering to make her own files available, she had the material transported to the Manuscript Division of the Library of Congress the day before I arrived in Washington in October 1998.

Hours of poring over letters, memos, drafts of briefs, and outlines for oral arguments left me enthralled. The issues Ginsburg addressed resonated personally and intellectually. The strategic sense, craft, and precision that went into her brief writing dazzled. And the relationship that emerged with one of her clients and his small son demonstrated a level of caring that was unmistakable. On my third day, during my lunch break, I phoned Maeva Marcus, then the Supreme Court historian, to thank her for her role in transmitting my initial inquiry about the missing papers to Justice Ginsburg. She immediately invited me to a meeting of the Supreme Court Historical Society that was scheduled for that same evening. The distinguished historian John Hope Franklin would be speaking, and if the Ginsburgs attended, I could express my appreciation to the justice in person. Spotting the couple at the front of the auditorium as the lecture ended, I offered a quick "thank you" before backing off so her conversation with Justice Souter could continue.

During the reception that followed, we had two further brief encounters, each initiated by the justice. As we talked about one particular case, she immediately volunteered that she had remained in close touch with her former client Stephen Wiesenfeld, some years later officiating at his son Jason's wedding ceremony. Having been immersed that morning in the files for a case known as *Craig v. Boren,* I mentioned how much I enjoyed the correspondence between "Dearest Amica" and "Ranger Fred," a.k.a. Fred Gilbert. (Ginsburg, who wrote the amicus brief, had showered Gilbert with legal advice punctuated by pithy ripostes to his jocular antifeminist jabs.) She mentioned that she and "Ranger Fred" had enjoyed a beer together the last time Gilbert had been in Washington. Later, as I was about to leave, she added, "If you have any questions about the cases, just ask."

I was already engaged in a half-completed project for the University of Chicago Press, so my editor John Tryneski suggested that I first complete an account of Ginsburg's litigation and then return to the Chicago manuscript. Neither of us could have envisioned at the time how vastly the Ginsburg project would expand—nor that one of California's all-too-frequent wildfires would consume my home, all my research, and both manuscripts in 2008. (Fortunately, a former research assistant had retained a prior draft of some of the Ginsburg chapters.)

. . .

BETWEEN 2000 AND 2006, I had six interviews with the justice as well as occasional correspondence. To say that she helped clarify aspects of litigation for a nonlawyer is an understatement. As our interviews pro-

ceeded, I yearned to understand the formative experiences and relationships that had shaped her sense of identity and formidable intellect—and,
not least, her legendary self-discipline, rigor, and tenacity. Who inspired
a young Cornell coed in her sophomore year to envision a life in the law
at a time when women in the legal profession were marginalized and the
feminine mystique reigned? To what experiences could I attribute the
vision of gender equality that she brought to her litigation twenty years
later? It must surely have involved a more expansive vision than scholars
in the 1980s and 1990s had been prepared to acknowledge.

In making an appointment for one of our interviews, I suggested
we focus on her early years in Flatbush. The justice made it quite clear
that she had no appetite for revisiting the adversity that shadowed her
Brooklyn origins. Yet she tolerated questions that had not been submitted in advance, responding in her characteristically deliberative fashion,
punctuated by long pauses as she formulated responses. We had no written agreement in advance about what could or could not be included
in those interviews or what I might publish. Perhaps none was needed
because we agreed that she would read for factual accuracy what have
now become the introductory chapters (1–6) that precede her ACLU
years (chapters 7–13). Despite a certain wariness in our relationship, we
proceeded much more comfortably over time as the focus moved on to
her college and law school years and the challenges of combining career
and family. I also interviewed members of the justice's immediate family.
On one occasion when the memories of mother and daughter conflicted,
the two talked. It was agreed that Jane's version of her dating experience
would prevail.

I understood at the time that I had no letters or a diary from Ginsburg's early life, which gave her unusual power over an account by a
biographer. I was also aware that we all construct our past—that memory is filtered and interpreted over time. I tried to compensate in the
first chapters by going back to the same question again if she answered
obliquely or—on my first try—not at all. I took into account silences
and tried to read between the lines, noting the remarkable consistency
of her recollections in interviews done by others. I tried to fill in gaps
with recollections where I could of those who knew her at the time. Yet
the legal analyst Jeffrey Rosen put it best when he described the justice
as "always everywhere and just out of reach."

. . .

IT WAS ONLY AFTER completing my draft of the first thirteen chapters that I came to appreciate that I still had an unfinished narrative. By the end of the 1970s, Ginsburg's thinking on constitutional change, reproductive rights, gender justice, and affirmative action had evolved. Yet conservative pushback against equality stalled further advances on the Court. Her transition from advocate to judge was not accomplished easily, despite widespread support for her in the feminist and liberal legal community. At the time, only one woman sat on the federal bench, despite President Jimmy Carter's desire to increase the number of women and minorities following passage of the Omnibus Judgeship Act in 1978. Ginsburg's nominations, first to the prestigious U.S. Court of Appeals for the District of Columbia Circuit in 1980 and then to the Supreme Court in 1993, were replete with high drama.

Extending my narrative by focusing on key equal protection cases during Ginsburg's tenure as justice does not capture the full range of her judicial contributions. But my discussion does allow readers to see where her fingerprints on legal doctrine are clearest. The book's longer chronological span also provides a view of the full arc of Ginsburg's life and career, breaking new ground in exploring the origins and development of her distinctive approach to the law. She has been at the center of America's epochal and ongoing struggle for more inclusive citizenship—a struggle that has animated a range of "rights" movements from civil rights and women's rights to gay rights and immigrants' rights. Ginsburg's story, deeply rooted in the exodus of Jews from Eastern Europe and Russia to the United States, is also part and parcel of the social and political history of America from the depression-ridden 1930s to the tumultuous present.

. . .

SEVERAL THEMES ARE illuminated through the narrative of Ginsburg's life. First is the sheer difficulty of the struggle for equality under the law. Legal challenges that wind up in the Supreme Court may be won. But much may also be lost along the way as opponents nibble away at what was once presumed to be settled law. A lawyer may craft a brilliant brief for her plaintiff, as Ginsburg did in 1972. That brief could have

helped the justices understand the harm to women created when stereotypical assumptions about women's "natural" role as mothers are incorporated into law. But the case was declared moot. The Court's action
with respect to one group can have a negative impact on legal strategy
used for another. Justice Powell's ruling on affirmative action in *University of California Board of Regents v. Bakke* (1978) contained language that
doomed implementation of a strategy that Ginsburg had proposed that
would have offered "a more capacious vision of discrimination's meanings, effects, and remediation," embracing both gender and race.

A second theme is the dynamic interaction between progressive
social movements and the conservative countermovements they trigger, all amply evident in the many compromises forged by the justices
over the years. Social movements can mobilize and change public opinion, influencing members of the Court and thus shaping constitutional
interpretation, as Ginsburg's feminist advocacy attested. But progressive
movements also tend to generate countermovements that shape public
opinion in their own way. For example, as popular views on affirmative
action shifted in the 1990s and conservative public-interest law firms
sought out potential clients for test cases, the University of Michigan's
admissions policies came under attack for discriminating against white
applicants. Ginsburg's powerful dissent in *Gratz v. Bollinger* (2003) documents why color-blind justice—championed by judicial conservatives
since 1980—continues to constitute injustice for many African Americans and Hispanics.

A third theme is found in the dynamics of the Supreme Court itself,
with its changing personalities and competing approaches to the law.
Traditionally, members of the modern Court have tended to focus on
constitutional text, original meaning, and the historical intentions of
those who framed and ratified the U.S. Constitution while also taking into account case law, custom, legislative intent, and common
sense. Many justices have also understood the Constitution to be a *living* document, encompassing fixed principles—freedom of speech and
of the press, the right to a speedy and efficient trial, the right to vote,
and the right to equal protection of the law and due process, among
others. These principles have been applied to situations that changed
dramatically over time. But attention to precedents (stare decisis) was
expected to ensure stability. While justices, many of them Republican,

have varied in their views, only recently has the Court become so polarized that five Republican-appointed justices line up repeatedly against their four Democratic-appointed counterparts. Nor did originalism hold sway—the view that the only acceptable method of interpreting the U.S. Constitution is to apply "the text and original meaning of various constitutional provisions" as understood by its authors in 1787.

A central organizing principle for the Reagan Justice Department's assault on what it regarded as a liberal federal judiciary and, more especially, the Brennan Court, originalism as an approach to constitutional interpretation has more recently been aggressively embraced, most notably by Justices Antonin Scalia, Clarence Thomas, and Neil M. Gorsuch. More important, originalism in theory, which aimed at neutral interpretations of the Constitution, differs from the practice of originalism by justices who tend to ignore those portions of the Constitution, especially the Reconstruction Amendments, that conflict with contemporary conservative values. Thus, the Warren Court, from which Ginsburg drew inspiration as a law student, was not the Burger Court, before which she argued. Nor was the Rehnquist Court, to which she was appointed, the Roberts Court, on which she now serves.

A fourth theme is the growing conservatism of the high court over the past five decades and the changing meanings attached to familiar labels. That Ginsburg, a centrist judge on the U.S. Court of Appeals for the D.C. Circuit from 1980 to 1993, is today ranked, along with Justice Sonia Sotomayor, as the most liberal member of the Court is telling. At a fundamental level, Ginsburg's distinctive jurisprudence has changed little. The Court, however, has changed, which also explains why some of her most notable opinions in recent years have taken the form of dissents.

. . .

ON A MORE PERSONAL LEVEL, a comprehensive biography of one of the most important figures in modern law in the United States permits exploring the experiences and relationships that inspired her passion for justice, her legendary advocacy for gender equality, and her distinctive jurisprudence. Not least, it demonstrates the formidable intellect, iron will, and emotional stamina that prompted Justice Souter to deem his former colleague a "tiger justice."

Essential to her desire to make We, the People more united and our union more perfect is her Jewish background. *Tikkun olam,* the Hebrew injunction to "repair the world," had profound meaning for a thoughtful young Jewish girl who grew up during the Holocaust and World War II. So, too, did the phrase above the entry to the first chambers that she occupied as justice—*Tzedek tzedek tirdof* (Justice, justice you shall pursue). Her mother, Celia, inspired her daughter's proto-feminism with stories of Jewish women of valor and her own admiration of Eleanor Roosevelt. Insisting that Ruth become independent, she provided sage advice and a model of great strength as she herself coped with terminal cancer. Ginsburg would attach her mother's circle pin to every suit lapel she wore when undertaking something in which she felt Celia would have taken great pride.

Faculty at Cornell University, her undergraduate college, also provided formative influences. Vladimir Nabokov sensitized Bader to the importance of words and their order in conveying an idea or image. Robert E. Cushman introduced her to constitutional law and the utmost importance of civil liberties, especially when national security fears predominate and Congress strays. He also honed her writing style, teaching her to convey substance accurately and economically. Milton Konvitz, who personified the legal scholar as activist, emphasized civil liberties and civil rights in his "American Ideals" course. Reinforcing the eighteen-year-old's dawning awareness that "a lawyer could do something that was personally satisfying and at the same time work to preserve the values that have made this country great," Konvitz convinced her that she could as well.

Her greatest enabler, however, would prove to be her college beau and beloved husband, Martin Ginsburg, even though cancer shadowed their lives. The dreaded disease took Celia two days before her daughter's high school graduation. It almost took Marty's life when they were students at Harvard Law School. In 1991, Ginsburg herself was diagnosed with rectal and colon cancer, requiring prolonged treatment and recovery. Then Marty's cancer reemerged in 2008. The following year, the justice underwent surgery for removal of a small pancreatic cancer. In June 2010, just after their fifty-sixth wedding anniversary, Marty succumbed to metastatic cancer. Though grief stricken, Ginsburg returned to the Court for the final day of the term, displaying steely self-discipline. Throughout those difficult years from 1991 to 2010, she never missed an oral argument, writing some of the most powerful dissents of her career.

Our yearly interviews ceased for a time after 2006, resuming yearly again in 2015. I deeply value the interactions that those nine meetings and our correspondence afforded. They inspired me and enriched the story I tell here about an individual who defines the word "indomitable." Throughout the years, her voice has retained—even sharpened—its characteristic moral clarity and passion, leaving its mark not only on law but on American society. Her commitment remains ongoing. And we as a people are the better for it.

PART I

Becoming Ruth

CHAPTER I

Celia's Daughter

June 27, 1950, should have been a day of triumph for an ambitious young girl just turned seventeen—the culmination of four years of outstanding academic achievement. It was graduation day at Brooklyn's James Madison High School. Ruth Bader had been chosen as just one of four students to speak for her eight hundred classmates. Instead, it was a day of wrenching grief.

Two days before, Ruth's mother, Celia, had succumbed to cancer after a four-year struggle. Ruth knew her mother had been waging a losing battle. Watching the physical deterioration of the parent who represented nurture and security, along with her father's silent grief, had been anguishing for the sensitive adolescent. Yet with Celia's encouragement, she won prestigious college scholarships, played in the school orchestra, and cheered on the football team as a baton twirler—never once revealing to her schoolmates the illness that shadowed the Bader household in Flatbush. By the end of summer, the ground floor of the modest gray stucco house at 1584 East Ninth Street stood vacant, a symbol of loss and abandonment following her mother's death and her father's emotional and economic collapse.

. . .

CELIA BADER GAVE BIRTH to her second daughter, Joan Ruth, on March 15, 1933, at Beth Moses Hospital in the borough of Brooklyn in New York City. (Ruth's first name was dropped in kindergarten when there proved to be too many other children who answered to Joan.) The Baders brought the infant back to their apartment in Belle Harbor, a town near the ocean in the borough of Queens, just as they had her older sister, Marilyn. The new baby, energetic from the start, kicked so much that Marilyn promptly dubbed her "Kiki." The name stuck.

The boroughs, like the rest of the country in 1933, faced an unprecedented economic depression. Factories lay idle. Construction had come to a standstill. The banking system had crumbled, wiping out the hard-earned savings of millions. One wage earner in four was laid off, and according to the U.S. Children's Bureau one out of five children was not getting enough to eat. As tax revenues dried up, teachers went unpaid. In other parts of the country, schools simply closed their doors. In the Red Hook section of Brooklyn, jobless men put up makeshift shacks of junked Fords and old barrels at the city dump dubbed "Hoovervilles" in derisive reference to President Herbert Hoover's economic policies.

Nathan Bader, Ruth's father, was no stranger to hard times. He had begun his own struggle to earn a living shortly after his arrival in New York as a shy thirteen-year-old Russian Jew from a town near Odessa. Denied admission to schools in the Old World because of anti-Semitism, he had attended only Hebrew school. His mother tongue was Yiddish until he learned English at night school in his new homeland. Nathan worked in his father's business, Samuel Bader and Sons, which specialized in inexpensive furs. By the 1920s, he felt financially secure enough to marry Celia Amster.

Celia, who arrived in New York City while still in her mother's womb, had been conceived in a little town near what is now Cracow, Poland. Growing up in a Yiddish-speaking household in Manhattan's Lower East Side, the primal homeland for immigrant Jews, she developed a passion for reading. Indeed, she so often walked down the bustling, crowded streets with her head buried in a book that on one occasion she tripped and broke her nose. Her father, recognizing that she was the most intelligent of his three daughters, had enlisted her help with his bills, which she wrote out in a mixture of English and Yiddish: for example, "one cabinet, gefixed" (repaired).

Though eager to continue her education, Celia had to settle for a commercial emphasis in her course work at Julia Richman High School, a massive brick building on East Sixty-Seventh Street. At least the training would spare her the fate of her older sister, Sadie, who worked in a sweatshop until marriage. Upon graduating at the age of fifteen, Celia found a job as a bookkeeper and secretary for a fur maker in the bustling, densely packed garment district, a roughly rectangular area of Manhattan ringed by West Thirty-Fifth and Forty-Second Streets and Seventh and Ninth Avenues, where a largely Eastern European workforce fueled the trade. The position allowed her to develop a familiarity with the industry, capitalizing on her innate business instincts and her ability to shrewdly assess people.

The personable and highly intelligent young woman had just the qualities that the shy, sentimental Nathan instinctively sought in a wife. Celia, according to her daughter, would always be the stronger partner in their new household, advising her husband on his business as well as other matters. After marriage, the couple joined the Belle Harbor synagogue. In 1927, two years before the stock market crash, Celia gave birth to their first child, Marilyn Elsa.

· · ·

THE DOWNWARD ECONOMIC SPIRAL after Black Thursday in October 1929 prompted many young couples like the Baders to delay having more children. But in the fall of 1932, a new baby was on the way. Three years later, economic recovery remained elusive. Despite the Roosevelt administration's many initiatives, the country remained mired in poverty and despair. The Baders were spared the worst hardships; however, in 1934, they faced a different kind of loss. Six-year-old Marilyn was fatally stricken with spinal meningitis. Though Kiki was too young to remember her sister, she later recalled how deeply her parents mourned Marilyn's death. Every month, in the cold of winter or the heat of summer, they trudged to the cemetery. On the anniversary of Marilyn's death, they went to the synagogue to recite the Kaddish, the traditional Jewish prayer of mourning. Marilyn's picture continued to hang over the headboard of the Baders' bed, making her a looming presence throughout Kiki's childhood. There is no way to measure the impact of parental grief on their surviving daughter or to know whether it contributed to her preternatural seriousness. Ruth herself, however, later remarked that she grew up with the very "smell of death," alluding to the cloud her sister's passing cast over the Bader household.

Hoping to ease the pain with new surroundings, Nathan and Celia moved to Brooklyn, though the neighborhood was less desirable than the one left behind in Belle Harbor. They soon discovered that sustaining a separate apartment even in Flatbush was economically impossible. Because Nathan's brother Benjamin had married Celia's younger sister, Bernice (Buddy), the Bader brothers and their wives decided to share the downstairs of a two-family house in Flatbush until they could afford to live in separate houses on East Ninth Street.

Though the move to Flatbush was primarily initiated as a response to grief, it eventually turned out to be fortuitous. Flatbush was one of Brooklyn's six original colonial towns. Over the years, it had been transformed into a semi-urban area with a Jewish population that by 1930 was rapidly approaching the million mark, the largest concentration of urban Jews in the world. Yet the Jewish community was anything but homogeneous. Groups differed in culture, wealth, and religious affiliation as well as in origin—Western European, Eastern European, and Middle Eastern. Brooklyn's Syrian Sephardic Jews—a minority within a minority—maintained their traditional ways and food preferences as well as their Arabic language. In contrast, the many Eastern European Ashkenazi Jews tried hard to assimilate. After achieving some modest economic success, most moved out from the Lower East Side and from more crowded Brooklyn neighborhoods like Williamsburg and Brownsville to escape the congestion and shabbiness along with the weight of old-world strictures. If not quite the suburbs, the move brought more grass and open space.

As a sign of their newfound freedom, Jews of Nathan and Celia's generation often strayed from Orthodox Judaism with all its rules and rituals. Many chose to forgo Sabbath services, leaving Brooklyn's houses of worship half-empty on Saturday mornings. Sloughing off vestiges of their cultural and ethnic distinctiveness, they took pride in their "Americanness"—their ability to speak English, to wear American clothes, to have an education beyond the Talmud, and to escape the historical cycle that had locked even the most ambitious sons into the ghetto.

Yet at the same time, even those who were secular clung to cherished parts of their tradition—lighting candles for Friday dinner, keeping kosher kitchens while their children were young or eating only kosher meat and poultry, and observing the more important religious holidays, notably the high holy days from Rosh Hashanah through Yom Kippur. Those needing a synagogue for the holy days had plenty of choices;

more than half of all the synagogues in New York City had a Brooklyn address. Some in the community relished the sense of belonging that came from hearing a Yiddish radio station playing popular dramas such as *Bei tate-mames tish* (Round the family table) or musical programs like *Yiddish Melodies in Swing*—though not Celia, who saw Yiddish as the language of the Old World. Instead, the Bader family listened to *The Goldbergs,* a weekly comedy-drama created by the talented writer and actress Gertrude Berg. Playing the warmhearted Bronx matriarch Molly Goldberg, Berg guided her radio family and neighbors through the challenges of assimilating and simultaneously maintaining their roots as Jews while coping with the travails of the Great Depression and World War II. Mrs. Goldberg was an "amalgam of Jewish aunts, [mothers], and grandmothers," Kiki later recalled. However, she hastened to point out that her own mother "did not yell out of the window" in their working-class neighborhood, as did Molly Goldberg.

Flatbush in the 1930s and 1940s was home not only to Jews but also to Italians, Irish, and a smattering of Poles who lived on the same tree-lined streets, abutting busy Coney Island Avenue and Kings Highway. Each ethnic group was secure in its own identity, but that did not negate tensions among them. Anti-Semitism in the immediate neighborhood of East Ninth Street was not a major problem, although it certainly existed. Two elderly Catholic women living on the same block as the Baders clung to the belief that if a Jew came into the house, especially for lunch, it would bring bad luck—a superstition they transmitted to the boys for whom they served as foster parents. Other children on the street repeated stories that matzo was made from the blood of Christian boys and called Kiki and her Jewish friends "kikes." Nonetheless, a measure of tolerance prevailed in the neighborhood of modest homes and apartments.

Both homes and streets served as children's playgrounds for games of "red light, green light," giant steps, jump rope, jacks, and marbles. Before and after games, youngsters and especially their teenage siblings, gathered in nearby candy stores and soda shops to spend their twenty-five-cent weekly allowances on Cokes, egg creams, comic books, movie magazines, and an occasional newspaper.

What bound the citizens of Flatbush together was a sense of neighborhood solidarity and an intense yearning to be solidly middle class. Even if the Great Depression had thwarted their own youthful dreams, they could transfer hopes and aspirations to their children. Weathering the strains of the worst economic crisis the country had ever experienced, they nurtured a disproportionate share of the twentieth century's most distinguished citizens—many of them Jews. George Gershwin, Aaron Copland, Alfred Kazin, Norman Mailer, Mel Brooks, Woody Allen, Beverly Sills, Barbra Streisand, Milton Friedman, and Sandy Koufax would become household names. So would that of Nathan and Celia Bader's daughter.

. . .

NATHAN, A QUIET, GENTLE MAN, was an attentive and loving father but no disciplinarian. Celia had a far greater impact as a parent, in part because of her strong personality, keen intelligence, and high expectations. Perhaps, too, because those were the qualities her daughter chose to honor, characterizing her mother as "strict and loving." Celia had cut short her own formal education, not just because of a lack of money, but also because of conventional assumptions about the place of women. At that time, Jewish families commonly sacrificed the futures of their daughters to ensure that a son might attend a prestigious school and enter a high-status profession as his birthright in the New World, benefiting other members of the family with his upward mobility. Celia, therefore, had gone to work to support herself and help enable her older brother Sol to attend Cornell University.

Ruth insists that her mother accepted her fate, content with the many friends she so easily made. Yet Celia's extraordinary efforts to secure for her own daughter an education equivalent to Sol's suggest understandable ambivalence. College, Celia believed, would help Kiki achieve the independence and autonomy that came with being able to support herself economically until she made a "suitable marriage" or, in a worst-case scenario, if "anything happened" to a spouse. With only one daughter left, Celia determined that this lively little girl with intelligent eyes and dark blond hair should learn to "love learning, care about people, and work hard" at whatever she wanted to accomplish. As a good *baleboosta* (housekeeper and manager), Celia always pulled all the furniture into the middle of the room to make sure that the cleaning woman scoured every corner. She would now apply that same boundless zeal and perfectionism to Kiki.

Keeping her surviving child healthy was her first concern. The galoshes came out if storm clouds threatened. Heavy stockings were a part of Kiki's winter wardrobe. At the first sign of sniffles, the little girl was kept home from school. Though Kiki regarded her parents' cautionary measures as excessive and burdensome, she did not resist. Aunt Buddy had explained how her parents blamed themselves for Marilyn's fatal illness. Celia, especially, was convinced she might have done more to keep her older daughter healthy. Kiki claimed that she was never made to feel that she had to make up for her parents' loss. But she likely internalized the feeling nonetheless. Keenly aware of their grief, she patiently tolerated Celia's anxieties, complaining only if she felt her mother was excessively strict. Celia, in turn, often urged Kiki to shower special affection upon Nathan in an effort to dispel his lingering sadness.

Sharing her own love of literature and the performing arts was, for Celia, essential. Kiki's most pleasurable memories were of curling up in her mother's lap while Celia sang to her or read aloud from Robert Louis Stevenson's *Child's Garden of Verses* or A. A. Milne's poems about Winnie-the-Pooh and his assorted animal friends who inhabited the Wood. There was something magical about listening to a story unfold

Ruth Bader at age three, 1936, taken at her aunt Sadie (Sarah) Bessen's house in Neponsit, New York. Neponsit is next to Jacob Riis Park; Bessen's house was a block from the beach and the Atlantic Ocean.

in which the characters coexisted harmoniously in a peaceful haven while being enveloped in the comfort and security of maternal devotion. The world of Pooh was a reassuring one where happy outcomes were the rule. Moreover, Kiki adored Milne's ingenuous use of rhyme and meter. Sound and sense were perfectly matched in the rollicking rhyme of "James James Morrison Morrison Weatherby George Dupree," where parental control is comically inverted and James Morrison leads his mother home on a leash. Another favorite was Lewis Carroll's nonsense poem "Jabberwocky." The sounds intrigued even if Kiki had to struggle for the meaning.

As Kiki grew older, mother and daughter embarked on their "Friday afternoon adventure"—a trip to the neighborhood library. As soon as Celia felt comfortable leaving her child alone, the avid young reader picked out her three books for the week while her mother had her hair done. Kiki also created her own stories, providing dramatic readings to her younger cousins. A youngster with a voracious literary appetite, she was soon drawn to fictional role models whose achievements provided inspiration. Fascinated by the French classics *Nobody's Girl* and *Nobody's Boy,* she reveled in the mysteries of *The Secret Garden* and the adventures of *Mary Poppins. Little Women* elicited instant identification with Jo— Louisa May Alcott's feisty tomboy heroine. Jo's quest for autonomy and success in the larger world beyond family made her a model for generations of young girls eager for some endorsement of independence and ambition.

In contrast, Kiki found the Nancy Drew detective series less engaging, although she liked the fact that Nancy herself was brave, resourceful, and "smarter than her boyfriend." But even if Nancy Drew was allowed to "do something" in the world—a possibility that appealed mightily to her young Flatbush reader—accounts of sleuthing could not compete with the myths, preferably Greek, that Kiki began to devour around the age of eight. Sagas of gods and goddesses of the ancient world enthralled her.

The urgency with which she read was not unusual. For girls who had few high-achieving female figures in their immediate circle to emulate, childhood reading opened up imaginative space, providing role models with whom they could identify passionately—an "envisioning of their own destiny." Undoubtedly, Kiki caught glimpses of her future self in

*Ruth's mother,
Celia Amster Bader,
age forty-four, 1946.*

her beloved Greek deities, especially Pallas Athena, the goddess of reason and justice who ended the cycle of violence that began when Agamemnon sacrificed his daughter Iphigenia. It was Athena who created a court of justice to try Orestes, ushering in the rule of law.

But what she treasured most about her pantheon was what admirable substitutes Greek gods and goddesses made for all the saints worshipped by her closest friend, Marilyn De Lutio. The daughter of an Italian family living two doors down from the Baders, Marilyn regularly invited Kiki to dinners of spaghetti and meatballs and to Mass at St. Brendan's on East Twelfth Street. Despite her friend's frequent attendance, Marilyn worried that Kiki might not get into heaven because she did not believe in Christ. Ruth dismissed such worries, yet she mightily envied her Catholic neighbors having all those saints when she only had one invisible God.

Kiki's pantheon also included Anne Frank. Reading one of the diary entries, she was deeply impressed by the following passage:

> One of the many questions that have often bothered me is why women have been, and still are, thought to be so inferior to men. It's easy to say it's unfair, but that's not enough for me; I'd really like to know the reason for this great injustice!

Men presumably dominated women from the very beginning because of their greater physical strength; it's men who earn a living, beget children, [and] do as they please. . . . Until recently, women silently went along with this, which was stupid, since the longer it's kept up, the more deeply entrenched it becomes. Fortunately, education, work and progress have opened women's eyes. In many countries they've been granted equal rights; many people, mainly women, but also men, now realize how wrong it was to tolerate this state of affairs for so long.

Celia seldom missed Eleanor Roosevelt's column, "My Day," in the *Brooklyn Eagle* and shared with her daughter the respect and admiration she felt for the First Lady, who used her position to champion the poor and the disenfranchised. Amelia Earhart became another of Kiki's heroines. A pilot, adventurer, and proto-feminist, Earhart impressed Kiki mightily with her bravery in flying her plane solo across the Atlantic.

Celia also introduced her daughter to women who demonstrated what it meant to be Jewish, American, and female. These were women of valor, Celia explained, by virtue of their courage and humanity. Emma Lazarus, whose words were etched on a plaque at the base of the Statue of Liberty, not only celebrated the United States as a beacon of freedom but also illuminated the importance of the Zionist struggle, advocating the return of oppressed Jews to their ancient homeland.

And there was Henrietta Szold, the founder of Hadassah, the largest women's Jewish organization in the United States. Kiki's esteem for this beloved woman would later intensify when she learned Szold's views on who should say the Kaddish—the mourner's prayer that in Orthodox Judaism could only be recited by men.

Celia talked in especially glowing terms about Lillian Wald, the influential founder of the Henry Street Settlement on Manhattan's Lower East Side, who roamed filthy, overcrowded tenements to provide medical care to the sick and the poor. These were all women whose actions embodied the Jewish imperative of *tikkun olam* (repairing the world), pursuing justice and compassion and helping others.

. . .

CELIA ALSO TAUGHT by example, using a Jewish orphanage in Brooklyn, the Pride of Judea, to impress upon Kiki that even her own very modest economic advantages obliged her to share with those less privileged. Every year on March 15, Celia and her sister Bernice would buy huge containers of ice cream—"bricks" with strips of vanilla, chocolate, and strawberry—and hold Kiki's birthday party at the orphanage so the other children could take part. Although the birthday girl longed for a regular party like her school chums, she never complained, recognizing how much the children enjoyed the treat. A capacity for empathy as well as an appetite for achievement was becoming ingrained in the young girl.

Jewish parents saw summer camp as a haven from diseases like polio, as well as a place to reinforce ethnic identity, social contacts, and middle-class status. The easily accessible Adirondacks contained clusters of children's camps in an area where visiting parents could find accommodations—a feat not always possible in other parts of the Northeast in hotels and resorts where Jews were unwelcome. (Kiki would always remember a sign she had spotted on the lawn of an inn in Pennsylvania: "No Dogs or Jews allowed.")

Celia's brother Sol Amster and his wife, Cornelia, a public school teacher, owned and directed Camp Che-Na-Wah for girls and Camp Baco for boys on Lake Balfour near Minerva, New York. Kiki knew that Che-Na-Wah bore the name of a Native American "princess." She had no idea that the designation represented a conscious attempt to connect campers to a preindustrial landscape, promoting a cross-race identification with a more "primitive" culture. Nor was she aware that Che-Na-Wah was one of the more prestigious camps for Brooklyn girls. What she did know was that new friends, sports, and campfires awaited.

Kiki was an avid camper from the age of four until she "retired" as a counselor at eighteen, with summer in the Adirondacks being an annual ritual from 1937 through 1951. The sight of rustic buildings, the smell of the country air, the sparkle of the small lake, and especially the serenity of the high mountains and forests were experiences to be savored. At Che-Na-Wah, she discovered a love of horses and the water. Riding and, much later, waterskiing would become her favorite sports as an adult. Camps like Che-Na-Wah emphasized more than sports and the usual arts and crafts, using activities for campers to develop relationships with each other and, more important, with their Jewish heritage. Seated around the campfire, the girls were exposed to national and international news as well as the importance of *tzedakah* (charitable giving). Sharing with less fortunate Jewish children was reinforced by an annual camp bazaar that raised funds for various charities.

As conditions worsened in prewar Europe, the focus of charity shifted from hunger among American Jews to the plight of oppressed Jewish communities abroad. Among the suffering were relatives in Europe, desperate to escape the lengthening reach of Hitler and find a friendly haven—in the United States, in British-controlled Palestine, or increasingly in any country that would provide them with refuge from the abyss of Nazi fury. When Kiki was a young camper in the late 1930s, some of the campers themselves were refugees. But the empathy that Che-Na-Wah directors wanted for these new arrivals and their families was not always forthcoming. The German Jewish newcomers seemed a bit convinced of their own superiority, Kiki and her U.S.-born counter-parts concluded. Parents, no doubt, saw it as a replay of the traditional disdain that German Jews had long held for their Eastern European counterparts—the *Ostjuden.*

Many of the campers—Kiki included—remained indifferent to news flashes from Europe, where national borders changed with surpris-ing frequency. But by 1947 indifference gave way to avid attention—at least on details involving Britain's royal nuptials. Che-Na-Wah's young teens lapped up news that the bride-to-be had saved ration cards in order to purchase the white satin for her wedding gown. If events such as Princess Elizabeth's impending marriage to Prince Philip earned higher audience ratings from Kiki and her peers than had the shattering glass of Berlin's *Kristallnacht,* it did not mean that the camp's mission had failed. Owners and staff, like parents, had wanted to spare children knowledge of the Final Solution. Campers were told to leave radios at home, and staff burned newspapers after reading them. At meals and in the cabins, counselors were told to "studiously avoid all war talk." Even parents were instructed not to mention the war on visiting day. At the time, many adults thought that the camps that held relatives were forced labor camps, not death camps. That Hitler planned to exterminate all European Jewry seemed incomprehensible, even to journalists who had received confirmation as early as 1942.

Despite their own apprehensions during the war years and the challenges of dealing with food and transportation in wartime, the owners and staff at Che-Na-Wah, as at Camp Baco, adhered to their mission: to impart to campers a combination of *tzedakah* with Jewish identity in a relatively secular setting. It was a formula that Sol Amster and his sister Celia, like many in their community, believed would allow youngsters to negotiate the currents of life in the United States, affirming their identity as both good Jews and patriotic Americans.

· · ·

WHEN THE TANNED CAMPER RETURNED home at the end of each summer, other activities beckoned. Family outings to Neponsit meant a swim at the beach because Aunt Sadie's house sat on the ocean block. Frequent trips to the Brooklyn Academy offered a series of children's plays to which the Baders subscribed for Saturday matinees. There were occasional operas for children, which the youngster adored. Celia even organized a trip into Manhattan to attend the ballet at City Center. And, of course, there was school.

Kiki attended Brooklyn Public School 238, a square brick building a little over a block away from home. For such an avid reader, first grade offered no challenge. But second grade, in which the children were taught to write, was a different matter. Her teachers insisted that she use her right hand—an ordeal for Kiki, who, like her mother, was left-handed. When she received a D in penmanship for her effort, she resolved never again to write with her right hand. Nor was she enthralled reading about Tom and Jane or Dick and Jane in grade school. "[T]he boy was out there climbing trees, riding bicycles, and the little girl was sitting there in a pink party dress," she recalled. "And I was thinking to myself, I would rather be climbing trees than sitting in the pink party dress." There were no pink dresses at P.S. 238 on Fridays. For school assembly on Fridays, Kiki, like the other girls, wore her white shirt, blue skirt, and red tie, while the boys were decked out in white shirts and blue pants topped off with the requisite red tie.

After school, piano practice and homework were top priorities. Beginning with a local teacher for basics, Celia later engaged the music director from camp, who had once been a close associate of George Gershwin's. The studio in which he gave lessons was in Manhattan on

West Ninety-Fifth Street near the Thalia Theater. If Kiki's talent was not all that she and her teacher might have wished, her dedication to three hours of practice a day as a young girl in an effort to master her technique was impressive. Moreover, early training primed the youngster for a lifelong appreciation of opera and the arts, as well as providing a musical outlet through which she could express her emotions.

Nathan and Celia, though not devoutly observant, were also intent on instilling in their daughter a profound sense of her heritage. Jewish celebrations and rituals punctuated the year. On Friday nights, Celia lit Shabbat candles and recited the brief prayer and each spring changed the dishes for Passover. Seder was celebrated at the home of Nathan's parents—a long, noisy meal with the extended Bader family that combined prolonged reading from the Haggadah with gay songs and much laughter. Kiki loved the time when, as the youngest child, she got to ask the traditional question: "Why is this night different from all other nights?" The rest of the ceremony was spent answering her question. During Hanukkah, all the grandchildren returned to Grandfather Bader's home to receive Hanukkah *gelt*—$1 each. Such rituals, which centered on the home, were as much an observance of ethnic identity and continuity as they were of religion. The exception was Kiki's aunt Sadie, who, Celia explained, had been born in the Old World of *Yiddishkeit*. For Sadie, observance of *kashruth* (Jewish dietary rules) and adherence to Orthodox tradition and practice, with its patriarchal underpinning, were all consuming.

Wherever the Amsters and Baders stood on the Orthodox-secular continuum, they agreed that the escalation of anti-Semitism in Europe and the United States demanded that American Jews reinforce a positive sense of Jewish identity and community. Nathan and Celia enrolled their daughter in Hebrew school. Here she could receive systematic training in religious texts, absorbing ideals of justice and equality grounded in religious principles as well as the Hebrew language and Jewish history and culture. Over the years, Kiki attended a variety of schools, ranging from Reform to Orthodox, before ending up at the East Midwood Jewish Center, an imposing Renaissance-style Conservative synagogue and community center on Ocean Avenue.

Kiki knew that at this critical juncture in history, being a Jew *and* an American citizen had never been more important. The whole family participated in Grandmother Bader's effort to learn to write her name and master the answers to questions that would be on her citizenship exam. Growing up in a shtetl, she had never attended school. Yet she deeply impressed her granddaughter by how diligently she studied and how intensely proud she was when she could answer the questions on the exam in her broken English.

· · ·

EVEN WITH HEBREW SCHOOL and piano lessons, there was always ample time and energy for play. Kiki had grown up with her cousin Richard; the two families moved into different houses on the same block in 1939, when the children were in first grade. These constant playmates considered themselves more like twins than cousins. They went roller-skating together, rode their bicycles, and joined in the neighborhood games that were interrupted only by their mothers' admonitions to come inside for piano practice, homework, supper, or bed.

As the two grew older and joined the Ninth Street "gang," "play" became more dangerous, particularly after the youngsters and their Eighth Street rivals began hurling rocks at each other. When Celia found out about the intensity of the rivalry, she declared with unmistak-

Ruth at age ten with her cousin and playmate Richard Bader, 1943.

able finality that there would be no more rock throwing. Her sternness had its desired effect on a daughter who vividly recalled her mother's response when she, as a small child, had continued tossing a tomato back and forth to Richard, despite orders to stop. The inevitable splat on the kitchen floor occurred. Richard had escaped punishment from his mother. Celia had not been so forgiving.

Kiki also remembered the time she came home with her first and only B on her report card. She had just been skipped to a higher grade at school, and the math test involved long division, a subject her former teacher had not yet covered. But Celia would accept no excuses. As another Brooklyn child recalled, if there were Bs, "the whole house went into mourning." Kiki had promised herself that she would never again bring home anything less than straight As. English, history, and social studies classes she breezed through, but math was never a favorite. Studying, however, absorbed only a fraction of her energy. Climbing garage roofs became her next caper.

Recognizing how quickly this budding adolescent was growing up, Celia made quite explicit her goals—education and independence. For Kiki, this meant more than getting top grades. Nourished by her reading of achieving women, she knew she wanted to "do something" with her life. What she would do, she had no idea; however, as she matured, she was sufficiently self-aware to know that she had an ambitious and competitive streak and that college was part of her future. Celia, who determined that her daughter would not be a subway scholar who commuted daily to a less prestigious public college, had been saving money for tuition at an elite private institution.

As the economy began to improve in the early 1940s, she made small deposits into five local savings banks for Kiki's education. Having lived through the crash, when banks closed their doors and customers' deposits vanished, she was unwilling to entrust all her savings to a single institution. Nor, apparently, did she count on Nathan to come up with the tuition.

· · ·

IN THE MEANTIME, conditions abroad had quickly deteriorated as Hitler pursued the Third Reich's brutal quest for dominance. Then came news of the Japanese bombing of Pearl Harbor on December 7, 1941. War came when Kiki was only eight years old.

She was too young to appreciate how much wartime production would revitalize the Brooklyn naval yard, which eventually employed seventy thousand workers toiling around the clock. Nor did she recognize how strongly defense work would breathe new life into the ailing local economy, securing Brooklyn's rank as the fourth-largest industrial city in the country. But as hostilities persisted, she became keenly aware of the well-being of a "dear elder cousin," Seymour, who had been inducted into the army after Pearl Harbor. Stationed in the Pacific, he had become a constant source of anxiety to family members. She was also old enough to understand the distressing news on the radio and to be frightened by film clips of the war. Like many youngsters during those years, she remembered evening air-raid drills, war bonds, and the ration stamps that were required at gas stations and butcher shops.

Along with her classmates, Kiki tended a "victory garden" at school, knit squares that would be incorporated into afghan blankets for the troops, and collected tinfoil from chewing gum wrappers so the aluminum could be used in the manufacturing of armaments. On "stamp day," students used part of their allowance money to purchase twenty-five-cent stamps to paste into a savings bond book that could be used to purchase bonds supporting the war effort. While the boys became instant experts on various warplanes, spending hours drawing aircraft like the B-17, Kiki admired posters of "Rosie the Riveter" and the strong, active women who had moved into factories to make the United States the "arsenal of democracy." Like other youngsters, she used Victory Mail purchased at the local post office to write to Seymour, no doubt unaware that the letters, once mailed, were microfilmed and sent overseas, where they would be reproduced and censored for sensitive information, before finally being handed on to the men to whom they were addressed.

At the war's end in 1945, Kiki, now twelve, had vivid memories of momentous events. FDR, the only president she had ever known, suddenly died in April at his retreat in Warm Springs, Georgia. The news plunged Brooklyn into mourning. For many in the borough, the grief could not have been more intense had a member of the immediate family died. The Bader home was an exception. Celia's admiration for the First

Lady was not matched on her husband's part by reverence for FDR. As a small-business man, Nathan disliked the extensive government regulations associated with the New Deal. Although Celia's political leanings were toward the Democratic Party and Nathan's toward the GOP, neither wife nor husband was highly partisan. Believing that two terms were enough for any president, they had voted for Wendell Willkie in 1940, knowing he, too, was an internationalist.

In May, Nazi Germany surrendered, inspiring total jubilation in massive V-E Day celebrations across the country. The Baders, like many parents, spared their daughter *Life* magazine's horrific photographs of the emaciated survivors of Auschwitz and other death camps. But there was no escaping newsreels of mushroom-shaped clouds over Hiroshima and Nagasaki in August. Awe gave way to horror as Kiki grasped what human suffering the bombs inflicted on the Japanese, casting a pall over forthcoming V-J Day celebrations. Then she breathed a sigh of relief when news arrived that Seymour would be coming home.

After six years of war, death marches, and the Holocaust, the late president's hope for a new world organization dedicated to the preservation of peace and human rights was a part of the Roosevelt legacy to which Kiki and her parents fully subscribed. Realization of world governance might actually occur with the founding of a new international organization to promote peace and security. The Baders' universalist sentiments were shared by over 80 percent of Americans who supported U.S. membership in the United Nations. Celia and her daughter closely followed Eleanor Roosevelt's efforts on behalf of the adoption of the Universal Declaration of Human Rights, which the former First Lady lauded as "the International Magna Carta for all men everywhere." Two months after Mrs. Roosevelt had been chosen to head the UN Commission on Human Rights, Kiki, now a thirteen-year-old eighth grader and editor of her school's newspaper, the *Highway Herald,* wrote her own editorial:

> Since the beginning of time, the world has known four great documents, great because of all the benefits to humanity which came about as a result of their fine ideals and principles.
>
> The first was The Ten Commandments, which was given to Moses

while he was leading the Israelites through the wilderness of the land of Canaan. Today people of almost every religion respect and accept them as a code of ethics and a standard of behavior.

Up until the thirteenth century, conditions under the kings of Europe were unbearable for the commoners. Taxation was high, living conditions poor and justice unknown. It was then, in 1215 A.D., that the barons and peers of England met and drew up a charter called The Magna Carta. After forcing King John to sign it, the document was declared the governing law of the land. This gave the English peasants the first rights ever granted to them.

When William of Orange, a Dutchman, was offered the English throne, his chief ambition was to use the military powers of Britain to aid his beloved Holland in its war with Spain. In accepting this offer, he had to grant certain concessions to the English people. So, in 1689, he signed The Bill of Rights. This limited the King's powers and gave much of the government control to Parliament, another important stride in the history of the world.

The Declaration of Independence of our own U.S. may well be considered one of the most important steps in the shaping of the world. It marked the birth of a new nation, a nation that has so grown in strength as to take its place at the top of the list of the world's great powers.

And now we have a fifth great document, The Charter of the United Nations. Its purpose and principles are to maintain international peace and security, to practice tolerance and to suppress any acts of aggression or other breaches of peace.

It is vital that these be assured, for now we have a weapon that can destroy the world. We children of public school age can do much to aid in the promotion of peace. We must try to train ourselves and those about us to live together with one another as good neighbors for this idea is embodied in the great new Charter of the United Nations. It is the only way to secure the world against future wars and maintain an everlasting peace.

Endorsing the formation of the United Nations and its Universal Declaration as the latest development in the evolution of human rights

Ruth, aged thirteen, at her Hebrew school confirmation at the East Midwood Jewish Center. She is seated to the left of Rabbi Harry Halpern, and her friend and future college roommate Joan Bruder is on the right, 1946.

beginning with the Ten Commandments and the Magna Carta, the precocious author signaled her enduring attention to history and support for human rights.

Parallel experiences were also occurring at her Hebrew school. Levi Soshuk, a Jewish educator and Zionist who worked with young people, taught at the East Midwood Jewish Center as well as at Abraham Lincoln High School. A master at capturing the idealism of teenagers with his vision of a progressive new land of Israel where Jews and Arabs could peacefully coexist, he told stories of the first aliyah, or immigration, of Jews to Palestine. It was an intellectually inspiring cocktail for a young teenager developing her own view of postwar possibilities at a time when "Americans suddenly seemed to stand beholding a new heaven and a new earth." Graduating in her white robe on confirmation day in 1946, Kiki Bader carried home her prize for "best" in Hebrew school.

· · ·

MOVING ON to academically oriented James Madison High School meant traveling to Bedford Avenue. With eight hundred students in attendance, two different shifts cycled through classes each day. The student body was about 60 percent Jewish, because many of the elementary school Catholic students were siphoned off by parochial schools. Among the faculty, an unusually high percentage of instructors had Ph.D. degrees. Unable to find jobs in colleges and universities as enrollments shrank during the Depression—and because of anti-Semitism—they had taken positions at James Madison, which they intended to hold until retirement. Generations of young high school graduates became the beneficiaries.

Kiki quickly proved that she was smart enough to be selected for the elite honor society, musically talented enough to be awarded a cello position in the school orchestra, and popular enough to be elected to the twirling squad and booster society. As one of the "go-getters," she wore her black satin jacket with its gold lettering while selling tickets to football games. Smart, pretty, and popular—she dated frequently—she seemed a model American teenager. Only later did she acknowledge that she studied the cello merely to qualify for the back row of the orchestra and that the baton twirling and booster society were de rigueur for

Ruth leading religious services at Camp Che-Na-Wah, in the Adirondacks, New York, which she attended each summer from 1937 to 1951. The camp was owned by her uncle Sol and his wife, Cornelia Amster. Ca. 1948–50.

anyone aspiring to be "in." If truth were told, she had no interest whatsoever in high school football, although as a dutiful twirler she attended every game, despite chipping her front tooth on a baton. Dodgers games, which the entire high school attended on "Dodgers Day" every spring, were no less "boring." Even in those unformed teen years, when adolescents routinely try on and discard diverse identities, she had recognized an ill fit.

More enduring aspects of her personality emerged elsewhere. At camp, she volunteered to serve as the rabbi for Friday night services. She relished speaking in public and found the singing of Hebrew chants with their Eastern European melodies "inspirational." More important, she actually enjoyed the responsibility of conducting the camp service. Such opportunities for Jewish girls were infrequent in an age before bat mitzvahs became commonplace.

Her obsession with intellectual achievement also stood out at James Madison, which had more than its share of bright, college-bound students. Her scores, her guidance counselor advised, might earn her admission to Swarthmore, Wellesley, or Barnard. And of course, she would apply to Uncle Sol's alma mater, Cornell University. Classmates who knew her best found the teenager "modest" about her academic accomplishments, although some students thought her to be "annoyingly competitive, too aggressive by half." "Pushy" even, said one. But her old friend and fan the former D.C. Superior Court judge Richard Salzman firmly disagreed, insisting that his childhood neighbor and schoolmate was "popular, personable, and serious." She belonged to "all the right groups," he recalled, and excelled academically "without giving the impression of studying"—a prerequisite for any teenage girl who valued peer group acceptance in those prefeminist years.

. . .

WHAT OTHER STUDENTS, including Salzman, did not know was that Kiki Bader's mother was waging a losing battle against cervical cancer. Their classmate's silence and rigid compartmentalization of her life were hardly surprising. A mother's prolonged illness marked the family as abnormal in the eyes of other teenagers in the postwar years; "cancer" was an unspoken word and death a taboo subject. Celia's cancer, diagnosed in 1946 during her daughter's freshman year at high school, required surgeries and weeks of hospitalization. Kiki managed her time carefully because every minute counted; trips to and from Beth Moses Hospital took an hour each way.

Soon the days settled into a dreary routine: school, the subway trip to the hospital, where she met her father, a visit with her mother, dinner at the cafeteria near the hospital. Then it was back home, to rise again in the morning and return to classes. Illness so dominated the Baders' lives that neither father nor daughter had much inclination to discuss anything else, especially their shared pain.

The glum routine and depressing reality of her mother's illness propelled the guarded teenager to look for ways to escape temporarily. The Brooklyn Academy provided a place to release tears "without coming away feeling sad." She could suspend grief when absorbed in concerts or engrossed in films like Laurence Olivier's *Henry V.* Long walks in Central Park on the way to her piano lessons helped, especially when combined with visits to museums. Music also provided relief. She would plunge into Chopin's preludes, a series of twenty-four short pieces that cover a vast range of expression, from the opening homage to Bach's "Well-Tempered Clavier" to the gaiety of a Polish mazurka, to the apocalyptic D minor. Playing allowed her to immerse herself for hours in music from melancholy to wildest anguish to peaceful serenity. Grief, no doubt, also contributed to Kiki's conviction that she could not give up smoking. She had smoked her first cigarette at thirteen when a school chum dared her to inhale without coughing. She took the dare and became hooked, to the great dismay of her mother, who dared not fuss too much about the unfortunate habit that father and daughter shared.

Celia, too, knew her days were dwindling, yet she never insisted on her daughter's company. Rather, she encouraged Kiki to keep up with friends and high school activities in the hope that they would help blunt the impending loss at home. Nonetheless, Kiki stoically clung to Celia's bedside as much as a busy teenager could, acutely aware that the disease was taking its inexorable toll. She knew it pleased her mother to see her studying. And her mother had many things she wanted to share.

One of Celia's most frequent exhortations was "Be a lady." Kiki knew that for her mother, the term "lady" was a "most honorable one," implying much more than the usual upper-middle-class admonition to observe good manners, behave properly in the company of young men, and refrain from sex before marriage. Being a lady meant holding fast to one's "convictions and self-respect." It implied self-control—restraining not only erotic desire but also anger. Such admonitions, often uttered to children of those who have been targets of discrimination, weighed heavily upon the consciousness of a daughter already well schooled in self-discipline.

Although Celia lived to see the much-anticipated letter of acceptance from Cornell—she had asked her brother Sol to write on Kiki's behalf— cancer overtook her in the spring of 1950. An aggressive round of radiation treatment that her doctors had prescribed did nothing to relieve her suffering and made her violently ill. Having learned only the week before that her daughter had been chosen as one of a select few graduates to be on the "Roundtable Forum of Honor" that would present commencement remarks, she died at the age of forty-seven on Sunday, June 25. The burial took place on Monday, and on Tuesday, graduation day, Kiki stayed home with her father. Her teachers later delivered her medals to her home.

Celia had managed to hold on long enough to provide the essential guidance and role model that her daughter needed at a critical phase in her development. Unlike most adults at the time who "protected" children from knowledge of a parent's fatal illness, she spoke openly about the impact of her death. She especially urged Kiki to look out for her father. Celia's strength and candor thus spared her daughter the worst aspects of "mother loss"—the adult depression and anxiety disorder that psychologists believe disproportionately afflicts children, particularly daughters, who lose their mothers before age seventeen. Yet no amount of preparation could blunt the devastating pain and waves of inconsolable grief that engulfed father and daughter.

. . .

SITTING SHIVAH, the customary seven days of mourning when family and friends gather to recite the Mourner's Prayer, might have functioned to ease the family's feelings of desolation by reaffirming the belief of the mourners. Instead, tradition only intensified Kiki's despair. Ten men were required to form a quorum, or minyan, to say prayers for the dead. The fact that women did not count in this patriarchally inspired Orthodox practice incensed the incipient feminist in Kiki. As the daughter of a woman who never underestimated what women could accomplish, she found it appalling that Celia's own sisters would countenance what their niece could only regard as an insult to her mother. Yet she felt she had to acquiesce. Sadie, she knew, was rigorous in adhering to the rituals of Orthodox Judaism, and Bernice, the youngest and prettiest of the three sisters, was no rebel.

As the somber, sorrowful sounds of the Kaddish surrounded the mourners, Kiki's deeper grief at her mother's death took over. Yet the emotions inspired by the incident lingered, becoming a turning point in Kiki's decision to become a secular Jew. Many years later, she would quote from Henrietta Szold's response, written in 1916, to a caring offer made from a man in the community to say the Kaddish for her mother:

> It is impossible for me to find words in which to tell you how deeply I was touched by your offer to act as "Kaddish" for my dear mother. . . . [I] appreciate what you say about the Jewish custom [that only male children recite the prayer, and if there are no male survivors, a male stranger may act as substitute]; and Jewish custom is very dear and sacred to me. [Y]et I cannot ask you to say Kaddish after my mother. The Kaddish means to me that the survivor publicly . . . manifests his . . . intention to assume the relation to the Jewish community that his parent had, [so that] the chain of tradition remains unbroken from generation to generation. . . . You can do that for . . . your family, I must do that [for mine].

Reflecting on her own mother, Kiki declared, "She was the strongest and bravest person I have ever known."

· · ·

ON ONE MATTER, however, Kiki was deeply torn: what to do about her father. Celia had suggested that Kiki carefully consider Barnard, where she had been accepted, which was only a subway ride away. Relatives, concerned about Nathan, lobbied for the prestigious women's college, hoping she would come home every weekend. But Celia had always talked about Cornell. And Sol, as an alumnus, had hired Cornell students as waitresses at the guest lodge at his camps in the Adirondacks—coeds who told his niece "great things" about the university. Kiki managed to convince herself that it was Cornell that her mother had really wanted her to attend. She and her father had already been through so much pain together; living with such consuming grief was suffocating. Yet she felt a keen sense of guilt for putting her own needs first.

At least she could help her father financially. The tuition money Celia had so laboriously saved in her five accounts totaled $8,000—a remarkable sum given the time and circumstances and worth many times more in contemporary purchasing power. Kiki reckoned that with New York State Regents and Cornell scholarships to cover tuition, she could make almost enough money from various jobs to cover her room, board, and other necessities. Taking out the small portion of Celia's savings that she calculated she would need to make up the difference, she turned over the rest of the nest egg to her father. Despite a burgeoning consumer-driven economy, she realized that the small retail business Nathan and his brother Isidore had carried on after their father died was struggling as larger, more fashionable department stores took over and families moved to the suburbs. Nathan's grief and depression, compounded by the loss of his wife's astute counsel, proved overwhelming. It was only a matter of months before Nathan Bader Inc. closed its doors, leaving its owner, no longer a provider, with an overwhelming sense of failure.

His daughter, on the other hand, had the future. Before she departed for her summer job as camp counselor, she and a Flatbush friend, Joan Bruder—also on her way to Cornell—met by chance on the train station platform. The giddy anticipation with which they talked about college made their meeting too memorable for time to erase. "Kiki asked me to be her roommate," Joan recalled. "We had known each other from Hebrew school, having gone to different high schools. I was so flattered and excited that she would ask me. It was a wonderful moment."

While Kiki was at camp, a letter arrived from Aunt Buddy relating her efforts to find a place for Nathan to live. She had found a small apartment in a house farther out on Long Island in Lynbrook. Apart from its minimal cost, the apartment had just one advantage—proximity to her own family in Rockville Centre. Once they had removed his few belongings, the apartment in the house on East Ninth Street was rented to another family. Even Nathan's ties to the Belle Harbor synagogue were severed. Unable to pay his dues, he was denied his customary seat for the high holy days.

For Kiki, this last affront to her father's pride hit hard, reinforcing not only her growing alienation from religious practice but also a new steeliness in her resolve. The synagogue's action, she believed, went against the spirit of justice and compassion that was supposed to be at the core of Judaism. She would honor her heritage and its ethical teachings and values in which she had been immersed since childhood—but that was it.

· · ·

THE RUPTURE WITH THE PAST now complete, Kiki's world had vanished—and with it, the last vestiges of childhood. Yet Celia would remain a guiding presence throughout her daughter's life. As an accomplished adult at the absolute pinnacle of her profession, she would look at her mother's photograph as she left her office each day and say to herself, "She would have been proud of me."

CHAPTER 2

Cornell and Marty

In August 1950, Kiki and her father packed her luggage into his aging Chevrolet for the trip to Cornell. Her trunk and skis had to be shipped ahead. As the car headed farther upstate toward Ithaca, the greenness of the landscape was overpowering—far more like the countryside above Lake George, where she had spent so many summers as a camper, than the streets of Brooklyn. The prospect of being one of nine thousand students at a distinguished university in the midst of a dramatic postwar physical expansion could have seemed daunting. Yet the seventeen-year-old felt no sense of apprehension, only an awareness of new possibilities beckoning.

· · ·

AS THE CAR HEADED UP State Street, father and daughter soon found themselves in the middle of Ithaca's business district, where a colorful gaggle of small shops and stores lined the streets. There was Rothschild's Department Store, the Corner Book Store, movie theaters, banks, various specialty-clothing stores, jewelry shops, and the Ithaca Hotel—home to the "Dutch Kitchen," a favorite haunt of undergraduates. Like most American towns, Ithaca had its five-and-ten-cent stores: Kresge's, Newberry's, and Woolworth's. As the car headed to Cascadilla Gorge and climbed East Hill toward the campus, she could see Cornell itself towering on her left. Turning onto College Avenue brought her past rooming houses in Collegetown and over Triphammer bridge to the north side of Fall Creek and a group of dormitories. Here stood Clara Dickson Hall, a huge Colonial-style brick building to which freshman women had been assigned. Nearby Balch Hall, where she would live her sophomore and senior years, would be her only real home for three of her next four years.

Dickson, the largest residential hall in the Ivy League, had rooms arranged in clusters so that a single, double, and triple together shared a single bath. Ruth, who had already agreed to room with her friend Joan Bruder, discovered her suite mates were all Jews. Perhaps, as her new friend Irma Rubenberg suggested, the university wanted to make minorities feel at home. The girls joked that they had been put together "so that we wouldn't contaminate the others"; gentiles were at both ends of the corridor, Ruth recalled. Their sardonic humor was not entirely misplaced. Quotas limiting the number of Jewish students in prestigious eastern universities had been in place since the mid-1920s, thinly concealed behind phrases like "regional distribution," "social balance," and "harmony." Jews had influenced campus organizations and culture at Cornell by 1950, yet they still were not fully accepted socially.

Such overt avowals of anti-Semitism had waned in the aftermath of World War II. Yet even as more Jews moved into new neighborhoods, attended college, entered prestigious professions, and achieved a middle-class lifestyle, barriers remained. Summer resorts, private clubs and schools, and sororities and fraternities remained segregated—evidence of the more genteel expression of prejudice on display as soon as rush season began.

Over the summer, Ruth had made friends with two Cornell "Tri-Delts" who also worked as counselors at Camp Che-Na-Wah. Yet the much-anticipated invitation to visit the Tri-Delt sorority house never arrived. The social distance between Jew and gentile, institutionalized in separate fraternities and sororities until the 1960s, was "rigid," Ruth wryly recalled. Even at the student union's Ivy Room, the center of 1950s campus life, the two groups tended to sit on opposite sides of the room— Jews on the left, non-Jews on the right, insists the Cornell alumnus Jon Greenleaf.

Whatever the degree of social distancing between the two groups— experiences and memories vary considerably—the young women living in adjoining rooms in Dickson quickly bonded. Because they shared similar backgrounds, the chemistry among them was instantaneous. These new best friends did everything together, even inventing a name for themselves based on the first letter of each first name—*K* in Ruth's case for Kiki. Ruth, they agreed, while possessing a well-developed sense of privacy, was "easy to live with. Any lingering grief over her mother's death she kept inside." Her father, whom Joan Bruder described as a "nice, quiet, gentle man," inspired in his daughter a keen sense of duty, friends observed. Initially, however, the group was more interested in acclimating to college life than gaining insights into each other's past, though they would remain good friends for life. There were new experiences to share: classes in which students answered to "Miss" Bader or "Miss" Zicht, Saturday night parties where couples danced the Lindy between slow dances, football weekends, and the really serious romance.

First on the agenda of new experiences were the myriad rules that surrounded college women in the 1950s. According to the *Cornell Desk Book,* coeds were expected to attend classes wearing skirts with sweaters or blouses (usually with Peter Pan collars). Jeans and Bermuda shorts should be reserved for "picnics, house parties, and geology labs." Sensible flat shoes and socks were mandated; penny loafers or saddle oxfords sufficed. Depending on the occasion, dating required anything from "casual dresses and suits to cocktail dresses and formals." White gloves and hats were obligatory for church or luncheons. Style shows, written up in the student newspaper, the *Daily Sun,* provided further demonstration of appropriate attire. Finally, Cornell coeds were expected to be "well-groomed" at all times.

Women students on North Campus took their meals in the dormitory and dressed for dinner. Observance of proper manners mattered: no one was permitted to leave the table before everyone had finished. Ruth's slow eating proved agonizing for dinner partners eager to rush off for their boyfriends' phone calls. Those going out for the evening met their dates in the dorm parlors. Male visitors, denied access to their girlfriends' rooms, had to be out of North Campus dormitories by 10:30 on weeknights.

Curfews were part of the regulation of courtship that universities provided in lieu of absentee parents. Nonmarital sexual behavior in all forms—a national preoccupation in the early Cold War years—focused especially on women. It was the unfortunate college girl who lacked the moral rectitude and self-control to protect her reputation by "drawing the line" for her more sexually ambitious male partner. The ultimate taboo—premarital pregnancy—was abhorred in middle-class white gentile families but evoked even greater stigma in Jewish circles.

· · ·

THE EARLY WEEKS passed quickly. Part-time work, intended to supplement Ruth's scholarship, required full use of her well-honed organizing skills. She was determined to catch up on aspects of her education that could not yet match those of her prep-school classmates. They knew all about art and could identify the period and style of painting and often the artist. By contrast, Ruth's lack of knowledge signaled not only an educational deficiency but the full pleasure of "seeing" important works of art she had begun to explore in Manhattan's great museums.

Yet in the 1950s, being a brainy, arts-conscious, achievement-oriented coed who also enjoyed the company of the opposite sex posed problems. Appearing more intelligent than a potential date was hazardous to one's social life. Because a noisy dorm was no place to study, Ruth found out-of-the-way classrooms, specialized libraries, and even empty bathrooms in campus buildings where she could work without being seen. A bathroom in Goldwin Smith Hall became a favorite. "I knew some pretty obscure libraries on the Cornell campus" as well, she later remarked, explaining, "The most important degree for you to get was Mrs., and it didn't do to be seen reading and studying." Even among other women, studying was frowned upon, especially if bridge players needed a fourth hand.

Suite mates quickly learned that while Ruth would conceal her studying, she would modify neither her academic priorities nor her determination to stick to them. When she studied in the dorm, she sat cross-legged night after night reading intensely while they played cards and chatted. Only after condensing her notes to index cards, condensing the index cards, and then memorizing the contents would she allow herself to relax and go out for a movie. "A dedicated student? Yes; a nerd? Absolutely not," insisted one of her closest companions.

The work had its own joys. Some of Ginsburg's courses were memorable, and the professors even more so. She adored her European literature class, taught by the Russian-born Vladimir Nabokov, one of the twentieth century's great writers, whom she found a "marvelously amusing" and wonderful teacher. Nabokov's love of words, especially the sounds of words, she found remarkable. One of the advantages of the English language, he pointed out, was that its adjectives come before nouns, thus focusing the reader's attention first on the description of the person or object. Contrast that with a language like French, he suggested, where the first word encountered is normally the noun, with the adjective following, as in *cheval blanc* (horse white). The first color you think of upon hearing *cheval* is brown, but in English by the time you get to "horse," you already see it as white.

She could still remember a quiz on *Bleak House:* "When you first meet 'Peepy,' what do you see?" The obvious answer was that Peepy had his neck trapped in an iron railing and could not extract his head. The response Nabokov sought was that the little boy had his "unnaturally *large* head" caught. Using these adjectives, he explained, allowed Dickens not only to heighten the discomfort of the neglected Jellyby child but also to evoke the misery of childhood in nineteenth-century England.

Words and word placement, Nabokov explained, conveyed impressions to the reader, painting vivid word pictures. Dickens had opened *Bleak House* with just such an image—the deep fog that blanketed Lincoln's Inn Hall and all of London. In great literature, Nabokov insisted, words were to be savored—a lesson Ruth took to heart as the class read Jane Austen, Flaubert, Gogol, and especially Tolstoy.

Yet when it was time to declare a major, she chose not to focus on

Vladimir Nabokov, who taught at Cornell between 1948 and 1959. He sensitized Ruth to the importance of word choice and placement and inspired her love of Russian novels.

literature. A major in political science (government at Cornell) offered more employment possibilities. The relatively minimal course requirements would also make it possible to take additional courses in music and art history. The excellence of the government faculty provided a further incentive. Clinton Rossiter and Mario Einaudi had world-class reputations, and Robert Cushman, an expert on American constitutional law and civil liberties, enjoyed a reputation as a top-notch teacher. To complement Cushman's course, she planned to enroll in a much-touted exploration of the philosophical and intellectual underpinning of the Constitution taught by Milton Konvitz, an exceptional scholar, teacher, and activist in the School of Industrial and Labor Relations and the Law School.

· · ·

AS SOON AS RUTH ENROLLED in Cushman's constitutional law class, it became apparent that student, professor, and subject were an instant fit. "Scary smart," in the words of one classmate; "she seemed to have a natural ability to be logical and reasoned, and not let emotions get in her way," said another. A close friend and classmate reflected many years later, "Logic and reason were always basic to Ruth's style of thinking. She entered college with that aptitude, just as she brought with her a high level of intellectual discipline and of self-discipline." These qualities no doubt played a part in the bonding of student and teacher. When Ruth asked Cushman if he would supervise further study and work with her on her writing, he agreed.

If Nabokov had sensitized Ruth to the importance of words, Cushman taught her the importance of conveying substance accurately and economically. Get rid of the clutter, he advised. Spare, clear prose should be her goal. The reader should never have to read a sentence more than once, he insisted. His eager pupil absorbed his message, just as she had Nabokov's instructions on how to use language to paint "word pictures," unaware that she was acquiring precisely the writing skills that would distinguish her future briefs. As the 1924 Democratic presidential candidate, John W. Davis, one of the most highly regarded corporate lawyers of his day, had advised, "If you want to win a case, paint the Judge a *picture* and keep it simple."

Cushman also offered Ruth work as a research assistant, stimulating

Robert E. Cushman, professor of government at Cornell from 1923 to 1957 and an expert at American constitutional law. His mentoring encouraged Ruth's deep appreciation of civil liberties and her respect for lawyers who defended them.

in her a lasting fascination with constitutional law and a powerful appreciation of civil liberties, which were his passions as well. They talked at length about McCarthyism, and Cushman asked her to follow the latest blasts of the House Un-American Activities Committee (HUAC) and the Senate Internal Security Subcommittee. Alan Barth's columns and editorials in *The Washington Post,* the newspaper offering the most extensive coverage of McCarthyism, soon became daily fare. In contrast with Barth's reasoned, measured prose, *Red Channels,* a right-wing tract that exposed purported Communists in radio and television, offered alarmist warnings. Yet Ruth consumed each page as devoutly as any entertainment figure who had ever belonged to a left-leaning political group listed by the attorney general. Cushman also put her to work on a library exhibit that included not only books targeted by McCarthyites but also book burning throughout the ages. In doing so, he no doubt informed her that the government had demanded that the university provide reading lists containing material on communism, only to be told that to obtain reading lists, one must be enrolled in the course.

As Cushman talked about the essential American values and fundamental freedoms guaranteed by the Constitution that were being destroyed in the zeal to protect national security, he spoke with admiration about civil libertarians who fought back. None garnered greater respect than the small band of lawyers who defended those charged with disloyalty. They understood that legal restrictions based on political beliefs and associations affected not just target groups, such as Communists, but all Americans.

Civil liberties and civil rights were also central to the "American Ideals" course offered by Konvitz. A man of enormous energy and broad learning who combined a Ph.D. in philosophy with a law degree, he used the Torah, Plato's works, and other texts to illuminate the intellectual underpinnings of the Constitution. Konvitz also personified the legal scholar as activist. He had worked for the National Association for the Advancement of Colored People (NAACP) Legal Defense Fund in the 1940s as the principal assistant to Thurgood Marshall on cases involving police brutality, lynching, and segregation. Expanding the scope of his activism to the international arena, he would write a constitution for the African country of Liberia in addition to numerous books on civil rights and civil liberties.

Ruth found this erudite rabbi's son much too scholarly and intimidating to approach after class. Yet he clearly accomplished for her one of the things for which he was renowned as a teacher: challenging students to figure out where they stood on the important issues of their time and

Milton Konvitz, professor of constitutional labor law, personified the legal scholar as activist. His course on American ideals nourished Ruth's hope that she could become a lawyer who worked to preserve the nation's highest values.

helping them to discover their own power to act. Konvitz, Ruth recalled, reinforced her new awareness that "a lawyer could do something that was personally satisfying and at the same time work to preserve the values that have made this country great. . . . [This] was an exciting prospect for me," she acknowledged. More important, he nourished her hope that someday she could become a lawyer engaged in the same enterprise. At the end of her sophomore year, the eighteen-year-old added her name to the list of students signing up to take the legal aptitude exam (LSAT) in her junior year, a primary requirement for admission to law school.

The youthful decision did not sit well with family members who feared she would be unable to support herself as a lawyer. Becoming a school-teacher like her aunt Cornelia was the only option Celia and Nathan had envisioned. However, a brief stint in a classroom at Ithaca High School had convinced the Baders' intellectually demanding daughter that public school teaching was not for her. How could she possibly teach from a textbook that treated the causes of the Spanish-American War in such a biased fashion? In Ruth's mind, Celia's emphasis on achievement and independence effectively overrode specific vocational categories.

. . .

IN THE MEANTIME, there were other aspects of campus life to engage. Active in the Women's Self-Government Association, she sat on the student-faculty Committee on Academic Conduct for the Liberal Arts College that handled plagiarism cases. One of the faculty members on the committee for whom she also worked part-time became so impressed by her "integrity, sense of responsibility and tact" that he wrote to Harvard Law School on her behalf. "That [Miss Bader] . . . should be selected to the College Administrative Officers as one of three undergraduates to serve . . . is, itself, testimony to the general esteem in which she is held. I think it is fair to say," he noted, "that Miss Bader does not seek leadership or positions of influence; they are thrust upon her because her strength of character and intelligence are quickly recognized by others. Personally," he observed, "she is attractive, friendly, dignified, and modest almost to the point of reticence. She is not, however, one who evades decision or action when they are required. There are few young women of Miss Bader's age whom I would describe as serene and wise, but I think those adjectives are entirely fitting in her case."

Ruth's leadership of a group concerned with careers for women proved equally revealing. She was convinced that she had classmates at Cornell who felt alienated from society's expectations—the same alienation expressed by a despairing Wellesley College student who scratched into the metal wall of a library carrel the words

Study hard
Get good grades
Get your degree
Get married
Have three horrid kids
Die, and be buried.

Yet with the exception of her close friends, the professional ambitions of most Cornell coeds, she discovered, were limited to finding a husband with the requisite degrees.

Why, she wondered, did the university, which was presumably devoted to promoting the intellectual development and independence of all of its students, do nothing to counter an ethos so harmful to Cornell women? Admitted to the college in a ratio of one to four, they had to have a higher grade point average than their more numerous male peers. Yet the sole expectation was marriage. Nor were such expectations confined to the university. Her closest friends were leaving Cornell as soon as they became engaged. Joan Bruder was the first to go. Her parents, assuming their daughter's future was assured once she married a Harvard man, saw no reason to continue paying Cornell tuition when she could finish her studies at a less expensive school closer to home. Others in the close-knit group soon followed suit. But not Anita Zicht and Irma Rubenberg, who stayed the full four years, Rubenberg marrying one of her teaching assistants, Edward Hays McAlister, and acquiring a Ph.D. of her own.

At the time, neither Ruth nor her counterparts on other campuses understood how ideological and structural constraints—codified in postwar public policy initiatives from Social Security to the GI Bill and the Federal Housing Administration—extended the gendered segmentation of the workforce and social welfare policies in ways that limited aspiration and choice for young women. The early 1950s was the heyday of the feminine mystique, the term that Betty Friedan would later coin to describe the fierce pressure that pushed middle-class daughters in the Cold War years into early marriage and domesticity—gentiles and Jews alike. Indeed, as Jewish men recaptured the role of provider, the first status symbol on the Lower East Side, as elsewhere in the United States, became a non-employed wife. Marrying a young man with strong financial prospects thus became a vocational ambition consistent with living the postwar American dream.

Young women who did aspire to a professional life faced challenges that few fully comprehended. There was the initial hurdle of admissions quotas. Schools that trained students for law, medicine, or other traditionally male professions had quotas that limited the number of women to a maximum of 10 percent. Once through the needle's eye, the token women admitted faced further obstacles in securing scholarship money. Jobs for which they trained were in even shorter supply. For those who secured employment, the biggest challenge still awaited: combining career and family in a society that offered scant support to women who tried to do both.

· · ·

PREOCCUPATION WITH STUDIES and the multiple challenges of a career did not preclude participation in the lighter side of campus life. To relax, Ruth played the piano (Gilbert and Sullivan operettas were favorites), rode horseback, went to the movies, pledged Alpha Epsilon Phi, one of two Jewish sororities at Cornell that had its own array of activities, and participated in the Big Red Revue, the annual student-produced musical talent show. On many occasions, she just "hung out" with girlfriends, though she was no stranger to the campus party scene.

Never at a loss for dates, Ruth maintained a special relationship during her freshman year with a Columbia University Law School student from Paterson, New Jersey, whom she had met at summer camp. During holiday breaks in Lynbrook, where she stayed with Aunt Buddy and Uncle Ben, she spent as little time in her father's spare apartment as she could manage; being there only intensified the pain and guilt. Instead, she and her boyfriend went into Manhattan, where they could enjoy a full day in the city together.

There was also another man in her life—Marty Ginsburg, a Cornell

An engagement photograph of Martin Ginsburg, who had finally won over his future life partner, taken by a professional photographer (unknown) in Rockville Centre, New York, 1953.

Ruth during her senior year at Cornell, when the couple announced their engagement, in 1953.

undergraduate from the class of 1953. Marty, who spotted Ruth on campus, persuaded his fraternity brother and roommate who dated her close friend to arrange a blind date. Because several of Ruth's friends often partied at Tau Delta Phi, where Marty was an enthusiastic member and bartender, the "date" was easy to set up. The intermediaries agreed that because Marty had a girlfriend at Smith College and Ruth a boyfriend at Columbia Law School, the two would be "safe" company for each other during the week. On Sunday evenings, the two had dinner at a nearby restaurant where other diners could glimpse Marty's head bent down to catch the words of the small dark blonde next to him. Though firm friends and constant companions, they were not yet a "couple."

In his college days, Martin D. Ginsburg was the clever, supremely self-confident son of a prosperous vice president of the Federated department store chain. After growing up in Rockville Centre, Long Island, where he shared his mother's avid love of the links, he became a member of Cornell's varsity golf team. However, his passion for golf was soon matched by his interest in his new "friend" with whom he had long, absorbing conversations "about anything and everything." After asking what courses she was taking, he signed up for the same ones. "Ruth was a wonderful student and a beautiful young woman," recalled Marc Franklin. "Most of the men were in awe of her, but Marty was not. He's never been in awe of anybody."

· · ·

AT FIRST GLANCE, the couple seemed dissimilar. He was tall with tightly curled blond hair; she was tiny and utterly feminine in appearance. Not only were their economic backgrounds different—hers exceedingly modest, his far more affluent—so were their personalities. Marty was as ebullient, witty, and gregarious as Ruth was serious, reserved, and self-contained. He appeared to be carefree; she had abiding concerns about her father. Both enjoyed sports, but she loved the more solitary challenge of horseback riding, which tested her own skills. He was an avid golfer in a game that was directly competitive and social. Both were intellectually gifted. Marty relied on his native intelligence and aptitude scores to overcome his less than stellar grades. Ruth would graduate with highest honors, a Phi Beta Kappa key, and the top ranking among women in her class (a Cornell man beat her for the top spot).

Yet these seeming opposites knew what attracted them to each other. It was certainly not Ruth's unforgettable blue plaid coat, which Marty thoroughly disliked, but rather her "intellectual luminosity" that drew him to her. Add to that a smile of such "stunning radiance" that all her friends found it remarkable. She, in turn, expressed delight in Marty's superb mind, outgoing personality, boundless confidence, and utterly irrepressible sense of humor. Though he failed to pull his weight in their study group on constitutional law, he had been the only student in class to answer correctly Nabokov's quiz about the Jellyby child's "unnaturally *large* head."

Ruth soon replaced the girlfriend at Smith in Marty's affections, but she hesitated about making the relationship a romantic one. If things did not work out, she could lose her most cherished companion. Perhaps she worried that Marty knew her too well. Her insecurities and self-doubts had been apparent to her closest friends in high school. Or she might well have felt that a student who was social chair of Tau Delta Phi, cut classes, and dropped his chemistry major when labs interfered with golf practice showed insufficient concern for his future. Whatever the source of her apprehensions, her persistent suitor had banished all doubts by her junior year.

The couple could be seen together constantly. The twosome walked around Beebe Lake only a short distance from Balch Hall on paths that other lovers had long since made smooth. The lake, resplendent in the fall against the colorful foliage of the maples, was magical in winter when frozen. On a sunny day with snow and the ice buildup on Triphammer Falls sparkling in the background, it became a winter paradise. Marty's gray Chevrolet carried the absorbed pair still farther. They drove along the narrow forty-mile shore of Cayuga Lake, aware, as Ruth put it, that they shared "an intense intellectual and emotional connection." The two also discovered common interests in addition to their love of classical music.

Politically, they were appalled by McCarthyism, which hit close to home. In September 1950, Professor Philip Morrison, a brilliant theoretical physicist at Cornell, had been singled out in the newsletter *Counterattack* as a "member or supporter of various Communist-like activities." A month later, Senator Joseph McCarthy accused Morrison of belonging to subversive organizations. A 1951 report of the House Un-American Activities Committee cited him among those associated "with the current communist peace offensive." Though the American Peace Crusade had not yet appeared on the attorney general's list of subversive organizations, Morrison was an impassioned spokesman. A former graduate student of Robert Oppenheimer's at Berkeley, Morrison had not only worked on the Manhattan Project but actually driven the plutonium-based bomb from the Los Alamos laboratory to the remote desert site west of Alamogordo, New Mexico, where he assembled it for the trial explosion and later helped load another on the *Enola Gay*. Among the first American scientists sent to Hiroshima and Nagasaki to inspect the horrific damage, he returned with a tenacious dedication to nuclear disarmament and peace.

Morrison, like many politically concerned students in the 1930s, had joined the Young Communist League as an undergraduate at Carnegie Institute of Technology and then the Communist Party but drifted away soon after Pearl Harbor. Like many in his Berkeley circle, he saw himself as pulling the New Deal to the left. But his association with such distinguished African Americans as Paul Robeson and W. E. B. Du Bois (both party members) and his opposition to the Korean War and participation in the World Peace Rally in Washington, along with the citation by HUAC, generated negative press coverage for Cornell. Subpoenaed by the Senate Internal Security Subcommittee in 1953, Morrison talked about his own activities; however, he refused to name others. Calls for the physicist's immediate dismissal poured in from outraged trustees, among them B. F. Goodrich's president, John Collyer, as well as other alumni who viewed communism as the paramount threat to national security. For a university with a strong tradition of academic freedom, a politically active student body, and a campus newspaper that closely followed both the Korean War and McCarthyism, there was no escaping the cross fire, especially when Professor Marcus Singer, another popular professor, received a subpoena from HUAC.

Singer, a highly regarded neurobiologist and the first scientist in the United States to induce limb regeneration in frogs, spoke openly about a Marxist study group he had joined in the 1940s while at Harvard, as well as his break from the party in 1945. "My loyalties always were and always will be with my country," he explained. "We were not subversives, sir. We didn't follow only slavist policy. We were intellectuals. We were scholars. We were pursuing a right." But when pressed to provide names of other members of the group, Singer refused, claiming "his honor and conscience" would not allow him to inform.

Indicted for contempt in 1954, Singer, like Morrison, was relieved of his teaching duties but allowed to continue his research. Unlike their less fortunate counterparts at other colleges and universities, neither was fired. Nevertheless, the episode—anguishing for the defendants, especially Singer, who lacked the support from his department that Morrison enjoyed—left a deep imprint on students who collected funds for Singer's trial. Marty and Ruth lamented that constitutional guarantees of freedom of speech and assembly no longer seemed to matter.

. . .

YET EVEN THE DEEP SHADOW of McCarthyism could not repress the couple's delight in each other. When they were enrolled in the same courses, Marty's natural competitiveness created a challenge satisfying to both as he tried to outscore her. "He was the only guy I ever dated who cared whether I had a brain," she declared, adding emphatically,

"He was just so damn smart." They were determined to share careers, although they were not yet sure in what field, so that "there would be something [to] talk about together," someone to "bounce ideas off of," and each would know what the other was doing. Whatever they did, Marty insisted, they would do it together.

Ruth encouraged Marty to choose law, too. Yet despite his lapsed chemistry major, he had not entirely ruled out medicine. Business school was also a possibility, but Harvard Business School would not admit women, and his bride-to-be refused to settle for the substitute provided by Radcliffe's Management Training Program. The two programs, she concluded, were simply not equivalent in what they offered in training and prestige—a harbinger of the kind of equality-conscious assessment that would mark her later career. That left Harvard Law School because Ruth had no interest in medicine. Marty followed her lead.

By Christmas vacation, the couple had become engaged, to the delight of her relatives who rejoiced in her obvious happiness and good match. Now that she was to be married, they could finally relax about her decision to go to law school and concentrate instead on the engagement party. Aunt Buddy chose the legendary Plaza Hotel as the perfect setting for a glamorous occasion. The future bride's Cornell roommates focused less on the neoclassical splendor of the Persian Room than on how "radiant" their friend looked. Her blue outfit brought out the blue in her blue-green eyes. Marty's pals remembered the bride-to-be as "that serious, blonde woman" who had little interest in small talk and expressed with "constant clarity" what was truly important to her. Ruth, who loved to dance, found her best partner not in her fiancé but in her future father-in-law. "He was the very best dancer I've ever danced with," she declared.

Marty's enthusiasm for dual careers suggested that he was an extraordinary suitor—a man ahead of his time. But how to explain his proto-feminism? According to his fiancée, neither of them thought about social conventions concerning men's or women's roles. The difference of which they were most conscious, she insisted, had to do with being a Jew or gentile. Nor did Ruth think her future mother-in-law was responsible for her son's progressive attitudes. Perhaps it was his enormous self-confidence that allowed him to see life as full of possibility rather than as a set of constraining gender norms. More likely, the future groom was simply secure enough, smart enough, and ardent enough to figure out what it would take to win the hand of his lady. He was prepared to follow through long term, negotiating whatever it would take to make the relationship work.

Ruth's first thought was to start their life together as soon as possible. She had completed all her required courses for graduation by the end of her junior year and was ready to move out of her sorority house and on to her legal education. Perhaps she could double register her senior year, enrolling at Cornell Law School, along with the first-year law students. She could then graduate with her Cornell class and join Marty and his second-year class at Harvard Law the following fall. But Harvard

Ruth and Marty after their engagement party held in the Persian Room of the Plaza Hotel, New York City, December 27, 1953.

dashed that plan. The first year had to be done in Cambridge, not Ithaca. Despite the initial disappointment, compensations awaited. She would move out of the sorority house into one of the senior dormitories where, as her freshman suite mates Irma Rubenberg and Anita Zicht recalled, personal friendships readily crossed religious and ethnic boundaries. A full year at Cornell would allow her to explore more art history, music, and literature. There were also other exceedingly pleasant discoveries, among them Marty's parents.

· · ·

THE SENIOR GINSBURGS, Morris and Evelyn, lived in the upscale community of Rockville Centre on Long Island. Their spacious home was situated at the edge of the Rockville Centre Golf Course and Country Club, from which they, as Jews, were barred. Thirty-seven Dogwood Lane had a vibrancy that the small downstairs apartment in Flatbush had lacked during Celia's long illness. The Ginsburg residence resounded with the sounds of Marty's lively younger siblings and the constant talk about golf by parents and son.

Morris, Ruth soon learned, had gone from a stockroom boy with an eighth-grade education to vice president of Federated Stores, a department store chain. A prominent figure in business as well as community circles, he was a risk taker and an institution builder. The new synagogue and the Cold Spring Country Club both counted him as a founding member. Marty's father, Ruth soon concluded, "was really a wonderful individual: very bright, very handsome, very enterprising, very, very outgoing." He was also an "absolutely superb listener." In fact, "Father," as she would soon call him, would say, "I know what I know. If I go somewhere and talk about myself, I don't learn anything. If I listen to other people, more likely than not, I will find out something I didn't know." Listening, Ruth decided, was not only an art but a mark of intelligence.

These parents, so different from her own, immediately reached out to the serious young woman who had given their son new motivation, recognizing that she was the best thing that had happened to him. This was no small compliment coming, as it did, from Evelyn, who was as wrapped up in her only son as she was in her daily golfing. Quickly incorporating Ruth into the family, Morris and Evelyn immediately offered her the emotional support and encouragement that her own father had been too devastated to provide. Morris used his connections to find his future daughter-in-law summer work in the shop of Abraham & Straus, a retail chain that had a Long Island store. He also got Nathan a job as a haberdasher in a Flatbush store, managing to help him without offending his pride.

When Marty telegraphed his parents, asking them to book passage for two for June 24, 1954, on an ocean liner for Europe, Morris and Evelyn knew that a wedding was at hand. Everyone agreed that the Ginsburgs' Long Island home was the perfect place for the ceremony. By limiting attendance to relatives—eighteen in all—the couple could save on wedding costs, traditionally paid by the bride's family, and could instead have an extended honeymoon abroad, which the groom or his family traditionally underwrote.

The marriage took place on June 23, 1954, shortly after the bride's graduation from college. Ruth had indeed found her "life partner," a man so much in love with her and so talented and blessed with self-confidence that he would never be threatened by his wife's accomplishments. She also acquired, somewhat to her surprise, a bridesmaid when Claire, Marty's younger sister, decided to walk down the stairs behind Ruth and stood under the chuppah (wedding canopy) just as the ceremony was about to start. Though Celia was not there to embrace her daughter, Ruth had gained exceptionally devoted in-laws. As substitute parents, they would use money at their disposal to help the newlyweds do things they could not otherwise have afforded to do.

The elder Ginsburgs, in turn, had gained an older daughter with far more ambition and determination than suggested by either her glamorous engagement photograph or its quintessentially 1950s counterpart, the demure sweater-clad bride-to-be, her eyes cast down decorously. Evelyn even took her new daughter aside on her wedding day and placed in her hand a pair of earplugs. Explaining the secret of a happy marriage, she advised, "It helps sometimes to be a little deaf." Ruth took note of the advice, coming as it did from the woman whom she now called "Mother." Sealing her membership in the Ginsburg family, Evelyn and Morris made their wedding gift to their daughter-in-law a set of golf clubs.

The honeymooners left for a long automobile tour of Western Europe. Armed with the bride's notes from her art history courses, they drove through England, France, Switzerland, and Italy, stopping wherever there was something she particularly wanted to see.

. . .

THE COUPLE'S RETURN BROUGHT an abrupt change of scenery as they traveled from Paris to New York to Lawton, Oklahoma. When the Korean War heated up, Marty figured that if he had to serve in Korea, he would go as an officer and reluctantly signed up for another two years in ROTC. In the waning weeks of the war, he received orders to report to Fort Sill, Oklahoma, the principal artillery base in the United States. Law school would have to be deferred for two years—a diversion that proved to be a blessing in disguise. "We had nearly two whole years," Marty recalled, "far from school, far from career pressures, and far from relatives, to learn about each other and begin to build a life."

At artillery school, Lieutenant Ginsburg proved to be a natural at gunnery. Given his expertise at math, trigonometry came easily to him. And as an avid golfer since the age of twelve, he knew how to gauge his mark. As his wife recounted, "He would look at the target as the last shell burst and say, 'It's a five iron away.' His ability to judge distances and adjust fire power was phenomenal," she recalled. "He ended up the top man in his class at the artillery school." Indeed, he was so good as a cannoneer that rather than being sent overseas, he was assigned to teach gunnery for the remainder of his tour of duty.

For the next two years, home was Artillery Village. Using housing for married officers, along with other facilities on the post, seemed a little like living in a socialist state, observed the new Mrs. Ginsburg. The couple resided in an attached house subsidized by the U.S. Army, shopped at the commissary for food (sold at lower prices than off the base), bought liquor that was not otherwise available in a dry state, received medical care for a minimal fee from a post doctor, swam at the Officers' Club in an Olympic-size swimming pool, and played golf on a decent course at no cost. Other Ivy League graduates provided a circle of good friends. The only drawback was that there were few jobs available for wives.

After working briefly as a clerk-typist at the post supply office, Ruth took a comparable job in the Social Security Office in Lawton. She was overqualified, but no matter; they needed the income. And it offered an opportunity to better the shabby treatment of Native Americans in the area, if only she could figure out how. Sensitized to prejudice and to the plight of those less fortunate by her childhood orphanage treks, she found the treatment of African Americans and Indians appalling. Needy Indians seeking benefits were routinely turned away by Social Security workers. The reason cited was inadequate proof of age. Many lacked birth certificates because Native American births often were not recorded. A catch-22, it allowed bureaucratic regulations to mask prejudice and deny legitimate need.

Ginsburg's sense of justice was deeply offended that an agency of the government, created to help citizens, should treat those seeking help so inequitably, not to say callously. It was "just plain old nastiness," she concluded. Because the whole matter lay beyond her control, she could not help making it the topic of dinner conversation. Birth dates on fishing licenses or drivers' licenses should be acceptable substitutes, she decided. So she quietly certified those who were otherwise qualified.

At home, the couple shared cooking responsibilities, with Ruth on duty during the week and Marty taking over on weekends and for guests. In the late spring, the bride's cousin Richard sent Marty an English-language copy of the legendary French chef Auguste Escoffier's cookbook, knowing precisely which of the new Mrs. Ginsburg's talents needed vast improvement. Marty reckoned that if he could perform lab experiments in chemistry, he could follow directions in a cookbook. After all, his mother had never been a cook either, though she had taught her daughter-in-law a few essentials. Beginning with basic stocks, he worked his way through much of Escoffier's repertoire, never suspecting that he would one day be as renowned for his culinary talent as for his mastery of tax law and his ability to put together corporate mergers. What he did know was that there would be fewer dinners of his wife's overdone pork chops and gray tuna casseroles.

After dinner, the newlyweds often spent their evenings reading aloud to each other from Pepys, Tolstoy, Dickens, and even Spinoza, although the philosopher was tougher fare. Tolstoy, Nabokov's favorite author, was Ruth's first choice. The couple also took a correspondence course in accounting—a skill the budding tax expert in the family wanted to acquire—and they entertained guests. One of Marty's fellow officers remembered many evenings in which the three would discuss cases his host recalled from his first year at Harvard Law. Equally memorable was

Ruth's total involvement in the discussions. She had visited Marty's Saturday classes on occasional trips to Cambridge during her senior year at Cornell and found the Socratic question-and-answer dialogue between professor and students invigorating.

Often the couple listened to opera, borrowing records from the collection at the post's library. Toscanini's recording of *La traviata* had long been a favorite of Ruth's. When the Met went on tour, the pair drove to Dallas for a weekend of performances. In preparation, the two studied librettos and played and replayed the music for a month beforehand. For Ruth, it was the continuation of a well-established love affair with opera. Marty's grandfather had worked in an opera house in Odessa, Russia, and his parents held season tickets for the New York Metropolitan Opera. Ruth pursued the subject with such emotional and intellectual passion that she would one day be photographed as a "supernumerary" in a Washington National Opera production of *Ariadne auf Naxos,* Richard Strauss's tale of a party hosted by the richest man in Vienna. Costumed in an elegant white nineteenth-century gown and headdress, she and other guests at the party watched a comedy troupe perform an opera based on the story of the grief-stricken Ariadne, who had been abandoned by her lover on the Greek island of Naxos. That memorable evening, however, was well in the future. More immediate was an event for which she was far less prepared—childbirth.

· · ·

THE MONTHS OF WAITING had more than their share of anxiety. A local physician in Lawton, detecting complications, advised terminating the pregnancy. A telephone conversation with Evelyn and Morris immediately quashed that possibility. Evelyn took charge, setting up an appointment for her daughter-in-law with an excellent ob-gyn during the couple's brief Christmas trip home. They returned to Oklahoma with the understanding that the expectant mother would fly to Rockville Centre in June, a month before the anticipated date of birth. Marty flew in briefly for the birth of their daughter, Jane, on July 21, 1955.

Though the new mother cradled her baby, nothing she did kept Jane from crying incessantly, leaving Ruth desperate for sleep. After five weeks with Evelyn and Morris, she concluded she had to get back to her husband. A local pediatrician finally advised the young mother to dilute

The newlyweds during Ruth's pregnancy, Fort Sill, Oklahoma, fall 1955.

the last of the many formulas she had tried by cutting it in half. The crying stopped instantly. For Ruth, who had no firsthand experience with infant siblings, even knowing where to bathe her daughter when she returned was a puzzle—one that her more knowledgeable husband easily solved by proposing the kitchen sink. From the moment of Jane's first immersion in a warm bath, she was exposed to her parent's world of culture. When Marty got up for the baby's two o'clock feeding, he played classical music, hoping that Jane would drink in a love of Mozart and Beethoven as she sucked on her bottle.

As Ruth cared for her daughter, she thought carefully about her own future. With their days at Fort Sill nearing an end, she had to make a critical decision. She and Marty had agreed on shared careers before their marriage, and that was what she desperately wanted. But in an era when motherhood was thought to involve intense and exclusive devotion to one's children, she wondered if she could still pursue a demanding professional life as a lawyer. Celia's devoted mothering was firmly implanted as a model.

Did she really have an aptitude for the law? True, she could write with great precision, analyze problems clearly, and argue effectively, but was that enough? What were the alternatives? She loved music, but her ability as a pianist was modest. As for her real passion, opera, her recurrent nightmare was that she was onstage, her mouth opened for her great aria, and the sounds that came out were not the mellifluous tones she anticipated but her own hopelessly inadequate voice. Clearly a musical career was not an option. Moreover, her original desire to use the law to make a difference had powerful appeal. But could she do it with a child?

Family discussions helped clarify her dilemma. Nathan still feared his daughter would be unable to support herself as a lawyer. Morris was quite confident that his son would be an adequate provider. If his daughter-in-law chose to stay at home with her baby, he assured her, no one would fault her decision. On the other hand, if she *really* wanted to be a lawyer, Morris advised, a child should be no obstacle. She should stop feeling sorry for herself and go for it.

Evelyn added her support. Giving up a golf game in order to be with her first grandchild would be no sacrifice, especially when the couple returned to New York. Ruth would soon discover what an extraordinary mother-in-law she had. Evelyn "was just there when I needed her," Ginsburg recalled, and she never interfered or made emotional demands.

The elder Ginsburgs also contributed in other ways. When Harvard Law School found out that the Miss Bader to whom they awarded a scholarship was now Mrs. Ginsburg, she was asked to supply her father-in-law's financial statements. Ruth was incensed. "If a male student were in a comparable situation, would the Law School ask for the financial statement of the wife?" She seriously doubted that the Law School would revoke his fellowship when he married, holding his wife's father financially responsible. Though the implication might have been unintentional, the request also implied that her position as a wife was more relevant than her own merit as a student. But because there was nothing she could do to alter the ruling, she gratefully accepted Morris's offer to pay her tuition. Eventually, she came to appreciate Harvard's position that need should take precedence, though she continued to insist that it was fundamentally "wrong not to treat married men the same way"— another early indication of what was to become a lifelong commitment to gender equality.

The ever-supportive Morris simply regarded payment of his daughter-in-law's tuition as an emphatic vote of confidence in her future as a lawyer. Nor were tuition payments the extent of his aid. When Ruth began searching for housing near the Law School, Morris and Evelyn saw no reason why the young couple should have to make do in a dingy, dark Cambridge apartment when, with some financial assistance, they could afford more attractive accommodations. Once his daughter-in-law found a suitable apartment, Morris promptly provided the couple not only with additional money for rent in an apartment building on Garden Street but also with a credit card for gasoline and a charge card for the best restaurant in Boston. "A remarkable man, he never made us feel obligated," Ruth recalled admiringly. "It was a matter of sharing with the family when Father and Mother felt we needed their help the most. They were always wonderfully generous and supportive, never worrying about accumulating a large estate after they died."

Marty, enthusiastic as ever about their dual career path, delighted in moving his family back to the East Coast in the summer of 1956. He would now be able to resume his own studies, and his wife would be one of nine women in a class of 552 students. *She* would make the *Harvard Law Review,* he told friends. Ruth listened quietly, grateful for her husband's confidence. Yet she understood why Marty's classmates dismissed his prediction. Her sex, diminutive stature, and motherhood did not accord with the image of the academic supermen who typically ran the prestigious journal.

Did she really have the intellectual horsepower to make it in the nation's top law school? she wondered. The dean of the Law School had already greeted the first-year class with his customary warning: "Harvard Law School has no glee club. The next three years are mine."

CHAPTER 3

Learning the Law on Male Turf

When the Ginsburgs arrived back in Cambridge, Erwin N. Griswold was already halfway into his twenty-one-year stint as dean of Harvard Law School (HLS). He was a short, stocky midwesterner with an authoritative, gruff manner, and his reputation as a "giant of legal history," a master of tax law, and a gifted administrator and fund-raiser extended far beyond the Law School quadrangle. His domain included Langdell Hall, Austin Hall, which housed the august James Barr Ames Courtroom, where the Ames competition was held, along with the Gropius-designed dormitory at Harkness Commons. That it constituted "the legal equivalent of Mount Everest" provoked debate at Yale. But Harvard's dean, along with his faculty, remained supremely confident that the school yielded to none in its preeminence at turning out graduates who could "think like lawyers."

· · ·

TEACHING FIERCELY PROFESSIONAL STANDARDS to the nation's finest—which, as recently as 1950, had meant men only—did not fit easily in 1956 with the reality of an HLS student in a skirt with a fourteen-month-old baby in tow. Indeed, the nine women in the first-year class might well have wondered if, in Griswold's mind, Harvard Law students still came in only one sex. Although the school had begun admitting women on his watch—one of the last to do so in the nation—there was not a single woman on the faculty. Soia Mentschikoff, the first woman to teach in the Law School for a year as a visiting professor, had come and gone—the academic equivalent of Rosie the Riveter, whose contribution was no longer required at war's end.

Erwin Griswold, dean of Harvard Law School from 1946 to 1967.

Illustrative of the chilly climate that would persist during years of tokenism for women, Griswold routinely fixed his penetrating gaze on each first-year woman, asking, "Why are you at Harvard Law School, taking a place that could have gone to a man?" He posed the question each year at an obligatory dinner of blandly stewed chicken and lima beans hosted by his wife, Harriet, at the couple's home in Belmont. Seated in a semicircle in the living room, along with a handful of faculty members and guests, each new woman feared the dreaded moment when she had to respond with a suitably profound answer. In retrospect, Ginsburg charitably termed the no-win question "an attempt at humor," ignoring the sexism implied. At the time, however, she regarded the entire episode as a source of acute embarrassment.

Ginsburg's anxiety was further heightened because of who else was there. Her escort was an eminent visitor from Columbia Law School, Professor Herbert Wechsler, former chief legal adviser to the U.S. judges at the Nuremberg trial of Nazi war criminals and a key contributor to the final Nuremberg judgment. As a highly successful expert in both constitutional and criminal law, Wechsler would win a landmark Supreme Court victory in 1964 for *The New York Times* in a First Amendment case that substantially enlarged the freedom of the press. Meanwhile, he burnished his reputation as a distinguished scholar who engaged with the real world. His current preoccupation involved compiling a model penal code for the American Law Institute that would guide state legislatures in the process of rewriting their criminal laws. How, Ginsburg wondered, would she, a "lowly first year student," dare to make small talk with such an illustrious dinner partner? Wechsler, who was her professor of criminal law, seemed to combine "the power and mien of the Greek gods Zeus and Apollo." How could she possibly converse with him intelligently?

To make matters worse, when she stood up to respond to the dean's question, she forgot that she had a full ashtray in her lap. "I watched in horror as butts and ashes spilled onto the Griswolds' carpet," she recalled. "But the host seemed not to notice. Then I managed to mumble something about my husband being in the second-year class and thinking it important for a wife to understand her husband's work."

At the time, Ginsburg wanted only to say something "that would not be considered confrontational"—something that would not call more attention to herself than she already had attracted by creating that "dreadful" ash-covered spot on the carpet. She succeeded inasmuch as her answer did not provoke. It was perfectly pitched to the ethos of an era in which a wife of a successful man made his career advancement her career goal. But it could hardly have provided comfort to the dean if, as Ginsburg now maintains, he hoped to elicit answers that would convince the holdouts on the faculty who still doubted the wisdom of admitting "the second sex"—the interpretation that the dean himself provided in his memoir.

Whatever Griswold's intention, Ginsburg's response to the infamous question was not the whole truth. Nor was that of a bolder classmate who replied, "Dean Griswold, there are nine of us; well, really only eight because Ruth Ginsburg doesn't count for this purpose. There are 500-odd of them. What better place to get a man?" Clearly the gruff, reserved dean, with his stern expression, had not succeeded in creating an occasion where the token women felt free to voice their own aspirations, even if his motivation was as untainted by sexism as he claimed. Ruth Bader had wanted a legal education so *she* could make a difference. Promoting Marty's career was a gratifying but secondary objective.

. . .

NOR WAS THIS the only hint that the Law School, like the rest of the university, still remained male turf. Cornell's library had separate entrances for men and women, but Lamont, the undergraduate library at Harvard where old periodicals were kept, was designated for men only. The restriction meant little until Ginsburg's second year, when late one night she needed to use the collection of aging magazines and journals to check a footnote in an article. She pleaded with the guard to bring the journal to the door; she just needed to take a look at it, she explained. He refused. In the end, she had to ask a male classmate to do the job.

And there were other annoyances. The men bestowed derogatory nicknames upon their female classmates. Ginsburg's were "Ruthless Ruthie" and, she later learned, "Bitch." "Better Bitch than Mouse," she responded. Some professors, who normally ignored the women in their classes, would periodically hold "Ladies Day." The attitude of the faculty members engaging in this sport, Ginsburg remembers, was "Let's call on the women for comic relief." The male students bought into it, laughing and stamping their feet. A similarly insidious activity involved filling in the names of women to denote incompetent parties in hypothetical cases. If the case involved rape, there was no waiting until "Ladies Day"; they were interrogated about the most intimate details—an experience that Ginsburg was spared. In an era when sexual harassment was unnamed and professorial authority unchallenged, female students, no matter how embarrassed, concluded they were being trained to keep their wits intact and emotions under control.

Though the professors with whom Ginsburg studied did not indulge in such sport, she was always aware that the few female students stood out; they could never slouch down in their seats behind a taller class-mate or hide in the back of the room as men could. Ginsburg's visibility, she believed, made it imperative that she always be prepared. It was not that she minded being asked questions; she found the Socratic method of teaching law "tremendously engaging." Dialogue between professor and students proved much better than sitting passively through a dull lecture. Even when another student was responding, the constant inter-change kept her mind from wandering. As faculty laid out the complex-ity of contracts, torts, or civil procedure, she recognized immediately that some of her professors were extraordinary, spicing their interroga-tion with wit and timing.

What she did wish for was a women's room in Langdell Hall. If nature called, she made a "mad dash" of nearly a block to Austin Hall. Built in 1883, the building contained an overheated janitor's closet that had been converted to a bathroom. Asbestos dripped from the ceiling. An inconvenience under ordinary circumstances, the distance proved agonizing during an exam when every minute counted. After frantically running the circuit, she would fervently hope that there would be no repeat trip until the exam was over.

Yet despite the testosterone-charged atmosphere pervading the institution—and the scarcity of bathrooms for women—Harvard Law had much to offer its students intellectually. The school stood at the epicenter of a shift in the approach to law, lawmaking, and especially judicial review. The method later came to be known as "process theory" or "process jurisprudence." Ginsburg's thinking would be profoundly affected.

· · ·

PROCESS THEORY, which dominated legal thinking at the time, was first and foremost an offshoot of legal realism, a movement of the 1920s and 1930s, whose mother church was Yale. Legal realists rejected the notion that law consisted of formal rules that could be automatically applied. Instead, they insisted, social, political, and economic forces influenced the legal system. In turn, private and public law shaped societal conditions. Contrary to what law schools had long taught, law was not a matter of fixed rules, nor were judges totally neutral, especially in cases where the law was not clear. Such thinking captivated lawyers, especially New Dealers, who felt that law at the time was out of touch with society and the modern world. Yet few were prepared to carry legal realism to its ultimate conclusion—to say that law was *just* politics, or economics, or the personal whim of judges.

Such reluctance was dramatically reinforced by the perversion of law by totalitarian regimes before and during World War II, as well as by the challenges of the Cold War. Surely law involved more than the whims of a Hitler or Stalin. Could the necessary criteria be developed to ensure that judges would reach decisions objectively, not subjectively? These questions, though systemic and jurisprudential in nature, had been addressed by Justices Holmes and Brandeis when they defended freedom of speech against government repression and an overzealous citizenry during World War I. For legal scholars after World War II searching for a way to inject some standards into legal realism, the questions were paramount.

The emerging civil rights movement soon pushed the issue beyond academia into intense public debate. In moving the Supreme Court to its landmark decision in *Brown v. Board of Education* (1954), civil rights advocates cut to the core question. Was it right for a majority of Supreme Court justices to engage in judicial activism when the two elected branches of government failed to carry through long-overdue reforms? Could their decision be reconciled with democracy? Should the Supreme Court even make policy on civil rights? If so, how could it articulate policy change in a way that would be grounded in the law itself and, therefore, *legally unassailable*?

These questions were particularly tough for a generation of legal scholars who, haunted by memories of an activist conservative Court until 1937, were naturally suspicious of an unconstrained judiciary. Yet these same scholars were also New Dealers wedded to the regulatory state and liberals bent on protecting and enhancing fundamental rights. For them, the challenge became, how could judges play a role in progressive social change without assuming an illegitimate role as a third legislative chamber and inviting a negative response from other political institutions and the public? Could courts extend constitutionally guaranteed rights *and* maintain the integrity of the legal process?

Henry M. Hart Jr., a Harvard Law School alumnus and member of the faculty since 1934, came up with some answers. Steering a fine line between "the two great peaks" of legal formalism and legal realism, Hart emphasized that judges could not make decisions simply by articulating their own policy preferences. Rather, he argued, decisions had to be the result of a *process* of reasoned elaboration of neutral principles, building from authoritative starting points such as statutes, statutory purpose, and judicial precedents. Without this process, the courts would lose legitimacy. Astute lawyers, Hart proposed, would recognize that the decisions being handed down were insufficiently grounded in the law and compromised by poor craftsmanship.

Between 1947 and 1953, Hart gained renown for having "the most carefully worked-out theory of law to appear in teaching materials of that period." With a former student and colleague, Albert Sacks, he continued to revise and expand his course on legislation, and by 1956–57 the pair had produced their landmark text, *The Legal Process: Basic Problems in the Making and Application of Law.* Placing less emphasis on adjudication per se, Hart and Sacks focused on "legislation, negotiation, mediation, arbitration, and management."

More than just a welcome curricular innovation, the substance of the course allowed Hart and Sacks, along with others such as Columbia's Herbert Wechsler, Yale's Alexander Bickel (another Harvard Law School alumnus), the University of Chicago's Philip Kurland, and the legendary judge Learned Hand to contribute to a significant debate on constitutional law throughout the 1950s and 1960s. Process jurisprudence was just reaching its formative peak when Ginsburg arrived at Harvard. Her first year, 1956–57, coincided with the production of Hart and Sacks's landmark text, which, though unpublished, was widely circulated.

· · ·

GINSBURG KNEW that she was intellectually and politically at the right place. Most of the Harvard Law School faculty believed in a dynamic, problem-solving government that respected the law. Like a good many of their counterparts on other law school faculties, they were moderate to mildly left of center: New Deal Democrats, for the most part. The legal process theorists among them generally welcomed the rights-oriented egalitarian thinking of the Warren Court—with two strong provisos. First, the chief justice and his more liberal colleagues must maintain a proper relationship with the other branches of government. Second, their decisions must rest on both articulate, reasoned constitutional analysis and careful legal craftsmanship.

On some key Warren Court decisions, such as *Brown v. Board of Education,* they were prepared to make allowances. Griswold had served as an expert witness for Thurgood Marshall in litigation leading up to that landmark case. Many Harvard faculty members were committed to racial equality—most in principle, a few in practice. Hart had his only child in an integrated public school, while Sacks remained closely identified with the civil rights movement for most of his life. Although both men applauded *Brown,* the two never fully absorbed the extent to which the most critical legal development of the decade—and the insurgency

behind it—undermined basic assumptions of legal process. In rejecting state statutes separating the races, African Americans challenged the
very assumption that legislation is arrived at rationally and objectively.
How, they asked, can law be presumed legitimate and binding when it
fails to serve the interests of *all* citizens?

If stability and consensus dominated the vision of process advocates,
partially obscuring the reality of inequality, process theorists were not
alone. Liberals generally in the 1950s had little room to maneuver once
the Left had been discredited by McCarthyism. Calling attention to
malfunctions in the polity put them at risk of attacks from the Right,
dulling their zest for fundamental change. Issues, once a matter of public debate, disappeared from the radar screen—among them, women's
equality.

Ginsburg suspected few on the Harvard Law School faculty had ever
given gender much thought, yet she was not deterred. A faculty member
she trusted on the issue, Abram Chayes—his wife was a Yale Law graduate who had taken the women in the class of 1959 under her wing—
reassured her that the small number of women at Harvard was the result
not of sex discrimination but of self-selection. The pool of qualified
applicants, Chayes explained, was tiny because it was well known that
women with a law degree had great difficulty finding jobs. Temporarily
satisfied with that explanation, Ginsburg treated the affronts directed
at women students as "petty annoyances." The words "problem" and
"anger" had been effectively banished from her vocabulary under Celia's
tutelage—making her, like many young women of her generation, initially acquiescent when confronted by what, in retrospect, was clear evidence of gender discrimination.

Minimizing sexism proved easier than managing her own doubts
about her ability in the presence of so many high achievers. Particularly
memorable was the presence of a remarkable classmate who had come to
Harvard Law for a year as a Nieman fellow in journalism. The first day
of her civil procedure class, he spoke "brilliantly." Initially intimidated,
Ruth confided to Marty at dinner, "If that's what they're all like, I'll
never make the grade in this place." But Marty was reassuring, and his
wife resolved to match the standard set by the future *New York Times*
legal analyst and columnist Anthony Lewis.

At times, the fierce competitiveness permeating the Harkness dormitories and Langdell Hall became almost too intense for some students to bear (legend had it that if one light went on in Harkness in the middle of the night, others immediately followed). But Ginsburg was not among them. She knew she could always retreat to her garden apartment, located in the residential complex just behind the Radcliffe College dormitories. The short walk home was pleasant—just the right distance from the Law School.

Fortunately, the demands of parenting proved easier to handle than she had feared. Her earlier queries about sitters had yielded the information she needed. Told that a young couple in Cambridge with a two-year-old were divorcing and giving up their nanny, Ruth wasted no time. "A wonderful New England grandmother type" took care of Jane until four in the afternoon when "Mommy" came home. Mommy then became a master of diversion techniques as she played with the energetic toddler until it was time to tuck her snugly in bed after her bedtime stories. Then began a long evening of study. Preparing for Benjamin Kaplan's civil procedure class became a pleasure.

Kaplan provided Ginsburg with a model of a superb law professor. A brilliant legal thinker who, as a young lieutenant colonel, developed the legal theories framing the indictments used by the Supreme Court justice Robert H. Jackson at the Nuremberg war crimes trials, Kaplan later served as reporter to the Advisory Committee on Civil Rules for the Judicial Conference of the United States. He was a "wise, witty" wordsmith extraordinaire, and his mastery of Socratic teaching kept his students engaged but never humiliated, Ginsburg recalled. He "would often rephrase the answer crisply, shoring up the responder's confidence and strengthening the grasp of the entire class." Questions as to which cases courts are empowered to decide, how cases are presented and processed, and the effects of judgments had never been a turn-on for first-year students. But Kaplan's new casebook, which began with an overview of the various phases of litigation, allowed her to grasp how the rules of civil procedure functioned to secure "the just, speedy, and inexpensive determination" of controversies. Under his guidance, cases and hypotheticals came alive. By the end of the course, she was hooked. Civil procedure would remain a major interest of Ginsburg's, and Benjamin Kaplan's mastery of the field would continue to guide her. So would his emphasis on precision and craftsmanship.

Not all her professors and classmates elicited the admiration she accorded Wechsler and Kaplan. But Ginsburg labored steadily, her days lightened only by her intervals in the park with Jane and their evening playtime together. Then "Mommy's" law books were reopened. The months of hard work were enlivened by the camaraderie of the classmates in her study group. Often their shared grappling with the complexities of law was eased by Marty's excellent dinners, sometimes topped off with a chocolate soufflé for dessert.

Weekends provided a break in the routine: dinner out was followed by theater; tickets were sold on campus at a discount. Opera took precedence when the Met's traveling company came to Boston. There were also small parties, the Ginsburgs often arriving with Jane in tow. As word of Marty's culinary talent spread, the couple began entertaining friends.

The only unsettling aspect of this regime was that Ruth had no clear sense of how well she was doing; there were no papers, no grades, no progress reports, just the looming end-of-the-year finals, which consisted of "long, hypothetical fact-situations, with the instructions to spot the legal issues, specify the relevant legal rules, and apply them." Surrounded by students whom she considered so extraordinarily intelligent, Ginsburg, like many first-year students in this "law school as boot camp" environment, worried about her class standing. Moot court, which was considered very important at Harvard, had not gone as well as she had hoped. Her oral argument was fine, but the student judges had given her brief a low grade. Dismayed, Ruth had asked her torts professor, Calvert Magruder, to read it. To her immense relief, he replied that her argument was very plausible and that she had done a good job. The commendation was reassuring, coming as it did from someone with such a distinguished record as a U.S. District Court and Appeals Court judge. Her more astute classmates had no doubts about the ability of the young woman they remember as above all "intelligent."

· · ·

IN FACT, when ratings were released at the end of her first year, Ginsburg turned out to be very near the top of her class. She could credit her success to her own intellect and to the unrelenting pursuit of excellence first encouraged by her mother. She also had another essential asset that she was the first to acknowledge—the aid of an adoring and ever-supportive husband. Marty shared the shopping, cooking, and other household and child-care chores. More important, she insisted, he "believed in me more than I believed in myself." As she explained, "He was always so secure within himself that he never regarded me [and what I might accomplish] as a threat." What she might also have added was that he provided an intellectual sounding board off which she could freely bounce ideas, confident that she would get honest, constructive feedback.

There was also one other factor that might have indirectly contributed to her success, though it did not occur to Ginsburg at the time—the age-old connection between Judaism and the law. The Torah (the five books of Moses) functioned as the original constitution for Jews. In the centuries following their exile from the land of Judea, rabbis and scholars in scattered Jewish communities had to figure out how to apply the Torah and its multiple commandments to seemingly insoluble problems of law and ritual. How could a common standard of behavior be maintained in the face of new sociopolitical, economic, and technological developments?

The result was the Talmud—a body of debates and opinions emphasizing legal argumentation based on the precedent of Mosaic law. Issues were examined from every possible angle, though room was always left for further interpretation in the face of ever-changing circumstances. The pattern of thought and methodology used to create the Talmud two millennia ago is remarkably similar to the kind of thinking demanded in law schools today. Ginsburg herself later elaborated on this theme in the introduction to a book about her Jewish predecessors on the Supreme Court. "For centuries," she explained, "Jewish rabbis and scholars have studied, restudied, and ceaselessly interpreted the Talmud, the body of Jewish law and tradition developed from the scriptures. These studies have produced a vast corpus of Jewish juridical writing that has been prized in that tradition."

Ginsburg never had the intensive Talmudic training given to boys in the Orthodox tradition. Yet religious practice inevitably gives direction to larger arenas of values, attitudes, and behaviors, shaping distinctive thought patterns in a particular culture—even in individuals who never studied Jewish law. Jewish humor, for example, is full of "takeoffs" on the reasoning process used in Talmudic disputes. Ginsburg's natural

aptitude for reasoned and logical argument was almost certainly reinforced by aspects of her background that made it easy to "think like a
lawyer."

That she could indeed think like a lawyer was not lost on her classmates. As her fellow student Thomas Ehrlich observed, "Through the
quiet force of her mind, Ruth seemed better able than the rest of us to
take a problem, to break it into its component parts, to examine each
part, and to put the problem back together again—solved." That, he
added, "was what Harvard Law School was all about, at least in those
days, and Ruth could do the drill with more precision, style, and grace
than the rest of us. . . . I really loved law school," he continued, "and I
think Ruth did too."

. . .

WHATEVER THE SOURCES of Ginsburg's success, one of the benefits
of standing near the top of her class was a coveted place on the *Harvard
Law Review*. "Making" the *Law Review* was no small accomplishment;
working on the prestigious student-edited legal journal was a passport to
future accomplishments. Just as it guaranteed greater attention from the
faculty and recognition of special status by other students, so it served as
a prerequisite for judicial clerkships, a professorial appointment, or other
elite positions upon graduation. Both Ginsburgs were delighted with the
news. Ever the proud spouse, Marty offered to keep Jane at his parents'
home on Long Island while his wife returned to Cambridge two weeks
early from summer recess to start work on the *Law Review*.

Once the academic year began, classmates glimpsed Ginsburg hard
at work on the third floor of Gannett House, while Jane crawled up
and down the worn stairs. The new cohort on the editorial staff quickly
discovered that serving on the *Harvard Law Review* was a full-time job.
First, they were told to check out the advance sheets—reports of decisions
from state and federal courts—and identify cases that might be worth
writing about in a case note. Then the editor gave each new reviewer a
topic to investigate and report back on what had previously been published and whether it merited a note in the *Harvard Law Review*. If the
answer was yes, the prelim writer must explain how the subject might
be redefined so as to focus on matters not previously covered. Next was
the actual writing of case notes. Then, once the next issue was assembled,

The 1957–58 Harvard Law Review *staff, Ruth Bader Ginsburg far right, second row from top.*

everything had to be meticulously checked and rechecked for possible errors as a first printing and then a second one were readied for the final copy.

Payoff for all this work came in the company gathered at Gannett House. Ginsburg discovered that her fellow staffers—who included Richard Goodwin, future special assistant to John F. Kennedy and Lyndon B. Johnson; Indiana University's fifteenth president, Thomas Ehrlich; and Jack Friedenthal, a noted expert on civil procedure and evidence—provided admirable intellectual stimulation, "all . . . one could want." Though sometimes "a bit stuck on themselves," they were "thoughtful, amusing," and generous—ever ready "to share notes, insights and outlines." They, as much as the experience and prestige, were what made being on the *Law Review* such an "all consuming" enterprise.

Other benefits included encountering a different side of the dean. The preeminent guide and inspiration for the *Law Review,* "the Gris," who was always "in and out of the library stacks turning out lights," was each issue's first and most avid reader. His concerns extended to more than his insistence that each new issue be promptly delivered to his office on the tenth of the month, never later. Griswold's dedication to legal scholarship and the most exacting editorial standards made him a "constant if intangible presence in the office." His exactitude, reflected in the demands of the review's editors, made precision second nature, as indeed it became for Ginsburg. Her ability to spot errors "down to the last comma" made her a much sought-after partner with whom to proofread, especially because a long session at the Ginsburgs' apartment often ended with one of Marty's culinary treats.

· · ·

GINSBURG'S SECOND YEAR BROUGHT another intellectual delight— enrollment in Albert Sacks's section of the legal process course. Sacks, Ginsburg discovered, not only believed in equal opportunity for women but also was an inspiring and humane teacher. He never used his section to humiliate or ridicule students. Rather, he treated all members of the class with patience and respect, conveying even the most complicated matters with consummate skill. He illuminated "the nature, uses, limits and interrelationships of different legal processes through stories of spoiled cantaloupes and a spoiled heir, non-litigious employees, burnt

Albert Sacks, another master teacher, who introduced Ginsburg to legal process theory during her second year at Harvard Law School, 1957–58.

bundles, a bashful principal, and dozens more," she recalled. As a professor, the man had "clearly mastered the art of keeping a class alert and engaged" as he demonstrated that the law is "accountable to reason, not fiat." Institutional architecture and procedure mattered, he emphasized, and could be subjected to systematic analysis.

More significant, Ginsburg realized she could now see "the legal universe in fuller scale"—what Sacks and Hart considered the purposiveness of law. The role of multiple lawmaking bodies—their institutional design, jurisdiction, procedures, and relationships to one another—now made perfect sense. She could appreciate the interactive linkages among these institutions and how those connections, in themselves, limited the role of the federal courts. The importance of process in crafting decisions of the courts was also crystal clear. It stood to reason that decisions, even if morally "right," would have no staying power if marked by sloppy craftsmanship, subjectivity, or doctrinally ungrounded activism. The long-term impact of rulings depended on judges' abilities to persuade by the force and excellence of their reasoning. Otherwise, the courts would be undermined by a loss of respect by first-rate lawyers. As Hart told his class, Fats Waller summed it up best: "T'aint Whatcha Do (It's the Way Whatcha Do It)."

"Spellbinding is not an exaggerated description of my appreciation of 'Legal Process,'" Ginsburg recalled. It "guided my thinking about the law." And how could it be otherwise? Thomas Reed Powell spoke not only for himself but for his colleagues when he said, "My emphasis is on process, process, process, on particulars, particulars, particulars, on cases, cases, cases, on the contemporary court, on resolving competing considerations, on watching for practicalities not likely to be expressed in opinions, in which the court pretends that the case is being decided by its predecessors rather than by itself."

But there was more to the appeal of process jurisprudence than the enthusiasm with which it was embraced by Ginsburg's professors. Process jurisprudence was part of the larger intellectual culture of the 1950s. Disillusioned with the ideologies and mass fanaticism that had ravished Europe as well as by anti-Communist excesses at home, scholars in various disciplines looked to the American past. What, they asked, made the American experience "unique"? Minimizing fissures in the national fabric, they focused on consensus in a pluralistic society based on shared democratic values and agreement on the fundamentals of government and the economy. Leadership of the free world demanded an orderly, benign polity, and economic growth promised a larger piece of the pie for everyone.

If the status quo reigned, it was not for long. The conflict-ridden 1960s destroyed the illusion of consensus. Abuses of state power, violations of civil rights and civil liberties, and other inequities of "the affluent society" could no longer be minimized. The sociopolitical conditions underlying the legal process approach eroded. Legal scholars on both the Right and the Left began critiquing basic assumptions of its founding thinkers, notably their optimism and consensus orientation—a practice that had its counterpart in other disciplines.

Yet, as a noted student of American jurisprudence points out, the men with whom Ginsburg studied were not primarily concerned with explaining how the law is. Rather, they focused on "how it ought to be." Regardless of how it might appear to work in reality, "law, from the process perspective," writes Neil Duxbury, "must always be understood in the light of the faith: that is, as an institutionally autonomous activity founded in reason." Other scholars agree that it is the normative appeal of process theory—Hart and Sacks's "optimistic view of citizens as interdependent and law as purposive"—that accounts for its continuing appeal today. Certainly for a young Ruth Ginsburg, attuned by temperament and training to reason and restraint, the appeal of the *ideal* of law, combined with her interest in procedure, made legal process irresistible.

· · ·

THE INTELLECTUAL EXCITEMENT generated by Sacks and her *Law Review* comrades gave way to other concerns in early December 1957 when Marty was involved in an automobile accident. Recovery was quick, but very shortly thereafter he discovered a lump while showering. The concerned couple asked a young doctor, a resident at Massachusetts General Hospital who lived in their building, to perform an examination. He urged Marty to get an appointment immediately with a distinguished urological surgeon at Mass General, Dr. Wyland Leadbetter. The diagnosis was testicular cancer; surgery would have to be followed by massive doses of radiation. The first operation, scheduled immediately after midyear exams in January, would remove the tumor; a second surgery would remove the lymph nodes into which the cancer had spread—four nodes, as it turned out. For Ruth, the words had a painfully familiar ring. The disease that had taken her mother now threatened to take her husband.

Despite the intense emotional stress, Ruth pushed ahead stoically, just as she had done in high school during the long years of Celia's illness. As she held Marty's hand tightly in the hospital, she told herself that after losing her sister and her mother to fatal diseases, *she would not lose her husband; she simply would not let death win again.* This time she would be lucky: Marty would survive. Somehow, through this ordeal, she would once again hold things together. She had the innate toughness. And she had learned during her high school years how to compartmentalize and produce under circumstances that were life threatening for the person she loved most.

Taking charge, she urged her mother-in-law, who had left her own family to help, to return to Long Island. Then she added Marty's share of the household chores to her own. To keep her husband abreast of his classes, she chose a person in each of his courses to keep track of assignments and use carbon paper to make an extra set of notes, which she passed along to the patient. Friends provided bedside tutorials. In order to type Marty's third-year paper while keeping up with her own workload, Ruth was at her book-covered dinner table when her family went to bed; sometimes she was still working when they awoke in the morning. During the day, she was simply too busy to think, "What if he doesn't survive?" and that was how she wanted it.

"We took each day and lived it as best we could," she would say in retrospect, adding, "I grew confident in my ability to juggle that semester." Later she confessed that nights without sleep had made it hard to stay awake in less interesting courses. The psychic toll she kept to herself, as she had following her mother's death.

Meanwhile, her *Law Review* comrades knew only that she got her assignments and turned them in promptly, exactly as Ruth wanted it. As Ronald Loeb recalled, "While she was always cordial and helpful, Ruth was also very effective and efficient. We always had the sense that she organized her time carefully, unlike the rest of us *Law Review* 'bums' who hung around the office all hours of the day and night, complaining about how much work we had to do. While we weren't close friends," he continued, "I certainly don't think I would have forgotten anything as important as Marty's cancer, had she told us about it. But I didn't know Marty then, and I am sure she considered it a private matter, though we surely would have tried to be supportive had we known."

"What I do recall vividly," Loeb added, "is that she set a standard higher than most of us could achieve, but we didn't resent it. She never missed class; was always perfectly prepared; her *Law Review* work was always done on time; she was always beautifully dressed and impeccably groomed; and she had a happy husband and lovely young daughter. And she was always friendly and helpful to the others of us on the review. I think we all had a secret crush on her, although none of us would have admitted it." What Loeb did not realize was that it was the fraternity of *Law Review* "bums" whom Ruth would later credit with helping "me stay on my feet" during the ordeal.

Despite outward appearances, meeting the almost superhuman standards her friends observed while simultaneously dealing with Marty's illness and her own intense anxiety must have been agonizingly difficult. As his recovery progressed, she would later acknowledge that her sense of relief was beyond measure. Her husband had not only survived but, with only two weeks of classes, had made his highest grades ever, graduating magna cum laude. Ruth modestly attributed Marty's success to classmates—his and hers—who had rallied around them, serving as note takers and tutors. It was a display of support, she later noted, that totally belied Harvard Law students' reputation as ruthless competitors.

As for herself, she believed Marty's illness had revealed how much she could accomplish under pressure. She also credited her husband's cancer with changing her life permanently in at least one respect. It made her confront the reality that she would always work; she had a child she might have to support on her own. In fact, Ruth did not need Marty's illness to enhance her commitment to work. Her mother had already seen to that. Beyond her many admonitions to her daughter to be independent, there had been a silent message—that Celia herself would have been far happier working outside the home had a working wife not been thought in those days to reflect badly on her husband's ability to support his family.

Fortunately for Celia's daughter, the role of sole provider was avoided, though it would be several years before Marty received a clean bill of health. When asked about his wife's courage, endurance, and academic accomplishment during his illness, the former patient expressed no surprise. Ruth's performance, he insisted, was precisely "what I had come to expect of her." How much the experience had deepened their love and dedication to each other required no elaboration.

. . .

BY THE CLOSE OF RECRUITING SEASON, Marty had an offer from the Manhattan firm of Weil, Gotshal & Manges, where he had successfully clerked the previous summer. When nothing comparable emerged in Boston, where the couple had hoped to stay at least until Ruth's graduation, the Ginsburgs moved to New York in the summer of 1958.

In working with the future chief judge of the U.S. Tax Court Theodore Tannenwald Jr., Marty Ginsburg discovered his true passion—structuring financial deals to minimize tax costs. In three and a half years—a remarkably short time—he would race to partnership and lay the foundation for his reputation as one of the top tax lawyers in the country and a specialist on mergers, acquisitions, and buyouts. Among friends, he would become as renowned for his sense of humor and exquisite gourmet cooking as for his "creative, deeply intelligent" approach to tax and business issues. During much of his subsequent career, he would also combine private practice with academic appointments at the law schools of New York University, Stanford, Columbia, and finally Georgetown. As if all that were not enough, he added behind-the-scenes consultation with the IRS and the Treasury Department, service on numerous professional boards and committees, professional writing, and of course plenty of golf.

Ruth, meanwhile, coped with the impending move to New York. Could she complete her remaining year at Columbia while receiving her degree from Harvard? She realized that she was asking for special treatment, but she wanted to keep the family together, as she explained to Griswold, hoping he would understand. She did not want to have to speak of her reluctance to ask a husband whom she had nearly lost to cancer to move to New York alone, even if only for a year, when his final prognosis was still so uncertain. Nor would she put into words the psychic impact of the ordeal that they had undergone. But the vice-dean to whom she first made her appeal denied the request, and Griswold refused to overrule him. She had "not made out an adequate case of exigent personal circumstances required for such permission," she was told.

With a summer clerkship already lined up at Paul, Weiss, Rifkind, Wharton & Garrison, a venerable and prestigious New York firm, Ginsburg immediately arranged a transfer to Columbia, where she soon won designation as a Kent scholar—one of five in the class of 1959.

Word of her arrival preceded her. "We heard that the smartest person on the East Coast was going to transfer, and that we were all going to drop down one point," said Nina Appel, a Columbia classmate and later dean of Loyola University Law School in Chicago. Dropping down a point was a small price to pay to add another woman to the token eleven in the class, Appel concluded, especially one with whom she could eat brown bag lunches in the "dark and dank basement lunchroom next to the lockers" in Kent Hall, then the location of the Law School.

Appel found her new classmate, as a person and as the good friend she soon became, to be "quiet, serious, conscientious, and committed." Rejecting the notion that Ginsburg was shy or humorless, Appel emphasized "serious." Ruth, she added, embodied "great character and integrity

Ruth and Martin with their daughter, Jane, aged three, at Martin Ginsburg's parents' house in Rockville Centre, New York, 1958.

as well as innate modesty. Our conversations," she recalled, "even on social occasions, were mainly about the law; after all, we were two of twelve women in a rigorous, highly competitive program with 341 men. That we were ambitious and competitive was a given." She might also have added that she and Ruth were developing a professional identity as well—a process that for women, especially in male-dominated professions, required the personification of seriousness. That Ginsburg was also highly competitive came as no surprise to her old Flatbush neighbor and classmate Richard Salzman. When he saw his former school chum heading to class, he remembers thinking, "God, it's Ruth and she's gonna be first again."

Ginsburg promptly signed up for the noontime seminar on federal courts and the federal system co-taught by her former criminal law professor Herbert Wechsler and Gerald Gunther, a young Harvard Law alumnus whom Columbia had hired to teach constitutional law and federal jurisdiction. Students described the course, already oversubscribed, as "grueling." And Wechsler they considered "notorious" for posing long, complicated, multipart questions. Yet Ginsburg, her old schoolmate recalled, replied with equally long, complicated, multipart answers. "Then, like a coda, she would add a polite mention of factors Wechsler had left out," Salzman recounted.

Wechsler, who, like Hart and Sacks, was a leading process scholar, did not disappoint in their second encounter. He did upset Ginsburg, however, with his Holmes Lecture at Harvard that year, "Toward Neutral Principles of Constitutional Law." Wechsler criticized the Warren Court's reasoning in its famous school desegregation decision, among other rulings. He insisted that *how* justices decided cases was as important as *what* they decided. Despite her training in process theory, she would not concede that the process of decision was *always* as important as substance, as Wechsler seemed to believe. Still, she found her former professor to be as "awesome and inspiring" as ever. Hart and Wechsler's *Federal Courts and the Federal System* proved to be "the most engaging text assigned in my law school years." The course she described as "extraordinary."

Praise flowed in both directions. Ginsburg impressed Wechsler; she had an even greater impact on Gunther. Describing her as a "sensitive young student" of unusually "somber demeanor," Gunther would always

remember how transformed she could become by "one of the most radiant smiles that I have ever encountered." Not least, she "possessed a
mind second to none," he insisted. "Penetrating," "thoughtful," "open
minded," and "fair," Ruth, he concluded, was also "exceedingly modest."

Such traits earned Ginsburg the loyalty of her classmates on the
Columbia Law Review. Knowing she had earned a place on the *Harvard
Law Review*, the editor offered her a position as a "professional courtesy."
Staff members soon discovered that their new colleague was "friendly,
unassuming, and had a good sense of humor." As Edmund Kaufman
recalled, "Ruth never referred to how things were done at Harvard; she
just fit in perfectly and pitched in immediately." In addition to being
a "superb editor" of work that second-year students were turning out,
she also displayed "a zeal for scholarship, craftsmanship, and inclination
toward perfection." That, combined with comparable qualities in a couple of other key editors, yielded some of the best issues that the review
had ever published. Kaufman's sentiments, shared by law review staffers
at both Harvard and Columbia, were a tribute to Ginsburg's friendliness
and helpfulness—qualities that both Celia and thirteen years at summer
camp had undoubtedly nurtured. True to predictions, when grades were
announced at the end of the year, she had tied for first place in her class.

· · ·

OFF CAMPUS, Ginsburg discovered that social life did not revolve
around the Law School as it had in Cambridge. Some students lived
in boroughs distant from the campus and returned home at the end of
the day. The city itself was a distraction for many, as indeed it became
for the arts-loving Ginsburgs. The student in the family found time to
play hostess to Marty's younger sister, Claire, whom she delighted in
introducing to Manhattan's teeming restaurants and movie theaters.
Nor was the youngest member of the family neglected. Happily situated in Greenhouse Nursery School, conveniently located next to the
Law School, Jane flourished—so much so that Ginsburg could not resist
teaching her to read.

Following Celia's example, mother and daughter not only read stories
together but trooped off to children's plays. Nor could any child of this
opera-loving couple go unexposed to her parents' musical passion. At
an Amato performance of *Il trovatore,* Ginsburg recalled, "Jane stood

up in the middle, screaming at the top of her lungs because she felt she could do as well as the soprano on the stage." Perhaps she had rushed her daughter a bit—at least where grand opera was concerned. But it was hard not to be overzealous, given her own love of music. Introducing Jane to the arts was part of Ruth's definition of being a good mother, honoring the memory of her own mother in the process.

New York was an opera lover's paradise. Marty's parents had provided a subscription to the Metropolitan Opera upon their son's return to the city, and the young Ginsburgs attended religiously during the season. Arranging for one of their many Barnard College sitters to stay with Jane at the apartment at 404 West 116th Street, Ruth also occasionally attended rehearsals at the City Center, where Julius Rudel conducted the New York City Opera with another Brooklynite holding center stage— the ebullient soprano Beverly Sills. Now and then the couple squeezed in an evening at the theater.

· · ·

AT COLUMBIA'S GRADUATION CEREMONY, as Ginsburg walked forward to receive her diploma, her four-year-old daughter broke the solemnity of the occasion. "That's my Mommy," the little girl proudly shouted. There was no mistaking Jane's sheer delight upon spotting her mother amid the sea of gowned law school graduates in the class of 1959.

For her part, Ginsburg treasured both of her loves—the intense pleasures of family and her boundless passion for the law.

· CHAPTER 4 ·

Sailing in "Uncharted Waters"

A job offer should have been a foregone conclusion for a student tied for first place in the graduating class at Columbia Law School. Serving on the law reviews of both Harvard and Columbia and clerking successfully at a premier New York law firm were just icing on the cake. Such superb credentials typically guaranteed offers from top Wall Street firms or a coveted clerkship with a judge on a federal appeals court. Even an invitation to clerk with a justice at the Supreme Court should have been a possibility. The candidate believed she had all the prerequisites right down to the impeccably tailored black suit her mother-in-law had given her to wear for interviews. Poised for success, Ginsburg was caught off guard when job hunting did not go as anticipated.

. . .

THE FIRST SURPRISE CAME from Paul, Weiss, Rifkind, Wharton & Garrison. Knowing she had done excellent work the previous summer, she fully expected an offer. But the partners, who apparently believed that having an African American woman (Pauli Murray) as a fairly new associate was sufficient advertisement of the firm's commitment to diversity, showed no interest in hiring another woman.

Interviewing at Columbia with well over a dozen other firms, Ginsburg felt dismay when only two responded with an invitation for a second interview. Neither made an offer. To describe this turn of events as "depressing" was an understatement. The anguish of rejection was consuming. What had she done wrong? In the job market, as in law school, merit was supposed to prevail. Why was she being rejected?

Explanations varied. Being Jewish did not help. White-shoe firms were reluctant to hire Jewish applicants. Even Paul, Weiss, Rifkind, Wharton & Garrison, the only "balanced" firm at the time, preferred WASP applicants in order to maintain its Jewish quota of no more than 50 percent. So did Jewish firms yearning for broader social acceptance.

Sex and motherhood, the rejected candidate soon discovered, were her downfall. Clients, she was told, would be uneasy with a woman. Other members of the firm too might feel uncomfortable. Or, *she* would be ill at ease in such a masculine environment. The underlying message was always the same: "We don't want women." And they certainly did not want a young mother. When a senior partner needed affidavits for an unexpected motion, she would likely be out tending a sick child. How could she, with all of her family obligations, possibly have time for the informal social activities that generated client contacts?

Concerns about work-family conflicts had plausibility. But more was involved. Potential employers automatically equated "lawyer" and "male." Lawyers, they unconsciously assumed, came with all the archetypal "male" traits. As an attendee at the Association of American Law Schools Conference in 1971 observed, "What were women lawyers after all? Simply soft men. The rough-and-tumble, knock-down-drag-out adversary confrontations would continue, as always," he concluded, "with hard men center stage."

Viewed through these lenses, Ginsburg—with her small size, soft voice, youthful image, and feminine appearance—did not measure up. Add to that her self-characterization at the time as "rather diffident, modest and shy"—traits that upon first encounter obscured her innate toughness, work ethic, and drive to excel. Male recruiters assessing Ginsburg could easily conclude that, irrespective of sex, her persona did not comport with the image of a potential rainmaker—a lawyer with the self-assurance, charisma, and track record to attract new and profitable clients to a firm.

In sum, ethnicity, sex, and motherhood trumped other attributes. "To be a woman, a Jew, and a mother to boot," Ginsburg remarked in an often-repeated quotation, was just "a bit much" in 1959. She might have been able to surmount the first two impediments, she coolly speculated, but not all three. This restrained analysis—offered to an interviewer writing about successful women attorneys—belied her acute disappointment at the time. Only years later would she acknowledge that the experience remained seared in her memory as one of the most devastating developments of her entire career. The rejections gnawed away at her sense of professional identity and competence.

. . .

FORTUNATELY FOR GINSBURG, the Columbia professor Gerald Gunther thought her intellectual credentials merited a clerkship. Having himself clerked for the renowned judge Learned Hand of the U.S. Court of Appeals and then for Chief Justice Earl Warren, Gunther understood the professional payoffs awaiting young lawyers who held such coveted positions. He was also aware of the sheer hard work, "awesome responsibility, and complete subservience" required in the master-apprentice relationship that characterized a clerkship. As the faculty member charged with the responsibility for finding clerkships for the few graduating students the faculty deemed worthy of the honor, Gunther took up Ginsburg's cause. His target: "that small group of very good judges" in New York City who would be inclined to take his recommendation seriously.

Making the rounds at Foley Square in lower Manhattan, where the U.S. Court of Appeals for the Second Circuit was located, Gunther turned initially to Learned Hand, who was Ginsburg's first choice. Because she had studied under the leading process theorists at both Harvard and Columbia, Ginsburg would prove a lively discussion partner as well as an indispensable assistant, he promised. Yet despite Gunther's praise and assurances, the judge flatly refused. A gentleman of the old school, he knew that it was highly impolite to curse in front of a lady, and he had no intention of censoring his salty language.

Gunther then called every federal judge in the Southern District. Only two would agree to an interview, and one declined to make an offer. How could they function when their only clerk would be constantly running home to tend to her daughter? they asked; it was just too chancy. One of the two, Judge Edmund L. Palmieri, whose second clerk had been Jeanne Silver of Yale, had additional concerns. He stayed late in the office. What would his wife and daughters think about his working into the evening with such an extraordinarily attractive young woman?

Gunther was astonished by the response. A Holocaust survivor, he thought he understood prejudice. As a recent Harvard Law graduate, he

Gerald Gunther, who made possible Ginsburg's clerkship upon her graduation from Columbia Law School and remained her friend and champion throughout her career.

had seen firsthand the bias against the pioneer women in his class. But the gender fissure was not going to become a crater for Ruth Ginsburg if he had anything to do with it. Judge Palmieri was a devoted alumnus of the Law School; perhaps that tie could be exploited. Contacting Palmieri, Gunther threatened never to recommend another clerk from Columbia if the judge refused to give Ginsburg a chance. When Palmieri began to waver, Gunther added carrot to stick. If she did not work out, he promised, she could easily be replaced by a particularly talented young man from her class; though the young man was already employed, Gunther had persuaded his firm to release him if need be. Thus reassured of a backup, the judge relented and agreed to meet Ginsburg.

Unaware of the extraordinary measures to which Gunther had gone, Ginsburg simply assumed that Palmieri relented because he had two young daughters who he hoped would themselves be treated fairly one day. Several of Palmieri's other clerks later expressed doubts that their boss could ever have been so obdurate. But Gunther stuck to his account, insisting that Palmieri's resistance dissolved only after he met with Ginsburg. The two hit it off immediately, just as Gunther had anticipated. The job was hers.

. . .

GINSBURG FOUND THE JUDGE to be "a model European-style gentle-man," fluent in both French and Italian (Palmieri's wife was French). Enamored with opera, he was also a connoisseur of fine food and wine. Ruth discovered the judge had a daily routine that she promptly adopted. Every day at four o'clock, the two would walk, chatting about everything from testimony given at a trial, to the cast of the Met performance that evening, to good inexpensive restaurants, which Palmieri urged Ruth and Marty to try.

That judge and clerk worked so well together, and enjoyed each other's company, was due in no small measure to Ginsburg's characteristic preparation. She knew that the judge's cases were mostly civil cases and some garden-variety criminal cases, with less frequent criminal antitrust matters thrown in. Rarely did he deal with political issues. She also knew that he was fair, ruling without regard for social status or income. Having read everything she could find that Palmieri had written, she mastered the nuances of his writing style before she reported for work. It was important that the judge be comfortable with what she drafted for him. She learned just as quickly to decipher Palmieri's handwriting, a feat none of his prior clerks had managed to accomplish.

The elaborate preparation paid off. Once the judge decided what position he wanted to take on a particular case, he simply told her, "This is what I want to do and these, basically, are my reasons. You write it." Often he would ask, "What's the law?" Such queries sent Ginsburg rushing off to research relevant precedents and to compose an appropriate memorandum or opinion. District court was a fast-paced operation. Cases and motions covering a huge range of issues had to be dealt with quickly. In order to dispel any lingering concern that family obligations might prevent prompt completion of her responsibilities, she over-compensated. "I worked probably harder than any other law clerk in the building," Ginsburg recalled, "stayed late sometimes when it was necessary, sometimes when it wasn't necessary, came in Saturdays, and brought work home."

. . .

DURING GINSBURG'S SECOND YEAR as a clerk, one incentive for finishing work on time—or carrying anything remaining home with her—was the opportunity to share a daily ride uptown with Judge Palmieri and Judge Learned Hand, who lived near each other. The great jurist, "the most revered of living American judges," according to *The New York Times,* had delivered the Holmes Lectures her second year at Harvard before a rapt audience. With over fifty consecutive years on the bench, the elderly Hand's health had begun to fail, but his mind was as sharp and his language as pungent as ever.

Ginsburg would sit in the backseat while this aging lion with his strong jaw, piercing eyes, and bushy eyebrows held forth in the front. On occasion, he would serenade his traveling companions with Gilbert and Sullivan; on other rides, he would pose questions like "If you could be born anytime in history what time would you pick?" Sometimes the topic was literature; at other times, it was shoptalk. Throughout, Hand punctuated the conversation with curse words unfamiliar to the young woman in the backseat. One evening she finally screwed up the courage to ask the judge why he had used his purple language as an excuse not to hire her but never censored himself on their rides home from the Foley Square Courthouse. In his rich, deep voice, he replied from the front seat, "Young lady, here I am not looking you in the face."

Ginsburg's second year brought other opportunities as well. Palmieri's assignments carried ever-greater responsibility. Yet he also permitted her considerable freedom once she had fulfilled her obligations. In her spare time, Ginsburg sat in on trials presided over by other judges, spending as much time in various courtrooms as she could. In the criminal division of the U.S. Attorney's Office, she confirmed the fact that indeed there were no female lawyers or clerks. She was not persuaded by the argument that such work was inappropriate for women. Gender discrimination aside, she remained deeply impressed with the justice dispensed in the federal judicial system.

Palmieri, in turn, gained an enduring appreciation of his clerk and found himself charmed by Ginsburg's young daughter. He frequently told the story of the group of Wall Street lawyers from well-known firms who came unannounced to his office one day to present a paper they had prepared. As they later told him, they thought that Ruth, who the judge agreed looked barely eighteen, was his daughter and that Jane, who sat drawing pictures, was her little sister. This charming family scene dissolved into utter confusion when Ginsburg asked in her most professional tone, "Gentlemen, what is your problem?" She then followed with an incisive analysis of the paper that left the judge's visitors awestruck. They had never expected such legal acumen from the soft-spoken, diminutive young woman whom they took to be Miss Palmieri.

Ginsburg, the judge later averred, was one of the three best law clerks he ever had. "She even show[ed] up on weekends," he proudly announced, though he himself rarely did. Privately, he praised her competence and charm, which, he noted, had been evident from the outset. He also mentioned two additional qualities that she had manifested "in many subtle and delicate ways" in their close professional association: loyalty and affection.

· · ·

AS GINSBURG'S TIME with Palmieri wound down, Albert Sacks phoned his former Harvard student to say that he wished to submit her name to Justice Felix Frankfurter for consideration as a clerk. Because the justice was as renowned for being supportive of his clerks as he was critical of his brethren on the Court, Sacks no doubt thought that a clerkship with Frankfurter would be ideal for Ginsburg. She certainly could handle the incessant grilling to which Frankfurter subjected his clerks. And because he had made his own passage from Vienna to New York's Lower East Side to Harvard Law School and on to Washington's inner circle, he surely would not hesitate to hire a fellow Jew. More important, "the Little Judge," as his clerks affectionately called Frankfurter, was widely known to be a staunch believer in merit. In 1948, he had chosen William Coleman, the first African American law clerk in the Court's history. The justice, Sacks believed, might now in 1961 set another record—this time breaking the gender barrier.

Ginsburg basked in this gesture of confidence from a professor she so admired. Though she knew Sacks frequently placed clerks with Frankfurter—the justice always recruited from Harvard, where he had taught for twenty-five years—she was dubious from the outset that he would go for a woman, especially the mother of a young child. Further, he had only one precedent—a woman whom Justice William O. Douglas had appointed as clerk in 1944 as a wartime expedient. The odds, Ginsburg calculated, were not in her favor.

Sacks was at his most persuasive. Ginsburg's intellectual stature was every bit the equal of previous Harvard graduates, whom Frankfurter found entirely satisfactory. Moreover, she was always impeccably dressed and groomed and never wore pants, which he knew Frankfurter detested on women. Yet the peppery justice simply would not budge. He was, as his biographer has observed, "a person of paradox and contradiction."

. . .

THOUGH HARDLY SURPRISED by the decision, Ginsburg still needed a job. Palmieri swung into action, phoning law firms and writing letters attesting to his clerk's ability. Just as important, he assured potential employers that motherhood had presented no barrier to her full commitment to work. Offers soon followed. But before Ginsburg could settle in at her desk at Strasser Spiegelberg, she received an intriguing call from Hans Smit, the founding director of Columbia Law School's Project on International Procedure. Could they meet for lunch at the Harvard Club?

"How would you like to write a book on the Swedish legal system?" her tall Dutch-born host asked. Momentarily stunned, Ruth replied, "Tell me more." Part of the new Project on International Procedure, Smit explained, involved surveying foreign legal systems so that American lawyers could understand how other systems worked. Projects on French and Italian law were already under way. Studying the Swedish legal system now seemed appropriate, because the Swedes had adopted a new code of procedure. In place since 1948, it combined the basics of the continental system with what the Swedes saw as the best of the Anglo-American tradition of common law. The study had yet to move forward because of the difficulties posed by the Swedish language.

Would she consider coming to work for the project as a research associate while learning Swedish? The project would provide a tutor, Smit promised. There was also funding for her to stay in Sweden as long as she needed once she had acquired the necessary linguistic skills. Topping off the package, he promised the opportunity to co-author a book with a prominent appellate judge in Lund, Anders Bruzelius. The judge's daughter, Karin, had been a Kent scholar at Columbia. Everything Smit had learned about the father suggested that the two would be a good fit. Intrigued, Ginsburg promised to consider the offer.

She and Marty carefully weighed the pros and cons. Ruth knew that law firms disliked granting leaves of absence, and she could not afford to take an international assignment without one. To learn to read and write Swedish would require at least a year; learning to speak it properly would likely take even longer. Yet writing a book appealed to her scholarly bent. And Smit, with his cosmopolitan background, expertise in comparative law, and outgoing personality, promised to be a most engaging associate.

But what about family? If she took the job, it would involve two long stays in Sweden. Marty, who was working furiously to earn his partnership, would only be able to join her on vacations. She would miss him dearly. Yet at the age of twenty-eight, she needed to find out if she could manage on her own with a child. The opportunity proved "irresistible."

Securing a two-year leave of absence from Strasser Spiegelberg, Ginsburg began a yearlong effort to master both Swedish law and the language. Her language instructor turned out to be a Columbia undergraduate who had learned Swedish when performing as the principal male dancer for the Royal Swedish Ballet. Their almost daily lessons—spiced with ballet gossip—became a welcome relief from a steady diet of Swedish law.

In the meantime, Ginsburg set to work on the Project on International Procedure. Ever the apt student, she discovered that Smit, who was only a few years older, rewarded her hard work in ways for which she would be eternally grateful. By her own admission she was much too self-effacing at the time, and job rejections had done nothing to enhance her self-confidence. Smit not only promoted his protégée to associate director but encouraged her to develop a public image commensurate with her ability. Inviting Ginsburg to lecture to his civil procedure class for a week, he urged her as well to publish her work in law journals. He also eased her into the comparative law circuit, introducing her to other scholars in the field as well as refining her taste in food and wine.

Recalling their work together, Smit observed, "Ruth is basically a reserved person, quiet but with a steely determination. When she sets her mind to do something, she does it and superbly." Convinced that he, too, had made the right choice, Smit joined the list of scholars and teachers whose mentoring would have a lasting impact.

. . .

BY THE LATE SPRING OF 1962, travel plans were in place. She would fly to Sweden alone so Jane could complete the last six weeks of first grade at the Brearley School. The Ginsburgs had enrolled their daughter in the elite private girls' school at the insistence of the Brearley alumna and Yale Law graduate Antonia "Toni" Chayes, who, with her husband, Abe (Professor Abram Chayes), had befriended the token women at Harvard Law School. The two women had stayed in touch. Brearley, Toni counseled, was top-notch academically. Because tuition payments left no money to cover a private car service, the Ginsburgs moved downtown to Seventy-Ninth and York so that mother and daughter could walk to school before "Mommy" headed uptown to work. The housekeeper would assume that task—and others—in the six-week interval before Jane and Marty arrived in Sweden.

When Bruzelius met Ginsburg for the first time, the tall Swede could hardly believe that this diminutive young woman was to be his co-author. But a few weeks together demonstrated the aptness of Smit's pairing. Ginsburg delighted in the way things were working out. She had Harvard professor Benjamin Kaplan's publications on comparative systems of civil procedure, especially his work on Germany, on her desk, a fully equipped three-bedroom house in Lund, superb university child-care facilities for Jane, and English-speaking colleagues and friends, thanks to her father-in-law's networking. Though Marty's two-week vacation sped by much too quickly, Ruth readily admitted to a certain satisfaction in being able to function so well on her own.

The following year she delayed the trip until Jane's school year ended. Waiting in Stockholm was an apartment for visiting scholars at Wenner-Gren Center. The handsome capital city, set on an archipelago of islands, was only an hour's train ride away from Lake Bråviken. There she found a country home that functioned much like an American summer camp for Jane. With her daughter safely situated, Ginsburg could focus on her work. And work she did, almost completing the book that she and Bruzelius were co-authoring.

There were also professional benefits. The Project on International Procedure marked the beginning of a keen interest in comparative law that would bring Ginsburg prestigious assignments: membership on the editorial board of *The American Journal of Comparative Law,* the Europe Committee of the American Bar Association (ABA), the board of directors of the American Foreign Law Association, and, in 1969, an honorary degree from Lund University for her contribution to the study of Swedish law.

More important than the immediate professional payoff was the long-term international perspective that Ginsburg acquired. She understood that differences in legal systems in constitutional democracies have to be taken into account. Yet differences should not prevent American legal practitioners from discovering what "good minds abroad" have to say about shared critical issues, she maintained. While decisions of foreign courts had no binding authority in the United States, she ardently believed that if American lawyers and judges refused to be enlightened by their counterparts abroad, they could not expect to be heeded in an increasingly globalized world. Unwillingness to learn from others not only was wrongheaded but diminished U.S. influence internationally.

Long hours of summer light had illuminated more than the Swedish landscape—more even than the merits of other legal systems. Set off as well was the greater gender equality Swedes enjoyed. Prior to the 1960s, Swedish feminists and the Social Democrats had focused on helping women combine work and family roles. Their efforts did not escape Ginsburg's immediate notice. Day-care arrangements for faculty children at Lund University far surpassed anything comparable in Manhattan, where she had found only two nursery schools where Jane might be enrolled. Women made up 20 percent of Swedish law students, not a token 4 percent as in the United States. Observing a judge on the bench who appeared to be about eight months pregnant provided yet another eye-opener, as did Sherri Finkbine's much publicized abortion in Sweden.

A married mother of four, Finkbine had taken the drug thalidomide for symptoms of morning sickness, only to discover subsequently the high probability that the fetus would be severely deformed. Finkbine's Arizona doctor had recommended a therapeutic abortion and she and her husband agreed, but he then declined to perform the procedure, fearing he would be liable for criminal prosecution. Following Finkbine's flight to Sweden, Ginsburg questioned the criminalization of a medical procedure in the United States that seemed so fully warranted. Sweden's health-care and child-care policies, she concluded, were in every way more attuned to the needs of women and families than were those in her own country.

Yet even the excellent services provided by the state did not suppress a fundamental question. Why, asked Eva Moberg, the editor of the women's journal *Hertha,* should married women have two jobs, one domestic and one nondomestic, when their male partners had only one? There was nothing about the act of childbirth that required her to be the one to continue to do the feeding, diapering, and caring for the child until she or he became an adult. "We ought to stop harping on the concept of 'women's two roles,'" Moberg wrote. "Both men and women have *one* principal role, that of being people."

Ginsburg followed the heated debate unleashed by Moberg in the Stockholm *Daily News* as the young feminist carried her argument further. Predicting that the day would come when women no longer had the exclusive "right to choose" between home and a career, both men and women, she contended, would have the same options and the same obligations toward society. Whether Moberg's American reader realized she was witnessing a new stage in Swedish feminism is unclear. What did impress her was that "every cocktail party in the country . . . was consumed with talk of" Moberg's article.

Based on a new four-year multidisciplinary study of women's work and family life, Swedish and Norwegian social scientists had concluded that culturally constructed roles—stereotypical assumptions about the proper role of men and women—imposed constraints on both sexes that penalized individuals and impoverished society. The roles and responsibilities of men as well as women would have to change with men sharing equally in parenthood if both sexes were to have "the right to be human."

About to return to New York, Ginsburg would follow from a distance Sweden's new government-appointed commission to study women's issues and propose policies to promote equality between the sexes. By 1969, the commission's proposals became part of the Social Democrats' official Equality Program under Prime Minister Olof Palme. Though she claimed to tuck away the opening salvos for gender equality once back in Manhattan, *jämställdhet,* as it was referred to in Swedish, had become imprinted in Ginsburg's consciousness as firmly as "Sverige" (Sweden) had been stamped on her passport.

. . .

REFLECTING ON HER PROFESSIONAL FUTURE upon her return to New York, Ginsburg had second thoughts about her decision to join Strasser Spiegelberg. Partnership positions in large firms were (and are) a mark of power and prestige in the legal world. Yet did she really want to be stuck in the routine of having to work for the next twenty years on someone else's project? And how about the eventual responsibility of bringing in business for the firm? She had always found the rigors of legal scholarship enticing. Enthralled by the law and its processes, she enjoyed sorting out legal intricacies. Perhaps she could teach after a stint in private practice. Law schools, she knew, allowed their faculty to engage in some litigation in addition to teaching. When a questionnaire surveying teaching interests of recent graduates arrived from Harvard Law School, she added her name, then dismissed the matter, but not before sharing the possibility with her good friend and Columbia mentor Gerry Gunther.

Shortly thereafter, Professor Walter Gellhorn at Columbia called. What, he asked, was she, a Columbia graduate, doing on a Harvard list of potential Law School faculty? His curiosity had been piqued, he explained, because he had a job for her. No, it was not at Columbia, New York University, or Fordham, as Ginsburg had hoped, though Gellhorn would later admit that in view of her credentials it should have been her alma mater. Rather, the opening was at Rutgers Law School in Newark, which had just lost its only minority faculty member, Clyde Ferguson, to the deanship of Howard University Law School. Because Ferguson taught civil procedure, an opening now existed for which she was qualified. Gunther, who had indicated that Ruth might be interested, had already contacted Eva Hanks—then Eva Morreale, another Columbia graduate, whom Rutgers had hired the previous year with the encouragement of Ferguson. Hanks lived in the city, Gellhorn continued, and she had agreed to come by the Ginsburg apartment for a chat. Realizing how little she knew about Rutgers, Ginsburg welcomed the visit.

Hanks assured her future colleague that she would welcome another woman. The Law School had a good dean, Willard Heckel, a thoroughly left-liberal faculty, and a new building on the way, and it was making a real effort to attract minority students. This was a tenure-track job from which she could commute back and forth from Newark to the city. Knowing women held only eighteen tenured academic posts in law schools in the entire country, Ginsburg gave her visitor her curriculum vitae and other materials to present to the Rutgers search committee.

Offered the position, Ginsburg now had to make a decision. She had really wanted at least five years' experience in a Manhattan firm before teaching. But would another offer to teach come her way? Could she afford to pass up a bird in the hand? If she took the offer, how would she get litigation experience? Did the Rutgers faculty even want her? Or had they made the offer to a woman only because they failed to find another African American?

After talking it over with Marty, Ruth decided to accept. Yet she was troubled by the pay discrepancy she had discovered—not just between Columbia and Rutgers but also within the Rutgers Law School faculty. She would be earning less than her male colleagues with comparable qualifications. When she confronted the dean with the discrepancy, Heckel replied that she was now at an underfunded state university. Furthermore, she had a husband to take care of her, so it was only fair that she receive a lower salary than a man with a family to support. Heckel, a kindly man, seemed strangely indifferent to the new federal law mandating equal pay, Ginsburg observed. As a new hire on a yearly contract, she resolved not to push the issue—at least not yet. Better to bide her time until other female faculty at Rutgers were prepared to file an equal-pay complaint. In the meantime, she was grateful for a schedule that made it possible to meet her new responsibilities comfortably.

Ginsburg found even more to appreciate in Eva Hanks. Although the wary males on the faculty always referred to the two as "the girls," Hanks assured the newcomer that the respect of her colleagues would come in time. The various inequities—including pay—were simply part of the price of admission paid by women entering the halls of academe in the 1960s. Just do your job well, Hanks advised, and try not to get sucked into the political battle between the traditionalists who want to teach law the customary way in the standard courses and the innovators who insist on adding "law and" courses—law and economics, law and sociology, and so on. The battle also extended to research, Hanks explained: traditional legal research versus empirical research. Ginsburg, seeing merit in both positions, decided to tread cautiously on what would prove to be highly polarized terrain.

. . .

WHEN CLASSES BEGAN in September 1963, Ginsburg quickly settled into the routine of teaching. Determined to make use of every minute of her time, she read her mail on the subway to Penn Station from her apartment on the Upper East Side, even though she had three changes along the way, making it such a nerve-racking commute that she had nightmares about not making the connections. During the train ride to Newark, she reviewed the day's lectures. On the return trip, she immersed herself in academic journals, going over the latest articles on civil procedure and comparative law. The trip was grueling, especially on a daily basis.

Then, in early 1965, the thirty-two-year-old professor learned that she was pregnant. She was ecstatic. She and Marty had been told after his cancer treatment that they could have no more children. Conception seemed a near miracle. But along with the happiness came inevitable concerns. Given the massive doses of radiation that Marty's reproduc-

Ginsburg with her daughter, Jane (aged ten), July 1966.

tive system had sustained, Ruth worried whether the fetus would escape unaffected. And what about the impact of the pregnancy on her career? During Marty's military service in Oklahoma, she had applied to be a Social Security claims examiner at a GS-5 level. When she revealed her pregnancy, the personnel officer promptly demoted her to a GS-2, explaining that a pregnant woman would be unable to travel to Baltimore for the necessary training session. Furthermore, if she took a job as a typist, she would be expected to leave work before giving birth and not return. At the time, she had rationalized the incident as "just the way things are." Nonetheless, the memory rankled.

Still on a year-to-year contract, she resolved not to be so naive this time and risk losing her job as soon as her pregnancy showed. Until the renewed contract was in hand, she would disguise her expanding figure in oversize clothes borrowed from her mother-in-law. And she certainly would not tell her colleagues that she was expecting. She and Hanks were careful to save their conversations for the railroad station or for the city. Her joy, along with any minor physical complaints, she would also reserve for Manhattan. In just a few months, the semester would be over.

Among friends, the Ginsburgs reveled in anticipation. Joan Bruder Danoff, Ruth's old Cornell roommate, noted how she "glowed" throughout her pregnancy. "You were the very essence of motherhood," declared Ruth Lubic, the wife of a law firm associate of Marty's. Enrolling in a Lamaze class taught in a West Side apartment, the expectant mother learned how to cope with labor without sedatives. "Prepared to the hilt," Ginsburg was struck by the contrast with her first pregnancy a decade earlier, when she had been unprepared for giving birth.

On September 8, 1965, a very pregnant Ginsburg produced a healthy baby boy. It was "one of the happiest days of my life," the relieved mother proclaimed—a triumph over illness and death, especially for Marty. The beaming couple named their blond-haired son James Steven.

· · ·

THERE WAS LITTLE TIME to hold this miracle baby, observe his facial expressions, or feel his tiny hand clasped tightly around her finger. Within the month, Ginsburg was back at Rutgers. Her teaching obligations for the next academic year included not only her accustomed course on civil procedure but also a new course on comparative law and another on conflicts of laws and federal jurisdiction. Fortunately, it meant only one new preparation each semester. Yet planning classes took time, especially because her lectures were carefully typed. Ginsburg also knew she must not let the demands of research take second place. She already had several publications to her credit: the book she had co-authored with Bruzelius on Swedish civil and criminal procedure and their English translation of the Swedish Code of Judicial Procedure, as well as journal articles. Yet more publications were needed if she wanted to move up the academic ladder. Moreover, it had to be significant new work, which meant a major investment of what was now in shortest supply—time.

Ginsburg was accustomed to working late into the night long after Marty had gone to bed; however, the months following James's birth brought a level of sleep deprivation that she apologetically appeased by dozing off during the quieter parts of an opera. A new baby was only part of her growing family-care workload. Her father, Nathan, who had been badly injured in an automobile accident, had to be moved into the Ginsburgs' recently acquired apartment at 150 East Sixty-Ninth Street until he recovered. Because there was no guest room, Nathan and all his hospital gear wound up in Jane's bedroom, much to the dismay of the ten-year-old, who wanted her own space. Though fully aware that her daughter was "miserable" at the addition of a temporary roommate, the beleaguered mother felt she had no alternative.

Trapped by the needs of two generations, Ruth set up a nursing schedule, grateful that Marty's income permitted as much outside help as possible. But when gaps appeared in the schedule, it was she who had to juggle her calendar to be at home with her ailing father because Marty was caught up in the treadmill of his practice. Yet she never con-sidered a leave of absence during these intensely demanding months. Ever the realist, she knew that asking for special consideration could jeopardize her prospects for tenure. Male colleagues would likely assume that a woman with family obligations would be unable to pull her weight as a scholar, teacher, and involved member of the profession. She was undoubtedly correct in her assessment, but it did nothing to alleviate the strain in the apartment. Add to that commuting daily, teaching a full course load, preparing for new classes, and dealing with tenure pressure. The ultimate juggler, she had never underestimated how much she could handle. But now she felt overwhelmed.

. . .

IN THE DAZE of the months that followed, the dedication of Rutgers Law School's new headquarters in 1966 provided an unexpected boost. Chief Justice Earl Warren and two associates (Justices William Brennan and Abe Fortas) arrived in Newark. When right-wing activists circled the block venting their outrage at the Supreme Court, the worried host, Dean Heckel, suggested that perhaps he should call for greater police protection. But Justice Brennan, the primary speaker, objected. "Leave them undisturbed," he urged the dean. "They are just exercising their First Amendment rights." Warren and Fortas, whom Brennan had persuaded to accompany him to his home state, concurred.

Brennan's courage and wisdom that day made an indelible impression on Ginsburg. Like so many of his admirers, she found the justice's qualities of mind and heart inspiring. Moreover, Brennan's many opinions for the Court, along with his detailed commentary, added up to an astonishing level of productivity. Just thinking about the man and the example he provided restored Ruth's spirits whenever she felt exhausted and worried about whether she had taken on too much.

The hard-pressed young mother needed every bit of inspiration she could find as the semester dragged on. Together she and Evelyn went to great lengths to see that Jane did not feel totally overlooked with a new baby competing for the family's attention and a convalescent grandfather occupying her bedroom. Ginsburg's outings with her daughter, like her own many years earlier with Celia, were more likely to include arts institutions than department stores. "I schlepped Jane to every children's theater, to concerts, operas, Gilbert and Sullivan productions, and Rodgers and Hammerstein Broadway shows," Ginsburg recalled. When Jane was eight, Ruth had taken her to the Metropolitan Opera to see *Così fan tutte*. Playing the record a month ahead of time so that the music would become familiar, she sat down with her daughter and went through the libretto so that the youngster would know the lines. Clad in a velvet jumper made especially for the occasion and seated in the front row of the balcony so that she would have a clear line of vision, Jane, according to her mother, had "loved it." Acknowledging that as a working mother she probably "overcompensated on weekends," she remained nonplussed at her daughter's assertion that when she grew up, she was going to be just like "Nana," who had never worked outside the home.

A career-oriented mother and Jewish parents made the ten-year-old stand out at an exclusive school like Brearley with its elite WASP clientele. Her mother's weekend cultural expeditions, a trip with her parents to the nation's capital—nothing alleviated the young girl's sense of discomfort with her outsider status. Even a tour of historic sites around Washington had to be interrupted for a morning at the Court so that her parents could be admitted to the Supreme Court bar. Jane sat through the oath taking of new attorneys and a bit of a dull tax case before deciding she had endured enough. As she walked out of the courtroom, her parents hastily followed, knowing that the Supreme Court Building was no place for a youngster to be wandering around alone. Unable to return, Marty and Ruth entirely missed the civil rights case they had so wanted to hear.

Not until her high school years would Jane finally feel less an anomaly. The ninth grade brought more students of working mothers, though she had long had as a classmate Emily Heilbrun, the daughter of Carolyn Heilbrun, a professor of literature at Columbia. Heilbrun's mysteries, written under the pseudonym Amanda Cross, were devoured by Jane's mother, along with those of Dorothy Sayers. But nothing, the teenager felt, could overcome the ultimate marker of difference—being a Jew. Despite her blond hair, which she thought made her look more like the other girls, her application to dance classes attended by schoolmates came back wait-listed. Her parents took the message to mean "no Jews wanted." Jane adamantly refused to let her mother reapply. A few years later, when she attended her first Brearley dance, Jane confided to her mother that she had a good time and met a very nice boy. "What is his name?" Ruth asked. Jane provided a first name. "And what is his last name?" Jane responded with what was obviously a WASP surname. Her mother, who had dated Christian boys in high school and college, replied, "Well, don't expect him to call; his parents won't allow him to." To Jane's regret, the prediction proved all too accurate.

Thursdays, when the housekeeper was off, Ginsburg worked at home. Her physical presence, however, did nothing to improve relations between mother and daughter. Ruth's strictness contributed to the tension, just as Celia's had done. Jane resented the frequent admonitions to "stand up straight," "clean up your room," "do your homework," and "try another draft of your English essay." Sloppy writing was as intolerable to Jane's highly disciplined and overextended mother as a messy room. The strain in the household apparent, Jane asked if her parents' shouting signaled the breakup of the Ginsburgs' marriage. Ruth responded reassuringly, attributing Jane's anxieties to the divorce of parents of a child in a nearby apartment.

Jane later acknowledged that, to put it mildly, she had not appreciated her mother's tenacity on matters of posture, tidiness, or diet. "I was a resentful child and a spoiled brat," she confessed. "Mother is tremendously sentimental, but she could also be somewhat austere. When I did something bad, which happened often, my dad would yell, but my mother would be real quiet, and I'd know she was very disappointed in me." Recalling her mother's eagle eye for candy wrappers in the wastebasket, she added, "Her searches and seizures of my childhood debris showed that Fourth Amendment principles held no place of honor in our household order." Although she subsequently felt grateful for Ruth's demanding standards, at the time they were a source of considerable friction between mother and daughter.

While Jane could be exasperating at times, she had a keen sense of humor. Sent to summer camp—an experience, which, unlike her mother, she thoroughly disliked—Jane failed to send the obligatory letter home each week. Chided for not abiding by camp rules by a mother who wrote to her daughter every single day, Jane posted her envelope the following week. Upon opening it, her parents found a newspaper clipping about the post office's misplacement of a seventy-year-old letter. Their daughter's ingenuity alone was worth a smile, if not the giggle Ruth usually reserved for Marty's jokes.

No wonder, then, that during the early years, when his hardworking wife's time was stretched so perilously thin, Marty considered it his job to inject some playfulness into her life, enlisting his daughter in a dinner-table game. Jane's job was to count the number of times either of them could succeed in saying something or telling a story that would make her mother smile. So caught up did Jane become in the game that she later produced a booklet titled "Mommy Laughed."

· · ·

AS THE END of the 1965–66 academic year finally approached, Ginsburg had done more than survive. She had two new courses at Rutgers under her belt and a seat on the editorial board of *The American Journal of Comparative Law,* along with additional articles and an edited book on trade regulations in the Benelux countries (Belgium, the Netherlands, and Luxembourg). Accordingly, promotion to associate professor proceeded on schedule. The hardworking mother and scholar could now relax, but only momentarily.

Asked to teach a course in comparative law at New York University in addition to her regular Rutgers courses, she agreed, hoping it would culminate in an offer of a faculty position. In the middle of a lecture, a note was thrust into her hand. Stopping in mid-sentence, she glanced down. "Son ingested Drano; taken to nearest hospital." Flying out of the door onto Washington Square, she made a mad dash, at first to the wrong hospital. Finally, the distraught mother learned that James, now two years old, had sampled some of the white granules in a container that he found under the kitchen sink. Fortunately, the housekeeper had rushed him to the emergency room before calling his parents.

As Marty and Ruth gazed down at the blistered mouth of their son, they wondered whether the disfigurement would be permanent. "Deep burns distorted his face," Ginsburg recalled, "charred lips encircled his mouth—a tiny, burnt-out cavern, ravaged by lye." Tests revealed that James had not actually ingested any of the Drano. Within days it was clear that the child would survive, though months would pass before his parents learned that the scars would not be permanent.

The accident marked one of the lowest points of Ginsburg's adult life. Yet she subsequently recounted the event in the same dispassionate style with which she related the trauma of job rejections. The housekeeper, she insisted, did precisely what she herself would have done. In private, however, she agonized over the fact that she was not there when the disaster struck. Was her son paying the price for her career? Most of her guilt stemmed from failing to remove the Drano from the toddler's reach. How could she have been so remiss? "She absolutely doesn't forgive herself," Jane perceptively noted. The compassion Ginsburg gave so freely to others she did not extend to herself; self-forgiveness had not been one of Celia's lessons.

. . .

INDEED, THE HARD-PRESSED WORKING MOTHER often felt that as a two-career couple with children she and Marty were sailing in "uncharted waters." Aware that his wife's career was still very much a work in progress, Marty lined the dining room with bookshelves to accommodate part of his law library, dictating equipment, and growing collection of cookbooks so that he could at least work at home at night. But the demands that came with his soaring reputation prevented his doing more to balance parenting responsibilities. Were the indispensable housekeeper to suddenly quit, they both knew that "Nana" would

Ginsburg watching the end-of-term student show at Rutgers School of Law in Newark, New Jersey. She was one of two women on the law faculty, from 1962 to 1973.

pitch in temporarily. After Nathan recovered from his accident, he, too, helped, taking James to Central Park most Sundays. But there were times when even Ginsburg's formidable juggling skills were tested.

The Law School was yet another proving ground. Ginsburg knew that she was a knowledgeable teacher, expert in her subject matter. But her no-nonsense manner and slow, unexpressive delivery did not make for memorable classroom performances. "For the good students, she was a wonderful teacher," said her colleague Frank Askin. "A lot of the weaker students got bored and went to sleep." In the beginning, her colleague Eva Hanks recalled, "she clung to the lectern almost as if she were afraid of the students." What did come across was the remarkable intensity with which she talked about the law. Students seized upon it instantly as the feature they would caricature at their annual spoof of the faculty. Imitating Ginsburg at the lectern, her student counterpart talked on earnestly, oblivious to the fact that articles of clothing were being removed one by one until she was left lecturing in her undergarments. Colleagues and students roared with laughter, though Hanks, who thought the students never knew where to draw the line in these events, declined to attend.

The two had an unspoken understanding, Hanks recalled. "We never sat together at a faculty meeting, and we had coffee together only at the Newark train station or in the city." Even in their conversations, "family responsibilities were mentioned only indirectly. . . . We knew we needed to be seen as autonomous professionals." Downplaying their otherness as women in a male-dominated environment, in which they were expected to play by rules not fully disclosed, was not easy. Asked what their Rutgers colleagues thought of Ginsburg, Hanks replied without a pause, "They misread her. She was so petite and so soft-spoken, they never realized how tough she was."

Marty knew, of course. He also knew that his hardworking spouse needed all the support he could offer. While managing the pressures of his own flourishing career, he tried to provide breaks that would go beyond their frequent opera evenings, thrilling as those were when singers such as Leontyne Price, Franco Corelli, and Marilyn Horne made their triumphant debuts. Whisking the family off to vacation spots helped, allowing Ruth to experience the exhilaration of waterskiing, though she often brought work along as well. There were also frequent short trips related to Marty's corporate tax practice that allowed the couple to escape to luxury resorts for a few days of combined work and relaxation without the children. Friends with whom they dined on such junkets discovered that Ruth's leisurely eating habits had not changed since her first year at Cornell. "World Wars, Court calendars, 'Gandhi,' [and] Davis Cup matches can be completed before you will finish an appetizer," they teased.

Yet while the children were still young, she was reluctant to miss an evening meal at home, despite the presence of a live-in housekeeper. As a working mother, it was a way of "being there" for her family. Moreover, having dinner with Jane and James, while classical music played in the background and the family members talked about their day, was part of the Ginsburgs' definition of good parenting. Another part was not clinging to the children too tightly, especially as they grew older.

When Jane reached ninth grade, her parents agreed that because she so disliked summer camp, they should search for an alternative that would be completely different from her Manhattan routine. To Ginsburg's delight, she managed to locate a family on the outskirts of Annecy, France, with whom Jane could live for the summer. The mother and her five children met the essential criteria: "They spoke another language, lived in a different culture, and were not intellectuals." Returning for two more summers, the teenager improved her fluency in French each year to the delight of her parents, who breathed a sigh of relief at having finally solved the problem of their daughter's school vacations. For Jane, these summers marked the beginning of a love affair with France so intense that as a mother herself she would insist on speaking French with her own children.

· · ·

WITH JAMES NOW ENROLLED at nursery school at "Little Dalton," the elite private school for boys, his mother felt she could add new commitments. The most critical of these was volunteering her services to the New Jersey affiliate of the American Civil Liberties Union (ACLU), a venerable organization that had also become heavily engaged in championing civil rights. A national body, the ACLU had affiliates in most states that represented clients whose civil liberties or civil rights had allegedly been violated.

James Ginsburg ("my golden-haired boy," said Ginsburg of him) circa 1968, 1969, in the garden of Ginsburg's mother-in-law, Evelyn Ginsburg, Rockville Centre, New York. Standing near James, Erica Landau, the daughter of friends from Cornell days.

But why would this workaholic professor and mother take on yet another job? Obviously, working with the New Jersey affiliate would serve as an opportunity to gain the much-needed litigation experience she had forfeited by taking a teaching position. But there were also other considerations. In the wake of World War II, American Jews had begun a major effort to use the law to protect and extend civil liberties, not only through their own defense groups, but also through nonsectarian organizations like the ACLU. As the fight against anti-Semitism became a fight for human rights, Jewish lawyers played a leading role as activists in the liberal movement's effort to use the law as a tool for justice that was substantively humane. In part because of their efforts, along with those of lawyers from the NAACP Legal Defense Fund and other such groups in the liberal legal network, the courts during the 1960s had acquired new luster as ultimate protectors of human rights. For that generation of law professors, affiliation with the ACLU was also a form of public service.

Ginsburg's sympathies with the rights revolution had never been in doubt. But only after quickly climbing the academic ladder from associate professor in 1966 to full professor with tenure in 1969 and the award of an honorary degree from Lund University did she feel that she could afford even minimal participation. It was not that she had been indifferent to events reshaping American society during the tumultuous 1960s. How could one not be intellectually and emotionally engaged when in 1968 alone the Vietcong's Tet Offensive sent sixteen hundred American soldiers home in body bags and eight thousand more with wounds? Protests were erupting like wildfire, consuming university campuses; a maverick candidate had forced a sitting president in his own party to renounce a second term; and assassins' bullets had struck down both Martin Luther King Jr. and Robert Kennedy.

Yet through the agony and tumult, Ginsburg's focus had remained on her high-wire act, perilously balancing career and family. Beyond matters relating to her professional and personal life, causes—even highly deserving ones—had to yield. Never in her most ambitious dreams did it occur to her that responding to a New Jersey nurse's complaint against the army might open the door to a more demanding career. Nor could she imagine what might conceivably trigger the transition.

CHAPTER 5

The Making of a Feminist Advocate

T
he times, they are a-changin','" the folksinger Bob Dylan pro-
phetically sang in 1963. And Ginsburg was changing as well. She
began the politically turbulent 1960s as an ambitious academic
and a deeply caring, perfectionist mother who had zero tolerance for
sloppy writing and messy rooms. She would end the decade as a legal
activist intent on dismantling old gender distinctions in law that denied
women—and in some situations men—equal citizenship. It was "one of
the great turning points of my life," she would later reflect.

In retrospect, Ginsburg's embrace of feminism seems to have been an
easy fit for a woman who, in many respects, "walked the walk" before
the street was named. Nevertheless, adopting a feminist identity is a
process—one in which her own life experience intersected with a larger
historical canvas colored by the past and stretching well beyond the
United States.

· · ·

"NEW POLICIES REMAKE POLITICS," political sociologists observe.
The same might be said of law. Earl Warren and the Supreme Court on
which he served as chief justice from 1953 to 1969 had given new vigor to
efforts to protect the civil liberties and civil rights of groups previously
considered on the margins of society—members of the Communist
Party, African Americans, Chicanos, nonbelievers, welfare recipients,
even criminals. Spurred by advocates of President Lyndon Johnson's
Great Society from above and by the demands of ordinary citizens from
below, the rights revolution became a swelling tide over the course of the
1960s.

Powering the surge were advocacy groups eager to use the legal process to enhance the rights of populations that politicians had traditionally ignored. Though cramped by the severe political and governmental repression of the McCarthy years, progressive organizations of all kinds—from the leftist National Lawyers Guild to the more centrist ACLU and NAACP's Legal Defense Fund, along with new environmental groups—provided a burgeoning support structure. Funding, organizational backing, networking, and talented lawyers eager to change the law—all prerequisites for the slow, expensive process of litigation—enhanced the possibility of winning.

Central to the ferment were women motivated by growing frustration with sex-based discrimination in law and society. In 1963, union women celebrated passage of the Equal Pay Act. A goal throughout the 1950s, the bill had been passed as a concession to male unionists, who were fearful that wages might be undercut by employers hiring cheaper female workers. That same year a former labor journalist who in 1952 had written a "remarkable manual for fighting [gender-based] wage discrimination" for the United Electrical Workers—the most radical American union in the immediate postwar years—published her first book. An instant best seller, Betty Friedan's *Feminine Mystique* tapped into the strong undercurrent of discontent felt by many educated middle-class women during the 1950s and 1960s. Though Ginsburg, who had escaped the snares of suburban domesticity, found Friedan's analysis limited, she shared the author's feminist sympathies.

Far more significant was the Civil Rights Act, which Congress passed one year later. An urgent response to the struggle for racial justice convulsing the South, the Civil Rights Act of 1964 provided comprehensive legislation covering voting rights, public facilities, and employment. Title VII, which dealt with employment, outlawed discrimination on the basis of sex as well as race, obliging the federal government to undertake an "affirmative" program of equal employment for all employees and job applicants. The government was also to create the Equal Employment Opportunity Commission (EEOC) to monitor compliance with the law. The commission, which initially regarded the sex-discrimination provision as a "fluke" inserted by opponents to block passage of the bill, was astonished when 25 percent of the complaints the first year came from women. When these complaints were ignored, women working within the EEOC contacted the Michigan Democrat Martha Griffiths, who had worked to keep "sex" in the bill and was determined to see the new law enforced in its entirety.

When the EEOC failed to live up to its mandate, Griffiths lambasted the agency on the House floor only a few days before the 1966 meeting of the Conference on the Status of Women. Conference participants who were most upset at the EEOC's inaction decided to act on the advice of black women in the agency, who argued that if women had a civil rights organization as adept at applying pressure as the NAACP, the EEOC could be made to take gender-related discrimination seriously. Before the day was out, twenty-eight women, including Betty Friedan, who happened to be in Washington, founded the National Organization for Women (NOW).

At its organizational meeting in October, at which Friedan was elected president, NOW called for "full participation of women in the mainstream of American society exercising all the privileges and responsibilities thereof in equal partnership with men." To that end, its Bill of Rights, adopted in 1967, called on Congress to pass an equal rights amendment, demanded that the EEOC enforce antidiscrimination legislation, and urged federal and state legislators to guarantee equal and unsegregated education. To ensure women control over their reproductive lives, NOW called for removal of penal codes denying women contraceptive information and devices as well as safe, legal abortions. To ease the double burden of working mothers, it urged legislation that would ensure maternity leaves without jeopardizing job security or seniority, permit tax deductions for child-care expenses, and create public, inexpensive day-care centers. To improve the lot of poor women, NOW urged reform of the welfare system and equality with respect to benefits, including job-training programs.

By the time the head of the New Jersey affiliate of the ACLU approached Ginsburg in July 1970, a resurgent feminist movement with roots spreading out across the nation was clearly in the making, not only in the United States, but abroad.

. . .

BUT WHY GINSBURG? Stephen Nagler, executive director of the busy New Jersey affiliate, knew that the Rutgers Law School professor was already effectively handling the problem of Nora Simon. A discharged army lieutenant and nurse, Simon had been denied the opportunity to reenlist, though her marriage had been annulled and her baby surrendered for adoption. Jobless, Simon had appealed to the New Jersey affiliate. Diana Rigelman, a Rutgers Law School student working at the affiliate that summer who had just completed Ginsburg's first-year course in civil procedure, turned to her professor. An "ice woman"— precise, scholarly, and professional—in Rigelman's eyes, Ginsburg was just the kind of female lawyer that the army would take seriously. Neither Rigelman nor Nagler knew why the case held such appeal for Ginsburg. But handle it she did. As an expert in civil procedure, Nagler reasoned, Ginsburg should know something about how courts operated. In any event, it made sense to ask a woman to handle "women's" problems. If the implicitly sexist reasoning left something to be desired, the decision proved to be inspired.

Because of her own experiences, Ginsburg found she could readily relate to her clients' circumstances. For the former Cornell coed who had concluded that the educational experience offered by Radcliffe's Management Training Program did not match that of Harvard Business School, it was an easy stretch to support the young girl who wanted to attend all-male Rutgers College, not Douglass, its female counterpart. Ginsburg was genuinely moved as she listened to Eudoxia Awadallah, a teacher who told her that she had been required to take an unpaid leave once her pregnancy began to show, a common requirement of school boards at the time. Women like Awadallah reminded her of her own pregnancy-related job problems. How could she not relate to the employee of the Lipton Tea Company who wanted to enroll in the company health insurance program for her entire family because the benefits it offered were more generous than those offered by her husband's employer? But female employees at Lipton could get group insurance only for themselves, not a spouse or children.

As the mother of a bright daughter, Ginsburg could also identify with the parents of the eleven-year-old girls barred from Princeton University's Summer-in-Engineering Program on the grounds that their daughters would distract the sixth-grade boys for whom the program was intended. Had Jane been denied the benefits of a comparable program offered by

Columbia or New York University, she and Marty would have been no less incensed. Such discrimination hurt, especially at a time when less than 2 percent of the nation's engineers were female.

Empathy aside, Ginsburg had never had the slightest intention of becoming an expert on discrimination law and equal protection analysis. Nor did she expect her female students—and a few males—to clamor for a course on women and the law. Yet for law schools and their faculties, as for other institutions under scrutiny by student activists, the 1960s was no ordinary time.

Students, mostly left-liberals, attacked faculty hierarchy, the grading system, the curriculum, and more. Black law students wanted increases in African American students and professors. In New Haven, the question of whether the Black Panther Bobby Seale could get a fair trial spilled over to Yale Law School, where young Hillary Rodham and Bill Clinton were students. Women had their own concerns.

In 1967, small groups of young white women had met in Chicago and New York. Veterans of the black freedom struggle, the leftist Students for a Democratic Society, and the antiwar movement, they demanded rights and liberation not just for victims of racism, poverty, and colonialism but also for themselves as women. In part, theirs was a generational revolt against the highly gendered lives their mothers led; in part, it was a visionary effort to transform power, politics, and the private sphere of family and sexuality. Though many of these 1960s radicals wanted much more than "bourgeois" rights, some of the brightest made their way to law school.

At Yale, these young feminists bemoaned the fact that Professor Fred Rodell held one of the Law School's most popular classes at Mory's, an all-male club. Less than seventy miles south, at New York University, a first-year law student, Janice Goodman, just back from Mississippi, where as a member of the Student Nonviolent Coordinating Committee she had been working to register black voters, stood in line to buy the weighty casebooks she needed for classes. Told by the second-year student next to her, Susan Deller Ross, that the Law School awarded its most prestigious scholarship, the Root-Tilden, to men only, the two agreed to form the Women's Rights Committee to protest. Their second objective was to get a course on women and the law into the curriculum at a time when no law school in the country offered such a course. Putting together a syllabus of sorts themselves, they finally persuaded the Law School to pay a faculty member $500 to preside over the course in the fall of 1969. Then Goodman and another member of the NYU Women's Rights Committee, Mary F. Kelly, took the train to Newark to meet with Ginsburg and their Rutgers sisters in law. Diane Rigelman and other Rutgers students added their pleas. Ginsburg could not resist.

· · ·

TO MEET THE NEEDS of both students and her ACLU clients, Ginsburg realized that she would have to learn more about women's legal status. A few months earlier, she had combed through federal court decisions and law school journals. She discovered that she could read the entire body of U.S. legal literature on the subject in a single month. The paucity of the material was an eye-opener.

Ever inquisitive, Ginsburg pushed her reading back into the years before the American Revolution. Under the old system of domestic law that prevailed in seventeenth-century England, the concept of coverture dictated a set of rules and practices that linked married women to the state through their husbands. "Covered" with her husband's civic identity, a wife, while entitled to economic support, had no legal or political rights of her own. Because she lacked an independent legal identity, there were relatively few constraints on what her spouse might do with her body, her property, her earnings, and her children. Since a wife's political interests were considered identical to his, she and her unmarried women relatives were denied the right to vote, nor did they have the right—and obligation—to sit on a jury. In practice, these common-law restrictions varied across race, region, and class in the early years of the American Republic. What few exemptions did exist with respect to holding property or making contracts were difficult and expensive to obtain.

New laws, enacted primarily during the second half of the nineteenth and the early twentieth centuries, gradually ate away at coverture. By the 1920s, in the aftermath of the long struggle for suffrage, women in the United States were able to own property, sue and be sued, vote, and in some states serve on juries. Yet the concept of coverture remained a powerful legal convention. As late as the 1960s, Ginsburg discovered, states still allowed husbands to control the bodies of their wives. The legal concept of marital rape did not yet exist. In Connecticut, where it was illegal to prescribe, distribute, or use birth control devices, women could not even determine how many children they might bear—assuming the law was enforced. In many states, husbands still controlled much of their wives' earnings and determined where the family lived. Women had no choice on so personal a matter as whose surname they would bear upon marriage. Even where coverture did not explicitly dictate the letter of the law, it cast a long shadow.

Hoyt v. Florida (1961), a Supreme Court case that Ginsburg long believed should have been decided differently, provided a perfect example. As late as 1960, an all-male jury had convicted Gwendolyn Hoyt, a battered wife, of second-degree murder for killing her husband. Hoyt's attorneys argued that the trial was unfair because no women were included in the jury. Florida's assistant attorney general, however, successfully defended his state's law exempting women from jury duty. Hoyt, he argued, had been tried by her peers because the larger jury pool had included names of women who had volunteered their services.

Writing for the Florida Supreme Court, Judge E. Harris Drew observed that the obligation for jury service conflicted with women's primary obligations to home and family. "Whatever changes may have taken place in the political or economic status of women in our society," he wrote, "nothing has yet altered the fact of their primary responsibility, *as a class,* for the daily welfare of the family unit upon which our civilization depends." The Warren Court, though initially divided 6–3, decided unanimously to uphold the Florida decision, including the basis for its jury-exemption statute. Justice John Harlan wrote, "Despite the enlightened emancipation of women from the restrictions and protections of bygone years and their entry into many parts of community life formerly considered to be reserved to men, woman is still regarded as the center of home and family life."

Neither the decision nor Harlan's comment surprised Ginsburg. Judge Drew and Justice Harlan were merely generalizing on the basis of their own communities, where, as the historian Linda Kerber notes, women were expected to be home to cook their husbands' dinners. Ginsburg acknowledged as much. "They can't help being influenced by their own life experience," she observed. Yet more than gender-role stereotypes were at play. There were also vestiges of coverture in the rationale offered to explain why there were no women on the Tampa jury. Women, it was assumed, discharged their obligations to the state for public service by their private service to husband and family. The consequences for women like Gwendolyn Hoyt were disastrous.

Hoyt, Ginsburg believed, had been denied by an unenlightened judicial system the opportunity to be tried by a jury of her peers. Why was it so hard to comprehend that women had to serve on juries on the same basis as men for Hoyt to have a fair trial? she wondered. To exempt women as a class from one of the fundamental obligations of citizenship, Hoyt's lawyers had charged, was anachronistic. Ginsburg could not have agreed more, especially when no law sanctioned restrictions. She was also convinced that women and men, like blacks and whites, have different life experiences, which is why the Court had decided that a black man could no longer be tried by an all-white jury. Biological difference was not what was at issue. Rather, it was what the world made of skin color. The fact that men and women, like blacks and whites, were treated differently created an operative difference that needed to be taken into account. It was that simple, she believed—and that complicated.

. . .

EVEN MORE TROUBLING than the vestiges of coverture was the persistence of nineteenth-century notions of womanhood, particularly the idea that the "weaker sex" required special safeguarding. Mirroring the preconceptions of their society, legislators and judges alike had allowed differential treatment that often worked to disadvantage women, all in the sincere belief that women actually benefited from such treatment. This conviction, sometimes referred to as "judicial paternalism" or "judicial patriarchy," had received its classic formulation in 1908.

In a celebrated decision in *Muller v. Oregon* (1908), the Court ruled unanimously that Oregon's maximum-hours legislation was an appropriate health measure for women workers but not for men. Women, the justices reasoned, suffered greater physical vulnerability because of their reproductive role, which set them apart from men, who should be free to contract their labor. "Differentiated by these matters from the other sex," the decision read, "she is properly placed in a class by herself, and legislation designed for her protection may be sustained, even when like legislation is not necessary for men, and could not be sustained." The decision was rightly praised at the time for upholding urgently needed labor reform for Oregon's non-unionized women workers. But it relegated all women legally to a separate class.

Even the passage of the Fair Labor Standards Act in 1938, which set a national minimum wage and maximum hours, did not immediately make the *Muller* rationale legal deadwood. The courts continued to treat women as members of a special class while treating men, in most circumstances, as individuals under the law, keeping alive the old trope that the two sexes inhabited separate spheres. Moreover, legal language persistently reflected gender stereotypes. The belief that differential treatment always benefited women, Ginsburg found, showed little sign of weakening.

In 1948, the Court in *Goesaert v. Cleary* had upheld a Michigan law excluding women from tending bar without the "protecting oversight" of a male owner, unless the woman in question was the wife or daughter of bar owners. According to Justice Frankfurter, "The Constitution does not require legislatures to reflect sociological insight, or shifting social standards." The ruling seemed particularly egregious to Ginsburg for two reasons. First, the statute had been initiated in a self-interested manner by a male bartenders' union eager to reduce competition from women. Second, Valentine Goesaert, the widow of a bar owner, brought the suit because she could not maintain the family business financially unless she and her daughter could continue working in the bar following her husband's death.

For Ginsburg, the conclusion was obvious. Gender discrimination—differentiation that combined stereotypical understanding of differences between the sexes with chivalrous (and often condescending) attitudes toward "the ladies"—pervaded the law, coloring other aspects of the Court's understanding of equal citizenship.

. . .

EQUALITY, as a principle of constitutional law set forth in the Fourteenth Amendment, meant that all persons similarly circumstanced should be treated alike under the law. That much was undisputed. But the popular and legal meaning of what it meant to be "similarly situated" or "similarly circumstanced" had varied historically. Race, for example—which had long been considered something fixed and essential—was in fact a fluid, shifting category.

Given this understanding, it followed that groups deemed not to have been "similarly situated" in the past could no longer be treated differently under the law. Thus, the Court began to closely examine laws and regulations discriminating between individuals on the basis of race, subjecting them to "strict" scrutiny. Did they violate the equal protection clause of the Fourteenth Amendment or, if federal laws were involved, the due process clause of the Fifth Amendment? Where skin color or other physical features such as hair once *seemed* to be evidence of an essential difference, justices by the 1950s could now view blacks and whites as similarly situated persons with a constitutional guarantee of equal treatment under the law.

But the Court balked at doing the same for the sexes. Ideology and social custom had made male and female bodily distinctions appear more important than any shared human characteristics. So deeply ingrained were divisions between the two sexes in time and space that women and men did not seem interchangeable.

The Nineteenth Amendment, the one place in the Constitution that mentions women specifically, might have transformed the legal relationships between men and women long before the 1960s had its full potential not been undermined by a narrow interpretation. Even the amendment's core guarantee—the right to vote—was, in the Deep South, denied to many poor white women and men. Impediments were devised such as the poll tax, literacy tests, and the grandfather clause, which had originally been designed primarily to disenfranchise African Americans. In fundamental ways, Ginsburg concluded, women—irrespective of race, religion, or economic status—simply were not yet legally full citizens.

The Warren Court, the most liberal Court in the twentieth century, had done nothing to remedy women's inferior legal status. Nor was the record of the lower courts on sex discrimination any better. Some of the prevailing laws that discriminated on the basis of sex seemed to Ginsburg to be not just unfair but absolutely "senseless." A Wisconsin statute, for example, allowed male barbers to cut the hair of men and women alike while female hairdressers could only snip the hair of women. "How," she wondered, "have people been putting up with such arbitrary distinctions? *How have I been putting up with them?*" The whole picture was simultaneously appalling and endlessly "fascinating." The more she read, the more engrossed she became. This was a denial of human rights as described in the Universal Declaration of Human Rights (1948).

· · ·

UNDERSTANDING HOW LAWS that purported to protect women's interests but in fact served to limit their civil rights and liberties also enabled Ginsburg to see how the law held the key to change. Using the equal protection clause on behalf of African Americans, as well as other groups, the Warren Court had potentially made itself the extender of federal safeguards to all citizens. In this new climate of rights-based litigation, might the Fifth and Fourteenth Amendments yet prove to be the emancipatory tool for women that nineteenth-century feminists had hoped they would be? Members of the President's Commission on the Status of Women had debated the question throughout the early 1960s, but efforts to find a suitable case to test the Court languished. If good cases could be found to which the Court would respond positively, sex-discrimination law could conceivably become a whole new field of study. By refocusing her research, she could be in the vanguard. The more Ginsburg thought about the possibility, the more excited she became. In a very real sense, this opportunity had fallen into her lap like one of James's soccer balls. She resolved to move the ball toward the goal with all the speed and intellectual agility she could muster.

· · ·

WHEN GINSBURG PROPOSED her new course titled "Women's Rights: Sex Discrimination and the Law," she undoubtedly knew that at NYU a male faculty member had responded that the Law School might as well teach a course on the law of the bicycle as a course on women and the law. But at Rutgers, Dean Heckel proved receptive. In response to previous student requests, he had encouraged Rutgers Law School faculty to expand the curriculum with new courses on civil rights, civil liberties, urban poverty, and legal representation of the poor. Likewise, programs in clinical education already included constitutional litigation, urban legal problems, consumer problems, environmental law, and prisoners' rights. So why not women's rights? Because Ginsburg had decided to make sex-based discrimination her new research specialty, Heckel could be confident that she would do the job well.

By 1970, Ginsburg had her course but no casebook—one of those thick, heavy volumes of relevant cases and commentary that are basic to instruction in every legal field. As she put together a mimeographed packet, she exchanged material with other trailblazers. Eleanor Holmes Norton, the assistant legal director at the ACLU, had been hired by NYU as an adjunct to teach a similar course the previous year. Barbara Bowman (who would later use Barbara A. Babcock as her professional name) had just agreed to commute weekly from Washington, where she worked as a public defender, to New Haven to teach Yale's new course before moving west to Stanford University. Ann Freedman, inspired by Sue Deller Ross and her sisters at NYU, had created a course with other women law students at Yale before graduating and planned to commute to Washington to teach a similar course at Georgetown University.

Ross, who had just joined the legal staff at the Equal Employment Opportunity Commission in Washington, had been promptly recruited by law students at George Washington University to create a course there together with Gladys Kessler, now a judge on the U.S. District Court for the District of Columbia. Kenneth Davidson offered a course at SUNY Buffalo initially to undergraduates and law students. And Leo Kanowitz at the University of New Mexico, who had just published his new book, *Women and the Law* (1969), an eye-opening call for change, extended the locale of these courses beyond the East Coast. Women at Berkeley's Boalt Hall were not far behind, persuading a lawyer from the Legal Aid Society of Alameda County to come to Berkeley, until the tenured faculty member and future dean Herma Hill Kay agreed to take over the course.

When this vanguard shared reading assignments, they were doing more than creating syllabi; they were defining a field. Just what ought to be covered under the generic label "Women and the Law"? Sex discrimination as reflected in constitutional law, criminal law, employment law, public accommodation, education, family law, and abortion constituted the core. But what else? How much history was essential? Should proposals for changing the law be included? To what extent should changes in U.S. law be linked to those occurring in other countries?

Most texts, they knew, were prepared by law professors aiming for objectivity. To what extent should feminist insights be included in their teaching materials? If the entire approach was to be feminist, shouldn't they lay out their viewpoint at the beginning of the course? Should they stick to cases and statutory materials, or should they try to get at the underlying causes of sex discrimination? How much should be included about cultural expectations? Was there some guideline on including material from other disciplines? Should selections from feminist classics be added? How about the first great feminist treatise, Mary Wollstonecraft's *Vindication of the Rights of Woman* (1792), or, better yet, John Stuart Mill's essay *The Subjection of Women* (1869)? How could one top Ginsburg's favorite Mill quotation? "The principle which regulates the existing social relations between the two sexes—the legal subordination of one sex to the other—is wrong in itself, and now one of the chief hindrances to human improvement . . . It ought to be replaced by a principle of perfect equality, admitting no power or privilege on the one side, nor disability on the other." There was always Margaret Mead's *Sex and Temperament* (1935). What about more recent feminist writings? Questions vastly outnumbered answers.

Energized by the exchanges, Ginsburg brimmed over with plans. To class discussions of general reading assignments, she would introduce a comparative dimension, taking note of gender-equality innovations in Sweden and elsewhere. She would also emphasize the toll extracted from men as well as women by sex-based discrimination. Examples were plentiful: the Illinois father who applied for custody of his illegitimate children after the death of their mother, only to learn that under Illinois law his claim to custody was no better than that of a stranger; the young Oregon man convicted of criminal conduct for living with a woman receiving public assistance (had he been a woman or she a man, no crime under Oregon law would have been committed); and the bachelor denied a federal income tax deduction for dependent care for the nurse he had engaged to attend his invalid mother (which would have been available had he been a daughter).

She also added a research component to her course, requiring each student to work on a project in a frontier area of the law. Not only would participants gain the exposure to socially relevant issues they craved, but Ginsburg could acquire much-needed data for her New Jersey sex-discrimination cases. Why not add a symposium on "women and the law"? Such a conference would help establish Rutgers's leadership in the new field as well as her own. She could introduce it with a quotation from John Stuart Mill, provide a comparative side-glance at policies affecting women in other countries, especially Sweden, and conclude with what she regarded as key items for the feminist agenda in the United States. Topping her list were vigilantly enforced equality of opportunity in employment and education, reproductive rights, and child-care facilities. In addition, Ginsburg added tax reforms to abolish "the marriage penalty" and allow deductions for child-care expenses.

When the response to the Rutgers symposium proved overwhelmingly enthusiastic, Ginsburg joined the students' efforts to create a new journal covering developments in the area of law "that especially affect women as women." In 1971, the *Women's Rights Law Reporter* published its first issue with an advisory board that constituted a Who's Who of early feminist lawyers and their allies: Eleanor Holmes Norton, then with the New York City Human Rights Commission; Pauli Murray, a founding member of NOW and ACLU board member; Ann Freedman, co-organizer of the Yale Law Women's Association and one of several co-authors with the Yale Law School professor and feminist Thomas Emerson of the much-cited article on the Equal Rights Amendment; Bernice Sandler of the Women's Equity Action League; Faith A. Seidenberg of the National Organization for Women; Nancy Stearns of the Center for Constitutional Rights; and Arthur Kinoy, civil rights strategist and Rutgers Law School professor who in 1966 founded the Center for Constitutional Rights with his fellow radical and law partner—the rambunctious, controversial, and ever-present William Kunstler.

The excitement, the challenge—the "sheer gutsiness" of it all—Ginsburg found "invigorating," though the effort clearly took a toll. A neighbor who often dropped by the Ginsburgs' apartment while Marty was preparing dinner observed that Ruth usually looked exhausted by the time she arrived home. Fatigue aside, Ginsburg knew that she was at the forefront of an entirely new field of study that could reach beyond the academy, reinforcing the momentum for change. Hectic schedules left little time to envision a future when the generic label "women and the law" would give way to feminist jurisprudence. For now, it was exhilarating enough just to know that new research, teaching, and professional activities meshed so completely with her own convictions.

. . .

MEANWHILE, GINSBURG and a few like-minded colleagues, spurred on by feminist students, had become convinced that a single course on women and the law was only one piece of the pie. Broader questions about the place of women in law schools and in the profession demanded answers in order to buttress proposed changes. The findings were not encouraging.

Female students were still few and far between. As late as the 1960s, an institution as prestigious as Berkeley's Boalt Hall failed to admit enough women even to fill its puny 10 percent quota. Women who did gain admission to law schools confronted animosity from male classmates, demeaning treatment from insensitive professors, and the near absence of female faculty who could act as role models and mentors. The hostility was such that a third-year student at Harvard Law reported that of the seven women in her first-year section in 1969 five found it necessary to see a psychiatrist regularly. Most toughed it out without professional help, though war in Southeast Asia added to the pressure. As a Yale student reported, "Given Vietnam, there was certainly a sense, and it was articulated some of the time, that it was bad enough that we were in school, but [worse] . . . we were taking the place of a man who . . . had to go to Vietnam."

Difficulties persisted after graduation, as students at NYU discovered from inquiries to their legal sisters elsewhere. In April 1970, women from seventeen different law schools as far south as Duke and as far west as Berkeley gathered at NYU. Resolving to put pressure on law school placement officers to deny offending firms the use of school facilities for interviews, they agreed to report incidents of sex discrimination by firms in their respective areas. Women who did manage to get hired often received lower pay and fewer promotions than their male counterparts. A mere 3 percent of the legal profession in 1970, they were scarcely represented in its higher ranks. Of the 2,700 lawyers employed by forty top law firms in six major cities, only 186 were women. Of almost 10,000 judges, fewer than 200 were female, and most of those were in courts of limited jurisdiction where they lacked upward mobility. Integration of women into the legal profession, Ginsburg and her allies concluded, had proceeded with about as much deliberate speed as racial integration in southern schools in the wake of the *Brown* decision. That would have to change.

Yet despite her new equality-oriented endeavors, Ginsburg had yet to identify herself as a feminist. Then she read Simone de Beauvoir's *Second Sex*. A feminist classic, first published in 1949, the book sparked an intellectual epiphany—the "click" moment that feminists refer to when the full force of feminism's powerful ideology came alive. One of the first works in contemporary Western culture that attempted to understand how and why women were socially constructed as inferior to men, *The Second Sex* offered insights that Ginsburg found "overwhelming," just "staggering."

Concepts of sex, sexual difference, internalized oppression, and woman-as-a-fluid-rather-than-a-fixed reality were presented by the French philosopher in a manner that Ginsburg had never previously considered. De Beauvoir had shown her a new way of looking at women and of understanding how they were oppressed. "There was a passion that suddenly gripped her," recalled Ruth's Rutgers friend and colleague Eva Hanks. "I remember her telling me that she was so affected by the book that she crawled into bed with Jane and read parts of it aloud." In fact, "she was so excited and talked to lots of colleagues about the book. She sort of caught fire. . . . She . . . found her goal or passion starting with that book." To emphasize the point, Hanks noted, "Even the men in the department noticed the change in Ruth. It was unmistakable."

. . .

BUT NOT ALL FEMINISTS were as analytically compelling as de Beauvoir. The shrill rhetoric, disruptive tactics—and what, in a moment of self-criticism, a radical feminist called the "hippy-yippy-campy" quality of more extreme elements of the women's liberation movement—struck Ginsburg as counterproductive. She was a woman for whom the word "moderate" "dangled from her wrist like an ID bracelet." Polarizing language, ideological fractiousness, and confrontational tactics simply did not appeal to her. Yet as a student of history, she was too astute not to recognize both the basis for radicals' anger and the fact that their media-savvy protests could make the demands of moderates more acceptable. Moreover, she fully agreed with the central insight of radical feminists— the distinction between sex (biology) and gender (culture).

"Woman," she had learned from Mill, de Beauvoir, and the Swedes, is a social construct. Society defines women and men through the unconscious acceptance of gender norms and constraints that naturalize difference and exclusion. It follows, therefore, that women—and men—could change that construct and themselves by changing institutions and practices. That was what Sweden's "right to be human" was all about. As for the conviction that a woman's most basic right was the right to consent to pregnancy, she believed that, too.

For Ginsburg, the words in the "Bill of Rights" of the newly organized National Organization for Women, stressing the right of women to "full participation in the mainstream of American society now, exercising all the privileges and responsibilities thereof in truly equal partnership with men," struck the loudest chord. She believed in equal privileges; she believed just as strongly in equal responsibilities; and in her private life she had always taken for granted the principle of equal partnership. She and Marty had based their marriage on the premise that shared work-family roles permitted both partners to share the burdens and joys of domestic life and the professional world alike.

. . .

GINSBURG'S FEMINIST CONSCIOUSNESS HAD, in fact, been long in the making and bore the distinctive imprint of her personal history. Celia, most importantly, with her insistence on independence and achievement, had provided a role model of a strong, intelligent, and competent woman. Prefiguring the adult feminist was the young reader who was deeply impressed by Anne Frank's indictment of gender inequality and the high school student who passionately objected to all-male minyans when sitting shivah after her mother's death. Other experiences also registered: early job rejections, pregnancy discrimination, exposure to Sweden's more gender-equitable society and the accompanying ideology of *jämställdhet,* pay disparities for women law faculty, sex-related barriers affecting her New Jersey ACLU clients, and discovery of how penalizing stereotypes saturated the law. Add to these the complaints from women law students about professors who acted as though the legal world was still an exclusive men's club. How could they not react to such blatantly gender-biased statements in textbooks as the assertion that "land, like woman, was meant to be possessed"?

And there was more. There were meetings in which she voiced an idea, only to have it attributed to one of the men present, or irritating professional occasions when "Mrs. Ginsburg's" qualifications were limited to "wife and mother of two." Marty—or any other male lawyer for that matter—would never have been introduced with reference to his family relationships rather than his professional credentials. Yet it happened to her with annoying frequency. Though she tried hard to keep her sense of humor, such introductions violated her sense of identity and demeaned her professionalism. There were also all those meetings to which she was invited that were held at clubs to which "men only" were admitted. She now made it a matter of principle to call such inappropriate rules to the attention of the meeting's organizers, trying, of course, to make her position clear without arousing resentment or animosity. In this personal evolution, the process of radicalization was cumulative and strikingly thorough.

Ginsburg's feminist identification, once acknowledged, proved deep and abiding. She truly believed that if gender barriers erected by law and culture could be removed and supportive social policies implemented, women would function as men's full equals in the nation's social, political, and economic life. The wisdom of Sarah Grimké's plea, which she liked to quote, rang as true to her in 1970 as it did when the noted abolitionist and equal rights advocate first proclaimed it in 1837: "I ask no favor for my sex. All I ask of our brethren is that they take their feet off our necks."

Feminism, Ginsburg knew from the outset, really was an international phenomenon. She could rattle off specifics. The UN General Assembly had already adopted its "Convention on the Elimination of Discrimination Against Women." Both halves of a divided Germany had legalized women's legal status as men's equals. France, Israel, Sweden, and the Soviet Union had taken steps to provide new mothers with greater job security and compensation for loss of earnings during pregnancy-related illnesses and childbirth. Sweden had implemented programs to attack gender coding of jobs and revised its tax policy to permit individual taxation. Norway, Sweden, and the Soviet Union had ultimately concluded that "administrative inconvenience," cited as the reason why married women could not retain their birth names, was really no barrier. In Switzerland, women had finally been granted equal voting rights in federal elections, and there were encouraging signs in places as distant as China and Senegal.

This was a movement about human rights that she had to be part of. Here was her chance to "do something."

<hr>

CHAPTER 6

Seizing the Moment

· · ·

Asked later how she became a cause lawyer, Ginsburg replied that "it was all a matter of being in the right place at the right time." But it was much more than that. "Chance," aptly observed a Nobel Prize winner, "favors only those who know how to court her."

· · ·

MELVIN WULF, the legal director of the national office of the ACLU in Manhattan, arrived in Newark to visit Frank Askin, who taught constitutional law at Rutgers Law School. When they concluded their business, Askin asked his guest if he would like to stop by the office of Ruth Ginsburg. She had told him that the two were summer camp acquaintances. Wulf was delighted: this must be Kiki Bader from Flatbush, whom he remembered well as an ebullient Che-Na-Wah camper. As a sixteen-year-old former camper turned waiter, Wulf, who had starred in the camp's big production of Gilbert and Sullivan's *Patience,* had been assigned a table of twelve-year-old girls—among them, the spirited and vivacious Kiki.

The woman Wulf encountered in Newark was now a slim, suntanned, and conservatively dressed law professor busily preparing for class. What struck him most was how completely the remarkable exuberance of the youthful, breezy camper had been transmuted into mature restraint. The woman he engaged in conversation had a serious bearing and considered style of speaking. One could almost see her mentally formulating every word—attributes, Wulf could assume, that had been honed during years of playing on male turf.

The adult Ruth's quiet, unassuming demeanor only partially con-

cealed her relentless will and astonishing capacity for work. Even more
effectively hidden was her ambition, a trait admired in men but considered so inappropriate in women at the time that most female professionals worked hard to keep it invisible.

Within minutes, it became clear to these former campers how much
their lives had diverged despite their common Columbia law degrees.
Wulf, who started out on the national ACLU's two-person legal staff in
New York, was never one to miss a new area of rights activity. In 1961,
he co-authored with Ruth Calvin Emerson, wife of the Yale professor
Thomas Emerson, an amicus curiae (friend of the court) brief in *Poe
v. Ullman,* a Connecticut birth control case that helped lay a constitutional basis for privacy in matters related to marital sexual expression.
As ACLU legal director, he devoted his considerable energies to leading
the organization into the legal vanguard of the civil rights struggle. Then
came the Vietnam conflict. A passionate foe of the war, Wulf included
antiwar resisters in the ACLU's defense efforts, despite initial dissent
within the organization.

The timing of the reunion proved fortuitous. In the fall of 1970, the
new executive director of the ACLU, Aryeh Neier, had come up with an
important project. Neier, the former head of the organization's innovative New York City affiliate, was, at the age of thirty-three, the youngest
national executive director in the organization's history. He was also one
of its most outspoken and resourceful. Convinced by the Warren Court
that "nothing was beyond the reach of litigation," he saw the ACLU's
successful grant-supported special civil rights project of the 1960s as a
prototype for others. Why not extend full citizenship rights to *all* rights-
disadvantaged groups? A special project on women's rights, he proposed,
should be the next step. For Neier's plans to proceed on schedule, the
ACLU needed a director and chief litigator for the nascent Women's
Rights Project, preferably a good litigation strategist with some courtroom experience.

When Wulf and Ginsburg parted, neither could have anticipated how
soon they would reconnect, thanks to the help of her devoted spouse.

Sitting at home one night in late October 1970, reading the weekly
publication of rulings by the tax courts, Marty Ginsburg walked over
to his wife's desk. Read this case, he urged her. Charles E. Moritz, Ruth
discovered, was a traveling salesman for a book company who lived with

Melvin Wulf, legal director of the national office of the ACLU from 1962 to 1977, whom Ginsburg had known when they were summer camp acquaintances.

his eighty-nine-year-old invalid mother in Denver, Colorado. Unable to care for her while at work, Moritz, a bachelor, hired nursing help. When tax time rolled around, he attempted to deduct a portion of what he paid the nurse. The Internal Revenue Code allowed an income tax deduction in such circumstances for never-married, employed daughters but not for sons. The IRS denied him the deduction. Claiming sex discrimination, Moritz pleaded his own case before the U.S. Tax Court, which upheld the IRS's original ruling. When she finished reading the facts of the case, Ruth's response was just what her husband anticipated: "Let's take it." Here was the first of the essential test cases she needed—if they could persuade Moritz to appeal within the required ninety days.

What both Ginsburgs saw, apart from Moritz's personal plight, was a classic example of sex discrimination based on stereotypes that cut both ways, denying fair, equal treatment to men as well as women. Refusing Charles Moritz a tax deduction could be understood as a violation of the constitutional guarantee that neither the federal government nor the states could treat similarly situated citizens differently—in this case, never-married, employed men and women. But would the court of appeals see it this way? Sex-discrimination cases had always been brought by women and fared poorly in the courts, though recent developments were a bit more encouraging.

· · ·

INITIATION OF A TEST CASE, especially with a male plaintiff, would not be easy. When the Ginsburgs set to work on a brief, it was clear that two points were essential. First, they needed to illustrate why Charles Moritz's plight constituted sex-based discrimination. Second, because the case involved federal rather than state law, they would have to show why and how the equal protection component the Court had read into the due process clause of the Fifth Amendment applied to Section 214(a) of the tax code. There were also other pressing matters to consider—not the least of them, Ruth's inexperience as a litigator. Marty, a veteran petitioner in tax cases, would act as co-counsel, handling all aspects of the case relating to the Internal Revenue Code. But first Moritz had to be persuaded to let them appeal the case.

Marty made the contact; Moritz was dubious. He could not imagine why any legitimate lawyer would want to pursue the case when so puny a sum was involved—under $300. Marty patiently explained the notion of a test case, assuring Moritz that he would be under no obligation to pay any lawyers' fees. Because even appearing to solicit business was considered unethical by the American Bar Association in 1970, the couple needed an institutional sponsor.

Mel Wulf, Ruth calculated, was not likely to pass up a case that was "as neat a craft as one could find" to test sex-based discrimination against the Constitution—a description that she knew would recall the lyrics Wulf sang in the camp's production of the Gilbert and Sullivan operetta *Ruddigore*. If the tax court ruling could be overturned, she assured the ACLU legal director, an "important foothold" would be "secured for women's rights cases." Adding that she had spoken to Norman Dorsen, she reported that the ACLU's general counsel was enthusiastic. Dorsen had also promised to take up with Wulf the possibility of making *Moritz* an ACLU case. The Ginsburgs would act as co-counsel at no charge if only the ACLU would cover the costs. It was not that she and Marty were unable to pay the expenses, she explained. Rather, she needed the ACLU's backing. "We will take the case to the Tenth Circuit, and if our achievement is not glorious there, we will make a valorous try at the Supreme Court." Flattered no doubt that she remembered his stirring entry in *Ruddigore* when the chorus sang, "From the briny sea / Comes young Richard, all victorious! / Valorous is he— / His achievements all are glorious!" Wulf gave his assurance within three days.

Though Ruth now had the endorsement of the national ACLU, she still had no client and, of course, no brief. Moritz preferred to move cautiously. It took a series of phone calls and finally a letter from Marty on the firm letterhead of Weil, Gotshal & Manges to persuade him to go ahead with the appeal.

In midwinter, the Ginsburgs left the city for a two-day trip to draft the crux of the argument, a "docketing statement," which she sent to Wulf. He replied that it met "the high standard to be expected of one who was early exposed to the rigorous discipline of Camp Che-Na-Wah." The government, also impressed, offered to settle. Moritz declined, holding out for a legal precedent, as had been agreed with the Ginsburgs.

Ruth now set to work on the brief, consulting with Dorsen, whom she had known since her days on the *Harvard Law Review*. In turning to Dorsen, she gained the advice of a "master strategist" and superb brief writer who was currently serving as lead advocate for the ACLU in the famous 1971 Pentagon Papers case. An ardent supporter of the ACLU's use of strategic cases to introduce the judiciary to critical issues in need of consideration, he had just testified before the Senate Judiciary Committee on behalf of an equal rights amendment. Ginsburg had every reason to believe that Dorsen's judgment mattered a great deal. In April 1971, upon completion of the brief, she received the resounding endorsement from Dorsen that she had hoped for. His pronouncement that *Moritz v. Commissioner of Internal Revenue* was "one of the very best presentations I have seen in a long time" was just what the untested brief writer needed to hear.

. . .

AS THE PLANE LIFTED OFF the runway at LaGuardia en route to Denver, where the Ginsburgs would appear before the U.S. Court of Appeals for the Tenth Circuit, Ruth reviewed her argument. The tax court had determined that Moritz had no basis for his discrimination complaint, because Congress had denied all never-married, employed men an exemption. The Denver resident had not been arbitrarily singled out; therefore, his constitutional right to due process had not been violated. To get that ruling overturned, the Ginsburgs faced an uphill battle. The federal courts had never found a provision of the modern Internal Revenue Code unconstitutional.

Norman Dorsen (second from left) is toasted by (from left to right) Alan Reitman, Roger Baldwin, and Aryeh Neier of the ACLU in December 1976, after he was elected president.

To succeed, Ruth resolved to make three points clearly and convincingly: first, that Section 214(a) of the Internal Revenue Code drew a line based solely on sex; second, that Congress had no legitimate rationale for writing the code in such a fashion; and finally, that doing so deprived Charles Moritz of his constitutional right to equal protection. Specifying that any woman could qualify for a tax deduction for the care of an incapacitated dependent parent while denying that deduction to a never-married, employed man, she would insist, constituted unwarranted differentiation on the part of Congress. Nothing in the legislative history of Section 214(a) or in what was known about biological differences between the sexes could provide a rational basis for such a distinction. The rule not only violated contemporary notions of fair and equal treatment; it also ignored the Fifth Amendment's due process clause, which had been interpreted to encompass a guarantee of equal protection of the law and of security from arbitrary treatment. Charles Moritz, she would plead, deserved to be granted "the constitutional guarantees of due process and equal protection that apply to all *persons,* a class in which men and women share full membership."

In the oral argument, the Ginsburgs agreed, style would count as much as content. The case would have to be made narrowly with no overreaching claims for gender justice. Instead, she determined to paint the plaintiff's plight so vividly that from even the briefest description Charles Moritz's voice would emerge as a real person—a skill harking back to Nabokov's word pictures, which she would continue to hone in future cases. Legal arguments on Moritz's behalf would be supported with case citations in the brief. And never, never, she vowed, would she be threatening or emotional. Rather, she must lead the judges to the desired judgment in a way that would be comfortable for them. Moritz deserved to win. But her larger goal remained that of establishing equal protection as a viable weapon with which to attack sex discrimination in the law.

. . .

AS THE COUPLE BECAME ACQUAINTED with their client over dinner in Denver, Ruth was impressed by Moritz, who seemed to be a man of great integrity. At the hearing the following day, Marty began. He explained to the three judges the tax issues involved in the case and responded to questions, which soon spilled over into constitutional matters. Quickly realizing that he was intruding into his wife's territory, he turned to Ruth. Answering every question, the novice litigator made precisely the points she had planned. But whether the Ginsburgs had convinced the panel remained to be seen; the decision would not be handed down for nearly eighteen months.

In the meantime, Ginsburg hoped to use the *Moritz* brief as a prototype for another sex-discrimination case, *Reed v. Reed*. If the Supreme Court chose to hear the case, the ACLU would be involved, and she could then approach Wulf about writing the brief. What she did not know at the time was that the ACLU had a feminist past. Nor was she personally acquainted with the women on the national board—Dorothy Kenyon, Harriet Pilpel, and Pauli Murray—whose advocacy of feminist issues within the ACLU had so effectively paved the way for her own role and to whom she would later pay homage.

. . .

NONE HAD BEEN MORE STALWART than Dorothy Kenyon, a pathbreaking feminist advocate who gained national and international recognition for her work on behalf of equal rights in the 1930s and 1940s. Resident feminist gadfly on the ACLU's national executive board for over forty years, she chaired its Women's Rights Committee. Opposing discrimination against married women during the Depression and advocating equal pay and employment practices in the years after World War II, she made the issue of equal jury selection her own. In the midst of the civil rights struggle, when her committee was renamed the Equality Committee, Kenyon argued that women's equality could not be ignored. By the time she wrote the ACLU's first amicus brief in *Hoyt v. Florida* (1961), she was convinced that legal classifications based on sex were rooted in archaic stereotypes about both sexes, reinforcing women's second-class citizenship, and must be updated. Describing herself as "a Cassandra crying out in the ACLU wilderness against the crime of our abortion laws and man's inhumanity to women," the now white-haired Kenyon had formed a troika in the 1960s with the new board members Harriet Pilpel and Pauli Murray to move the ACLU into the forefront of a resurgent feminist movement.

As counsel to Planned Parenthood and later the ACLU, Pilpel had participated in every significant birth control case since 1936. A significant player in the legal wing of the new abortion law reform movement, in 1964 she and Kenyon succeeded in getting the ACLU to study state abortion laws. With the Court's decision in *Griswold v. Connecticut* (1965), which protected marital partners' use of contraception as a constitutional right of "privacy," she encouraged efforts to expand *Griswold* so as to make the termination of a pregnancy a rights issue. She and Kenyon led the effort to persuade the ACLU to endorse a woman's right to an abortion during the first three months of pregnancy.

Pauli Murray—whom Kenyon and the civil rights leader James Farmer brought onto the board in 1965—proved an equally powerful ally on sex discrimination. A multitalented woman whose life was a lesson in the harmful effects of discrimination based on race, sex, and sexual preference, Murray had been a law student at Howard University in 1944 when she attached a letter to her senior thesis on dismantling race-based segregation. "Now," she asked her adviser, "how do I go about killing 'Jane Crow'—prejudice against sex?" Awarded a Rosenthal Fellowship for further study at Harvard Law School, she was rejected because of her sex. By the time she had earned a master of law degree at Berkeley's Boalt

Dorothy Kenyon, Pauli Murray, and Harriet Pilpel— advocates of feminist issues and members of the ACLU national board—provided the groundwork and inspiration that Ginsburg would build upon.

Hall, published a book Thurgood Marshall described as the bible of civil rights lawyers, and completed a doctorate in jurisprudence at Yale, she had the answer to her question.

When she and Kenyon had completed their section of the brief on Alabama's exclusion of blacks and women from juries in *White v. Crook*, Murray inserted into the appendix of the brief a prepublication copy of an innovative article that she had just co-authored, provocatively titled "Jane Crow and the Law." In it, she and Mary Eastwood, a lawyer at the Department of Justice (DOJ), argued that the eradication of sex-based discrimination in the law deserved the same commitment and resources that had previously been aimed at discrimination based on race.

Their argument, that women and African Americans had been subjected to strikingly similar forms of subordination, relied primarily on sociological sources. Reasoning by analogy, the pair was careful to acknowledge critical differences. Yet they maintained that in essence the two forms of discrimination were comparable and their histories interrelated. Similar myths and mechanisms—including the law—had perpetuated the inferior status of both groups.

"Sex" as a valid basis for legal classification had implications comparable to the "now discredited doctrine of 'separate but equal'" with respect to race, the pair contended. The willingness of the Supreme Court, however, to apply the equal protection clause to race-based discrimination but not to sex-based discrimination was a failure of the courts and not of the Fourteenth Amendment, which could easily encompass all forms of arbitrary discrimination.

But to follow the NAACP's strategy in *Brown* by challenging various forms of sex discrimination under the equal protection clause with well-developed arguments and carefully coordinated amici briefs, as Murray and Kenyon envisioned, required an intermediate step. Partnership between the emerging women's movement and the ACLU would be essential. As a member of President Kennedy's Commission on the Status of Women and a founding member of NOW, Murray set to work.

To bring the ACLU into the feminist camp, she had to persuade the organization's Equality Committee and ultimately the ACLU board to expand their own understanding of discrimination. A passionate and persistent advocate, Murray prevailed after a three-year effort. Critical support came from key colleagues on the executive board as well as from feminist delegates from ACLU affiliates. In 1970, she and Kenyon—now ill with cancer—presented the ACLU leadership with a far-ranging resolution that called for the pursuit of a "dual strategy" consisting of equal protection litigation as well as passage of the ERA. They also demanded organizational advocacy of a woman's right to control her own body, including the right to abortion, sterilization, and also protection from involuntary sterilization—a position that Pilpel, now vice-chair of the ACLU, ardently supported. The "troika," as Kenyon referred to herself and her two allies, had done its work.

In September 1970, the board of the foremost organization of civil libertarians in the nation overwhelmingly endorsed the ERA by a vote of 52–1, thus fully embracing the feminist movement. The ACLU's president, Aryeh Neier, also proposed a special project on women's rights. The new initiative was a fitting tribute to two indomitable women. Kenyon would not live to celebrate the project's first Supreme Court victory, while Murray would break new barriers in 1973 as a seminarian and future Episcopalian priest. But together with Pilpel and stalwart feminist affiliates and male allies in the ACLU leadership, they created a rare opportunity—an institutional base in a venerable and aggressive civil liberties/civil rights organization for an ambitious advocate eager to create law curtailing sex discrimination. Though Ginsburg would build on their arguments, she had yet to make that base hers.

· · ·

IN APRIL 1971, with the school year soon to end, Ginsburg contacted Wulf. Reminding him that she had volunteered to write the appellant's brief in *Reed v. Reed* should the Supreme Court agree to hear the case, she sent along a copy of the *Moritz* brief. At issue in *Reed* was an Idaho law stipulating, "Where there are several persons equally entitled to

The ACLU's president, Aryeh Neier, appointed Ginsburg to the first directorship of the Women's Rights Project, 1972.

administer the estate of a person dying intestate, males must be preferred to females." The equal protection argument that she had used in
her *Moritz* brief could be applied as well to *Reed,* she noted. Her letter
ended with a tantalizing question: "Have you thought about whether it
would be appropriate to have a woman co-counsel in that case???" Wulf
and Ginsburg understood each other perfectly. "*We* will write the brief,"
he replied.

As the two worked together on the brief during the summer of 1971,
Wulf grew to appreciate Ruth's legal acumen, sound judgment, and
precision. Her research, he concluded, was "impeccable"; she had even
included in the brief two recent decisions from the West German Constitutional Court that had rejected sex-based preferences. She did so, she
explained, not because she expected the U.S. Supreme Court to follow
blindly the lead of its European counterparts. Rather, the justices should
know what other high courts were doing about sex discrimination.

Ginsburg lacked experience as a litigator. But after reviewing the
brief, Wulf concluded that she was just the right person to realize the
potential of the proposed Women's Rights Project. Dorsen and Neier
agreed. She had the academic credentials, the ability, and, above all,
the ambition—that essential "fire in the belly." Dorsen recalled, "At the
time, Ruth had not yet managed to conceal fully her feelings about her
personal experiences with discrimination; there was still some rawness
there." But that, he acknowledged, only fed her determination.

· · ·

IF SHE ACCEPTED the directorship of the Women's Rights Project,
Ginsburg knew that she would have advantages that advocates in other
feminist legal organizations lacked. Foremost was the opportunity to be
part of a long-established human rights organization. "Civil liberties," she
explained, "are an essential part of the overall human rights concern—
the equality of all people and the ability to be free." And the ACLU has
long been a player in such historically important cases as *Scopes, Sacco
and Vanzetti,* and *Scottsboro.* An impressive string of Supreme Court victories over the years had heightened the ACLU's influence over U.S. law
and public policy. Its record of success before the Warren Court over the
decade from 1954 to 1964 had placed the organization at the vanguard of
a broad range of critical social issues, redeeming its compromised record

during the McCarthy era. ACLU litigators—among them Dorsen, Marvin Karpatkin, and the venerable Osmond Fraenkel—had extraordinary expertise, making them invaluable mentors. Not to be discounted was funding and a national network of affiliates.

A start-up fund of $50,000 from the ACLU, combined with a small grant (eventually $100,000) from the Playboy Foundation, would soon create a pool of financial resources for litigation greater than what was available either to NOW or to the Women's Equity Action League (WEAL), another feminist advocacy group. And additional grants seemed possible, given the ACLU's long history of foundation support. As director of the Women's Rights Project, she would have a staff—however small—and resources to take her cases as far as the courts allowed. With access to relevant cases from across the nation generated by affiliates, she could choose those she judged most likely to win.

In addition, the position would thrust her into the mainstream of a new kind of advocacy. In the 1960s and 1970s, the ACLU's newer ventures were transforming the venerable organization, like other specialized public-interest legal organizations, into what came to be known as cause lawyering. A radical departure from traditional law firms, where attorneys engaged in remunerative work for individual and corporate clients along with a little pro bono representation, cause lawyers were free to align their values and practice. Unencumbered by the constraints of established firms, they could actually do something about a cause in which they believed.

A protean and heterogeneous enterprise, cause lawyering stretched the conventions of legal practice. Advocates chose cases most likely to maximize legal gains for the cause itself, even if that left some of them vulnerable to the charge that they might be putting cause above client. They also engaged in activities other than litigation, encouraging public education as well as remedial legislation—an essential activity in Ginsburg's view. As anyone following the Swedish prime minister Olof Palme's Social Democrats knew, substantive equality required not just legal victories but extensive legislative efforts as well.

The number of female lawyers involved in cause lawyering was high—not because they were necessarily more altruistic than their male counterparts, but because they had fewer professional options. Also, as women, they could finally "speak truth to power." That fact alone helped compensate for the long hours, heavy workload, and other inconveniences associated with cause lawyering.

· · ·

BEFORE JOINING THEIR RANKS, Ginsburg needed to get in place another piece of her professional life. She had always yearned to be at a first-rate law school that did not require a commute that literally generated nightmares. She had begun exploring new venues shortly after her promotion to full professor at Rutgers. Though she had spent a semester as a visiting faculty member at New York University Law School in the spring of 1968, no offer of a permanent position had followed due to a hiring freeze. But there would soon be other options, thanks in good part to the federal government.

In 1970, the Nixon administration extended affirmative action to universities. As with businesses holding federal contracts over $50,000, universities had to formulate affirmative-action plans for hiring minorities and women with goals and timetables. Specific numbers or quotas were not mentioned, but employers had to set "reasonably attainable targets" and make a "good faith effort" to hire individuals on the basis of merit or risk cancellation of government contracts.

With the "old boy" tradition of job placement under federal scrutiny, it was no accident that Ginsburg received an invitation from Harvard to join the Law School faculty as a visiting professor for the fall semester of 1971. In the academic world, visiting professorships often serve as a trial marriage: host faculty and visitor can size up each other and decide whether they want to tie the knot. But as Ginsburg soon discovered, commuting to Cambridge for classes—in addition to her regular teaching at Rutgers—was not an optimal situation for a job candidate eager to be at her best. One day, when a Harvard faculty member told her as she was walking to class that he would be attending to observe her teaching, her heart sank. She was so exhausted from staying up most of the night to finish a brief that she felt fortunate just to remain standing upright. As the fall semester wound down, Ginsburg met with her old champion Albert Sacks, now the Law School's dean. Sacks urged her to continue teaching through the spring, allowing the faculty more time to decide whether to offer her a permanent position.

Ginsburg declined. Harvard had weathered its own annus horribilis in 1969, when police and student protesters faced off in Harvard Yard. At the Law School, students had a long list of grievances, over which faculty were divided. But it was not just the legitimacy of student discontent and its remedies that eroded the old sense of community that had flourished at Langdell Hall. By 1970, two new schools of legal thought had taken over: Chicago-style law and economics on the Right and critical legal studies (CLS) on the Left. Sacks might now be the school's chief administrator, but process theory had been pronounced "dead." In its wake, "Crits [CLS] and their enemies waged aerial dogfights over legal philosophy, while grim trench warfare went on below over admissions, appointments, and curriculum," declared an astute observer. Knowing that proposed female and minority faculty appointments would be casualties in this ideological minefield, Ginsburg had sensibly surmised that her future lay elsewhere. She had learned her lesson at Rutgers, where she and Eva Hanks had received a divided vote for tenure from a deeply fragmented faculty. Also, she had her eye on Columbia.

· · ·

SO DID THE OFFICE of Civil Rights (OCR). Old timers on the Columbia faculty—some of whom were actually still quite young—complained vehemently, as did their Harvard counterparts, that the absence of women on the Law School faculty did not constitute a problem. Nor did the fact that the male-female ratio among law students had remained ten to one for the last thirty years merit concern. As one veteran member of the Columbia Law School faculty put it, "It really wasn't sexism so much as just not wanting to change the club-like atmosphere that prevailed." Such sentiments were not confined to the Law School, as university-wide hearings on the status of women made clear in 1970. Nor did it mean that Columbia's record was worse than that of its counterparts elsewhere. According to *The New York Times,* thirty-six universities and colleges holding federal contracts, including Columbia, were soon to be charged with sex discrimination. An investigation of Harvard had already begun.

With the clock running, the gentlemen's clubs of the country's most prestigious law schools began scrambling. Michael Sovern, the popular new dean of the Columbia Law School, called a faculty meeting for the purpose of selecting a woman. Hans Smit had talked about hiring Ruth

Ginsburg for years, but to no avail. Though her name was not on the short list of possibilities to be discussed, Smit had copies of Ginsburg's résumé put around the table in front of each chair before the meeting began. Attached was a letter from a Rutgers colleague whom Smit had told, "Don't try to make her out to be a great lecturer. Just talk about her command of her subject." The letter, a paean to Ginsburg's scholarly expertise, had the desired impact. Because various members of the faculty had taught the candidate, she was a known quantity. And one thing they "knew": this woman was no militant feminist likely to create problems. She had no record of faculty activism at Rutgers. So Ginsburg it would be. Back in his office, Sovern picked up the phone.

Could she attend a cocktail party to which the entire law faculty had been invited, Sovern asked. "We're not going to ask you to show and tell," he said, referring to the usual faculty job interview, where prospective candidates were expected to sell themselves to their hosts. "We want you . . . and we are having a friendly gathering to persuade you to accept our offer." Ginsburg happily accepted. Keenly aware of the role of the OCR, she knew that the doors of Greene Hall had not opened in a spontaneous acclamation of the importance of her scholarship and her riveting lectures. But neither did she sell herself short. If she could reach an arrangement with the Law School and the ACLU that would allow her to divide her time between the two, she could well have the best of both worlds.

Marty realized that this was a critical moment in his wife's career. He had done his best to share the responsibilities of parenting, but Ruth had borne much the heavier load during the years when he was racing to partnership and building a name for himself. Now he could afford to do more.

The children were also growing up. A much happier Jane was now in high school and would soon be off to college, probably the University of Chicago. A staunch feminist, she could appreciate what her mother wanted to accomplish. And the housekeeper would be on hand to help with James. A bright, high-spirited, exceedingly talkative, energetic six-year-old, he loved music, math, and soccer but found it difficult to focus on school subjects that were not among his favorites. The towheaded youngster also had a seemingly unrivaled talent for engaging in escapades. His various capers brought frequent calls from the prestigious

Dalton School summoning his mother. Frustrated by the fact that she was always the one who had to meet with school authorities, Ginsburg finally told the principal, "This child has two parents. Please alternate calls." As she had anticipated, the principal had second thoughts about interrupting Marty, and she was now spared frequent trips. Also, she felt she no longer had to overcompensate for being a working mother by taking her lively son to every cultural event for children in Manhattan, as she had done with Jane.

At the age of thirty-eight, it was now her turn to make her mark outside legal academia. Her husband and daughter would back her completely. While Marty could not promise the outcome of the cases so key to her equal protection argument—*Moritz* and *Reed*—what he lacked in certainty, he made up for in confidence. In little more than a year, his wife had found cases and developed an equal protection argument that involved not just an effort to rid the law of sex-based classifications but "a far richer theory," notes the legal scholar Cary Franklin. Involved as well was the constitutional limitations on the state's power to enforce stereotypes. In addition, she had secured offers to be the ACLU's leading women's rights advocate and Columbia Law School's first female full professor in its 114-year history. A woman who believed that "if you want something badly enough you find a way," Marty knew, was not to be underestimated.

. . .

IN JANUARY 1972, *The New York Times* carried the headline "Columbia Law Snares a Prize in the Quest for Women Professors." The accompanying article called Ginsburg's appointment a "major coup" for the university. Congratulatory letters by the dozens flowed in on legal letterhead and on the personal stationery of old friends and classmates. A former student at Brooklyn Public School 238 inquired if Columbia's "prize" was indeed the Kiki Bader whom he remembered as having "very blonde hair and a lovely flashing smile and of course being very bright." Jack B. Weinstein, a judge on the U.S. District Court of Appeals, added his congratulations along with the observation that "our procedure group is now truly extraordinary." Judge Palmieri, who was reportedly buying up all the copies of *The New York Times* he could find, expressed his great delight along with a fatherly admonition—"don't work too hard." Senator George McGovern, whose presidential candidacy had won Jane Ginsburg's ardent support, sent his congratulations along with an emphatic denunciation of gender discrimination.

Columbia's president, William J. McGill, was also quick to convey his pleasure in what would be the first of many exchanges between the two. "A number of lawyers downtown, a large number of the Law School faculty, and my old friend Jennifer McLeod at Rutgers have told me how lucky we are," McGill wrote, "and I'm prepared to believe it. . . . I should also add that I was ready to say all these things even before I read the wonderful publicity about you in the *New York Times*. After that, you can have almost anything, even my office!"

Responding graciously, Ginsburg was nevertheless a bit miffed when McGill noted that with her appointment the Law School had now met half of its affirmative-action target. The comment offended Ruth's sense of merit. She knew she had the right credentials and she had certainly paid her dues professionally. Lund University in Sweden had awarded her an honorary degree in 1969, along with the traditional tall pleated hat and a much-cherished gold ring, the only ring she wore. Surely, she

Ginsburg began teaching at Columbia Law School while also serving with the ACLU, 1972.

had earned her place on the faculty. But sensibilities on both sides were raw in the tension-filled atmosphere of Columbia in 1971–72.

. . .

MCGILL HAD TAKEN ON the formidable task of knitting back together a financially strapped university in the wake of a radical student takeover and long-standing tensions with its African American and Puerto Rican neighbors in Harlem and Morningside Heights. Then he discovered that he had a gender problem as well. A report compiled by Columbia Women's Liberation on the paucity of women on the faculty at Columbia and their near absence in the senior ranks had made its way to the desk of J. Stanley Pottinger, head of the Civil Rights Division of the Department of Justice.

Struck by the report's juxtaposition of the number of women earning advanced degrees and the number employed in a breakdown by department, Pottinger had asked Columbia for employment data sorted by race and gender. When his requests were repeatedly ignored, Pottinger—who was under intense pressure from women's groups to enforce government guidelines—concluded that the charges had merit and the university's administration was stonewalling. Notified in November 1970 that $33 million in federal contracts were at risk, the embattled McGill took notice. With no admission of guilt for past discrimination, over the next year the university put together an affirmative-action plan that called for the hiring of almost nine hundred women and minorities over a five-year period.

If McGill's satisfaction with Ginsburg's appointment was colored by the difficulty of meeting the plan's goals in a time of financial stringency, the response of her new colleagues was perhaps no less tinted. The male culture of the professional schools was strong. Some saw affirmative action simply as an abuse of federal power; others feared that it would lead to deteriorating academic standards. Jewish professors, remembering when top universities used quotas to limit the number of Jews admitted and hired, were especially alarmed. At the Law School, most members of the faculty had doubts as to whether a woman—any woman—could lecture effectively to large groups of law students. Even Ruth's old friend Walter Gellhorn raised a skeptical eyebrow.

But the new dean, Michael Sovern, was determined to push forward, promoting two female administrative assistants to vice-deans, hiring Ginsburg, and taking half of the enormous men's room on the first floor of Greene Hall and converting it into a women's room. When asked what to do with the urinals, he suggested filling them with flowers.

Aware of the varying sentiments that prevailed in this all-male preserve, Ginsburg resolved to teach her lecture course on civil procedure with her customary rigor and authority. In her small seminars on sex discrimination and conflict of laws, students could get to know her better. Many, she hoped, would discover in her what she as a student had found in Harvard's Al Sacks—a caring, fair teacher who coupled "accessibility with demanding standards of precision in thought and expression." As her only female colleague at the Law School, Harriet Rabb, who ran an employment-discrimination clinic, noted, Ginsburg's "commanding and authoritative air in class" masked a "shy, gentle, incredibly nice person" with a healthy sense of humor.

Ginsburg hoped that initial concerns about her teaching would disappear in time. But showmanship in the classroom was not her forte, and "dazzling" was a description to which she had never aspired. Nor did she expect to be "one of the boys." There was no time—or desire— for schmoozing. What she treasured about these new colleagues was their professional self-confidence and lack of factionalism. Just being on the faculty of one of the top three law schools in the nation eased the insecurity that had gnawed at some of her Rutgers colleagues, feeding their often-acrimonious disputes. Moreover, the intellectual power of the Columbia Law School faculty was impressive. Michael Sovern, its brilliant and principled dean, had the vision and leadership qualities that would later earn him the presidency of the university. Having such good minds available for practice sessions, where she could present an argument she intended to make before the Supreme Court, would sharpen her performance. Even those colleagues who failed to share her litigation goals would provide incisive questions, objections, and suggestions. In the meantime, new avenues of activism were opening.

· · ·

INDEED, the ink was scarcely dry on Ginsburg's contract when the request came to please do something about a recent labor cut at Columbia that involved the dismissal of twenty-five maids and not a single janitor. She promised to look into the controversy, even though she was still teaching at Rutgers. The maids, she discovered, were overwhelmingly poor women of color who were sole providers for their families. Less upset about pay inequities than employment security, they knew that their jobs were quite literally the only thing that stood between them and welfare. When Transport Workers Union Local 241 proved reluctant to support its female members, feminists in the Columbia Women's Affirmative Action Coalition reached out. Two of their members had been meeting with President McGill about the coalition's input into the university's Affirmative Action Plan when the firings occurred. Both young lawyers, they offered to represent the maids at no charge and promised to file for a preliminary injunction from the court to stop the layoffs.

Ginsburg was brought into the dispute by Janice Goodman, the NYU Law School student who had approached her about teaching a sex-discrimination course at Rutgers and now acted as an attorney for the maids. Hoping that a resolution could be achieved before the matter went to court, Ginsburg contacted the university's vice president, Joseph Nye.

When Nye welcomed the Law School's newest faculty member to his office, she politely reminded him that Columbia was already in violation of Title VII of the Civil Rights Act of 1964 and perhaps the Equal Pay Act as well. After all, maids and janitors did basically the same work. Yet the seniority system was rigged so that every maid would have to be let go before the first janitor could be fired. Surely, she suggested, a more gender-equitable solution could be found that would spare the university a legal defeat. Nye explained that the union set up the system under which the maids had been fired, and the university must maintain good relations with its unions. Implying his hands were tied and assuring his visitor that Columbia was well represented by a downtown firm, he next said, Ginsburg recalled, "Now, dear, wouldn't you like a cup of tea?"—a signal that the discussion was over.

Nye, however, had underestimated his visitor, seemingly unaware of the expertise her ACLU post confirmed or the constituency she represented. (Ginsburg had kept her future dean Michael Sovern in the loop, so she could claim the support of the law faculty.) Shortly after her meeting with Nye, Gloria Steinem, Bella Abzug, Susan Steinberg Danielson, and other feminist notables declared their solidarity with the maids at a well-attended press conference on campus. Heartened by their new allies, the laid-off workers believed that the union might be reconsidering. The university, on the other hand, gave no sign of accommodating.

Nor was this Columbia's only gender war. The newly organized University Senate's Committee on the Status of Women was at the same time battling against salary discrimination, while women students were complaining that dining requirements at the university facilities were less restrictive for men than for women. Students also protested that the gym reserved all its tracks for male runners, leaving women to the streets of Morningside Heights. And so it went. Her alma mater, Ginsburg concluded, seemed further behind the curve in dealing with issues of discrimination than Rutgers, which had far fewer resources at its disposal. In letters to McGill, she shared Rutgers's policies, impressing upon the president the need to investigate and respond promptly to "reasonable" requests for gender equity so as to spare Columbia "unnecessary publicity" and perhaps ensuing legal confrontations. McGill responded positively to the spirit of Ginsburg's letters but offered little substance.

One thing seemed certain: the problems of dismissed maids would have to be determined by the court. When that day arrived, the chief counsel of the EEOC spoke in favor of a stop order. Singling out women for dismissal violated equal employment practices required by the Civil Rights Act, he explained. The union promptly backed away from the seniority system established in its contract with Columbia, leaving the university the sole defendant. In September 1972, the personnel office finally ordered that the layoffs be handled through attrition. In the end, not a single maid was fired, Ginsburg later noted with considerable satisfaction.

It was not just the maids in Transport Workers Union Local 241 who found advocates. In signaling to McGill that problems of discrimination should be resolved in-house, Ginsburg sent a further message: *she* would not be silent on matters of gender equality at Columbia.

Mounting a Campaign

· CHAPTER 7 ·

A First Breakthrough

A heady transition in affiliations under way, Ginsburg eagerly awaited the impact of the Court's ruling on the case she had worked on the previous summer, *Reed v. Reed*. As soon as she learned the facts of Sally Reed's case, Ginsburg grasped its potential.

Cecil and Sally Reed had each held custody of their adopted son at different times, Sally when Richard (Skip) was small and Cecil when he was a young teenager. Skip had recently been living with Sally, who realized that her son made his regular weekend visit with his father's second family with great reluctance. One fateful weekend, Skip telephoned his mother, begging to cut the visit short and come home. When she reminded him that Cecil had visiting rights and that he must stay, Skip went to the basement of his father's house and shot himself with a hunting rifle from Cecil's gun collection. The wound proved fatal.

Sally, grief stricken, felt Cecil bore some responsibility for the boy's death. Taking charge of her son's few belongings—a small savings account that she had established, consisting of several hundred dollars for college tuition, together with a clarinet, phonograph records, a guitar, and clothing—she applied to the court on November 6, 1967, to be the administrator of Skip's estate. Cecil filed soon after, convinced that his former wife was "too dumb" to do the job and that he had the law on his side. Idaho law stipulated that "of several persons claiming and equally entitled to administer, males must be preferred to females."

When the court rejected Sally's request, she strenuously objected. A housewife of very modest means, she had earned a living after the divorce by ironing, baking, babysitting, and looking after disabled people in her small Boise home. Furious that "a woman could be stepped on like this," she found her way to Allen Derr, a forty-three-year-old Boise attorney.

Derr agreed to take up her cause. His empathy for the underdog had been awakened during World War II by the racial discrimination he had witnessed against his African American corpsmen. When he returned to college stateside, his sense of racial injustice was further fueled when his college fraternity wanted "to take in colored pledges" and alumni objected. The incident prompted him in the early 1950s to spend four years traveling around the country to see that Tau Kappa Epsilon chapters could admit whomever they wanted. Making a connection between racism and sexism had been easy for a father of an eleven-year-old daughter, Derr recalled. He agreed to appeal Sally Reed's case to the Idaho District Court.

The district court decided in Sally's favor. Her sense of vindication was short-lived, however. Cecil appealed, and the Idaho Supreme Court overturned the district court's decision in November 1970. The law did discriminate against women, the judges acknowledged. Nonetheless, it furthered the state's "legitimate interest" by alleviating the need for hearings by the probate court to determine which parent was better equipped to serve as administrator. Because the legislature's preference for male administrators was "rationally related to a permissible government objective"—that is, administrative convenience—the statute did not violate Sally Reed's constitutional right to equal protection. The judges also asserted that the legislature's assumption that men were generally better qualified than women to administer estates was not totally "without basis in fact."

· · ·

THE ACLU BECAME INVOLVED in *Reed v. Reed* when its veteran general counsel, Marvin Karpatkin, spotted a report in *Law Week* on the Idaho Supreme Court's decision and called the case to Wulf's attention. *Reed* could be the turning-point case, predicted Karpatkin. As a member of the Equality Committee, he knew how intensely Kenyon and Murray wanted to bring an equal protection case before the Court. Clearly, the amount of the estate was minuscule. Nor was the particular form of sex discrimination involved high on the feminist agenda. But at the very least, Karpatkin advised, a strong brief challenging the statute could serve to educate the Court on gender discrimination in the law.

Wulf wasted no time. Upon learning that Sally Reed lacked resources

*Sally Reed and her Boise attorney
Allen Derr in 1987—sixteen years
after the* Reed *decision, the first case
in which the Supreme Court rejected
sex-based discrimination.*

to carry the case further, the ACLU's legal director offered assistance, which Derr promptly accepted. Wulf then filed a jurisdictional statement explaining why the U.S. Supreme Court should consider the case, following up with a reply brief that rebutted Cecil Reed's plea as to why the justices should not do so. Now it was up to the high court to decide whether to hear the case. There was no guarantee that *Reed* would be reviewed, because appeals are often dismissed summarily "for want of a substantial federal question."

In April 1971, Wulf got the green light. He and Ginsburg could now proceed on Sally Reed's appellant brief. Working with them were four women law students: Diana Rigelman, who had worked with Ginsburg at Rutgers to get the formerly pregnant, now divorced, Nora Simon back into the army; Mary F. Kelly and Janice Goodman of NYU, who had helped persuade Ginsburg to teach her course "Sex Discrimination and the Law"; and Ann Freedman, the driving force behind Yale's course "Women and the Law" and a member of the advisory board of the Rutgers *Women's Rights Law Reporter*. Creating a preliminary draft that, in Goodman's words, "would educate the court on everything," especially the relationship between race and sex discrimination, they dumped it in Ginsburg's lap. When they saw her final version, they found it barely recognizable. Ginsburg had translated into compelling constitutional arguments the philosophical and sociological indictment of sex stereotyping made by cutting-edge rights movements.

. . .

AS GINSBURG AND WULF had worked together to determine the brief's content, their first question involved strategy: What level of scrutiny should they argue for? Because the relaxed "rational basis" test was still the norm in 1971, the customary procedure would be to argue that the Idaho statute calling for male administrators did not meet the standard of "reasonableness" in terms of promoting a legitimate government objective; therefore, Sally Reed's constitutional right to equal protection of the law had been denied. In addition, the brief could indicate why the Court needed to toughen the standard of review, requiring proof that distinction on the basis of sex was not just "reasonable" but "necessary." Alternately, they might begin by arguing for a tougher standard of review. But if they reversed order, how much emphasis should be placed on the need for strict scrutiny?

The Court first spelled out the meaning of "strict scrutiny" with respect to racial discrimination in a 1944 case concerning the detention of Japanese Americans during World War II. "It should be noted to begin with," the majority opinion in *Korematsu* stated, "that *all legal restrictions* which curtail the civil rights of a single racial group *are immediately suspect*. This is not to say that all such restrictions are unconstitutional but rather that *courts must subject them to the most rigid scrutiny*." Relying heavily on *Korematsu,* Thurgood Marshall and NAACP attorneys had succeeded in raising the bar for racial classification from a reasonableness test (*Plessy*) to requiring strict scrutiny (*Brown*). Under that more demanding standard, attorneys general for the next three decades had to demonstrate that laws that discriminated either against or for a group to whom strict scrutiny applied were not merely "reasonable" but "necessary" to achieving an important governmental objective.

If strict scrutiny of sex-based classifications could be achieved, it would not dictate identical treatment of men and women, Ginsburg

believed. Rather, it would require careful examination of all laws pre-
scribing differential treatment to ensure that lawmakers had not relied
on outdated stereotypes and assumptions, which had long served as a
rationale for women's subordinate legal status, much as they had for
African Americans. But the Court's readiness to perform that examination, especially when it involved pregnancy-related discrimination,
would require considerable education. Fortunately, what was at issue in
Reed was merely Sally Reed's competency to do a job.

. . .

THE IMMEDIATE QUESTION WAS how to organize the brief. Should
she begin with the argument that the Idaho law failed the rational basis
test and then make the argument for strict scrutiny? Or should she do
the reverse? Ginsburg and Wulf finally decided that if strict scrutiny
was to be the ultimate goal, the sooner the justices began associating it
with "sex-based discrimination," the better. As a fallback position, she
would then argue that the Idaho law failed to meet even the rational
basis standard.

Having taken over the writing of the brief, Ginsburg quickly cut to
her core argument for strict scrutiny, relying heavily on Pauli Murray's
parallel between race and sex discrimination. Sex and race were each
"congenital, unalterable trait[s] at birth with no necessary relationship
to talent or ability to perform," she insisted. Why should Idaho mothers who sought to administer a child's estate be automatically treated
as a separate—and legally inferior—group simply because of their
sex? For women, that was no more conducive to equality than it had
been for African Americans who were accorded separate—and legally
inferior—treatment because of skin color. The fact that discriminatory
estate administration was hardly comparable to the ills inflicted by racial
oppression was not Ginsburg's point. Rather, use of the analogy with its
powerful moral claim was a strategic device that she, like other feminist
lawyers, would initially employ in order to gain judicial recognition of
previously unrecognized harms to women. To clinch the argument, she
provided abundant examples from American history, recounting numerous situations in which struggles for racial justice and women's emancipation connected.

Ginsburg then moved on to her less controversial position. Cecil and Sally Reed were "similarly situated" individuals in that each was capable of administering a son's estate. The Idaho law favoring men over women as estate administrators was therefore unacceptable because the Fourteenth Amendment stipulated that states could not deny citizens "equal protection." Further, Ginsburg argued, the sex-based distinction bore no "reasonable relationship" to the government's stated interest, which was efficient administration of estates. Any administrative efficiency gained by eliminating court hearings on which parent was better qualified did not meet even the "reasonable" or "rational relationship" test—especially when balanced against Sally Reed's fundamental right to an evenhanded application of governmental action under the equal protection clause.

Assuming that the Court would continue to apply the rational basis test in *Reed,* irrespective of her argument for tighter scrutiny, Ginsburg astutely inserted wording from a 1920 tax case involving a fertilizer company, *Royster Guano v. Virginia,* that she and Marty had used in *Moritz.* The case reeked of seabird excrement, she and Marty joked, but the ruling offered the most suitable language. A sex-based classification, she quoted, "must be reasonable, not arbitrary, and must rest upon some ground of difference having a fair and *substantial relation* to the object of legislation so that all persons similarly circumstanced shall be treated alike."

Another key element of Ginsburg's strategy, which she had also used to great effect in *Moritz,* was to discredit powerful gender stereotypes. Underlying the injustice in *Reed* were the fundamental common-law disabilities at the foundation of the American legal system—the denial of married women's rights to contract, sue, and hold property in their own names. Ginsburg then wove together demographic and economic developments as well as cases in which both lower courts and the Supreme Court had departed from such "antiquated" precedents and stereotypes.

In sum, she concluded, the line drawn by the 1864 Idaho legislature subordinating women to men without regard for the capacity of the individual "creates a 'suspect classification' requiring close judicial scrutiny." Legislative distinctions based on sex, "for purposes unrelated to any biological difference between the sexes, ranks with legislation based on race, another congenital, unalterable, trait of birth." With this incorporation of two decades of litigation by Thurgood Marshall and the NAACP's Legal Defense Fund, Ginsburg made her final pitch for "a clear affirmation from the Court that sex *per se* is a suspect classification."

· · ·

IN ADDITION TO Wulf and Ginsburg, the brief's list of authors included the names of Allen Derr, Pauli Murray, and Dorothy Kenyon. None of the three had written a word of the eighty-eight-page brief. Yet few were more deserving than the two remarkable women whose lives and work had made the argument possible. As Ginsburg later explained, "My generation owed them a great debt, for they bravely pressed arguments for equal justice in days when few would give ear to what they were saying." They "kept the idea—and the hope—alive."

The brief bore other evidence of Ginsburg's distinctive imprint. Revealing her sensitivity to judicial actions in constitutional democracies other than her own, she mentioned two decisions from West Germany's Constitutional Court voiding laws privileging males over females. As she later explained, "I thought it fitting to inform the Court that Constitutional Courts abroad, created after World War II, were taking seriously equality norms written into post-war Fundamental Instruments of Government." Feminists in the United States were "not simply riding the coattails of the African American civil rights movement," she added. Rather, we were "part of a movement for change that transcended national boundaries [and racial and] . . . ethnic identification." When the four research assistants looked at what Ginsburg had done with their notes, they marveled not only at the extent to which her knowledge of the law far exceeded theirs but also at how much more radical her feminism was than they had realized.

· · ·

OTHER ASPECTS OF the case's preparation went less smoothly. Both the amicus brief submitted by the National Federation of Business and Professional Women's Clubs and the joint brief provided by the American Veterans Committee and NOW turned out to be consistent with the ACLU's brief that Wulf had sent. But that was not true of the one prepared by the Corporation Counsel of the City of New York, which asked for heightened scrutiny only secondarily. "Such favors I don't need," Wulf grumbled. Far more important, disagreements emerged when Wulf turned to the question of who would deliver the oral argument.

. . .

GINSBURG WAS DETERMINED from the beginning to have a female attorney—someone with the presence, authority, and experience to forestall "the locker-room humor" that some of the justices had indulged in during *Phillips v. Martin Marietta,* a Title VII sex-discrimination case argued several months earlier. Wulf agreed. The woman he had in mind was Eleanor Holmes Norton. As he explained to Sally Reed, "There is . . . the very important symbolic value of having a woman argue your case." Norton "is a national figure—both on behalf of civil rights and women's rights—and is one of the most persuasive lawyers I know."

Norton, with her keen legal mind, commanding presence, and intense commitment to equality, was indeed a natural choice. A civil rights activist and Yale Law School graduate, she had clerked for the much-respected Philadelphia jurist A. Leon Higginbotham Jr., a federal district judge, before joining the ACLU in 1965 as assistant director in charge of litigating First Amendment cases. In her first Supreme Court victory, she had defended the right of a white supremacist to hold a rally in Maryland. A successful defense of Alabama's governor George Wallace's right to hold a rally at New York's Shea Stadium soon followed.

Highly regarded as a principled and very effective civil rights and civil liberties lawyer, Norton as an African American feminist also shared Kenyon and Murray's eagerness to bring a sex-discrimination case relying on equal protection to the high court. That she had left the ACLU in 1970 to head the New York City Commission on Human Rights posed no problem. But Sally Reed's lawyer had other ideas.

. . .

DERR HAD BEEN DETERMINED from the outset to present the oral argument himself. He had donated his time and money pursuing the litigation when chances for victory were slim. At the Supreme Court level, however, the ACLU had paid the filing fee, written the jurisdictional statement and the briefs, and paid the printing costs. But as the Idaho attorney later remarked to Sally Reed, "You . . . know that I so sincerely believed in this case." The oral argument, she agreed, was his to make.

Wulf appreciated Derr's early commitment to the case, his understandable sense of proprietorship, and his eagerness to capitalize on a rare opportunity to argue before the high court. But the ACLU legal director also understood the need for expert knowledge of the legal issues, especially once the justices began raising questions during oral argument. Their interrogations—often penetrating and, at times, even brutal— were designed to help them become better informed in areas with which they were less familiar and, therefore, less likely to have developed strong views. On such occasions, it helped to have a veteran Supreme Court litigator with a string of successful oral arguments. And as Wulf knew well, experienced appellate advocacy was even more critical in a test case in a new area of sex discrimination where the Court was being asked to reverse not only a lower court decision but also the century-old notion that differential treatment was, for the most part, benign. In short, the ACLU legal director was convinced that while it was difficult to win a case on the basis of the oral argument, Derr could easily lose it. Ego should not be allowed to trump experience and expertise, jeopardizing their common objective—victory.

Wulf was correct in his assessment. But the conflict was inherent in the ACLU's practice of picking up cases its affiliates had not originated. Local lawyers who had been with the case did not relish being replaced. With time running out, Wulf had resorted to the painfully blunt language that was his trademark. The brief that Derr had filed before the Idaho Supreme Court on Sally Reed's behalf, wrote the exasperated Wulf, was simply "awful." It demonstrated "total ignorance" of the equal protection clause and of cases involving sex discrimination. A Supreme Court case, he reiterated, demanded expert oral argument.

Acknowledging finally that there was no possibility of changing Derr's mind, Wulf advised the Idaho attorney to start preparing by reading every case and article cited in the ACLU brief. "Study the brief and try to understand it, and when you stand up before the Supreme Court, make damn sure you know our brief backwards and forwards." Argue that the Court "must apply the rigid scrutiny test in sex-discrimination cases—Point I of our brief," he instructed. "Since your only excuse for arguing the case is because you want to, let me make it perfectly clear that we expect an expert performance." The advice was counterproductive.

. . .

ON THE DAY OF the oral argument, Derr had risen to take his place at the front of the bench. To his credit, he had not wavered when asked about laws that discriminated in favor of women, such as protective labor legislation or draft exemptions. Laws should not treat men and women differently where biological difference did not matter, he insisted, as in the cases of two similarly situated individuals such as Sally and Cecil Reed. As he continued, it became painfully apparent that Derr could not stand up to the barrage of questions from Burger and especially Douglas, Brennan, White, Blackmun, and, not least, Marshall, always a tough interrogator. The Idaho lawyer lacked not only sufficient command of the relevant body of law but also the precision of statement that could be expected from a repeat player at the Court.

Cecil Reed's counsel, Charles Stout, followed with his argument. Having few new points to make, he noted that Idaho women had long had the vote. Had they wanted to change the law preferring male administrators, they could have done so at any time.

The oral argument in *Reed* "may have been one of the worst in the history of the Supreme Court," Wulf fumed, after hearing a firsthand report from Janice Goodman, who described Derr's performance as a "total humiliation." Justice Blackmun agreed. Taking brief notes on each oral argument in his tiny script, he characterized Derr's performance as "the worst oral argument" he had ever heard. Other appraisals were in the same vein, although Ginsburg insisted that Stout's was worse.

Wulf had remained confident that *Reed* could still be won on the basis of the brief, which he labeled "sensational." Neier had agreed, later noting that all Ginsburg's briefs were "simply superb pieces of legal argumentation." Equally impressed, Congresswoman Martha Griffiths termed the brief "great," adding, "If Mrs. Reed does not win, I am going to resign from the human race."

Ginsburg, however, had remained uncertain that the brief would prevail. Then, on the train ride back to New York on November 22, 1971, the day the decision was announced, she spied a banner headline in the

evening paper of a fellow commuter. "My first reaction was total ela-
tion," Ginsburg later recalled. "I could hardly hold back the tears of joy."

. . .

A UNANIMOUS COURT, speaking through Chief Justice Burger, reversed the decision of the Idaho Supreme Court, using for the first time
ever the equal protection clause to strike down a statute that differentiated on the basis of sex. "To give a mandatory preference to members of
either sex over members of the other, merely to accomplish the elimination of hearings on the merits, is to make the very kind of arbitrary
legislative choice forbidden by the Equal Protection Clause," the justices
declared.

When Ginsburg read the full opinion, she noted that in striking down the offending statute, the Court had not gone nearly as far
toward doctrinal change as she and Wulf had hoped. In continuing to
use the rational basis test, the ruling stopped short of holding laws that
drew distinctions between the sexes inherently suspect. The narrowness
of the decision was no more than could realistically be expected, even
though Wulf told Derr it was the result of his poor oral argument. There
were simply too many other factors. Burger and his more conservative
colleagues were no doubt reluctant to get the Court embroiled in yet
another struggle for equality—this time involving gender. Unlike the
1940s and 1950s, when the justices felt compelled to take the lead on
racial discrimination because Congress and the president would not,
the representative branches of government were already tackling gender inequality. The Senate was about to join the House in dropping the
Equal Rights Amendment into the legislative hopper of all fifty states.

There were also other considerations that would not have gone
unnoticed by the justices. In November 1971, the country was already
rocked with controversy over recent Court-mandated affirmative action
for workers, Court-mandated busing of schoolchildren, and Court-
sanctioned publication of the Pentagon Papers. There was also a decision
pending on what would prove to be the most controversial and divisive
issue on the Court's docket for the foreseeable future—decriminalizing
abortion. To move faster on gender equality would only fuel the furor
over liberal judges and judicial activism.

Nonetheless, Ginsburg believed, subtle but significant movement could be found in the shift of language in the *Reed* decision. No longer would the Court require a government interest be "rationally" related to a sex-based classification; now the Court would require it be "substantially" related. Burger had picked up on the language of the 1920 equal protection case that Ginsburg had quoted in her brief. Was the change in wording mere coincidence? Or was it a signal that the justices really were headed in a new direction?

The press, quick to report the decision as front-page news, shared her uncertainty. The *Detroit Free Press, The Kansas City Times,* and *The Dallas Morning News,* among others, characterized the decision as a positive step, noting there was still a need for the ERA. *The New York Times* editorialized that if the Supreme Court were to follow up *Reed,* interpreting the " 'equal protection of the laws' in a modern manner," the Fourteenth Amendment could "do as much for the feminine [*sic*] majority" as it had for racial minorities. The *Los Angeles Times* agreed, as did *Newsweek* and *Time,* although the reporter for *Time* observed that the decision "falls far short of announcing a broad general principle."

Ginsburg's assessment was closest to that of *The Boston Globe,* which called the outcome "a smidgen of equality." Publicly, she characterized the decision as "a small, guarded step." Legal scholars concurred, uniformly lamenting that the Court had missed an opportunity to elaborate on basic issues such as "fundamental rights," "strict scrutiny," "suspect classifications," and "compelling state interest." Ruth's former mentor Gerald Gunther provided the most astute analysis in his assessment of the Court's 1970–71 term for the *Harvard Law Review.* The justices, Gunther believed, were groping for a standard in equal protection cases somewhere between rational and strict scrutiny.

Privately, Ginsburg had additional concerns. With the ERA before Congress, longtime amendment advocates would cite *Reed* as evidence of the failure of the Court to ban sex-based discrimination outright—which it was, even though to expect such a dramatic reversal so soon would have been naive. However, to ignore the positive elements in *Reed*—the fact that a unanimous Court for the first time ever had found a sex-based classification in violation of the Fourteenth Amendment, and might do so again—would undercut the value of the case as a precedent in future litigation.

Ginsburg's concerns were not unwarranted; *Reed*'s ambiguous and cryptic reasoning was reflected in the lower courts' inability to come to a consensus about the role of the Court in equal rights legislation. The lower courts agreed that *Reed* had a substantial impact on sex-based litigation but differed as to how the ruling should be applied. Some used it to strike down sex-based legal classifications, as did the U.S. Court of Appeals for the Tenth Circuit in ruling for *Moritz*. Others applied *Reed* narrowly, differentiating sex-based discrimination from discrimination based on pregnancy.

Concentrating on every signpost, Ginsburg breathed a sigh of relief when evidence of *Reed*'s impact emerged in a footnote by Marshall in *San Antonio Independent School District v. Rodriguez* (1973) and in a majority opinion by Brennan in *Eisenstadt v. Baird* (1972). At least two justices, it appeared, viewed the *Reed* ruling as a turning point. Elated, Ginsburg exulted to Wulf, "What *Reed* has wrought! Who said it wouldn't make waves?" And this was just the beginning.

CHAPTER 8

Setting Up Shop and Strategy

A s Ginsburg made her way downtown from her Columbia office on 116th Street, where she spent her mornings, to the ACLU's national headquarters at the building it was subleasing from the Johns Manville Corporation, her agenda remained daunting. The Women's Rights Project had "no files, no staff of our own, no office space, no money except for the ACLU's initial contributions and a couple of very small grants." Setting up a functioning legal office in short order would be difficult enough. Creating a litigation strategy that would shape new legal doctrine on sex discrimination posed an even more daunting challenge.

· · ·

WHAT SHE DID HAVE at the outset were assurances from Neier that funding for the project would be a top priority. He had long had his eye on the Ford Foundation. Though a leading supporter of civil liberties and civil rights, Ford had recently bypassed the ACLU. The foundation's president at the time, McGeorge Bundy, former national security adviser in the Kennedy and Johnson administrations, bluntly stated why. The organization had defended "draft dodgers" during the Vietnam War. No amount of discussion would bring Neier and Bundy to closer agreement over the rights of those who opposed the war. Yet after ignoring women in its equal opportunity initiatives throughout the 1960s, Ford was fast becoming "the premier philanthropy dealing with feminist issues." Susan Berresford, the foundation's young program officer for national affairs, had approved funding to underwrite women's rights litigation in Cleveland. Might Ford agree to do one in New York as well?

At the meeting to discuss the ACLU's funding proposal, Ginsburg was at her most persuasive. Berresford responded positively—but with a critical reminder. According to foundation policy, not a penny of Ford money could be spent on litigation involving abortion. The Rockefeller Foundation, which had a long-standing interest in population control, should be their target. Neier did not like such a restricted understanding of what constituted women's rights. Nor did Ginsburg. Yet Neier did not want to reject Ford's first ACLU grant. The money involved would provide a major supplement to the smaller, controversial grant from the Playboy Foundation. Because Neier and Ginsburg had both agreed that the project's first priority must be equal protection litigation, perhaps the ACLU could live with the reproductive rights restriction. Ginsburg, who generally regarded Neier's judgment as "terrific," agreed. He was one of the most institutionally innovative and active executive directors at the ACLU in years and an ardent supporter of its women's rights initiative.

. . .

STAFFING WAS NEXT on the agenda. In February 1972, Wulf had hired Brenda Feigen to direct the Women's Rights Project along with Ginsburg and to help with educational and outreach aspects. A Vassar graduate and a member of the Harvard Law class of 1969, Feigen had become a committed advocate for women's rights by the time she received her law degree. Moving quickly into the New York feminist network while studying for the New York bar, she soon became national vice president of NOW for legislation, an ardent lobbyist for the ERA, and a collaborator with Gloria Steinem in the founding of *Ms.* magazine. Her networking skills, telegenic appearance, and legal training, Wulf calculated, would make her ideal for the outreach dimension of the Women's Rights Project. That she also loved a good fight was certainly no disqualification in his eyes. In ideology, style, and contacts, he believed, she could serve as a balance to the far more reserved, consensus-oriented Ginsburg, whose legal network did not include the A-list New York feminists with whom Feigen rubbed shoulders.

Because there were no funds to hire a legal staff, Ginsburg continued the practice she had followed with her New Jersey ACLU cases—enlisting research assistants from among the best of her students at Columbia, along with volunteers from New York University, Yale, and Rutgers. Her sex-discrimination seminar provided another possibility.

Brenda Feigen, who worked closely with Ginsburg in the early years of the ACLU's Women's Rights Project.

Law students had long complained that their studies bore too little relevance to real litigation. Working on the project's cases would thrust them into the trenches, making it a win-win arrangement for the ACLU and its apprentices. Young feminist attorneys in the city might also be willing to jump in temporarily if given an opportunity to contribute to what might be landmark cases.

Ginsburg's calculation proved correct. Student recruits, once aware of their professor's demand for "getting it right and keeping it tight," including the dotting of every i, edited and reedited work assignments, circulating drafts among themselves before daring to turn in a copy marked "first draft." Ample compensation for their diligence was the knowledge that they were contributing to the work of a leader whom most considered extraordinary. She, in turn, sweetened the pot. The student who contributed the most to a case accepted by the Court would win a trip to Washington and a seat next to her at counsel table during oral argument. But before these self-styled "daughters of Ruth" could stake their claim to the prize, they had to have space in which to work.

The ACLU's move to the grand old Johns Manville building solved the problem. Feigen found a huge space set off by a small hallway that could be partitioned into many smaller offices. She promptly posted a bright yellow sign that proclaimed, "WOMEN WORKING."

. . .

IF FEIGEN'S SIGN ADVERTISED what would be a central feature of the new project, Ginsburg's experience as a working mother heralded another. Remembering how quickly she had been forced to leave her newborn son in order to teach during the fall semester—James's birth date fell on September 8—his mother decided that a woman-friendly work site must be one in which a nursing mother could bring her infant to the office. The policy, she anticipated, would undoubtedly elicit complaints about "a lack of professionalism" in Women's Rights Project precincts. What she had not expected were new demands from ACLU staff to bring their pets to the office if infants were to be allowed.

As far as Ginsburg was concerned, it was all about making work sites a place where women—and men—could fulfill family obligations as well as practice legal skills. Breaking down gender boundaries that denied women the rewards of work and men the rewards of parenting was a basic tenet of *jämställdhet*. The project's work would get done, infants notwithstanding. And it did, though upon entering project offices for the first time, Jill Goodman, expecting a typical legal workplace, described what became a combined nursery and law office as "wild."

"Wild" was no doubt the word that came to Roger Baldwin's mind as well. The venerable lawyer, who had so personified the ACLU in its early years, was a child of the Victorian era, having graduated from Harvard in 1905. Upon opening the door of a project office to discuss a legal matter, the elderly gentleman found the lawyer he had come to see breast-feeding. The scene, he later admitted, made him feel he needed an invitation to enter this female "*sanctum sanctorum.*" Though reassured of his welcome, Baldwin had been doubly confounded when the new mother proved eager to discuss business while her baby nursed.

. . .

THAT THE POLICY STUCK WAS indicative of Ginsburg's relationship with a staff whose loyalty she won in her own inimitable fashion. Her arrival at the office, usually around eleven o'clock, was typically preceded by an earlier telephone call to Feigen. To Feigen's greeting of "Hi, Ruth. How are you?" came not even a perfunctory "Fine, thank you" or "How are you?" Instead, Ginsburg asked, "Have you read the advance sheets yet?" or "Did you read about the new case the Court has decided to accept?" Ruth's "head is in the law, and sometimes in the opera," Feigen observed.

Yet she and other associates quickly learned not to equate the director's single-minded focus with coldness or indifference. As another close associate recalled, "We whom she mentored quickly learned that her reserve was merely that; it was not chill, nor was it a lack of interest in us as human beings. She'd speak easily with us about the villains of the world, the bench, the bar, and even the feminist community, who put stumbling blocks in our way." And she took note of "special events in our lives," hosting a surprise baby shower or birthday party topped off with a culinary treat from Marty.

Ginsburg also expressed her caring by sharing a glimpse of her own life. "[She] spoke to us about her private life and ours," said one, "allowing us to see that analysis had a place in our private life just as emotions did in our professional lives. We did not understand [at the time] what an utterly remarkable workplace she created for us." And with good reason. As law students or recent graduates, they were not yet fully immersed in a professional culture in which "personal" and "professional" were sharply divided and "reality" neatly fit into legal categories. Ginsburg, who never accepted the notion that analytical skills were solely a male attribute, embraced feminism's understanding of how the gendered division of "private" and "public" had limited women's intellectual and vocational possibilities. Sharing her understanding with her ACLU "daughters" came naturally to a woman whose mother had shared with her own daughter. And if their work-focused leader seldom laughed, there was on occasion that "rare, radiant smile" that Ginsburg's former professor Gerry Gunther had discovered could light up a room.

One of Ginsburg's Columbia students recalls a telephone call from the Dalton School informing Ginsburg that her son lacked the requisite book bag. When questioned as to why, the youngster had replied that his lawyer-parents were much too busy to supply him the bag. His mortified mother explained that James had never informed her of the requirement. She would see to it immediately. When Ginsburg put down the phone, she relayed the incident with a wry smile and resigned shake of the head that M. E. Freeman felt communicated volumes about the daily challenges of trying to balance family life with professional commitments, especially when both parents were as deeply involved in their work as were Ruth and Marty.

It was not just their mentor's role balancing that her young apprentices appreciated but the rigor and judgment she brought to their collective enterprise. "I don't know if I fully understood the significance of the case I was working on," Freeman later reflected. "I just wanted to do my very best to please Ruth." She could be intimidating at first, they uniformly agreed. She was positively "scary" because she was so "meticulous," Jill Goodman explained. Ruth worked so hard that she almost seemed to be "a different species." "We were all in awe of her."

Yet there was a significant part of this new undertaking to which they did not contribute. Assessing the new Court, sizing up potential litigation problems, and developing a strategy were tasks that Ginsburg saved for herself.

· · ·

ONE OF THE FIRST MATTERS the novice litigator had to consider was the Court itself. With the retirement of Chief Justice Earl Warren and the resignation of Abe Fortas in 1969, and then the illnesses and retirement of Hugo Black and John Marshall Harlan in 1971, the composition of the Court had changed dramatically. Warren's replacement as chief justice, the Republican Warren Burger, provided the kind of law-and-order advocate that President Richard Nixon had promised, as did the nomination of Harry Blackmun, a hardworking moderate conservative who got the Fortas seat.

Then, in October 1971, the president nominated Lewis F. Powell Jr. and William H. Rehnquist as replacements for Black and Harlan. Powell, a tall, slim, aristocratic Virginian and former president of the American Bar Association, was much respected for his probity, compassion, moderating instincts, self-restraint, and unfailing graciousness. Deeply suspicious of ideology, he was concerned to "preserve a place for all considerations" in making a judicial decision. But precisely what did this mean? A swing vote perhaps? More important, where would this cautious centrist stand on gender equality as law and social policy?

By contrast, Ginsburg had little doubt about where the invariably outspoken William H. Rehnquist stood. At first glance, he seemed to epitomize the kind of strict constructionist that Nixon had pledged to nominate. For principled conservatives, strict construction had long meant judicial restraint and caution—narrow rulings tailored to the facts in a particular case. For Nixon, however, strict construction meant reading the Constitution as embodying his political agenda. Nowhere in that agenda was there a call for the extension of rights—what judicial conservatives scornfully referred to as "liberal activism" epitomized by the Warren Court, a code word for social and cultural changes they deplored. As one of Nixon's staffers optimistically wrote in a memo to the president after the confirmation of his last two nominees, the White House "has all but recaptured the institution from the Left," halting "much of its social experimentation" and making it "an ally and defender. . . . [of our] values and principles."

Though the assessment proved premature, the highly intelligent Rehnquist did not disappoint his backers. He turned out to be a conservative activist willing to sacrifice strict construction in order to shift the law toward the political right. Specifically, this meant limiting the powers of the federal government, expanding the rights of private property owners, and cutting back on the rights of criminal defendants, among others—a process, first set in play by Nixon, that would come to fruition in the twenty-first century with the Rehnquist and Roberts Courts.

At the time, however, Ginsburg knew only that the rights of minorities and women were not part of Rehnquist's vision of what the Constitution required. As a clerk to Justice Robert H. Jackson, he had drafted a memo to his boss arguing against *Brown* and the integration of racially segregated schools. And as assistant attorney general, he had testified ambivalently for Nixon's support of the Equal Rights Amendment. In an internal memo, he said of ERA supporters, "I cannot help but think that there is also present somewhere in this movement a virtually fanatical desire to obscure not only legal differences between men and women but insofar as possible physical distinctions between the sexes. I think there are overtones of dislike and distaste for the traditional difference between man and woman in the family unit, and in some cases, very probably a complete rejection of woman's traditionally different role in this regard."

Such views could hardly be described as sympathetic to feminism, despite Rehnquist's long friendship with his Stanford Law School class-mate Sandra Day O'Connor. The ACLU had made its doubts clear when the organization publicly called for the Senate to defeat the Rehnquist nomination, breaking a half-century tradition of never formally oppos-ing a nominee for public office.

· · ·

AS A LEGAL SCHOLAR, Ginsburg was too astute to think that the jus-tices could be neatly categorized politically or jurisprudentially. Labels, while convenient, often proved imprecise for a variety of reasons. A particular justice might be "liberal" in terms of protecting freedom of speech but "conservative" on the rights of criminals. The Court's center of gravity could shift with a new appointment, transforming a former "conservative" into a "moderate." Or, as Blackmun would demonstrate, a "centrist" could over time move decisively to the left. But of one thing she was certain: the present Court she was about to confront was not the one that had existed just four years earlier. In addition to the four Nixon appointees, it included the moderate-to-conservative Potter Stewart and Byron White.

Stewart, a dissenter from some of the famous Warren Court deci-sions and a strong adherent of stare decisis—the doctrine that precedent controls—was a capable centrist and a source of institutional stability. A justice whose first concern was how rulings of the Court would work in the real world, he had voted with the liberals on issues involving freedom of expression and racial integration. And he had been a vote for *Reed*. White, a Kennedy appointee, was hard to categorize. An individual of great legal intellect, he put forth no larger interpretation in his many decisions, deciding each case on its own merits. On criminal law issues, he tended to be conservative, though his conservatism could never be taken for granted. His votes on civil liberties varied with the issue; on cases involving racial discrimination, he sided with the liberals. White's vote Ginsburg would aim to win, though she was less confident about Stewart.

But her basic concern remained. How would the centrists on the Burger Court—Powell, Stewart, and possibly Blackmun—respond to sex discrimination?

. . .

AS GINSBURG THOUGHT ABOUT the challenge, she realized that her starting point in one respect differed dramatically from that of the litigators for the NAACP Legal Defense Fund. Marshall would have been hard put to find an African American—male or female—who thought that blacks as a group had benefited from different treatment. "Different" when race was involved had always meant inferior. On the other hand, many women actually believed that sex-based distinctions invariably favored them.

The conviction that different treatment was preferential treatment and that it involved more than long-standing practices was best captured in the assertion of the Eagle Forum's Kathleen Teague: "A constitutional right" to be treated "like ladies" is a right "which every American woman has enjoyed since our country was born." Never mind that Teague's statement was inaccurate. Racial and class distinctions had always defined which women counted as "ladies." Even "ladies" enjoyed no constitutional exemption from the obligations of citizenship. Teague's certainty—wholly unsubstantiated by fact—was evidence of what the historian Alice Kessler-Harris has aptly termed "gendered imagination," those gendered habits of mind around which ideas of fairness are constructed and social policies built.

Nor were women alone in this regard. Such habits of mind were found among men as well. Ginsburg had only to recall recent Senate debates over the ERA, where male opponents had refused to move beyond inherited gender definitions. Senator Samuel J. Ervin Jr. of North Carolina was a case in point. An ardent champion of civil liberties (though not civil rights), a judge who had resigned from the bench because he felt that every time he sentenced a felon, something good in him died, Ervin "was very bright," recalled his fellow senator Birch Bayh. Yet "Sam did not in his heart of hearts understand the kind of problems that women were facing. [He] . . . just couldn't see it."

Neither did many of his male contemporaries. "The response I got when I talked about sex-based discrimination," Ginsburg recalled, was, "What are you talking about? Women are treated ever so much better than men. They can work if they wish, or stay home if they choose. They can serve on juries, or decline jury duty, if selected. They can avoid military service, or they can enlist."

Justices—along with other like-minded decision makers—would have to "reconsider attitudes and values they have held all their lives," she concluded. But how could she persuade a group that was mostly "white, well-heeled, and male" to abandon deeply embedded preconceptions about the sexes that seemed to them commonsensical? At the very least, she needed a litigation strategy that took into account the Court's prior antidiscrimination experience.

. . .

EEOC GUIDELINES ABOUT WHAT constituted sex discrimination might have alerted the justices to the problem of using sex as an inappropriate proxy for other characteristics. Especially helpful was the agency's emphasis on detection of broad generalizations about men and women that failed to take into account the capacities of a particular individual. But with only one EEOC case having reached the Court thus far, she could not assume much familiarity with EEOC guidelines.

A strategy building on race-discrimination law, as she had done in *Reed*, rested on an obvious parallel to race-based discrimination, to which the justices could relate. But what about areas where the race-sex analogy did not fit smoothly? While blacks and whites were always interchangeable, there were clearly situations, especially those involving reproduction, where the two sexes were not the same.

Here she would have to show that laws purporting to be "protective" of women as an extension of their childbearing capacity could actually be harmful, undermining the rights of individual women. Regulations forcing women to give up positions in the workforce early in their pregnancies, when they were still capable and willing to work, demonstrated the kind of sex-based stereotyping that disadvantaged female employees and undermined the role women play in society. Similarly, restrictions on access to contraceptives, to procedures for terminating unwanted pregnancies, and to temporary disability coverage for childbirth were forms of sex-based disadvantage. Clarifying precisely when biological differences between men and women *mattered*—and when they did not—would be a major problem.

An even greater challenge would be to get the Court to understand that even if a law omitted sex distinctions, it was not necessarily gender neutral in impact. A statute or regulation that seemed gender neutral at first glance might actually affect men and women quite differently. Recognizing disparities in outcome would be no less key to promoting gender equality than it had been in advancing racial equality. Otherwise, the realities of women's lives—the actual constraints they faced—would simply be ignored.

As she reflected on the task at hand, Ginsburg realized that she had a major educational effort ahead. A delicate assignment, it would demand great patience, utmost tact, "constant dialogue, [and] constant persuasion," she concluded. Not least, it would require a fully developed litigation strategy. Here she would rely on the example set by Marshall, whose efforts "inspired."

. . .

MARSHALL HAD BEGUN his campaign against laws sanctioning racial subordination in a variety of areas—school segregation, lynch laws, and Jim Crow laws. Carefully negotiating the support of local communities that supplied plaintiffs, NAACP litigators developed cases on significant issues. Adroitly adapting to changing circumstances, they developed a strategy in which they used victories cumulatively to set up favorable precedents, moving ever closer to more difficult issues. In this way, Marshall and his team had succeeded in making a major transformation in legal doctrine seem not only appropriate but almost inevitable. Precedents already established, supported by the weight of national opinion, allowed the Court to transform constitutional jurisprudence on race.

But after conversations with Marshall's associate Jack Greenberg, Ginsburg realized that in adopting Marshall's strategy as her own, she would face critical differences. Control and coordination of cases had been relatively easy for Marshall, especially in the early days of litigation when there were few African American lawyers in the South. Most were personal friends of his. In addition to Marshall's own legal expertise and legendary political prowess, the NAACP was usually the only game in town. As the civil rights movement grew, developing different groups and tactics, the NAACP's legal defense team remained its premier litigator. For the man known as "Mr. Civil Rights," serving as traffic cop for litigation had posed scant problem.

Ginsburg's situation differed. A carefully orchestrated case-by-case approach could serve an educational purpose, enlightening the public as well as judges and legislators as to what constituted wrongful differential treatment. But even if the ACLU proved to be the best-funded and most active litigator in the feminist movement, she had no authority to act as gatekeeper with respect to other organizations, deciding which cases should be appealed to the Court and which should not. Given the likelihood of a growing number of gender-equality cases initiated by other groups and individuals with a differing agenda, securing an orderly progression of cases would prove impossible.

The best way to attempt to prevent weak or untimely cases from slipping through, Ginsburg concluded, would be to join the boards of other feminist litigation groups such as NOW, WEAL, and the Women's Legal Defense Fund. That could promote the personal contacts and communication that might harmonize efforts, though, as Neier later noted, Ginsburg would constantly have to persuade others to conform to her strategic thinking.

Marshall had yet another advantage. When attacking racial discrimination, NAACP lawyers had been able to say that the Reconstruction-era framers of the Fourteenth Amendment clearly intended African Americans—at least African American men—to have some kind of equality, even though the precise nature of that equality remains a matter of dispute. For women's rights litigators, by contrast, reliance on the equal protection clause of the Fourteenth Amendment was more problematic. Efforts of Reconstruction-era feminists to persuade their Radical Republican allies in Congress to define citizenship in terms of sex as well as race had failed. In the absence of "original intent" by the amendment's framers, it would be harder to persuade some members of the Court to extend the equal protection clause to women, holding laws that discriminated on the basis of sex to the same strict standard of scrutiny as laws that discriminated on the basis of race, color, national origin, or religious creed.

It would also take time for enough precedents to accumulate to bring about significant legal change, especially for women whose legal disadvantage was compounded by race, class, and/or sexual preference. "Justice," as Justice Benjamin Cardozo had said, "is to be wooed by slow advances." Or as the prominent legal scholar Cass Sunstein put it, "nudges" rather than "earthquakes." Further, she had no guarantee that a favorable judicial and political climate would persist, allowing time for a cumulative string of victories. Clearly, she would have to keep strong cases coming before the Court at a rapid pace.

. . .

BUT WHICH CASES to litigate? An array of possibilities awaited, thanks to her old Harvard dean, Erwin Griswold, now U.S. solicitor general. After the favorable ruling on *Moritz*, Griswold had stunned Moritz's lawyers by petitioning the Court to review the decision. Why? the Ginsburgs puzzled. The case itself had no continuing importance. Congress, in fact, had changed the offending provision, although not retroactively, even before the case was decided. Griswold, however, had realized that the judges' decision in the Tenth Circuit cast doubt on the constitutionality of a long list of federal statutes. Attached to his petition was an Appendix E containing *all* of the provisions of the U.S. Code that differentiated on the basis of sex—a monumental accomplishment, because there were no computers in law offices at the time. The only way the solicitor general could have generated his list, the Ginsburgs concluded, was by using computers at the Department of Defense (DOD).

Griswold, at the top of his game, had clearly foreseen that feminist-inspired legal challenges would arise. In fact, he had previously corresponded with the ACLU's Pauli Murray about the very strategy that Ginsburg would implement, hence his resort to the DOD's computers. In printing out Appendix E, he provided "a treasure trove" by identifying precisely which laws were vulnerable. Surely he had to know that as co-counsel for Charles Moritz, Ginsburg would receive a copy of the petition.

Though Ginsburg never fully penetrated Griswold's intentions, she now had choices to make. There were the obvious unacceptable precedents that she hoped to overturn: *Muller v. Oregon, Hoyt v. Florida,* and *Goesaert v. Cleary.* It was only a matter of finding the right cases to challenge them. Certain cases, she reasoned, were best avoided. Challenges to veterans' preference would not likely fare well in the wake of the Vietnam War. Social Security cases, on the other hand, were a logical target. Regulations involving benefits, formulated at a time when fewer women spent most of their adult lives in the workforce, were saturated with gender stereotypes. Some provisions were so patently unfair to working women and their families that they begged to be challenged. Moreover, any additional expense resulting from a decision favorable to an ACLU plaintiff would come out of public, not private, funds.

Whatever the cases finally chosen, Ginsburg knew she must insist on certain qualities. The cases had to have "good facts"; that is, they must involve ordinary people whose unfair treatment could easily be recognized. Moreover, each case chosen would have to be specific and narrowly defined, yet incrementally more demanding, so as to take the Court's reasoning ever closer to strict scrutiny. In addition, she resolved to look for cases that she could take over at the federal district court level. She could then be confident that all bases were covered and that her case was rock solid if a loss forced her to seek review in the Supreme Court or if a win required that she defend against an appeal by the government. Either way, the appeals process from a federal district court would be the most direct route to the high court.

· · ·

BUT HOW TO INCREASE the likelihood of a favorable ruling? In deciding to put cases posing constitutional questions on the Court's agenda, cause lawyers know that justices look for a green light from the public, other branches of government, and the interpretive community—legal scholars, respected journalists, and others who influence their thinking. Extending rights to women, Ginsburg realized, was no exception.

Growing public approval of gender equality would be important for three reasons. First, justices do not live in a vacuum oblivious to the message of social movements. What the public perceives as reasonable and fair plays a role in judicial decisions. Second, precisely because the elected branches of government are more reflective of the popular will, the Court takes into account the actions of Congress and the executive to confirm that all three branches are moving roughly in the same direction. Finally, the interpretive community plays an important role in building momentum for consideration of new constitutional issues. All three factors seemed to be moving in the right direction.

Over the preceding decade, polls had revealed a slow but dramatic shift in public attitudes on gender equality. By 1972, a substantial majority of Americans had come to agree that women indeed suffered sex-based discrimination. Less than a third of the population (31 percent of men and 25 percent of women) saw no need for a change in women's status.

Equally important, the move toward gender equality had acquired tangible form in Congress. Passage of the Equal Pay Act (1963) and prohibition of sex discrimination in Title VII of the Civil Rights Act (1964) was followed by Title IX of the Education Amendments Act (1972). Moreover, the EEOC was about to win a major settlement with the corporate giant American Telephone and Telegraph (AT&T). The executive branch also appeared to be serious about equity in the workplace—at least when the "New Nixon" emerged.

Most symbolic among governmental actions was the overwhelming vote in Congress on March 22, 1972, for passage of the Equal Rights Amendment, barring sex-based discrimination in federal as well as state statutes. In the months immediately following, twenty-two states rushed to ratify nearly two-thirds of the thirty-eight needed for the amendment to become part of the Constitution. Both congressional action and the early ratification count should reassure the justices that they were not "radicals in robes," usurping the prerogatives of other branches of government.

Another related development had to do with the greater involvement of women in the law. Though a somewhat tangential factor in the eyes of the Court, their growing, if still small, numbers served as notice of change, reinforcing awareness that inequality between the sexes was more than an excuse for demonstrations by women's liberationists with arresting names like the Furies, Cell 16, and WITCH (Women's International Terrorist Conspiracy from Hell). There were now more feminist lawyers, more women as clerks at the Supreme Court, more legal scholarship on sex discrimination, and more cases involving sex discrimination in the lower courts. In 1971 alone, nine well-respected law journals published a total of eighty-four articles relating to the subject of sex discrimination. Five journals devoted entire issues to the topic.

Changes in the law school population alone were unmistakable. A scant 4.5 percent in 1967, women's share had risen to 8 percent three years later. In December 1970, the nation's law schools had opened their doors to women following nondiscrimination orders issued by the Association of American Law Schools (AALS), as well as by the American Bar Association. Women had doubled their enrollment to 16 percent by 1973. With federal legislation and guidelines forbidding sex discrimination finally on their side, women in the legal profession could well exceed the number of men by the twenty-first century. For those enrolling in the 1970s and 1980s, women's equality zoomed to the top of their rights agenda, as the vibrancy of the newly organized National Conference on Women and the Law attested.

Ginsburg applauded the burgeoning activism of this younger generation of women lawyers. Led by senior scholars such as Herma Hill Kay, they would file the cases in the lower courts, write the briefs, and provide the scholarship that would ultimately capture the courts' attention. Yet she was convinced that still more needed to be done outside feminist circles to heighten judicial awareness.

· · ·

SEPTEMBER 1972 ARRIVED, and with it the ACLU's biennial meeting with affiliates in Boulder, Colorado. Much had changed since the Ginsburgs' last visit to Denver, when they had argued the *Moritz* case. She had made her presence felt at Columbia, put in place a support structure for what Neier would call the most "clearly planned" litigation strategy in his tenure at the ACLU, and secured the Court's consideration of two new cases for which she had great hopes, *Struck v. Secretary of Defense* and *Frontiero v. Richardson*. Yet there was one thing that had not changed—a reluctance to talk about herself. When it was Ginsburg's turn to speak to the delegates in Boulder, Neier watched in amazement as this small, resolute woman talked about the project and future cases with great clarity but with absolutely no reference to herself. Yet for all her diffidence, she displayed new vigor and authority.

Taking a break from the conference, Ginsburg and Feigen went horseback riding. Galloping across the flat countryside outside Boulder, "Ruth rode freely, almost wildly, but always in control," Feigen observed. Here was someone who played as hard as she worked. Equally telling was the control she exerted—whether over a galloping horse or a fledgling legal unit about which she felt she "was making it up" as she went along "pretty much on her own."

The woman who "began as 'The World's Greatest Living Authority on Section Umpty-ump of the Swedish Civil Practice Act in Relation to Section Ump-Umpty of the FRCP [Federal Rules of Civil Procedure]'" was turning into "a tiger for the Cause"—"a quiet tiger, a moderate, sensible tiger, but a fearsome tiger" nonetheless, observed a genial male friend.

PART III

Learning Under Fire

"The Case That Got Away"

Stationed in an evacuation hospital in Vietnam, Captain Susan Struck had directed her nursing staff under sniper fire and grenade explosions. Her record as a nurse and manager was unblemished. Then, in September 1970, her superiors learned that she was pregnant. Shipped back to McChord Air Force Base in Washington a month later, she immediately received her discharge orders. Air force regulations mandated dismissal of a pregnant woman, even at the officer level, unless she opted for an abortion—a procedure readily available on some military bases.

Struck, an unmarried Roman Catholic, felt she could not have an abortion. Instead, she hoped to carry her pregnancy to term, surrender the baby for adoption, and then resume her military career, using only her accumulated leave time for the birth and recovery. Unfortunately, the air force had a backup rule: "The commission of any woman officer will be terminated with the least practical delay when it is established that she . . . [h]as given birth to a living child while in a commissioned officer status." Facing immediate discharge, Struck turned to ACLU lawyers in the state of Washington to secure a stay of her discharge until the case could be heard by the U.S. District Court for the Western District of Washington.

In the meantime, she gave birth on December 3, 1970, to a daughter, whom she cradled in her arms before surrendering the baby to her adoptive parents. Two months later, Struck learned that the district court had ruled against her, judging the air force's regulation constitutional. Appealing the decision to the U.S. Court of Appeals for the Ninth Circuit, she hoped for a reversal, only to learn in November 1971 that a divided appeals court had upheld the lower court's ruling. She had only one recourse left—the Supreme Court. Her lawyer, Robert Czeisler, a member of the ACLU's Washington affiliate, turned to Ginsburg.

· · ·

AFTER CAREFULLY REVIEWING the file, Ginsburg thought "long and hard" about the case and the issues it presented. The problem, she believed, had little to do with the obvious physiological differences between the sexes, though these could hardly be ignored. Rather, it lay in the vulnerability to various forms of pressure that sexual relations often create for women in their childbearing years—pressures to give up needed jobs when pregnant, to have a pregnancy terminated involuntarily, or to carry an unwanted pregnancy to term against one's best judgment. When such pressures take the form of statutes or regulations, the law becomes by its very nature sex-based, penalizing women.

Allowing air force personnel who became fathers to remain in the military, rewarding them with bonuses for reenlisting while forcing out women who became mothers, provided a clear-cut example of sex differentiation based on old stereotypes. Furthermore, it constituted an invidious distinction between similarly situated individuals—Susan Struck and the father of her baby—who were co-partners in the conception. *Struck,* Ginsburg concluded, was a paradigmatic case of sex discrimination.

Persuading nine men to see it that way—some of them veterans of an all-male military—would be a long shot. *Muller*'s legacy, that women's childbearing capacity required special treatment, still retained a powerful hold. Judges had difficulty seeing the ease with which protection becomes restriction. Added to that was the military's argument that full battle readiness demanded the very regulations that Susan Struck contested. The ERA's history was no help, either. Feminist architects of the ratification strategy, beginning with Pauli Murray and Mary Eastwood, had previously conceded that the prohibition against sex discrimination should not apply to laws relating to unique physical characteristics, such as pregnancy. Endorsed by Bella Abzug, Betty Friedan, and other movement leaders, the exemption was a pragmatic concession to opponents' fears. Worries that the ERA, by requiring equal treatment of men and women, would invalidate criminal rape laws and maternity benefits

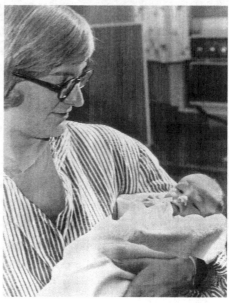

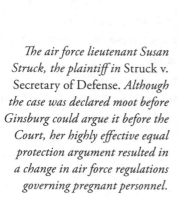

The air force lieutenant Susan Struck, the plaintiff in Struck v. Secretary of Defense. *Although the case was declared moot before Ginsburg could argue it before the Court, her highly effective equal protection argument resulted in a change in air force regulations governing pregnant personnel.*

had surfaced repeatedly during congressional debate over the proposed amendment.

Ginsburg understood the qualification, as initially intended by Murray and Eastwood, to be a narrow one, subject to careful judicial scrutiny—an understanding shared by Thomas Emerson of Yale Law School, lead author of the definitive study of the ERA's potential impact. Otherwise, the "unique physical characteristics" exception would open the door to the old rationale of difference that was at the very core of sex discrimination.

The case had another compelling aspect. Susan Struck's plight involved abortion, the military's way of dealing with pregnant women in uniform who wanted to remain in the armed forces. Pregnancy-related regulations—whether by the states severely restricting abortions or by the military requiring them as condition for remaining in service— clearly reflected a cluster of stereotypical gender assumptions about women's "natural" role as mothers. Historically, that meant "protecting" future mothers by automatically relegating them to the domestic sphere and their traditional role as caretakers.

Yet mothering, Ginsburg and her feminist legal sisters recognized, imposes real limitations on women—on their ability to acquire a good education and/or marketable job skills, pursue satisfactory employment, or participate in politics or other pursuits associated with full citizenship status in our society. Female citizens may choose motherhood, devoting themselves exclusively to the nurture and care of their children in a spirit of self-sacrifice. They may even consider mothering the most fulfilling experience of their lives. Or they may seek to combine mothering with other identities and activities, using whatever arrangements their circumstances permit to make the combination possible.

The state, however, must not force women to go down one track or the other: either to forgo or to assume motherhood. To do so, Ginsburg maintained, amounted to coercion in the guise of "protection"—sex-based discrimination and, especially for women on the wrong side of the race and class divide, subordinate citizenship status. On the principle of non-coercion, she would remain adamant.

. . .

WHEN GINSBURG FILED the *Struck* petition to the Supreme Court in 1972, she did so at a decisive moment. Termination of a pregnancy had moved from an intimate private decision to passionate public debate, from legislative halls to courtrooms, and ultimately to the high court in little more than a decade. Until the mid-nineteenth century, abortion was not considered a criminal offense if performed before "quickening," which occurs in the second trimester of pregnancy. By 1910, every state except Kentucky had banned abortion at any stage of pregnancy with the exception of "therapeutic" procedures performed to save the life of the mother. Yet abortions had never stopped. In the years after World War II, women of means and influence either left the country or got referrals by their private physicians to competent practitioners. Poor women, especially women of color, were less fortunate. In New York City, nearly half (42.1 percent) of the total maternal mortality in the 1960s could be traced to botched illegal abortions.

Appalled by the deadly results, public health officials found allies who also recognized the need for change. Doctors wanted freedom to exercise their professional judgment in the care of their patients without being second-guessed by overzealous prosecutors. Concerned clergy, therapists, and psychiatrists experienced frustration at the limited options available to those they counseled. Though motivated differently, advocates for decriminalization united in their intent to reform and ultimately to repeal repressive statutes.

Turning first to state legislatures in the 1960s, reformers proposed a model code drafted by the American Law Institute. With the approval of hospital committees, doctors could use therapeutic exemptions to perform abortions for rape, incest, fetal deformity, and the physical and mental health of the mother. Spurred by broad media coverage of the thalidomide scare and discovery of rubella-related fetal defects, legislators in California, Colorado, and North Carolina adopted reform laws in 1967. But the slow pace of liberalization and the red tape associated with petitioning hospital committees, combined with the paucity of legal abortions actually performed in states that did relax their abortion statutes, generated frustration. With legislative reform stalled in other states, reformers turned to repeal—an approach that gained further momentum with the resurgence of feminism.

Objecting to the gender paternalism of regulations intended to shield doctors, NOW's president, Betty Friedan, insisted, "There is only one voice that needs to be heard. . . . The right of [a] woman to control her reproductive process must be established as a basic and valuable human civil right not to be denied or abridged by the state." In articulating a woman's right to decide, feminists made clear that abortion was no longer a public health problem. Nor was it about liberating women from motherhood. Rather, it was about women's "self-determination"—their freedom, equality, and dignity as citizens.

With the development of a legal argument with which to challenge restrictions, the struggle over abortion moved into courtrooms. Initial lawsuits focused on doctors, contesting prosecution on the grounds of vagueness. Feminist lawyers in New York and Connecticut, seeking to educate judges and the public alike, enlisted women as petitioners, using their stories to communicate the consequences of stringent statutes. In the process, they expanded the list of constitutional prohibitions violated: a woman's right to privacy, to liberty, to equal protection, and to freedom from cruel and unusual punishment (for engaging in sex). Although the New York case became moot when the legislature narrowly voted for repeal, challenges in other states proceeded through the courts.

With conflicting decisions on abortion mounting in the lower courts, the Supreme Court agreed in 1971 to hear two cases. One, *Roe v. Wade,* challenged an 1854 Texas ban that permitted abortion only to save the life of the mother. The other, *Doe v. Bolton,* targeted Georgia's "reform" statute, which eased restrictions to allow the procedures in limited circumstances under strict qualifying conditions.

. . .

THE PRIMARY BRIEF for *Doe v. Bolton* had arrived on Wulf's desk while Ginsburg was at work on the *Reed* brief. Thanks to the efforts of Dorothy Kenyon and Planned Parenthood's Harriet Pilpel, the ACLU had long been among the organizations at the forefront of the effort to liberalize abortion restrictions. Margie Hames, a member of the ACLU national board, led the Atlanta team that successfully challenged the Georgia statute. Wulf, sharing the brief with Ginsburg, asked for her assessment.

After careful reading, Ginsburg concluded that the Hames brief did not measure up. The problem lay not in the basic argument: that the state had no compelling reason to interfere with a woman's decision about whether to carry a pregnancy to term. Rather, what she found troubling was the level of craftsmanship in a brief submitted by the ACLU. It ought to be equivalent in quality to the work produced by the best private firms, she maintained. The argument for the right to terminate a pregnancy also needed firmer constitutional ground in which to anchor women's claim.

What troubled Ginsburg was that the authors of *Doe v. Bolton,* like the young Texas attorneys Sarah Weddington and Linda Coffee, who had initiated *Roe v. Wade,* had chosen to ground their argument in "privacy"—the right to marital privacy, found in *Griswold v. Connecticut* (1965), protecting the use of contraceptives free from state interference. But the privacy rationale, even when tied to due process, could constitute a problematic base on which to rest women's reproductive freedom. The right to privacy was not part of the text of the Constitution. An equality argument based on equal protection, especially if carefully crafted, could have at least provided an additional textual anchor, Ginsburg believed. As the controversy over *Brown* and school integration had demonstrated, strong textual anchoring in the Constitution was essential if a landmark decision was to have staying power.

. . .

STRUCK NOW SEEMED PROVIDENTIAL. Might she use the opening provided by *Reed* to establish a sex-equality approach to reproductive rights that could serve as a precedent for attacking other forms of
pregnancy-related discrimination, perhaps even abortion regulations?
A sex-discrimination argument had made some headway in the lower
courts and at the EEOC, thanks to the leadership of Wendy Williams
and Sue Deller Ross, though not nearly enough. Yet the more Ginsburg
thought about it, the more convinced she became that bringing reproductive rights under the equal protection umbrella placed them precisely
where they belonged. And she knew a well-crafted brief could influence
judicial thinking.

Timing would be critical. Oral arguments in *Roe* and *Doe* had taken
place on December 13, 1971. But when the Court met in conference to
discuss the two cases, there had been little agreement on either one.
When Justice Blackmun's initial draft of a decision proved lacking the
following May, a decision was made to have the cases reargued before a
full Court following the seating of Justices Powell and Rehnquist. With
the date set for reargument on October 11, 1972, all three cases would
now be heard in the same term.

. . .

THE *STRUCK* ARGUMENT, Ginsburg knew, would need to be carefully
constructed. Equal treatment, the right to sexual privacy and autonomy,
and free exercise of religion were all involved. Two goals stood out. First,
to make clear how sex-based classifications based on societal assumptions about pregnant women as a group penalized individual women
like Susan Struck. Second, to illuminate the larger pattern of sexual
subordination created by regulations embedded with stereotypes about
pregnancy, childbirth, and mothering. Throughout, she would have to
underscore the critical point that equality demanded carefully discerning when and how different treatment infringed on the equal citizenship stature of women. Downplaying the "unique" aspect of childbirth
required equating pregnancy-related disability with other forms of temporary disability.

The argument opened with a clear statement: "Until very recent years, jurists have regarded any discrimination in the treatment of pregnant women and mothers as 'benignly in their favor.' But in fact, restrictive rules, and particularly discharge for pregnancy rules, operate as 'built-in headwinds' that drastically curtail women's opportunities," impelling them "to accept a dependent subordinate status in society."

The air force's claim that its pregnancy regulations vindicated a "legitimate and compelling interest"—discouraging pregnancy and maintaining a fighting force—had to be rejected, Ginsburg argued. As applied, the regulations denied Captain Struck equal protection of the law and substantially infringed upon her right to autonomy in deciding whether to bear a child.

Proceeding first to pregnancy discrimination, Ginsburg acknowledged that in the event of any temporary medical disability, removal from a combat zone was entirely appropriate. Yet for every other temporary medical disability, including drug addiction and alcoholism, the air force encouraged reporting, rehabilitation, and reassignment. That pregnancy was the only temporary disability warranting mandatory discharge, she contended, constituted a flagrant example of sex discrimination.

The presumptions behind such a regulation had far less to do with military readiness, Ginsburg argued, than with prejudice against women and traditional notions about motherhood. The idea that a woman who becomes pregnant is so disabled that she must immediately leave her job, be confined to home to await childbirth, and thereafter devote herself to child care was—to say the least—outmoded and disadvantaging. It denied women—many of whom were handicapped only during the weeks immediately before and after delivery—the "opportunity for training and work experience during pregnancy, and in many cases, for a prolonged period thereafter."

More damaging still, Ginsburg asserted, was the "Draconian" regulation denying female military personnel the opportunity to return to active duty after giving birth. Automatic involuntary discharge of an officer not only deprived her of her career and benefits but further denied her what she most needed: protection of her right to work to support herself as she had in the past and to receive further training and advancement. Women, whether military or civilian, do not work for "pin money," Ginsburg pointed out; they were often the sole source of support for themselves and, in some cases, their families. Regulations that disregarded this reality compelled women to settle for inferior employment and/or economic dependency.

Furthermore, the underlying rationale for the air force's regulations seemed to defy logic. Immediate, involuntary dismissal was hardly necessary to further the air force's purported goal of battle readiness. Maintaining battle-fit personnel, she pointed out, was routinely accomplished by rotating personnel in and out of a combat zone. Rotating out a pregnant officer was no different from reassigning a male suffering temporarily from an injury or alcoholism. Recovery time for the new mother was, in fact, considerably shorter.

Nor was the air force's secondary goal of discouraging pregnancy accomplished by singling out for automatic discharge *only* those women who gave birth. Female air force personnel who underwent abortions or whose pregnancies ended in miscarriage suffered no penalty, nor did the servicemen, married or single, who fathered a child. On the contrary, military men with children received financial incentives for staying in the service. Likewise, the air force's argument about the burden of more paperwork imposed if regulations were changed could not be considered a viable defense. The Court had already made clear in *Reed* that administrative convenience was not sufficient justification.

Finally, Ginsburg took on the matter of abortion itself. Regulations that required women to terminate a pregnancy in order to pursue an air force career denied them the right to personal autonomy and free exercise of religion in making a decision in accordance with their moral and religious beliefs. Because no similar burden was placed upon male personnel, who were co-partners in conception, the regulation was sex-based.

In sum, the brief concluded, the regulations that violated Susan Struck's constitutional right to equal protection could not be sustained even on a rational basis. If disability was the issue, she was less of a burden to the service than reported drug addicts or alcoholics in uniform. If morality in terms of sexual behavior was the issue, her male partner was equally culpable, yet fathering a child brought no adverse consequences.

. . .

A MODEL OF EFFECTIVE ADVOCACY, the brief was remarkable in other respects as well. It dispelled later criticism of Ginsburg's vision of equality as a limited formalistic one in which men and women are treated the same. She neither emphasized women's distinctive role as child bearers nor ignored it. Nor did she totally reject classifications that differentiate men and women. Rather, she asked that the Court recognize *how* classifications that incorporate traditional sex stereotypes work to deny women opportunity. It was on the long-term effect of air force practice and how it contributed to the perpetuation of women's subordination as a group that she focused. What also made the brief notable was its date. In 1972, Owen Fiss had not yet written his classic article on subordination in which he proposed shifting the emphasis in equal protection cases involving race from classifications to social practices that disadvantage the group. And it would be another seven years before Catharine MacKinnon applied a subordination perspective to the sexual harassment of working women. Prescience, however, is not always rewarded.

· · ·

GINSBURG'S OLD HARVARD DEAN, Erwin Griswold, was now the solicitor general. That alone signaled that the air force would be well represented. His office attracted some of the best young legal talent around, guaranteeing that the government's brief would be a strong one. What she did not anticipate was that Griswold would advise the air force to change its regulations and grant Captain Struck a waiver. It was a smart move on Griswold's part—one that took the long view, as Ginsburg would later acknowledge. It put an end to Struck's mandatory discharge for pregnancy and restored her military career. It also ensured that the case would now be dismissed.

Ginsburg was thus deprived of her first chance for a Supreme Court victory in the 1972–73 term, in what was to have been a pairing of cases. More important, she had lost her opening wedge in an effort to get the Court to understand pregnancy discrimination as sex discrimination. Gone too was any hope of using *Struck* to nudge the justices closer to a view of reproductive freedom as an issue of liberty and equality. The clock had run out.

· · ·

ON JANUARY 22, 1973, with flags in the capital flying at half-staff to mark former president Lyndon Johnson's death, the Court finally announced its decisions in *Roe* and *Doe*. Consensus had not come easily. The justices had no intention of simply making abortion available upon demand. Rather, they struggled at length over when in the course of a pregnancy a woman's right to an abortion should give way to the state's concern for protection of fetal life. Trying to accommodate his colleagues' various concerns, Justice Blackmun had finally come up with a draft that satisfied seven of the justices (Brennan, Marshall, Douglas, Stewart, Powell, Blackmun himself, and Burger).

Constitutionally, the opinions in *Roe* and *Doe* were grounded in privacy undergirded by substantive due process (liberty). Blackmun, writing for the majority, conceded that the right to personal privacy was not explicitly mentioned in the Constitution. Nevertheless, a long line of decisions recognized its existence, whether in the Fourteenth Amendment's due process clause or the Ninth Amendment's reservation of unspecified rights to the people. That right is broad enough, Blackmun wrote, "to encompass a woman's decision whether or not to terminate her pregnancy." "However, it is not unqualified," he continued, and it has to be balanced by the state's interest in protecting both the health of pregnant women and "the potentiality of human life."

To accommodate these divergent interests, Blackmun—who had previously served as counsel to the Mayo Clinic—adopted the trimester system. In the first trimester, abortion was to be a matter of medical judgment by the pregnant woman's physician and could be performed free from state interference. During the second trimester, doctors might perform abortions under certain conditions specified by the state, so long as maternal health was the top priority. In the final trimester, the state could place the interest of the fetus over the right of the woman to an abortion, banning the procedure except when the life or health of the mother was at risk.

In a shorter opinion in *Doe*, the Court struck down Georgia's narrow range of therapeutic exemptions, declaring that advance permission from a hospital's physicians committee was unnecessary, as was the acquiescence of two doctors in addition to the woman's own physician. Further, abortion could not be restricted to a hospital if other licensed institutions satisfied health standards.

Dissenting, Justice White, in a terse, passionate statement, called the decision an "exercise in raw judicial power." Nothing in the language or the history of the Constitution, he contended, justified privileging the convenience of the woman over the potential life of the fetus. Rehnquist also had strong objections. The Court, he agreed, had overstepped its authority. The right to privacy on which the majority had based its decision, he charged, was not the "liberty" protected by the Fourteenth Amendment. The "sweeping invalidation of any restriction on first trimester abortion" amounted to judicial legislation.

. . .

FOR CHAMPIONS OF ABORTION LAW REPEAL, the rulings were an occasion for celebration. The *Roe* decision, especially when combined with *Doe,* was "far broader in scope than anyone expected," exulted the chairman of the National Abortion Rights Action League (NARAL). "It scaled the whole mountain," Pilpel declared in an interview. "We expected to get there, but not on the first trip." Legal scholars, even those who agreed with the outcome, were less ecstatic. *Roe* was long on medicine, many concluded (Ginsburg among them), but woefully short on law.

Public reaction to the decision was predictably divided. As the abortion law reform movement had gathered momentum during the 1960s, polls showed that by the end of the decade a majority of Americans—64 percent, including a majority of Roman Catholics—believed that "abortion should not be a matter of the law but should be left to the prospective parents and their doctor." But apart from circumstances involving a woman's health, serious fetal defects, or rape, there was little consensus on repeal in the broader public.

Catholic bishops had led the initial resistance to liberalization of abortion laws by state legislators in the late 1960s. Inflamed in particular by New York's vote for repeal in 1970, abortion opponents had already formed a successful countermovement in state after state. In the 1972 presidential elections, abortion had become a partisan issue. President Nixon's strategy to woo Catholic voters and "Middle Americans" away from the Democratic Party identified his Democratic presidential challenger, George McGovern, as the "Triple-A candidate" who favored abortion, amnesty (for draft dodgers), and acid (legalization of LSD and other narcotics). The longtime Republican conservative Phyllis Schlafly linked abortion, the ERA, women's lib, and federally funded day care as the bête noire of American women and mothers.

In the wake of *Roe,* the antiabortion movement exploded. What feminists understood as a woman's right to make a decision about whether to bear a child free from government coercion, others saw as an exercise in moral laxity, female self-indulgence, and abdication of maternal responsibility. Though resistance had been evident in earlier legislative battles, it was not until the mid-1970s that opposition really took off. Right-wing organizers successfully channeled concern about the decline of traditional morality, "the family," and the nation into a large, angry, and increasingly partisan antiabortion coalition.

. . .

RECALLING THE BACKLASH against *Brown* and the attempt to undermine it both at the state level and in Congress, ACLU leaders realized immediately that they would have to stay on top of new legislation attempting to chisel away at abortion rights. They also had to be prepared, if necessary, to litigate. Anticipating a barrage of cases designed to nibble away at *Roe,* Neier had promptly asked his Women's Rights Project director to take them on. Ginsburg politely declined. There was the matter of funding for the Women's Rights Project, specifically the Ford Foundation's ban on abortion-related litigation. Her own equal protection litigation was just getting started, and the project already had plans under way to expand its number of cases. There was also the matter of staffing. Her tiny legal office could not take on more suits, especially given the demands of ACLU affiliates. And finally, there was her unrelenting schedule.

The solution, they quickly agreed, was a separate Reproductive Freedom Project that could devote itself entirely to the defense of *Roe.* It was the only feasible option under the circumstances. Given her decidedly mixed feelings about *Roe,* Ginsburg must have breathed a sigh of relief—one so large that she now no longer recalls Neier's request.

. . .

ROE WAS "the single most important litigation advance of the decade," she would later write to Isabelle Katz Pinzler in 1979. But like many of her feminist legal sisters, Ginsburg deplored the medicalized nature of the decision, which appeared to have been written with physicians' autonomy, not women's, as the primary concern. The Court should have "placed the woman alone rather than the woman tied to the physician at the center of its attention," she would subsequently suggest. The brethren, she felt, had construed the issues too narrowly. The conflict "is not simply one between a fetus' interests and a woman's interests, narrowly conceived, nor is the issue state versus private control of a woman's body for a span of nine months." Also in the balance, she emphasized, is a woman's right to make autonomous decisions about sex and parenting that affect "her full life's course," echoing her point in *Struck* about the long-term impact of pregnancy-related regulations on equal citizenship.

Ginsburg also questioned Blackmun's trimester approach. What would happen to women who, for whatever reason, failed to get to a doctor before the end of the first trimester? Also, what would happen to a woman's right to terminate a pregnancy as fetal technology progressed, making it possible to sustain fetal life outside the womb at earlier and earlier stages of pregnancy? Then there were her persistent concerns about the fragile textual backing for privacy upon which *Roe* rested, deriving as it did from what many legal scholars had regarded as sloppy jurisprudence in the earlier *Griswold* decision. Anchoring the abortion right in the equal protection guarantees of the Fifth and Fourteenth Amendments, she firmly believed, would have made the decision much less vulnerable to legal and political undermining.

Nor was it only the weak constitutional grounding in privacy that worried Ginsburg. As someone trained in process theory, she had a keen appreciation for the interaction of lawmaking institutions, the importance of preserving respect for judicial review, and the Court as an institution. The sweeping decisions in *Roe* and *Doe,* she believed, challenged all three. The justices could have simply invalidated the Texas law, the most extreme in the nation, and not taken on *Doe.* That would have given the public the chance to adjust to *Roe* while leaving state legislatures the opportunity to work out regulations in dialogue with their constituents. Laws that proved too restrictive could then have been challenged so that the Court might proceed incrementally, giving the public more time to adjust. As written, she feared, *Roe* would become ever more vulnerable as backlash intensified, threatening the institutional legitimacy and authority of the Court itself—an outcome that a narrower decision might have made less likely.

. . .

OTHER PROMINENT LEGAL SCHOLARS—Sylvia Law, Catharine MacKinnon, Rhonda Copelon, Reva Siegel, Robin West, Cass Sunstein, Kenneth Karst, and Laurence Tribe—agreed with Ginsburg for the most part about the missing equality component in *Roe*. "The rhetoric of privacy, as opposed to equality," Law forcibly stated, "blunts our ability to focus on the fact that it *is women* who are oppressed when abortion is denied."

At the time, however, such reservations were muted in the feminist legal community—at least in print—as Siegel has insightfully pointed out. Advocates of the ERA had refrained from talking about the sex-equality dimension of the right to abortion while ratification of the amendment was pending. To do so, they feared, would play into the hands of right-wing antifeminist activists like Schlafly, who linked the ERA to abortion, suspension of rape laws, gay rights, and every other threat she could imagine.

But by 1976, it was harder to keep silent as state after state rejected public funding for abortion for poor women. Beginning with *Maher v. Roe* (1977), the Court ruled that the protected right against state interference in seeking abortion did not require state and local governments to pay for abortion. Antiabortion opponents in Congress, seeing a green light, quickly inserted an amendment banning the use of federal funding to pay for abortions for indigent women, even in cases involving rape and incest, unless the pregnant woman's life was at stake.

The Court considered the ban in 1980 (*Harris v. McRae*). In its defense, lawyers argued that due process stopped the government from intruding into a fundamental liberty of the people, but nothing more. It was, in short, a "negative" liberty. Consistent with that understanding and the precedents established in *Maher,* the Court ruled once again that *Roe* prohibited government from interfering with a woman's privacy where abortion was concerned; it did not, however, require the government to pay for the procedure. Medicaid (which funded all other medically necessary procedures) was an "entitlement," not a right—a statement that baffled Ginsburg.

The majority's rulings "defy reason," she concluded, as did Justices Brennan, Marshall, and Blackmun. How could the right to choose mean anything to women who, for financial reasons, had no choice? Better than most, Ginsburg knew that privacy theory and liberty theory guaranteed negative liberty in that they focused on what the government could not do. She also knew that the concern exhibited by feminists and their legal sisters in the pre-*Roe* years, targeting the disparity in access to abortion between rich and poor women, had not become a part of *Roe*.

. . .

ONCE THE DEADLINE for ratification of the ERA expired in 1982, Ginsburg and her feminist legal allies no longer felt compelled to keep their views on the limitations of *Roe* to themselves. But the abortion-rights scene had also changed. By 1982, Catholics, Protestant fundamentalists, and the New Right had energized antiabortion forces with new numbers, tactics, and political reach. *Roe* had become a make-or-break issue for political candidates and judicial nominations—arguably, the defining issue in the culture wars. Pro-choice leaders, beleaguered by antiabortionists whose tactics included not just picketing but also bombings of clinics and assassinations of physicians and clinic staffers, found any criticism of *Roe* suspect. As Kate Michelman of NARAL observed, Ginsburg's "criticisms of *Roe* raise concerns about whether she believes the right to choose is a fundamental right or a lesser right."

Ginsburg's alternative scenario, as to how a narrower decision might have played out at the state level, also prompted rejoinders. The pre-*Roe* legislative record, she was reminded, did not justify her confidence that reform could have been accomplished at the legislative level had the Court's ruling been less sweeping. Even in her home state of New York, only a gubernatorial veto by Nelson Rockefeller had kept abortion legal in the months immediately prior to *Roe*. In fact, her view of legislative liberalization was "simply and utterly wrong," stated the legal historian David Garrow.

Blackmun, always on the defensive where *Roe* was concerned, conceded that Ginsburg had "a valid point of view" with respect to her sex-equality approach but insisted that she "pick[ed] at Roe." For someone writing in the 1980s, her line was "an easy one to take," he acknowledged, but not in 1972–73. Noting that "she wasn't on the firing line at the time," he characterized her response as "a professor's appraisal twenty years after"—a condescending reference to law professors whose job it is to assess Supreme Court decisions. He later elaborated, adding that "Justice Douglas [who had written the majority opinion in *Griswold*] was all for privacy and this was the road to take at that time."

Mark V. Tushnet, Justice Marshall's clerk in 1972–73 and a distinguished constitutional scholar, agrees. The Court had barely begun to recognize women's equality interests as constitutionally significant, he noted. Inserting a women's equality theory in *Roe* "would have been regarded in 1973 as outside the bounds of professional respectability—as, indeed, were the advocates who were actually making such arguments. . . . How could those men (the gender here is one of the points) actually have done anything different?"

Neier makes a similar point, noting that when the New York City affiliate of the ACLU took its stand on abortion in 1965 and when Roy Lucas began his effort to define abortion as a privacy right in the aftermath of *Griswold,* there was a "virtual absence of judicial protection for women's rights. . . . Even if we had had the consciousness . . . that emerged a few years later, I doubt we could have gotten anywhere."

Yet equality talk was in the air. An equality argument had been made in connection with antiabortion laws in New York and Connecticut as well as in an amicus brief for *Roe* prepared by Nancy Stearns on behalf of the group New Women Lawyers. Stearns, in fact, had advanced a particularly strong equality claim based on the Nineteenth Amendment as well as the Fourteenth Amendment. NOW also provided an amicus brief along similar lines, as had the American Association of University Women (AAUW) and other groups. Most significantly, Judge J. Edward Lumbard, part of a three-judge panel for the Second Circuit, had invalidated the Connecticut abortion statute using an equality argument.

Both Justices Blackmun and Powell were aware of Judge Lumbard's decision. But as Blackmun's biographer Linda Greenhouse has pointed out, "There was a disconnect between what the Court heard in *Roe* and what it chose to say." Had the decision come a few years later, once Ginsburg had been given the opportunity to argue other sex-discrimination cases, Justice Brennan might well have added an equality claim rooted in equal protection. But it is difficult to imagine that as early as 1972 another outcome was possible—not that legal scholars have not tried.

. . .

GINSBURG, HOWEVER, clung to the belief that if only the justices had heard *Struck* before deciding *Roe* and *Doe,* they might have dealt with reproductive issues differently. Wishful thinking was a possibility she later acknowledged. But there is no doubt that the incorporation of the sex-discrimination approach into *Roe* would have had profound consequences for reproductive laws, especially since sex-equality juris-prudence was still in its formative state. More apparent, too, might have been the gendered dimension of reproduction and why women, not the state, must bear the burden of choice—a view toward which the Court would move in *Casey* (1992) (though with significant concessions to the states and a nod to women-protective arguments).

. . .

SUBTLETIES OF THE LAW were not what "*Roe* rage" was about. For right-to-lifers who felt "as though they had been disowned by their coun-try" by a decision that negated their values, it was all about the "unborn" and their rights from the moment of conception. "Fetal rights" and "fetal personhood" swiftly became the new slogans du jour for abortion opponents. The rhetorical shift was calculated to enhance the status of the fetus to equal protagonist in the conflict—"babies." An obvious ploy, it prompted a rueful letter to Ginsburg from an old Rutgers friend. "I have nightmare visions of the fertilized egg being named a person [in terms of the law] before female adults are," wrote Phyllis Zatlin Boring. Lamenting the progress of the ERA's ratification, Zatlin's "nightmare visions" only confirmed Ginsburg's determination not to let her next case get away.

CHAPTER 10

A "Near Great Leap Forward"

Sharron Frontiero, a physical therapist at Maxwell Air Force Base Hospital in Montgomery, Alabama, had married her fiancé in 1969 in their hometown of Gloucester, Massachusetts. Returning to the base with her new husband, the twenty-three-year-old lieutenant opened her air force paycheck. She thought there must be a mistake. Her male colleagues received increased housing allowances when they married, but she had not. Her husband, Joseph, a navy veteran, was now a full-time college student. They needed the larger housing allowance as well as medical and dental benefits for him. The personnel office, she assumed, would surely correct its mistake.

There had been no error. Lieutenant Frontiero could not legally secure a housing allowance, much less medical benefits for her husband, unless he was her "dependent." By most standards, he was; Sharron's yearly salary of $8,200 provided nearly three-quarters of their family income. But a federal statute stipulated that a married female member of the armed services could receive spousal benefits *only* if she demonstrated that she was contributing more than half of her husband's living expenses. Joseph received a monthly veteran's payment of $205 from the navy under the GI Bill and earned $30 a month working part-time as a night watchman, putting him over the limit.

For nearly a year, the frustrated lieutenant went through air force channels, trying to rectify the situation. It was the principle of the thing that so infuriated her. To have different rules for married men and women in the service was just wrong. "Our idea," she explained, "was that men don't depend on women and women don't depend on men. Men and women depend on each other." But despite her formal complaint, nothing changed.

Claiming discrimination on the basis of sex, the Frontieros turned to Joseph Levin Jr., a local attorney who had lectured to a Huntingdon College class that Joseph Frontiero had attended. A civil rights lawyer, Levin was about to join Morris Dees to found the soon legendary Southern Poverty Law Center. He understood immediately what was at issue. Described by Dees as "bright" and "tireless," Levin had never questioned the racial practices of his native state until the Ku Klux Klan burned a twelve-foot cross on the lawn of his Jewish fraternity house. The cross burning was a protest against an editorial in the University of Alabama student newspaper written by a fraternity brother who criticized Governor George Wallace's refusal to let black students enroll at the University of Alabama. The open hatred was an eye-opener for a college student who had gone through junior high school oblivious to the significance of the Montgomery bus boycott.

After receiving his law degree and serving a two-year army stint, Levin had returned to Montgomery, where he soon exchanged the boredom of his father's commercial practice for a partnership with the fearless Dees. Specializing in what the two young trial lawyers anticipated would be major civil rights cases, they planned to use fees from their paying clients to support exciting pro bono cases like Sharron Frontiero's.

Levin's first task was to convince the Frontieros that the air force would be too concerned about appearances to retaliate by transferring Sharron to some remote post. Only then did the couple agree to sue. He then argued the case before a three-judge panel for the Middle District of Alabama. The panel consisted of two giants of civil rights enforcement, Judges Frank M. Johnson Jr. and Richard T. Rives. It was Johnson and Rives who had struck down Montgomery's bus segregation law and also handed Dorothy Kenyon and Pauli Murray their victory in *White v. Crook* (1966).

But this time the two men could not agree. Judge Johnson wanted to rule for Frontiero, but the cryptic wording in *Reed,* handed down while the three-judge panel—Johnson, Rives, and Judge Frank McFadden— was in the midst of deliberations, did not help. Rives was more impressed by the Court's rejection of strict scrutiny. The panel ruled by a two-to-one majority that the sex-based classification sought in *Frontiero* bore a rational relationship to the purpose of the law, which was to save the government money and time. By assuming that most wives of servicemen would be economically dependent, the government was spared the expense of processing proof of dependency. (The cost, however, would have been offset by savings achieved by withholding benefits for husbands such as Joseph Frontiero, who were only partially dependent.) Sharron was dumbfounded by the decision, but Levin remained confident, encouraged by Johnson's strong dissent. This was not the end, he promised.

. . .

LEVIN THEN APPROACHED the ACLU for help in appealing the case to the Supreme Court. Wulf and Ginsburg responded immediately. *Frontiero,* an ideal equal protection case, would also provide an opportunity to extend to women in the military the same guarantees regarding compensation that the Equal Pay Act and Title VII accorded civilians. Should the Court elect to hear *Frontiero* and should the ACLU win, the cost to the government would be modest. Better yet, the stage would be set for other cases involving Social Security benefits, where equalization would entail far larger sums. Not least, the case offered another opportunity to argue for strict scrutiny. If a majority was not yet ready to move to the higher standard of review, Ginsburg would urge the Court once again to adopt the language she had proposed in *Reed.* A rule must have "a fair and substantial relation to the object of the legislation so that all persons similarly situated shall be treated alike."

But first, arrangements had to be nailed down with local counsel. At Levin's request, Ginsburg, collaborating with Feigen, would handle the jurisdictional statement without assistance from the Southern Poverty Law Center. She would also prepare both the brief and the reply brief. And she, not Levin, would present the oral argument in Court, Wulf insisted.

After the Court granted review, Wulf checked with the civil rights lawyer Charles "Chuck" Morgan, who had previously headed the ACLU's Southern Regional Office and was now in charge of the Washington office. Morgan, who knew all the players, was not encouraging. Levin would want to argue the case on narrow grounds, ignoring strict scrutiny, Wulf reported. They would have to make it unmistakably clear that at the Supreme Court level, the ACLU would be in charge.

Ginsburg and Wulf believed that they had reached an agreement

*Lieutenant Sharron
Frontiero and her
husband, Joseph (1973),
who challenged sex-based
differentials in military
benefits in* Frontiero v.
Richardson. *Ginsburg's
advocacy before the Court
persuaded four justices
but not the critical fifth to
make sex-based laws and
regulations subject to strict
scrutiny.*

with Levin and, by extension, his assistant, Charles Abernathy, a third-year Harvard Law School student and editor of the *Harvard Civil Rights–Civil Liberties Law Review.* Because the Alabama duo, still in their twenties, had offered to help with a preliminary draft of the brief once the Court accepted the case for review, Ginsburg mailed a copy of the *Reed* brief's strict scrutiny argument and a tentative outline for *Frontiero,* along with relevant chapters from her forthcoming casebook on sex discrimination. She also suggested that amici briefs be solicited from the Women's Law Fund, a Cleveland-based project of the Ford Foundation, NOW, and other groups. Then, with her usual dispatch, she set to work on the appellant brief.

The response from Montgomery was not reassuring. Levin dismissed amici briefs as unnecessary, indicating that the case would be better served by maintaining a "Nixonian low profile." Nor was he inclined to make the argument for strict scrutiny. However desirable it might be in principle, he insisted, it would not be needed to win *Frontiero.* Abernathy, while admitting that he needed help gathering statistical data, agreed. "It was not a good strategy to invite the 'Burger Justices' preoccupation with decisions that had a revolutionary impact on the courts," he wrote. "Given the nature of your suggestions up to now, I think our arguments are at a higher level of sophistication than you suggest, and that, of course, makes me a bit reticent in incorporating your suggestions into the brief." As Ginsburg wryly noted on another occasion, "Some things don't change—today's members of the *Harvard Law Review* seem as impressed with their own superior understanding as the crew I knew and loved." At the time, however, she felt far less charitable.

The situation was rapidly deteriorating. Levin informed Wulf that he and Dees had decided to present the oral argument themselves. "It's our first opportunity to argue a case before the Court and we have grown very attached to this particular case over the past couple of years." A dismayed Ginsburg responded, emphasizing the importance of having a woman argue the case. "I am not very good at self-advertisement," she wrote, "but I believe you have some understanding of the knowledge of the women's rights area I have developed over the past two years." Levin shot back that neither her sex nor her expertise mattered "one iota." "I find myself trying to determine at exactly what point in time we allowed ourselves to become 'assistants' in our own case," he added, declaring that he and Dees would proceed without the ACLU. Ginsburg, hackles up, fired back, telling Levin that he had "made [her] temperature rise." If all he wanted were suggestions, she added, he could have read the previously mailed chapters of her forthcoming text. "Frustrated"—the word she later chose to describe her emotions—hardly captured Ginsburg's feelings at the time.

· · ·

TRY TO GET LEVIN'S CONSENT for an ACLU amicus brief, Wulf advised. If he agreed, the Women's Rights Project could remain in the game. Levin consented. But it was now the end of October, and there was little time left. With the help of Feigen and her husband, Marc Fasteau, also a Harvard Law graduate, Ginsburg completed the amicus brief by December.

Levin meanwhile put the finishing touches on his own brief. Narrowly focused, his argument was designed to win for the Frontieros by demonstrating that the law at issue could not withstand rational scrutiny. Whether the Court should apply a higher standard of review to sex discrimination was "a question that need not be reached in the present case," Levin noted, adding that "a sex classification needn't always be suspect."

Ginsburg agreed that the law in question could not pass the rational relationship test. But, unlike Levin, she had more than one fish to fry. First, she wanted to expose the remnants of coverture in the stereotypes of male breadwinner/female dependent that underlay the assumption that military wives should automatically receive benefits while husbands rarely would. Second, she hoped to demonstrate why strict scrutiny was appropriate.

She began her brief by surveying women's legally and historically inferior status, as she had in *Reed*. Again she demonstrated how the many laws that had seemed to offer special protection to women when originally designed in fact ultimately acted to hinder them. Again she drew on Pauli Murray's race-sex-discrimination analogy, explaining that sex bore no more relationship to ability than skin color and, like race, merited stricter scrutiny. The justices also should appreciate how much the lower courts needed the definitive guidance that a higher level of scrutiny would provide.

Ginsburg then turned to Sharron Frontiero's plight, explaining why the specific legislation dealing with military benefits that disadvantaged Frontiero could not be justified by administrative convenience. Like *Reed* and *Stanley,* another sex-discrimination case where the Court had rejected administrative convenience as a rationale, the statute challenged did not pass even the rational relationship test. There was really no reasonable justification for denying Sharron Frontiero and her sisters in uniform equal pay and allowances, she concluded.

As to remedies, the Court could refer the matter to Congress to repair in future legislation. But should the justices choose to go that route, benefits would be denied to *all* dependents, which was hardly the intent of Congress. Surely the preferable remedy, Ginsburg proposed—as she had in *Moritz*—was judicial action extending benefits to *both* sexes. Judicial extension—an idea she had picked up in conversation with her old mentor and friend Gerry Gunther—could be regarded as a kind of judicial legislating that encroached on congressional prerogatives. But cutting off benefits for men in the military—the only other alternative until Congress acted—was surely not what lawmakers had originally intended, she argued.

Clear, concise, and tightly reasoned, Ginsburg's amicus brief ultimately wound up in *Landmark Briefs and Arguments of the Supreme Court of the United States*. That it did so was no surprise to her colleagues. Feigen was awed by Ginsburg's knowledge of and adroit use of history as well as the eloquence of her language. "I have never had an experience like the writing of our *Frontiero* brief," she recalled. Kathleen Peratis, who would soon take over the title of project director, responded similarly. "I had written briefs before," she remarked, but working on a brief with Ginsburg was "a new experience. Every sentence, every citation, had to make a point. No citation was ever allowed in which the case had been eroded by some other decision. The legal scholarship had to be impeccable and the language a model of clarity [and precision]"—a standard, the ACLU litigator Norman Dorsen noted, that Ginsburg invariably met. Clearly, in Peratis's words, "She made her very high standards the norm for all the work of the project."

But would Ginsburg's amicus brief persuade Levin to reconsider strict scrutiny? Sending him a copy, she pointed out that her brief differed "substantially" in approach and substance. Though not fully persuaded, he agreed to a joint reply brief addressing points made by government attorneys, which she would write and he would file.

Ginsburg relished the task. It allowed her to attack the solicitor general's arguments with respect to Congress as well as the use of outdated legal precedents. Not least, the reply brief provided another opportunity to argue for suspect classification. The government lawyers, she wrote, had no clear evidence of the original intent of Congress. In all likelihood, the nation's legislators had relied on prevailing gender stereotypes, which the Court had already rejected in *Reed*. To argue that military personnel matters should be left to Congress was inappropriate because the issue in question was constitutionality, a matter that only the Court could decide.

Finally, she took issue with the government's insistence that sex distinctions should not be considered suspect unless the ERA was ratified. "In sum," Ginsburg concluded, "appellants"—Frontiero and her sisters in the services—"submit that designation of the sex criterion as suspect is overdue, provides the only satisfactory standard for dealing with the claim in this case, and should be the starting point for assessing the claim."

. . .

NEXT CAME PREPARATION for oral argument—a momentous event for any first-time advocate appearing before the Supreme Court. Ginsburg and Levin, finally, had agreed to divide the thirty minutes. But no decision had been made as to who would say what or for how long. The challenge for Ginsburg was a double one. She could distill a brief of over seventy pages into a ten- to fifteen-minute presentation. But to be effective, she needed to be so familiar with the material and so certain about the points she had to make that she could jump agilely back and forth between her prepared presentation and responses to questions from the bench. Reducing her notes to a brief handwritten outline, Ginsburg prepared strong opening and concluding sentences, hoping to make her key points in whatever order she could.

Without agreement from Levin, there was no opportunity for a moot court rehearsal. He finally consented to a meeting at ACLU headquarters in Washington with Chuck Morgan as arbiter. Trying to make the best of a bad situation, Ginsburg told herself that arguing with co-counsel the night before their big day in Court would at least keep her from worrying about her own performance. Despite the evident tension, the two attorneys finally agreed that Levin would speak first with Ginsburg to follow.

. . .

THE MORNING OF JANUARY 17, 1973, dawned crisp and cold. After finishing her usual exercise routine drawn from the Canadian Air Force Exercise Manual, Ginsburg showered and had breakfast. Dressing carefully, she put on her mother's jewelry—antique gold earrings and a matching circle pin that she attached to her suit jacket. Wearing Celia's jewelry had become a custom on significant occasions. Her first oral argument before the Court surely qualified—an accomplishment in which her mother would have taken pride. But neither the jewelry nor her impeccably tailored reflection in the mirror eased the mounting anxiety. Deciding to forgo lunch, lest her queasy stomach betray her, she concentrated on her argument until it was time to leave the hotel.

Located at 1 First Street NE, the west-facing Supreme Court Building sits, along with the neighboring Library of Congress, across the street from the Capitol. As Ginsburg approached, she was reminded how much it looked like a pristine Greek temple with its fluted Corinthian columns and pediment. The inscription carved into the frieze above the main entrance—"Equal Justice Under Law"—seemed especially appropriate. Once inside the Court, she was too preoccupied to appreciate the grandeur and symbolism of her surroundings. She and Feigen were escorted along marble floors of the Great Hall past busts of all the former chief justices to the front of the courtroom, along with the government's lawyers. Ginsburg immediately noted Marty's reassuring presence in the section reserved for the Supreme Court bar, located just behind the counsel table. The two women took their seats along with Levin at the "desks" where lawyers for the two sides sit, actually a single, long table bisected by the lectern.

Red benches set aside for members of the press were behind them and to their left. Another set of red benches on the right were reserved for guests of the justices. An additional collection of black chairs in front of those was meant for officers of the Court and visiting dignitaries. As they looked toward the bench, the clerk of the Court, responsible for the administration of the Court's docket, was to their left, while the marshal of the Court, who acted as the timekeeper for each session, sat to the right of the bench.

When the heavy red velvet draperies parted behind four marbled columns, the nine black-robed justices filed in, taking their seats in order of seniority in the high-backed black leather armchairs behind the mahogany bench. Chief Justice Burger took his place at the center with the senior associate justices on either side. At the end of the bench, the marshal stood up from his desk. Dressed in formal morning clothes, he somberly intoned the traditional words: "The Honorable, the Chief Justice and the Associate Justices of the Supreme Court. Oyez! Oyez! Oyez!" Attorneys newly admitted to the Supreme Court bar took their oath—the same oath that she and Marty had taken years ago when they were sworn in.

· · ·

ON THIS PARTICULAR WEDNESDAY, the court would hear arguments in four cases, the last of which was *Frontiero v. Richardson*. Levin led off. His voice a monotone, he began to make the basic points in his brief, arguing that the sex-based statutes denying Sharron Frontiero spousal benefits failed the rational basis test. His sentences were punctuated with pauses and stammers as though words sometimes had difficulty coming out of his mouth. He had barely started when the questioning began. Did the Frontieros' case apply only to civilian spouses? Did Levin's income figures come from a "median head count of Armed Forces males"? Was the military 98 to 99 percent male? The questions seemed to catch him off guard, and he struggled to answer. He tried to stick to his argument, but as he was answering yet another question, he suddenly realized he was already two minutes into the time promised his co-counsel.

Ginsburg now had no more than ten minutes to make her case. As Levin said "Professor Ginsburg," she moved to the microphone, adjusting it downward. Chief Justice Burger acknowledged her, "Mrs. Ginsburg." She preferred "Ms." but said nothing, aware of "the many butterflies in my stomach." Standing ramrod straight, she began speaking clearly, "Mr. Chief Justice and may it please the Court." The first sentence was hard to get out, but looking at the nine men seated before her, she realized that she had a captive audience in the most important court in the land. With a new surge of power, she explained why sex-based laws and regulations especially should be subjected to the highest standard of scrutiny. Her Brooklyn-inflected accent remained, but the ever-present pauses in the middle of a sentence were now absent, replaced with a confident tone with emphasis added on key words.

Pointing out the erratic fashion in which lower courts were ruling on sex-discrimination cases, she emphasized the need for the high court's guidance. Moving on to the similarity of sex-based and race-based discrimination, she carefully elaborated on Murray's classic statement, answering questions before they were asked. Addressing the objection that the equal protection prescription had been designed to address the problems of blacks, not women, she observed that not just race but national origin and alien citizenship had been made suspect classifications. "The newcomer to our shores was not the paramount concern of the nation when the Fourteenth Amendment was adopted." If the amendment could embrace ethnic diversity, was it not capacious enough to include women?

Clearing her throat, Ginsburg took aim at the government's argument that women as a majority had little need for suspect classification in order to secure equality, countering with evidence to the contrary. Neither in the past nor at present had their greater numbers brought them equal treatment. Citing examples of discriminatory practices sanctioned by law and society, she argued that though the forms of discrimination were now subtler, sex-based discrimination was no less stigmatizing. The appellee's argument—that "no close scrutiny of sex-based classifications is warranted . . . unless and until the Equal Rights Amendment comes into force"—she pronounced "unsatisfying." Because the "notion of what constitutes equal protection does change . . . clarification of the application of equal protection to the sex criterion . . . should come from this Court."

Nearing the end of her list of reasons why strict scrutiny was appropriate, Ginsburg concluded with her favorite quotation from the nineteenth-century abolitionist and feminist Sarah Grimké: "I ask no favor for my sex. All I ask of our brethren is that they take their feet off our necks." She then quickly summarized her argument. Astonishingly, not a single word from the bench interrupted her statement.

· · ·

"INCREDIBLE" WAS Feigen's admiring summation of Ginsburg's performance. "Ruth spoke eloquently without a note, never pausing except for inflection. . . . You could have heard a pin drop." But how to account for the highly unusual silence from the bench? Marty shared Feigen's apprehensions. Were the justices politely letting his wife go through the motions? Ruth attributed the silence to indifference; they just "weren't interested" in what she had to say. What none of the three could have anticipated was the impact on Justices Blackmun and Marshall.

Blackmun, who regularly graded lawyers arguing before the Court, privately gave Ginsburg a C plus, noting that she was "very precise" but too "emotional." He disliked "emotion"—a quality he found overabundant in both her *Reed* and *Frontiero* briefs, though precisely what he meant by the term is unclear. (The *Reed* brief he also termed "mildly offensive and arrogant," though admitting that Sally Reed's lawyers nonetheless had the stronger argument.) Why Blackmun was so offended by "emotion" is unclear. Certainly, he would not hesitate to appeal to feeling in his future dissent in *DeShaney v. Winnebago County,* which included the famed lines "Poor Joshua! Victim of repeated attacks by an irresponsible, bullying, cowardly, and intemperate father."

According to his biographer Linda Greenhouse, Blackmun had a hard time understanding the feminist movement, despite the accomplishments of his wife and daughters. The litigation effort Ginsburg had mounted made him "wary and a little grumpy." Perhaps he was put off by the Grimké quotation. More likely, he saw "emotion" in any discussion of women's longtime legal disadvantages. As he had made clear in his notes on the *Reed* brief, he had no use for historical background as argument and hoped any mention of it could be avoided by the justices themselves—a predilection he clearly discarded in *Roe.*

Blackmun also made a further notation. Next to Ginsburg's name he wrote "J"—his abbreviation for "Jew." Did the designation reflect the midwestern provincialism of a self-styled "country boy"? Or did he associate Ginsburg's ethnic and cultural background with negative stereotypes?

Marshall had a very different reaction. Initially willing to let the decision of the court of appeals stand, he had voted against hearing the case. But Ginsburg's argument apparently convinced him. Not only should the decision be overturned, he decided, but strict scrutiny might now be an appropriate standard for sex-based as well as race-based discrimination.

· · ·

NEXT, SAMUEL HUNTINGTON SPOKE for the government, delivering a twofold argument defending the statute in question. Differential treatment, he contended, achieved administrative efficiency and was a reasonable governmental object. Measured by the rational basis standard, which was the appropriate standard, the law did not constitute a violation of equal protection. The argument—precisely what Ginsburg had anticipated—generated so many interruptions from the bench and so much murmuring among the justices that at times it was difficult for those in the back of the room to hear Huntington's responses. To whom did the statute apply? To whom did it not apply? And more to the point, what did it cost?

Once the questions subsided, Huntington tried to distinguish his case from *Reed*. No statistical evidence supported the Idaho statute's underlying assumption that men were better administrators of estates, whereas the government had statistical data indicating that "most" military women did not have economically "dependent" husbands. Again the justices peppered him with queries about what administrative benefits might actually be gained by the government. Huntington gamely tried to respond. But he was forced to acknowledge that he could not back up his premise that administrative efficiency was the reason for specifying differential treatment.

· · ·

FOLLOWING THE SESSION, the co-counsels parted. Ginsburg turned to compliment Huntington on his presentation, delighted that he, too, had made the argument for extension. Then, to her great surprise, she suddenly realized that the short, stocky man with glasses standing before her was none other than "the Cris," the solicitor general himself. She had always thought that her former Law School dean saw her as a nuisance because of her two visits to his office with family-related requests—encounters that invariably underscored her anomalous status as a woman. Yet Griswold shook her hand enthusiastically. Although she could not recall his precise words, she distinctly remembers that from that day forward he was much friendlier to her. With his initial congratulatory handshake, he seemed to be signaling that he finally accepted her as "a member of the club." For the young woman whom he had challenged in 1956 to explain why she was taking the place of a man, the long-deferred recognition was gratifying.

· · ·

AFTER A BRIEF VISIT with a friend at Georgetown Medical School, it was time to catch the flight home. Marty was staying in Washington overnight. Feigen proceeded to escort Ruth back to the shuttle with all of the casebooks in tow. Marty knew that his wife's navigational skills were imperfect at best and she seemed a bit numbed by the experience.

The SCOTUS, 1973. Standing L–R: Justice Lewis Powell, Justice Thurgood Marshall, Justice Harry Blackmun, Justice William Rehnquist. Seated L–R: Justice Potter Stewart, Justice William Douglas, Chief Justice Warren Burger, Justice William Brennan, Justice Byron White.

He also knew that she attached great importance to being at home for dinner with the children, or at least to say good night.

· · ·

WHEN THE JUSTICES MET in conference to discuss *Frontiero,* the chief began by saying that he saw no parallel with *Reed.* In his view, Congress definitely had the right to draw lines on the basis of sex in the military. As usual, Burger, for all his dedication to the Court and to the judiciary, rambled on, unable to exert the leadership and persuasive power that had so distinguished his predecessor. (In notes taken at a later conference Blackmun wrote, "CJ keeps yapping.")

Most of Burger's colleagues, who spoke in order of seniority, objected. Constitutional guarantees of equal protection, they contended, must take precedence in a situation where no vital military matter was at stake. Douglas, Brennan, Marshall, White, Powell, and Stewart were all prepared to reverse the district court's decision. Blackmun was undecided. Only Rehnquist stuck with the chief. Seeing that there was a clear majority in favor of reversal, Burger then proposed that they handle *Frontiero* as they had *Reed*. The Court would strike down the particular laws at issue. Brennan, Douglas, White, and Marshall, each of whom had been impressed by Ginsburg's argument for strict scrutiny, wanted to go further. But with the exception of Rehnquist, they accepted Burger's proposal.

The chief justice then delegated the opinion to Douglas, who, as the senior member of the majority, passed the assignment to Brennan. Having avoided a decision of strict scrutiny, the chief probably felt that Douglas's decision to let the ultra-persuasive Brennan draft the opinion was safe.

Brennan directed one of his clerks, Geoffrey Stone, to prepare a draft indicating that the statute did not pass muster under the most lenient standard of review, but to avoid taking a position on "suspect" scrutiny. Stone objected. If the Court was going to subject sex-based classifications to a higher standard of scrutiny, it ought to come out and say so. The two debated the merits of the approach, and Stone decided to prepare an alternative draft, which he assumed they would discuss the following day. By the time Stone arrived at Brennan's chamber the next morning,

William J. Brennan Jr., a preeminent strategist and the most influential liberal justice of the twentieth century, 1956–90.

the justice had made his decision. He sent around Stone's alternative, proposing a broad constitutional ban on sex-based discrimination. In his covering memo, Brennan noted that Douglas and White preferred the "suspect" criterion, as did he. A flurry of other memos followed. With positions now fully revealed, the stage was set for negotiation.

. . .

WHITE HAD ALREADY RESPONDED, noting that he and Marshall both thought the Court had moved beyond a rational basis test in *Reed*. "In any event," White added, "I would think that sex is a suspect classification, if for no other reason than the fact that Congress has submitted a constitutional amendment making sex discrimination unconstitutional. I would remain of the same view whether the amendment is adopted or not."

Powell replied that he saw no reason to consider whether sex was a "suspect classification" in this particular case. "Perhaps we can avoid confronting that issue until we know the outcome of the Equal Rights Amendment," he added, echoing the government's point. Stewart, who had recently indicated to Brennan that he might be amenable to consider sex a suspect classification in connection with another case, replied that while he was prepared to overturn the lower court's ruling on *Frontiero*, he agreed with Powell. Sex-based discrimination, in his judgment, was more complicated than race-based discrimination. Laws discriminating on the basis of sex that appeared to benefit women, he acknowledged, often failed to do so in practice. But he, too, was not yet ready to conclude that gender distinctions were always invidious, arbitrary, or irrational.

Blackmun, who especially in his early years on the Court experienced great self-doubt about his votes, was going through his usual "Hamlet-like approaches" as he tried to justify his decision. Equal protection cases concerning strict scrutiny of laws involving legal foreign-born U.S. residents had recently been decided. Upon reading the brief, he had assumed the same course would be followed with women as with noncitizens. But when Powell and Stewart held back, he found himself conflicted. His *Roe v. Wade* opinion, released five days after oral argument in *Frontiero*, elicited far more personal criticism and vitriol than he had anticipated. He was loath to become the swing vote in a decision that would fundamentally change legal doctrine on sex discrimination.

. . .

BRENNAN, UNFAZED, persisted in his search for a fifth vote. He knew that his alternative, if accepted, would effectively usher in the ERA. But he saw no reason to wait for the remaining states in a matter of civil rights, especially because eleven states had already voted against ratification and four more were likely to do so within the next month or two. The trend in state legislatures, Brennan pointed out in a memo to Powell, had become not to ratify and even to rescind prior votes on ratification. As a good Virginian, he must surely be aware that his home state had rejected the ERA and that the additional votes required for the amendment to become part of the Constitution were proving elusive. "I therefore don't see that we gain anything by awaiting what is at best an uncertain outcome," Brennan ventured. Whether or not ratification succeeded, "we cannot ignore the fact that Congress and the legislatures of more than half the States have already determined that classifications based on sex are inherently suspect." For the Court to act with such evidence of majority approval, he continued, could hardly be considered a raw exercise of judicial power.

But Powell, who was being wooed as Brennan's fifth vote, was reportedly put off by the language of the second draft, which sounded too "women's lib" for his taste—as, evidently, had parts of Ginsburg's amicus brief and oral argument. More to the point were the facts Brennan cited about legislative foot-dragging on ERA ratification. What Brennan considered evidence to support strict scrutiny, Powell saw as a reason not to make sex discrimination suspect. If states were rescinding their votes for ratification and others were failing to ratify, the better part of wisdom should be to wait for the final count. Concurring in the judgment in *Frontiero* but not on a higher standard of scrutiny, he then circulated his own draft.

Burger, reacting to the " 'shuttlecock' memos," sent Brennan a blunt reply: "Some may construe *Reed* as supporting the 'suspect' view but I do not." At some point, he added, "I will perhaps join someone who expresses the narrow view expressed by Potter [Stewart], Harry [Blackmun] and Lewis [Powell]." Upon receiving Powell's draft, Burger signed on, noting that his own endorsement was meant as a "puny effort to mute the outrage of 'Women's Lib.'" Rehnquist still dissented.

On the question of strict scrutiny, the count was now 4–4, with Stewart holding the deciding vote. Stewart disagreed with the Griswold-Powell argument that the pending ratification precluded the Court from acting, but he also disliked equal protection cases. They invariably put the Court in a position that elicited charges of judicial legislating. As a judicial minimalist, he thought it far better for the Court to decide case by case, striking down laws one at a time, letting precedent build, and then delivering the ultimate blow. Besides, he, too, was confident that the ERA would be ratified, despite the warning signs noted by Brennan. Urging his colleague not to publish the alternative draft as a plurality opinion without his vote, Stewart argued that it would be harder in subsequent decisions for him to join the Brennan four without appearing inconsistent to outsiders.

Brennan declined to wait. He was convinced that strict scrutiny was the proper approach. He had come so close—so very close—to writing another landmark ruling. If only Warren or Fortas had been on the Court, he later lamented to his clerks, he could have won. His former colleagues would not have been so intimidated by charges of judicial legislating. And Warren would have seen to it that they achieved "the right result."

. . .

WHEN THE DECISION WAS DELIVERED on May 14, 1973, Brennan, writing for a four-member plurality—including Douglas, White, and Marshall—declared the sex-based military laws unconstitutional. Rehnquist was the lone dissenter. Burger joined Powell's concurring opinion along with Blackmun. Stewart issued a separate one-sentence concurring opinion. Attacking classification by sex, Brennan noted that stereotypes—whether about the economic dependency of wives or husbands or any other characteristic—frequently bore no relation to a particular individual's situation. "Statutory distinctions between the sexes often have the effect of invidiously relegating the entire class of females to inferior legal status without regard to the actual capabilities of its individual members," he stated.

As for the government's contention that the classification was rational in that it saved the government time and money, Brennan declared, "The Constitution recognizes higher values than speed and efficiency."

In denying husbands of female members of the armed forces the same benefits provided to wives of male personnel, the laws had denied similarly situated individuals equal protection. The four justices also suggested that they might go further on strict scrutiny, declaring that "classifications based upon sex, like classifications based on race, alienage, or national origin, are inherently suspect and must therefore be subjected to strict judicial scrutiny."

Sharron Frontiero and her counterparts in the military had won a resounding victory. "The law came in like a great white knight for me," the former lieutenant later exclaimed. "We could have tried to change public opinion, but the law came in and changed reality." The author of her amicus brief, on the other hand, had reason to be disappointed. She had lost her appeal for strict scrutiny, though she had come agonizingly close.

· · ·

GINSBURG WOULD NOT LEARN the full extent of the maneuvering on the high court until 1979, when Bob Woodward and Scott Armstrong published *The Brethren*, based on their confidential discussions with law clerks. But close reading of Powell's concurring opinion yielded a strong hint. Writing as if the majority opinion were the alternative draft, Powell attacked "the Court" for preempting "by judicial action a major political decision." From that statement, Ginsburg could surmise two things. First, Powell must have written his response when it appeared that Brennan had a majority for strict scrutiny, which would have made the remaining state votes on ratification of the ERA unnecessary. Second, Stewart, or possibly Blackmun, was the swing vote that eluded Brennan's grasp. Otherwise Powell's concurring opinion, with its attack on his colleagues, made no sense.

The popular press and other interested observers might not have shared Ginsburg's sensitivity to the politics of the Court's opinion, but they clearly understood the case's importance. The *Frontiero* decision generated a warm letter of thanks to Brennan from the chairperson of the Defense Department's Advisory Committee on Women in the Services. There were also handwritten notes from women who, even though they had no family members in the military, nonetheless wished to thank the justice for what the decision might mean for their daughters and granddaughters. The press showered him with bouquets as well. *The Washington Post* and the *Los Angeles Times* both deemed the decision front-page news, while *The New York Times* declared the "decision fell just short of a major triumph for the women's rights movement." *The Boston Globe* quoted Ginsburg's statement that the *Frontiero* decision was "the most far reaching and important ruling on sex discrimination to come out of the Supreme Court yet." Her sentiments were also echoed by *U.S. News & World Report*.

Legal journals agreed that the decision was a significant advance for women's rights in that four justices had opted for strict scrutiny in so short a time. Yet there were troubling aspects of the case. The lack of a fifth vote meant that the Court had now made a constitutional ban on sex discrimination in the form of the ERA the only option. Also, in interrogating Levin and Huntington, the justices had betrayed an eagerness to get at the hard costs involved. This line of questioning suggested that several might have been willing to uphold the statutes had the government provided better data supporting a legitimate economic rationale for differential treatment. However, most reviewers, echoing Gunther's earlier assessment of *Reed,* agreed that at the very least *Frontiero* made clear that "the old 'minimal' scrutiny of sex classification" was "dead."

. . .

GINSBURG'S REACTION WAS MIXED: pride in what she called this "near great leap forward," but regret at the lack of a majority to secure strict scrutiny. Publicly, she made every effort to emphasize the case's historic significance. Privately, she believed Brennan had overreached. As the master builder of a majority, he knew better than most that the number of votes was what counted. "Five" was the most important word in the Court, he told his clerks every year, holding up his hand, fingers outstretched.

. . .

DISAPPOINTED THOUGH SHE WAS, Ginsburg looked ahead, keeping in mind the prediction of her former mentor and friend Gerry Gunther. In his assessment of the Supreme Court's 1971 term, Gunther was no doubt aware of the prevailing tendency of the Court to reject overbroad rules and imperfect proxies that did not take into account exceptions in areas ranging from the First Amendment to voting rights. The Burger Court, for the most part, he concluded, was prepared to expand the scope of the equal protection clause *so long as it could find some middle ground short of strict scrutiny.* If Gunther's assessment was correct—and *Frontiero* indicated that it was—then it would be even more imperative, Ginsburg reasoned, to take a "middle ground" approach, one that would move the Court as close to a standard of strict scrutiny as she could get.

In the future, her briefs would have to be further targeted to the swing voters in the center of the bench—Stewart, Powell, and Blackmun—whose grasp of sex-discrimination complexities was less sure than that of Brennan and his allies. They assumed that applying a more rigorous standard meant that sex-based distinctions would *always* be found invidious, arbitrary, or irrational. Exceptions were hard to grasp, she acknowledged, in part because the right case illustrating an exception had not yet presented itself, and in part because thinking in terms of sexual difference had become so naturalized. As Powell had written, "If and when it becomes necessary to consider whether sex is a suspect classification, I will find the issue a difficult one. Women certainly have not been treated as being fungible with men (thank God!)."

If skeptical justices could see how gender categories adversely affected men, then they might perceive more easily how women were harmed. She had a new Social Security case for a retired widower she was eager to pursue. For an advocate whose ideas about gender equality had been shaped by the Swedish ideology of *jämställdhet,* using a male plaintiff to show how gender discrimination could simultaneously harm both a man and a woman was an easy decision.

CHAPTER II

Coping with a Setback

A s the national upheaval of Watergate unfolded in Washington
and the ten-year travail in Vietnam neared an end, a reporter
in search of other stories turned to the Women's Rights Project.
To spice his account, he asked for personal anecdotes about Ginsburg.
"There are no anecdotes," he was told. Ruth is "almost pure work." How
could she not be as her responsibilities mushroomed and her litigation
agenda came under threat?

· · ·

GINSBURG'S PARAMOUNT OBJECTIVE during the 1974–75 term was
taking two new Social Security cases through the federal district courts,
both of which were destined for the high court. One, a Social Security benefits case, involved a widowed father and his infant son. For
those justices just beginning to recognize gender discrimination against
women, *Wiesenfeld* would demonstrate that it could cut both ways. Neier
had additional plans for the head of what was fast becoming the nation's
premier feminist litigation unit. He invited Ginsburg to serve as ACLU
general counsel—one of three—and to stand for election to the national
board. She welcomed her new role as general counsel. Working with
the ACLU heavyweights Norman Dorsen and the "marvelously wise"
Osmond Fraenkel would not only be an enviable learning experience
but also give her a hand in shaping every aspect of the ACLU's litigation
program. Campaigning for a seat on the national board, on the other
hand, was not her métier.

Local ACLU affiliates were inundating the New York office with
requests for advice on their cases. It was Feigen's job to advise the affiliates on priorities and keep them informed on pending cases, the impor-

tance of follow-up litigation, and legislative lobbying. But her intense involvement in litigating against compulsory sterilization and working on ERA ratification proved all consuming. Ginsburg wound up not only responding to questions from the affiliates about litigation but also updating the press about new cases, responding to law students writing case notes for their law journals, and answering "every nut from Waukegan who writes in with his problems," as a Columbia colleague dryly noted. But with a full teaching schedule at Columbia, even she recognized that she had to have backup.

With a grant from the Rockefeller Foundation, Ginsburg created the Equal Rights Advocacy Project at the university, which would work in tandem with the Women's Rights Project. New apprentices from the second- and third-year classes would provide research assistance for the massive report newly requested by the Commission on Civil Rights as well as for briefs. They would also draft memoranda and court papers, communicate with parties and cooperating lawyers, and serve with faculty members at Columbia as moot court judges. Those who contributed substantially to cases reaching the Court would get the promised seat at the counsel's table during oral arguments.

For students like Lynn Hecht Schafran, who felt that she and her classmates had too many classes unrelated to the way the law is actually practiced, the chance to work with "a real live plaintiff" for the Equal Rights Advocacy Project was a dream job. Better yet, it came with the opportunity to work with a professor whose litigation would make history, though, as M. E. Freeman readily admitted, "I didn't fully understand the importance [of some of the things I worked on] at the time."

Neier also applauded the arrangement. But he worried about Ginsburg's unwillingness to campaign for a seat on the ACLU's national board of directors. When she was introduced at the board meeting, her performance almost drove him to distraction. Candidates for the board usually had no trouble touting their credentials. But Ginsburg refused to utter a single word about her qualifications. Convinced that she would have to talk about herself if requested to discuss her cases, Neier asked her to describe her litigation agenda. She provided information about her various cases with great animation and enthusiasm, but always in terms of what the ACLU did or planned to do, never in terms of what she had done or might do. Amazed that anyone so qualified and ambitious could be so extraordinarily self-effacing, Neier breathed a sigh of relief when she nonetheless won a seat on the board in what he wryly noted was a "rare display of good judgment" on the part of the ACLU electorate.

But before the new general counsel and board member could return to her Social Security litigation, Ginsburg found herself saddled with a case she fervently wished would disappear.

. . .

MEL KAHN, a Florida widower, had persuaded his local ACLU chapter to challenge an 1885 Florida law that provided a property-tax exemption of up to $500 for widows, for the blind, and for the totally disabled but not for widowers. When the Dade County tax assessor refused him the exemption, which would have netted him $15, he claimed to be a victim of sex discrimination. The court found in his favor, agreeing that he had been denied equal treatment under the "basic rights" provision of the Florida Constitution. The Florida Supreme Court overturned the decision, ruling that the state had properly used the tax exemption to reduce well-known income disparities between the sexes. Kahn's attorney, new to the ACLU, appealed, unaware that he needed prior approval from the national office. Reading in *Law Week* that the Supreme Court had granted probable jurisdiction, Wulf and Ginsburg were stunned.

The timing could not have been worse. *Kahn v. Shevin* disrupted her strategy of leading the Court to a fuller understanding of gender discrimination in a carefully chosen sequence of cases. Women were not directly disadvantaged by the Florida exemption. Worse still, *Kahn* was a case of reverse discrimination. The Court was just beginning to think about the issue of reverse discrimination with respect to race, where whites claimed to have been penalized by affirmative-action programs intended to benefit African Americans and other nonwhite minorities. It was entirely too early to broach this thorny issue in relation to gender. The justices were not yet equipped to distinguish between *benign* discrimination—action targeted for limited duration to a specific group to compensate for specific past disadvantages and ameliorate injustice—and *paternalistic* discrimination based on old stereotypes that perpetuated inequality. The two forms of discrimination could be easily confused or conflated in the hands of a skilled lawyer.

If the ACLU lost, she predicted, *Kahn* would reinforce the idea that women required different (special) treatment to protect them, thereby giving new justification to the very stereotypes that the ACLU had chosen to attack. Government lawyers, intent on maintaining the status quo, would have a fresh precedent to use in future cases involving other forms of protection. *Kahn* was "big trouble."

Wulf and his associates agreed. But the Court had already accepted the case, setting oral argument for February 1974. A resigned Ginsburg called William Hoppe, Kahn's Florida attorney, to ask if she could help. But how to argue the case? "I'll give you a gold medal if you can suggest any route other than equal protection for widower Kahn," she wrote to a friend.

Early sex-discrimination cases, including her own, had relied on the race-sex analogy to alert justices to comparable harms inflicted by stereotyping. But the last thing Ginsburg wanted to do was elicit comparison of the harm suffered by Mel Kahn with that inflicted on African Americans. Avoiding the analogy, she would try to expose how antiquated gendered stereotypes underlying the law for both sexes penalized individuals.

The paradigm of male providers and economically dependent wives that informed the 1885 law, she would argue, had no basis in biology and was no longer tenable. In 1973, wives earned more than their husbands in over 7 percent of families, despite the disadvantages that women continued to suffer in the labor market. "Although discrimination against women persists and equal opportunity has by no means been achieved, women simultaneously have been placed on a pedestal and given special benefits. Both discrimination against, and special benefits for, women stem from stereotypical notions about their proper role in society." Florida's tax exemption, which rested on stereotypes, was sexually discriminatory by being both over- and underinclusive, benefiting affluent widows while disadvantaging widowers of limited means like Melvin Kahn. Moreover, the exemption bore no rational relationship to the state's objective of countering discrimination against women because female heads of household were not included. When the December holiday break arrived, she carried case material to Puerto Rico, where the family was vacationing, determined to stay in her hotel room until she finished the brief. Only then would she put on her water skis and allow herself the physical exhilaration of skimming over the ocean at great speed without losing control.

. . .

ON THE FAMILY'S RETURN to New York, the sun-bronzed attorney sent a copy of the appellant brief to Gerald Gunther. What should she emphasize in the oral argument? she asked. Gunther termed the brief "a fine job—strong throughout." Ginsburg, having become persuaded by her argument in the course of writing the brief, was delighted. Surely the Brennan four, who had favored strict scrutiny in *Frontiero,* would agree that the Florida tax exemption should not rest on a sex-based classification, even if widows as a class were more needy than widowers. But persuading Powell, Stewart, or Blackmun would be difficult in a case where the benefit seemed so harmless—"just a little boost." Also, tradition weighed heavily in favor of allowing states and localities large leeway in devising their tax laws.

Oral argument would require especially careful preparation—all the more so because *Kahn* had been scheduled for Monday, February 25, 1974, to precede *DeFunis v. Odegaard,* the first test of affirmative action to reach the Court. The core question in the *DeFunis* case was, what kind of special treatment—if any—based on racial and ethnic classification might pass constitutional muster? Was there a difference between benign discrimination (intended to end the vestiges of slavery and the economic disparities created by decades of government policies intentionally benefiting whites only) and invidious or negative discrimination (for example, exclusion of earlier generations of African Americans from professional schools)? If race merited strict scrutiny, must policies be color-blind? Given the sequencing of the two cases, Ginsburg speculated, the justices might well ask, if race-based preferences were permissible for blacks, why shouldn't sex-based preferences, such as widows' tax exemptions, be acceptable for women? The Court would presumably be interested in consistency, given the extent to which race and sex discrimination had been analogized in *Reed* and *Frontiero.*

. . .

A LITTLE MORE THAN a year had passed since Ginsburg's Supreme Court debut. As she again approached the Marble Palace on this wintry mid-Atlantic day, she hoped that members of the Court would prove to be as attentive as she assumed they had been when she argued *Frontiero*. But it was not to be.

Bombarded by questions before she had barely begun, Ginsburg was caught in precisely the line of questioning she had hoped to avoid. Was she arguing that sex "ought not to be treated as a suspect classification"? Knowing that she lacked a fifth vote for suspect classification, she had not asked for it. Trying to respond and then move on to her key points, she replied, "I have not yet found any such [sex-based] classification in the law that genuinely helps. From a very shortsighted viewpoint, perhaps, such as this one, yes. But in the long run—no . . . [Women] are the only population group that today still faces outright exclusions and restrictive quotas . . . [T]he notion that they need special favored treatment because they are women, I think, has been what has helped to keep women in a special place and has kept them away from equal opportunity for so long." Going on to quote Title VII, she pointed out that the single woman head of household who never marries is most harmed by the statute in question.

Not until the rebuttal did Ginsburg finally have the chance to address the relationship between race and sex discrimination. Justice Blackmun asked, "How would you distinguish *Kahn* from *DeFunis*?" Both women and blacks, she replied, had been subject to a long history of legal and political discrimination. Race-based compensatory treatment, at issue in *DeFunis,* was a current measure intended to foster equality by increasing minority presence in professions that had long excluded them. By contrast, the "preferential" treatment accorded women by Florida's antiquated law reflected a view of women as men's wards—as the dependent, disabled sex. It was hardly intended to promote marriage equality and women's participation in life beyond the hearth. Quite the contrary, it reinforced the kind of stereotyping that limited individual choice and equal opportunity.

By the time Ginsburg had made her point, Justice Douglas was no longer present, having slipped away from the bench for the remainder of the argument. Ginsburg was unconcerned. She knew that he had been favorable to women's rights in the past. Surely she had made her point so clearly that someone of Douglas's acumen would have seen the logic of her argument.

Her unease had to do with the other justices whose queries indicated that they did not yet understand why a sex-based classification might be objectionable when most of the women who benefited from the exemption were economically disadvantaged. Their problem, she realized, had in part to do with the analogy with race-based discrimination. When compared with the harm inflicted by Jim Crow laws, the impairment suffered by women because of Florida's tax law paled in significance. Consequently, her effort to point out the paternalistic discrimination inherent in the statute seemed much too fine a point for the men in the middle. Blackmun, for example, pronounced her argument "too smart."

· · ·

WHEN THE MEMBERS of the Court met in conference, the lineup was predictable—with one glaring exception. Brennan, White, and Marshall were prepared to reverse the lower court's decision. Douglas, however, joined Burger and Rehnquist in upholding the widows' exemption under the old rational basis test, arguing that "women as widows are largely destitute." Blackmun, expressing "discomfort" with the "rationality" of Florida law's stipulation of widowhood rather than need, was inclined to reverse. But it was a tax statute. He, along with Stewart and Powell, thought it hopeless to try to bring logic to tax law—federal or state. The vote to uphold the statute prevailed.

· · ·

WHEN THE CONFERENCE on *Kahn* ended, Douglas, as the senior justice in the majority, was left to write an opinion affirming Florida's differential treatment of widows and widowers. Ordinarily, he turned out his opinions quickly, often scribbling the first draft with minimal substantive input from his clerks. In this instance, however, he began by asking his law clerk Ira Ellman questions about the case. Ellman initially failed to understand why he was being interrogated. Was the justice disturbed by the illogic of voting for strict scrutiny in *Frontiero* and *DeFunis* and then voting to deny the equal protection claim in *Kahn*? Douglas finally managed an explanation several days later. Unlike Brennan, he confessed, he was not overly concerned with doctrinal consistency. What troubled him most was memory of his mother's experiences as a widow. "He didn't want to endanger the tax break that Florida gave to widows," Ellman recalled.

Aware that he had only one day to produce a draft, the apologetic clerk turned "a gender discrimination claim . . . into a tax case." Expanding on the premise that the rationale for the statute was the economic gender gap, he cited Labor Department statistics that confirmed the lower earnings of women, on average, compared with men. Loss of a spouse, he argued, would typically be worse for a widow than for a widower who would presumably continue working when his wife died. Tax relief, therefore, cushioned the impact of spousal loss for the sex most in need of a financial cushion. The draft "was short, if not sweet," Ellman recalled, and Douglas took it. Having written an opinion for *DeFunis* that reflected great insight into the conflicting values at play in affirmative action, the ailing justice apparently felt his work was done.

When Douglas circulated his *Kahn* opinion, Marshall and Brennan dissented, explaining that they found the law overly inclusive because wealthy as well as poor widows benefited. They would have joined the majority in upholding the Florida law if it had been means-tested so as to exclude affluent widows. Only White was prepared to declare any tax break available to one sex but not the other in violation of the Fourteenth Amendment. If the purpose of the law, as the Douglas opinion asserted, was to alleviate past discrimination, then the law should have applied to "all those widowers who have felt the effects of economic discrimination, whether as a member of a racial group or as one of the many who cannot escape the cycle of poverty," White declared.

· · ·

WHEN THE COURT RELEASED its ruling on April 24, Ginsburg's reaction was "amazement and disappointment." She could understand that Brennan and Marshall might fear that they would seem inconsistent if they upheld race-based preference in the form of affirmative action for blacks while denying sex-based preference in the form of a tax exemption for widows. But she found Douglas's vote absolutely baffling. He had flatly rejected race-based compensatory treatment in *DeFunis*, claiming that it "stigmatizes" blacks, yet upheld sex-based compensatory treatment in *Kahn*. Apparently, he thinks "it's 'benign' to rank widows with the blind and totally disabled," she grumbled. His opinion, she lamented, "is a disgrace from every point of view. I'm ashamed of Stewart for associating himself with such sloppy work."

Though Ginsburg would stand by her assessment of the majority opinion, she softened her judgment of Douglas upon receiving a letter from an Emory University Law School student who was preparing a case note on *Kahn*. Read Douglas's new autobiography, *Go East, Young Man,* the student urged. The justice's father, Ginsburg learned, had died when young Bill was five, leaving a widow and three children to endure years of poverty in central Washington. Douglas, his older brother, and his younger sister worked odd jobs throughout their youth to keep the family afloat. Clearly the experience had made an indelible impression on the justice, as his clerk later verified.

But even this additional insight did little to ease Ginsburg's acute disappointment. A ruling that put women in the same category as the blind and the disabled she found totally unacceptable. She was reminded of a comment allegedly made by Harvard's president, Nathan Pusey, when the Vietnam draft call was at its height. Harvard, he is said to have lamented, will "be left with the blind, the lame, and women." The classification in *Kahn,* she reiterated, was "barely distinguishable from other products of paternalistic legislators who regarded the husband more as his wife's guardian than her peer." Moreover, it "reinforced the role-typing that so often placed women 'not on a pedestal but in a cage.'" Indeed, she lamented, *Kahn* might be the greatest blow to the concept of equal treatment since *Hoyt*.

Nor was she comforted by the outcome of other gender-related decisions reached in the 1973–74 term. *Schlesinger v. Ballard* (1975) upheld a military ruling that seemed to favor female naval officers by granting them a longer time to achieve promotion under the navy's new "up or out" policy. But the sex-based barriers that necessitated special treatment in the first place were ignored. Similarly, the Court rejected the Cleveland Board of Education's mandatory maternity leave rule that left otherwise fit teachers idle and unpaid, but not on the equal protection grounds that the case had been argued. And in another pregnancy case, *Geduldig v. Aiello*, six members of the Court agreed that excluding pregnancy-related disability from California's 1974 Unemployment

Insurance Code was not sex-based discrimination inasmuch as it was a physical condition—not gender—that was the basis for exclusion.

That the Court would strike down statutes having a negative impact on women (*Reed* and *Frontiero*) while upholding those that favored women (*Kahn* and *Ballard*) ignored the complexities of how inequality is constructed and maintained. Such reasoning, Ginsburg insisted, was naive and optimistic—a "Panglossian" rationale. Resorting to damage control, she resolved to do what she could to blunt the impact of *Kahn,* treating it as an aberration occasioned by a tax issue in her article titled "Gender in the Supreme Court" for the University of Chicago's *Supreme Court Review.* In her forthcoming lecture tour as Phi Beta Kappa Visiting Scholar, she vowed not only to explain *Kahn* but also to discuss "the pregnancy problem" and promote ratification of the ERA at every stop.

. . .

MEANWHILE, Ginsburg's sparsely furnished office at Greene Hall became a mecca for students. Women in the first-year law class jumped from 8 percent of the class in 1970 to 20 percent in 1972–73 and then to 32 percent by 1980. A bright, motivated, feisty lot, they flocked around the only tenured woman on the faculty, finding much that appealed. Unlike the few other women in the profession in the early 1970s who so conformed to its masculine norms that they seemed to be little more than "male impersonators," Ginsburg proved to be a role model for women such as Diane Zimmerman. Highly accomplished, Ruth "did not hide" her femininity and family. Nor did her restrained, low-key demeanor conceal a kind, thoughtful, deeply caring individual.

"I think I took every course Ginsburg offered," recalled Jane Booth, "and I really struggled with law school, especially my first year. I remember my initial impression in our big civ[il] pro[cedure] class." She was an "extremely knowledgeable, highly analytical lecturer, who had an example to answer any question we might ask." She was never "off-the-cuff." More intellectual than some of her colleagues, "she didn't see it as part of her role to entertain." In small sex-discrimination seminars, however, she caught fire as she talked about "litigation strategy, timing, the importance of knowing civil procedure so that you never had a case dismissed for procedural reasons, and, of course, precision. . . . Her great gift to us was her perfectionist standards." Getting trained by Ginsburg, Booth added emphatically, "was the best legal experience I had in my three years of law school. . . . She brought out the very best in all of us, never once implying that we had to adopt her [workaholic] lifestyle." What is remarkable, Booth continued, is that "Ruth kept tabs on us long after we graduated. I once got a letter from her consisting of a single question: 'Why are you still working for that jerk?' I knew she was telling me it was time to move on."

Women were not the only students who gravitated toward Ginsburg. Gerard Lynch also claimed her as role model—"someone [who], while being a legal academic, could have an impact on the world."

. . .

AS THE LAW SCHOOL'S REPRESENTATIVE on the University Senate, Ginsburg had suggested a comprehensive pay equity review. Designed to identify sex-based discrepancies, the review revealed, among other inequities, a differential in the university's retirement plan. Women received a lower monthly payment because, on average, they lived longer than men after retirement. That payment inequity, Ginsburg concluded, should not go unaddressed.

The university claimed that it was powerless to change a policy decided by the Teachers Insurance and Annuity Association, the insurer for many private universities and colleges. But having heard the "our hands are tied" response from the administration in connection with the layoff of Columbia maids, Ginsburg wasn't buying.

Turning to her female colleagues, she persuaded Chien-Shiung Wu, an internationally renowned physics professor and former member of the Manhattan Project, to host a tea party at her apartment near the campus. With Madame Wu's apartment secured, Ginsburg sent handwritten invitations to top female administrators and all the senior women on the faculty—hardly an arduous task because there were only eleven compared with over a thousand men.

One of the eleven, Carol Meyer, a professor in the School of Social Work, attended the event with initial reservations. Upon arriving, however, she was reassured by "a diminutive woman with black hair, tied with a huge bow." Ginsburg, Meyer recalled, "was gracious and funny and clearly in command as she told us her purpose in bringing us together."

The result was a suit against Columbia with some one hundred female faculty members and administrators as plaintiffs. While some called the legal action an act of disloyalty to the university, the dean of the Law School, Michael Sovern, came to her defense.

. . .

ASKED WHY she constantly took on increasing responsibilities, Ginsburg stated simply that she was just doing what the job demanded. But in fact, she had two jobs as well as editorial board duties for the *American Bar Association Journal* and *The American Journal of Comparative Law,* membership on key committees of the ABA, the Association of the Bar of the City of New York, and the Association of American Law Schools, along with meetings of the boards of the many feminist legal organizations on which she sat.

Her children and husband had long ago adjusted to her night owl schedule. When James awakened at five o'clock one morning and wandered out of his bedroom half-asleep, seeing his mother still fully dressed at the dining room table, a cup of cold coffee at her side, did not surprise. He knew that when his dad went to bed around midnight, his mother had to leave her desk in the bedroom and move all of her papers onto the dining room table. There she labored away, sustained by coffee and, according to Jane, ice cream or a box of prunes. As one of her associates later noted, she "could accomplish more between 10 p.m. and midnight than I could all day." Except that she seldom stopped at midnight.

. . .

THE ACUTE DISAPPOINTMENT over *Kahn* eased; Ginsburg was ready to revisit the Court during the 1974 fall term, confident that she had her life under control. At home, she had her usual full-time housekeeper. Jane was racing through the University of Chicago, poised to graduate in three years. At the ACLU, Kathleen Peratis, an impressive young Californian, now bore the title of director of the Women's Rights Project. Handling the day-to-day administration, she absorbed the founding director's exacting standards and learned quickly to heed her advice on litigation strategy. Yet, as Peratis was the first to point out, "Ruth, while never heavy-handedly imposing her views, . . . remained very much

Kathleen Peratis, who worked closely with Ginsburg, took over day-to-day administration of the Women's Rights Project, freeing Ginsburg for other ACLU responsibilities. The two women have remained close friends.

at the helm." Adhering to Ginsburg's advice, the two women bonded so closely that Peratis named her first daughter Ruth. Ginsburg later recalled, "I could say a word to her and she would understand."

Free now to focus on the cases that could secure the ACLU's reputation—and her own—Ginsburg was confident that her years as a rookie at the Court were over. If her future litigation proceeded as she hoped, the equality train, derailed by *Kahn,* would soon be "back on track."

· · ·

THE RAILROAD METAPHOR was apt. With the nightmare of Watergate finally at an end, liberals expected to move forward with an unfinished agenda following a Democratic sweep in the 1974 elections. But the seismic plates of politics were slowly shifting. More than she could have known at the time, losing *Kahn* would prepare her for a Court and a country increasingly divided in the decades ahead.

PART IV

Moving Forward

CHAPTER 12

Getting Back on Track

Edna Stubblefield, a nineteen-year-old African American woman from the little Tennessee town of Paris, had gone to a bar where she encountered a rival for her boyfriend's affections. Words between the two women escalated into a brawl in which Edna stabbed her adversary. A call went out immediately for help, but the first ambulance driver refused to go into the area known locally as "black bottom." In the long wait for medical assistance, the victim bled to death. When the police arrived, Stubblefield was arrested and, in her subsequent trials, convicted of first-degree murder.

In the early 1970s, the Henry County Jury Commission still systematically excluded blacks from jury service and provided exemptions for any white woman who did not wish to serve. That meant that Stubblefield was denied the opportunity to have a jury of her peers. Yet the Tennessee Court of Criminal Appeals rejected her appeal, as did the Tennessee Supreme Court. With only one appeal remaining, her lawyers had turned to the Women's Rights Project.

Ginsburg, distressed by the multiple forms of discrimination Stubblefield had endured, responded immediately. If the Court agreed to hear the case, she could pick up where Dorothy Kenyon and Pauli Murray had left off in *White v. Crook*—the 1966 ruling that allowed African Americans to serve on juries. Striking a blow to jury exemptions, yet another form of "benign" discrimination, would undermine the *Hoyt* image of women "as the center of home and family life" as the justification for excluding women from jury service.

To Ginsburg's great dismay, the high court had refused to hear Stubblefield's appeal. Although the criminal court of appeals had reduced her crime to second-degree murder, both the conviction and the jury-exemption law remained unaffected. Fortuitously for Ginsburg, a test case had emerged in Louisiana—a state that also required women to preregister for jury service—which Ginsburg could take over.

. . .

HEALY V. EDWARDS HAD BEEN transformed into a class-action suit in 1973. Some plaintiffs were women who claimed that in a state where females represented less than 5 percent of the jury pool, they would be disadvantaged should they be charged with a crime. Others objected to the sign-up requirement for women seeking inclusion in the jury pool. Male plaintiffs contended that exemptions for women burdened men with excessive jury service.

Ginsburg was delighted by the range of plaintiffs and the fact that each group had standing. That is, each group involved in the case had such a strong personal stake in the outcome that the Court could be confident that the lawyers for both sides would present the strongest and sharpest arguments possible. Furthermore, all of the groups had been denied due process of law and equal protection under the Fourteenth Amendment. Female plaintiffs, as she pointed out in her brief, were especially vulnerable. Empirical studies indicated that male-dominated juries awarded lower damages and stiffer sentences to women. With respect to juries, men and women were not simply interchangeable. To assume they were—and thus to exclude women—"deprives a jury of a perspective that may be important," Ginsburg contended, moving to the crux of the issue.

Citing precedent, she referred to *Ballard v. United States* (1946), where the Court had ruled that jury pools must include women to be considered a fair cross section of the community. The five-member majority had elegantly laid out why both sexes must be included: "The thought is that the factors which tend to influence the action of women are the same as those which influence the action of men—personality, background, economic status—and not sex. Yet it is not enough to say that women when sitting as jurors neither act nor tend to act as a class. Men likewise do not act as a class. But, if the shoe were on the other foot, who would claim that a jury was truly representative of the community if all men were intentionally and systematically excluded from the panel?" Putting the issue bluntly, Douglas, who wrote for the majority, concluded,

"[T]he two sexes are not fungible. . . . The exclusion of one may indeed make the jury less representative of the community than would be true if an economic or racial group were excluded." While African Americans (and later the Court) would take issue with the last point, Douglas's observation that the two sexes are not interchangeable and that both are needed to create a representative jury pool was precisely the point that Ginsburg wanted to make.

The problem was that *Ballard* involved *federal* court jury selection—a matter over which the Supreme Court exercised supervisory power. *Hoyt,* on the other hand, involved the power of the *states* to regulate jury membership. To overturn a state law, a ruling of constitutional dimensions would be required. Fortunately, there was the *Reed* ruling in which a sex-based classification established by state law had been rejected for similarly situated individuals. That, Ginsburg would argue, was precisely the issue in Louisiana's jury-exemption law. Hence there were compelling reasons for the district court to hear the case.

. . .

WITH THE INITIAL STEPS completed, Ginsburg began thinking more about the brief. She had already put students in the Equal Rights Advocacy Project to work collecting information on every case since *Hoyt* involving jury service by women. There was the *Stubblefield* argument on which to draw.

As the *Healy* brief took shape, it took the form of a vigorous and carefully documented attack on the core assumption behind the women-only exemptions—that women are constantly preoccupied with and absolutely essential to home maintenance and child care. In 1973, 50 percent of married women with school-age children were in the workforce as well as 70 percent of widowed, divorced, or separated mothers. Jury service, therefore, "would not constitute a disruption of a pattern of continuous child care but rather absence from their employment."

If concerns for child care were the primary legislative objective, the Louisiana law should not then exempt childless women or women whose children were cared for by others, nor should it ignore men who were responsible for the care of young children. Instead, exemptions should be awarded on an individual basis to persons of either sex who demonstrated that jury service might create real difficulty. In sum, the sex-based classi-

fication was "appallingly overbroad" with respect to women, "stereotypi-
cally underinclusive" with respect to men, bore no rational relationship
to any legitimate state objective, and was, therefore, an unconstitutional
denial of equal protection.

The issue, Ginsburg emphasized, was not whether jury duty imposed
an undue burden on women; both sexes found it burdensome. Rather,
the point was that "jury service is not only a right, it is a statutory
duty and a citizen's duty"—a statement she would later reiterate in her
Supreme Court brief. Exempting women from jury service assigns them
to inferior citizenship status by assuming that as a class they are incapable of shouldering the same civic rights and responsibilities as men.
There was nothing "benign" or harmless about that!

· · ·

IN JULY 1973, Ginsburg flew to New Orleans to make her oral argument before the federal district court of appeals. The heat and oppressive
humidity did not affect her keen awareness of what was at stake. The
Louisiana jury system she challenged was virtually identical to that of
Florida, which the Supreme Court had upheld twelve years earlier, making the outcome risky. What feminist legal advocates regarded as sterile
precedent could be viewed by tradition-minded jurists as binding law.
And then there was *Kahn* to worry about—a precedent that encouraged lawyers defending jury exemptions for women to link them to tax
exemptions for widows and term them "benign." Yet New Orleans–born
jurists such as Skelly Wright, John Minor Wisdom, and Alvin Rubin had
made history in the federal court by enforcing the law of the land with
courage, compassion, and powerful legal scholarship despite cross burn-
ings designed to intimidate. She could only hope they would bring to
sex-based discrimination the same clarity they applied to race.

As she stood up to make her argument, Judge Rubin intervened.
Asserting that her brief spoke for itself, he asked if she had any points she
would like to make concisely. Taken aback, Ruth was torn by conflicting emotions: sheer delight that the court had found her brief compelling *and* strong disappointment that she would not be able to display
her mastery of the issues. After a short statement she left, knowing that
she had raised a fundamental question—not about jury systems per se,

but rather about the pace of legal change. How soon can precedents be overturned?

. . .

SHE HAD HER ANSWER promptly. On August 31, the three-judge panel announced its decision. Written by Judge Rubin with his customary economy and clarity, the decision declared *Hoyt* obsolete and no longer binding. Dealing with the question of whether women and men were alike or different and what difference, if any, difference should make, Rubin cut to the core. Women and men were different, he wrote, but not in the rights and obligations of citizenship. "Females, as individuals, bring to juries 'qualities of human experience' entirely different from those of males, and a diversity of temperament among themselves, completely heterogeneous. Their absence from jury selection panels," he explained, "is significant not because all women react alike, but because they contribute a distinctive medley of views influenced by differences in biology, cultural impact and life experience, indispensable if the jury is to comprise a cross-section of the community."

Ginsburg was delighted. Rubin's statement captured the issue perfectly. But how would the brethren respond to his dismissal of *Hoyt* as "yesterday's sterile precedent" that "courts need not follow"?

. . .

WHEN LOUISIANA APPEALED the decision, the Supreme Court agreed to hear *Edwards v. Healy* in combination with *Taylor v. Louisiana,* even though Louisiana was already in the process of revising its jury-exemption statute. *Taylor* involved Billy Taylor, a recently convicted felon who had been found guilty by an all-male jury and given a death sentence for aggravated kidnapping. (Wielding a butcher knife, he had abducted and raped a woman in front of her daughter and grandson and robbed all three.) Taylor's lawyer, William King, searching for some technicality that would allow him to appeal the case, seized on sex-based exemptions. His client, he claimed, had been denied a jury consisting of a fair cross section of Louisiana citizens. Because the two cases would be heard in tandem, Ginsburg and King coordinated their respective briefs and oral arguments.

Appearing before the Court on October 16, 1974, eight months after she had argued *Kahn,* Ginsburg sat quietly as Louisiana's assistant attorney general, Kendall Vick, made his case. Vick tried to convince the justices that the case was moot because Louisiana was in the process of adopting a new constitution. Because the new constitution provided that every citizen, regardless of sex, could serve on a jury, Vick pressed the Court to find the case moot. But he failed to convince. Even if, as one justice argued, *Healy* became moot, "the same issue exists in the next case [*Taylor*] where there can be no question of mootness." Mootness, Vick was told, could not compromise the larger "equal protection matter" at stake.

When Ginsburg's turn came, she was barely able to finish her opening statement before interruptions began. Was this to be *Kahn* redux? The first question went to the heart of the equality debate. Were women the "same" as men and therefore fungible in terms of the law or were they sufficiently "different" to require different treatment? Did women really *need* to be on juries for the accused to have a trial of peers because "the new theory was that there is very little difference between men and women"? she was asked.

Ginsburg refused to be trapped by these seemingly mutually exclusive alternatives. She understood that the answer was far more complex than that suggested by relying on binary opposites of sameness and difference. She could have noted that while in many respects the two sexes are the same and can be treated the same, there are circumstances in which a gender-neutral outcome requires differential treatment. But that response would have opened up a line of questioning that she had no wish to pursue. She responded by reminding the Court that Justice Douglas had written in *Ballard* "that the two sexes are not fungible; that the absence of either may make the jury even less representative of the community than it would [otherwise] be."

Asked about the present status of the ERA, she replied that there were still five states to go in addition to the two states that had rescinded while only three had ratified. Eager to steer the discussion away from ratification, she returned to the basic arguments of opposing counsel with respect to jury exemptions.

Addressing first the question of administrative convenience, she reminded the Court that it had declared in *Reed* that administrative convenience did not justify gender-based classification. She then turned to the argument that the exemption of women contributed to family stability. If concern for dependents was the issue, women-only exemptions were overbroad because they included childless women, women with adult children, and women with the means to provide substitute caregivers. Fifty-nine percent of Louisiana's total adult female population had no children under eighteen, and of the 41 percent with children under eighteen 37 percent were in the labor force.

Why did she treat *Hoyt* "fairly cavalierly"? she was asked. That was not her intention, she responded respectfully. Ginsburg then skillfully made two points. First, at the time of the *Hoyt* decision the Court had reasoned that the voluntary system could work if Florida made a good-faith effort to try to get women to serve. It was now clear, as Justice Douglas had noted, that this approach had not worked. Second, women's labor force participation had risen in the interim, and working mothers were not taken into account in consideration of jury exemption in *Hoyt*, nor were unemployed women who did not have child-care obligations.

Another question on *Kahn* quickly followed. Ginsburg grasped the implication instantly. Shouldn't the law on jury exemptions for women be guided by *Kahn*, which provided tax breaks for widows? Justice Brennan had already handed her the answer when he verified her interpretation of the *Kahn* decision as a tax case. The relevance of *Kahn*, she replied, was that the Court had always allowed the states larger leeway for line drawing in tax codes.

Returning to *Hoyt*, she argued, "The focus on women jurors caused the Court to lose sight of what should have been the primary focus." Gwendolyn Hoyt was a battered woman. "Her crime was committed after an altercation in which she claimed her husband had insulted and humiliated her to the breaking point." Convicted of second-degree murder, Hoyt believed that "women jurors might better understand her state of mind when she picked up a baseball bat and administered the blow that led to litigation." The Court, Ginsburg continued, "had not focused on the denial of equal protection and due process to Mrs. Hoyt; the focus was on the benign classification of women as jurors rather than the unfairness to the litigant." Viewed in that light, "the overriding consideration really should not be the burden or the benefit of jury service to prospective jurors, but the fairness of the system to litigants."

Though other questions followed, Ginsburg's statement on *Hoyt* had made an impact. The Court could now "hear" the argument that had been made—but not heard—in 1961. When she concluded her summation, Chief Justice Burger added, "I am not sure you need any defense, Mrs. Ginsburg, but your brief and argument was much less cavalier toward *Hoyt* than the three judges of the Fifth Circuit." It was a compliment of sorts, coming from a chief justice who in 1971 had offered a letter of resignation to the president when he learned that Nixon was toying with the idea of nominating a woman to the Court.

• • •

DECIDING *TAYLOR* FIRST, eight justices agreed that Billy Taylor had been denied his right to a jury representing a cross section of the community. By this time, *Healy* had been rendered moot by an amendment to Louisiana's constitution putting women on juries on the same basis as men. But the arguments in *Healy* had been clearly understood. Writing for the majority in *Taylor*, Justice White declared, "We think it is no longer tenable to hold that women as a class may be excluded or given automatic exemptions based solely on sex if the consequence is that criminal jury venires [panels] are almost totally male. . . . If it was ever the case that women were unqualified to sit on juries or were so situated that none of them should be required to perform jury service, that time has long since passed."

Marshaling sociological and statistical data as well as judicial precedent, White explained why women were sufficiently different from men to make their absence from a jury significant, yet sufficiently like men that they should not be exempted from jury service. Rehnquist provided the lone dissent, arguing that Taylor's trial was fairly conducted and that while it might be reasonable to conclude that the Louisiana jury system was an anachronism, it was not the duty of the Court to enforce upon the states its perception of modern life. The notion that some "flavor" is lost if one sex is excluded, he noted, "smacks more of mysticism than of law."

Rehnquist's dissent aside, Ginsburg was thrilled with the news, though the taste of victory was bittersweet inasmuch as Billy Taylor rather than Edna Stubblefield had been the beneficiary. Indeed, the Court's refusal to hear the *Stubblefield* case grated more than ever. Though she never spoke about the inseparable relationships of race, class, and gender as "intersectionality," Ginsburg fully grasped how disadvantage was compounded for women who were poor and black.

To all but die-hard exemptionists, it was clear that *Taylor* marked a turning point. Yet only five years later, Ginsburg would have to repeat her arguments in a case involving the state of Missouri, where, as in Tennessee, legislators refused to heed the brethren. *Duren v. Missouri* (1979) would be another win. However, it was not until 1994 that the Court finally recognized that the equal protection clause fully protected the rights of both sexes not to be discriminated against in jury selection.

When the Court ruled on *Taylor,* Ginsburg thought she detected a hint of more rigorous scrutiny in the future. Justice White, writing for the majority, had stated that "weightier reasons" than "merely rational grounds" were necessary to justify sex-based classification. That hint boded well for her Social Security case, *Weinberger v. Wiesenfeld,* which she had originally intended to follow *Frontiero.*

. . .

STEPHEN WIESENFELD, a self-employed computer consultant in Edison, New Jersey, and his wife, Paula, a high school math teacher and Ph.D. candidate, were expecting their first child. Married in 1970, they had decided to try an alternative family lifestyle. Paula would pursue a career in school administration once she received her degree, and Stephen would take on household chores and child-care responsibilities. But anticipation turned to grief when Paula died during childbirth from an embolism, leaving her distraught husband with their newborn son, Jason.

After bringing the infant home from the hospital, Stephen tried to find a suitable caregiver. When none proved satisfactory, he decided to continue with the couple's original plan. He would care for the baby with a little help from relatives, though at some financial sacrifice. Because Paula had been the principal breadwinner in the family, working until the day she gave birth, Stephen applied to Social Security for survivors' benefits for Jason as well as child-care benefits that had long been available to widows with infants. Jason was declared eligible, but no checks would be forthcoming for his stay-at-home dad. Stephen's claim for benefits payable to a surviving spouse entrusted with the care of a child had been rejected; only women were entitled to "mothers' benefits," even if the father had to forgo employment in order to stay home with the child.

In November 1972, after reading a story in the New Brunswick *Home News* about widowed men, Stephen wrote a letter to the editor describing the inequity in his situation. "TELL THAT TO GLORIA STEINEM!" he concluded. The letter caught the eye of a Rutgers Spanish instructor, who forwarded a clipping to Ginsburg.

Here was her perfect follow-up to *Frontiero,* a case that brilliantly illustrated how gender discrimination against either sex ultimately harmed men as well as women. Stephen Wiesenfeld was being penalized in a way that a woman who had just lost her husband and principal wage earner would not be—simply because of the old male breadwinner/female family caretaker model of marriage. Likewise, Paula was not being treated as a full-fledged wage earner entitled to benefits for her family. That women and men should be able to function as both full labor force participants and as fully involved parents was basic both to Ginsburg's own family life and to her feminism. "It's a great case," she replied, "and we will certainly take it if Mr. Wiesenfeld agrees."

Stephen consented. Ginsburg, assigning the case to students in the Equal Rights Advocacy Project, had reassured her client that she would "get to work" on the plea "as soon as I get over my first argument in the Supreme Court (*Frontiero*) scheduled to be heard on January 17th." Never one to rely solely on judicial remedies, she also wrote to the Michigan congresswoman Martha Griffiths, a member of the Women's Rights Project board of advisers, urging her to introduce amendments to Social Security laws that would equalize benefits. Because the ACLU would be challenging federal law, Ginsburg arranged with Jane Lifset, a former Rutgers student and a practicing attorney in New Jersey, to act as co-counsel for the necessary filing in the federal district court of New Jersey. The plaintiff's claim was that the law violated the due process clause of the Fifth Amendment. Ginsburg then asked two of her students to draft a memo in support of a motion for summary judgment, which she would pass along to Lifset for comments. By mid-February 1973, the complaint was ready to be filed.

Eager to call attention to the case, Ginsburg dashed off a letter to the *New York Times* reporter Lesley Oelsner, who had written a lengthy story on Ginsburg's appointment to the Columbia Law School faculty.

In a "thank you" note to Oelsner for her story, Ginsburg had promised to send information on future Women's Rights Project cases that might provide good copy. She now enclosed a draft of the *Wiesenfeld* complaint, explaining that the legal point was "significant" and that the facts of the case made it "particularly appealing." "Do you think you can arrange to have the *Times* do a feature story on the case to appear the day after the complaint is filed?" Ginsburg asked. "I can give you twenty-four hours notice of the filing date."

· · ·

IN MID-MARCH, she learned that the federal district court in New Jersey would hear the case and that it had been assigned to Judge Clarkson S. Fisher, who was tied up in a protracted Vietnam draft resister's case in Camden. But good news came with bad. The three judges on the district court, she learned, were "very conservative." Moreover, attorneys for the government would almost certainly argue that the statute passed the "rational" relationship test. A "valid public purpose" was served, they would likely contend, inasmuch as it compensated for past employment discrimination against women. Widows were typically underemployed relative to men or, if employed, earned less. Therefore, they needed additional protection for themselves and their children. In addition, they would surely point out the financial cost to taxpayers of a decision in Wiesenfeld's favor.

Ginsburg honed her counterargument carefully. First, she would point out that the law reflected precisely the kind of gender stereotyping that the Court had already rejected in *Frontiero.* Second, it constituted discrimination for which there was no governmental justification, compelling or otherwise. Third, it violated a wage-earning woman's right to equal protection. And last though by no means least, it deprived Jason Wiesenfeld of the care of his only parent. The loss of a mother was no small matter for Ginsburg, who was fast forming an enduring friendship with Stephen and Jason.

Months went by without a hearing date. During the wait, she had celebrated *Frontiero,* worked on *Stubblefield* and *Healy,* reworked the *Wiesenfeld* brief, and reassured Stephen—and herself. There were so many inequities for women under Social Security, most of which were not susceptible to judicial attack. She simply had to win the first of the few that might be amenable to legal correction. Finally, in June 1973, a hearing date was set. "Hallelujah!" she exulted. She and Stephen arranged to meet on the train en route to Trenton.

. . .

MEETING HIS ATTORNEY in person for the first time, Wiesenfeld described her as "small, frail, and absolutely sure of herself." She had reassured him no matter which side lost, the case would be appealed. Yet upon completing the oral argument, Ginsburg was a bit less optimistic about the outcome than she appeared to her client. Judge Fisher and his associates seemed troubled, among other things, as to why a man holding three university degrees would choose to stay at home and care for his son. Because opposing counsel had emphasized the financial cost that equalization would entail, the judges also made clear their misgivings about the hefty price tag.

Seeking to diminish their concerns, Ginsburg had explained that the toll on the Treasury would not add up to anything like the $20 million or more annually that the government had estimated. That inflated figure was based on the assumption that *every* eligible widower would elect to provide child care. Most widowers would choose to work rather than babysit, although what most men would do was not at issue. This case, she repeatedly insisted, involved Stephen Wiesenfeld. As for the concern that the judiciary would be usurping a legislative function, Congress was indeed considering corrective legislation, but nothing had yet passed. Whether such responses were convincing was an open question.

Increasingly apprehensive about the outcome, Ginsburg considered starting action on a case similar to *Wiesenfeld* in another district. It might be prudent because one never knew which case might come before the Court first.

Stephen also worried. In district court, the government lawyer had argued that because he now had a lucrative job as a technical consultant to an engineering firm, the case should be dismissed. If he gave up his job to save the case, what new line of work would allow him maximum time with Jason, pay enough salary to qualify for Social Security, and enable him to reinvest any profit in the company? With the Arab oil embargo looming, he would sell Fuji bicycles from a storefront near the Rutgers campus, keeping the stock in his garage. He then notified Ginsburg that he was no longer employed at his $1,500-a-month job at Cyphernetics. Ginsburg, assuming he had lost his job, asked one of her students to prepare an affidavit to the effect that he was now unemployed. Though the core issues in the case remained unchanged, Stephen's economic circumstances now closely resembled those of widows whom the original drafters of Social Security had in mind.

Stephen never told Ginsburg what he had done, knowing she would never have asked him to change his lifestyle to save her case. The affidavit, she was later convinced, played "a key role" in securing what finally proved to be a favorable decision. "A weird opinion," she concluded, upon reading the three-judge ruling in December 1973, "but considering the conservative composition of the bench, a minor miracle that we prevailed without a dissent." As expected, the government appealed. "It should be much easier to preserve the victory in the Supreme Court than it was to get it in the first place," she assured Lifset. But she would soon have cause to reconsider.

. . .

IN APRIL 1974, the Court delivered its *Kahn* decision. The solicitor general was the Yale legal scholar Robert Bork. An urbane, witty conservative, Bork had achieved national notoriety the previous October, when, in what came to be known as the "Saturday Night Massacre," he fired Archibald Cox, a former solicitor general who, as special prosecutor in the Watergate scandal, had demanded that President Nixon turn over the incriminating secret tapes. Bork could be counted on to use the Court's willingness to uphold differential treatment in *Kahn* to buttress the government's claim for differential treatment in *Wiesenfeld*. "Mothers' benefits," like "widows' tax exemptions," government lawyers would argue, had been designed for women who, because of economic discrimination, were financially disadvantaged. Classification by sex, in this instance, was "benign."

To counter the argument, Ginsburg knew she would have to neutralize *Kahn*. Her own brief would have to convince the Court that *Frontiero* provided the better precedent. "We will simply have to do our best to overcome bad precedent," she told Stephen. On the positive side, she could expect another strong amicus brief from the Center for Constitutional Rights. Her students in the Equal Rights Advocacy Project, who had worked on the case since the outset, would also be helpful, especially M. E. Freeman. In addition, she had the assistance of Kathleen Peratis, who had taken over as director of the Women's Rights Project.

. . .

WORKING FROM AN ELEVEN-PAGE OUTLINE, she began documenting the many limitations of the key provision of the Social Security Act her client was challenging. Not only did it highlight the gender stereotypes that denigrated women's efforts in the economic sector, denying them equal citizenship. It also discounted the parental status of the surviving spouse and father, disadvantaging children by denying them the personal care of their only parent. Furthermore, the provision encoded a model of the single-earner family that no longer corresponded to reality for millions of dual-earner couples.

Skillfully undercutting the arguments of the government, she demonstrated that the law did not relate fairly to its legislative purpose—providing for the families of deceased workers—nor did it operate to compensate women for past economic discrimination, as the government argued. On the contrary, it exacerbated past discrimination by denying working women the same level of benefits provided to their male counterparts.

Anticipating the budgetary argument, Ginsburg reminded the Court that it had previously ruled in *Reed* and *Frontiero* that fiscal economy could not be achieved by "invidious exclusions" of persons guaranteed equal protection of the laws by the Constitution. In a further effort to neutralize *Kahn,* she pointed out that "while special deference may be due to state policies on issues of local concern, such as state taxation and zoning, latitude for under-inclusive classification is less broad when a wholly federal and employment-related benefit is in question."

Then she turned to the section on remedial action, making her usual argument for extension. If the Court found the gender line in the survivors' benefit provision unconstitutional, benefits must be not taken away from widows but extended to widowers. Such action would be consistent with the larger legislative purpose—protecting families of deceased insured individuals. Yet she knew the argument was problematic.

Only rarely had the Court ever extended the scope of a law it found unconstitutional, so there were few precedents. Further, such action could be seen as legislating on the part of the judiciary. A further complication was the money involved. With a little help from Gerry Gunther, she had developed a viable argument for extension, which she had used in *Moritz* and *Frontiero*. But no funds were involved in *Moritz* inasmuch as the IRS took the initiative in changing the tax code. In *Frontiero,* a restrictive quota severely limited the number of women in the military. Hence those with dependents were so few that providing them the same benefits as military wives could easily be accomplished within the Pentagon budget. *Wiesenfeld,* by contrast, would require extending benefits to widowed fathers. That could cost more money than Congress had authorized, thus making the Court hesitant to follow through.

Gambling, Ginsburg opted for extension. Defense of a male plaintiff could not be allowed to jeopardize, even briefly, benefits desperately needed by poor women.

. . .

ON A COLD JANUARY DAY IN 1975, Ginsburg left her Washington hotel for the Court. Upon leaving, she passed a woman walking her dog. Ruth immediately recognized the great opera star Maria Callas, whose vocal and dramatic skills, as well as her personal life, had made the diva a familiar figure. Recalling evenings at the Met when Callas had brought down the house with her dazzling arias in *Tosca* and her more recent concert at Carnegie Hall, Ginsburg took the sighting as a good omen.

Now considered a "repeat player" at the Court, she entered with Wiesenfeld, who watched as she sat down at counsel's table. In this "awesome" setting where everyone stood as the justices entered and took their seats, "she seemed so small," he recalled. M. E. Freeman, who sat at counsel's table with her mentor, found her attention fixed on the brethren. Justice Douglas, felled by a stroke, was absent. Wendy Webster Williams, who had slipped over to the Court from George Washington University Law School, focused on Ginsburg's performance. "As soon as Ruth uttered her first sentence about Stephen Wiesenfeld, the widowed father being denied benefits, Jason Wiesenfeld being denied the care of his only parent, and Paula Wiesenfeld being denied the protection afforded a male wage carner, I knew she had it."

But before Williams's hunch was confirmed, Ginsburg had to undercut two points made by the government's attorney, Keith Jones. First, that Social Security was insurance, not compensation for work, and that Congress, therefore, was not obliged to provide female wage workers the same benefits as those available to males. Second, that the restriction to "widows only" was done in order to compensate women for their inferior position in the marketplace.

Laying out the case with her customary precision and authority, Ginsburg not only rebutted the government's position but made a powerful argument of her own. As in *Frontiero,* she remained uninterrupted. Finally, she was asked how long benefits for children had to be paid. She confessed that she did not know why the age limit had been set at eighteen, whereupon a brief discussion ensued about the age at which children could live on their own. The question, Ruth assumed, was stimulated by another case under consideration, *Stanton v. Stanton,* in which the issue was the constitutionality of a Utah law requiring parents to support a daughter only until the age of eighteen but a son until twenty-one.

Eager to cut short any diversion from her list of key points, Ginsburg used much of her remaining time to remind the Court that there was an income limitation on child-care benefits. For any earnings of the parent beyond $2,400 per year, $1 of benefit is removed for every $2 earned. Moreover, she explained, the parent receiving the benefit must be performing the child-care function. Wrapping up on schedule, she rushed out of the Court in order to get back to New York for a two o'clock class.

Having exchanged the counsel's bench for a lectern in a matter of hours, Ginsburg answered a few questions and then went right into her lecture. Two of her students marveled at the sense of duty that propelled her to return so quickly. No other professor on the law faculty, they insisted, would have argued before the Supreme Court in the morning and rushed back to Columbia for afternoon classes, passing up an opportunity to network in Washington over lunch. But family dinner had priority.

. . .

WHEN THE JUSTICES MET in conference, they were split. Burger, Rehnquist, and most likely Blackmun were prepared to reject Ginsburg's argument. Brennan, who had been assigned the majority opinion, had already put his first female clerk, Marsha Berzon, on the case. Picking up

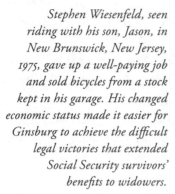

Stephen Wiesenfeld, seen riding with his son, Jason, in New Brunswick, New Jersey, 1975, gave up a well-paying job and sold bicycles from a stock kept in his garage. His changed economic status made it easier for Ginsburg to achieve the difficult legal victories that extended Social Security survivors' benefits to widowers.

on a cue that Ginsburg had inserted in the brief, Berzon researched the history of the statute. To Brennan's delight, she learned that Congress had intended the law to provide for children, not widows. Writing what became the key section of the opinion, Berzon notes that it lent a "new perspective" to the justices' considerations. Brennan could now get all nine votes.

When Ginsburg read the telegram on March 19 informing her of the unanimous decision, her eyes filled with tears of joy. The next day *The New York Times* carried a front-page story and photograph of a smiling Stephen Wiesenfeld holding three-year-old Jason, who had the telephone receiver at his ear. The headline proclaimed, "Justices Back Widowers' Equal Rights." And indeed, they had.

Writing for the Court, Brennan declared that the Constitution "forbids the gender-based differentiation that results in the efforts of female workers required to pay social security taxes producing less protection for their families than is produced by the efforts of men." The notion that men are more likely than women to be primary wage earners is not without empirical support, he noted. But the Court emphatically rejected the government's *Kahn*-based argument that the gender distinction in Social Security law was intended to compensate widows for the disadvantages women experienced in the labor market. Rather, Berzon's extensive legislative research revealed that Congress's original intention was to allow mothers to stay home with their children. Limiting protection to children with a surviving mother rather than a surviving father, the opinion continued, served no valid legislative purpose at the time. Now, however, the provision was archaic in the light of women's contemporary labor-market participation and overbroad in its assumption that men cannot provide parental care.

Critical, too, was the fact that the Court had opted for extension. That it did so meant that the justices were "legislating a bit," Ginsburg admitted, but only tentatively. Ultimate authority to recast or scrap the law in question still remained with Congress. Privately, she would come to regard her success in persuading the Court on extension in *Frontiero,* and especially *Wiesenfeld,* along with four future benefits cases, among her more important accomplishments. Those cases "made the law" on extension versus invalidation, she noted with pride.

Although there was no reference to strict scrutiny in the decision, the unanimity of the Court was clearly a sign of progress. In effect, the *Wiesenfeld* judgment substituted the functional description "sole surviving parent" for the gender classification "widowed mother" employed in the statute. She also noted with pleasure the Court's focus on legislative purpose—that is, that children deprived of one parent should have the personal attention of the other. The rigor with which the justices had examined legislative intent provided some assurance that future cases involving a "benign" gender classification would not get by without close inspection of the actual purpose of the legislation. The succession of cases—*Frontiero, Taylor, Wiesenfeld,* and ultimately *Stanton*—suggested that the justices were now prepared to reject legislative line drawing based on outmoded gender-role stereotypes, particularly in relation to the workplace. The equality train that had seemed derailed by *Kahn,* she concluded, was now definitely "back on track."

Yet there were miles to go. The Court still had not specified where it placed gender discrimination on the equal protection spectrum. In fact, Blackmun, in his *Stanton* opinion overturning sex-based age differentials in the context of child support, concluded that under any test—"compelling state interest, or rational basis, or something in between"—Utah's distinction between males and females was invalid. But if strict scrutiny were not an option for a majority, could they agree on a test that was "something in between" to which they would adhere? A question for another term—now it was time to celebrate.

. . .

THE GINSBURGS HELD a victory party at their New York apartment, leaving some ACLU staffers confounded by the fashionable address and the sight of hired staff passing out hors d'oeuvres and drinks. The hostess, however, was less concerned with the reaction of her colleagues than with her guests of honor—Jason and Stephen Wiesenfeld. James and his mother had previously gone shopping to buy some of James's favorite childhood books for Jason. Neither mother nor son could have anticipated that their three-year-old guest would one day ask a future Supreme Court justice to perform his wedding ceremony, as, many years later, would Stephen.

CHAPTER 13

Moving Forward on
Shifting Political Ground

After the turbulent 1960s, the Watergate scandal, and a humiliating exit from a divisive war, celebrating the two hundredth
birthday of "one nation, indivisible, with liberty and justice
for all" challenged bicentennial planners. Spectacular fireworks, ringing church bells, and tall ships sailing into Manhattan's harbor helped
temporarily. But the reality of a sluggish economy and mounting inflation fed fears that the American dream was ending. Public intellectuals fueled the sense of national decline, lamenting the erosion of civic
culture, the nation's "failure of nerve" internationally, the "decline of
paternal authority," and the "culture of narcissism." In the heartland, the
televangelist Jerry Falwell called for a return to God, patriotism, and the
patriarchal family.

The cultural and political mood of the country was shifting. At
the 1976 Republican convention, conservative delegates secured major
changes in the platform. Planks were approved calling for a constitutional ban on school busing and abortion, enactment of a constitutional
amendment to protect the right to life of unborn children, and the
nomination of judges who "respect traditional family values." Pro-ERA
Republican women and their allies narrowly averted a plank that would
have withdrawn the party's historic endorsement of the amendment.

Ginsburg, who had spent the summer teaching and traveling in
Europe, was too astute to dismiss evidence of backlash. Publicly, she
maintained that *Wiesenfeld* put the equality train back on track. Privately, she confided to Catherine East, "I don't think we will see from
this Supreme Court an articulated advance in theory [strict scrutiny].

Wiesenfeld and the Louisiana jury case demonstrate that the Court is in fact moving in a different direction." Cases from *Craig v. Boren* to *University of California Board of Regents v. Bakke* would confirm the accuracy of her prediction. The Court's attentiveness to social and cultural divisions roiling the country and the conservative political ascendancy those fractures helped generate made winning her two cases on the fall docket an imperative.

· · ·

THE FIRST OF THE TWO CASES, *Craig v. Boren,* had a long history. In December 1972, Fred Gilbert, a recent Harvard Law graduate and Tulsa-based attorney, had filed a suit in the U.S. District Court for Western Oklahoma challenging a statute that mandated a sex-based difference in the drinking age. Women in the state could buy near beer (beer with low alcoholic content) at eighteen; men had to be twenty-one. The initial complaint had been dismissed by the three-judge district court in 1973. The law at issue, the court had ruled, was a valid exercise of state power under the Twenty-First Amendment, which gave the states full authority to regulate commerce in liquor. Gilbert immediately appealed to the Tenth Circuit.

Before the three-judge panel could reach its decision, the original plaintiff, a politically aware nineteen-year-old Oklahoma State student, had turned twenty-one. To avoid rendering the case moot, Curtis Craig, a freshman fraternity brother, stepped in as co-plaintiff along with Carolyn Whitener, the hardworking co-owner of Honk 'n Holler, a curbside convenience store in Stillwater, Oklahoma. But the change in co-plaintiffs did not alter the outcome. In 1974, the Tenth Circuit handed down its ruling. Sex-based age classification for purchasing near beer served a rational purpose: the promotion of traffic safety. Males between eighteen and twenty-one had a much higher incidence of arrests for drunken driving as well as a higher number of vehicular accidents than their female counterparts. "Fed-up with the whole thing," Gilbert was ready to throw in the towel when he appealed to the ACLU.

Ginsburg knew that the cause of thirsty fraternity boys was a frothy one. Yet *Craig v. Boren* could strike a blow against *Goesaert v. Cleary*. The 1948 decision denying Michigan women the opportunity to be bartenders ranked high on her list of outdated precedents. More important, a favorable decision in *Craig* could clarify the heightened scrutiny standard that the Court appeared to be using in recent sex-discrimination cases—that "something in between" to which Blackmun had referred. She urged Gilbert to appeal.

. . .

WHEN THE COURT AGREED to hear the case, Ginsburg assured the Tulsa attorney that the ACLU would pick up all printing expenses for a jointly written brief. There was only one condition—that she would have final approval of its contents. As for the oral argument, "in view of your long, hard efforts in this case, the day in court surely belongs to you if you want it," she wrote. If he preferred to do the brief himself, she would provide an amicus brief and advice. Immensely relieved, Gilbert "implore[d]" Ginsburg's presence at the table for oral argument. As for a joint brief, time and distance dictated separate efforts. Gilbert could not have envisioned the useful advice, much less the attention to detail, that the mail from New York would bring over the next six months.

By the end of January 1976, their correspondence had become playful. Addressing Ginsburg as "Dear Amica," this self-styled male chauvinist signed off as "Ranger Fred." Banter aside, Ginsburg instructed, "We don't have 5 votes for suspect classification so play that down. Urge instead 'heightened scrutiny' as evidenced in *Reed, Frontiero, Wiesenfeld,* and *Stanton.*" And "don't remind Brennan that in *Frontiero* he copied from *Sail'er Inn* without acknowledging the source." Finally, she urged, "stay away from conclusive presumption argument in view of *Weinberger v. Salfi.*" Further, Ginsburg encouraged the insertion of highlights from her *Craig* amicus brief. She also volunteered to track statistics on traffic safety and drinking habits in New Jersey.

As appreciative as Gilbert was of this display of expertise, he confessed that he was "beginning to feel like the superfluous male loitering around the delivery room (who nevertheless eagerly awaits his consort's next installment)." Two weeks later he sent his own brief with apologies for having run out of time before he could do the necessary cutting and polishing. "I think I succeeded in excising everything that could be prejudicial to your other litigation," he added, referring to *Goldfarb*. "Your brief makes many strong points effectively," Ginsburg assured him, "and should serve well enough for the purpose at hand."

Her own amicus brief, a typically taut and persuasive argument, acknowledged that Oklahoma did indeed have broad authority under the Twenty-First Amendment to regulate the sale and service of alcoholic beverages. The amendment did not, however, insulate the state from review of legislation resting on overbroad generalizations concerning the drinking behavior, proclivities, and preferences of the two sexes.

The age differential might appear to benefit young women, she acknowledged. But the only two post-*Reed* cases in which the Court had countenanced sex-based differentials, *Schlesinger* and *Kahn,* had involved legislation justified as compensating women for "past and present economic disadvantage." Surely, Ginsburg argued, "the concept of 'compensatory' or 'rectificatory' gender classification does not encompass the solace 3.2 [near] beer might provide young women . . . about to encounter an inhospitable job market." On the contrary, the differential was but another manifestation of old gender norms.

Countering the statistical data on arrests, traffic deaths, and injuries used by Oklahoma officials to establish the state's objective, she pointed out that drinking preferences and proclivities also varied by ethnicity and social class. To limit the sale of beer on the basis of ethnicity would be regarded as invidious. Sex-based line drawing was no less inappropriate. Quite simply, she contended, the statistical proof on which the lower court relied "utterly failed to demonstrate the supposed legislative objective."

With respect to precedents, neither of the two Supreme Court decisions cited by Oklahoma officials provided "reinforcement" for the state's case. The first, *California v. LaRue* (1972), upheld state prohibition of nude dancing and explicit sexual acts in establishments licensed to sell liquor by the drink. "But whatever support the Twenty-First Amendment provides for state action explicitly and precisely directed to the co-mingling of live sex and liquor, that brand of 'sex' is not the issue in the case at bar," she continued. As for *Goesaert,* even the three-judge district court had avoided reaching back to this outdated ruling, which was "overdue for final burial." In sum, the Oklahoma law constituted a sex-based classification that "could not survive review whatever the appropriate test: rational basis, strict scrutiny or something in between."

Leaving nothing to chance, Ginsburg's letters continued after the briefs were filed. Too much was at stake, she pointed out, to allow *Craig* to go down on procedural grounds. It could be argued that Carolyn Whitener, co-owner of the Honk 'n Holler, lacked standing because she, unlike her would-be male customers, had not suffered a denial of equal protection. Urging Gilbert to be prepared to address that point persuasively, citing ample precedents, Ginsburg enclosed a memo presenting the case for standing for Whitener. And do submit the reply brief she had authored, she reminded Gilbert.

. . .

HER SECOND CASE, scheduled for oral arguments on the same day as *Craig,* targeted survivors' benefits in Social Security law. The prototype had initially been prepared for Edgar Coffin, a retired New Jersey police officer whose situation resembled Stephen Wiesenfeld's—minus the child. Before retirement, Coffin had enjoyed earnings on a par with his wife, Edna. However, she had a higher pension and Social Security payments—income he was not entitled to as a survivor when she died. As in the case of Paula Wiesenfeld, the law denied Edna Coffin equal protection and provided no survivors' benefits to her husband. The case seemed tailor-made for Ginsburg. But "sometimes the best laid plans go awry," she recalled, "and this one did." Three weeks before the judges ruled in *Coffin,* the U.S. District Court for the Eastern District of New York decided a parallel case, *Califano v. Goldfarb.* Thus, *Goldfarb* moved ahead of the others in the Supreme Court's docket.

Knowing she would have to play the hand she was dealt, Ginsburg consoled herself with the knowledge that the facts were straightforward. More important, the case had been well handled by Nadine Taub, a Yale Law graduate who headed the Women's Rights Litigation Clinic at Rutgers Law School in Newark.

Leon Goldfarb, a Russian-born seventy-year-old resident of Queens, had attempted to collect Social Security survivors' benefits upon the death of his wife, Hannah, who had worked for twenty-five years as a secretary in the public school system. While such benefits were paid automatically to a surviving widow, Goldfarb's application was denied. As a widower, he was expected to prove that his deceased wife had supplied three-fourths of the family income (all of her own and one-half of his), which was not the case. The injustice of the requirement rankled.

"We earned that money; we gave it every month," he insisted, so "there shouldn't have been strings attached to it."

Using the *Coffin* brief as a template, Taub, Peratis, and Ginsburg crafted the *Goldfarb* brief. Worried that because Leon Goldfarb, unlike Edgar Coffin, had a pension of his own and might be considered a double-dipper, Ginsburg focused on his wife, Hannah. Personalizing the injustice suffered by all working women who paid Social Security taxes for years and then were denied the same protection for a surviving spouse afforded their male counterparts made the brief more compelling.

On October 5, Ginsburg returned to the Supreme Court chambers to present *Craig* in the morning and *Goldfarb* in the afternoon. Seated next to Gilbert at the counsel's table, she hoped "Ranger Fred," as she confided to her secretary, would stay "on the straight and narrow." As expected, Gilbert's oral argument elicited a good deal of laughter from the brethren—his hyperbole simply couldn't be contained, even by Ginsburg. Nevertheless, her presence at counsel's table signaled that much more than beer drinking was on the line as Gilbert was the first to acknowledge.

"Dearest Amica," he later wrote, "Your presence, by my side packed considerable psychological clout, enough clout, along with your good sportsmanship and scholarly contributions to qualify you for the 'One of the Boys Award' from the 'Machismo Law Society of the Tulsa University Law School.'"

"Dear [Ranger] Fred," she replied, "I am sending you copies of August Strindberg's writing." The multitalented Swede had always had a troubled relationship with women. "It may help you understand," she wrote, "that Truth is not necessarily that which is asserted by two (male) witnesses."

· · ·

GINSBURG, as well as court reporters, noticed the shift in mood after lunch as the Court turned to *Goldfarb*. Deputy Solicitor General Keith Jones led off. Replaying one of the government's arguments in *Wiesenfeld*, Jones contended that Congress had originally ordered different treatment for widows in order to compensate for women's economic disadvantage. As *Kahn* demonstrated, the Court had long sanctioned such preferential treatment. Unlike *Wiesenfeld,* which denied all benefits to surviving fathers with minor children, the statute challenged by *Goldfarb* merely required proof of financial dependency. Given that so many women were dependent on their husbands and that so few husbands were dependent on their wives, requiring a support test for men only served a valid government interest in administrative convenience. In other words, the rational relationship test had been met.

Had economic relationships changed so appreciably since the 1939 amendments to the Social Security Act that husbands were no longer breadwinners and wives no longer stay-at-home homemakers? If that were so, Jones argued, Congress should change the law. In the meantime, however, to abandon the support test and automatically provide benefits to widowers would cost the government an estimated $447 million a year in Social Security payments. *Goldfarb,* like *Craig,* was not about women but about men who were trying to ride "the skirt-tails" of the women's rights movement, Jones concluded.

· · ·

GINSBURG FOLLOWED. Speaking in her usual precise fashion, she conceded that the Social Security law automatically guaranteeing survivors' benefits for widows appeared at first glance to operate benignly in favor of women. Yet in practice, she argued, working women and their families were harmed by stereotypical assumptions about men's role as breadwinners and women as stay-at-home dependents or pin-money wage earners. Legislative history indicated that lawmakers had never intended a needs test as a criterion for benefits. Rather, they had equated the terms "widow" and "dependent." Unlike the Florida widows' tax exemption in *Kahn,* which hurt no women, the disparate treatment dictated by Social Security law actually disadvantaged those wage-earning women who paid Social Security taxes.

Ginsburg had barely begun her opening statement before Justice Stewart and then Justice Stevens (Justice Douglas's replacement) peppered her with questions about anti-male bias. Ginsburg readily acknowledged that sex-based line drawing was a sword that could cut both ways. Many of the laws that appeared to discriminate against men, she insisted, also discriminated against women inasmuch as they reflected gender stereotypes that disadvantage women such as Hannah Goldfarb. Should the same or a different constitutional standard apply to the two sexes? Stevens asked. His question was just what Ginsburg had hoped to avoid. If she answered directly, she risked losing the vote of Powell, who simply could not envision a single standard that took into account sex-related difference only when it genuinely mattered.

Convinced that easy solutions on the part of the Court precluded recognition of "deeply entrenched discriminatory problems," she declined to answer. Laws that discriminated against either sex generally had an "invidious impact against women," she replied. Stevens persisted. "But your answers always depend on . . . finding some discrimination against females. You seem to put that in every answer." Ginsburg responded, "I have not yet come across a statute that doesn't have that effect." "If there were one," Stevens continued, "you would say it should be tested by a different standard, I take it." If there were such a statute, Ginsburg replied, "I would have to reserve judgment on what the answer would be. In any case, I have not come across such a statute in my—" Cutting her off in mid-sentence, the frustrated Stevens kept pushing. The tense dialogue continued until Ginsburg finally managed to return the discussion to *Goldfarb*.

But she was not off the hook. What about *Kahn*, she was asked, where women specifically benefited? The purpose of *Kahn*, she replied, had been to cushion the impact of spousal loss on the sex for which that loss imposes a disproportionately heavy burden. Was that not also the purpose of the Social Security provision that Goldfarb was contesting? Ginsburg responded that a tax break of $15 to benefit widows (the issue in *Kahn*) did not have the same impact as Social Security benefits so large that their availability could sway decisions as to which spouse should be the primary breadwinner.

The exchange then turned to options for redressing the Social Security law and to the cost involved. Ginsburg insisted, "It is impossible to rationalize a gender criterion allocating benefits on the ground that it is cheaper to proceed that way." Concluding, she restated the basic issue: "Appellee Goldfarb respectfully requests that the judgment [of the district court in his favor] be affirmed, thereby establishing that under the equal protection principle women workers' national social insurance is of no less value than is the social insurance of working men."

. . .

PRESS REPORTS OF THE ORAL ARGUMENTS focused less on the primary issue in *Goldfarb* than on Stevens's interrogation and Ginsburg's responses. Knowing that Stevens was looking for a universal standard, she regretted in retrospect that she had not quoted the justice's own previous words. Once questioned about racial discrimination, he had responded that he would go beyond "merely a color-blind remedy in certain circumstances." Still, he added that his judgment would always be "a function of the kind of factual situation disclosed by the particular case." It was an approach Ginsburg knew to be equally appropriate for gender-discrimination cases. Why hadn't she used it? Under the bombardment of questions, it just had not occurred to her to reply to the former Chicago judge with his own words.

Hindsight was of no more use than predictions about future outcomes. As she was well aware, there were complicating factors, notably *Califano v. Webster.* In this case, William Webster, upon his retirement in 1974, challenged a provision of the law that allowed different formulas for calculating a retired wage earner's average monthly wage, which was the basis for determining the amount of old-age benefits to be received by retired workers. This law, eventually phased out in 1972, had been enacted by Congress in the 1950s to rectify women's unequal pay. Originally, a formula was put in place that allowed women to drop three more low-earning years than men. A three-judge U.S. District Court for the Eastern District of New York had then ruled in Webster's favor: the 1972 change should be retroactively applied. Faced with the prospect of having to pay as much as $17 billion to some nine million retired men, the government had appealed.

The outcome in *Webster* deeply concerned Ginsburg, knowing that the ghost of *Kahn* still hovered. Too many members of the Court still had problems recognizing the difference between *malign* and *benign* gender discrimination. A majority might view *Goldfarb* and *Webster* as similar examples of gender discrimination against men and blend the two together because both involved Social Security. If that occurred, the huge price tag involved could then lead the Court to decide both cases in favor of the government. Initially, Ginsburg had tried to avert that possibility by demonstrating how the two cases differed. She ultimately averted any discussion, believing it to be too diversionary. But that did not alleviate her anxiety.

. . .

WHEN THE COURT MET in conference a few days after the oral arguments on October 5, the chief led off, turning first to *Craig*. This case, he maintained, was an isolated incident that should be dismissed on procedural grounds. Because Curtis Craig had turned twenty-one after the Court agreed to hear the case, his claim was moot. The question before the Court was whether Carolyn Whitener had standing, and he thought not. If, however, his colleagues thought she did, then he was prepared to find for Whitener, provided the majority opinion was narrowly written.

There was no consensus among the other justices. Blackmun and Powell were inclined to follow the chief's lead: dismiss on the standing issue and, if other justices disagreed on standing, find for Whitener on the merits of the case. Rehnquist predictably took the most conservative position: dismiss on standing and support Oklahoma should the Court decide the dispute. Brennan, Marshall, White, Stevens, and Stewart were prepared to find for *Craig*, but as in *Frontiero* the old split over the standard to be applied reemerged. Brennan, Marshall, and White were still prepared to adopt strict scrutiny. Stevens agreed that "some level of scrutiny above mere rationality has to be applied," but he was unclear as to what that level should be. Stewart, whom Brennan had tried so hard to convert to strict scrutiny in *Frontiero,* still hesitated to go beyond the rational basis test.

Because a clear majority existed for overturning the Oklahoma law, Brennan, the senior member of the majority, assigned himself the opinion. He could always write a narrow opinion overturning the law in question. But in both cases, the real issue was the standard of review, and Brennan, like Ginsburg, hoped for more. Unfortunately, with barely three other justices sharing his preferred position—that Whitener had standing, that the Court should rule in favor of Craig, and that the standard of review should be one of strict scrutiny—the master consensus builder faced an uphill battle. Rehnquist would clearly dissent. Burger, Blackmun, and Powell, while more sympathetic on the merits of the case, were not willing to raise the standard of scrutiny. Could he write a draft that would satisfy himself, Marshall, and White—all of whom wanted strict scrutiny—*and* persuade Stevens and Stewart or perhaps one of the other holdouts to sign on?

After several drafts and many accommodations, Brennan crafted an opinion that provided the "something else" that Ginsburg had sought in earlier cases—an intermediate standard of scrutiny that lay between the rational basis test and strict scrutiny. Clearly there were compromises along the way. Brennan, Marshall, and White settled for an intermediate standard. Stevens got what he wanted. Stewart came aboard as hoped. And, most surprising, Powell and Blackmun, who had initially been prepared to dismiss *Craig,* reversed their positions entirely when presented with a standard that they understood as not requiring them to strike down all sex-based classifications. Brennan's discussion of why Whitener had third-party standing would also prove important for future cases. Burger joined Rehnquist in dissent.

Brennan's majority opinion, acknowledging that the purpose of the Oklahoma statute was to promote traffic safety, concluded that statistics cited to validate sex-based classification were unconvincing and insufficiently related to the state's goal, as the *Craig* team had argued. Then he turned to the main issue. Articulating the review standard on which the Court had operated since *Reed* in 1971, albeit somewhat erratically, the majority held that "classifications by gender must serve *important* governmental objectives and must be *substantially related* to achievement of those objectives." Concurring and dissenting opinions openly referred to a new "middle-tier" standard.

. . .

WHEN THE CONFERENCE then turned to *Goldfarb,* the chief justice, favoring the government's position, wanted to overturn the district court's ruling. Brennan, Marshall, and White, viewing *Goldfarb* as a logical extension of *Wiesenfeld,* strongly disagreed and voted to affirm. Powell, Stewart, Stevens, and Blackmun also voted a "tentative affirm," in part because they were reluctant to overturn so recent a decision as *Wiesenfeld.* Because there seemed to be a clear majority in favor of affirming, Brennan again chose to reserve the majority opinion for himself.

When he circulated a draft opinion, it was clear that his majority was in peril. Stevens insisted that a law discriminating against men, although prima facie invalid, could find sufficient justification in *Kahn.* Stewart was on the fence, though he complimented Brennan on "a remarkably fine job." Given *Wiesenfeld,* "the result it reaches is close to unanswerable." Still, he added, he was having "some second thoughts" about *Wiesenfeld* and would, therefore, wait to read the dissenting opinion before making a final decision. Blackmun, too, declined to join until he could see Rehnquist's dissent. When the Rehnquist dissent was circulated, Burger signed on immediately, declaring in his high-handed way that it "should convince the most ardent equal protectionist," which of course it did not. Blackmun, also concerned about preserving *Kahn,* followed the chief in joining the Rehnquist dissent. The count in favor of affirming was now 4–3 with Stewart and Stevens still undecided. Then Stevens circulated a memo saying that he would write an opinion concurring with the majority, acknowledging that he had engaged in "considerable backing and filling." With Stewart joining the dissent, the count settled at 5–4.

Ginsburg's fears were put to rest with a phone call on March 2, 1977, from Justice Marshall's law clerk and her former student, David Barrett, who conveyed the *Goldfarb* decision. Brennan's plurality opinion affirmed that a sex-based classification dividing the adult population into breadwinning males and dependent females for purposes of survivors' benefits operated to the disadvantage of wage-earning women. Stevens, in his concurring opinion, focused on the discrimination against surviving male spouses. He, too, concluded that the law had never been intended to redress labor-market discrimination against women, as the government had claimed. The fact that men were disadvantaged by the equation of "widow" and "dependent" was "the accidental by-product of a traditional way of thinking about females." He also pointed out that the government paid out $750 million per year to widows who were *not* dependent on their husbands—a sum much larger than any money the government saved by not screening women for dependency.

The four dissenting members—Rehnquist, Burger, Blackmun, and Stewart—argued that the classification functioned benignly inasmuch as the model of breadwinner male/dependent female still reflected the reality for many couples. Further, the automatic qualification of widows, but not widowers, was administratively convenient for the government.

· · ·

IN A BRIEF UNSIGNED OPINION issued the same day, the Court ruled against William Webster, as Ginsburg had so ardently hoped. The Social Security benefit calculation establishing a more favorable formula for retired female workers than for retired males was seen as differential treatment in the interest of gender equality. In this instance, Congress, attempting to address past discrimination against women workers in the form of lower wages, had used a sex-based classification for a specific, tightly defined, compensatory purpose. The remedial end matched legislative intent and did not hinder the general rule of gender neutrality and equal treatment.

Ginsburg rejoiced. Finally, the Court had been able to distinguish between appropriate sex-based classification, as in *Webster,* and inappropriate sex-based classification, as in *Goldfarb*—a distinction that would prove critical if feminist lawyers were to use affirmative action effectively for women. To celebrate, she brought cookies, baked by Marty, to her sex-discrimination class. "After North Carolina's nay vote on E.R.A., we needed that report to lift our spirits," she later wrote to Barrett. Her immediate response to the *Goldfarb* victory, according to Barrett, was even more exuberant. He reported to Brennan's law clerk, Gerard Lynch, that Ginsburg had exclaimed that she felt like kissing the good justice—which in fact she would do many years later when she visited Brennan in the hospital shortly before his death. In the meantime, Lynch wrote, "Save at least a handshake for the draftsman."

He also enclosed the *Webster* opinion that he had drafted. "I was wondering what you'd think of it," he wrote. "I attempted to confine legitimate 'benign' discrimination pretty narrowly, throwing in a plug for absolute equality and yet preserving the possibility that truly compensatory programs can be clearly identified." At any rate, he continued, "the job was done without benefit of briefing [because the case had been disposed of summarily—without briefs or oral argument], and I suspect that *to the extent the Court really believes what the opinion says,* it may be of considerable importance."

Ginsburg's response was immediate and appreciative. "The *Webster* opinion," Ginsburg wrote to Lynch, "leaves a corridor for genuine compensation without offering encouragement to lower courts tempted to seize on *Kahn* and *Schlesinger v. Ballard* whenever confronted with a gender classification. . . . Had I been assigned the task, I could not have done it better."

Expounding to ACLU affiliates as well as the press on the importance of the three decisions, Ginsburg underscored the heightened-scrutiny standard. When asked by the senior editor of the *Harvard Law Review* for an article on the rulings, Ginsburg offered to meet with him when she was in Boston. She also referred him to comments she had written in the possession of Professor Laurence Tribe. She could not resist adding that the incoming Harvard Law School student Jane Ginsburg, who would be arriving in Cambridge around Labor Day, was "also familiar" with the cases "and precedents leading up to those decisions." No one aware of the nightly discussions around the Ginsburg dinner table doubted the accuracy of that statement. Undeniable, too, was the pride reflected in being part of the first mother-daughter team in the history of Harvard Law School.

· · ·

DESPITE THESE LATEST RULINGS, feminist jurisprudence was at a crossroads. The Court had made progress. Yet legal analysts agreed that intermediate scrutiny represented at best no more than a "qualified" victory for the women's rights movement. Determining whether a statute in question was "substantially related" to "important government interest" was clearly subjective. And there was no indication of what factors should enter into such a determination or how those factors should be weighed. Unless the Court clarified further, the distinguished legal scholar Kenneth Karst predicted, intermediate scrutiny "will remain a mask for an unexplained process of adjudication." In principle, of course, the ERA should remedy the problem. But there was the rub.

Only one more state had ratified in 1977, leaving the count three short of the required thirty-six. The legitimacy of rescission was also undecided. Supporters—Ginsburg included—would push successfully to extend the ratification deadline to June 30, 1982. Yet extension only generated charges that ERA supporters were fixing the rules. Their narrow loss in North Carolina, a critical state, proved prophetic. Nor was the dramatic slowdown in ratification the only setback for equality advocates during the Court's 1976–77 term.

The brethren's "ostrich-like" responses on pregnancy discrimination brought another disappointment. Before *Geduldig v. Aiello* had reached the Court in 1974, feminist lawyers already had Title VII cases moving through the lower courts, among them *General Electric v. Gilbert*. The company refused to cover workers whose disabilities arose from childbirth or pregnancy in an otherwise comprehensive disability plan that included vasectomies and hair transplants. The lower courts ruled that the company's actions represented a clear violation of Title VII of the Civil Rights Act. Ginsburg had teamed up with Sue Ross, author of the original EEOC guidelines in 1972, to prepare an amicus brief. But GE's lawyer had two aces in the hole. The first was letters indicating Congress in 1964 and the EEOC in 1965 did not believe that Title VII covered pregnancy. Second was Justice Stewart's statement in *Geduldig* that pregnancy discrimination could not be termed sex discrimination because it did not apply to members of the relevant class (nonpregnant women). Only Brennan and Marshall dissented from a ruling that held discrimination related to pregnancy was not sex discrimination under Title VII.

Dismay did not begin to capture feminists' reaction to what Ginsburg described as a "disaster." "Women's Rights Movement Is Dealt Major Blow," declared *The New York Times* in its front-page headline. *Gilbert* also had serious legal ramifications for women other than pregnant workers. In embracing *Geduldig*, Rehnquist reinforced the idea that sex-discrimination claims could prevail if—and only if—there were opposite-sex comparators (men/women). Supporting this narrow, formalistic definition of discrimination, he provided a faulty reading of Title VII's meager legislative history. Both opponents and supporters of adding "sex" to Title VII agreed that inclusion would change traditional gender roles in the family and public sphere, as the legal scholar Cary Franklin has made clear. What Rehnquist created in *Gilbert* was an "invented tradition" that would thus make it difficult for a plaintiff charging sex discrimination in other situations where employment practices impeded women's job opportunities—sexual harassment, for example.

As if that were not enough, the Court dealt pregnant women a further setback—one that, unlike pregnancy disability, would not be remedied by future congressional action. In two closely related cases involving abortion, the Court held that denial of federal Medicaid funds for poor women seeking abortion, except in the narrowest of circumstances, did not violate equal protection. As Powell stated in his majority opinion in *Maher,* such policy "places no obstacles—absolute or otherwise—in the pregnant woman's path to an abortion." Aghast that Powell's conclusion could be so detached from the realities of the lives of poor women, Ginsburg believed it to "defy reason." Yet she also understood where the problem lay.

. . .

SEX-EQUALITY LAW RESTED on what feminist advocates realized from the start was a partial and imperfect analogy to race. Beginning with Pauli Murray's Jane Crow article, they had used the race-sex analogy to highlight the similarity of race-based and sex-based stereotyping. Both were expressions of prejudice embodied in the law that, without any adequate justification, restricted the capacities and autonomy of a subordinate social group.

But the analogy also had limitations. While Social Security benefits claim cases were relatively straightforward, cases involving pregnancy-related discrimination had proved problematic from the start. Race discrimination required dealing with comparable groups. Thus, justices looked for opposite-sex comparators uncomplicated by reproductive difference. Hence Stewart's clever crafting in *Geduldig* as *pregnant and nonpregnant persons* (which included women) had enabled a majority to decide that pregnancy discrimination was not sex discrimination. Likewise, equal protection cases compelled comparison of the relative harms experienced by women and racial minorities, revealing the inadequacy of direct comparison. For justices in the middle, the claims of Mel Kahn or Leon Goldfarb, for example, fell far short of the tragedies inflicted on African Americans by Jim Crow.

Affirmative-action cases proved equally difficult for lawyers and judges to draw applicable parallels on account of race and sex. Because women as well as racial minorities still faced deeply entrenched discriminatory patterns in education and employment, feminists had embraced affirmative-action claims as another route to gender parity. In employment, for example, full-time female workers earned on average only slightly more than 60 percent of men's wages. Top management positions were a male preserve. Small businesses, eager to cut costs, seldom provided pregnancy disability, flextime, or parental leave. Yet with the exception of minority women, neither women in general nor disadvantaged racial and ethnic groups were well served by lumping their problems together for affirmative-action purposes.

Ginsburg had sensitively addressed both the similarities and the divergences in the race-sex analogy in her 1975 article "Gender and the Constitution." As a group, she noted, women needed no special consideration in admissions to educational institutions. Historical circumstances for the two groups diverged. Sex-discrimination remedies in universities, she suggested, might focus on "eliminating institutional practices that limit or discourage female participation." Employment discrimination, on the other hand, adversely affected both groups; hence, the same remedies applied—numerical goals in training, hiring, and promotion. The work-family bind, she hastened to add, not only required parents willing to share work-family responsibilities but also legislative measures, among them quality child care.

If the race-sex analogy had become a double-edged sword for feminist litigators, as *General Electric v. Gilbert* so clearly demonstrated, Ginsburg knew she could ill afford to let the analogy flounder. With affirmative action her best hope for addressing gender inequality in the workplace, forward motion hinged on the outcome of a new race-based affirmative-action case, *University of California Board of Regents v. Bakke,* slated for the Court's 1977–78 term.

For defenders of affirmative action, *Bakke* was a nightmare case. Allan Bakke, a white male NASA engineer, had his application to the University of California's new Davis Medical School rejected twice. The school's admissions program set aside 16 percent of its slots for "disadvantaged" applicants whom Bakke outscored. Claiming "reverse discrimination," he filed suit. The Medical School's two-pronged admissions system violated both the Constitution's equal protection guarantee and the Civil Rights Act. The same strict scrutiny that applied to racial classifications designed to disadvantage minorities, his lawyers argued, should also be applied to programs that gave them advantages. Lawyers for the university countered that strict scrutiny should be reserved for classifications that disadvantage "discrete and insular minorities," not programs that sought to further the opportunity of groups historically excluded. When Bakke won in the California Supreme Court, the University of California appealed.

Ginsburg immediately grasped the central legal problem. How, under the equal protection clause, could the strict scrutiny applying to racial classifications be reconciled with race-based affirmative action? If she reversed the race-sex analogy, she could use emerging sex-equality jurisprudence as a model for addressing the problem of race-based affirmative action. *Craig* provided the less exacting standard of scrutiny than did strict scrutiny. And the Court's reasoning in *Webster* offered both a way to distinguish between beneficial and harmful classifications and an indication that the justices would accept carefully tailored remedial programs designed to overcome generalized discrimination. By reversing the race-sex analogy, she sought to offer not only a strategy for *Bakke* but also "a more capacious vision of discrimination's meanings, effects, and remediation" that would embrace both sex and race.

Brennan, too, had seen the advantage. Writing for himself, Marshall, White, and Blackmun in *Bakke*, Brennan had drawn upon sex-discrimination cases as a useful equal protection parallel. Intermediate

As a scholar in residence at the Rockefeller Foundation institute in Bellagio, Italy, Ginsburg enjoyed unaccustomed leisure to think and write during the summer of 1977.

scrutiny, applied to racially based affirmative-action plans, could allow for carefully tailored programs designed to compensate for past discrimination. But Powell, whom Brennan had carefully courted for his fifth vote, disagreed. "[T]he perception of racial classification as inherently odious," Powell insisted, "stems from a lengthy and tragic history that gender-based classifications do not share." The Court "has never viewed gender-based classification as inherently suspect or as comparable to racial or ethnic classification for the purpose of equal protection analysis."

Burger, Rehnquist, and Stewart, following Stevens's lead, maintained that the University of California, Davis Medical School's explicit racial quota violated Title VI of the Civil Rights Act, thus avoiding any discussion of the standard of review appropriate for affirmative-action programs under equal protection. Powell, casting the deciding vote, as he had in *Frontiero,* wrote the opinion. His decision—to which none of his fellow justices signed on—rejected the UC Davis preferential admis-

Ginsburg and Justice Thurgood Marshall (1978) at Berkeley Law School's Boalt Hall, where they judged a moot court competition. Ginsburg was a fellow for the spring semester at the Center for Advanced Study in the Behavioral Sciences at Stanford University.

sions program for minorities because of its use of racial quotas. Insisting that all claims of racial discrimination—whether brought by blacks or whites—must be subject to strict scrutiny even if the discrimination proved "benign" (compensatory), Powell thus backed Bakke's admission to the Medical School. Nevertheless, in a nod to the Brennan four, the courtly Virginian conceded that race, ethnicity, and poverty could be among the many factors considered by institutions seeking "diversity" among students and faculty in order to enrich academic dialogue and achieve a "robust exchange of ideas." *Bakke* was hailed as a "Solomonic" compromise by some; both Bakke and affirmative action (in some form) had won. Yet Powell's decision, like all compromises, contained elements that each side opposed.

Ginsburg was not the only legal scholar and advocate in 1978 who wondered what this tortured decision from a fractured Court really meant. Alert to the troublesome implications of Powell's race-gender comparisons, she immediately raised questions at the annual meeting of the American Bar Association meeting in August and elsewhere. "Did Justice Powell mean preferential treatment for women ordered by a government agency should be less vulnerable to challenge in court than preferential treatment for racial and ethnic groups saddled with 'a lengthy and tragic history' of adverse discrimination? That seems an anomalous position," she noted. "Did he mean, on the other hand, that courts should have a higher tolerance for official discrimination against women than such discrimination against racial and ethnic minorities?"

Other feminist legal scholars were less charitable as they highlighted the shortcomings—historical as well as analytical—of his approach to gender. Powell kept the old race-gender analogy, "alive and well . . . circumscrib[ing] the recognition and remediation of inequality," concluded Serena Mayeri. That was just what Ginsburg's more capacious reformulation, along with that of the Brennan four, had sought to avoid.

. . .

AS GINSBURG WAS ALSO acutely aware, much of the larger feminist legal agenda remained unaccomplished. It was not just the future of sex-based affirmative action that hung in the balance after *Bakke*. So did standards for challenging disparate impact; that is, legislation that at first glance appeared not to discriminate between the sexes but in fact had a negative impact on women. In race-based cases involving disparate impact, plaintiffs previously had only to establish evidence that the law in question impacted blacks and whites differently. Then, in a 1976 case, the Court had raised the ante. To establish an equal protection violation, there had to be proof that the state acted with a discriminatory intent. Ginsburg worried that the majority might also extend motive review to sex-based challenges involving disparate impact.

As it happened, an apt case, *Personnel Administrator of Massachusetts v. Feeney,* was making its way through the courts. *Feeney* involved a challenge to a Massachusetts law giving absolute lifetime preference to veterans applying for high-level civil-service positions. Long after World War II, the military had maintained a 2 percent quota on female enlistment, thereby restricting the number of women who could later qualify for the preference (and then only for pink-collar jobs such as switchboard operator or secretary). For nonveterans like Helen Feeney, who aspired to senior positions, the experience of repeatedly acing the civil service exam, only to be bypassed by a much-lower-scoring male, proved infuriating.

Yet no matter how devastating the impact of such preferences on women's employment opportunities or how supportive she might be of the young Massachusetts ACLU attorney pursuing Feeney's suit, Ginsburg found it hard to be optimistic about the outcome. The Court's newfound commitment to legislative motive, when compounded by a reluctance to acknowledge unconscious bias, would make it exceedingly difficult to prove that lawmakers in the Commonwealth of Massachusetts had *intended* the lopsided result created by a "facially neutral" statute.

Indeed, without the explicit constitutional commitment that ratification of the ERA would provide, Ginsburg found it hard to predict how equal protection litigation on a whole variety of gender-related issues would fare in the 1978–79 term. The Court had moved beyond the most obvious examples of explicit discrimination, lending credence to those who argued that her equal protection victories demonstrated that the amendment was no longer needed. Furthermore, Justice Brennan, her most reliable ally, was ailing. More troubling still, Allan Bakke's win, if followed by a loss for Helen Feeney (which occurred), could signal a discouraging new trend. A majority of the current Court was not only prepared to apply strict scrutiny of programs designed to remedy past discrimination of minorities and women. The more conservative members were also loath to apply the judicial scrutiny necessary to detect latent biases in legislation having a discriminatory impact on those same groups. The dual impact of unfavorable rulings in these two cases could amount to a shift in equal protection doctrine that would likely serve to perpetuate rather than erode race and gender stratification.

There were, to be sure, other legal issues to pursue such as sexual harassment. The "social and economic pressures" that fostered feminism's resurgence, she believed, would continue to exert pressure on decision makers over the long term. But in the short term, conservatism, never a marginal factor in American life, had become a potent groundswell. As new conservative foundations and "public interest" law firms increasingly took the offensive in the "battle for control of the law," the constitutional understandings for which Ginsburg and her allies in the liberal legal movement had struggled would be powerfully challenged. If she were ever to move the equality principle further, Ginsburg concluded, it would have to be from the other side of the bench.

PART V

Becoming Judge and Justice

CHAPTER 14

An Unexpected Cliff-Hanger

A little more than a year after a former Georgia governor won the White House in 1976, *Ms.* magazine portrayed a pregnant Jimmy Carter on the cover. The eye-catching design underscored feminists' expectations that Carter, in return for their vigorous support during his campaign, would do for women's rights what Lyndon Johnson had done for civil rights. The thirty-ninth president must continue to deliver on his promises to appoint women and minorities to high-level positions in his cabinet, federal agencies, *and* the judiciary.

Passage of the Omnibus Judgeship Bill in 1978 put women and minorities back on the front burner. Eight years in the making, the legislation's primary goal was to address long-standing backlogs and delays on the federal bench by expanding the federal judiciary by one-third. Of the 152 new judgeships, most (117) would be for the ninety-four district courts, with the remainder (35) going to the twelve circuit courts. Beyond creating a larger judiciary to handle the pressure on the federal bench, the Omnibus Judgeship Bill incorporated consideration of merit—the candidate's character and experience—into the nomination process. Most important, the bill guaranteed that a strong effort would be made to fill the new positions with qualified women and members of minority groups—a matter that Carter took seriously. At the White House signing ceremony in October, the president noted the "almost complete absence" of women and minorities on the federal bench. (Only 11 women out of a possible 505 served as federal judges.) Pledging "more than token representation" among his nominations, he promised quality as well as numbers—nominees who "possess and have demonstrated commitment to equal justice under the law."

. . .

GINSBURG HAD CONSIDERED the possibility of a career move as soon as Carter was elected. Solicitor general would have been her dream job. But as she waited at the Department of Justice for an interview, both she and the African American candidate waiting with her knew it was not to be. A long list of qualified white men who had served the party during its eight-year exile from the White House were available. Attorney General Griffin Bell, no progressive, dutifully included a few women and minorities on his list of judicial candidates for the president. He himself preferred nominees who shared his background in large corporate firms. But such firms had never been welcoming to women and minorities, denying them the experience Bell sought from a candidate.

The Omnibus Judgeship Bill now created new opportunities, as both Ginsburgs were keenly aware. They had just spent a semester in Palo Alto, California, which afforded them time to contemplate the future. Marty, who frequently taught a course in tax law at New York University, had served as a visiting professor at Stanford Law School while Ruth held a fellowship at the Center for Advanced Study in the Behavioral Sciences. Her project had been an account of her equal rights litigation, but as she wrote, she realized the story was unfinished. Nor could it be completed given the signs of conservative resurgence. Marty was now prepared to exchange his partnership at Weil, Gotshal & Manges for a chaired professorship, preferably at Columbia, while doing everything possible to promote a judgeship for his wife. Jane, meanwhile, had made the *Law Review*—the first mother-daughter combination to do so in Harvard's history—thrilling both parents, especially her mother. Now twenty-three, Jane was ready to launch her own career. The ever-energetic James would be completing eighth grade at the Dalton School, making it a good time for a transition.

Ginsburg had her heart set on Foley Square, home of the U.S. Court of Appeals for the Second Circuit, where she had once clerked for Judge Palmieri. On January 15, 1979, she turned in the questionnaire for prospective nominees to the Second Circuit, along with another for the U.S. Court of Appeals for the D.C. Circuit as a backup. The start of a complicated process, she had little inkling of just how anxiety-ridden the next eighteen months would be.

. . .

GINSBURG KNEW THAT a federal judgeship would have been out of the question without the merit selection system. But she also knew that she could count on other factors to work in her favor. By 1979, feminists in the Carter administration—"femocrats," as the political scientist Sally Kenney would later call them—had come to occupy key executive posts. Barbara Babcock, the first woman professor at Stanford Law School and a friend of Ruth's from feminist legal circles, had been named assistant

Ginsburg with her daughter, Jane, at Harvard Law School, 1978. Behind them is Herma Hill Kay, dean of Boalt Hall. Ginsburg and Kay were likely there to attend a conference on women and the law.

*Ruth, Jane, and James Ginsburg vacationing on the Caribbean island of
Mustique in 1979.*

attorney general for the Civil Division. One of her tasks was to generate names of strong female judicial candidates. But as Babcock quickly
discovered, identifying the women who would make good federal judges
was not the problem. Getting them nominated and confirmed was considerably more difficult. Elevating a woman over a highly qualified man
who had paid his dues to the party meant "thwarting the ambition of
those identifiable, faithful, and deserving men." Fortunately, Babcock
had a tenacious and effective feminist ally in Margaret McKenna, the
deputy White House counsel. McKenna's boss, Robert Lipshutz, shared
his deputy's commitment to a racially and gender diverse federal bench.
Roe v. Wade advocate Sarah Weddington, who served at the White
House as special assistant for women's interests, had the president's ear,
as did the shrewd First Lady, Rosalynn Carter.

"Insider" strategic knowledge together with effective lobbying by
"outsider" feminist groups combined to create a network that, for the
first time in the nation's history, offered a real chance for a racially and
gender diverse judiciary. Ginsburg's own recent appointment to a blue-
ribbon advisory committee for the Second Circuit inspired a measure of

confidence. She considered herself on good terms with Judge Lawrence Walsh, a former president of the American Bar Association, who chaired not only the advisory committee but also the merit selection committee. Her affiliations with numerous women's and progressive organizations, especially those engaging in feminist litigation, provided a natural constituency. Norman Dorsen, then president of the ACLU, and others, had written strong letters. And she was confident that she could demonstrate her command of constitutional law. But when she arrived for her interview with the selection committee for the Second Circuit, an unpleasant surprise awaited.

After introductions by Judge Walsh, the all-male panel began with their questions. They were not what she had anticipated. Business lawyers all, the committee members quickly discerned that Mrs. Ginsburg lacked familiarity with securities law. With a reprimand for her inexperience, they ended the interview. "You were as close as I've ever seen you to frazzled and dejected," the journalist Nina Totenberg later recalled, reminding her friend of their conversation during a shared cab ride to Columbia a couple of days after the interview.

Ginsburg doubted that her lack of experience in securities law was the main reason her application had failed. Rather, she speculated, "there was an unholy alliance between people who didn't want me on and people who didn't want [Constance Baker] Motley," the former civil rights advocate turned highly accomplished district court judge for the Southern District of New York, who also hoped to move up in the Second Circuit. If by "unholy alliance" she meant men on the committee who preferred their judges to sport a prior Wall Street affiliation rather than that of the NAACP and the ACLU, then her speculation proved correct. As Carter noted in his diary on January 30–31, 1979, "Mrs. Ginsburg [has] been a matter of some controversy." She was considered "excessively liberal." Instead, the nomination went to Amalya L. Kearse, the first African American partner in the major corporate firm Hughes Hubbard & Reed, whom Ginsburg later described as "a natural."

. . .

REGROUPING, she now set her sights on Washington. As a New Yorker, she would never have thought to apply to the U.S. Court of Appeals for the D.C. Circuit had she not received an invitation directly from former

Senator Joseph Tydings, who chaired the selection committee. Fortuitously, her old dean Erwin Griswold, the former solicitor general, also sat on the committee, which she hoped would help. Gerald Gunther, with whom she had long conversations at Stanford, was familiar with the D.C. Circuit, as the U.S. Court of Appeals for the District of Columbia was commonly known, added his encouragement. The court had a progressive reputation under the leadership of Judge David L. Bazelon, whose landmark rulings on behalf of the mentally ill had put him at the forefront of the intersection of science and law, and in a series of conflicts with Chief Justice Warren Burger. Other judges, among them Skelly Wright, who had played a critical role in promoting racial desegregation in his native South, added to the liberal luster attached to the circuit. As the court responsible for reviewing the decisions and rule making of many government agencies, the D.C. Circuit actually offered a better fit for Ginsburg than did the Second Circuit. Admittedly, administrative law was not an area in which she had specialized. But then neither was constitutional law when she first began her litigation. She knew she could learn. And it was well known that the D.C. Circuit had served some of its judges as a stepping-stone to the Supreme Court.

Ginsburg's supporters in the legal and feminist communities swung into action. NOW's Legal Defense Fund, the Women's Equity Action League, and the National Women's Political Caucus (NWPC) all lauded her candidacy. Local chapters signed petitions. Letters poured in from Griswold, Palmieri, Gunther, and Wechsler. Columbia's executive vice president and former Law School dean, Michael Sovern, together with his Law School successor, Albert J. Rosenthal, touted Ginsburg's intellectual capacity and judicial temperament, especially her objectivity and moderation as an advocate. Distinguished members of the bar association, among them Chesterfield Smith and William Spann, wrote as well.

When names of eight nominees went to the White House, Ginsburg made the cut. But so did Patricia Wald, an impressive public-interest lawyer, who had strong backing in Washington's feminist circles and had served as Carter's assistant attorney general for the Office of Legislative Affairs. So, too, did Abner Mikva, a liberal Chicago lawyer and five-term Illinois congressman, who had served on both the House Ways and Means Committee and the Judiciary Committee. The night before the list went to the press, Tydings phoned Ginsburg to report that Wald and Mikva would get the two slots created by the Omnibus Judgeship Bill. Then he added reassuringly, "There are going to be more vacancies in the D.C. Circuit and you are going to get one of the appointments."

. . .

IN JUNE, when the Court wound down its 1978–79 term, Ginsburg could point to two additional decisions advancing gender equality. Alimony was now to be available to husbands as well as wives (*Orr v. Orr*). Also, unemployed female breadwinners were now entitled to the same unemployment benefits as their male counterparts (*Califano v. Westcott*). Though she had argued neither case, her extensive guidance on the brief in *Califano v. Westcott* paid off. "I'm elated about *Westcott*," she confided to Gerry Gunther. "Not a peep, even from Rehnquist, on the sex discrimination issue," she said of the 5–4 vote. "On the extension remedy," she noted, "the vote was close." But a majority agreed to extend welfare coverage to Cindy Westcott, recognizing that a wife's past earnings might qualify her rather than her husband as unemployed head of household. At least all the justices acknowledged that "[Justice] Harlan in *Welsh* is the starting point [for extension]," Ginsburg added—acknowledging once again that it was Gunther who had suggested she start with *Welsh* in her efforts to persuade the Court to remedy sex-discriminatory statutes by extending benefits to the excluded sex.

Delight over the *Westcott* victory, however, could not offset Ginsburg's disappointment that there was still no move to the bench at hand. She had written to Barbara Babcock in early June, enclosing copies of recommendation letters for Babcock's use:

> Mike Sovern's [letter] notes my "international reputation as a civil procedure scholar," and my honorary degree from Sweden's Lund University for my Swedish civil procedure studies. Chesterfield Smith's is altogether glowing, and notes our association in ABA activities. Andy Lowenfeld's stresses my scholarly inclination "in the related issues of federalism." Al Rosenthal's and Jack Greenberg's stress general intellectual ability. [Enclosing a résumé, she noted:] I have deleted most of my feminist affiliations. [Finally, she added:] Respected people likely to give me high marks include: Erwin Griswold, Al Sacks, Bernard Segal (Philadelphia), John P. Frank (Phoenix), and Bill Spann

(Atlanta). A month ago, Larry Tribe mentioned he had strongly recommended me to Tim Kraft.

But sterling recommendations from elite lawyers downplaying Ginsburg's advocacy and attesting to her scholarly bent and balanced judgment were still not enough—at least not for someone as potentially
controversial as the ACLU's premier feminist litigator whom some
opponents also regarded as personally lackluster, drone-like, and elit-
ist. Attorney General Griffin Bell, while committed to carrying out the
president's instructions on diversity, had a narrow definition of merit and
frowned on advocacy of any kind. In addition, Ginsburg's rejection by
the Second Circuit selection committee was held against her by some.

As *The New York Times* observed of the new federal judicial nominations, politics remained a major factor. The two new nominees to the
D.C. Circuit—both liberals—provided cases in point. Wald, whose
career more closely resembled Ginsburg's, had a varied résumé. But it
included a stint in the Justice Department in the Johnson administration and, more important, an appointment by Carter as assistant attorney general in charge of legislative affairs. Two years of intense exposure
to staffers on the Hill as a member of the administration had, as Wald
pithily observed, "sanitize[d] my prior liberal do-gooder record" as a
public-interest lawyer. Further, she had the confidence of the attorney
general. Mikva, in addition to his impressive legal credentials and experience in private practice in Chicago, had major political bona fides from
the start. Previously a senior partner of the former Supreme Court justice Arthur Goldberg and a veteran of ten years in the Illinois House of
Representatives, he had years of service in the U.S. Congress under his
belt as well as strong backing from Peter Rodino, the powerful chair of
the House Judiciary Committee. A man who radiated confidence and
ability, Mikva would later serve as a counselor to President Clinton and
political tutor to his fellow Chicagoan Barack Obama.

. . .

LONGING FOR "some time in far off places," Ruth packed her bags for
Taiwan. Her relish for international travel—a firsthand look at other
legal systems, some teaching abroad, topped off with a round of major
music festivals—was fast becoming a summer routine. The Taiwan trip

would be a nice break for Marty, who had just accepted an appointment at Columbia as the Beekman Professor of Law. Both needed a temporary escape from the pressure of judicial nominations.

The previous summer Ruth had visited China as part of an American Bar Association group invited to observe the legal system evolving in the aftermath of the Cultural Revolution. While the differences in China's legal procedures proved stark, she found her distinguished travel companions, such as Chesterfield Smith, stimulating.

Taiwan promised to be more Westernized than the mainland. But on the island to which General Chiang Kai-shek had fled when the Communists took over mainland China in 1949, military tribunals exercised authority over civilians, creating a potential for human-rights abuses. From Taipei's Grand Hotel, the Ginsburgs made the usual rounds of official visits. Her most impressive encounter proved to be with Yao Chia-wen, a young lawyer "of extraordinary courage, energy, and talent" who "almost single-handedly" established a legal aid program in Taiwan. "Far from being 'a leftist sympathizer,'" she would write upon his arrest a few months later, "he simply believes a healthy Government should hold elections, put up with criticism, [and] allow parties other than the KMT [Kuomintang] to form." Yao, not the government, she insisted, was the "genuine patriot." Upon learning of his arrest, which she read about in *The New York Times* in mid-December, Ginsburg contacted Norman Dorsen, a member of the board of the New York–based Lawyers Committee for International Human Rights. Along with other human rights groups, the committee unsuccessfully sought clemency for Yao, who received a twelve-year prison term.

When Ginsburg returned home in mid-July, encouraging news awaited. Nine members of the Congressional Women's Caucus— including Elizabeth Holtzman, Patricia Schroeder, Barbara Mikulski, and Geraldine Ferraro—had sent a joint appeal to Carter and top White House officials on Ginsburg's behalf. More letters of support poured in from other friends in high places. Barbara Babcock sent a copy of her letter to her new boss at the Justice Department, Attorney General Benjamin Civiletti, asking him to take Ginsburg's candidacy seriously. "She's brilliantly qualified for the appellate bench; I don't know a better writer and analyst. But more importantly for political purposes, she is a symbolic figure in the women's legal community." "It will be viewed as a slap in the face," Babcock emphasized, if "a woman who is so well-qualified and, more than any woman applicant in the country, has 'paid her dues,' is not chosen." But there was little supporters could do until Judge Bazelon, whom Babcock had been nudging to take senior status in the hope that Ginsburg would get his seat, decided to retire.

Once Bazelon's decision created a vacancy, Ginsburg's White House backers resumed their campaign from the inside in tandem with Susan Ness of the NWPC's Legal Support Caucus, who rallied outside organizational support. But the numbers on the bench Carter believed most important to increase were African Americans. When the White House announced Judge Bazelon's replacement on December 6, it was not Ginsburg who got the nod but Harry T. Edwards, an African American specialist in labor law and arbitration at the University of Michigan and chairman of the board of Amtrak. Ginsburg's name had been passed over for the third time.

. . .

THEN, IN LATE NOVEMBER, fate intervened. Judge Harold Leventhal suffered a fatal heart attack after a brisk game of tennis. At the White House, Benjamin Civiletti, the new attorney general, Frank Moore, the president's congressional liaison, and Weddington met to discuss remaining judicial vacancies—three, in particular. The attorney general, Weddington recalls, was not in favor of Ginsburg as Judge Leventhal's replacement. If she was not good enough for the Second Circuit, why put her on the D.C. Circuit? But after a lengthy discussion during which Weddington agreed to two of the names, a reluctant Civiletti finally consented.

Fearing that the attorney general's reluctance did not bode well for Ginsburg, Weddington now had to find a way to hold him to his promise. Confident that Carter would support Ginsburg's nomination, she phoned the anxious candidate on December 6. The attorney general had not yet met with the president to formally seek the nomination, Weddington confided, but she assumed that he would do so promptly, once the standard American Bar Association and FBI background checks were completed. Then she rushed downstairs to the Oval Office to tell the president that she had revealed Ginsburg's selection. Just as she anticipated, news leaked to the press, with whom she had cultivated

Sarah Weddington, Roe v. Wade advocate and a special assistant to President Carter, whose support of Ginsburg's nomination to the D.C. Circuit proved critical.

good relations, generating both a front-page story in *The Washington Post*—"Feminist Picked for U.S. Court of Appeals Here"—and excited responses from well-wishers.

Richard Bader, now the executive director of the American Shakespeare Theatre, wrote to his childhood playmate and cousin Kiki to congratulate her on her achievement. "Bravo! Bravo! Bravo!" applauded Pauli Murray, who wrote that she was as happy about the news as "a puppy dog with two tails. A better appointment could not have been made." John P. Frank, a distinguished civil rights lawyer and former scholar at Yale Law School, agreed. "What a splendid Christmas gift to the country and to a cause we both hold dear," he wrote. Harvard's Laurence Tribe added his own note of congratulations: "We'll all be the better for your confirmation."

While these bouquets lifted Ginsburg's spirits, the letters Weddington sought needed to be addressed to the White House. Without such pressure, she feared Civiletti would delay, which, in fact, he did. Weeks passed with no action. The president, beset by riot-inducing gasoline shortages, soaring inflation, the Soviet invasion of Afghanistan, the plight of fifty-two American hostages in the American embassy in Iran, and competition from Edward "Ted" Kennedy for the nomination, had other concerns. But in an election year, Ginsburg and her supporters could ill afford to wait.

Spurred by Susan Ness, founder and director of the Judicial Selection Committee of NWPC, nearly a dozen leaders of women's organizations sent a telegram in mid-January 1980 to the White House. Why had nothing yet been done about Ginsburg's nomination? "Time is of the essence," they wrote. "It is crucial that we have an opportunity to discuss with you the devastating and long-term implications of the administrations [*sic*] failure to move quickly and decisively with her nomination." When there was no reply, the organizations' leaders were livid.

. . .

WAS CARTER'S SUPPORT on women's issues wavering? He had, after all, endorsed a Court decision denying federal funding for abortions in *Maher v. Roe.* He had allowed his closest aides to redefine the job of the White House assistant Midge Costanza, who hosted a group of thirty presidential appointees—all women—to protest his stand on the *Maher* decision. And he had fired Bella Abzug as chair of the National Advisory Committee for Women because of her open opposition to his budget priorities. NOW's president, Eleanor Smeal, who chose to believe the worst about the president's commitment to the appointment of women judges, issued a press statement in which she refused to endorse Carter's bid for renomination. Increasing the number of female judges to 5 percent was "no big thing," she scoffed.

Her broadside angered the president and dismayed more politically savvy feminists, who had a far better grasp than Smeal of the obstacles to selection of the relatively small number of qualified women in the pipeline. Alarmed that Ginsburg's nomination might be caught in the cross fire, the NWPC's Susan Ness and her colleagues turned to Weddington. But she was in no position to help.

Civiletti, annoyed with Weddington for phoning Ginsburg without his permission, forced her to backpedal. Then, on February 2, the National Public Radio journalist Nina Totenberg reported that the attorney general was holding back the nomination because he had been upset by Weddington's role in leaking Ginsburg's selection. Five days later, Ginsburg received a call from Civiletti assuring her that she would get the nomination once background checks were completed. But it would be another two months before the president finally provided his signature—time enough, as it turned out, for conservative opposition to surface among congressional Republicans angered by what they saw as the partisanship of Carter's judicial selections. While nominations for judgeship positions had always been a partisan process, Carter had unwittingly made the process more political by introducing "merit" into the mix.

Word had already reached the press of grumblings from the Senate office of South Carolina's archconservative Strom Thurmond, where an aide dismissed Ginsburg as a "one-issue woman." Ohio's representative John Ashbrook, latching onto Ginsburg's support for the Equal Rights Amendment, questioned the ability of this "militant feminist" to judge impartially. Illinois's congressman Philip Crane declared that a woman with Ginsburg's views on the ERA and other issues "could bring about a vast revolution" in society as a federal judge. Such charges were typical of the kind of apocalyptic rhetoric then popular with ERA opponents. "Godless feminism" seemed to be replacing "Godless communism" in the lexicon of social conservatives. Ginsburg feared the worst.

She knew the Mikva and Wald nominations had both drawn fire in Congress. The National Rifle Association took aim at Mikva for his support for gun control in Illinois. "Pro-family" forces, angered by Wald's championing of children's rights, charged that she was "anti-family"— news indeed to a mother of five who had stayed at home with her children for a decade. The accusations derailed neither nominee. But right-wing organizations, alarmed that the progressive D.C. Circuit could gain yet a fourth liberal, showed no sign of letting up.

Letters on Ginsburg's behalf from notable legal scholars and lawyers had deliberately downplayed her feminist credentials, emphasizing instead her expertise in civil procedure and comparative law. But would such reassurances be sufficient in the waning days of the judicial sweepstakes when the nomination was not yet official? Ginsburg tried to keep her anxiety under control, but the months of waiting had taken their toll. To be described as a "militant feminist" with "a fetish which dominate[d] her viewpoint on almost every aspect of the law" was a calumny she felt she could not ignore. Thinking more letters from respected legal scholars might help, she asked Herbert Wechsler to write again.

When the ten new women nominated to the federal bench gathered for a gala celebration at the former ambassador W. Averell Harriman's elegant Georgetown home on March 11, Ginsburg was not among the honorees. Finally, however, on April 8, Civiletti called to say that the president had signed the nomination. With the public announcement three days later, the reality that she would indeed become a federal judge finally took hold.

· · ·

YET THE DRAMA WAS not over. First, a date had to be set for a confirmation hearing before the Senate Judiciary Committee. Ted Kennedy, who chaired the committee, needed time away from Washington to campaign against Carter in the Democratic primaries. Once hearings were finally set for June 4, preparations could begin in earnest.

Delighted that his wife had received the American Bar Association's highest rating for prospective judges, Marty appealed to influential friends and clients to help set up appointments for Ruth to meet with key members of the Judiciary Committee. Ira Millstein, a senior partner

President Jimmy Carter congratulating Ruth Ginsburg after her nomination to the D.C. Circuit in 1980.

at Marty's old firm who knew Orrin Hatch, called the Republican senator and arranged a long lunch for the three of them. Just come with an open mind, he suggested. When Hatch left the table, he was aware of Ginsburg's strong commitment to gender equality but convinced that she was fair-minded and nonideological. Combining visits to the Capitol with house hunting, the couple settled on an apartment in the Watergate with quick access to the Kennedy Center for the Performing Arts and a school for James. Georgetown Day School promised a fresh start for the fourteen-year-old. For Marty, one of the country's preeminent tax law experts, the exchange of a professorship at Columbia for one at Georgetown University Law Center proved easy. And the rapidly expanding Washington office of Fried, Frank, Harris, Shriver & Jacobson readily offered him the challenge of creating its tax department.

When Ginsburg returned to the Capitol for her confirmation hearing, she came with carefully prepared answers designed to downplay her role as an advocate. When questioned about her expertise as a trial lawyer, she responded that her experience in appellate advocacy was extensive and her work as a law professor made her well prepared for a judgeship. "Appellate judging has much in common with legal scholarship," she responded. "There is time for reflection, research, and for collegial exchange." Questioned about biases she might have formed during her activist years that might hamper her objectivity, she responded that she had cut any affiliation with organizations such as the ACLU. Suggesting that her loyalties lay mainly in academia, she explained, "That style of work and thought comes to me more naturally than the role of an advocate." What Ginsburg had not anticipated was testimony from a representative for United Families of America, Sandy McDonald, who urged the committee to look for a more "balanced" candidate—one whose judicial interpretation would not endanger the family, as would such an avowed feminist.

Mild compared with the opposition launched against Wald and Mikva, McDonald's testimony had little impact. On June 17, 1980, the Senate Judiciary Committee voted 8–1 to recommend Ginsburg for the judgeship; South Carolina's conservative Strom Thurmond cast the only negative vote. Full Senate ratification swiftly followed. "After many anxious weeks, the clouds cleared," Ruth wrote to a friend.

On a warm sunny day in Washington in late June, Judge Skelly

Wright swore in the newest judge of the D.C. Circuit. As Marty beamed, Gunther talked about the qualities of temperament and judgment that Ginsburg brought to the court. The many photographs taken at the party that followed in September afforded ample opportunity to glimpse the "dazzling smile" that Gunther recalled about the reserved young woman he had once taught at Columbia.

. . .

COMPARED WITH THE STRESSES Ginsburg endured in her previous career as a professor of law and general counsel of the ACLU, life on the court of appeals passed in relative calm. The process of settling into her new job was made easier by the warm welcome she received from her new colleagues—not only Patricia Wald, Abner Mikva, and Harry Edwards, but also such veteran judges as Skelly Wright, Edward Tamm, and Malcolm Wilkey. At first, the workload seemed intimidating. While three-judge panels were assigned to each case, Ginsburg quickly learned that judges worked as individuals, assisted only by three clerks. The challenge was to persuade the other members of the panel. Given the variety of cases, as well as her own exacting standards, her workdays seemed endless—a perception best captured by James in a poem for his mother's fiftieth birthday in 1983:

SONNET FOR JUDGE

Hi ho, hi ho, it's off to work you go:
Eleven thirty A.M. is the time.
In chambers what you do I do not know;
It must be great since we don't eat till nine.
We call and plead but never any luck
You still have one opinion left to read.
Patiently waiting, Dad and I are stuck.
You arrive and without a fuss we feed.
After dinner you march up to your room;
(Once we've cleaned the dishes from which we fed)
You go up there with coffee and with prune.
And by seven A.M. you get to bed.
On three hours' sleep you're not always fun.
But that's okay, says thy sweet loving son.

At first her clerks found their boss intimidating, though in some situations unexpectedly informal. One young clerk recalled that his first meeting with the judge occurred at a Roy Rogers fast-food restaurant populated by hungover truck drivers. But soon other hallmarks of the Ginsburg style became evident: her attention to the particulars of cases and contexts, refusal to judge prematurely, and insistence on arguing each case on its merits. Treating her opinions as she had her briefs, she made use of her clerks' contributions. In the beginning, however, she shredded their drafts, insisting on writing and rewriting her own opinion until every word conveyed precisely what she intended. "A meticulous writer," her former clerk Michael Klarman recalls, "we all felt like we learned a ton about writing from her."

Striving to meet Ginsburg's demanding standards generated rewards for her clerks not unlike those she had bestowed on her ACLU associates and apprentices: sensitivity to the challenges of combining work and family, supportive mentoring, small gifts brought back from travels, and invitations to Marty's gourmet dinners. Such invitations meant

Ginsburg with Marty at the Greenbrier resort in West Virginia, 1972.

Now judge for the U.S. Court of Appeals for the District of Columbia Circuit, 1980.

not only exquisite cuisine but welcome exposure to the wit of the host. Marty would phone his wife's chambers many evenings asking if "the Great One" was in, recalled Klarman. "He was the funniest person I have ever known. The two of them were an extraordinary duo. She was so straight and serious. And he would just crack you up, often at her expense (though their deep affection and respect for each other could not be missed)."

Marty was not the only one aware of the personality quirks that made his wife seem somewhat "otherworldly" to her staff. After a crash through a barrier gate, Marty soon discovered his wife's safety—and that of others—were best enhanced if he drove her to work. On the golf course when she stood bowed over a putt for an unusually long time, he had finally walked over and said, "I believe you're supposed to face East." The judge's secretary recounted an exchange with her boss the day of the parade down Constitution Avenue celebrating the Redskins Super Bowl victory. Ginsburg had inquired what the noise was about. Her secretary replied, "The Redskins won the Super Bowl." "What's the Super Bowl?" Ginsburg asked.

Klarman, an ardent baseball fan, had his own memorable encounter with the judge, who as a young schoolgirl had found the Brooklyn Dodgers games boring. "I asked for a day off to go to Baltimore for Opening Day of the baseball season to celebrate the Orioles' World Series win the year before. She thought I was crazy, and I'm sure I sunk in her estimation as a result. She didn't care what we did with our time as long as we got the work done, which made her a great boss. And she would have totally understood it if it was Opening Night of the Opera season. But baseball? Really?"

In the arena on which Ginsburg focused her attention—the courtroom at 333 Constitution Avenue, NW—her careful preparation and precision stood out. Each question, posed in that distinctively clear voice, had been carefully thought out in advance, the Washington attorney Alan Morrison observed. "Her rigorous interrogations were devoid of sarcasm or off-the-cuff comments." But anyone who displayed sloppy thinking or tried to obfuscate the real point confronted "a tiger on the bench." Clerks, members of the bar, and colleagues on the bench agreed that the former ACLU advocate quickly turned into "a judge's judge," one whose analytical rigor earned respect even from those with whom she vehemently disagreed.

Not surprisingly, she generally proved sensitive to equal protection claims advanced by minority groups that were traditional victims of discrimination as well as by organized labor within the unique statutory framework under which federal employees operated. A staunch defender of free speech rights on the airways as well as freedom of information, she wrote a leading decision applying the *New York Times v. Sullivan* "actual malice" standard of libel and also authored an opinion limiting the FCC's power to regulate the broadcast of nonobscene but "indecent" speech. She dissented in a First Amendment case from a decision upholding the Reagan-Bush administration ban on aid to any foreign family-planning organization that furnished abortion counseling or referral. And she sided with protesters in *Community for Creative Nonviolence v. Watt*, ruling that a "sleep-in" by the homeless in Lafayette Square was expressive conduct fully protected by the First Amendment, though she was later reversed by the Supreme Court. She also wrote a strong majority opinion in a decision that limited the discretion of the executive branch to deny tourist visas on political grounds.

On separation of powers, she authored a strong dissent when the

296 · RUTH BADER GINSBURG

D.C. Circuit ruled that the independent counsel law was unconstitutional. Ginsburg argued that the law did not violate the separation-of-powers doctrine, but instead maintained the system of mutual checks and balances that is "the genius of our Constitution." Her dissent was later upheld by the Supreme Court in *Morrison v. Olson.*

On religious freedom and separation of church and state, she proved to be an eloquent defender of religious freedom. For example, in 1984 a D.C. Circuit panel upheld an air force ban preventing an Orthodox rabbi and clinical psychologist, Simcha Goldman, from wearing his yarmulke while on duty and in uniform *inside* the mental health clinic on the base. Goldman requested an en banc hearing so that all of the judges, not just a panel of three, would decide his case. The hearing was rejected, but Ginsburg cast a dissenting vote. She was less sympathetic, however, to a member of the Ethiopian Zion Coptic Church in *Olsen v. Drug Enforcement Administration.* Carl E. Olsen argued that if Native Americans could enjoy the religious freedom to use peyote as part of their traditional worship, he should be allowed under the First Amendment to smoke marijuana. Ginsburg's opinion brought up the vast demand for and abuse of marijuana in the United States when compared with peyote. Further, for Native Americans, use of peyote outside rituals is sacrilegious, while the Ethiopian Zion Coptic Church teaches that marijuana should be smoked continuously throughout the day.

In her opinions on health, safety, and the environment, whether they involved lead paint or nuclear energy, she could be counted on to enforce agency compliance to the law when the law was clear. And in her opinions on searches and seizures, criminal procedure, rules of evidence, and prisoners' rights, she did what she customarily did: read statutes, studied precedents, and then applied the law without regard for ideology. On criminal law, attorneys faced tough questions, but she also took great care to see that the rights of the accused were protected. Overall, she distinguished herself as a moderate.

. . .

JAMES'S PERCEPTION NOTWITHSTANDING, his mother's life was not all work. During her first years on the D.C. Circuit, she became keenly aware that social relationships crossed partisan lines. It was a tradition she continued. Ginsburg's young clerks could understand her strong friendship with Harry Edwards and his wife, with whom the Ginsburgs attended opera, golfed, and shopped when attending judicial conferences abroad. Ruth and Marty had, in fact, severed their membership in a prominent country club that had changed its rules so that the Edwardses, as African Americans, could no longer belong. What her liberal clerks puzzled over mightily was her friendship with the highly conservative Antonin Scalia. Nor could they understand why she became so very friendly with Robert Bork and his daughter.

What her clerks might not have realized at the time was how much their judge enjoyed matching wits with members of the conservative legal pantheon. She also valued their respect for her intellect and judicial collegiality. Such relationships helped cement the reputation she had chosen to establish on the bench.

Chastened by her rejection for the Second Circuit, Ginsburg took a different path from that of her more predictably liberal colleagues, positioning herself to the right of Wald, Mikva, and Edwards. In the 1984 *Dronenburg* case, for example, Bork had written a "rambunctious" ruling that James Dronenburg, a petty officer in the navy, could not contest his dismissal without back pay because his consensual homosexual conduct was not protected by the right to privacy. Bork had not held back on his contempt for the right to privacy. Nor had the panel (which included Scalia) addressed Dronenburg's equal protection claim. Liberal members of the D.C. Circuit, perturbed by Bork's opinion, thought that the military's treatment of homosexuals deserved serious equal protection analysis. In a vote on whether to rehear the case before the full court of appeals, Ginsburg voted with Bork, Scalia, and other conservatives. The case, they agreed, had been appropriately decided under the Supreme Court's summary concurrence with an obscure district court opinion. Because Ginsburg's preference was to stick to settled law, she might well have assumed that any ruling in Dronenburg's favor would be overturned by the Supreme Court. But gay rights activists expressed disappointment that she had not yet embraced them in her equal protection jurisprudence. Other commentators also noted an unwillingness to take on the Court or colleagues that was not shared by other federal judges such as Richard Posner, Amalya Kearse, and Patricia Wald.

Whatever her calculus in the *Dronenburg* case, as more Reagan and Bush nominees joined the D.C. Circuit, a centrist position clearly

The Ginsburgs vacationing in St. Thomas in the Virgin Islands, December 1980.

accorded with Ginsburg's moderating instinct just as it had years earlier on a polarized Rutgers Law School faculty. A 1988 survey would conclude that "she voted 94 percent of the time with Reagan appointed Laurence H. Silberman—86 percent of the time in non-unanimous cases—while agreeing with Patricia Wald, a fellow Carter appointee, only 55 percent of the time and in only 38 percent of the time in non-unanimous cases." As a judge, she seemed to feel constrained to be "a judicial priest" rather than "a judicial prophet," the legal analyst Jeffrey Rosen concluded. But Joel Klein pointed to another factor: she had become "the sole unifying force on an otherwise fractious circuit court." Appealing for a temperate, collegial brand of decision making in speeches and in print, she deplored the divisive behavior and personalized attacks favored by her more combative colleagues.

There was also no denying that the middle represented astute positioning on the part of an appeals court judge who correctly surmised that by the time the next Democrat reached the White House, the requirement for a "liberal" justice would have a different look. By 1991, Ginsburg had jumped to the top in a survey of "leading centrists" likely to be considered for the Supreme Court. Perhaps less well known now by the public than she had been as litigator, she had thoroughly secured her reputation as a thoughtful, fair judge, renowned in judicial circles for her intellectual rigor, caution, and collegiality.

. . .

IN THE MEANTIME, the Washington years had also been about family, especially with a graduation and a wedding in the wings. While the Ginsburgs were still living in New York, Jane had fallen in love with the executive editor of the *Harvard Law Review,* George T. Spera Jr., a magna cum laude graduate of Princeton. After a year of clerking following graduation, the couple had become engaged with the full approval of the Ginsburgs, who were untroubled by the prospect of an interfaith marriage (Spera was a Roman Catholic). Ruth lit up at the very mention of her expanding family and delighted in shopping for a wedding gown with her daughter. She and Marty soon became the proud grandparents of Paul and Clara Spera as Jane made her way to full professor at Columbia Law School and received a doctorate of law with high honors from the University of Paris. George's flexibility and willingness to share child care enabled Jane to combine career and family successfully, much to Ruth and Marty's delight. When Paul and Clara came to Washington to visit "Tata" and "Bubbe," as the children called their grandparents, it was Marty's chocolate chip oatmeal cookies that became the dessert du jour. For years, he had the two children convinced that the statue atop the dome of the Capitol was of him.

Meanwhile, James, after the usual round of college visits with his mother, had followed his older sister to the academically intense University of Chicago. After receiving his undergraduate diploma, he decided during his second year in law school that becoming founder and president of Cedille Records, a classical label he had started in college, trumped going into the family business of lawyering. Remembering their son's avid record collecting since he was seven, and his love and command of music, his parents were fully supportive, given their own devotion to opera. An old Cornell friend and fellow tax lawyer, Carr Ferguson, with whom Marty and Ruth had shared the elder Mrs. Ginsburg's box at the Met, recounted how utterly absorbed Marty was in music—"its

Ruth and Marty with
their first grandchild,
Jane's son, Paul, 1987.

construction, nuance, emotion, and the artistry of its performance. . . .
For Marty as for Ruth, music was as sustaining as food." With James as
with Jane, the apple had fallen close to the tree.

Marty, renowned for his mastery of the tax code, had played a major
role in the General Motors buyout of Ross Perot's Electronic Data Systems Corporation in 1984. When approached by Perot, he had hesitated
because his firm represented several competitors. While technically not
a conflict of interest, Marty thought "it looked unseemly." But his long
friendship with Perot and the intellectual challenges the mergers presented were tempting.

Marty had agreed to take the job but at no pay. He then extricated
Perot from an unhappy corporate marriage, saving him a great deal of
money. His work so pleased his client that two years later a deeply appreciative Perot offered to endow a chair in taxation in his honor. Marty
and Ruth had deliberated so long as to where the chair should go, Perot
told them that he was giving it to Oral Roberts University. Upon hearing that, Marty promptly said Georgetown University but explained to
Perot that it was bad luck in the Jewish tradition to name something for
someone while the person was still alive. So income from the endowment was designated for books for the library until Marty's death.

In the meantime, Marty wore his many accomplishments lightly, summing up an impressive résumé by saying he accepted lecture invitations "in warm climates" and had written a "ghastly number" of tax articles. A few years later, the American Bar Association's Section of Taxation presented him with its Distinguished Service Award. He responded that in 1970 he had performed only "one distinguished service": taking the Tax Court advance sheet on Charles E. Moritz to Ruth. Her successful appeal of that case, he pointed out, had led to her career shift from "diligent academic to enormously skilled and successful appellate advocate—which in turn led to her next career on the higher side of the bench."

As friends of the couple had known for some time, when the next seat on the Court became available, with a Democrat in the White House, Marty would do his utmost to make sure that his wife was a candidate. Now "sanitized" after thirteen years on the D.C. Circuit—to use Patricia Wald's term for her own transformation from public-interest lawyer to judge—Ginsburg was prepared to move on, her principles intact.

CHAPTER 15

The 107th Justice

Given the opportunity to make the first nomination to the Court by a Democratic president since 1967, when Lyndon Johnson named Thurgood Marshall, Bill Clinton told aides he wanted to hit a "home run" with his nominee—a person to whom people would respond with "Wow." But the process of filling Justice Byron White's seat bore all the marks of the initial White House disarray, presidential indecision, and Republican-imposed constraints that marked the administration's first year in office. Nevertheless, when Clinton strode to the lectern in the Rose Garden that bright June day in 1993, accompanied by a small woman in a cobalt-blue suit and large sunglasses, he had a winner.

Introducing his nominee as a pathbreaking attorney, advocate, and judge, he described Ruth Bader Ginsburg as "one of our nation's best judges, progressive in outlook, wise in judgment, balanced and fair in her opinions." Hailing her pioneering advocacy on behalf of gender equality, he predicted that she would be "an able and effective" architect for consensus building on the Supreme Court, just as she had been on the court of appeals. "In the months and years ahead, the country will have the opportunity to get to know much more about Ruth Ginsburg's achievements, decency, humanity and fairness." Then he added in closing, "Ruth Bader Ginsburg cannot be called a liberal or a conservative. She has proved herself too thoughtful for such labels."

Feeling the power of Ginsburg's moving acceptance speech moment, a senior official thought to himself, this is not one of those statements that falls into the category of "Rose Garden Rubbish." Later that day, Clinton dashed off a note to his nominee: "You were terrific today—the American people who saw you must have been as moved by your state-

*President Clinton as Ginsburg accepts her nomination to the Supreme Court,
June 14, 1993.*

ment as all of us were. . . . I'm glad my wife met your granddaughter and
I wish I had met your mother."

Meanwhile, the press had its opening. ABC News's Brit Hume asked
if Clinton might disabuse the public of what seemed like a "certain zigzag
quality in the decision-making process." The president angrily retorted,
"How you could ask a question like that after the statement she just made
is beyond me." As he turned his back on Hume and walked Ginsburg
back to the White House, George Stephanopoulos, the president's young
director of communications, thought, "Brit just didn't know how right
he was." Editors of *The New Republic* chose to focus not on the process
but on the outcome. "Clinton deserves unstinting credit," they exulted.

· · ·

WHEN HE FIRST LEARNED of Justice White's resignation on March
19, the president began his search for a highly qualified political figure with real-world experience and a "big heart." Under the direction
of James Hamilton, who had handled the vetting for cabinet members,
an outside team of seventy-five lawyers began collecting information.

The president had turned first to the brilliant orator and three-term New York governor Mario Cuomo, who had been at the cutting edge of the Democratic Party. But Cuomo's indecisiveness kept the White House dangling until the governor finally declined. George Mitchell, the respected Senate majority leader and a former federal district judge from Maine, also quickly declined. So did Richard Riley, the former governor of South Carolina and Clinton's secretary of education, who frankly acknowledged that as a "mediocre country lawyer" he was not up to the job. But Secretary of the Interior Bruce Babbitt, the former governor of Arizona, was still a possibility, as were several federal judges.

By early June, the list had narrowed to a few names: Babbitt and three federal judges. Clinton first considered and then rejected his good friend the distinguished judge Richard Arnold of the Eighth Circuit. The nomination of another Arkansan, Clinton feared, would set off charges of "cronyism." He then focused on Babbitt, only to have fellow Democrats in Congress as well as environmentalists vigorously lobby to keep the secretary of the interior in his current position. Political aides agreed. The president needed a strong supporter in the red states of the intermountain West. Also, Orrin Hatch, the ranking Republican on the Senate Judiciary Committee, indicated that Babbitt would have a hard time getting confirmed, having angered senators from western states with his environmental program. Knowing that any political figure would generate opposition from Judge Robert Bork's New Right Judicial Selection Monitoring Project, set up to screen Clinton's judicial nominations, the president turned next to two federal judges: Stephen Breyer and Ginsburg.

Breyer, a genial pragmatist who served as chief judge of the First Circuit in Boston, had the strong endorsement of Senator Edward Kennedy. A specialist in administrative law, he had extensive experience on Senate committees during the Watergate prosecution and, more recently, as chief counsel to the Judiciary Committee, which earned him a thumbs-up from Hatch. On Thursday, June 10, members of the White House counsel's office flew up to Boston for intensive vetting. Clinton summoned him to the White House for an interview, but not to go over specific cases Breyer had decided. Rather, Clinton wanted to get a better sense of Breyer's judicial philosophy and outlook and how he might bring together a divided Court.

Breyer, who regularly biked from his home in Cambridge to his office in Boston, had an accident requiring Thursday's initial vetting to take place in the hospital. The discomfort of a punctured lung and broken ribs, compounded by a subsequent long, jarring train ride to Washington the next day, put him off his game during his private lunch with the president. In addition, an earlier background check had revealed that Breyer had neglected to pay Social Security taxes for an elderly housekeeper. The White House conveyed that information to key members of the Judiciary Committee, who reported that the lapse should not preclude his nomination. But coming so soon after the "nanny" problems that had derailed Clinton's first two nominees for attorney general, Zoë Baird and Kimba Wood, White House aides were eager to avoid appearing to apply a double standard. For all of Breyer's impressive credentials, the two men were "not on the same wave-length," Clinton told aides on Friday night. The discussion turned to Ginsburg.

The White House staff, hoping for a younger justice who might outlast Clarence Thomas, viewed the sixty-year-old Ginsburg as an unlikely candidate. Some of her associates, familiar with her avoidance of small talk, acknowledged that she could seem "remote and bookish," which did not augur well for her ability to bring other justices around to her position. Despite reservations about Ginsburg's personality that had surfaced early, there was no denying that her opinions were passionate and principled. Joel Klein in the White House counsel's office had distilled exhaustive research on Ginsburg into a nine-page, single-spaced personal and legal profile ten days earlier. Ginsburg's judicial philosophy, wrote Klein, "appears to be an unusual synthesis of the experiences that have shaped her life: her background as a pioneering woman lawyer and advocate for gender equality, as an academic proceduralist, and as a thoughtful federal appellate judge. Despite a deserved reputation for rigor and caution—as opposed to judicial 'activism,'" Klein continued, "Ginsburg's approach to cases is fundamentally pragmatic, displaying little enthusiasm for rigid, abstract rules as theories."

In his concluding analysis, he described the judge as "an accomplished advocate, respected scholar and eminent jurist, highly esteemed for her forceful mind and dedication to the law." Her campaign of court challenges in the 1970s "left a lasting imprint on legal doctrine and American society. It may be a reflection of how far we have come," he acknowledged, "that these triumphs seem taken for granted today," noting criticism of Ginsburg by women's groups for her critique of *Roe*. In the 1980s and 1990s, he continued, "Ginsburg's sense of fairness and meticulous attention to the case at the bar have made her an influential respected 'swing vote' on the D.C. Circuit. In constitutional adjudications, Ginsburg has advocated a cautious role for federal judiciary, but one which does not lose sight of the circumstances in which litigation has arisen."

The reservations about *Roe v. Wade* articulated in her 1992 Madison Lecture and her vote against rehearing the *Dronenburg* case, Klein acknowledged, would likely be negatives for women's groups and gay rights activists, who wanted the president to nominate a strong champion of *Roe* and privacy rights. But her nomination would bring "needed religious and gender diversity to the Court" and "would be perceived in many quarters as a departure from the use of ideology as the primary consideration in Supreme Court nominees." As a consensus builder, she would "likely bring to the Court the rigor and intellectual energy necessary to persuade the Court's decisive center."

Two unsolicited documents arriving that day from Senator Patrick Moynihan impressed the president. They were already in the pile of material on Ginsburg, but Moynihan wanted to make certain that Clinton read them that day. The first was a strong letter on her behalf from Michael Sovern, who had become president of Columbia University, to Moynihan. Attached was a separate note from Sovern to the senator that said, "Pat, She's the real thing." The other was a copy of a speech that the former solicitor general Erwin Griswold had made to the Supreme Court in 1985 on the fiftieth anniversary of the building in which he singled out three advocates for their contribution to changing the law: the NAACP's Charles Houston and Thurgood Marshall and the ACLU's Ruth Bader Ginsburg. As the decision came down to the wire, Klein summed up the view of the White House counsel's office: "Judge Ginsburg's work has more of the humanity that the President highly values and fewer of the negative aspects that will cause concern among some constituencies." On the evening of Saturday, June 12, with Breyer still in town, Ginsburg—in Vermont for a wedding—received a summons to the White House.

Returning from Vermont in casual clothing, she was reluctant to meet the president without changing. The White House counsel, Bernard Nussbaum, told her not to worry: Clinton would also be dressed informally because he was returning from the golf course. On this particular Sunday, however, the president had opted to attend church instead. Ginsburg was taken aback as Clinton approached her in his "Sunday best" navy-blue suit, shirt, and tie.

Despite this perceived faux pas, the potential nominee turned a thirty-minute interview with Clinton into a winning ninety-minute conversation. We discussed "anything and everything," Ginsburg explained afterward. "Sometimes there's just a chemistry between two people, and I liked him very much. I talked about my childhood, my teaching constitutional law, women's rights litigation." Clinton, having done his homework, asked in turn about a variety of cases—a couple in business law, some of the ACLU cases she had litigated, and a dissent in which she supported the right of Jewish military officers to wear yarmulkes while on duty. "I just wanted to hear her talk," he explained, in order to get a feel for her thinking. What struck him especially was how interwoven her earlier life experience was with her work and the difference she had made in people's lives in those ACLU years—and how self-effacing she was. "Tremendously impressed," Clinton said of his reaction to his nominee. A resolutely principled individual, he concluded, she had sterling credentials, a brilliant mind, and the empathy for ordinary folk that he so valued—"someone who viewed government in terms of the way it impacted people's lives."

Clinton knew she would also have the approval of key Republican players—an imperative for an ambitious yet realistic young president elected with only 43 percent of the popular vote and with a health-care bill he wanted to pass. In November 1991, *The American Lawyer* had named Ginsburg one of the nation's leading centrist judges. Indeed, her record on regulatory issues on the D.C. Court indicated that she had sided more often with Republican-nominated fellow judges than with her Democratic colleagues. True to her training in legal process, she was considered "a paragon of judicial restraint." That is, someone who tended to resolve cases on narrow procedural grounds, preferring small incremental steps to bold assertions of judicial power in order to preserve the legitimacy of the outcome. Judicial minimalism, Clinton knew, was then considered to be the best defensive strategy at the time for putting a brake on the conservative activists on the Court who were vigorously striking down progressive legislation. Further, minimalism encouraged justices to focus on the particularities of the case at hand rather than make sweeping pronouncements that get too far ahead of elected branches of government and the public in making law.

Some liberals, Clinton rightly anticipated, would be deeply disappointed that his nominee was no Marshall or Brennan. As a graduate of Yale Law School, he understood their dismay at the conservative legal movement's considerable efforts to dislodge legal liberalism. He also shared their concern about the erosion of the Court's commitment to civil rights and civil liberties. Yet he was confident that he had made a superb choice. Ginsburg's reputation as a centrist with a liberal bent and her emphasis on collegial decision making squared with the president's own inclination for accommodation and a place at the ideological center. She would decide cases on their merits, he believed, work with conservatives when possible, and "stand up to them when necessary."

Clinton conveyed his decision to Bernard Nussbaum, Joel Klein, and other key participants in the White House counsel's office late Sunday afternoon. After attending a barbecue for members of the press corps and watching the NBA game between the Chicago Bulls and the Phoenix Suns go into three overtimes, he dialed Ginsburg from the White House kitchen at 11:30. A bad connection through the White House operator forced the president to ask her to hang up. He dialed the number himself from his residence. "If I'm going to propose, we might as well have a good line. I am going to ask you to accept this position tomorrow. I feel good about this." A stunned Ginsburg, thinking of their earlier conversation, responded, "Oh, there is so much I wanted to say. I felt I didn't say anything." Clinton reassured her: "You did fine. Just speak from your heart and mind tomorrow." Around midnight the president called Breyer, telling him he expected him to be a major contender for the next seat on the Court, and chatted with Babbitt. Next, he phoned key senators: Mitchell, Joseph Biden, Hatch, Kennedy, and Moynihan, and tried to reach Bob Dole.

On Sunday morning, a White House aide had arrived at the Ginsburgs' Watergate apartment. But before the vetting team could begin its work, Marty served them a Tuscan lunch of cannellini beans, canned tuna fish, and lemon juice. Only after did the accountants from the administration make their way upstairs with Marty to go over his meticulously assembled tax records, documenting the couple's net worth at between $3.2 and $6.7 million. They also made sure that undocumented household help had not been hired and that the housekeeper's Social Security taxes had been fully paid. Downstairs in the living room, Nussbaum and Ginsburg went over personal and legal matters. Having vetted more than a hundred judges in his career, the associate White House counsel Ron Klain claimed he had never met anyone who was as well prepared as the Ginsburgs. "Marty had everything," Klain said. But, in fact, it was Ruth who handled the family financial information.

Meanwhile, *The New York Times* had already arrived with the announcement of the nomination in banner headlines. The *Times* described the nomination as a "surprise selection," noting that the president's decision had "stunned lawyers and jurists, and even many Administration officials" who had anticipated two days earlier that Breyer would get the nod. The *New York Post* trumpeted, "Pat Was Key to Top-Court Pick," and that a Brooklyn girl had won, also reporting the next day that Ginsburg and Moynihan had chatted about the Brooklyn Dodgers.

· · ·

IN HER QUEST for the nomination, Ginsburg also had more than a little help from a devoted spouse. Though Justices White and Blackmun were known to be thinking about retiring at the time of Clinton's election, a potential nominee could not be perceived as promoting herself for White's seat. To do so openly would have been seen as a breach of decorum. Members of the federal bench—and certainly the Court— like to maintain the public fiction that their nominations occur devoid of any campaigning. So Marty had quietly taken the initiative, realizing that he would have to act quickly. He knew that federal judges lacked the visibility of politicians like Cuomo and Babbitt. More important, he recognized that a nomination to the high court does not occur without behind-the-scenes efforts from supporters.

The place to start, he decided, was with his wife's natural constituency—the women's movement organizations that had spearheaded her nomination to the D.C. Circuit. Arranging a meeting with the heads of prominent feminist organizations, he found that his trial balloon sank like a stone. Marty attributed the palpable lack of enthusiasm to a ruling in which Ruth had participated three years earlier that rejected a case brought by the Women's Equity Action League, an organization that lobbied for educational opportunities for minority groups. Ginsburg had served as a member of WEAL's advisory board for four years, and the decision on the case seemed to WEAL loyalists at odds with her prior commitment to the organization. But the problem involved more than the WEAL case, more even than a much earlier case involving a sailor who challenged the military's prohibition on homosexual conduct.

The outcry from pro-choice circles following her Madison Lecture at New York University two years earlier had not helped. Taking issue with grounding the right to abortion in privacy rather than equality once again, Ginsburg had also questioned the sweep of *Roe v. Wade,* arguing that the law is best changed in "measured motions" rather than in "doctrinal limbs too swiftly shaped" (and hence unstable). Had the Court simply ruled on the more extreme Texas law at issue, giving the states more time to liberalize their laws, some of the discord, she suggested, might have been averted.

As insight into the judicial thinking of a potential nominee, the lecture hit the mark. As a comment on backlash to *Roe,* the aim was off. The legal historian David Garrow pointed out that Catholic-led backlash against abortion law reform predated *Roe* and that the movement for reform in the states had faltered by the time *Roe* and *Doe* reached the Court. Moreover, the influx of evangelical Protestants into the antiabortion movement had not occurred until almost twenty years later. (Even President Clinton would make a point of distancing himself from Ginsburg's backlash analysis while emphasizing her very strong commitment to reproductive rights.)

Yet the prior rulings Marty believed to be problematic, even when compounded with the prolonged fallout from the Madison Lecture among pro-choice leaders, were insufficient to explain the negative response to his initial foray with leaders of feminist organizations. What he might not have fully appreciated is the change that had occurred within feminist circles in the fifteen years since his wife first initiated her move to the bench.

As the feminist legal community—like the larger women's movement—fractured in the late 1970s, the unity of strategy and tactics that

Ginsburg had struggled so hard to maintain dissolved. Divisions quickly emerged among feminist legal practitioners over whether pregnancy could be accommodated within an equality framework or whether it required special treatment. Equality feminists predominated in drafting the bill that became the 1978 Pregnancy Discrimination Act. But by 1987, the two sides were pitted against each other in oral arguments over a California law mandating maternity leave for women, *California Federal Savings and Loan Association v. Guerra*. Equality feminists argued leave should be extended to men in the form of paternity leave.

In the legal academy where activism and scholarship intertwined, a new generation of feminist scholars critiqued its predecessors in much the same way that daughters often end up criticizing their mothers, but with an ideological twist. Focusing on the limitations of equality legal theory, more perceptive critics acknowledged the significant constraints Ginsburg had faced and the considerable tactical skill she displayed in dealing with them. But others were less charitable, glossing over distinctions between Ginsburg's vision of equality and that of the Court. Characterizing her litigation as assimilationist in outlook, insistent on formal equality, and inadequate for accomplishing the legal changes that would benefit most women, many of these "daughters" in academe claimed that equality advocates opened doors only for those with the resources sufficient to play by men's rules. They also faulted Ginsburg's use of male plaintiffs and her focus on classifications that could be characterized as burdening both men and women.

In the 1980s, during Ginsburg's years as judge, the search for new perspectives rapidly accelerated. For some legal theorists, the psychologist Carol Gilligan's relational theory offered promise. In her influential study of adolescents' moral development, Gilligan had highlighted women's capacity for nurture, empathy, and preservation of relationships. Accordingly, cultural feminists scrutinized aspects of the legal system that reflected male values and priorities. Few went as far as Robin West, who claimed that modern legal theory was "essentially and irretrievably masculine" in its valorizing of freedom and autonomy and devaluation of connectedness. West's critics were quick to point out the biological essentialism underlying her claim. But while cultural feminism came perilously close to resurrecting the old Victorian ideology of separate male and female spheres with its gender-distinctive attributes against which Ginsburg had fought, others critiqued equality feminism on different grounds.

Catharine A. MacKinnon, whose book *Sexual Harassment of Working Women* (1979) gave legal content to the concept of sexual harassment as sex discrimination, which the courts could accept, offered a systemic explanation of women's legal status originating in sexuality and male dominance. Her clear, compelling elaboration of substantive equality in the context of male hierarchy offered new ways to understand the prevalence of sexual violence and the persistence of women's subordination, as well as the inadequacy of equality remedies for gender discrimination. Legal understanding of equality, MacKinnon pointed out, means treating like persons alike and according the right to demand equal treatment only to similarly situated persons. Women, therefore, have no claim to equality in contexts where for reasons of biology or social fact they are not "the same" as men. The focus of the court, she argued, should not be on whether differential legal treatment is based on real (as opposed to stereotypical) differences between the sexes. Rather, it should be on whether the law perpetuates the subordination of women (a concept that Ginsburg had advanced in 1971 in *Struck*).

MacKinnon also offered a highly influential critique of formal equality and other liberal mainstays like privacy and consent, which failed to protect women from sexual violence. Other feminist legal theorists focused on minority women, pointing out the error of making white, middle-class, heterosexual women the unstated norm for all women, including the most disempowered. Subordination, feminists of color such as Kimberlé Crenshaw argued, involves intersectionality. That is, multiple forms of oppression—race, ethnicity, class, gender, and sexual orientation, as well as other factors such as religion and nationality—intersect in ways in which each exacerbates the consequences of the other.

This vibrant and diverse explosion of new theoretical approaches in the law—cultural, hierarchal, and intersectional—brought concern for different issues such as sexuality, sexual violence, and pornography. New understanding of how the legal structure itself was part of the system that enforced gender inequality heightened the challenges legal feminists faced. None of these developments negated Ginsburg's pathbreaking accomplishments. Yet collectively these new critiques served, if only temporarily, to diminish the significance of her contributions in what became a much larger debate among legal scholars about the value of liberal legalism.

Ginsburg reached the same conclusion. Never one to mince words in private, she initially confined her acerbic comments to close friends. When she read Katha Pollitt's attack on Gilligan and other difference feminists in *The Nation,* she impulsively sent Pollitt a fan letter. But that was after she addressed her critics directly in a keynote speech at a 1988 symposium titled "Feminism in the Law" held at the University of Chicago. She began her remarks by celebrating the recent and rich explosion in feminist legal theory. Then she reminded her audience that in 1971, when the ACLU Women's Rights Project was established, with the exception of the Nineteenth Amendment, "the Constitution remained an empty cupboard for people seeking to promote the equal stature of women and men as individuals under the law." Listing each of the many negative descriptions that "some observers" had applied to her litigation, she responded, "Such comment seems to me not fair. The litigation of the 1970s helped unsettle previously accepted conceptions of men's and women's separate spheres, and thereby added impetus to efforts ongoing in the political arena to advance women's opportunities and stature. An appeal to courts at that time," she continued, "could not have been expected to do much more."

Temperate in tone, Ginsburg left no doubt in her closing remarks that she regarded two aspects of legal feminists' intense examination of gender and law as unacceptable: "the [current] tendency to regard one's feminism as the only true feminism [and] *to denigrate rather than appreciate the contributions of others.*"

Feminist organizations outside the academy had also undergone changes in the Reagan-Bush years as leaders confronted a dramatically altered political context that put them on the defensive. It was not just the demise of the ERA. The failure of the U.S. Senate to ratify the Convention on the Elimination of All Forms of Discrimination Against Women (CEDAW) that President Carter had signed and twenty nations would ratify by 1981 further disappointed. The Reagan administration had also reduced the number of women in upper-level positions in government, ending the insider-outsider links that had so enhanced the effectiveness of feminist organizations in the Carter years. Other administration-inspired reverses followed: pullback in the enforcement of Title IX, virtual elimination of the Women's Education Action Project in the Department of Education, attacks on comparable worth, elimination of foreign aid to overseas health organizations for birth control purposes, a halt on enforcement of affirmative-action regulations, and dwindling federal and state resources for agencies that aided women.

Policy shifts found reflection in popular culture. The *Wall Street Journal* reporter Susan Faludi's *Backlash* persuasively documents the covert attack on feminism waged during the 1980s. Conservative politicians and media outlets—hostile to the clearly overblown perception of women's increased access and the resulting loss of status for men—set out to turn back the clock. The destructive rhetoric tried to convince women that feminism was the primary cause of everything from chronic health problems to paralyzing loneliness and alcoholism and, in fact, their own worst enemy. Yet nothing so dramatized the hostility to changes associated with gender and sexuality as did the virulent attacks on abortion clinics, many of which had emerged as a result of feminist networks. Law enforcement officials estimated that "by 1990 abortion clinics had experienced 8 bombings, 28 acts of arson, 28 attempted bombings or arson, and 170 acts of vandalism." Women's rights groups placed the estimates even higher.

Thus, from the standpoint of some in the legal academy and others in the organizational trenches, Ruth Bader Ginsburg—pioneering sex-discrimination strategist and litigator of the 1970s—had by 1993 morphed into an outmoded supporter of formal equality, safely ensconced behind the bench and detached from the fray.

Had the feminist leaders whom Marty consulted glimpsed his wife's clippings file on feminist legal perspectives and on gender issues during her years on the D.C. Circuit, they might have concluded that her commitment to substantive equality remained intact. Or perhaps not, considering the reputation she had acquired as a judge who prized relationships with conservative heavyweights such as Scalia and Bork. Marty could only agree with the economist John Kenneth Galbraith, who cynically observed, "Nothing is so admirable in politics as a short memory." More than a witty aphorism, he needed advice.

He found it only in former clients such as the New York financier and philanthropist Leon Levy, but more particularly in Stephen Hess and

William Josephson. Ruth's cousin Beth Amster had married Stephen Hess, a veteran staffer in the Eisenhower and Nixon administrations and an adviser to Presidents Ford and Carter. Now a research professor of media and public affairs at Georgetown University, Hess had superb contacts in the media as well as with former staffers with whom he had worked, especially Daniel Patrick Moynihan. Josephson, a retired partner at Fried, Frank, Harris, Shriver & Jacobson, the firm with which Marty was affiliated when the Ginsburgs moved to Washington, had been a longtime friend and partner of Sargent Shriver's and had headed Shriver's vice presidential campaign when he ran with George McGovern in 1972.

Marty also approached Senator Moynihan, chair of the Senate Finance Committee, in April. Moynihan admired Ruth's pioneering victories for gender equality. He had been the first to call when she was nominated to the D.C. Circuit with an offer to sponsor but had deferred to New York's senior senator, Jacob Javits. But Moynihan was not yet ready to commit. Marty then turned to Stuart Eizenstat, former chief domestic policy adviser for President Carter. The White House, Eizenstat counseled, would expect letters from legal academics, Ruth's other natural constituency. Wasting no time, Marty began by contacting people who had championed his wife's candidacy in the past: her former professors Gerald Gunther and Herbert Wechsler; Michael Sovern, the president of Columbia University; and distinguished members of the American Bar Association who supported her for the D.C. Court, such as Chesterfield Smith, and Norman Dorsen, with whom she had served as general counsel for the ACLU. Other familiar names were women in legal academe: Vivian Berger at Columbia, Herma Hill Kay at Berkeley, Barbara Babcock at Stanford, Sylvia Law at NYU, Patricia King, Sue Deller Ross, and Wendy Williams at Georgetown, and Nadine Taub at Rutgers. Also included were Kathleen Peratis and Janet Benshoof.

Benshoof was an apt choice. One of *The National Law Journal*'s "100 Most Influential Lawyers in America," a MacArthur fellow, and the founding director of the Center for Reproductive Law and Policy, she verified Ginsburg's long-standing commitment to reproductive freedom in an enthusiastic endorsement. Fourteen letters from members of the New York University Law School faculty, who had heard Ginsburg's Madison Lecture, conveyed their "distress that her remarks at NYU had been misconstrued as anti-choice and anti-women." Thirty-four letter writers in all during April and May from notables such as Ann Richards, governor of Texas, kept Ginsburg in the running—along with strong advice from Attorney General Janet Reno to choose a woman.

Then, at the end of April, Marty received an unexpected call from Moynihan. The senator explained that he had been on a flight to New York on Air Force One when asked by the president for a recommendation for the Supreme Court vacancy. Pressed for a response, Moynihan had provided one name: Ruth Bader Ginsburg. Reporting that Clinton had replied, " 'The women are against her,' " Moynihan told Marty, "You best take care of it," and ended the call.

Realizing that in his initial probe of feminist organizations he might have perceived indifference where there was actual opposition, Marty phoned the White House counsel, Bernard Nussbaum. An old acquaintance from New York legal circles and a Columbia and Harvard alumnus, Nussbaum was playing a major role in the selection process, along with his associates, Vince Foster and Ron Klain. Nussbaum affirmed that leaders of three women's groups, including NOW Legal Defense Fund and NARAL, had sent a joint letter to the White House on May 19, which he faxed to Marty. Claiming that they wanted to clarify their stance, they stated that "at this stage of the process, we have not taken any position in favor of or in opposition to any candidate." There were "a number of superbly qualified women who would be excellent candidates" for the Supreme Court. What the letter did not say was whether Ruth Bader Ginsburg, one of the most distinguished lawyers and judges of her generation, was among them.

Keenly aware that "Washington is a sieve," Marty set to work. Contacting Stephen Hess with the news that Ginsburg's name was not on the list, he sent along copies of her Madison Lecture. Hess circulated the information to influential members of the press, acknowledging that he was a relative by marriage. The *New York Times* legal commentator Anthony Lewis titled an op-ed article "How Not to Choose," identifying himself as neither a supporter nor an opponent of Ginsburg's selection. He defended the kind of intellectual exploration exhibited in the Madison Lecture. In particular, Lewis documented the "knee-jerk" reaction of women's groups who opposed a former advocate who had won many of the important cases against gender discrimination. That he found "depressing." Next came Jeffrey Rosen's unsolicited assessment of potential nominees in the May issue of *The New Republic,* ranking Ginsburg as the top candidate with the strongest support from both liberals and conservatives.

On May 21, Barbara Flagg, a professor of constitutional law at Washington University Law School and a former Ginsburg clerk with whom Marty had conferred, sent a four-page letter to Harriett Woods, the two-term president of the National Women's Political Caucus, who led the Clinton administration's Coalition for Women's Appointments. Urging the NWPC to support Ginsburg's nomination, Flagg wrote,

> I've heard expressed some concerns about her views on the constitutionally protected right of privacy, especially as it applies to homosexuals and to abortion. I'm a law professor, a lesbian, and a former law clerk to Judge Ginsburg. . . . I want to assure you that I'm completely comfortable with, and confident of, her views on both issues. . . . I believe that if she were [a justice], our rights would be more secure than they are today.

As letters supporting Ginsburg's nomination continued to pour into 1600 Pennsylvania Avenue, the White House sent word to Marty to back off. But in the critical final days when Moynihan notified Hess that his office was having difficulty tracking down Griswold's speech to the Supreme Court lauding Ginsburg's advocacy, it was Marty who supplied the name of the person at the Court who was able to provide Moynihan with a copy that the senator then rushed to the White House.

Among the many articles on Ginsburg appearing in the days following the nomination, *The Washington Post* devoted one to Marty's endeavors on his wife's behalf, as did *The New York Times* and *The National Law Journal.* Downplaying his role, Marty explained the circumstances that had led to his solicitation of letters. He claimed to have acted without Ruth's knowledge, although she surely had some awareness of the campaign. She apparently read Flagg's letter to Harriett Woods for factual accuracy. Friends and relatives of the couple confirmed that Marty's effort to smooth the way for his wife's advancement was characteristic of the couple and their relationship. Marty had always been Ruth's greatest fan, they noted. Hess added, "It's a great love story." That it was—and one with a feminist twist. No other campaign for a seat on the Court had been spearheaded by a male spouse.

With Ginsburg's having the highest possible rating from the American Bar Association and no real opposition in sight, the three-day confirmation process promised to be subdued in contrast with the firestorm of partisan opposition that had divided the Senate and done in Robert Bork in 1987. Still more sensational had been the turn of events two years earlier in the widely televised Clarence Thomas hearings following Anita Hill's shocking testimony about sexual harassment. In the wake of intense criticism following the Thomas-Hill confrontation, the Judiciary Committee, chaired by the Delaware Democrat Joseph Biden, had been enlarged to include two women, the Democratic senators Dianne Feinstein and Carol Moseley Braun. Nonetheless, the White House and Moynihan, as Senate sponsor, were taking no chances.

Upon Ginsburg's nomination, Moynihan phoned Robert A. Katzmann, a former graduate student and highly talented legal scholar. Would he be willing to serve pro bono as special counsel to help prepare Ginsburg for the hearings, the senator asked, and take her on a round of office visits to members of the Senate? When Katzmann promptly agreed, Moynihan added, "Make sure she is always allowed to be herself." The injunction proved unnecessary. As Judge Harry T. Edwards had discovered when they served together on the D.C. Circuit, "Ruth . . . is always the same in whatever setting you encounter her. She does not posture for family, friends, acquaintances, or onlookers." Katzmann could have added, "Or for senators." The nominee made clear she had no intention of distancing herself from the ACLU or any other prior affiliations.

Carefully briefed before each meeting on the interests and likely concerns of the senator she was about to meet, Ginsburg and "team Ginsburg" (Ron Klain and Joel Klein from the White House counsel's office and Katzmann) made their rounds on the Hill. Ginsburg, recognized by admiring tourists, especially women, was immediately surrounded—a point duly noted by senators, who began having a photographer present to capture the occasion. The gracious nominee agreed to attend an ice cream social at the Capitol sponsored by constituents of the Republican senator Charles Grassley. Moynihan, who was busy with chairing the Finance Committee, received daily reports from Katzmann. The senator would then have a private word with the appropriate colleague on the

floor of the Senate, reiterating his strong support of Ginsburg. Nor did
Marty relinquish his role as adviser. Also briefed daily by Katzmann, the
latter was much impressed by Marty's brilliance, "keen sense of the big
picture, attention to detail, and unerring judgment." Meanwhile, Klain,
Klein, and Katzmann arranged extensive tutorials for Ginsburg in the
Old Executive Office Building, next to the White House, where she
prepared for confirmation hearings, complete with mock questions from
particular senators.

When the Senate Judiciary Committee convened on July 20 for the
first day of the hearings, the nominee arrived early with family and
friends in tow, including Jane's two children, seven-year-old Paul and
three-year-old Clara, along with Stephen Wiesenfeld, her former plaintiff in the *Weinberger v. Wiesenfeld* case. Calm and confident, she sat
at the table with Senator Moynihan. Ginsburg began by introducing
her family, displaying Paul's construction book titled "My Grandma Is
Very, Very Special," followed by a brief statement on her early life, which
The New York Times's Neil Lewis dubbed her "Flatbush strategy." Stating that she was there "to be judged as a judge, not as an advocate,"

*Ginsburg making the rounds of key senators' offices with Senator Joe Biden
prior to the confirmation hearings in 1993.*

she promised to follow the model of the former justice Oliver Wendell Holmes, who counseled, " '[O]ne of the most sacred duties of a judge is not to read [her] convictions into [the Constitution].' " Judges must remember their place in society, Ginsburg continued, indicating that she would not steer the Court beyond public opinion.

When questioned, the nominee demonstrated that she had mastered the rules of the confirmation game. For three days, she candidly discussed issues on which she had written while avoiding answers to anything that could be construed as likely to come before the Court in the future. Questioned about abortion, she used the plight of Captain Susan Struck to emphasize that a woman's right to decide whether to carry to term or end a pregnancy is central to her "life, to her well-being and dignity." Endorsing the right to privacy, she explained that she would have preferred to see *Roe v. Wade* grounded in equal protection and the concept of individual autonomy embodied in due process rather than in due process alone. Asked whether under equal protection the father would have an equal say in the decision, she replied, "It is her body, her life and men, to that extent, are not similarly situated. They don't bear the child." On gender equality, she maintained that despite the progress made by the Court, it remains important to have a statement against sex discrimination as part of the Constitution, because the Court had left the degree of scrutiny open.

Anticipating future cases, she declined to answer questions on the constitutionality of school vouchers or the rights of homosexuals, other than to denounce discrimination on the basis of sexual orientation. When pressed by senators on the death penalty, she held firm: "I am not going to say to this committee that I will reject a position . . . in a case [where] I have never expressed an opinion. I have never ruled on a death penalty case." Responding that her own beliefs were not relevant, she asserted that she would be "scrupulous in applying the law on the basis of the Constitution." Yet she did not shy away from expressing her position on questions bearing on other aspects of criminal law, whether about mandatory sentences or about a defendant's *Miranda* rights. Nor did she hesitate to offer insights into her views about freedom of speech and religion, separation of powers, statutory interpretation, and enumerated rights.

In the three days of hearings, the nominee conveyed how she

approached problems and made decisions, but she refused to be ideologically pigeonholed. As Elena Kagan, who served as counsel to the Judiciary Committee, observed of Ginsburg's "preternaturally controlled testimony," she deployed a "pincer technique" that worked well. When she chose to sidestep a question, she declined to answer, saying the "question . . . may well be before the Court again . . . and it would be inappropriate for me to say anything more," or she would respond that the question was posed too abstractly and she would have to have a specific case complete with briefs and arguments. How such an ardent advocate turned into a judge's judge—Biden's initial question—was a conundrum she left unanswered. As the legal analyst Lyle Denniston noted, it was not because the committee had failed to press. Senator William Cohen, a Maine Republican, had put the Senate's problem with the nominee to her bluntly midway through the hearings: "There is some suspicion in some circles . . . that you are basically a political activist who's been hiding in the restrictive robes of an appellate judge, and that those restrictions will be cast aside when you don a much larger garment."

Yet for all the grousing about her "stingy" testimony, Biden's unanswered question, and speculation as to whether she might come under the sway of her more dynamic friend Justice Scalia, Ginsburg won the unanimous support of the Judiciary Committee. The Democratic-controlled Senate quickly followed with its endorsement, voting 96–3, making the confirmation an "official lovefest." It was a tribute to the nominee's superb performance, to Moynihan's diligent and vigorous sponsorship, and, not least, to a Senate in which judicial nominations had not yet succumbed to party polarization.

On August 10, in the East Room of the White House, a beaming Marty Ginsburg held the Bible for his wife's oath of office as President Clinton looked on contentedly. A small cohort of colleagues, family, and friends were also present. Moving on to the Supreme Court for the investiture ceremony followed by a reception, Ginsburg was formally presented to her eight colleagues for the first time.

Of the men before whom she had argued in the 1970s, only three remained: Blackmun, Stevens, and Rehnquist. Blackmun, now eighty-four and the Court's most liberal justice, was expected to retire soon. Stevens, whom Ginsburg remembered for his sharp questions in the *Goldfarb* case, was still noted for his judicial restraint, independent streak,

Ginsburg's swearing-in ceremony with Clinton, Marty Ginsburg, and Justice Rehnquist, August 10, 1993.

white hair, and familiar bow tie. He continued to consider himself a conservative in the traditional sense by adhering to deeply rooted precedents of the past. But the Court had moved so far to the right during his long tenure that he now belonged to the liberal wing. Rehnquist—the most conservative of the three—had high marks from colleagues for his skill in running the Court as well as for his intelligence and amiability.

Among the newer members awaiting Ginsburg was Rehnquist's Stanford Law School classmate Sandra Day O'Connor, with whom she had traveled to Paris as part of a delegation of jurists. Potter Stewart's replacement, O'Connor had an instinct for strategic compromise that made her the powerful swing vote on the Court. Straightforward, energetic, and a born centrist, she belonged to Ginsburg's generation of women graduates from elite law schools who had been penalized because of their sex in early job searches. Denied a job at a major law firm, she had turned first to private practice and then to electoral politics, becoming the first female majority leader of the Arizona Senate and then a state judge prior to her nomination by President Reagan to the Court in 1981. Through the choices she had made, O'Connor had become a symbol of women's progress. Yet she had a far less robust vision of gender equality than did Ginsburg.

In the meantime, however, the new arrival appreciated O'Connor's warm welcome and her promise to share information on the Court's elaborate rules of protocol and decorum as well as on the personality quirks of its other members. For example, the most recently confirmed justice has special duties at conference meetings. Answering the telephone, pouring coffee, and opening the door to take messages Ginsburg knew she could manage. But the thought of having to keep a count of the votes on hundreds of appeals for review left the newest justice with the same feeling of insecurity that she remembered when taking her first practice exam at Harvard.

Two of the justices, Scalia and Thomas, she already knew from the D.C. Circuit, though Thomas's time there had overlapped her tenure only briefly. Scalia, as combative and captivating as ever, shared her love of opera, good writing, and New Year's Eve celebrations. But relishing Nino's wit and intellect did not mean that she appreciated the personalizing of his dissents. Nor did she agree with his originalist understanding of the Constitution. To treat the founding document like a statute whose words carried the same meaning they did in 1787 in Philadelphia no more accorded with Ginsburg's view of an initially flawed but evolving document than it did with Thurgood Marshall's view of the Constitution. But as Scalia would later confess, he was a "fainthearted originalist" compared with Clarence Thomas. Thomas, unyielding in his originalism, was far more prepared to jettison long-established precedents if they conflicted with his research on the eighteenth-century meaning of the text.

That left Anthony Kennedy and David Souter. Kennedy, despite his conservative instincts, had an expansive vision of personal liberty that led him to vote against clergy-led prayer at school graduations and eventually to write the majority opinions overturning Texas's sodomy law and Kentucky's use of the death penalty for juvenile offenders. But he could also be mercurial. In his conservative mode, Kennedy might just as easily apply his lofty rhetoric to advance opinions that seemed to his more moderate colleagues "to repudiate . . . common sense." Souter, the New England embodiment of that virtue, appealed immediately to

Ginsburg holding hands with grandchildren Clara and Paul Spera. Behind her from left to right, George Spera, Jane, Marty, and James Ginsburg, after her 1993 swearing in.

Ginsburg with his intellect, dry wit, and gentle, helpful manner. She would also discover that he was a prolific reader and a great storyteller on those rare occasions when she could persuade the reclusive justice to attend social events. A Republican nominee to Brennan's seat who became quite friendly with the man he replaced, Souter had a healthy respect for adherence to precedent, including *Roe v. Wade*.

After taking a second oath of office, Ginsburg put on her black robe, which she, like O'Connor, would soften with lace jabots. She then took the chair assigned to her by order of seniority. In her address after her investiture, she said, "I am a judge born, raised, and proud of being a Jew. The demand for justice runs through the entirety of the Jewish tradition. I hope, in my years on the bench of the Supreme Court of the United States, I will have the strength and the courage to remain constant in the service of that demand."

. . .

DECISIONS ABOUT WHERE Ginsburg would locate her chambers and how she would furnish them would prove at least as revealing as her testimony before the Judiciary Committee. Eschewing a first-floor suite that Clarence Thomas was about to vacate, she chose instead a more remote location on the second floor, consolidating a set of rooms previously used by retired justices. Here she could have her clerks close at hand and avoid the noise of demonstrators. Rejecting as well the massive desks used by her colleagues, she opted for a smaller one that better suited a woman barely five feet and weighing less than a hundred pounds. Above the doorway into her office hung a framed injunction from the Torah that read, "Justice, justice you shall pursue." Airy draperies framed the windows. The art—all modern—also set the office apart. A Josef Albers painting on loan from the National Museum of American Art punctuated the light gray walls with its abstract design.

On the surrounding bookcases filled with legal volumes and a smaller collection of publications on women and gender, she carefully arranged autographed photographs of opera stars such as Luciano Pavarotti, as well as a few family photographs. A shot of her with Justice Marshall when the two were judging a moot court at Boalt Hall at Berkeley in 1978 evoked fond memories. Another photograph showed her with President Carter. Celia's picture had pride of place on the desk. Directly across from the desk near the bookcase stood a white poster board replica of the Statue of Liberty customized by young Paul for his grandmother. On the bookcase behind the sofa, she had placed another photograph— one of her son-in-law, George Spera, holding Paul as an infant. Visitors to Ginsburg's chambers familiar with her vision of shared work and family roles quickly grasped that the photograph conveyed a message beyond that of the usual grandmotherly pride.

Meanwhile, work piled up. The Court had scheduled forty-six cases for argument with which the justices needed to familiarize themselves before the beginning of the fall term on October 4. In addition, some 1,619 new appeals for review, along with jurisdictional statements that had accumulated over the summer recess, had to be dealt with in September. Preliminary memos prepared by clerks helped. But each memo still had to be read carefully by members of the Court and, when in doubt, checked against the original documents.

When the term officially began, the newest justice felt a bit more at home, thanks to O'Connor. A cohesive force on the Court and an open, outgoing personality, she assumed the "big sister" role that Eva Hanks had played those first years at Rutgers. The two women bonded, despite their different backgrounds, personalities, and appearances. Only three years apart in age, O'Connor and Ginsburg had former clerks in common and saw each other frequently at performances of the Washington National Opera. Both women had grown children, successful husbands, highly privileged addresses, and a zest for traveling. Neither hesitated to confront issues that she considered important.

Lawyers arguing before the Court addressed both as "Justice O'Connor." Even Ginsburg's longtime friends the Harvard Law School professor Laurence Tribe and the ACLU's Bruce Ennis proved guilty, prompting the National Association of Women Judges to present the two justices with T-shirts shortly after Ginsburg's confirmation. One read, "I'm Sandra, Not Ruth"; the other, "I'm Ruth, Not Sandra." Though the confusion would persist throughout the time they served together, Ginsburg took it in stride. Judge Patricia Wald had preceded her on the D.C. Circuit bench. In the early years, lawyers had often confused the two.

The Marble Palace, however, required some adjustments. The justices' robing room had to change. Despite O'Connor's presence for twelve years, only after Ginsburg joined the Court was a women's bathroom installed. In the meantime, as for every new member of the nation's high tribunal, there was much to learn.

CHAPTER 16

Mother of the Regiment

W hen the October term began, Ginsburg eagerly awaited her first assignment. As a new justice, she anticipated an uncontroversial, unanimous decision. But to her great dismay, it turned out to be an intricate, difficult case on which the Court divided 6–3. Turning to O'Connor for advice, Ruth was told, "Just do it and, if you can, circulate the draft before he makes the next set of assignments. Otherwise, you will risk receiving another tedious case." If the advice was blunt, the reward was sweet. At the bench announcement summarizing the case, O'Connor slipped a note to Ginsburg. It read, "This is your first opinion for the Court. It is a fine one. I look forward to many more." An appreciative Ginsburg subsequently called O'Connor "the most helpful big sister anyone could have." It was no surprise that the two-time Ginsburg clerk Hugh Baxter felt that Ruth considered her relationship with Sandra to be more important than those with the other justices.

Settling in at the Supreme Court required more than setting up one's chambers and learning the duties of its newest member. Every change in personnel alters the dynamics on the Court. Understanding those dynamics becomes crucial if newcomers are to secure specific advantages from opposing colleagues. Ginsburg would undertake the process, which normally takes three to four years, with predictable caution. Like O'Connor, Marty eased the transition to the extent that he could. His legendary warmth, wit, and culinary skills were on full display at Supreme Court events that included lunches for spouses, thereby reinforcing his wife's reputation for collegiality. However, the legal markers that Ginsburg would put down in these early years were distinctly her own, reflecting concerns dating back to her ACLU years.

. . .

THE STAKES WERE HIGH. Despite the continuing decline of the old New Deal order, the triumph of free market capitalism, and the numerical ascendency of Republican nominees, the Rehnquist Court had not become the conservative juggernaut hoped for by ideologues on the Right. Its rulings signaled enhanced protection of property rights, increasing resistance to federal regulation, lack of sympathy for the rights of the criminally accused, and suspicion of race-conscious policies and civil litigation to establish them. But the Court was too deeply divided, ideologically and jurisprudentially, for the chief justice to shape the outcome to his own conservative views, especially on key social issues.

Justices O'Connor, Kennedy, and especially Souter had proven to be much less predictable than their nominating presidents would have preferred. O'Connor's flexibility, honed on the politics and political bargaining of the Arizona legislature, led her to a fact-based, contextual legal reasoning that prioritized accommodation over hard-edged rules. She also had an uncanny sense of public opinion that led her toward the middle. Kennedy's expansive conception of individual liberty, moral reading of the Constitution, and willingness to accept the social, economic, and legal changes wrought by the New Deal made him seem ideologically inconsistent from the standpoint of those adhering to a conservative legal agenda. In addition, international travel exposed him to European constitution experts whose views likely had a liberalizing impact. And Souter often voted with the liberals precisely because the New Hampshire native was a traditionalist, and the tradition that mattered to him was stare decisis. Adherence to precedents like *Roe* and *Bakke* had meaning for Souter not because previous justices had always been correct but because adhering to precedent promoted stability and predictability. As the legal scholar Mark Tushnet pointed out, all three centrists were representative of the vanishing moderate wing of the Republican Party, not the modern party that is hostage to the Right.

Not surprisingly, it was Souter, O'Connor, and Kennedy who had written the sixty-one-page draft that preserved the right to an abortion—though with limitations—in *Planned Parenthood v. Casey,* with Stevens and Blackmun making the majority. Rehnquist had accepted the defeat

The official informal group photograph of the Supreme Court, December 3, 1993. Seated on the left is Justice John Paul Stevens and on the right is Justice Harry A. Blackmun. Standing, from left to right, Justices Clarence Thomas, Antonin Scalia, Chief Justice William II. Rehnquist, Justices Sandra Day O'Connor, Anthony M. Kennedy, David Souter, and Ruth Bader Ginsburg.

with equanimity, but not Scalia. Always willing to give *Roe* a public burial, he responded with an angry dissent in which he was joined by Thomas.

Finding a place for herself in this deeply divided tribunal, Ginsburg once again sought a place in the middle. An active interrogator in oral arguments, she voted as a moderate, kept her dissents and concurring opinions narrowly focused, and became part of the majority whenever possible. Instead of following the liberal lead of Blackmun and Stevens, she found herself more often agreeing with Souter and Kennedy. Indeed, in cases involving civil liberties and civil rights, Justice Souter had a more liberal record than did Ginsburg initially. On criminal justice matters, she joined seven justices in upholding California's death penalty statute—a matter she and the other justices did not take lightly. In fact, she required clerks to visit Lorton prison in nearby Fairfax County, Virginia, in order to impress upon them the weighty issues the death penalty involved.

She also voted to allow federal district judges to order that executions of death row inmates be delayed until they could obtain attorneys to prepare habeas corpus petitions. On cases involving gender, where she might have been expected to be especially assertive in concurring opinions, she simply voted with the majority—with one telling exception.

The case (*Harris v. Forklift,* 1993) dealt with sexual harassment. Teresa Harris, a manager at Forklift Systems Inc., sued her male manager for sexual harassment under Title VII. Harris argued that her manager's inappropriate, offensive conduct created a hostile, abusive work environment. Hinting at her interest in reconsidering the standard of scrutiny used for gender discrimination, Ginsburg quoted rulings to the effect that the Court must require "an exceedingly persuasive justification" for a gender-based classification and that "whether 'classifications based upon gender are inherently suspect'" remained "an open question."

Over the years, intermediate scrutiny had been laxly applied, leaving lower court judges—and the justices themselves until O'Connor came

Ginsburg and Sandra Day O'Connor.

on the Court—too much wiggle room. The result was inconsistency and uncertainty. But how to make the standard tighter?

Strict scrutiny would have once supplied the solution to making classifications by gender inherently suspect. But in the wake of *Bakke,* strict scrutiny had also become problematic. In the Reagan-Bush years, conservatives, angered by affirmative action since the mid-1970s, pushed hard to nullify the civil rights measures of the 1960s by insisting that strict scrutiny apply to *any* legislation that took race into account. Redistricting plans designed to comply with the Voting Rights Act (VRA) had been successfully challenged. By 1995, conservatives also had the necessary votes in an employment affirmative-action case, *Adarand Constructors v. Peña.* Adopting Powell's position in *Bakke,* a majority held that strict scrutiny was the proper standard to apply to *all* remedial race-based government programs—state and federal—seeking to compensate for past discrimination. The pragmatic O'Connor, writing for the majority, was willing to allow some racial classification, provided it could meet

When Ginsburg followed O'Connor's practice of wearing a jabot with her robe, Rehnquist, not to be outdone by the ladies, began to wear gold stripes on his robe as chief justice in 1995. John Roberts did not continue the practice when he assumed the role in 2005.

the strict scrutiny test—a position that cost her the votes of Rehnquist, Scalia, and Thomas. Indeed, the case dispelled the assumption that strict scrutiny was "strict in theory, but fatal in fact."

Ginsburg was appalled at the negative implications of the 5–4 vote in a nation where racial discrimination and inequality tenaciously persisted. She joined Justices Stevens, Souter, and Breyer in a vigorous dissent that questioned the majority's failure to apply a less rigorous standard to programs designed to overcome the effects of past or present policies barring equal opportunity. She also signed on to another dissent by Justice Souter. Then, issuing her own dissent, she diplomatically praised O'Connor's elaboration of strict scrutiny as not " 'fatal' for classifications burdening groups that have suffered discrimination in our society." "Properly," Ginsburg wrote, "a majority of the Court calls for a review that is searching, in order to ferret out classifications in reality malign, but masquerading as benign." This last sentence, so evocative of Ginsburg as advocate, provided a further signal that as justice she was still searching for an evolving standard of scrutiny in equal protection cases—one flexible enough to salvage civil rights gains, especially affirmative action, yet consistently rigorous enough to unmask gender discrimination that slipped through with intermediate scrutiny. She did not have to wait long.

A much-publicized equal protection battle at the Virginia Military Institute (VMI) was making its way through the federal courts in Virginia. Whether women could be denied admission at VMI seemed of marginal significance on the eve of the twenty-first century, when women faced widespread economic problems and an epidemic of sexual violence. Yet this idiosyncratic case exposed a variety of issues: the social construction of gender, the narrow-mindedness of the lower courts, and the psychological pains of social change. If all went well, *United States v. Virginia* could validate Ginsburg's career as an advocate.

. . .

IN 1996, the long-brewing dispute over the all-male admissions policy at VMI arrived on the Court docket. Wrapped in regional symbolism— the gender system of southern chivalry, military tradition, century-old male-bonding rituals, and Lost Cause defiance—*United States v. Virginia* seemed anachronistic. Most American colleges and universities across the country—public and private, civilian and military—had already embraced coeducation and modernized behavioral assumptions and curricula by 1976, as had Oxford and Cambridge Universities in England. The remaining publicly funded single-sex institutions in the United States invited challenge.

. . .

THE RATHER FORBIDDING five-story neo-Gothic gray stone structure, fronted by a statue of General Thomas Jonathan "Stonewall" Jackson, shares the small college town of Lexington, Virginia, with another institution associated with a famous Confederate general. Washington and Lee University, VMI's more gracious brick and white-columned counterpart, had once had General Robert E. Lee as its president. Since the founding of VMI in 1839, the institute has had as its mission the development of citizen-soldiers. Young men, dressed in military uniforms similar to those worn by pre–Civil War cadets, drilled and marched to and from class and were provided training in military sciences, the liberal arts, and engineering. No ordinary college, VMI also required cadets to endure the isolation of "the post," the lack of privacy of its "barracks," and the harsh marine boot-camp requirements associated with VMI's infamous "ratline."

Freshman "rats" (the "lowest form of life") were at the beck and call of largely unsupervised upperclassmen who could barge into a room or a communal shower at any time, shouting, insulting, or ordering push-ups for a perceived infraction of the rules. The purpose of the system was to strip members of their individuality, break them down, and inculcate new values of honor, duty, and discipline achieved through communal suffering.

After seven months, first-year students experienced their final ritual as "rats," known as "breakout." First, they crawled together across twenty-five to thirty yards of cold, deep mud, created by water supplied by the Lexington Fire Department. Then they were told to climb up a steep, slick hill in the coldest part of winter as upperclassmen kicked them back, smearing mud into their eyes, ears, and mouth. The exhausted "rats" were supposed to keep struggling upward until someone finally extended a helping hand or foot to enable them to reach the top.

Those who survived the system—the attrition rate in recent years was around 25 percent—might have loathed the place during their first year. But for a century and a half, each graduating class had emerged intensely loyal to the institution that made them "VMI men." For this extended band of brothers, loyalty meant keeping the institute the way it was when they first experienced it. As Superintendent Josiah Bunting III, who headed the institute from 1995 to 2003, stated, "We think the things we did in 1890 and 1930 are still valid today."

Despite VMI's intense dedication to tradition, some things had changed. Unable to resist federal pressure, VMI admitted African Americans in 1968. Integration, however, did not occur seamlessly. In 1972, black cadets threatened to be absent without leave rather than attend a ceremony at which freshmen annually reenacted the charge of VMI cadets in 1864 at New Market, Virginia.

In the reenactment, the cadets were supposed to charge under the Confederate flag, an icon of Lost Cause ideology, as the band played "Dixie." The symbolism was more than some of the African American cadets could tolerate. They could not ignore the tones of white southern superiority, the distortion of Civil War causes, and the erasure of slavery, all present in the ceremony. Students narrowly voted to eliminate the flag (which it turned out their predecessors had not actually carried). But the change was overruled by a unanimous vote of the Board of Visitors, twelve of whose seventeen members were required to be VMI alumni, according to Virginia law. By the mid-1970s, the administration had managed to phase out Confederate symbolism and make attendance voluntary at the New Market ceremony by holding it after graduation rather than in the fall.

There was one thing, however, that alumni, administrators, and cadets agreed must not change. The institution, identified with Generals Stonewall Jackson, George S. Patton Jr., and George C. Marshall, would cease to exist if women were admitted. Turning boys into men required male bonding forged under physical and mental duress in a hypermasculine world.

If women could succeed as rats, what would that say about the "superiority" of "VMI men"? Much would be said in court about VMI's honor code governing a gentleman's conduct toward a lady as well as the institute's vaunted system. But little would make it into the litigation record about the latter's seamy underside. That is, the degrading, obscene remarks attached to women and anything perceived as feminine. Women were "the other" against which boys differentiated themselves in the process of becoming "VMI men." Though few of the institute's recent graduates (about 15 percent) entered the military or achieved the renown of the generals that VMI so revered, alumni remained a prominent and well-heeled presence in male-dominated fields such as engineering, business, and politics. A "network of connections" worth having, especially in Virginia, these sons of VMI demonstrated their success and loyalty by providing their alma mater with the highest per capita college endowment in the nation.

That some young women would seek admittance was predictable in an era when *U.S. News & World Report* ranked the institute high on its list of publicly supported liberal arts colleges. Though integration of the service academies had not come easily, female graduates of West Point, Annapolis, and the Air Force Academy had been entering the military for nearly two decades. Some thirty thousand to forty thousand women had been deployed to Iraq for Operation Desert Storm in 1991.

In 1989, the inevitable happened. A high school graduate from northern Virginia—her name still withheld—filed a complaint with the Office of Civil Rights at the Justice Department. It landed on the desk of Judith Keith, a trial attorney. Keith had had her eye on VMI for some time. A letter of inquiry about VMI's admissions policy promptly went out from the litigation section with a request for justification. Sex-based discrimination, VMI was reminded, violated Title VI of the Civil Rights Act and the Fourteenth Amendment's equal protection clause.

Soon, a firestorm erupted across the Potomac. Governor Gerald L. Baliles and his African American successor, Douglas Wilder, who had been kept out of Virginia's law schools in the 1950s because of his race, found themselves in a difficult position. Both thought VMI should comply with the Constitution as well as Virginia's own antidiscrimination statute, yet neither wanted to lose the support of the politically powerful VMI network. Public opinion in Virginia was divided. So, too, was the opinion among VMI faculty, but not within the far-flung alumni family. Union forces marching down the Shenandoah Valley had nearly destroyed the institute in 1864, burning its buildings to the ground. To bow to the federal government again, sacrificing a proud tradition of the all-male enclave, was unthinkable. "Better Dead than Coed" was how *The Washington Post* characterized the position of the institute's new superintendent and its cadets.

With the dispute now national news, the VMI Foundation hired the former attorney general Griffin Bell in 1990 to consult with its legal team headed by the VMI alumnus Robert H. Patterson Jr. When Bell indicated that he thought the institute could withstand a suit from the government, Patterson and his team filed suit "to prevent federal encroachment seeking to enforce unnecessary conformity to the state support of higher education in Virginia" and to ask that VMI's admissions policy be declared constitutional.

Having chosen to fire the first shot in the litigation battle, VMI's lawyers also selected their battleground shrewdly. They filed in the western federal district court in Roanoke, just down the highway from Lexington, where the judge's record suggested a more favorable ruling than seemed likely in the district court in Arlington, situated across the Potomac from Washington.

Presented with VMI's suit, which was not accompanied by one from the commonwealth, Justice Department lawyers responded. The institute was a state-funded school; its admissions policy was exclusionary; there were no activities—including the shaved heads, hazing, and constant surveillance involved in the "rat" system—in which women were unable to participate fully; and there was no similar program for women students available elsewhere in the commonwealth. In sum, there was no "exceedingly persuasive justification" that served "important governmental objectives" for keeping women out—language lifted straight from O'Connor's majority opinion in *Mississippi University for Women v. Hogan.*

VMI lawyers saw Washington radicals imbued with "political correctness" out to destroy not only a venerable southern institution but also single-sex education across the nation. They had an ally in Judge Jackson L. Kiser, a Reagan nominee to the Western District Court of Virginia, who had a history of refusing to recognize gender discrimination as an actionable cause. Comparing VMI's battle against the federal government to that of cadets against Union forces at New Market, Judge Kiser concluded that VMI served an important state educational objective by allowing for diversity in the state's offerings. The all-male admissions policy did not deny women access to specific programs, because Virginia Polytechnic Institute offered engineering courses as well as optional military training to both sexes. To admit women to VMI, according to Judge Kiser, would "distract male students from their studies," dilute the strength of the "adversative" method, water down physical fitness requirements, require modification of the barracks to create greater privacy, and, by their very presence, make "the very experience" the students sought no longer available. "VMI truly marches to the beat of a different drummer," he wrote, "and I will permit it to continue to do so."

The Department of Justice appealed, but did not expect to find a sympathetic ear on the notoriously conservative Fourth Circuit. The court's panel, in a ruling written by Judge Paul V. Niemeyer, sent the case back to Judge Kiser, giving the state three options. VMI could admit women, VMI could go private, or the commonwealth could create a separate institution for women with a less demanding physical program. Judge Niemeyer had offered little clarification as to what this third option would entail, other than that stereotyping and generalized differences about each sex were to be avoided.

The choice made was to create the Virginia Women's Institute for Leadership (VWIL) at Mary Baldwin College. A private liberal arts college, Mary Baldwin had once catered to young women from Virginia's best families until coeducation drew them away from its manicured grounds.

As the plan proceeded, Mary Baldwin students threatened to strike because their college was being used to subvert women's equality. Faculty deplored any move toward militarization of the campus. And the two facilities were simply not equal in terms of what they could offer a young woman desiring a VMI education. But that was to be the subject of the next trial, which began in February 1994.

Homing in on the two areas for which VMI was known—the military and leadership in general—Justice Department lawyers elicited an admission from Mary Baldwin's dean that the school had no tradition of military leadership and had made no effort to discover what was necessary for the development of such a tradition. The only concession to military training would be two to four hours a week of ROTC. ROTC students would be bused thirty miles to VMI for drills and participation

338 · RUTH BADER GINSBURG

in the newly created, largely ceremonial Virginia Corps of Cadets. The Confidence Building Program would provide training in self-defense and self-assertiveness. The college did not offer engineering or physics courses or a B.S. degree. As would also become clear, proportionally fewer of Mary Baldwin's faculty had Ph.D.s than did VMI's, faculty salaries were in the lowest 20 percent in the country, and the SAT scores of students at Mary Baldwin were a hundred points lower than at VMI. Finally, the college's financial future was uncertain.

Nevertheless, Judge Kiser, whose task it was to review the constitutionality of proposed parallel single-sex programs, seemed untroubled by the differences. The Fourth Circuit's ruling, as he interpreted it, meant that the programs need only be parallel, not equal. More important, as VMI's expert witnesses testified, female students had different pedagogical needs and learning patterns. Neither Judge Kiser nor VMI's legal team denied that *some* women might succeed under VMI's system. What neither they nor the court of appeals considered was whether the institute's hypermasculine approach—which West Point had rejected— was the best form of pedagogy for creating future male leaders. VWIL, Judge Kiser decided, was what women needed. Differences between the two institutions, he ruled, "are justified pedagogically and are not based on stereotyping." "If VMI marches to the beat of the drum, then Mary Baldwin marches to the melody of a fife," he concluded, "and when the march is over, both will have arrived at the same destination."

Once the U.S. Court of Appeals for the Fourth Circuit affirmed the ruling, the reaction was predictable. VMI supporters rejoiced, as did Virginia's political establishment. The Justice Department appealed.

. . .

AFTER THE COURT TOOK the case, a new administration submitted a brief calling for strict scrutiny of all gender classifications. Solicitor General Drew Days had made the decision to ask for strict scrutiny and his assistant, Cornelia Pillard, prepared the brief. It was a clear invitation to Ginsburg. VMI lawyers suggested that the government's sudden reliance on strict scrutiny was "tantamount to admission that VMI and VWIL 'can and should survive intermediate scrutiny.'"

Amicus briefs followed. Women's legal advocacy organizations and their counterparts in the civil rights movement supported the government's position, as did twenty-six private women's colleges, who argued that a decision in favor of the government would not threaten their existence as single-sex institutions.

Mary Baldwin College countered with an amicus brief for the defendants, as did several small colleges who were said to have VMI alumni on their boards. A brief by seven distinguished educators testified to opportunities offered by VWIL and the benefits of single-sex education. Self-styled conservative, pro-family groups such as Phyllis Schlafly's Eagle Forum chimed in. Resurrecting charges against the ERA, they predicted that a win by the government with strict scrutiny would mean the integration of bathrooms and school athletic teams, government funding of abortions, and same-sex marriages.

The amicus brief that would generate the most attention from the press and the Court bore the names of eighteen active and retired high-ranking female military officers. Collectively, these women had commanded intercontinental ballistic missile launch sites and army posts and had been shot down and held prisoner in Iraq. With palpable anger and accuracy, they drew on their experience to take aim at each of VMI's assertions as to why women should not be admitted.

· · ·

WHEN MORNING DAWNED on January 17, 1996, the streets in front of the Supreme Court were lined with spectators hoping to get seats to hear oral arguments, along with the media for whom space had been reserved. Deputy Solicitor General Paul Bender, a former classmate of Ginsburg's at James Madison High School and a magna cum laude graduate of Harvard Law School, represented the government. Theodore B. Olson, a "titanic" figure in conservative legal circles, had taken the case for VMI and VWIL. Though both men were veteran litigators at the Supreme Court, neither would distinguish himself on this occasion when pressed with tough questions from the bench. While Scalia's questions encouraged Olson's argument about single-sex education, O'Connor and the other justices appeared unpersuaded. As O'Connor reminded Olson, "We have to decide . . . whether Virginia can provide single sex education to just one sex, to just men."

The most dramatic moment in the argument came when Scalia pressed Bender as to why the United States thought VWIL was an inadequate remedy. The Court fell silent as the deputy solicitor responded:

[W]hat if a State set up a State law school in 1839, all for men, because at that time only men could be lawyers, and over 150 years it developed an extremely adversative method of legal education, the toughest kind of Socratic teaching, tremendous time pressures in exams, tremendous combativeness by the faculty, tremendous competitiveness among the students, and developed a reputation for that. And it was a place that was known as hard to succeed at, and a third or so of the people flunked out in the first year, and graduates of that school who survived the process became known as expert leading lawyers and judges in that State and Nationwide. And then as women came into the legal profession and started to apply to the school, to ask it to change its admission policy, the school made a judgment that most women wouldn't be comfortable in this environment, and the faculty would have trouble cross examining them in the same way they cross examine [men], and other students would have difficulty relating to them in the same competitive way, and so it's better not to let women into the school. What we'll do is, we'll set up a new women's law school, and it won't have the tough Socratic method. [I]t will have a much warmer, a much more embracing environment, and it won't have large classes with a lot of pressure. [I]t will have seminars, and it won't have tough exams, it will have papers, and things like that [laughter] and every woman has to go to that law school, and no man can, and no woman can go to the old law school. I think we all understand that that is not by any means equal treatment of women with regard to their access to the legal profession.

Bender had made a telling analogy. The justices were old enough to remember that they had studied law at a time when stereotypes and biases against women in the legal profession were strong. The two women on the bench—O'Connor and Ginsburg—had compiled distinguished records at top law schools, only to be denied employment by legal firms upon graduation.

. . .

WHEN THE JUSTICES MET in conference, Rehnquist led off with a vote to uphold the lower courts. He tended to agree with the Fourth Circuit argument that women would be better served by an alternative to VMI. Stevens voted against upholding the lower courts, as did the others with the exception of Scalia, though Kennedy indicated he might rethink his vote. There was no discussion of strict scrutiny, which had clearly become a two-edged sword. Thomas, who had a son at VMI, had recused himself, making the initial vote against upholding the lower courts 6–2. Because the chief was in the minority, Stevens apparently assigned the opinion to O'Connor. This should be Ruth's, O'Connor insisted, turning it down.

Eager to begin, Ginsburg set her clerks to work, instructing them to funnel their material to Lisa Beattie, whose earlier assignments had been to go through all the briefs and take notes during the oral argument. Beattie, working off a memo from Ginsburg, would be responsible for pulling together a draft. The two agreed that the case was about gender equality in public institutions, not the future of single-sex education. There had been no effort on the part of the government lawyers to confront the question of whether it was constitutional for a state to fund an institution premised on objectionable gender norms, so neither would the opinion. Nor would there be any mention of strict scrutiny, to which O'Connor and Kennedy would object. Further, it created too many problems for affirmative action. Rather, the draft would rely heavily on Justice O'Connor's wording in *Hogan* and—to keep Justice Kennedy's vote—on Kennedy's concurring opinion in *J.E.B. v. Alabama,* in which he stated that the Court's earlier cases had created "a strong presumption that gender classifications are invalid." Justice Stevens's concurring opinion in *Califano v. Goldfarb,* in which he condemned reliance on overly broad generalizations about the sexes, would also be cited. She would call instead for "skeptical" scrutiny of official actions denying rights and opportunities based on sex.

After her much-reworked draft circulated, Kennedy tentatively approved but also offered suggestions for changes. In her efforts to accommodate her colleagues, Ginsburg later recalled, she produced about fifteen drafts. Several "had an ending that I loved but we changed it because Justice Kennedy didn't like it." To her great delight, Rehnquist decided to change his vote and write a concurrence, leaving Scalia a very angry lone dissenter.

. . .

ON JUNE 26, 1996, Ginsburg read aloud to a packed courtroom portions of an opinion that would be termed "one of the Court's most important sex discrimination cases in years." Recognizing VMI's impressive record in producing leaders, she readily acknowledged that most women would not choose VMI's spartan barracks, constant surveillance, and punishing "adversative" system. But that was beside the point. "Generalizations about 'the way women are,' estimates of what is appropriate for *most women,* no longer justify denying opportunity to women whose talent and capacity place them outside the average description." Rights, as the Court had previously made clear, inhere in the individual, not the group. In the two years preceding the lawsuit, she noted, VMI had received, but not responded to, inquiries from 347 women. "Women seeking and fit for a VMI-quality education cannot be offered anything less, under the Commonwealth's obligation to afford them genuinely equal protection." "However 'liberally' this plan serves the Commonwealth's sons," she continued, "it makes no provision whatever for her daughters."

The state's alternative program at Mary Baldwin could be valuable for those students seeking its program, she acknowledged. But she dismissed the lower court's view that the VWIL and VMI programs were "sufficiently comparable" to satisfy equal protection requirements. Virginia had created a no more constitutionally acceptable alternative to VMI than had Texas when in 1946 it set up a separate school, which consisted of a couple of basement rooms, for Heman Marion Sweatt and other black law students to avoid admitting them to the flagship Austin campus. The tangible differences between VMI and VWIL in funding, military training, course offerings, and faculty salaries were not the issue. Reclaiming the Court's reasoning in *Sweatt v. Painter* (1950), Ginsburg emphasized,

More important than the tangible features . . . are "those qualities which are incapable of objective measurement but which make for greatness" in a school, including "reputation of the faculty, experience of the administration, position and influence of the alumni, standing in the community, traditions and prestige." Facing the marked differences reported in the *Sweatt* opinion, the Court unanimously ruled that Texas had not shown "substantial equality in the [separate] educational opportunities" the State offered.

Virginia's remedy, Ginsburg concluded, created "a 'pale shadow' " of VMI and "affords no cure at all for the opportunities and advantages withheld from women who want a VMI education and can make the grade." The concern, expressed by the Fourth Circuit, that it would be destructive to place men and women together at VMI reflected the same "ancient and familiar fear" that had kept women out of medicine, law, and other professions in the past. Noting that women had graduated at the top of their classes at West Point and Annapolis and that many were serving successfully in the military, she indicated that Virginia's fear for the future of VMI "may not be solidly grounded."

Her most pointed rebuke to the Fourth Circuit concerned its failure to correctly apply the standard requiring the state to demonstrate "an exceedingly persuasive justification" for an official action that treats women and men differently. Ginsburg traced the development of the standard back from *Reed* through *Craig* to *Mississippi University for Women v. Hogan,* and more recently *J.E.B. v. Alabama*. Under "today's skeptical scrutiny," she wrote, the justification for a sex-based classification must be "genuine, not hypothesized or invented *post hoc* in response to litigation. And it must not rely on overbroad generalizations about the different talents, capacities, or preferences of males and females." Nor could it substitute a standard such as "sufficiently comparable" of its own invention.

Perhaps most significant of her contributions was her clarification of how states may regulate "inherent differences" between men and women. They may do so in ways that are designed to include groups long denied full citizenship stature on equal terms in the life of the nation, but they may not do so in ways that perpetuate stereotyping and discrimination.

Rehnquist, in his concurrence, questioned Ginsburg's use of "skeptical scrutiny," fearing that a new verbal formulation would introduce an element of uncertainty into sex-discrimination analysis. Scalia, in a forty-page dissent, dismissed the majority interpretation of the equal protection clause as "invented," scolded his colleagues for shutting down VMI (which they did not), and predicted that public single-sex education nationwide was "functionally dead."

Ginsburg, however, had been exceedingly careful in crafting her opinion to make clear that the decision did not affect private single-sex schools. "Single-sex education," she wrote, "affords pedagogical benefits to at least some students." She went to great lengths to place Virginia's record of discrimination in the long historical narrative of women's rights litigation and women's history. Taking full advantage of the absurdity of earlier objections advanced for denying women admission to traditionally male educational institutions, she made clear that Virginia's claims were no more persuasive. "Sex classifications," she wrote, "may be used to compensate women 'for particular economic disabilities [they have] suffered,' . . . to 'promot[e] equal employment opportunity,'" and "to advance full development . . . of our Nation's people. But such classifications may not be used, as they once were, . . . to create or perpetuate the legal, social, and economic inferiority of women."

. . .

HAILED BY ADVOCATES of women's equality and bemoaned by supporters of VMI, the decision created a cascade of commentary in the press. Legal scholars parsed the meaning of "skeptical scrutiny." Did it ratchet up the standard of scrutiny to strict scrutiny, as the government had requested? Or was it just intermediate scrutiny by another name? How would the lower courts interpret it? Would the Court itself stick to a more muscular standard? For VMI, there was another question that the majority opinion did not address: What changes must it make to attract a critical mass of women?

One thing was indisputable. The decision, vintage Ginsburg, brimmed with precedents she had done so much to establish and that O'Connor had preserved. Marty cut out *The Washington Post*'s banner headline: "Supreme Court Invalidates Exclusion of Women by VMI." Framed, it hung outside the door of his office at Georgetown Law Center for years. *United States v. Virginia* changed the standard of review, admitted women to a bastion of sexism, and restored Ginsburg to the feminist pantheon, noted reviewers, who acclaimed her position. As one

Megan Smith going through the "ratline" at the Virginia Military Institute, 1998.

astute commentator noted, it "marked Justice Ginsburg's apotheosis, perhaps even more than her appointment."

Ginsburg readily acknowledged her delight. The Court's ruling, she believed, had achieved all that the Equal Rights Amendment would have. Moreover, it was precisely the decision she had wanted for her former client Susan Vorchheimer. "To me, it was winning the *Vorchheimer* case twenty years later." Though Philadelphia's (all-male) Central High was not a military school, the principle was the same. What she did not reveal was that her opinion echoed a decision she had made for herself at Cornell. When Marty contemplated applying to the male-only Harvard Business School, she had rejected what was then the Business School's pale shadow—the newly created Management Training Program at Radcliffe. Her reasoning at the time had been strikingly similar to that of the justices in *Sweatt*. The two institutions were not comparable in faculty, prestige, and alumni networks.

Aside from deferred gratification, what Ginsburg cherished most from the decision was a letter from a VMI alumnus. "I graduated from VMI in 1967," he wrote, "and I know a few young women today who are physically, intellectually, and emotionally tougher than I was over thirty years ago. If I could make it then, I know they can make it today. No need to thank you and the other justices who made VMI an open insti-

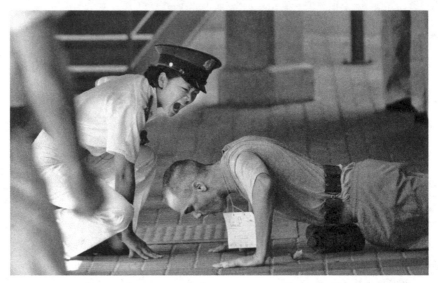

*Mia Utz, officer at the Virginia Military Institute, yelling at a "rat" during the
"ratline," 1998.*

tution." He continued, "You were only doing what obviously needed to
be done, but thank you none the less." Then, on April 13, 1997, he wrote
again and included a gift—a pin given at graduation to the mothers of
the class of 1967. "The pin enclosed was my mother's," he explained,
"she is dead now. We wanted you to have it. In an abstract way, you will
be 'mother' of VMI's first and succeeding women graduates. This pin
makes you an adjunct member of the VMI family. I am sure it would
have made my mother proud to know it is in your possession."

It was a gift the justice would treasure. As "mother" of VMI's first
coed class to graduate in 2001, she could take great pride in young women
like Erin Claunch and Kendra Russell. By the end of her third year
at VMI, Claunch ranked 15th academically in her class of 298, passed
the physical fitness test with a score better than the average for men,
and earned the rank of brigade commander, the second-highest honor a
cadet could achieve.

While access to VMI constituted a first step, it was perhaps a smaller
step than it was perceived to be at the time. Nothing was said in the
opinion about a method predicated on hypermasculine traditions, old
rituals and practices, and how it actively *constructed* female inferiority.
Indeed, Ginsburg almost seemed to be taking the institute's standards

at face value. "Kept away from the pressures, hazards, and psychological bonding characteristic of VMI's adversative training," she wrote, "VWIL students will not know the 'feeling of tremendous accomplishment' commonly experienced by VMI's successful cadets." Kendra Russell, like Erin Claunch, experienced such feelings of accomplishment. Yet as Russell aptly observed on graduation day, "This is still very much a boys' locker room."

VMI's determination to make as few adjustments as possible in making the transition to coeducation helps to explain the aptness of Russell's comment. Only because the institute's financial viability depended on the 30 percent of the budget coming from state funds did the Board of Visitors finally decide to admit women—and then by a one-vote margin. Many students and alumni remained intensely hostile to the slightest change that could be perceived as "feminizing" the institution, with some even resorting to hate mail.

But the fault also lay with the Justice Department. Its lawyers had never questioned the value of the "adversative" method or the assumptions of female inferiority embedded within it. Rather, the government's strategy from the beginning had been to challenge VMI's claim that men and women were so different the admission of women would change the unique benefits of the school. Tying VMI's rejection of women to false stereotypes addressed part of the problem. But it also obscured the other part—the way the institute's pedagogy degraded women. Passing remarks of some of the justices during oral argument implied that they were not die-hard believers in VMI's "adversative" methodology. Yet they were never fully exposed to its seamier side, given the narrowness of the argument.

VMI's failure to use the occasion to re-create the rigors of the institute in ways that would best train leaders for contemporary society thus surprised no one. Worse still, as Cornelia Pillard noted, "the way that the litigation anointed VMI's 'adversative' approach as valuable and special—which even the Justice Department and Supreme Court echoed rather than challenged—make it that much harder for VMI women to seek appropriate responsiveness from VMI now that it is their school, too."

Implicit in the critique of the Court validation of VMI's approach is criticism of Ginsburg that harked back to condemnation of equality tenets as access only. In writing her majority opinion, she had clearly made a number of strategic calculations and—in the course of writing fifteen drafts—concessions. There is no doubt that she understood the limitations of access and the need for institutional change. But given the constraints of the litigation record, she opted to place her faith in VMI women to bring about positive adjustments, just as the presence of feisty young women had done in non-supportive law schools in the 1960s. What clearly mattered most was keeping her majority and the tougher standard of scrutiny that she had articulated. *If* carefully applied in future equal protection cases involving new areas of the law, skeptical scrutiny *could* benefit far larger numbers of women across the United States.

But whether the Court would actually stick to the standard it had just endorsed was a gamble. The two women on the Court certainly hoped so. Time would tell.

· CHAPTER 17 ·

"I Cannot Agree"

The new century did not begin auspiciously for the Ginsburgs. Ruth was ill in the summer of 1999 when the couple left the island of Crete, where they had been teaching. Subsequently diagnosed with colorectal cancer, she recovered from surgery sufficiently to be back at the Court for the opening of the October term. But the dread disease, which had taken Celia's life and nearly cut short Marty's, was taken seriously in the Ginsburg family.

Radiation and extensive chemotherapy followed, reducing the weight of the diminutive Justice, who at her heftiest had barely weighed a hundred pounds, to the point that she looked as though a strong breeze might lift her aloft. While Marty prepared dishes that would tempt his wife's palate, Chief Justice Rehnquist eased her workload. Justice O'Connor, who had successfully battled breast cancer during the 1988–89 term, offered welcome advice on scheduling chemotherapy so that the worst side effects would not coincide with days she needed to be at Court. The advice, plus her own fierce determination to carry on, enabled Ginsburg to attend every single conference meeting during her painful chemotherapy regime. Coping with the nausea, other discomfort, and extensive fatigue sufficiently to be present at Court was a particular point of pride.

By November, she could look forward to the unveiling of her portrait that would hang in the Supreme Court. At least this was a much better likeness than the severe expression captured in the one for Columbia Law School, which she had asked to be taken down and stored. The ceremony, held at the D.C. Court of Appeals, would also provide a reunion with all her clerks as well as friends who had been asked to speak at the ceremony. Eschewing the elegant outfits Marty helped choose for their many embassy dinners as well as her usual well-tailored suits, she chose clothes more suitable for a patient recovering from surgery—a loose-fitting jumper and flat Mary Jane shoes.

With her good friend and former colleague Judge Harry Edwards presiding, the event began with witty and affectionate words from a man who identified himself as the person least likely to be expected to be paying tribute to Ruth Bader Ginsburg. "She's never going to make me a feminist," Scalia proclaimed. But he went on to praise the colleague who he had often claimed would be the one person he would want as company if he were marooned on a desert island. The wit and charm of his tribute proved a hard act to follow. Deborah Merritt spoke warmly and effectively for the many clerks seated in the front rows across the middle section of the court. Ruth's longtime friend and co-author Herma Hill Kay from Berkeley ably covered Ginsburg's career.

And Kathleen Peratis, a devoted ally during the ACLU years, spoke revealingly of the woman who spearheaded the Women's Rights Project and the deep ethical imprint that Judaism had left upon her. Though the honoree would later quibble about Peratis's focus on Judaism's influence, the celebration had lifted her spirits. But the same could not be said of developments on the equality front.

. . .

RACIAL AND GENDER JUSTICE, long linked, had inevitably become a hit-and-miss affair since the rightward-bound mid-1970s. It was then the Court ruled that to establish an equal protection violation, there had to be proof that the state acted with discriminatory *intent* in statutes that appeared on the surface to be race or gender neutral. "The result for women," noted a distinguished legal scholar, "has been to leave vast chasms of gender inequality unredressed in areas that 'ha[ve] always been' state law." Two new legislative initiatives, enacted during the Clinton years, had been designed to lift barriers that prevented women from competing as equals. The second now hung in jeopardy.

Passage of the Violence Against Women Act, or VAWA as it was commonly called, had not come easily. Sexual violence, whether in the form of rape, wife beating, or incest, had been transformed from a matter of private shame to an issue of public policy by radical feminists in the 1970s. Mustering evidence that these were not isolated acts attributable to lust or intoxication, younger feminists identified them for what they were—assaultive acts of power that crossed markers of nation, class, race, and ethnicity. They needed to be taken seriously. But despite their efforts, enduring cultural attitudes proved hard to change. By the end of the 1980s, U.S. statistics staggered. Every fifteen seconds, a woman was beaten by her husband or boyfriend. Every six minutes, a woman was forcibly raped. One-fifth to one-half of American women had been sexually abused as children, most by an older male relative. One out of every eight adult women in the United States—at least 12.1 million—had been a victim of forcible rape. Female college students remained especially vulnerable. Even in 2014, one of every four was sexually attacked before graduating, and one in seven raped—statistics that showed no sign of diminishing. Since 1974, the rate for rapes had risen nearly four times faster than the national crime rate. And despite changes in rape law in the 1970s and 1980s, reporting, arrest, and conviction rates showed no detectable improvement. The rate for assault and other violent crimes against women also rose dramatically, while the rate for the same crimes against men dropped. Similarly, the murder rate for women aged sixty-five or older had climbed by 10 percent, while it fell in the same age-group for men by 4 percent.

Though men and boys were also victims of sexual violence, the data indicated that women and girls were targets for certain types of violence *precisely because of their sex.* Millions of women, therefore, lacked the physical security and freedom to compete as equals in an economy in which they could expect to be wage earners and often single parents for much of their adult lives.

· · ·

FOR SENATOR JOSEPH BIDEN, the issue had become personal. His wife, Jill, took courses for her graduate degree at night. When he suggested that she park in an illegal space because it was safer, she exploded with frustration at the way women's lives are governed by fear of violence. Soon after, a man with a hunting rifle walked into a university classroom in Montreal, divided the students by sex, yelled that the women were all "a bunch of feminists," and killed fourteen of them. Aware of the senator's feelings about such needless tragedies, Ron Klain, who had moved from the White House counsel's office to become Biden's chief aide, handed the senator an article from the *Los Angeles Times* connecting the Montreal murder of "feminists" to a gap in U.S. law. Federal law tracking hate crimes targeted only a "victim's race, ethnicity, religion, or sexual orientation." Thus, "if a woman is beaten, raped or killed because she is a woman, this is not considered a crime of hate"—a legal loophole "welcome to no one but the misogynist."

Impressed, Biden promptly sent another young staff lawyer, Victoria Nourse, to the Library of Congress to figure out what Congress could do. Start by looking at the issue of marital rape, he instructed, a social problem he had tried unsuccessfully to address a decade earlier. Nourse returned with information that shocked them both. Some states, including Delaware, had extended the marital-rape exemption to become a date-rape exemption, downgrading a "rape charge if a woman was a man's 'voluntary social companion.'" Biden was even more troubled by this modification in policy, because he and his wife were raising a young daughter in Delaware. Convinced that state action had proven inadequate, Biden reached out to feminist groups and NOW's lead lawyer,

Senator Joseph Biden formulating a bill to make violence against women a federal offense, 1994.

Sally Goldfarb, who in turn called Catharine MacKinnon. "If Biden wants to do something for women," MacKinnon responded, "he should recognize rape and battering as federal sex-discrimination claims."

After weeks of hard work, Nourse, following MacKinnon's instructions, found inspiration in the Civil Rights Acts of 1871 and 1875. Designed to reduce Klan violence and civil rights violations against newly freed slaves, both statutes empowered the federal government to prosecute individuals who infringed on the rights of others. Though much of the legislation had been subsequently gutted by a reactionary Court, one part of the 1871 act survived: giving injured parties the right to sue violators in federal court. Nourse had her key. She could target gender-motivated violence by giving victims the right to sue their attackers for damages in civil court.

· · ·

THE FIRST VAWA BILL CAME to the Senate on June 19, 1990, with the overwhelming endorsement of attorneys general from states across the Union. For Biden and his staff, the great surprise came not when grateful women stopped him on the street to tell him their stories but when his civil rights initiative received almost immediate resistance from the chief justice. As the head of the federal court system, Rehnquist had ordered a financial impact study, assessing the potential cost of new legislation. The study, which had assumed that a shockingly high rate of women would sue, claimed that more than fourteen thousand new cases would be added to the federal caseload at a cost estimated to be three times greater than the costs for cases brought under the Civil Rights Act of 1991.

Rehnquist further tipped his hand in 1991, appointing a gender-balanced committee of four judges to assess the bill and report to the Judicial Conference of the United States, which he, as chief justice, chaired. After conferring with Nourse and Biden, the committee reported that they would work together to tighten the civil rights portion of a bill so as to secure a more realistic impact assessment. But that was apparently not what Rehnquist wanted. According to Judge John F. Gerry, the committee was to convince Congress of the bill's negative impact on the caseload of the federal courts. Judge Gerry's personal view was that with VAWA's passage the federal courts would be turned into domestic violence courts, creating "chaos."

Such a forecast seemed widely at odds with Biden's reassurances to the committee. But Judge Gerry's understanding of Rehnquist's intent proved correct. The chief, in his year-end report to the Judicial Conference, opposed any congressional addition of work to his courts unless it was "critical to meeting important national interests." Combating a continuing pattern of violence against women apparently did not qualify. In a speech to the American Bar Association, Rehnquist acknowledged that he was lobbying Congress against passage of VAWA. He urged the ABA to reconsider the measure as well.

If Rehnquist could sway the ABA, Biden worried that congressional support for VAWA might evaporate. Trying to interpret an intent (that federal courts would replace state courts as adjudicators of domestic relations cases) when it had been directly rejected by a bill's sponsor was bad enough in Biden's view. To do so before full debate had even occurred in both houses of Congress struck the senator as totally unacceptable.

Never known for his reticence, Biden fired back before the House Subcommittee on Crime and Criminal Justice, directly accusing Rehnquist of misreading the civil rights section as an invitation for women to flood the court with suits. Biden protested, "You cannot establish a cause of action under this bill by saying that, 'I am a woman; I have a bruise; ergo, I have a civil rights claim'—as the Chief Justice would lead you to believe." The senator then rebutted the claim that the civil rights remedy in Title III of the bill covered random crimes, pointing out that it applied only to those motivated by gender.

Looking for a counterweight, Goldfarb and her coalition leaders turned to the National Association of Women Judges. Its members, a moderate lot, were keenly aware of sexism and the problem of domestic and sexual violence. Goldfarb found the perfect liaison in Lynn Hecht Schafran, then a top official at Legal Momentum, NOW's legal arm, and a Ginsburg protégée with distinguished credentials. When prominent female judges failed to persuade the ABA's Judicial Administration Division not to oppose VAWA, Schafran knew just the woman on the ABA's Board of Governors who might be able to save the day.

Brooksley Born, a staunch feminist and partner at Arnold & Porter, was long familiar with ABA politics. After hearing her fellow board members (all men) assent to the Administrative Division's report opposing VAWA, she succeeded in getting the matter before the full ABA

House of Delegates. She explained that if the House passed the Administrative Division's resolution, the ABA would be on record as opposing civil rights legislation for the first time. Violence against women is endemic, she continued. The ABA must not urge the federal courts to close their doors. Her strategic plea carried the day.

Even with this small triumph in the ABA, the heavily male Judicial Conference remained opposed. Fortuitously, the gender-based committee had a new chair, Judge Stanley Marcus. Marcus, a Harvard Law graduate and a former Florida prosecutor, received a thorough and efficient briefing on the bill from Judge Mary Schroeder, who sat on the Ninth Circuit Court of Appeals, and the law professor Judith Resnik. Marcus and Schroeder worked with Nourse and Goldfarb to reshape the civil rights provision in ways that would assure the Judicial Conference that federal courts would not be overburdened. Fearful that the phrase "gender-based crime of violence" was too broad, they returned at MacKinnon's urging to "invidiously discriminatory animus," a phrase in the 1871 Ku Klux Klan Act that allowed the now-freed slaves to sue white attackers for violating their civil rights *if* they could show an attack was motivated by "some racial, or perhaps otherwise class-based, invidiously discriminatory animus." Using "animus" (meaning extreme prejudice) provided a way of linking VAWA to the civil rights language of the Reconstruction era and the promise of the Fourteenth Amendment.

. . .

AFTER NINE HEARINGS, a number of Senate Judiciary Committee investigative reports, and unwanted judicial interventions in what was the legislature's prerogative, the bill was reintroduced in the Senate in 1994. It made rape and domestic abuse a federal crime. It also made hundreds of millions of dollars available to local governments to help enforce their own sexual assault laws, as well as to aid victims. The provision, titled "Civil Rights for Women," allowed victims (male as well as female) of gender-motivated violence to sue their attackers in federal court for monetary damages, including punitive damages, irrespective of whether the offense had resulted in criminal charges, prosecution, or conviction. The bill also stipulated that federal courts had no jurisdiction over divorce or domestic relations cases—a matter on which Biden had assured critics from the outset. Relief under the civil rights remedy would be available *only* to those who were victims of a felony under state or federal law, not to all victims of sex-based violence—a significant limitation. And the plaintiff had to prove that the crime was due, at least in part, to animus based on gender (the social meaning of sex).

. . .

FOR CHRISTY BRZONKALA, VAWA's passage in September 1994 seemed opportune. Just eighteen, she arrived at Virginia Tech that fall. She had scarcely finished freshman orientation when two members of the varsity football team, Antonio Morrison and James Crawford, entered her dormitory and, when she declined their advances, pinned her down and raped her—Morrison twice, Crawford once. Feeling as if "her soul" had been "torn out," Brzonkala stopped attending classes and attempted suicide. While a Virginia Tech–licensed psychiatrist gave her antidepressants, no representative from the university had made more than a cursory inquiry as to why she needed treatment. Withdrawing from school, she made no charges until she returned to campus in early 1995. At a disciplinary hearing, Morrison admitted to sexual contact despite Brzonkala's objections. The university's Judicial Committee found Morrison, who boasted in the dormitory dining room that he "liked to get girls drunk so he could fuck the shit out of them," guilty of sexual assault and suspended him for two semesters. Crawford was acquitted. But for Brzonkala, the ordeal was far from over.

Morrison announced that he intended to challenge the verdict, in part because the Sexual Assault Policy had not been included in the 1994 Student Handbook. The university had already successfully defended itself in a similar case. Nevertheless, two female employees made the four-hour drive to Brzonkala's home that summer to convince her that it was technically necessary to have a hearing under the existing Abusive Conduct Policy. Student witnesses supporting Brzonkala's testimony had scattered over summer break. Further complicating matters, the university denied her access to the audiotape and other records while granting Morrison's lawyers full access.

Again sentenced to two semesters of suspension for misconduct, now described as "use of abusive language," Morrison appealed to higher officials at Virginia Tech who failed to notify Brzonkala. The provost found Morrison's sentence "excessive" compared with other cases and annulled it, thereby allowing him to return to campus in time for football season on a full athletic scholarship, as his coaches hoped. (Virginia Tech's football team ranked eighth in the country in 1995.) When Brzonkala learned in the newspaper of Morrison's plan to return, she again withdrew.

At no point in these proceedings did the university report Brzonkala's charges to the police. Rape, in fact, was the only violent felony that Virginia Tech did not automatically report. Although Brzonkala ultimately filed charges against Morrison and Crawford, the Montgomery County grand jury did not indict the two men. So in December 1995, Brzonkala, who had been recruited to the university as a student athlete, sued Virginia Tech for sex-based discrimination under Title IX of the Education Act, which mandated equal treatment in educational institutions receiving federal funds, including college athletics. She also sued Morrison and Crawford under VAWA.

. . .

BOTH SUITS, filed by lawyers from feminist groups and the Justice Department in federal district court in Roanoke, landed on the desk of Judge Jackson L. Kiser. The conservative states' rights champion, bent for so long on preserving VMI for men, would now rule on *Brzonkala*. True to form, Judge Kiser dismissed the suit against the university. The fact that Virginia Tech wanted Morrison back on its winning football team was not evidence of gender discrimination, he ruled. Nor was the university's failure to notify the police of the reported rape. Sensitivity to the feelings of rape victims, rather than bias, appeared to Judge Kiser to be the more appropriate explanation for Virginia Tech's inaction. Rejecting Brzonkala's claim that the institutional environment was a hostile one for her, Kiser seemed to suggest that she only feared that the environment "might become hostile in the future." As he read her complaint, no discrimination on the basis of sex had even been alleged.

However, when he turned to Brzonkala's case against Morrison and Crawford, Judge Kiser was surprised. Taking into account Morrison's lack of prior knowledge of the victim and his disparaging comment that she had better have no "fucking diseases," Kiser ruled that the assault had been a form of gang rape. It fit the wording of the civil rights provision of VAWA.

But then he turned to the constitutionality of the statute. He first cited *United States v. Lopez* (1995), a case in which the Court ruled that Alfonso Lopez Jr., who had walked into his San Antonio high school carrying a concealed weapon, could not be convicted under the Gun-Free School Zones Act, because Congress lacked authority for passage of the act under the commerce clause. Following the Court's reasoning in *Lopez,* Judge Kiser held that if a law banning firearms in a school zone went beyond Congress's power to regulate commerce, then surely rape was beyond the scope of the commerce clause as well. Nor, according to Kiser, could VAWA be sustained under congressional power to enforce the Fourteenth Amendment after a recent (1997) ruling in *City of Boerne v. Flores* that introduced a new test for deciding whether Congress had exceeded its Section 5 power to enforce the equal protection clause. Her case dismissed without trial, Brzonkala's pleas for justice had been denied.

Her lawyers appealed, as did lawyers for Morrison and Crawford. Briefs to the Fourth Circuit supporting appeals signaled the forces arrayed on both sides. Among those challenging the constitutionality of VAWA were the National Association of Criminal Defense Lawyers, conservative legal groups such as the Claremont Institute, the Center for Individual Rights, Phyllis Schlafly's Eagle Forum Legal Defense Fund, and the libertarian Cato Institute. VAWA supporters submitting briefs included the U.S. solicitor general, attorneys general of thirty-six states and Puerto Rico, Senator Biden, liberal legal scholars, international law scholars, human rights experts, organized labor, and a long list of women's organizations.

When the Fourth Circuit panel announced its ruling, Brzonkala enjoyed a fleeting victory. Two of the three judges held that the rapes themselves constituted a "hostile environment" and reinstated her claim against the university as well as her claims against Morrison and Crawford. Also agreeing on the validity of the statute, they held that Congress had sufficiently established the impact of gender-based crimes on interstate commerce with respect to lost work, lost productivity, lost mobility, and medical and other expenses. But after a strong dissent from the third member of the panel, Judge Michael Luttig, the conservative Fourth Circuit voted to take the case en banc, meaning all eleven judges would review the case.

This time, Brzonkala lost. While acknowledging that Congress had some latitude to act, the majority ruled that legislators had gone too far. Refusing to see women as active participants in the marketplace, the Fourth Circuit said that violence against women had only "an attenuated and indirect relationship with interstate commerce." (Never mind the future loss of wages represented by Brzonkala's decision to drop out of college.) Of far greater concern to the majority was the rationale used for VAWA, which could confer federal jurisdiction on other areas previously reserved to the states. Palpable throughout the decision was not only the issue of states' rights but the old specter that Schlafly had summoned up in the campaign against ratification of the ERA and that opponents of women's suffrage had used nearly a century earlier—the long arm of the federal government reaching into the family.

NOW's Legal Defense Fund, which represented Brzonkala, appealed, as did the Clinton administration. By the time the Supreme Court granted review, the case had become a cause célèbre.

. . .

GINSBURG WAS WORRIED. While VAWA had survived the test in other federal courts, both Rehnquist and Scalia had raised the specter of congressional regulation of "family relationships" under the guise of regulating "violent crime" in deciding the constitutionality of *Lopez,* the case cited by Judge Kiser. Despite a strong minority dissent, *Lopez* marked a dramatic reversal in Congress's power to legislate under the commerce clause. The Court's more right-leaning members had moved ahead on other decisions, carving out new immunities for states designed to limit the reach of federal policy. With both constitutional anchors for VAWA now weakened after a 1997 ruling in *City of Boerne v. Flores,* Ginsburg knew that the one vote determining its fate would be that of O'Connor. An ally on other gender-equality issues, the former Arizona legislator was a staunch new federalism advocate who believed that Congress should not address social problems that the states had fumbled.

. . .

ON A COLD, WINTRY JANUARY MORNING, lines began to form before dawn in front of the Court long before the doors opened to the public at 10:00 a.m. Meanwhile, members of the bar entered through a side entrance: NOW's Julie Goldscheid, who would make the first of the two arguments for VAWA, Sally Goldfarb, Victoria Nourse, Judith Resnik of Yale Law School, who, with Judge Schroeder, had worked so hard to provide Judge Stanley Marcus with the insight he needed to salvage the civil rights provision, and, not least, Senator Biden, who took his seat almost opposite Rehnquist.

Allotted the first ten minutes, Goldscheid argued that Congress was addressing "one of the most persistent barriers to women's full equality and free participation in the economy." Scalia immediately interrupted, dominating the questioning. Under her justification of VAWA's constitutionality, what, he asked, would prevent Congress from enacting a general crime statute on murder, rape, and robbery that would preempt state laws? Goldscheid reiterated that VAWA supplemented rather than usurped state authority; that attorneys general from thirty-six states had requested help; that the civil rights remedy was a response to discrimination, traditionally a matter of federal concern; and that the statute specified that traditional areas of state concern such as divorce, child custody, and equitable property distribution were left undisturbed.

O'Connor observed, "Well, presumably Congress could also, under your theory at least, legislate in those areas, too. If there's a bias against women and they're not receiving adequate alimony or it's not enforceable in court in the states, then it would have an effect on commerce. Would it not?" When Goldscheid began answering, Ginsburg jumped in to help out. "Make it just an alternative forum as here. You can bring your property distribution claim in state court or in federal Court. . . . But the case for marital distribution would also be based on discrimination, that is, a documented legislative history that shows that women are getting the short end of the stick in marital property distribution." But Ginsburg's intervention did not reassure O'Connor. Neither did Solicitor General Seth Waxman's emphasis on the importance of preventing perpetrators of domestic violence from crossing state lines or violating state protective orders. Scalia was having none of it.

When Michael E. Rosman, a litigator for the conservative Center for Individual Rights, took over, he, too, focused on the commerce clause. Unyielding in his insistence that *Lopez* precluded any regulation of non-economic activity, he argued that VAWA's civil rights provision lacked constitutional backing. An exasperated Ginsburg asked Rosman if he was challenging Congress's evidence that violence impeded women's economic mobility in the jobs that they could take and the times of day that they could work. He responded, "I'm not sure that Congress had any basis for believing it." Souter pressed hard to get Rosman to acknowledge that any part of the $3 billion drain on the economy created by medical expenses and lost wages could be attributed to animus-based violence. But Rosman refused. Interpersonal violence, he insisted, had always been left to the states—a claim that harked back to a time when slavery was considered a matter of interpersonal relations free from federal intervention.

Outside the Court next to the Washington headquarters of NOW Legal Defense, reporters stood around a shivering Christy Brzonkala and her lawyer, Martha Davis. Told that an attorney for one of her alleged assailants had suggested that her charges had been racially motivated, Brzonkala responded with an emphatic no. "When a woman is raped, she doesn't see a color."

Everyone knew that when the justices met in conference, O'Connor's vote would be decisive. The chief lobbied his longtime friend and law school classmate in a telephone call. States' rights trumped women's rights for the former Arizona legislator.

Rehnquist authored the majority opinion. Writing in broad strokes and employing reasoning that is sometimes difficult to follow, he rejected each of the two sources of constitutional authority on which Congress had relied. Not once were women mentioned other than Brzonkala, who, according to Rehnquist, claimed to have suffered "a brutal assault." In describing the assault, however, he omitted Morrison's language conveying animus—words too odious apparently to be in a Supreme Court opinion. Brzonkala's remedy, if she were to have one, according to the ruling, "must be provided by the Commonwealth of Virginia." The irony that she had already exhausted that option was not lost on the dissenting justices.

. . .

REHNQUIST IGNORED ENTIRELY what Justice Souter referred to as the "mountain of data" that Congress had collected showing the effects of violence on interstate commerce (which the gun-free law challenged

Christy Brzonkala and her lawyer, Martha Davis, after oral arguments in United States v. Morrison, *2000.*

in *Lopez* had lacked). Also ignored was a 1960s civil rights precedent in which the Court upheld under the commerce clause a statute outlawing racial discrimination in public accommodations based on evidence that had been largely anecdotal, as the dissent would point out. Instead, the chief cautioned that if the Court did not draw a line tightly between economic and noneconomic activity, Congress could enact legislation against other crimes of violence. The distinction between federal criminal law and the police power of the states would then be obliterated, as would be the states' control of domestic law.

But there was much that this slippery-slope reasoning failed to explain. Just how were states threatened by a federal law that (1) was supported by thirty-six states, (2) duplicated no state law, (3) provided federal funds to the states to help state law enforcement, and (4) provided merely a supplemental civil option while leaving state criminal remedies intact?

Then the chief justice turned to Congress's power under Section 5 to enforce the guarantees of the Fourteenth Amendment. Reaching back to discredited Reconstruction-era precedents when a conservative Court had thwarted a more equality-minded Congress on racial matters, he

concluded that the amendment applied only to state action. If state officials were failing, they should have been the object of VAWA, the ruling
concluded.

. . .

GIVEN THE REHNQUIST MAJORITY'S utter lack of deference to Congress, the outcome in *Morrison* was close to inevitable. Writing for the
dissent, Justice Souter charged that it was the majority that had overstepped, not Congress. The business of the courts was simply to determine whether Congress had a rational basis for its actions. Souter then
devoted three pages of his dissent to highlighting congressional findings, demonstrating Congress's rational basis for action. Never denying
the importance of federalist principles, he employed history, precedent,
and legal logic to dismantle the majority's reasoning. Breyer, adding an
additional dissent, identified key deficiencies in the majority's Section
5. "Why," he asked, "can Congress not provide a remedy against private
actors?" Although the text of the Fourteenth Amendment refers to states,
the Congress that enacted the amendment clearly intended its passage to
ensure the constitutionality of federal legislation against private as well
as state acts that deprived citizens of equal rights on the basis of racial
bias.

Breyer's point was strongly supported by scholars of Reconstruction.
Indeed, much of the unremediated violence directed against freed slaves,
the impetus for the amendment, was sexualized and directed at African
American women as well as men. The white men who in 1886 stripped,
tied up, and then brutally raped Rhoda Ann Childs with a pistol because
her husband served in the Union army, like those who attacked the wife
and daughter of a black Georgia Republican leader, were assaulting African American women as a way of retaliating for the actions of their
spouses. It was non-state actors who inflicted the violence. Congress,
in order to deal with problems that former Confederate states did not
adequately address, devised appropriate legislation in the Civil Rights
Act of 1871 and the Civil Rights Act of 1875. However, as white citizens,
northern and southern, moved to sectional reconciliation and white
supremacy a decade later, the Court overturned the Civil Rights Act and
other laws designed to secure some measure of racial equality. By curtailing Section 5 power, states thus regained the authority to legislate on

citizen-to-citizen equality rather than permitting the federal government to give that power to harmed individuals to enforce themselves through civil suits. It was no accident that Rehnquist had drawn on precedents from the 1880s rather than the 1870s.

. . .

FROM THE VIEWPOINT OF distinguished legal scholars such as Harvard professor Laurence Tribe, the ruling was a strong expression of judicial supremacy. " 'The court applied its own meta-test' to the legislative record," Tribe explained in an interview. "We don't care what the findings are, if accepting them endangers our vision of state sovereignty, our view of the architecture of our system." That test applied "even when the states are basically willing bystanders." "This decision," Biden added, "is really all about power: who has the power, the court or Congress?"

Others, such as Catharine MacKinnon, saw something more troubling in this new federalism—how it served the older ghost of racial and sexual terrorism. Setting her powerful dissection of the ruling against the historical backdrop of racial subjugation and federalism, MacKinnon pointed out that the states had done the least to protect African Americans' freedom and rights of citizenship. Making the states the sole avenue for women's equality repeated history. But this time it was all women, not former slaves, whom the courts had abandoned. *Morrison*, MacKinnon maintained, was a major battle in women's struggle for equality: a battle over the structure of the Union and the status of the sexes in civil society. It addressed ground zero for citizenship—physical security—and ground zero for women's human status: sexual inviolability. "At stake was nothing less than whether women are full citizens and full human beings: equals."

With customary brilliance, MacKinnon restored women's full citizenship to the center of the case, where it belonged, chiding the minority for not having done so sufficiently. According to MacKinnon, "Not one member of the Supreme Court argued that the rights the VAWA gave women were constitutional under the equality guarantee." She also raised—and answered—a fundamental question: Whose interest did the majority's notion of federalism serve?

That question would assume historic proportions in an election year like no other.

Catharine MacKinnon, noted feminist, legal
scholar, and strategist, who in 1979 established
the legal claim that sexual harassment is sex
discrimination.

· · ·

NEITHER GOVERNOR GEORGE W. BUSH of Texas nor Vice President
Al Gore, the leading contenders, generated great popular enthusiasm
during the presidential campaign. Many voters had soured on politicians
generally. Others, including some liberals, saw little difference between
"Gush" and "Bore," despite their sharply divergent positions on future
nominations to the Court. (Bush promised nominees cut from the same
cloth as Scalia and Thomas, while Gore named Brennan and Marshall as
models.) Republican stalwarts, however, cared passionately. It had been
eight years since they controlled the White House. And they had loathed
the Clintons from the day these two brilliant but flawed individuals
arrived in Washington. Conservatives' frustration at a failed Clinton
impeachment only intensified on Election Day. In Florida, where Bush's

younger brother Jeb occupied the governor's mansion and Republicans controlled the legislature, the race remained too close to call.

Two days after the election, Florida's mandated machine recounts cut Bush's narrow lead. The NAACP reported voter intimidation and irregularities in some northern counties along the panhandle bordering Alabama and Georgia, despite the Voting Rights Act of 1965. The media, however, focused on the frenzied maneuvering in Tallahassee as the postelection drama unfolded.

The dispute centered on poorly constructed ballots. On the Palm Beach County ballot, the voting holes between the columns failed to align the candidate's name clearly with the hole to be punched. Further, the lineup, which had always been Republicans first, Democrats second, and then third parties, this time listed Bush first, the independent candidate, Patrick Buchanan, second, and Gore third. Some Gore voters had inadvertently punched the hole designated for Buchanan. For the former Reagan adviser and right-wing commentator to win thirty-seven hundred votes in a Democratic stronghold—nearly twenty-seven hundred more than he received in any of Florida's other counties, struck even Buchanan as anomalous. Bewildered voters in Palm Beach "overvoted," punching more than one hole. Elsewhere ballots had "hanging chads" (tiny paper rectangles left hanging that voters were supposed to have pushed through) or "dimpled" chads (rectangles bearing the mark of the metal stylus)—"undervoting" in the parlance of the time.

With an estimated 175,000 votes in dispute, lawyers for both candidates swooped into Tallahassee, initiating a dizzying exchange of lawsuits. On November 9, Gore asked for a manual recount in four counties. Two days later, Bush lawyers, eager to keep their candidate's razor-thin lead from disintegrating, filed a request in the U.S. district court in Miami for an emergency injunction to halt the manual recounts. A partial recount in only four counties, they contended, violated the equal protection clause by weighting some votes more than others. When the Bush request failed in the Florida courts, he appealed to the Supreme Court. While the appeal was making its way through the federal courts, Secretary of State Katherine Harris, a Republican who co-chaired Bush's Florida campaign, interceded. Refusing to waive the November 14 deadline for localities to turn in their ballot totals, she ordered that manual recounts not be permitted.

Gore, along with county officials in the four counties that he hoped to win with a recount, challenged the decision. On November 17, the Florida Supreme Court ruled against Harris, extending the deadline for reporting to November 26. Bush's lawyers, viewing the ruling as an assault on Harris's lawful authority to certify the election, appealed for the second time to the U.S. Supreme Court. The Florida Supreme Court, they claimed, lacked the legal grounds to order the twelve-day extension. The two Bush appeals reached the Court on Thanksgiving eve, November 22, amid a full-scale attack on the Florida Supreme Court by the Bush campaign and House Republican leaders.

That the nation's highest tribunal would agree to become involved in a politically charged case grounded in state law at first seemed highly unlikely. Yet the following day the Court announced that it would hear *Bush v. Palm Beach County Canvassing Board,* Bush's appeal of the state court's decision extending the manual recount in the four counties. Bush's second appeal was temporarily denied; the court of appeals in Atlanta had not yet ruled. With only four votes needed to grant certiorari, there was no way to tell at the time whether the Court as a whole had concluded that the Florida situation was out of control.

The roller-coaster ride for the two campaigns continued. When the November 26 deadline for reporting arrived, Gore had an additional 567 votes from Broward County. Palm Beach County's addition to the Gore column, which came in ninety minutes late, was rejected. Miami-Dade was still counting, with more than 10,000 ballots yet to be reviewed. Harris officially certified Bush the victor with a margin of 537 votes. Gore's lawyers filed suit, knowing they were throwing a Hail Mary pass. But before they knew whether they had scored in the Florida courts, the Supreme Court weighed in.

During oral argument in *Bush v. Palm Beach County Canvassing Board,* the justices appeared to be divided. But on December 4, three days later, the Court announced its unanimous rejection of the Florida Supreme Court's twelve-day extension of the original November 14 certification deadline. The state court was also instructed to do a better job of explaining the rationale for the extension. Could it demonstrate that it took proper account of certain statutory and constitutional provisions governing federal elections? While nothing was said about Bush's assertion that the Fourteenth Amendment was relevant to the case, the ruling did call attention to an arcane provision of the U.S. Constitution. According to Article II, Section 5, presidential electors were to be appointed by each state "in such Manner as the Legislature" directed. That provision would end up being a core point—and a highly contentious one—as the Gore challenge to certification of the election tally worked its way up to the Florida Supreme Court.

On December 8, the Florida Supreme Court, composed entirely of Democrats, announced a sweeping and carefully crafted decision designed to pass muster in the high court. The recounts would continue in dozens of counties. Referring to a section of Florida law that said no vote shall be ignored "if there is a clear indication of the intent of the voter," the court ruled by a 4–3 majority that the certification by the Canvassing Committee was flawed. Nine thousand ballots in Miami-Dade alone, in which voting machines had failed to detect any vote for president, had never been hand counted. "Only by examining the contested ballots, which are evidence in the election context, can a meaningful and final determination . . . be made," the majority concluded.

But by what standards would the ballots be examined? The court did not say. Such matters had always been left to localities in Florida, as in the other states. The omission, however, did not go unnoticed by Bush's lawyers. That night they filed an appeal for an emergency stay blocking the recount, claiming it would cause their client irreparable harm. The final showdown had begun in what had become an increasingly bitter contest.

. . .

FOR THE HIGH COURT, accustomed to proceeding at a more measured pace, the compressed deadlines lent a surreal quality to the next two days. When the justices met in conference early Saturday morning on December 9 to consider the stay application and appeal in what had become *Bush v. Gore,* the recount had already begun in Florida. The liberals believed the Court had narrowly dodged a bullet with its unanimous ruling the previous weekend. They sat stunned as Rehnquist, Scalia, Thomas, O'Connor, and Kennedy voted to issue a stay. There was no compromise to be had. Justice Stevens authored a sharp dissent, which Souter, Ginsburg, and Breyer quickly signed. To stop the counting of legal votes, Stevens wrote, "the majority today departs from . . . venerable rules of judicial restraint that have guided the Court throughout its history." "Counting every legally cast vote cannot constitute irreparable harm," Stevens continued. "On the other hand, there is a danger that a stay may cause irreparable harm to [Gore and the Democratic challengers]—and, more importantly, the public at large—because of the risk that the 'entry of the stay would be tantamount to a decision on the merits in favor of the applicants.'" Stevens soberly concluded, "Preventing the recount from being complete will inevitably cast a cloud on the legitimacy of the election."

Publishing his dissent—an unusual act in itself—Stevens provided the public with its first glimpse of the division within the Court. But it was Scalia who inflamed suspicions of partisanship when he responded with a defense of the stay. The recount had to be stopped because it threatened "irreparable harm" to Bush "by casting a cloud on what he claims to be the legitimacy of his election."

Following a vote, the justices normally retreat to their chambers—but not this time. From accounts pieced together by the *New York Times*

Bush and Gore demonstrators clashed outside the Supreme Court, December 12, 2000.

legal affairs analyst Linda Greenhouse, the "shaken and demoralized" dissenters reached out to one another, fearful about the harm inflicted on the Court and the nation by what now seemed an inevitable outcome. Breyer, who had great faith in his ability to persuade, searched for a strategy that might sway Kennedy and conceivably even O'Connor.

The equal protection argument in the *Bush* brief had evolved into something new. The question was no longer whether it was constitutional to count votes in some counties but not others. Rather, it was whether the Florida court's recount order violated Bush's right to equal protection when counting standards varied from county to county. Breyer and Souter hoped that if they could convince Kennedy that the solution was to adopt a uniform standard for counting, they might be able to acquire the five votes needed to keep the recount going.

Before the justices took their seats for oral argument on Monday morning, the anticipatory buzz that preceded the last argument had turned into a "sullen hum." The same five justices so ostensibly wedded in *Morrison* to the primacy of states' rights and a narrow conception of the equal protection guarantee were now about to reverse their position.

Theodore Olson, a highly prominent Washington lawyer, launched into his argument. State legislatures, he claimed, not state courts, make the rules for presidential elections according to Article II of the Constitution. Justice Kennedy pointed out that courts interpret the words of legislation. Olson then argued that federal law prohibited Florida from changing the rule of vote counting after ballots had been cast. Kennedy responded, "I thought your point was that the process is being conducted in violation of the Equal Protection Clause because it is standardless." Olson's response gave Breyer his opportunity. "What would the standard be?" he asked. But Olson continued to dodge.

When Olson rose to give his rebuttal, Ginsburg cut to the core: "And there are different ballots from county to county too, Mr. Olson, and that's part of the argument that I don't understand. There are machines, there's the optical scanning, and then there are a whole variety of ballots. There is the butterfly ballot that we've heard about and other kinds of post-card ballots. How can you have one standard when there are so many varieties of ballots?" The question went to the heart of Olson's claim of an equal protection violation, but time ran out.

Yet nothing had changed. As the 5–4 vote confirmed, the majority had no intention of letting the Florida Supreme Court supervise a recount under any circumstances. The election was effectively over.

Surrounded by bright lights mounted on poles for television cameras in front of the Court, the justices worked on opinions into the early morning hours. Rehnquist turned in a quick draft that Scalia and Thomas joined. In ordering the recount, the opinion stated, the Florida Supreme Court had displaced the role of the state legislature in violation of Article II of the U.S. Constitution. But the ever-optimistic Breyer still clung to his proposed solution: send the case back to the Florida court with instructions to establish one statewide standard for counting. Breyer and Souter agreed that the Florida courts should determine whether the counties could complete such a recount before the Electoral College meeting on December 18.

Faced with such polarized positions, Kennedy and O'Connor came up with a mere twelve-page per curiam (by the Court) opinion, with which Rehnquist, Scalia, and Thomas concurred to create a majority. The opinion did little to explain the rationale for the ruling that the Florida Supreme Court violated the equal protection clause. But it did include a highly unusual passage: "Our consideration is limited to the present circumstances, for the problem of equal protection in election processes generally presents many complexities."

Ginsburg watched the jockeying among the majority, thoroughly disgusted by the distortion of equal protection doctrine. The Court had never indicated previously that election standards violated equal protection. Who were the purported targets of the violation? With early press accounts of violence and intimidation against African Americans in mind, she wrote that if there was any violation of equal protection, it was more likely to be by local and state authorities than the Florida Supreme Court. When Scalia saw the draft of her dissent, he sent a memo accusing her of engaging in "Al Sharpton" tactics about the election. This might have been one of those times when she felt like strangling her friend Nino. But exercising her customary restraint, Ginsburg chose not to fire back, omitting the reference to race from her opinion.

But as someone who had taught a course titled "Conflict of Law and Federal Jurisdiction," she did not mince words when she focused on the hypocrisy of Rehnquist, Scalia, and Thomas when it came to federalism. "Rarely has this Court rejected outright an interpretation of state law by a state high court," wrote Ginsburg. Yet three justices (Rehnquist, Scalia, Thomas) did just that by concluding that Florida had violated Article II of the U.S. Constitution. Their simple "disagreement with the Florida court's interpretation of its own State's law," she argued, "d[id] not warrant the conclusion that the justices of that court have legislated. There is no cause here to believe that members of Florida's high court have done less than 'their mortal best to discharge their oath of office,' and no cause to upset their reasoned interpretation of Florida law." Citing precedent, she noted that traditionally the U.S. Supreme Court defers to statutory interpretations by federal agencies, unless the agency transgresses a clear expression of congressional intent. "Surely," Ginsburg wrote, "the Constitution does not call upon us to pay more respect to a federal administrative agency's construction of federal law than to a state high court's interpretation of its own state's law."

The Court's lack of deference to state sovereignty in the dispute also undermined the majority's equal protection holding. Given widespread failures in voting methods and machine tabulation, Ginsburg argued, "the recount adopted by the Florida court, flawed though it may be," was no "less fair or precise" than the certification that had preceded that recount. Rather than demand a level of perfection that few other states could have attained, the Court should have deferred to the Florida Supreme Court's reasonable attempts to tabulate the vote as accurately as possible without imposing a December 12 deadline. "[O]rderly judicial review of any disputed matters that might arise," which the deadline foreclosed, impaired the state's effort to ensure equal protection for the majority.

Even more bitter were the words of the eighty-year-old Stevens, whose dissent became the most widely quoted language in the opinion. The majority's position, he wrote, "can only lend credence to the most cynical appraisal of the work of judges throughout the land," adding, "Although we may never know with complete certainty the identity of the winner of this year's Presidential election, the identity of the loser is perfectly clear. It is the Nation's confidence in the judge as an impartial guardian of the rule of law."

. . .

IT HAD BEEN a difficult year and a half since Ginsburg returned from Crete with colorectal cancer. After her surgery and chemotherapy, Marty told her to get a trainer because she "looked like a survivor of Auschwitz." She had gradually begun to regain her strength working with a fitness trainer at the Supreme Court gym, but she sorely needed what remained of the end-of-term recess. Having the Bush-Cheney team in control for what could be the next eight years did not bode well for the values and causes she cherished.

PART VI

Standing Firm

CHAPTER 18

Persevering in Hard Times

Ginsburg's apprehensions about the fate of the nation under Bush-Cheney materialized in ways she could not have imagined. Following September 11, 2001, the "Terror Presidency" emerged. In many ways, the country would never be the same.

In Afghanistan, bombing the Taliban government—a repressive Islamic fundamentalist group with ties to al-Qaeda—brought results. Some al-Qaeda leaders were captured or killed, and the operational effectiveness of the group was eroded. But Osama bin Laden remained elusive and dangerous, while a reckless U.S. invasion of Iraq in 2003 saddled Americans with nine years of combat. Some 4,488 young service people would return home in flag-draped coffins, while over 3,226 others were wounded.

Exacting a high price in both blood and treasure, counterterrorism irrevocably altered the lives of men and women who served their nation. Further, the administration's embrace of the war on terror as a means to expand executive power and the conservative agenda would impact the courts, Congress, and the military. Conservative policies of deregulation in environmental protection, health care, workplace safety standards, and the mortgage market, along with regressive tax policies, further eroded the welfare of those whose sons and daughters filled the military's ranks.

The toll seemed to be reflected in Ginsburg's bent head and frail frame, though, with Ginsburg, appearances are always deceptive. Her formidable intellect and sense of strategy remained intact. So did her continued adherence to founding principles such as separation of powers, checks and balances, and the right of habeas corpus—all differently interpreted by the administration. However, as the Bush-Cheney years ground on, the composition of the Court changed, and Marty's health faltered. The lone woman on the Court following O'Connor's retirement, Ginsburg seemed not just frail but forlorn. Yet her dissents acquired new power and edge at the very time when law seemed to many to have become a tool of power and humanitarianism was shelved.

. . .

FOR A JUSTICE whose first decade on the Court had been about expanding rights, the period of Bush's first term provided two important equal protection cases focused on gender. Only one provided a fleeting victory. The first, *Nguyen v. Immigration and Naturalization Service,* had involved a father, Joseph Boulais, and his son, Tuan Anh Nguyen, who were caught up in the complexities of the U.S. Code on conferral of citizenship to a child born to an unwed U.S. citizen. According to Title 8, Section 1409 of the U.S. Code, a citizen mother need only reside one year in the United States or its territories prior to giving birth in order to transmit citizenship to a foreign-born, nonmarital child. A foreign-born, nonmarital child of a citizen father, however, only becomes a U.S. citizen, retroactive to date of birth, if several additional conditions are met. The *Nguyen* case would test whether a majority of the Court would hold to the skeptical scrutiny of sex-based classifications set forth in *Virginia.*

Joseph Boulais, a U.S. citizen and veteran, fathered a child in 1969 with a Vietnamese citizen, Hung Thi Nguyen. Boulais left the boy in Vietnam until immigration to the United States proved feasible. In 1975, father and son were reunited in Houston. Boulais never formally applied for his son's citizenship, because Nguyen had been admitted as a refugee at the age of six. Nor did Nguyen apply before reaching twenty-one, the cutoff by which paternity must be established.

The issue came to a head when the twenty-two-year-old Nguyen pleaded guilty to a felony for sexual assault. As a result of his conviction, he faced deportation. He appealed to the Board of Immigration Appeals and secured proof of parentage based on DNA evidence, but he was denied because of his age. Father and son then challenged the decision in the Fifth Circuit, citing Section 1409(a) of the code as a violation of equal protection. When the court of appeals denied their petition, they appealed to the Supreme Court, citing Section 1409(a) of the U.S.

Code. In that statute, Ginsburg had quickly perceived the shadow of the old law of domestic relations (for example, the laws of bastardy and coverture), race privilege, and underlying injury to women embedded in the sex-based allocation of parental responsibility. Section 1409(a), she concluded, had no place in a modern-day constitutional democracy.

Yet she found herself in the minority when the case reached the high court. Kennedy voted with Scalia, Thomas, Rehnquist, and Stevens to find Section 1409(a) consistent with the equal protection guarantee. In his majority opinion, Kennedy justified sex-differentiating criteria on the grounds that more stringent requirements for citizen fathers were necessary. Essentializing the mother-child bond, he argued that unwed fathers did not enjoy the "unique" experience of a birthing mother that provides her with the potential to develop a meaningful relationship with the child. The different rules were there to ensure that an authentic parent-child connection exists through which the values of citizenship can be transmitted to the child.

O'Connor's strong dissent, to which Ginsburg privately contributed, challenged the majority's assumptions repeatedly. That the mother's presence at birth supplies adequate assurance that she will have an "opportunity" to develop a relationship with the child involving "real, everyday ties," while a father's absence at birth does not, rests on an overbroad generalization about sex, O'Connor admonished. The majority fostered the notion that men don't "naturally" have the same real and enduring ties to their children that women do, thereby perpetuating an unfavorable and false stereotype. As a result, the majority had failed to apply rigorous scrutiny as required by *Virginia* to the fit between the Immigration and Naturalization Service's account of governmental interests and sex-based classification required as a means to achieve it, debasing the "depth and vitality" of the Court's sex-discrimination precedents. Deeply disappointed that skeptical scrutiny had not had greater staying power, Ginsburg was also invested in the upcoming *Hibbs* case, which would again test the power of Congress to legislate its vision of what equality required.

· · ·

AT ISSUE IN *Nevada Department of Human Resources v. Hibbs* was the constitutionality of the Family and Medical Leave Act (FMLA). Passed in 1993, the act attempted to alleviate the work-family conflicts facing families—usually for, but by no means exclusively, women. Employers of a certain size were required to provide eligible employees job-protected unpaid leave for qualified medical and family emergencies. Eight years in the making and twice vetoed by President George H. W. Bush, the watered-down legislation still managed in some degree to enable women in the workforce to have children without jeopardizing their jobs, seniority, benefits, or promotions—a central goal of feminists in the 1970s—by combining the feminist quest for equal citizenship with the family values of the Reagan-Bush eras.

Like the Violence Against Women Act, the FMLA was grounded in the commerce clause and Section 5, the enforcement clause, of the Fourteenth Amendment. Anyone familiar with *Morrison* and the Section 5 jurisprudence of the Rehnquist Court could pinpoint the FMLA's vulnerability. In the eight cases in which the statute had been challenged in federal courts, judges in seven had concluded that the FMLA was not a valid exercise of Congress's Section 5 power to revoke the immunity that states enjoyed from private lawsuits. Only in the Ninth Circuit had liberal judges ruled that a private individual, William Hibbs, could indeed sue the State of Nevada for monetary damages for failure to fully comply with the statute.

Hibbs was working for the Nevada Department of Human Resources when his wife, Dianne, suffered severe injuries in a car accident. Hibbs applied for twelve weeks of unpaid leave under the FMLA in order to attend to his wife. While the request was pending, he learned that he might be eligible for paid leave under Nevada's Catastrophic Leave Program. But, unbeknownst to him, Hibbs's employer intended to count the Catastrophic Leave time against his FMLA leave time. After Hibbs received instructions to report to work, he declined, believing he still had time remaining on his FMLA leave. As a result, he faced dismissal charges and subsequently filed suit.

The stakes were high. Apart from the nearly five million state workers who would be affected, a ruling that the FMLA was *not* "appropriate" under Section 5, the enforcement clause of the Fourteenth Amendment, meant rejection of Congress's vision of what equal protection entailed. And that, noted the prominent legal scholar Robert Post, "would be a huge symbolic turn in American politics." The solicitor general also warned that ruling in favor of state immunity would be disturbing for civil rights enforcement generally.

Nevada's attorney general was confident that the Court's decisions upholding state sovereignty would prevail, given the new federalism of the Rehnquist majority. Yet when the vote count was a startling 6–3 to uphold the Ninth Circuit's decision, there was arguably less evidence of contemporary sex discrimination than had been presented in *Morrison* and in other recent cases. But Rehnquist, who wrote the majority opinion, took care to distinguish *Hibbs* from its predecessors. The FMLA, he explained, was "narrowly targeted at the fault-line between work and family—precisely where sex-based over-generalization has been and remains strongest." Twelve weeks of unpaid family leave for illness and emergencies, he wrote, was a remedy "congruent and proportional" to Congress's objective. It ensured "that family-care leave would no longer be stigmatized as an inordinate drain on the workplace caused by female employees, and that employers could not evade leave obligations simply by hiring men. Congress," he continued, " 'is not confined to the enactment of legislation that merely parrots the precise wording of the Fourteenth Amendment,' but may prohibit '*a somewhat broader swath of conduct, including that which is not itself forbidden by the Amendment's text.*' "

This strikingly broad interpretation was stunning, especially when coming from the man who, during Ginsburg's years at the ACLU, was the perfect example of a justice who just didn't "get it." After she joined the Court, he had questioned her as to whether Stephen Wiesenfeld had *really* stayed home to take care of the baby. But there was no doubt that Rehnquist had finally gotten it. In *Hibbs,* he had described the thirty-five years after *Frontiero* as a period of ongoing and institutionalized constitutional violations reflecting stereotypical judgments about mothers-to-be and mothers. In doing so, he limited the range of what could be attributed to "real sex differences" that can justify state action beyond what the Court had previously allowed.

Ginsburg's fingerprints were all over the ruling, so much so that upon reading Rehnquist's opinion, Marty asked, "Ruth, did you ghostwrite it?—it's remarkable." Her denial did not negate her persuasive power or the fact that the ruling embodied a message that she had long championed.

. . .

THE SUMMER OF 2005 had started off badly. The previous October, the chief justice had been diagnosed with an aggressive form of thyroid cancer. Months of radiation and chemotherapy had followed. With a tracheotomy that allowed him to speak through a hole in his neck, he finally returned to active participation on the Court in March. Defying expectation that he would have to resign, he hoped to hold on for another year. Justice O'Connor, however, had decided that she could not remain. Her husband John's Alzheimer's was progressing rapidly. Her sudden announcement in July of her intention to retire caught her colleagues on the Court, as well as the president, by surprise.

As tributes poured in to the woman whose critical swing vote had decided such crucial issues as abortion, affirmative action, and the death penalty, Ginsburg began coming to terms with the unwelcome reality of being the only woman on the Court. Although she and O'Connor had agreed on only 52 percent of the decisions handed down during their twelve years together, they shared multiple interests, including making the Court a more family-friendly work environment. And they especially delighted in demonstrating that women on the high court need not be

The Ginsburgs, 2003.

An ailing Rehnquist and his daughter Janet, July 10, 2005.

cut from the same cloth—one an outgoing member of the Cowgirl Hall of Fame, the other a passionate devotee of opera.

Though O'Connor always claimed that "a wise old man and a wise old woman reach the same conclusion," her very presence on the Court had a measurable impact on the gender sensitivity of the men with whom she served. Four of her male counterparts had increased their support of gender discrimination plaintiffs by as much as 26 percent. After Ginsburg's arrival in 1993, she and O'Connor had formed a solid partnership, writing a disproportionate share of the majority opinions on women's rights cases. Each could count on the other in the many sexual harassment cases brought under Title VII of the Civil Rights Act or under Title IX of the Education Amendments of 1972. Ginsburg built on O'Connor's ruling in *Hogan,* making eye contact with the woman who had salvaged sex-discrimination jurisprudence in the 1980s, and handed her the opportunity to read aloud her own majority opinion in *Virginia.*

The pair had worked together closely on the *Nguyen* dissent, which bore O'Connor's name. On a more personal level, Ginsburg would not forget the support offered by the senior justice in 1999 during her ordeal with colorectal cancer.

Two months later, just short of his eighty-first birthday, Rehnquist died, intensifying Ginsburg's sense of loss. His casket was placed in the

The members of the Supreme Court exit the Supreme Court Building heading toward the funeral services for the former chief justice William Rehnquist. From front to back, Justices John Paul Stevens, Sandra Day O'Connor, Antonin Scalia, William Kennedy, David Souter, Clarence Thomas, Stephen Breyer, and Ruth Bader Ginsburg.

Great Hall of the Court until the funeral on September 7, when a prestigious gathering of notables heard President Bush and Justice O'Connor
pay tribute. The Rehnquists and O'Connors had been friends in Arizona, even vacationing together.

For O'Connor, the chief's death weighed heavily, as did her departure from the Court. As the justices descended the steps from the Cathe-
dral of St. Matthew the Apostle, Ginsburg's head was bowed in grief.
She knew it was the end of an era. Sharp differences notwithstanding,
after a remarkable eleven years without a change in the Court's composition, a sense of family had emerged. Rehnquist, they agreed, would be
remembered for his superb leadership, acute intelligence, wry sense of
humor, poker-playing skills, and love of amateur theatricals.

But what resonated most deeply for Ginsburg was the humanity the
chief, too, had displayed during her bout with cancer—a disease that
had taken his wife. In his own terminal battle, his courage and determination offered an "exemplary" model of how to live and work pro-
ductively under great duress. Her sense of loss had doubled. Frequently
referring to her fondness for her "old chief," nearly two years later she
freely acknowledged how much she missed O'Connor and how deeply
sad she still felt.

· · ·

WITH TWO VACANCIES TO FILL, the Bush administration moved
rapidly. Withdrawing the name of Judge John Roberts, who had initially
been intended to replace O'Connor, the president nominated Roberts to
be the new chief justice. The rightward-leaning nominee had served in
both the Reagan and the George H. W. Bush administrations. Considered "the best Supreme Court advocate of his generation," Roberts had a
sterling reputation as a brilliant legal mind, master strategist, and excellent writer. Because he had been a member of the federal bench for only
two years, his scant judicial record provided little ammunition for opponents, though pro-choice activists took note of the fact that Roberts and
his wife were Roman Catholic. Promising minimalism, restraint, and
narrow opinions as he exuded charm and erudition, he won over many
Democrats but not Senators Barack Obama, Joseph Biden, Charles
Schumer, or Barbara Mikulski. Yet his confirmation was secure. The
youngest chief justice since John Marshall was nominated in 1801 would

take his place at the center of the bench when the October term began in 2005. Journalists predicted he could be presiding in 2040.

In January 2006, Roberts was joined by Judge Samuel A. Alito, the son of Italian immigrants and a conservative former prosecutor with a "law-and-order approach." Alito's refusal to consider *Roe v. Wade* "settled law," his deference to presidential power, and his consistent support of corporations deeply worried Democrats—and the ACLU. Yet Democrats could not muster the votes to defeat the nomination of a judge so highly qualified.

Though the newest justice had a reputation for being quiet and low-key, unlike the voluble Scalia, who craved the spotlight, Ginsburg suspected that his presence would swing the Court even further rightward. Steeling herself for what the Roberts Court held in store, she found her spirits plummeting in October, when it was confirmed that Marty had cancer again. To make matters worse, the most contentious issue possible had returned to the docket: abortion.

· · ·

IN 1995, Norma McCorvey, the original Jane Roe plaintiff in *Roe v. Wade,* had a religious conversion. Baptized in a swimming pool at a house in Garland, Texas, by the Reverend Flip Benham, a fundamentalist minister and national director of the antiabortion group Operation Rescue, she became a born-again Christian and an ardent antiabortion activist.

Benham also put her in touch with the Justice Foundation, a conservative legal foundation funded by the Texas physician and entrepreneur James Leininger that had handled McCorvey's suit challenging the case that bore her pseudonym. In support of McCorvey's suit, the Leininger-funded antiabortion group Operation Outcry collected more than a thousand affidavits of post-abortive women testifying to the guilt, depression, and self-destructive behavior experienced in the wake of their abortions. McCorvey's suit failed, but not the argument, which had been gathering steam throughout the 1980s and early 1990s despite growing evidence to the contrary in scientific and medical literature.

The affidavits gathered for McCorvey wound up in the hands of sympathetic legislators in South Dakota, Ohio, Louisiana, Mississippi, and Alabama, as well as the U.S. Congress. By 1996, the antiabortion

Justice Samuel Alito Jr. and Chief Justice John Roberts replaced Sandra Day O'Connor and Chief Justice William Rehnquist.

activist and author David Reardon had come up with a winning strategy for their use. Antiabortion forces, Reardon proposed, should co-opt the term "freedom of choice" and "reproductive freedom." Incorporating women's rights into the argument against abortion, he argued, would help convince "the middle majority" that it is the antiabortion movement that is *really* defending the right of a woman to make an informed choice to reproduce without the fear of being pressured into an unwanted abortion.

The gender-based reframing proposed by Reardon, combined with affidavits of psychological harm suffered by post-abortive women, had only to be topped off with gruesome imagery. Late-term abortions account for only 1.2 percent of the abortions performed in the United States. But one of the medical procedures used to perform what are notoriously called partial-birth abortions afforded an opportunity for graphic descriptions of intact dilation and extraction (D&E). The process involved the dilation of a woman's cervix to allow most of the fetus to emerge into the vagina intact rather than dismembering the fetus in utero by using forceps and other instruments. Physicians pointed to its advantages for certain women given their particular health conditions. Critics likened it to infanticide. Antiabortion activists and legislators now had a potent weapon with which to promote the nation's most "draconian" abortion ban yet.

Bill Clinton had twice vetoed a controversial federal ban because it did not create a statutory exemption for the pregnant woman's health. But with an antiabortion president in the White House and a Republican-controlled Congress, such vetoes were becoming a mark of Democratic administrations as the party system became increasingly ideologically identified. In 2003, the Partial-Birth Abortion Ban Act became the law of the land, even though a medical consensus did not exist. The statutes stipulated that up to a two-year prison term awaited a physician convicted of performing any abortion in which the death of the fetus occurs when "the entire fetal head . . . or . . . any part of the fetal trunk past the navel is outside the body of the mother, for the purpose of performing an overt act the person knows will kill the partially delivered living fetus."

The ban included no statutory exemption for the pregnant woman's health, saying that none was necessary—an omission that put the act on a fast track to the Court, which had ruled against a similar Nebraska statute only three years earlier. Dr. LeRoy Carhart and other physicians who performed late-term abortions sued to stop the act from going into effect. Dr. Carhart considered putting the state between the physician and the patient "an affront to medical practice." He still had memories of his rotation on the ward of Philadelphia General Hospital and the dozens of women he saw suffering from serious infections from botched abortions, some self-induced, in the years before *Roe*. When the plaintiffs won in the lower courts, Attorney General Alberto Gonzales appealed.

. . .

AS THE COURT PREPARED to hear *Gonzales v. Carhart,* Ginsburg feared the worst. The Court's abortion jurisprudence over the years had changed, reflecting growing attention to purported psychological consequences of abortion and increasing doubts about the decision-making capacity of women seeking the procedure. In 1983, the Court had rejected Akron, Ohio's "informed consent" regulation, finding that it was "designed not to inform the woman's consent but rather to persuade her to withhold it altogether." Barely a decade later in *Planned Parent-*

hood v. Casey, the Court still affirmed a woman's autonomy to determine her life course. The balance, however, had shifted.

A more permissive "undue burden" standard replaced strict scrutiny of restrictions. A legislature could regulate abortion for various purposes so long as it did *not* do so in ways that placed an undue burden on women. "We also see no reason," the majority had continued, "why the State may not require doctors to inform a woman seeking an abortion of the availability of materials relating to the consequences to the fetus, even when those consequences have no direct relation to her health." Informed consent requirements, twenty-four-hour waiting periods, and counseling services, according to the *Casey* majority, further "the legitimate purpose of reducing the risk that a woman may elect an abortion only to discover later, with *devastating psychological consequence,* that her decision was not fully informed." Thus the seeds of the women-protective argument had been planted in relation to abortion in marked contrast to all other medical decisions where it is assumed that the patient should, and ordinarily can, make the choice for herself.

The Court had narrowly overturned Nebraska's partial ban in 2000 (*Stenberg v. Carhart*), but not without creating bitter divisions among the justices. Justice Kennedy, who had always struggled with abortion, regarded O'Connor's and Souter's votes to overturn the ban as a betrayal of the compromise the three had forged in *Casey.* In a passionate dissent, he asserted that the ruling "contradicts *Casey*'s assurance that the State's constitutional position in the realm of promoting respect for life is more than marginal." Kennedy, the most reluctant member of the *Casey* troika, was not likely to soften his position that D&E was morally "abhorrent." And Alito was not O'Connor.

· · ·

THE 5–4 VOTE IN *Gonzales v. Carhart* fulfilled Ginsburg's fears. It reversed a thirty-year history in which the Court had never departed from the neutral position that *Roe* took with regard to the status of the fetus. Further, it banned a specific abortion procedure and wrote the health exception out of the law. Roberts, Alito, Kennedy, Scalia, and Thomas—all Catholics, as the press quickly noted—voted to uphold the Partial-Birth Abortion Ban Act. Writing for the majority, Kennedy noted that the act had none of the vagueness of the Nebraska ban. The majority's insistence in the Nebraska case that a statutory exemption be made for the woman's health was not necessary for Congress to include because there was "medical uncertainty" as to whether the banned procedure was ever necessary. Nor did the ban place an unconstitutional "undue burden" on women seeking a late-term abortion, prior to fetal viability. If a pregnant woman or her doctor decided to do so, they could go to court and apply for an individual exception. It was a recourse to which Ginsburg would object.

What the act did do, according to Kennedy, was express "respect for the dignity of human life." It also protected women from terminating their pregnancies by a method they might not fully understand and then later regret. "Respect for human life," he wrote melodramatically, "finds an ultimate expression in the bond of love the mother has for

Dr. LeRoy Carhart, who challenged the Partial-Birth Abortion Ban Act, departs the Supreme Court in Washington, June 28, 2000.

Protesters from both sides of the abortion issue face off outside the Supreme Court Building.

her child. . . . It is self-evident that a mother who comes to regret her choice to abort must struggle with grief more anguished and sorrow more profound when she learns, only after the event, what she once did not know: that she allowed a doctor to pierce the skull and vacuum the fast-developing brain of her unborn child, a child assuming the human form."

Kennedy's emphasis on ethical and moral concerns, the choice of language ("mother" and "child" rather than "pregnant woman" and "fetus"), the assumption that women's true nature was to be mothers, that they lacked decision-making capacity and required protection by the state, even the name of the legislation—all were straight out of the antiabortion movement's strategic playbook. Ginsburg strongly objected, as did Stevens, Souter, and Breyer. She had fought in the 1970s against women-protective arguments in jury exemptions and the workplace that in practice served to limit women's liberty and autonomy. She was not about to pull her punches now.

When the decision was announced, she made the unusual choice to read aloud her dissent from the bench. It was a way of connecting directly to the public, enlisting "We, the People" in a dialogue about a decision that she considered "egregiously" wrong. This was not the typical collegial dissent for which she was noted, but one permeated with uncharacteristic anger. Steely and stinging, she articulated every word for maximum effect, beginning,

> Today's decision is alarming. It refuses to take *Casey* and *Stenberg* seriously. It tolerates, indeed applauds, federal intervention to ban nationwide a procedure found necessary and proper in certain cases by the American College of Obstetricians and Gynecologists (ACOG). It blurs the line, firmly drawn in *Casey,* between pre-viability and post-viability abortions. And, for the first time since *Roe,* the Court blesses a prohibition with no exception safeguarding a woman's health.

Findings made after full trials in district courts, she noted, provided far more extensive medical and scientific evidence from "extraordinarily accomplished" experts on the safety and necessity of intact D&Es. According to those findings, it was indeed the preferred method for women with certain medical conditions, which she specified. "Today's opinion supplies no reason to reject those findings." It just "brushes [them] under the rug," offering instead "flimsy and transparent justifications for upholding a nationwide ban on intact D&E *sans* any exception to safeguard a woman's health."

Turning next to the central premise that the ban serves the government interest in preserving and promoting fetal life, Ginsburg exposed the gaping hole in the majority argument. The law saves not a single fetus from destruction, for it targets only "a *method* of abortion" that can be described as no more brutal than dismembering the fetus in utero. Introducing "moral concerns . . . untethered to any ground genuinely serving the Government's interest in preserving life" put the Court on a slippery slope that could lead to proscribing any type of abortion. "Our obligation is to define the liberty of all, not to mandate our own moral code," Ginsburg noted in a direct thrust at Kennedy.

Nor did she mask her frustration at the Court's invocation of "an antiabortion shibboleth" for which there is "no reliable evidence." In her words,

> Women who have abortions come to regret their choice, and conse-
> quently suffer from "[s]evere depression and loss of esteem." Because
> of women's fragile emotional state and because the "bond of love the
> mother has for her child," the Court worries, doctors may withhold
> information about the nature of the intact D&E procedure. The solu-
> tion the Court approves, then, is not to require doctors to inform
> women, accurately and adequately, of the different procedures and
> their attendant risks. Instead, the Court deprives women of the right
> to make an autonomous choice, even at the expense of their safety.
> This way of thinking reflects ancient notions about women's place in
> the family and under the Constitution—ideas that have long since
> been discredited.

The Court's allowance for challenges by an individual woman or her physician, Ginsburg continued, "jeopardizes women's health and places doctors in an untenable position" because the record documenting "medical exigencies, unpredictable in advance, may indicate to a well-trained doctor that intact D&E is the safest procedure."

"In sum," she bluntly concluded, "the notion that the Partial-Birth Abortion Ban furthers any legitimate governmental interest is, quite simply, irrational. The Court's defense of the statute provides no saving explanation. In candor, the Act, and the Court's defense of it, cannot be understood as anything other than an effort to chip away at a right declared again and again by this Court—and with increasing comprehension of its centrality to women's lives."

Wiping out any lingering reservations about her commitment to *Roe v. Wade,* she not only defended women's reproductive rights but grounded them in sex-equality principles, citing equal protection precedents—including decisions she had litigated or written.

· · ·

IN THE IMMEDIATE FUTURE, however, there seemed scant likelihood that Ginsburg's effort to rewrite *Roe* would prevail. Energized by their

Carhart victory, antiabortion forces stepped up legislative initiatives, persuading Republican-controlled states to adopt measures designed to limit freedom of choice under the guise of women-protective legislation. Parental notification, waiting periods up to seventy-two hours, invasive trans-vaginal sonograms, imposing constitutionally questionable restrictions on abortion clinics, and banning both private and public health insurance companies from offering abortion coverage in their plans were not without effect. By 2011, 87 percent of the counties in the United States had no abortion clinics.

In the years since, that number grew as antiabortion legislators imposed constitutionally questionable "women-protective" restrictions on clinics, forcing closings in Oklahoma, Texas, Louisiana, Mississippi, Alabama, and North Carolina. In Texas, a state with 5.4 million women of reproductive age, closing down clinics left women in the Rio Grande valley the alternative of traveling 240 miles to San Antonio or walking to Mexico. The demographic burden cried out for comment. "The closing down of clinics, the attacks on Planned Parenthood, amount to an attack on the health care available to poor women, particularly Black and brown women," wrote Kareem Abdul-Jabbar in a powerful essay in *Time*. By the time *Whole Woman's Health v. Hellerstedt*—the case challenging the Texas clinic closings—reached the Supreme Court in 2016, Google search data had revealed a "hidden demand for self-induced abortion" reminiscent of the era prior to *Roe v. Wade,* not only in Texas, but in fifteen other states where major barriers had been enacted.

Ginsburg's response was to step up summer speaking engagements in which she would urge young women to care more about reproductive rights and not take them for granted.

· · ·

THAT GINSBURG MIGHT FOLLOW her *Carhart* dissent from the bench—an act of theater intended to convey that the majority is not just mistaken but "profoundly wrong"—in the same term seemed unlikely. Yet the brief period of harmony that had characterized Roberts's first year as chief justice had vanished. Kennedy, whose thinking did not necessarily align with that of Scalia or Thomas, nonetheless provided conservatives with the fifth vote they needed to prevail not only on abortion restriction but also on racial integration in schools, the death penalty, faith-based programs, and wage equity. On May 27, 2007, Ginsburg would choose to dissent from the bench once more, making Lilly Ledbetter's name synonymous with discrimination against women in the workplace.

Ledbetter had worked for nineteen years as a manager at a Goodyear Tire and Rubber plant in Gadsden, Alabama, where she had been paid less than male managers for years—a discrepancy that she long suspected but of which she had no proof. Just before she retired as the only female manager, she received an anonymous note with salary information that showed she was making $3,727 a month, while the lowest-paid man in the department was being paid $4,286 for the same job. In March 1998, she filed a questionnaire with the EEOC. The commission, having long ruled that each pay period of uncorrected discrimination is seen as a new incident of discrimination, granted her the right to sue. In November 1999, she filed suit under Title VII of the Civil Rights Act and the Equal Pay Act.

At trial, Goodyear argued that Ledbetter was paid less because of a purportedly neutral merit system; she had not been recommended for merit raises in 1997 and 1998 because of her poor performance. Yet she had, in fact, won a "Top Performance Award" in 1996. Records presented by Ledbetter's lawyer showed that her pay was so low that it sometimes fell below the minimum set by Goodyear's pay policy for the job. Other women at the Gadsden plant also provided ample evidence of widespread sex discrimination. Ledbetter herself testified about the discriminatory attitude conveyed by the plant officials. The district court ruled for Ledbetter, and she was awarded $3.3 million in back-pay compensation and punitive damages. The U.S. Court of Appeals for the Eleventh Circuit reversed the verdict, holding that she had no case because she could not show intentional discrimination in her last pay-setting period six months prior to lodging her complaint with the EEOC.

When Ledbetter's lawyers appealed, the Bush administration rejected the EEOC's ruling and entered the case on Goodyear's behalf. The Court agreed to hear her case, because other federal appeals courts had accepted the EEOC's more relaxed view of the 180-day requirement. The question now hinged on the Court's interpretation of the requirement in Title VII of the Civil Rights Act of 1964. Whether and under what circumstances may a plaintiff bring action alleging illegal pay discrimination when the pay differential occurred outside the statutory limitations period of 180 days? Must the legal challenge be brought at the time employees are being discriminated against? Does the passage of time, absent new acts of *intentional* discrimination, effectively erase prior wage discrimination? Complicating the case further was a thicket of precedents, many amassed in the 1980s and less favorable to Ledbetter's claim, that the Court would have to sort through.

· · ·

WHEN ORAL ARGUMENTS BEGAN, Kevin Russell of Stanford Law School's Supreme Court Litigation Clinic tried to explain that it might take years for someone to find out that her paycheck was markedly less than other similarly qualified employees. Ginsburg jumped in to help him out. "Mr. Russell, I thought your argument was that . . . the spread in pay is an incremental thing. You may think the first year you didn't get a raise, 'well, so be it.' But . . . you have no reason to think that there is going to be this inequality."

The chief justice, his years as a corporate attorney coming to the fore, intervened on Goodyear's behalf, as did Alito. Under the plaintiff's theory, Roberts charged, companies would be liable for acts that were committed in the past. "I suppose all they'd have to do is allege that sometime over the past—I mean, it doesn't have to be 15 years," he said. "It could be 40 years, right—that there was a discriminatory act, in one of the semi-annual pay reviews I was denied this, a raise that I should have gotten." Wrong, replied Ginsburg. "If she's going to bring a case [alleging] I got a 2 percent raise, he got a 3 percent raise, her chances are slim." Then Kennedy raised the possibility that a company might have been sold between the time of the alleged discrimination and the lawsuit.

It was now clear that what Justices Roberts, Alito, and Kennedy saw as the practical aspects of how the law *should* operate would be a prime factor in the decision. Employers, they indicated, could hardly be expected to cope with trials at which evidence ran throughout the plaintiff's entire career. But what was equally clear is that Justices Ginsburg, Breyer, Stevens, and Souter were troubled by answers that allowed no avenue of redress for an employee who had unknowingly suffered gender-based pay discrimination at an earlier stage in her career.

With five votes in hand—Scalia and Thomas were givens—Roberts had exactly what he wanted: a civil case against a company in which the plaintiff's claim could be dismissed on procedural grounds. Such rulings reduce the number of potential future plaintiffs by making trial lawyers (and potential clients) think twice about filing a case. The "big guys" win without ever having to go to court. The next step in curtailing Title VII would be to limit the ability of plaintiffs to band together to sue in a class-action case. But Roberts and his fellow conservatives would have to wait until 1.5 million women working for a company known for its low wages, gender discrimination, erratic schedules, and illegal firings later filed suit in a blockbuster case against Walmart. In a 5–4 vote, the conservative majority determined that the hundreds of thousands of female workers suing Walmart did not have enough in common to file as a class. Hailed by business groups, the ruling sent a clear message: the larger the company, the more varied its job practices, and the less likely it will have to face a class-action claim based on race, sex, or other factors.

· · ·

IN THE MEANTIME, Alito, to whom the majority opinion in *Ledbetter* had been assigned, like any good lawyer, carefully selected precedents supporting his view of the ruling. "We apply the statute as written," Alito wrote. No "discrete act" of intentional discrimination occurred in the 180 days prior to Ledbetter's charge. Claims that earlier instances of pay discrimination had compounded over the years, resulting in smaller raises and a significantly lower salary than her male counterparts, he deemed irrelevant. "Current effects alone cannot breathe life into prior, uncharged discrimination."

Justice Stevens, delighted with Ginsburg's demolition of the majority opinion in *Carhart,* asked her to write the dissent in *Ledbetter.* Returning to the bench to deliver another oral rebuke, she began, "Title VII was meant to govern real-world employment practices, and that world is what the Court today ignores."

She then went on to explain clearly how pay disparities differ from other adverse actions to which the 180-day rule applies. Refusing to hire, firing, or failing to promote someone is each a discrete act that allows the employee to investigate and make a timely complaint. Pay disparities, by contrast, often occur, as they did in Ledbetter's case, in small increments that do not immediately arouse suspicion that discrimination is at work:

> Comparative pay information . . . is often hidden from the employee's view. . . . Small initial discrepancies may not be seen as meet for a federal case, particularly when the employee, trying to succeed in a nontraditional environment, is averse to making waves. . . . It is only when the disparity becomes apparent and sizable, *e.g.,* through future raises calculated as a percentage of current salaries, that an employee in Ledbetter's situation is likely to comprehend her plight and, therefore, to complain. Her initial readiness to give her employer the benefit of the doubt should not preclude her from later challenging the then current and continuing payment of a wage depressed on account of her sex.

Ginsburg turned next to the matter of precedents, pointing out that the majority had relied on the wrong ones. A further, close reading of congressional intent at the time Title VII was amended showed that "Congress never intended to immunize forever pay differentials unchallenged within 180 days of their adoption." Moreover, the courts of appeals in case after case had ruled that "each paycheck less than the amount payable had the employer adhered to a nondiscriminatory compensation regime" constitutes a fresh violation of Title VII.

She also scrutinized the Court's assertion that treating pay discrimination as a discrete act, limited to each particular pay-setting decision, is necessary to protect employers from the burden of defending claims arising from an employment decision in the distant past. "The discrimination of which Ledbetter complained," she pointed out, "is *not* long past." Rather, it was compounded with each pay period. Allowing employees to challenge discrimination that extends over long periods does not leave employers defenseless, she maintained, listing the various measures at management's disposal. Making clear "how far the Court has strayed from interpretation of Title VII with fidelity to the Act's core purpose," she concluded with an appeal to Congress to correct, as it had in 1991, "this Court's parsimonious reading."

. . .

THE U.S. CHAMBER OF COMMERCE, the country's largest business lobbying group, rejoiced—and why not? The Labor Department under Bush had already cut back enforcement in its Wage and Hour Division and tried to abolish the equal-pay initiative introduced by the Clinton administration. And with the president's new nominees on the Court, employers had prevailed in all four cases involving labor and employment issues in the 2006–7 term. In less than two years, the federal courts would apply the *Ledbetter* decision to some three hundred cases involving not only Title VII but also Title IX and the Eighth Amendment, exonerating employers from the consequences of discrimination.

For Ledbetter, now almost seventy, disappointment was all consuming. She had lost not only her case but her jury award. "I worked a lot of years doing the hard work and not to get paid as much as the men will affect me every day in the future" in the form of lower retirement benefits, she told reporters as she left the Court. Others echoed her dismay, calling the decision a "setback for women and a setback for civil rights." Workplace experts agreed, predicting that the ruling would have broad negative ramifications, narrowing the legal options for all workers. (In her dissent, Ginsburg had also noted that "the same denial of relief" would apply to those alleging discrimination on the basis of race, religion, age, national origin, or disability.)

Ginsburg's dissent could not be discounted. "Rarely in the history of the Court had a justice, speaking from the bench no less, called so directly on another branch of government to nullify a decision by her colleagues," noted legal commentator and author Jeffrey Toobin. Her ability to write in plain language that would allow the public to empathize with Ledbetter's plight had precisely the effect she intended. Within hours of the decision's announcement, New York's senator Hillary Rodham Clinton announced that she would submit a bill to the Senate to amend Title VII. The media picked up on Ledbetter's story and editorials endorsing congressional action quickly followed in *The New York Times,* the *Los Angeles Times, The Washington Post,* and other newspapers nationwide. Suddenly—very suddenly—the disappointed plaintiff had become Lilly Ledbetter, Democrats' cause célèbre.

. . .

AFTER THE SUMMER RECESS in 2007, the Court had one more opportunity to try to right the imbalance between liberty and security that had been produced by the war on terror. Warrantless wiretaps and internet intercepts were only part of the vastly enhanced domestic data-gathering effort that violated Fourth Amendment privacy precedents. Imprisoning captured members of the Taliban and al-Qaeda in Guantánamo Bay, Cuba, meant denying detainees (among them U.S. citizens) constitutional protections, including the century-old right to petition for habeas corpus.

In the 2004 oral arguments in *Rasul* and *Hamdi,* Ginsburg had asked Deputy Attorney General Paul Clement whether the government was torturing detainees at Guantánamo. He replied, "We don't do that." The very next day, the media was inundated with news of atrocities in Iraq in the U.S.-controlled prison of Abu Ghraib. The Court had tried again in 2006 in the *Hamdan* opinion, reminding the administration of such essential principles as checks and balances, separation of powers, habeas corpus protection for those held without trial, and judicial review. Yet

Taliban and al-Qaeda detainees held at Camp X-Ray, Guantánamo Bay, Cuba.

The photograph of Private First Class Lynndie R. England holding a prisoner on a leash at the Abu Ghraib prison created an international controversy regarding abuse and torture. Eleven soldiers, including England, would serve time in prison and be dishonorably discharged.

the administration took the ruling as no more than a mild slap on the wrist, even though the Court had made it clear that habeas corpus is a near-absolute guarantee of due process for those held in Guantánamo and can only be suspended by an act of Congress in response to an insurrection or invasion.

The White House then tried to outflank the Court with legislation to have trials by military commissions, virtually ignoring provisions in the Geneva Convention as well as those applying in U.S. military courts. The stage was now set for another showdown with the Court. But the Court procrastinated, despite the eagerness of Ginsburg, Breyer, and Souter to go ahead. It would take until June 12, the very last day of the 2008 spring term, for a majority to finally make clear to George W. Bush in *Hamdi v. Rumsfeld* that habeas corpus extended to prisoners at the American base at Guantánamo. As Kennedy stated, "the political branches . . . [may not] switch the Constitution on and off at will." Yet

much had been lost in the interim: presidential accountability, constitutional freedoms, and moral leadership. Not least was the squandering
of the international solidarity that the United States had enjoyed in the
wake of 9/11.

. . .

THE PAST DECADE, and especially the eight years of the George W.
Bush administration, had been difficult for Ginsburg. She had endured
much—her own bout with cancer and now the return of Marty's, the
loss of O'Connor and Rehnquist, the lonely years of being the only
woman on the Court. Not least were the defeats for equality that she
found so misguided—*Nguyen, Carhart, Ledbetter,* and more. But as was
her wont, she resolutely soldiered on, and along the way there were some
moments of great joy.

On November 1, 2008, she opened the door of her office chambers
to find the legendary mezzo-soprano Leontyne Price, now eighty-one,
kneeling on one knee before her. "What a joy," Ginsburg exclaimed,
beaming, clasping Price's hand between both of hers. At a luncheon at
the Court, which Ginsburg, Scalia, and Kennedy hosted, she told the
great singer that she and Marty had attended her spectacular 1961 debut
at the Metropolitan Opera in Verdi's *Il Trovatore,* at which Price had
received a forty-two-minute ovation, one of the longest in the Met's history. Ginsburg recalled how the spotlight had shone on Price's parents
when they were introduced between acts—a proud moment indeed for
an African American couple who struggled for so long as midwife and
carpenter-handyman in the predominantly black town of Laurel, Mississippi. Price, who was accompanied by her brother, a retired army general,
was visibly moved by Ginsburg's remarks, confessing, "I'm not going to
cry, though my mascara is starting to run."

During the luncheon, a string quartet that had been playing an
arrangement of opera arias began "Un bel dì vedremo" from Puccini's
Madama Butterfly. Cio-Cio-San, the tragic heroine, had been one of
Price's great roles. From her seat near the piano, Price began singing
softly at first and then in a much fuller voice to the final high B-flat. The
sound of her "gloriously familiar voice" had hushed conversation. Justice
Kennedy lifted a corner of his eyeglasses to wipe away what one listener
thought looked like a tear.

Justices Scalia, Ginsburg, and Kennedy joined the National Endowment for the Arts chairman, Dana Gioia (back row, left to right), in a photograph with the NEA Opera Honors awardees Carlisle Floyd, Leontyne Price, and Richard Gaddes (seated, left to right), 2008.

· · ·

THREE DAYS LATER, CNN called the election for Obama. The son of a white mother from Kansas and a father from Kenya who had spent his childhood in Indonesia and Hawaii had just become president-elect of the United States. In Chicago's Grant Park and surrounding streets, over 240,000 people began cheering, crying, screaming, dancing, and hugging total strangers. A brass band played "Happy Days Are Here Again" and car horns honked all along Michigan Avenue.

Amid the jubilation, a *New York Times* reporter interviewed members of the crowd as they waited for the victor to arrive. A young woman from the historically African American South Side observed, "Something has changed by going through this [election cycle] whether you are black or not." A young white man from the North Side imagined that "this is like what it would be for my generation if a gay president is elected." A middle-aged Hispanic woman concluded that "more than a racial barrier had been crossed. He may be black in color but . . . his thinking doesn't have color."

Barack Hussein Obama had become the embodiment of change in a nation eager for new beginnings.

CHAPTER 19

Losing Marty and Leading the Minority

I t was a frigid January day. The sun shone brightly as citizens poured into the nation's capital for the inauguration of the forty-fourth president. The crowd—two million strong—stretched all the way from the Capitol to the Washington Monument. When a tall, slender African American took the oath of office on the same Bible that Abraham Lincoln had used at his inauguration in 1861, the symbolism inspired some in the audience to hope that the election of a candidate whose mother hailed from Kansas, his father from Kenya, and his half sister from Indonesia signified the arrival of a new post-ethnic, multiracial order. Most pronounced was the collective yearning for a president who shared and would update the liberal political tradition that had shaped his party.

Ginsburg shared the excitement. James had alerted his mother to the eloquent community organizer turned politician even before he was elected to the Senate in 2004. When the Court subsequently held one of its rare dinners for members of the Senate, she had requested that the Obamas be seated at her table. As she got to know the couple, Ginsburg found the highly cerebral, pragmatic moderate senator to be *sympathique*—a French word conveying her highest form of praise. Yet others, who during the campaign had questioned Obama's citizenship, claiming he was born in Kenya, a Muslim, and a "socialist," remained convinced that he represented a threat beyond that posed by his recent Democratic predecessors, Carter and Clinton.

. . .

THE CHALLENGES AWAITING the new administration staggered. An economic crisis had wiped out savings and left fifteen million workers unemployed and an economy in recession. Something had to be done about a collapsed housing market, accelerating income inequality, and a global banking collapse. A broken health system demanded urgent attention as did escalating costs of ever more frequent climate-related catastrophes. A disengaged but combat-weary nation wanted its military personnel recalled from Afghanistan and Iraq at the same time that terrorist threats promised perpetual war. And despite protestations by some whites that racism had been conquered, America's "original sin" remained a powerful presence.

With Congress controlled by Democrats, Obama, a skilled policy maker, hoped for bipartisanship. But Republican opposition—honed in the House since Newt Gingrich clashed with Bill Clinton—had spread to the Senate as an increasingly ideological electorate became less inclined to trust members of the opposing party. A few days after the election, Republican minority leader Mitch McConnell assembled his caucus to lay out his strategy for obstructing and undermining the new president at every opportunity. Abetted by conservative interest groups, think tanks, right-wing media, and the Internet, McConnell would succeed in manipulating the rules of the Senate to block administration initiatives large and small.

Nor was the GOP establishment the only part of the Republican Party bent on opposition. Grassroots activists on the far right felt betrayed by the Bush administration's high-cost bailouts of banks. Resentful of a political class irresponsive to "average Americans" that failed to keep its word about reducing either the size of government or the national debt, they feared that Obama would continue the stimulus package and other expensive government programs, including a new health-care initiative. White middle-class, middle-aged, and elderly, they also believed that minorities, and especially immigrants, had not earned the right to government benefits to which productive citizens were entitled.

In rallying to "take their country back," many of these aggrieved insurgents had more in mind than the size of government and the exigencies of fiscal policy. The commander in chief was a black liberal intellectual, as was his attorney general. The majority leader of the House wore pearls. An openly gay Jew headed the powerful House Financial Services Committee, which appropriated funds for the Wall Street bailout. A thirty-eight-year-old, pregnant, unmarried Latina congresswoman proudly served her California constituents, and the daughter of Puerto Rican migrants would soon gain a seat on the Court. Even more telling, minority births would exceed those of whites in 2011. For those who still believed that the United States was a heterosexual, white, Christian country where men set the standard and subordinate groups stayed in their place, this was *not* change Tea Partiers could believe in.

Building on this grassroots momentum and claiming close ideological affiliation, professionally run right-wing advocacy groups such as FreedomWorks and Americans for Prosperity jumped in. Pushing their own billionaire-funded agenda, they called for reducing government regulations, privatizing Social Security and Medicare, and lowering taxes on businesses and the rich. Aided by complicit right-wing media, the augmented Tea Party movement, working together with the GOP, used a technologically sophisticated plan for redistricting following the 2010 census that packed conservative whites into Republican districts. The success of operation REDMAP enabled the GOP to wrest the House from Democratic control only two years after Obama's election, forcing the president to withdraw further stimulus to the economy and thereby prolonging recovery from the recession.

The extent to which racial dynamics stoked extreme partisan opposition is unclear. Americans generally disclaim the explicit racism of the pre–civil rights era. Yet the single-mindedness with which Republicans would oppose every major legislative proposal made by the first black president suggests that far more was at play than policy or partisan differences. The election of 2008 produced widespread racialization among many conservative whites that played out along partisan lines, as subsequent events and scholarship have amply demonstrated. Racial spillover reinforced hostile responses to critical administration programs, from the stimulus package, health care, and tax policy to Obama's eventual endorsement of same-sex marriage. To be clear, this is not to say that everyone opposing Obama or his policies was a racist. It is to say that after 2008 political divisions became much more influenced by racial considerations, as did mass politics. The result not only further compounded

Barack Obama is sworn in as the forty-fourth U.S. president, January 20, 2009.

the challenges the new president faced. The GOP's extreme partisanship combined with conservatives' mistrust in government, white nationalism, and xenophobia would also help enable Donald Trump's candidacy.

Ginsburg also found the early years of the new administration to be a trying time. Despite her friendships with Scalia and Souter, she still felt acutely O'Connor's absence. As the lone woman on the Court, she complained that her male colleagues' discourse seemed to have reverted to the prefeminist era of the popular television show *Mad Men*.

She had never felt more so than during oral arguments in April 2009 for *Safford Unified School District v. Redding*. Based on a tip from a classmate, Safford Middle School officials searched the backpack of thirteen-year-old Savana Redding for ibuprofen, which was not allowed on campus. Two female staff members then conducted a strip search without the consent of the girl's mother. Neither search found any contraband. Redding's mother filed suit against the school district claiming the second search violated her daughter's Fourth Amendment right to be free from unreasonable search and seizure.

During oral arguments, male justices failed to understand the perspective of the young girl, comparing her experience to that of changing into a swimsuit or gym clothes. Ginsburg, futilely attempting to remove the notion of triviality with which the argument was infused, pointed out that the young girl was forced to "shake [her] bra out, to stretch the top of [her] pants and shake that out." This could not be compared to changing for gym class. Breyer, missing Ginsburg's point, related his own experiences in the school locker room, stating that it was "not beyond human experience" for people to stick things in their underwear.

Unlike her colleagues on the bench, members of the press corps recognized Ginsburg's annoyance. Nina Totenberg noted how "the Court's only female justice bristled, her eyes flashing with anger," while Joan Biskupic described her as "openly frustrated." In a subsequent interview, Ginsburg explained, "Maybe a 13-year-old boy in a locker room doesn't have that same feeling about his body. . . . It's a very sensitive age for a girl. I don't think that my colleagues, some of them, quite understood."

Thanks to the press, the men on the bench got the message, ruling overwhelmingly that Redding's Fourth Amendment rights had been violated. Nevertheless, Ginsburg ardently believed that the Court needed another woman's voice. One small woman and "eight rather well-fed men" would hardly inspire young girls who wished to follow in the footsteps of their two history-making predecessors, she commented.

Political cartoon, September 19, 2014, reflecting the racism of right-wing Obamaphobes.

Foremost among Ginsburg's concerns was Marty's health. His devotion, brilliance, and irrepressible wit had been a constant in her life. Cancer, the scourge he had struggled against during his third year at Harvard Law School, had returned in 2006—this time as a tumor growing near his spine. Even standing to cook had finally become almost too painful for him to endure, although dinner was the one time when the couple could sit down and enjoy their nightly discussion of law over good food and wine. Both husband and wife were keenly aware that there were limits to how long Marty's doctors would be able to postpone the inevitable.

· · ·

AT THE END of the 2009 spring term, Souter announced plans for retirement. His utter distaste for the Roberts Court—"its disrespect for precedent, its grasping conservatism, and its aggressive pursuit of political objectives"—had swiftly mounted. The chief justice's maneuvering over the issue of campaign financing, which boldly raised questions not asked and not necessary to resolve, sealed Souter's decision.

Ginsburg understood Souter's intense frustration. Treating corporations as worthy of exercising First Amendment rights and counting the money they spent on political campaigns as speech that could not constitutionally be constrained by campaign finance laws limiting corporate contributions would wreak havoc on the political process. *Citizens United,* she was convinced, undermined the fundamental principle of democracy, especially at a time when the richest 0.1 percent have more wealth than the bottom 90 percent. There was also the critical issue of segregation in public education, on the rise since the 1980s and unconstrained by a conservative majority that disdained precedent. The impact was evident in the Seattle and Louisville rulings on integration plans in public schools. She had joined Breyer's passionate dissent. And then there was the *Heller* decision expanding an individual's right to bear arms—a ruling contrary to the view of the Second Amendment held by all the lower federal courts—that delighted the NRA and its right-wing supporters.

To make matters worse, Ginsburg received word in January 2009 that she had again been diagnosed with cancer. Fortunately, the malignancy had been detected at a very early stage, and the tumor was small—only about one centimeter. Yet undergoing the removal of even an early-stage pancreatic cancer—typically followed by radiation and chemotherapy—is arduous.

Scheduling the surgery at Memorial Sloan Kettering Cancer Center in New York in early February, the justice returned to Washington, managing once again to avoid missing a single oral argument during the spring term. Still, her delight at Jane's most recent honors for her global contribution to law on intellectual property could not obscure the side effects of her own extended treatments and the toll exacted by Marty's frequent visits to his doctors. Fighting cancer on two fronts had left Ginsburg exhausted and her formidable resolve depleted.

Then came a phone call from Marilyn Horne, the great mezzo-soprano. Horne told the justice that when she had been told of her own diagnosis of pancreatic cancer, she said to herself, "*I will live*. Not I hope I will live, but *I will live*." The effect of the call was invigorating, firmly implanting those three words in Ginsburg's mind. For months, they served as a mantra, constantly reinforced by Marty.

The president provided additional boosts. The first piece of legislation that he signed after sweeping into office with a Democratic Congress was

President Barack Obama, surrounded by lawmakers and Lilly Ledbetter, signed the Lilly Ledbetter Fair Pay Act, 2009.

the Lilly Ledbetter Fair Pay Act of 2009. Making it easier for a worker to sue for illegal wage discrimination, the act extended the 180-day statute of limitations so that each new paycheck was affected by an initial discriminatory wage decision. A copy of the bill, inscribed by Obama, now hangs in Ginsburg's chambers. Then, as a replacement for Souter, the president chose Judge Sonia Sotomayor, who he believed understood "how the world works and how ordinary people live."

· · ·

A CANDIDATE WITH a compelling life story, not unlike Ginsburg's own, Sotomayor had lost her father when she was only nine. Absorbing her mother's conviction that education offered the key to a better life, she made the transition from the Bronx to the Ivy League, thanks to affirmative action. Demonstrating her intellectual chops during her years at Princeton, she graduated summa cum laude before heading to Yale Law School. After working as an assistant district attorney in Manhattan and as a corporate litigator, Sotomayor served for six years as judge on the U.S. District Court for the Southern District of New York before moving to the Second Circuit.

Still, the nominee's strong qualifications did not guarantee a smooth confirmation. Opponents made much of a speech she had delivered at Berkeley in 2001, during which she suggested that "a wise Latina woman" might reach a better judgment than "a white man who hasn't lived that life." Ultimately, Sotomayor's record as a judge to whom facts and precedent mattered overwhelmed Republican claims that she was a reflexive liberal who made decisions based on empathy rather than law.

Confirmed on August 6, 2009, she received an especially warm welcome from Ginsburg, who thought all the fuss about the "wise Latina woman" remark had been "ridiculous." All judges are influenced by their life experiences, Ginsburg maintained, just as she herself had been. The newest member of the Court, she predicted, would indeed "hold her own."

· · ·

LESS THAN A YEAR LATER, Justice Stevens, still vigorous and sharp at ninety, announced his retirement, after almost thirty-five years on the Court. Solicitor General Elena Kagan proved to be a serious con-

Stevens (second from right) celebrates his retirement with (from left) President Obama and Justices Souter and Kennedy, September 8, 2009.

tender for his seat. She had grown up on Manhattan's Upper West Side. Her mother, an elementary school teacher, rigorously challenged young Elena, nourishing a fierce intellect, while her father inspired his daughter's love of opera and the law. After concluding her studies at Princeton, Oxford, and Harvard Law School, Kagan clerked for Judge Abner Mikva at the Court of Appeals for the D.C. Circuit and then for Justice Thurgood Marshall.

Following a stint as a professor at the University of Chicago Law School, she moved to the Clinton White House—initially as a member of the White House counsel's staff and then as a major adviser on domestic policy. When Republicans blocked her nomination to the D.C. Circuit, she returned to academia, using her superb teaching skills, deft political touch, and expansive personality to good advantage at Harvard Law School. Obama had lured the first female dean of his alma mater back to Washington as the first woman solicitor general.

Kagan's intellectual stature and caution in expressing her political beliefs made her confirmation possible. Yet the hearings did not go smoothly. Some Democrats disliked her support for executive power. Republicans complained that because she had no judicial experience, she was insufficiently prepared for a seat on the high court. Defenders pointed out that she had served as solicitor general—the "Tenth Justice," which gave her a deep understanding of the Court's work. Republicans also objected to her decision to bar military recruiters from Harvard Law School because of the military's "don't ask, don't tell" policy for homosexuals, which ran afoul of Harvard's antidiscrimination policy. Nevertheless, in August, the Senate voted to confirm 63–37.

. . .

GINSBURG FOUND the two new appointments "exhilarating." She had known both women previously, and neither was a "shrinking violet." Sotomayor would indeed prove a tenacious interrogator, displaying common sense and a keen sensitivity to injustice, especially in the criminal justice system. Kagan's brilliance, good judgment, sense of humor, and inimitable capacity for building bridges with those of different views also made her a force to be reckoned with. Someone who could see the big picture, she could become a fitting intellectual opponent for Roberts. Asked by Obama if she was happy with her new sisters, Ginsburg replied that she would be even happier if he would give her four more.

Sonia Sotomayor, Ruth Bader Ginsburg, and Elena Kagan pose together at Justice Kagan's investiture.

While the new justices added energy to the minority, the ideological balance of the Court remained unaltered. The five justices appointed by Republicans and the four by Democrats would continue to hold competing values on such issues as the balance of state and federal power, how best to pursue equality, the appropriate methods for interpreting the Constitution, and the role of the Court in a democracy.

One important change had occurred with Justice Stevens's retirement. In those cases where the chief justice was in the minority or when a dissent was required by the liberal quartet, Ginsburg, as the senior associate justice, would now assign opinions. Stevens had provided his replacement with a superb model of coalitional and intellectual leadership. Employing his position strategically, he had courted O'Connor and Kennedy to maximize the chances of getting five votes, assigning Kennedy the majority opinion in *Lawrence v. Texas,* a 2003 landmark decision invalidating bans on consensual sex between same-sex individuals. In other cases, Stevens himself wrote the opinion in order to keep Kennedy on board. When he wrote for the minority, as in *Bush v. Gore* and *Citizens United,* the veteran Stevens proved fierce in dissent.

Whether Ginsburg, who had more of a reputation as a loner, would be as persuasive as her predecessor had been with Kennedy seemed doubtful to the veteran Court analyst Jeffrey Toobin. Unlike O'Connor, who was a consistent compromiser and a gradualist during her years as the swing vote, Kennedy had in some areas moved closer to his impatient fellow conservatives, including cases involving reproductive rights. Referring to Kennedy's "flowery, discursive rhetorical opinions"—in contrast with Ginsburg's narrow, often dull ones—Toobin observed that the two justices were just not temperamentally harmonious. As the *Carhart* decision upholding the Partial-Birth Abortion Ban Act demonstrated, Kennedy's opinions could drive the famously restrained and ever polite Ginsburg to something close to rage.

But if Kennedy's vote proved elusive, she could move the Court—and the public—in other ways. Her seniority, formidable intellect, and nuanced understanding of legal issues would count for much. As her recent dissent in *Ledbetter* revealed, she had a gift for communicating the complex ramifications of the Court's rulings in simple language that could have a galvanizing impact on the broader public.

The greatest dissents, Ginsburg maintained, "speak to a future age" by becoming Court opinions and, gradually over time, the dominant view. Hence, she would try to persuade Breyer, Sotomayor, and Kagan that their dissents would be more powerful if they spoke in one voice rather than separately. She also resolved to make assignments fairly, retaining fewer for herself than had Stevens. Yet as the liberal anchor of the Court, she would write in closely watched cases.

. . .

IN THE IMMEDIATE FUTURE, however, plans for the fall term had to be put on the back burner as Marty's condition further deteriorated. During a hospital stay in early June 2010, his doctors at Johns Hopkins Medical Center reported that nothing more could be done. Marty managed to hold on for their fifty-sixth wedding anniversary. When Ruth arrived at the hospital on June 25 to bring him home, she pulled out the drawer next to his bed. In it, she found a yellow pad with a handwritten note.

6/7/10

My dearest Ruth—

You are the only person I have loved in my life, setting aside, a bit, parents and kids, and their kids. And I have admired and loved you almost since the day we first met at Cornell some 56 years ago.

What a treat it has been to watch you progress to the very top of the legal world.

I will be in JH Medical Center until Friday, June 25, I believe, and between then and now, I shall think hard on my remaining health and life, and whether on balance the time has come for me to tough it out or to take leave of life because the loss of quality now simply overwhelms.

I hope you will support where I come out, but I understand you may not. I will not love you a jot less.

Marty

. . .

ON THE FOLLOWING SUNDAY, June 27, Marty died at home of complications of metastatic cancer—hauntingly, almost exactly sixty years after Ruth's mother, Celia, had succumbed to the dreaded disease.

In a final protective act, he had taken from his wife the burden of the decision.

The next morning, the final day of the Court's term, an "ashen faced" Ginsburg took her seat on the bench to announce her majority opinion in *Christian Legal Society Chapter v. Martinez*—a ruling that said a Christian group at a public law school could not bar gay students. Marty, she believed, would have wanted her to be there. Stevens was retiring, and his colleagues had written a letter that Roberts read aloud. Stevens thanked his colleagues "and each of your spouses—present and departed—for your warm and enduring friendship"—a reference to Marty, whose death Roberts had announced at the beginning of the session. Ruth managed to control her tears during the session, though Scalia could not.

Burial took place in a private ceremony at Arlington National Cemetery.

. . .

IN THE WEEKS that followed, Ginsburg carried out not only every one of her speaking engagements but also Marty's, displaying remarkable emotional stamina, just as she had throughout his long illnesses. Despite her grief, she knew they had been exceedingly fortunate to have had so many years together. Even her former Columbia colleague Professor Henry Monaghan marveled at their long love affair: "In their gestures . . . you could just see!"

Family, always a source of great pleasure, now helped ease the pain. Jane, who not only shared Marty's culinary skills but exceeded her father's production of legal casebooks, came down from New York on a monthly basis to prepare food that could be put in small containers and stored in her parents' freezer. Otherwise, she feared that Ruth would revert to her old staples of Jell-O and cottage cheese. Mother and daughter shared their interest in law and family. Jane's son, Paul, who had graduated from Yale Drama School and trained at the Conservatoire National Supérieur d'Art Dramatique, was beginning his professional career as an actor in Paris.

Paul's feisty, talkative younger sister, Clara, whom Ginsburg had memorably introduced at her nomination to the Court as the first member of her family to meet Hillary Clinton, had followed in Jane's footsteps. Attending the Brearley School in New York and then the University of Chicago, she was majoring in Romance languages and literature while pursuing a variety of summer internships. After graduating with honors two years later, she would be off to Cambridge University to pursue two master's degrees, one in gender studies and the other in European literature and culture, and then back home for Harvard Law School.

Ginsburg knew that familiarity with France on the part of her Spera grandchildren was no accident. Jane had become a Francophile during that first summer spent living with a French family near Lake Annecy in lieu of summer camp. She had always spoken French to Paul and Clara and, as they became older, sent them to spend time with a French family in the summer. James would also expose his daughters, Mimi and Abby, in similar exchanges. It was one of the many ways in which Ginsburg's parenting style had been transmitted to her grandchildren.

James, in fact, also provided his mother with much to be delighted about—most especially his forthcoming marriage to Patrice Michaels. A lovely soprano and a former solo vocalist with the Chicago Lyric Opera, Patrice balanced national and international performances with a part-time job as lecturer and director of vocal studies at the University of Chicago. The elder Ginsburgs, aware that James's previous marriage had been an unhappy one, were convinced that this "unbelievably wonderful" woman would be the wife that they believed their son finally deserved. Patrice, they agreed, would also be a great help to James with his Grammy Award–winning classical recording company, Cedille Records.

Because this new blended family would include James's two daughters, Miranda (Mimi) and Abigail (Abby), as well as Patrice's two sons, Harjinder (Harji) and Satinder (Sat Nam) Bedi, from a previous marriage, new quarters were essential. Marty, knowing he had little time left, had purchased a new house for the couple in Chicago, following the example set by his own parents, who had helped financially when help was needed. Ruth would perform the wedding ceremony the day after Marty's memorial service on September 3. She would then officially become the step-grandmother of two handsome boys who, like their natural father, were Sikh. And there was also Derrell Acon. A protégé of Patrice's when she taught at Lawrence University in Wisconsin, Derrell had come from one of the most troubled areas of Detroit. He was now doing advanced studies in music at the University of Cincinnati College-Conservatory of Music. Very much part of Patrice's family, he would now become part of Ginsburg's as well.

For years, Ruth and Marty had made the Santa Fe Opera an essential part of their August agenda. This year George Spera called to say that he and James would accompany Ruth. Patrice also wanted to come and bring Derrell, and Abby refused to be left behind. Fortunately, a next-door neighbor of Scalia's offered his Tesuque adobe, with three and a half bedrooms, near the opera that could accommodate the justice's newly extended family. With the house also available in future years, Santa Fe would become the site of annual family gatherings, beloved by the justice not only for its music, museums, galleries, and surroundings but also for her growing circle of friends.

On conversational terms with many of the vocalists and staff, the justice had already developed a reputation not only as a "discerning, intelligent operagoer" but as one "keenly interested in new and unusual repertory" and new composers, according to the Santa Fe Opera's general director, Charles MacKay. Always accompanied by U.S. marshals and usually escorted to her seat in the orchestra section by MacKay, Ginsburg was often the recipient of small flurries of spontaneous applause when she entered. While respecting her privacy, operagoers sometimes stopped to thank her for a particular opinion or dissent.

That year there was also a stopover in Colorado Springs at the end of August for a meeting of the judicial conference for the Tenth Circuit bench and bar where she was joined by Beverley McLachlin, the chief justice of Canada's Supreme Court. After the formal speeches and dinner, the two justices took the stage for a "fireside chat" about their careers. Ginsburg's candor and humor had the audience "in fits of laughter" as she talked about her involvement in *Craig* as well as about some of the challenges she had faced as a working mother making her way through academia.

Returning home to Washington for Marty's memorial service and the wedding, Ginsburg knew that she could rely on her all-consuming job to help fill the void created by the loss, especially now that she was the leader of the liberal quartet. Her days were highly structured. Often former clerks who came to Washington invited her to join them for din-

Justice Ginsburg before the opera in Santa Fe with her grandson, Paul Spera, and friend Audrey Bastien, 2013.

ner. Despite the justices' often sharp disagreements and independent operating chambers, they could function as a family when challenges arose. They lunched together daily when the Court was in session, discussing not cases or controversial topics but rather museum exhibits, cultural events, or sports. Ginsburg, a ready participant in conversations that involved music and theater, turned silent on sports—just as her former clerk Michael Klarman would have expected. Sotomayor's unabashed enthusiasm for the Yankees—the Bronx Bombers—afforded a vivid contrast.

Members of the Court also celebrated birthdays, though, as Ginsburg wryly observed, many of her colleagues sang "Happy Birthday" off-key. She was especially touched to learn that the justices' wives, spearheaded by Martha-Ann Alito, had put together a collection of Marty's favorite recipes (with Jane's help). Along with photographs and tributes from children and close friends, the volume would be published after the memorial under the apt title *Chef Supreme*.

No longer battling the intense exhaustion that she had endured during Marty's last years, Ginsburg stepped up her own social and travel schedule. Nina Totenberg, legal reporter for National Public Radio and a friend since the justice's ACLU days, observed that without Marty's outgoing personality to rely upon, Ruth now engaged more in conversation, even when the topic was not the law. Ginsburg's genuine affection for Obama—and his fondness for his "favorite justice"—enticed her to the White House for a celebration of Hanukkah in December 2011.

One month later, during the Court's January recess, she flew to Egypt, accompanied by Jane, to consult with her Egyptian counterparts as they began the transition to a constitutional democracy after the fall of Hosni Mubarak. Then on to Tunisia, where the Arab Spring had begun, and finally back home for spring term featuring several criminal justice cases.

True to form, Ginsburg would use her expertise in civil procedure as well as her close attention to facts and context to ensure that the legal rights of criminal defendants were preserved. Lacking representation by veteran Court lawyers, defendants were frequently the victims of police and prosecutorial misconduct that lacked judicial supervision. Such was the plight of John Thompson, who had been wrongly prosecuted in New Orleans and spent fourteen years on death row before the reversal of his conviction. Prosecutors had withheld evidence. After Thompson was stripped by the Supreme Court of the damages he had been awarded, Ginsburg, joined by Breyer, Sotomayor, and Kagan, issued a compelling dissent. That five of her colleagues had been more concerned with protecting municipalities from civil rights suits than protecting the constitutional rights of Thompson and his unfortunate counterparts, she considered to be added cause for vigilance.

. . .

THE END OF THE FALL TERM 2012 marked Ginsburg's twentieth year on the Court. Milestones earlier in her tenure had been commemorated with symposia at which legal scholars highlighted her many contributions to equal protection doctrine, civil procedure, and comparative and international law.

Her distinctive jurisprudence had changed little during her second decade on the high bench. But the Court's long move to the right, together with Ginsburg's role as leader of the liberal minority, cast a judge and justice known for her judicial moderation and collegiality into the role of chief dissenter. Those familiar with the new passion, vigor,

The Ginsburg family following the wedding ceremony of James Ginsburg and Patrice Michaels. Standing, left to right: George Spera, Clara Spera, Paul Spera, and Jane Ginsburg. Seated: Satinder Bedi, Justice Ginsburg, James Ginsburg, Patrice Michaels, and Harjinder Bedi. On the floor: Abigail Ginsburg and Miranda Ginsburg, 2010.

and authority infusing her dissents in *Carhart* and *Ledbetter* wondered if her "inner liberal" had taken over, supplanting her adherence to the "middle way."

Ginsburg herself would quickly dismiss such speculation, and with good reason. Even as a pioneering liberal litigator calling for dramatic change in law and doctrine, she had approvingly quoted Justice Benjamin Cardozo's observation that "justice is not to be taken by storm. She is to be wooed by slow advances." Putting down path markers—"way pavers," Ginsburg called them—in a way that brings about gradual change in the law has pragmatic benefits as well. "Measured motions," she had always believed, assure that innovations in the law do not get so far ahead of public opinion that backlash becomes too powerful to contain.

Ginsburg's views on judging, shaped initially by process theory and honed by her experience on the appellate court, also had not changed. Fidelity to rules governing the litigation process as the surest way of protecting due process rights has remained constant since her days at Harvard Law School. So, too, her understanding of the role of the federal courts as protectors of constitutional rights. When approaching cases that raise issues of racial and gender discrimination or the use of stereotypes to define or restrict any group, she had seldom concealed her own strong views.

Nor had she ever been timid about dissenting if the majority ignored binding precedent, reached an unnecessarily broad result, or failed to accord appropriate respect to another branch of government or lower court. Throughout the Rehnquist years, however, she had approached decisions with caution and care, consolidating her reputation as a judicial moderate eager to promote consensus. Her dissents, like her opinions, had consistently revealed clear reasoning and a marked preference for calm, neutral language devoid of rhetorical flourishes, emotional appeals, or alienating critiques of colleagues' opinions.

· · ·

WHAT CHANGED DURING Ginsburg's second decade on the Court—apart from its composition—was her own level of frustration with continued conservative dominance. There had not been a definitively liberal majority since the Nixon years. Any hope of influencing Roberts and Alito on equality issues had withered in the 2007 school integration cases, when their adherence to color-blind solutions flew in the face of reality—expanding, not shrinking, de facto segregation. The "strained fury" of Breyer's twenty-minute dissent in *Parents Involved,* backed by Stevens's trenchant comments on Roberts's rewriting of the historic *Brown* decision, revealed the profound alienation of the Court's liberals.

Nor was it just the losses suffered by civil rights plaintiffs that alarmed Ginsburg. It was also the unprecedented loss of access to the courts by ordinary citizens. The class-action suits by consumers that had so effectively revealed the dangers of tobacco and asbestos in the 1990s ended in

2011 with the procedural hurdle erected by the Roberts majority in *Wal-Mart v. Dukes*. Ginsburg had fought back in another precedent-based dissent. She knew that it was not just the female employees at Walmart (many of them low-income minorities) who were the ultimate losers but also a large segment of the American public. Lacking the resources for sustained litigation against business and employers who they believe had wronged them, ordinary people would no longer have their day in court.

Judicial protection of the people's liberties had also been set back on First Amendment issues. The Roberts Court had acquired a reputation as a champion of unfettered free speech in *Citizens United*, when it held that corporations have First Amendment rights. But a closer look at subsequent cases told a different story. In *Holder v. Humanitarian Law Project*, Roberts required no factual findings as to whether the government's claims that the human rights group's activism supported terrorism and required censorship. That the government said so was enough for the majority. As a precedent, the ruling sent a clear signal: "[J]udges must defer, and then defer again, to the government when it seeks to justify bans on speech." Breyer, Ginsburg, and Sotomayor found that to be a dangerous message to send in an age of intensifying government surveillance, as Breyer's hefty dissent made clear. In subsequent decisions, prisoners, public employees, and students also found their First Amendment rights curtailed. The majority's "ham-handed categorical approach," Stevens (and Ginsburg) objected, made free speech either all (*Citizens United*) or nothing (*Humanitarian Law Project, Beard, Garcetti,* and *Morse*).

Well before she became de facto minority leader, Ginsburg's patience had worn thin. She was no longer willing to try to piece together another centrist compromise that violated her principles. Nor was she now inclined to cast her objections in the neutral, detached language that had generally characterized her dissents in the Rehnquist years. Gradually, her judicial voice acquired new authority, passion, and edge.

The change was amplified by the frequency of her oral dissents from the bench. Reading a dissent out loud "supplement[s] the dry reason on the page with vivid tones of sarcasm, regret, anger and disdain," risking "collegiality and decorum," observes Adam Liptak. During her first decade on the Court, Ginsburg exercised this "nuclear option" only six times. After 2006, the sight of the tiny black-robed justice rising from the bench wearing her "black and grim" dissenting collar and clutching her papers became a familiar sight—thirteen times between 2006 and 2015. At the end of the 2012 term, she actually broke a record for oral disagreement, speaking three times in one day, each time about equal rights. Nor was she the only member of the liberal minority to speak out more. Dissents from the bench were on the rise in the Roberts Court.

Because oral recordings are not available until the following term, the general public must rely on legal reporters and commentators to convey what is happening in the Court and why it matters. In the process, a dissent from the bench becomes amplified and a judicial portrait is painted. Like some of her predecessors, most notably Chief Justices Warren and Rehnquist, Ginsburg maintains good relations with the legal press, counting some of them among her closest friends. Her image became that of a liberal heroine—quite appropriately, as a *New York Times* tally of individual justices' voting records confirms.

When Stevens was asked about his own reputation as a liberal, he thought of Brennan and Marshall, who were on the Court when Gerald Ford nominated him in 1975. His own moderate views, he insisted, had not changed. That he now wore a liberal label was a measure of how far the Court had shifted to the right with the nomination of each new chief. Ginsburg could make a similar argument, pointing to the conservative majority. The Roberts Court had too often resisted modest corrections, discounted the Constitution, and diminished the role of the judiciary as the protector of the people's rights and liberties. Yet there is no denying she derives pleasure from the extensive coverage her more recent dissents have received. That they are also part of her legacy would become abundantly clear in the further honors that awaited.

. . .

YALE LAW SCHOOL WOULD observe the completion of Ginsburg's second decade on the Court in October 2012 with a symposium titled "Equality's Frontiers." Among the distinguished legal scholars celebrating her equal protection jurisprudence was Kenji Yoshino, the Chief Justice Earl Warren Professor of Constitutional Law at NYU School of Law. Paying Ginsburg the ultimate compliment at the end of his presentation, he said, "I regard her as the founding father of sex-equality jurisprudence. I leave it to her whether she would prefer to be referred to as a

The opera singer Plácido Domingo serenades Ginsburg as the two receive honorary degrees from Harvard, May 26, 2011.

founding mother, founding parent, or simply the founder." But, he continued, "I will not negotiate about returning to her the words of Chief Justice Marshall about some of the original Founding Fathers: 'No tribute can be paid to [you] that exceeds [your] merit.'" Ginsburg responded with her trademark modesty, paying tribute in turn to her predecessors who had worked for equal rights for women since the 1920s—among them, the Yale alumna Pauli Murray.

As much as Ginsburg appreciated the Yale symposium, it was an event the previous May that she especially treasured. In 1973, after her successful argument in *Frontiero,* Solicitor General Erwin Griswold, who as dean of Harvard Law School had refused to allow Ginsburg to count her year at Columbia toward her Harvard degree, had apparently prompted the Law School to offer her a Harvard degree. There had been a stipulation: she must return her Columbia degree. When she politely declined, Marty suggested that she hold out for an honorary degree. On May 26, 2011, she received an honorary doctor of law degree from Harvard. Sweetening the occasion, one of the seven individuals receiving the highest award that Harvard could bestow was the world-renowned tenor turned baritone Plácido Domingo. Domingo had sung "Happy Birthday" to the justice on her seventy-fifth birthday. As Ginsburg received her degree, he sang to her again. "Being so close to that great voice," she recalls, "was like having electric shock run through me." The photograph of the two of them on the podium, which she titled "Woman in Ecstasy," graces her chambers.

Life without Marty still had its wonderful moments. There would be more in the future as her legacy continued to be celebrated.

CHAPTER 20

Race Matters

Two of the most contentious race-conscious measures of the racially freighted Obama years hit the Court's docket in 2013—affirmative action and voting rights. Ginsburg at eighty would once again prove capable of delivering the judicial equivalent of a body slam at a time when the Court's conservatives seemed bent on denying equal protection to minorities.

· · ·

IN FACT, she had found her voice in a dissent ten years earlier in two cases involving affirmative action in higher education. Both originated at the University of Michigan (UM). In the 1990s, the university had actively pursued diversity through fellowships for black, Hispanic, and Native American students and minority-studies programs in order to raise the percentage of underrepresented minorities at the state's premier university. The administration's efforts succeeded. They also raised the ire of white parents whose children were being rejected, especially after a request filed with the Freedom of Information Act made public the university's affirmative-action policies.

Grutter v. Bollinger challenged the admissions policy used by the prestigious Law School on the Ann Arbor campus, while *Gratz v. Bollinger* disputed the policy used by the undergraduate College of Literature, Science, and the Arts. When O'Connor cast her vote with the liberal minority in *Grutter,* Ginsburg breathed a sigh of relief. The kind of forward-looking admissions policy endorsed by business and military leaders in their amici briefs would continue. The Law School, wrote O'Connor, could maintain its narrowly tailored race-conscious policy. Minority status was but one of several factors contributing to a "diverse and academically outstanding" class. Training society's future leaders from varied racial, social, and economic backgrounds promoted "a compelling state interest."

Ginsburg had anticipated that the narrow victory achieved by the Law School in *Grutter* would not be repeated in *Gratz*. The university's Office of Undergraduate Admissions compiled scores for each applicant based on the applicant's grade point average and five additional factors: the quality of the applicant's school; the strength of that school's curriculum; any unusual circumstances in the applicant's life; geographic residence; and alumni relationships. These scores were plotted on four separate grids: (1) in-state nonminority applicants; (2) out-of-state nonminority applicants; (3) in-state minority applicants; and (4) out-of-state minority applicants. Controversy had arisen over the lower standards applied to the preferred minority applicants. Two students with identical credentials would receive different results: the nonminority student would be rejected, while the preferred minority student received an acceptance.

Jennifer Gratz, the daughter of a policeman, had applied in 1997, along with 13,500 other high school seniors. The university could accept only 4,000 students—only 29.6 percent of those applying. Her application rejected, she filed a reverse discrimination suit against the university with the help of the conservative Center for Individual Rights.

In 1998, UM had discontinued its admissions grid system, replacing it with a "selection index." In order to create a diverse freshman class, the college adopted a point system that awarded points for grades, test scores, strength of the high school, quality of courses of study, place of residence, alumni relationships, personal character, the quality of the personal essay, socioeconomic disadvantage, athletic ability, and minority status.

Applications of underrepresented minorities automatically received 20 points on the 150-point scale as part of the university's efforts to admit a critical mass of minority students. While the percentage of minority students varied from year to year, it needed to be enough to avoid tokenism and isolation. A nonminority candidate who scored highly in other categories could easily accumulate more points than a minority applicant, as Ginsburg would point out. Nevertheless, the bonus proved fatal in the eyes of the Court's more conservative members.

In the *Gratz* oral argument, O'Connor took a dim view of the college's mechanized review process, as had Kennedy, who said it looked like "a disguised quota." Without an individualized review of each application like that provided by the Law School, the majority agreed that the undergraduate admissions policy was not tailored narrowly enough. The automatic 20-point bonus given to underrepresented minority applicants, Rehnquist wrote, had the effect of making "the factor of race . . . decisive," thereby violating strict scrutiny.

A disappointed Ginsburg issued a classic dissent, which Justice Souter joined. Taking issue with the Court's insistence that the same standard of review controls scrutiny of *all* official race classifications, she pulled no punches. "This insistence on 'consistency,'" she wrote, "would be fitting were our Nation free of the vestiges of rank discrimination reinforced by law. . . . But we are not far distant from an overtly discriminatory past, and the effects of centuries of law-sanctioned inequality remain painfully evident in our communities." Pointing out that large racial disparities continue to exist in employment, income, access to health care, and education, she cited data demonstrating that schools attended by almost three-fourths of black and Latino children were "poverty-stricken and under-performing institutions. . . . 'Bias both conscious and unconscious . . . must come down if equal opportunity and nondiscrimination are ever genuinely to become this country's law and practice.'"

Equal protection, Ginsburg insisted, required permitting government decision makers to "properly distinguish between policies of exclusion and inclusion." "Actions designed to burden groups long denied full citizenship stature" are not equivalent to "measures taken to hasten the day when entrenched discrimination and its after-effects have been extirpated. . . . To pretend . . . that the issue presented in [*Bakke*] was the same as the issue in [*Brown*] is to pretend that history never happened and that the present doesn't exist."

Acknowledging that "the mere assertion of a laudable governmental purpose . . . should not immunize a race-conscious measure from careful judicial inspection," she highlighted three points about the University of Michigan undergraduate admissions policy. First, the racial and ethnic groups to which the college was providing special consideration, she noted, "historically have been relegated to inferior status by law and societal practice; their members continue to experience class-based discrimination to this day." Second, there was no indication that the college adopted its current policy in order to limit any particular racial or ethnic group, and no places were reserved on the basis of race. Third, there was also no evidence that the college's admissions policy unduly restricted opportunities of students who did not receive the special consideration based on race. "The stain of generations of racial oppression is still visible in our society," she concluded, "and the determination to hasten its removal remains vital."

· · ·

GINSBURG'S EFFORTS to preserve race-conscious remedies had proven far more difficult once Roberts and Alito joined the Court. Former "foot soldiers" in the anti-affirmation-action crusade of the Reagan administration, they voted in race-related cases accordingly. "The whole point of the Equal Protection Clause," Roberts would famously declare, "is to take race off the table." Kennedy was less antagonistic to minority considerations than his four conservative colleagues; however, he lamented the relaxed application of strict scrutiny that O'Connor had applied in *Grutter*. Rigorous scrutiny, he insisted, must be applied to assure the *majority* of the fairness of the application process.

With possibly five justices opposed to affirmative action—a view that appeared to be widely shared by three-quarters of the American population—conservative advocacy groups had moved quickly. None proved more effective than the Project on Fair Representation, a one-man operation of Edward Blum, a former Texas stockbroker whose passion had become fighting race-based policies in the courts. Shortly after *Grutter,* Blum had discerned an opportunity at his alma mater, the University of Texas (UT).

· · ·

UT, LIKE OTHER UNIVERSITIES in the South, had closed its doors to African Americans as late as 1950, when the Court forced the Law School to admit Heman Marion Sweatt. Affirmative-action policies followed in the 1970s. However, as the color-blind "consistency" gathered steam, the conservative Fifth Circuit in New Orleans had rejected the university's race-conscious admissions policy in 1996. The enrollment of black students plunged from 5 percent to 2 percent of the student body. In response, the state legislature instituted a nominally race-neutral policy that automatically admitted students graduating in the top 10 percent of their high school class to a state university, although not necessarily to the institution designated as their first choice.

Under the Top Ten Percent policy, African American students admitted to the flagship campus at Austin came primarily from impoverished, segregated schools and neighborhoods. As the university's own surveys revealed, many understandably felt isolated, complaining that they were often the sole black student in a class. Once *Grutter* was decided in 2003, UT officials concluded they could do better, modifying the admissions process a year later. The underlying objective of the new policy was to admit African Americans from more privileged socioeconomic backgrounds in order to create greater variety in experience among black students and more future leaders for the state.

Admitting the top 10 percent of high school graduates still accounted for 80 to 90 percent of the in-state admissions for an entering class. For the limited number of places left, admissions officers reviewed each application individually, using two scores. The first allotted points on the basis of grades and SAT scores. The second, called a personal achievement index, awarded points for two required essays, activities, service, and "special circumstances." Under the new plan, black enrollment climbed back to 5 percent, where it had previously been under affirmative action. The university also committed itself to self-assessments every five years to determine whether minority consideration was still needed.

Yet any degree of race consciousness in admissions was too much for Blum and his financial backers. Casting about for a plaintiff, he learned that Abigail Fisher, the daughter of a friend, had been denied admission to the class of 2008 at the flagship Austin campus. Having failed to graduate in the top 10 percent of her high school class in the highly affluent, fast-growing Houston suburb of Sugar Land, the strawberry blonde claimed in a YouTube video (posted by Blum) that students with lower grades than she had been accepted. "[T]he only other difference between us was the color of our skin."

In fact, the university had offered provisional admission to forty-seven students with lower test scores and grades than Fisher's, and only five of them were African American or Latino. Left unsaid by her supporters was that UT had also turned down 168 black and Latino students with grades as good as or better than Fisher's. She was also offered admission to the Austin campus in her sophomore year if she achieved a 3.2 GPA at another Texas university.

Blum was still convinced that he had the right plaintiff. He quickly secured Bert Rein from the powerhouse Washington law firm Wiley Rein to represent Fisher in an equal protection suit against the University of Texas. When Fisher lost her case in the district court and again in the U.S. Court of Appeals for the Fifth Circuit, Rein filed a petition to the Supreme Court in 2011. The university protested that Fisher lacked standing because she had already graduated from another university in Louisiana and thus no longer had anything at stake in the case.

Conservatives on the Court granted a hearing, much to Ginsburg's dismay. To show such solicitude for the hurt suffered by Abigail Fisher while at the same time refusing to hear a case on racial profiling by the police—a practice that adversely impacted the lives of minorities on a daily basis—provided yet another example of how the right-leaning majority prioritized a conservative agenda at the expense of African Americans and Latinos.

Oral argument was set for October 2012. The importance of the case was underscored by the presence of the retired justices O'Connor and Stevens in the audience. When the justices took their seats, Kagan was notably absent. Having dealt with the case as solicitor general, she felt obliged to recuse herself. The remaining liberals—Ginsburg, Sotomayor, and Breyer—began questioning Rein. Precisely what about the current Texas policy failed to conform to the requirements set forth in *Grutter*? Rein claimed to have no problem with the race-neutral Top Ten Percent Rule. However, he saw no need for the personal achievement index used by the Austin campus. Race, he insisted, had become an "independent add on." Kennedy essentially agreed, asking Rein, "Are you saying that you shouldn't impose this hurt or this injury, generally for so little benefit?"

When Gregory Garre, a former solicitor general in the George H. W. Bush administration, rose to respond for the University of Texas, Roberts and Scalia immediately jumped in with questions designed to make the university's commitment to diversity look absurd. "Should someone who is one-quarter Hispanic check the Hispanic box or some different box?" Roberts asked. "What about one-eighth?" he persisted. Scalia piled on. Alito, returning to the question of "critical mass," asked what percent of the student body would have to be African American. Garre avoided the trap, aware that any figure he might have offered would be interpreted as an illegal quota. When the hour ended, it seemed clear that at least four justices, possibly five, were searching for a way to either eviscerate or overrule *Grutter,* dispensing with affirmative action altogether.

· · ·

NINE MONTHS PASSED with no word on the decision, inviting speculation about bitter divisions. As drafts circulated among the justices, an impassioned dissent from Sotomayor, fully backed by Ginsburg, caused Kennedy to rethink how far he was willing to go in overturning *Grutter.* As the term neared an end, a compromise was finally brokered that Sotomayor and Thomas could accept. (Thomas, like Sotomayor, was a beneficiary of affirmative action, but the two held polar opposite views of its value.)

Sidestepping the decisive victory sought by Blum and other opponents, the majority voted to toughen the level of strict scrutiny courts applied. *Fisher* was sent back to the lower courts to reconsider. Writing for the seven-member majority, Kennedy stipulated that colleges and universities must demonstrate that "available, workable race-neutral alternatives" do not suffice before taking race into account. Courts reviewing affirmative-action programs must also conduct "a careful judicial inquiry into whether a university could achieve sufficient diversity *without* using racial classifications." His sparse opinion offered no guidance for how this was to be done.

Breyer believed that the Court's minority had dodged a bullet, as indeed it had. Ginsburg, however, was supremely frustrated by her inability to persuade the Court to speak candidly in discussing the many forms discrimination takes. Issuing a lone dissent, she took exception to Kennedy's "Janus-faced logic" of allowing colleges and universities to value racial diversity yet tightening even further the requirements for taking race into account. Because the admissions policy at the Austin campus conformed both to Harvard's plan, which Powell had pronounced exem-

Abigail Fisher and Edward Blum outside the Supreme Court after oral arguments in Fisher v. Texas *in October 2012.*

plary in *Bakke,* and to that of the University of Michigan's Law School in *Grutter,* there had been no reason for the Court to take this case in the first place, she reasoned. She also took a swipe at the sophistry of the petitioner and her lawyer, who argued that the race-neutral Texas Top Ten Percent Rule and a race-blind holistic review of each applicant were the *only* alternatives available to the university. "I have said before and reiterate here that only an ostrich could regard these supposedly neutral alternatives as race unconscious. As Justice Souter observed in his *Gratz* dissent, the vaunted alternatives suffer from 'the disadvantage of deliberate obfuscation.'" Quoting directly from the legislature's own analysis of the Top Ten Percent Rule, Ginsburg pointed out that the plan had been adopted "with racially segregated neighborhoods and schools front and center stage."

Reading her dissent from the bench at the end of the term, Ginsburg underscored her dismay at the Court's further retrenchment in race-conscious remedies. When the Fifth Circuit again ruled in favor of the University of Texas, Rein appealed. The conservative justices put *Fisher* back on the docket for review in 2016, confident that next time they would secure the vote they wanted with a little help from Kennedy. If they succeeded, it would mean a reduction of the number of black and

Latino students at nearly every selective college and graduate program in the United States, with more white and Asian American students taking their place.

Meanwhile, the fate of the historic Voting Rights Act hung in the balance.

. . .

THE LANDMARK VRA OWED MUCH to the heroism of rank-and-file members of the civil rights movement and to the leadership of President Lyndon Baines Johnson. Nearly a century earlier, passage of the Fifteenth Amendment in 1870 had extended to black men, many of them former slaves, the right to vote and, with it, the chance to hold political office. However, the era of flourishing black political participation proved brief. The Republican presidential nominee Rutherford B. Hayes agreed to pull Union troops out of the South in 1877 in return for the electoral votes of Florida, South Carolina, and Louisiana. The North lost its moral edge and the political will to police the former Confederacy.

Never far out of line with public opinion, the conservatives on the Supreme Court of the day then proceeded to overturn many of the laws designed to protect the rights of former slaves. They also turned a blind eye to the major techniques of disenfranchisement, with the exception of the grandfather clause (which restricted current voters to those whose grandfathers had the right to vote before the Civil War). By World War II, the Court had begun lending a more sympathetic ear to plaintiffs charging violations of the Fifteenth Amendment; however, few African Americans who were denied access to the ballot box could afford the economic, physical, and psychological costs of prolonged legal action.

With no constraints from the Court, the White House, or Congress, a southern white elite—bent on securing political, social, and economic control—rendered black citizens politically powerless. Their methods included intimidation, violence, and myriad legal devices such as literacy tests, poll taxes, and whites-only primaries. In 1965, only 335 of the 15,000 voting-age black citizens of Selma, Alabama, were registered to vote, despite voter registration efforts by civil rights activists.

On March 7, 1965—a day that would later be remembered as "Bloody Sunday"—the Student Nonviolent Coordinating Committee leader John Lewis, Hosea Williams of the Southern Christian Leadership Conference, and the people of Selma made history. Beginning a five-day voting-rights march from Selma to Montgomery, the marchers were beaten and trampled upon by state police, some of whom were on horseback. Once national television networks showed camera footage of the ferocious violence inflicted on the marchers, voting rights became a national cause.

Personally sympathetic, President Johnson realized that restoring voting rights to blacks—a Second Reconstruction—would test his considerable political skills with Congress. He also knew he had no other choice. Congress had tried to insert strong voting provisions into the Civil Rights Act of 1957 and again into the Civil Rights Act of 1964. But segregationist Democrats had consistently watered down those provisions, leaving the poll tax and literacy tests in place.

To expand the vote, Johnson needed help from moderate Republicans, who could rest assured that their own constituents would be little affected. Appearing before a joint session of Congress and a national television audience of seventy million, the president made an emotional appeal for action. "It is wrong—deadly wrong to deny any of your fellow Americans the right to vote," he declared. "It is all of us who must overcome the crippling legacy of bigotry and injustice. And we *shall* overcome."

Facing a powerful coalition of southern Democrats and conservative Republicans, a bipartisan group of Democrats and moderate Republicans with strong backing from the White House succeeded four months later in passing what Johnson called one of the most monumental laws in the entire history of American freedom. The legislation sought to transform black southerners into "active participants in the governance process," as the distinguished liberal legal scholar Pamela Karlan later noted. The right to vote in a representative democracy had to have *instrumental* value, reflecting a fair chance for minorities to determine their policy preferences and ensure that their interests were protected.

The Voting Rights Act of 1965 sought to achieve this goal in several ways. Section 2, which closely followed the language of the Fifteenth Amendment, applied a nationwide prohibition against discriminatory voting practices and procedures. This included prohibitions against discriminatory redistricting plans, at-large elections systems, and voter registration procedures. Section 3 authorized federal courts to place states and political subdivisions under federal oversight of their voting practices. Section 4 established a "coverage formula" that provided legal criteria to determine whether a jurisdiction was subject to the requirements of Section 5 of the act. In turn, Section 5 provided a "preclearance requirement" under which (mostly southern) jurisdictions were required to submit any alteration of voting practices to the attorney general for approval. Any lawsuits against voting practices had to go directly to the federal court for the District of Columbia to determine whether the proposed alteration had a discriminatory intent or unintentional repressive effects.

. . .

A SUBSTANTIAL INCREASE in federal oversight, the act was supported initially by the Court and later extended by Congress in legislation signed in updated form by Presidents Nixon, Ford, and Reagan. From the outset, however, the VRA's larger goal—creating a more inclusive democracy through minority representation—came under assault. Eager to build the GOP in the South, Nixon and Reagan both quietly abetted efforts to let the act expire. Republican-nominated justices (Rehnquist, O'Connor, Scalia, Thomas, and Kennedy) further blunted the VRA's impact by insisting that the Justice Department prove not only the discriminatory effect of actions limiting the voting rights of minorities but discriminatory *intent* as well. Yet despite robust and persistent opposition, Congress expanded the act in 1975 to include language assistance for minorities and extended it again in 1982 for twenty-five years.

George W. Bush carried on the tradition of his GOP predecessors. His attorney general, John Ashcroft, staffed the Civil Rights Division with political appointees dedicated to thwarting the VRA's mission. He also hired as special counsel to the division Hans von Spakovsky—a man obsessed with the specter of voter fraud (as opposed to election fraud). Von Spakovsky, in turn, persuaded GOP officials in states under Republican control to follow up with voter-ID laws, cutbacks in early voting, curtailment of same-day registration, and other measures that disproportionately penalized minorities, students, and the elderly. Yet with the VRA set to expire a year before the 2008 presidential election, George W. Bush and his party did not want to shoulder the blame for the act's demise at a time when they needed black votes. In 2006, the Republican leadership on Capitol Hill pledged support for reauthorization.

Leaders on both sides of the aisle knew that disagreements were in store. Liberals had long believed that the provisions of the VRA did not go far enough to prevent voting-rights violations. Conservatives insisted it went too far. Much had changed since 1965, including demography. Robust two-party competition existed in parts of the South, especially urban centers. Most states with a significant minority population could boast a cohort of black elected officials at all levels.

While revisions of the VRA were clearly in order, the political will to undertake them was lacking. Civil rights were not high on the public's agenda during the long Iraq war. GOP ascendency in what had once been the solid South allowed Republicans, who in principle opposed the VRA, to be its beneficiaries in practice. Most important, any attempt to enlarge the coverage formula would invite debate about which members' present-day districts were more racist than others, destroying the bipartisan coalition in support of the VRA.

Compounding the political inertia were concerns about how the Court might respond. Since 1982, the Court had narrowed its view of Congress's power to enforce the post–Civil War amendments—the constitutional basis for the VRA's Section 5. Adherence to federalism and the Republican version of color blindness—hallmarks of the conservative majority—suggested that solicitude for the equality and dignity of states might well outweigh the rights of persons, especially persons of color, to effective representation and equal protection.

The House and Senate Judiciary Committees proceeded to hold extensive hearings, followed by debates in the full House and Senate. What emerged was evidence of a long list of voting-rights offenses, including but not limited to threatening students at a historically black college with prosecution if they tried to register; creating regulations making it more difficult to register; relocating polling places so that blacks and Hispanics would have to travel to remote or hostile venues in order to vote; and canceling elections or abolishing elected bodies just as black and Hispanic candidates were on the verge of gaining the majority of seats on a governing body.

With a legislative record amounting to more than fifteen thousand

pages, Congress concluded that the VRA had produced significant progress in eliminating the original barriers to ballot access. Nevertheless,
"second generation barriers constructed to prevent the minority from
fully participating in the electoral process" continued to exist, as did
racially polarized voting in the covered jurisdictions. Indeed, the majority of successful voter-discrimination lawsuits in the period up to 2006
had occurred in jurisdictions covered by Section 4.

In what appeared to be an impressive display of bipartisanship, the
House voted overwhelmingly for reauthorization, despite an earlier
rebellion by GOP legislators from the South whose crippling amendments failed. The Senate followed with a unanimous vote on July 20,
2006, and President George W. Bush signed the bill one week later.

But the aura of unanimity was, in fact, deceptive. As anticipated, the
reauthorization process had been a classic exercise in "political avoidance." The new version left intact most of the VRA's provisions. The
same areas remained covered, the Department of Justice retained its special place in the preclearance regime, and procedures for "bailing out"
with a record of good behavior remained unchanged. Section 5 had to be
reconsidered in fifteen years, even though the act was not set to expire
until 2031.

Still, after months of impassioned debate, the crown jewel of the civil
rights movement appeared to have been secured. Constitutional scholars
pointed to papered-over divisions about the VRA's meaning, especially
within the Senate Judiciary Committee, as possible pitfalls in the new
legislation. New fiats from the Court seemed likely, given the conservative majority's preoccupation with reducing race-conscious districting.
What no one anticipated was the election of Obama and the firestorm
that historic event would reignite.

. . .

TO SOME, Obama's election signaled that race no long mattered and
that the VRA was no longer necessary. It was indisputable that African
Americans and other minorities had voted in large numbers in 2008.
The Voting Rights Act, moreover, had played a crucial role in making
those votes possible. "If it weren't for the Voting Rights Act, there would
be no President Obama," noted Theodore M. Shaw, former president
of the NAACP Legal Defense and Educational Fund. Despite the elec-

tion of the first African American president, Shaw argued, one presidential election did not justify the removal of federal oversight. His equally wary Latino counterparts in the Mexican American Legal Defense and Educational Fund emphatically agreed. But their views were rejected by long-standing opponents of the VRA, who characterized Obama's election as a win in a politically "open market" that no longer required federal protection.

Thus far the constitutionality of Section 5 had gone unchallenged. However, immediately following reauthorization, Edward Blum decided to test the waters with a case from a tiny utilities district. When *Northwest Austin Municipal Utility District No. 1 v. Holder* reached the Court in 2009, Ginsburg sounded the alarm. Knowing how adept the chief had become at sowing seeds for major changes in seemingly small steps, she called the case "perhaps the most important of the term."

Roberts had worked hard in the Reagan Justice Department in 1982 to prevent the VRA's reauthorization. His aggressive questioning of Deputy Solicitor General Neal Kumar Katyal during oral argument in 2009 indicated his views had not mellowed, despite assurances he had offered during his nomination hearings.

When the justices met in conference, the Court was deeply divided. The chief finally secured a nearly unanimous majority for a narrow ruling for the utility company. In his formal opinion, Roberts began by paying tribute to the act's accomplishments. He also acknowledged that improvements may be "insufficient and that conditions continue to warrant preclearance under the Act." Then moving on to the larger question, he issued a warning: "The Act imposes current burdens and *must be justified under current needs.* The evil that Section 5 is meant to address may no longer be concentrated in the jurisdictions singled out for preclearance. The statute's coverage formula is based on data that is now more than thirty-five years old and there is considerable evidence that it fails to account for current political conditions." Extending Section 5 without updating the jurisdictions where federal preclearance of electoral changes is required, Roberts continued, "raise[s] serious constitutional questions" as to whether a statute conceived in 1965 is still warranted, given the progress the South has made.

In claiming that the VRA also differentiated among the states "despite our historic tradition that all the states enjoy equal sovereignty," Roberts imposed a new interpretation of the doctrine of equal sovereignty, which had long been understood to apply only to the terms on which states entered the Union, not to treatment of local evils that might have subsequently appeared. He also provided legal guidance to opponents of the act when he then declared that "a departure from the fundamental principles of equal sovereignty requires a showing that a statute's disparate geographic coverage is sufficiently related to the problem it targets."

Roberts's objection—that the Section 4 coverage formula singled out certain states for a weighty burden even though "the evil that Section 5 is meant to address may no longer be concentrated" there—was clearly heard in legal circles. Adam Liptak reiterated what Ginsburg had already grasped: that the chief justice had emerged as "a canny strategist, laying the groundwork for bold changes that could take the court to the right." The legal scholar Richard Hasen agreed, pointing to *Northwest Austin* as a prime example of "anticipatory overruling." Anticipating correctly that the Roberts majority would use *Northwest Austin* as a starting point in a decision overturning Section 4, the Columbia Law School professor Jamal Greene urged, "Remember that line ['the Act . . . must be justified under current needs'] if and when the constitutional issue returns to Court."

· · ·

WHEN CONGRESS FAILED to act, the ever-entrepreneurial Blum was ready. He had another case waiting. The Civil Rights Division had rejected a voting map in the town of Calera, Alabama, a white suburb of Birmingham located in the southwestern tip of Shelby County, only fifty-six miles from Selma. Dubbed "the heart of Dixie," Calera had accumulated numerous violations of the VRA over the years, as recently as 2008.

Bert Rein, the lawyer who had represented Abigail Fisher, filed *Shelby County v. Holder* in district court in Washington in April 2010. Turned down in district court, Rein appealed to the U.S. Court of Appeals for the D.C. Circuit. Losing again in a split decision, he appealed.

Presented with two cases challenging the constitutionality of Section 5, the Court agreed to hear *Shelby*. The question on which the justices would rule was whether Congress, in reauthorizing in 2006 Section 5 of the VRA using the preexisting coverage formula of Section 4, exceeded its authority under the Fourteenth and Fifteenth Amendments. Oral argument in this high-stakes showdown was set for February 27, 2013. The outcome would hinge on how the Court's right-leaning justices viewed Congress's power to enforce the two post–Civil War amendments.

. . .

ONLY A MONTH AFTER Obama's second inaugural, tourists making the rounds of Capitol Hill on a cold February morning could witness a study in contrasts. At the Capitol, a ceremonial unveiling of a statue of Rosa Parks, the lifelong civil rights activist who had ignited the Montgomery bus boycott, provided a celebratory occasion at which President Obama spoke. Across the street at the Supreme Court, African Americans stood silently holding signs reading, "Protect My Vote," as the doors swung open, allowing people waiting in line to enter.

As Rein began his argument about the changing South and the burden that preclearance procedures imposed on the "equal dignity" of the covered states, Sotomayor, Ginsburg, and Kagan pushed back. "Just think about this state you are representing," said Kagan, "it's a quarter black but Alabama has no black statewide elected officials. If you use the

Activists outside the Supreme Court as it prepares to hear Shelby County v. Holder.

number of Section 5 enforcement actions, Alabama would again be on the list. Under any formula that Congress could devise, it would capture Alabama."

Kennedy then intervened, pressing Rein to acknowledge that preclearance not only treated states differently but also infringed on state sovereignty and the "equal footing doctrine." Ginsburg protested. In a previous decision, the Court had not only upheld the VRA but also rejected the "equal footing" doctrine. But Kennedy persisted. If Congress is going to single out states, it should do so by name, rather than just reenacting the existing formula. Alito agreed, questioning whether discrimination is "a bigger problem in Virginia than in Tennessee, or a bigger problem in Arizona than Nevada."

When Solicitor General Donald B. Verrilli Jr. began his defense of reauthorization, Roberts asked the same question he had asked in *Northwest Austin:* "Is it the government's contention that citizens in the South are more racist than the North?" Verrilli responded that the government was not making that claim, rather that Congress had found that Section 5 was still needed in covered jurisdictions and only a "tiny fraction" of the proposed electoral changes submitted under the preclearance process had raised objections from the Justice Department.

Roberts and Alito remained unpersuaded. Kennedy, though at times indicating ambivalence, appeared increasingly skeptical. Scalia, in the most jarring comment of the morning, described reauthorization as the "perpetuation of a racial entitlement." Thomas, having previously indicated his willingness to overturn the law, maintained his customary silence.

When Rein returned to the stand for his brief rebuttal, he reiterated his argument that sufficient progress had been made in Alabama and the other covered states to justify restoring their full sovereignty. Sotomayor and Kagan zeroed in on the critical question: Who gets to make that decision—Congress or the Court?

The sharp ideological fault lines in the Court had rarely been exposed more dramatically, observed Robert Barnes of *The Washington Post.* Implicit in his observation was the extent to which conservative reaction to the civil rights movement had infused the spirit of Dixie into the Grand Old Party and ultimately the Marble Palace. While opposition to *Brown v. Board of Education* played out dramatically in the South, white resistance to racial advances was a national phenomenon. The article "Why the [White] South Must Prevail" appeared not in *The Birmingham News* or *The Atlanta Journal* but in the Manhattan-based journal *National Review,* founded in 1955 by the conservative intellectual William F. Buckley Jr. At issue for Buckley and fellow conservatives was not just school integration but something much larger. The civil rights movement advanced a vision of democratic government active in the pursuit of social justice that right-leaning individuals viewed as an extension of the New Deal and its egalitarian principles.

In order to achieve a rollback of the regulatory authority of the federal government, a resurgent political movement on behalf of states' rights became an imperative. Resurrection of the soft rhetoric of states' rights was an integral part of Richard Nixon's southern electoral strategy. When Ronald Reagan, the shining hope of the conservative movement, began his presidential campaign "to get government off our backs" in 1980, he made a stop in Mississippi at the Neshoba County Fair. Neshoba County, a white supremacist stronghold where three young civil rights activists—Andrew Goodman, Michael Schwerner, and James Chaney—had been murdered in 1964, still sheltered some of the conspirators. Reagan, who had opposed the landmark Civil Rights Act, spoke to the enthusiastic crowd on "states' rights," alerting the audience and the press alike that he and his party would stand with whites. George H. W. Bush and George W. Bush would follow Reagan's lead in promoting "color-blind" policies—a retreat from equality with more respectable connotations for suburban voters North and South who were turned off by extremism. By advancing Republican adherents of color blindness to the high court, the Bushes fortified a majority willing to elevate "state sovereignty" to the level of fundamental principle. *Shelby* was not just a measure of the metamorphosis that the party of Lincoln had undergone. It was also part of a conservative project to shred reforms designed to protect and expand democracy.

. . .

ON JUNE 25, 2013, the Court finally announced its decision in *Shelby County v. Holder.* Ignoring decades of law governing the Court's review of the Voting Rights Act, the five conservatives struck down Section 4's coverage formula, which had been used to determine the areas designated for federal oversight. While Section 5 still remained law, it had been rendered meaningless without Section 4. It was the most significant congressional act to date to be struck down under the rational basis standard of review.

Writing for the majority, Roberts proceeded, as predicted, with the statement in *Northwest Austin* that "the Act imposes current burdens and must be justified by current needs." In 2006, he wrote, Congress acted "as if nothing had changed." In fact, the Census Bureau indicated that African American voter turnout has come to exceed white voter turnout in five of the six states originally covered, with a gap in the sixth state of less than one-half of 1 percent. The paucity of enforcement actions under the act, the chief contended, constituted further evidence of the disconnect between stringent oversight of the covered area and current on-the-ground reality. Failure to update an act that departs so sharply from the "fundamental principle of equal sovereignty" of the states, according to Roberts, left the Court no choice but to declare Section 4 invalid. "Our decision in no way affects the permanent, national ban on racial discrimination in voting found in Section 2," he continued. "We issue no holding on Section 5 itself, only on the coverage formula. Congress may draft another formula based on current conditions."

Ginsburg knew full well that a hyper-partisan Congress beset by gridlock would be unlikely to draft another formula. Even if it could, there was no guarantee the formula would be upheld. Her powerful dissent, which Breyer, Sotomayor, and Kagan joined, did not mince words. Foremost, she reminded her right-leaning colleagues that the assessment as to whether the VRA should continue in full force was Congress's to make. Consistent with the post–Civil War amendments, it should have commanded the Court's deference.

Second, the struggle for fairness in elections was far from over. The intent of the Voting Rights Act, she emphasized, was not merely to put an end to various devices that impeded access to the ballot in 1965, as the majority seemed to have assumed. Rather, "the grand aim of the act is to secure to all in our polity equal citizenship stature, a voice in our democracy undiluted by race." That meant not only dealing with second-generation forms of discrimination but also maintaining the level of federal oversight that prevents backsliding in covered areas.

The majority, Ginsburg noted, had pointed to the paucity of enforcement actions under Section 5 as evidence that the act was no longer needed in the preclearance areas. It also acted as if registration and turnout were the whole story, ignoring the careful assessment of Congress based on legislative hearings. It also failed to engage evidence of persistent discrimination in covered areas. In addition, she pointed out, the majority had failed to recognize the continuation of polarized voting, which meant that minorities were at risk of being systematically outvoted and having their interests underrepresented in state legislatures. Had the Court been as diligent as Congress in studying the record, Ginsburg maintained, the majority would have also found that the case Congress made for retaining oversight of covered areas was solid. Evident as well was the fact that a number of jurisdictions that had "bailed out" since 1965, thereby permitting them to make voting changes without federal approval, which belied the majority's portrayal of the act as static.

It was not just the failure of the Court to do its job that Ginsburg so deplored. It was also the conservative majority's seeming failure to understand what that job entailed. The Court's responsibility, she pointed out, was not to decide whether Congress had chosen the perfect remedy. Rather, it was to decide "whether Congress has rationally selected means appropriate to a legitimate end." She also highlighted other disturbing lapses: the failure to indicate the standard of review as well as to address Shelby County's right to mount a facial challenge (one in which no application of the law is constitutional). "By what right, given its usual restraint, does the Court even address Shelby County's facial challenge to the VRA" when there is so much evidence of continuing violation in that state? "Leaping to resolve Shelby County's facial challenge without considering whether application of the VRA to Shelby County is constitutional or even addressing the VRA's severability provision, the Court's opinion can hardly be described as an exemplar of restrained and moderate decision making," she charged. "Quite the opposite. Hubris is a fit word for today's demolition of the VRA."

Hubris, she maintained, was also evident in the majority's "unprecedented extension of the equal sovereignty principle out of its proper domain—the admission of new States." The "sad irony of today's decision," Ginsburg concluded, "lies in its utter failure to grasp why the VRA has proven effective. The Court appears to believe that the VRA's success in eliminating the specific devices extant in 1965 means that preclearance is no longer needed. With that belief, and the argument derived from it, history repeats itself."

On June 25 in a somber, silent courtroom just before the term ended, Ginsburg read aloud a nine-minute summary of her *Shelby* dissent from the bench. Slightly changing the conclusion from her written version, she underscored the moral and jurisprudential chasm separating the Court's two sides. Invoking the words of Martin Luther King Jr., she said, "The arc of the moral universe is long, but it bends toward justice," and then added a qualifier, "if there is a steadfast commitment to see the task through to completion." She concluded, "That commitment has been disserved by today's decision."

This was the second time that the nation had lacked the moral edge and political will to make Reconstruction secure. It was the second time, too, that a conservative majority's exalted conception of the Court's power had functioned as an enabler for those who no longer chose to show concern for the historically excluded. History would indeed repeat itself, as Ginsburg predicted.

Texas promptly announced that a strict voter-identification law, which had been put on hold because of its discriminatory effects, along with redistricting maps would no longer be submitted for federal approval. In North Carolina, where Republicans had gained control of the governorship and both houses of the legislature for the first time since 1877, lawmakers acted with similar dispatch. Adopting new district lines and a voter-ID law, they also rolled back early voting and same-day registration. These were hard blows to the working poor and especially to the black churches that organized "souls to the polls" voting drives. Nor were racial minorities the only groups whose rights were being curtailed. Older citizens often lacked a driver's license that would serve as a form of identification. In university towns where students were likely to increase votes for Democrats, student IDs would no longer be acceptable.

"Disgusting," declared Rosanell Eaton, a ninety-four-year-old North Carolinian who had memorized the preamble of the Constitution in order to register in the days when the state had a literacy test. Agreeing, one of her contemporaries, Henry Frye, said, "It's not quite what it was a long time ago. It's more sophisticated." As eight other southern states followed suit, both Eaton and Frye could agree with William Faulkner's famous line: "The past is never dead. It's not even past."

. . .

RACIAL HIERARCHY AND POLITICAL POWER had always been far too deeply interwoven in the fabric of American life to be limited primarily to the areas of the Old Confederacy covered by preclearance. Republican-controlled states in the Midwest and the North had begun to tighten qualifications even prior to *Shelby*. Spurred by specious claims of voter fraud emanating from operatives in George W. Bush's Department of Justice, restrictions accelerated as evermore Republican-dominated states following the 2010 elections sought to keep minority constituencies from being able to vote. By 2016, a total of fourteen states had adopted restrictions on voting rights, earning the United States the dubious distinction of being the only mature democracy in the world that made it harder rather than easier for its citizens to vote.

CHAPTER 21

The Right Thing to Do

Two months after her dissents in *Fisher* and *Shelby*, Ginsburg stood at the Kennedy Center amid a glittering array of Washington's most influential arts patrons and philanthropists. The elegantly clad justice had not come to attend a musical event. Rather, she had come to perform a wedding—something that justices often do for close friends, relatives, and former clerks. Joining hands were her good friend the Kennedy Center's president, Michael M. Kaiser, and the economist John Roberts. With this simple ceremony, Ginsburg would become the first justice ever to perform a same-sex wedding. At a time when many states still stipulated that only a man and a woman could marry, her position on the Court conferred a powerful endorsement of the couple's equal standing in the law.

. . .

THAT THE INSTITUTION OF MARRIAGE had become an explosive civil rights issue for lesbians and gays seemed almost unthinkable. Only sixty years earlier, homosexuals had been denounced as "degenerates," "sex perverts," and "child molesters." Subjected to official witch hunts as well as unofficial violence, most had been forced into the "apartheid of the closet." Years of slow, painful struggle followed as a discriminated-against minority sought to acquire the basic rights of citizenship.

Leading the drumbeat against gay rights since the 1970s, the religious Right had aggressively increased the level, intensity, and political sophistication of the opposition, wielding major influence in the Republican Party. For those convinced that homosexuals are essentially different from heterosexuals and that marriage constitutes a legal union

The Right Thing to Do · 451

only between a woman and a man, same-sex marriage evoked a level of repulsion and fear of contamination that is visceral.

To persuade a majority of the Court to include civil marriage for same-sex couples within the framework of equal protection would thus require a total sea change in culture, politics, and the law. A story of inclusion, it demonstrates once again how social movements in dialogue with public opinion forge new understandings of the Constitution's meaning even as contestation continues. An apt coda to the story came in 2015, when two young gays posed for a celebratory photograph with a large cutout of Ginsburg. Her long legal effort to promote gender-neutral spousal roles had laid the base for the argument that same-sex couples were "perfectly capable of filling the purposes of marriage." When the high court heard its first oral argument on same-sex marriage, Ginsburg left no doubt where she stood on the issue.

· · ·

MARRIAGE EQUALITY WAS a relatively new priority for the gay liberation movement that emerged in the wake of the Stonewall riots in 1969. Lesbian feminists considered the institution oppressive. Gay men who relished sexual adventuring had little use for lifelong partnering. Those in committed relationships congratulated themselves on the greater gender-role flexibility characteristic of alternative unions. Political radicals found challenge enough in trying to dismantle entrenched privilege based on gender, race, class, and heterosexuality.

Resistance would soften during the 1980s as AIDS ravaged the gay community. Killing 150,000 gay men, the disease exposed countless more to the heartbreak of loss. Indignities compounded grief as state agencies, hospitals, funeral homes, insurance companies, and even probate courts refused to recognize the wishes of same-sex life partners—and often their financial contributions. Understandably, some in the gay community began to reconsider the legal benefits conferred by the state upon married couples.

A gay baby boom in the late 1980s and 1990s further inspired reassessment. Gay adoptions increased as new data became available indicating that children of gay and lesbian parents fared as well as did children of straight couples. Simultaneously, a greater use of donor insemination, sperm banks, and surrogacy allowed one and sometimes both members of same-sex couples to plan families cemented by blood ties as well as an emotional commitment. Parental responsibilities, in turn, generated additional demands for the greater legal protection afforded by marriage.

Marriage as a legal and social practice had also changed over two centuries. Courts and state legislators had reassessed criteria, ending coverture, permitting and then liberalizing divorce, and finally voiding bans on interracial marriage. By the late 1990s, only 56 percent of all adults in the United States were currently married, down from three-quarters in the early 1970s. The meaning of marriage throughout the industrialized world had clearly become less about procreation and more about long-term happiness and commitment. These developments, characteristic of all Western democracies where church-state relations were not deeply entrenched, meant that homosexuality and marriage—once thought to be antithetical—were converging.

Yet in a social revolution that encompassed organizations and individuals with competing strategies and ideologies, making same-sex marriage a top priority for lesbians and gays proved a hard sell. Some feared that "mainstreaming" the movement would blunt its radical edge. Others worried that the shift of focus might divert critical efforts to prohibit discrimination in employment and housing. The movement's legal arm argued that the courts were not yet ready to act favorably on litigation seeking marriage equality. The justices had waited to overturn homosexual state sodomy statutes in *Lawrence v. Texas* until 2003—long after the decriminalization of consensual sodomy had occurred in virtually all industrialized countries and in many states.

Yet *Lawrence v. Texas* had marked a watershed. For the first time the decision drew explicitly homosexual acts between consenting adults in private into the framework of constitutional rights. Justice Kennedy in his stirring majority opinion had written, "Liberty presumes an autonomy of self." It "gives substantial protection to adult persons in deciding how to conduct their private lives in matters pertaining to sex." Friends and foes alike jumped to the conclusion that *Lawrence* would now usher in marriage equality.

But when a judge in Hawaii concluded in 1993 that the law restricting marriage to a man and a woman constituted an unconstitutional sex classification, alarm bells went off in conservative organizations across the mainland. "A dream issue" for religious and social conservatives, the same Congress responsible for the Partial-Birth Abortion Ban Act passed the Defense of Marriage Act (DOMA) in 1996, making marriage a matter for federal regulation for the first time in the nation's history.

The act provided that no state was required to give full faith and credit to any law or judicial decision of another state recognizing same-sex marriage. DOMA further stipulated that marriage could only take place between a man and a woman. Referring to the traditional definition of marriage as the "bedrock of civilization," congressional testimony spoke of "hedonism, narcissism, depravity . . . and sin."

President Bill Clinton, who arguably had done the most for gay rights of any president in history up to that time, privately opposed the legislation. But he had been badly burned by his unsuccessful effort to lift the ban on gays in the military. Having vetoed the Partial-Birth Abortion Ban Act, he felt he had exhausted his supply of vetoes with a Republican Congress. If he failed to sign DOMA, he told his top adviser on gay rights, he would be "politically clobbered" in a year in which he faced reelection—a sentiment widely shared by Democrats voting for the bill.

Then, in 2003, the New England lesbian and gay legal advocate Mary Bonauto achieved a critical first victory for marriage equality in the Massachusetts Supreme Judicial Court, with a moving opinion in *Goodridge v. Department of Health* by Chief Justice Margaret H. Marshall. On November 18, 2003, the court ordered the commonwealth to begin issuing marriage licenses to same-sex couples within 180 days.

Opponents of marriage equality rushed to place measures on the ballot in 2004. Their aim was to put the issue beyond the reach of courts and legislatures by amending state constitutions to define marriage as a union between a man and a woman. It would be almost another decade before President Obama could issue a ringing call for marriage equality, linking Stonewall with Selma and Seneca Falls. "Our journey is not complete until our gay brothers and sisters are treated like everyone else under the law," he proclaimed in his second inaugural address, "for if we are truly created equal, then surely the love we commit to one another must be equal as well."

. . .

THE PRESIDENT'S DELAY WAS no surprise to his inner circle. As an Illinois state senator, Obama had signed a questionnaire in 1996 saying that he favored same-sex marriage. But as the Democratic candidate for the Oval Office in 2008, he could not afford to get out ahead of public opinion. Confining his support to other issues important to LGBT votes resulted in agonizing frustration for grassroots activists of marriage equality. But Obama genuinely believed that "We, the People"— movement activists, legal strategists, and an energized public—all have a major role to play in bringing about the social change necessary for historically marginalized groups to enjoy "equal citizenship stature."

Fortuitously, the president's hand was soon freed by the tsunami-like momentum that the gay rights movement was rapidly acquiring in popular culture, Democratic politics, and corporate circles. By 2012, Log Cabin Republicans, who had been lobbying for gay rights since the late 1970s, were joined in their push for marriage equality by a few prominent GOP figures such as Laura Bush and Dick Cheney. Thirty states now had antidiscrimination laws on the books, and nine provided same-sex marriage rights. National polls consistently showed that a majority of Americans, especially younger ones, supported marriage equality. Other nations led the way, and the U.S. Supreme Court might follow. Five months before his reelection, when Obama made his carefully nuanced endorsement, two cases had made their way to the Court's docket.

. . .

HOLLINGSWORTH V. PERRY HAD ALREADY achieved fame as the gay rights trial of the twenty-first century. A month after the passage of California's Prop 8 four years earlier, the Washington legal heavyweights Theodore Olson and David Boies, who had battled each other in *Bush v. Gore,* joined forces to challenge California's ban on same-sex marriage on federal constitutional grounds. Their bold move alarmed some gay rights legal advocates, who preferred a state-by-state strategy. An adverse decision by the Court could halt progress in all fifty states for the foreseeable future. Others objected to what they saw as "showboating" on the part of lawyers who had no prior connection to the movement. But Olson, who had won forty-four of the forty-five cases he had argued before the high court, had "neither the time nor the temperament" for qualms that might allow other federal lawsuits to reach the high court first.

Once Olson convinced progressive Hollywood backers who were funding the suit that the highly credentialed liberal litigator David Boies would act as co-counsel, events moved quickly. Having secured as plaintiffs two gay couples in committed relationships who claimed that Prop 8 violated their right to equal protection and due process, the high-powered legal duo filed an injunction in the U.S. District Court for the Northern District of California. Because neither Governor Arnold Schwarzenegger nor Attorney General Jerry Brown chose to defend Prop 8, supporters recruited the prominent trial and appellate lawyer Charles Cooper, who counter-filed.

Lawyers for both sides had hoped to expedite matters by moving directly to the Supreme Court, avoiding the expense and delays associated with a trial. But Governor Schwarzenegger objected. He remembered the chaos that had erupted in 2004 when San Francisco's mayor, Gavin Newsom, unilaterally issued marriage licenses to same-sex couples, only to have the California Supreme Court void those unions as contrary to state law. Then, in May 2008, when the California Supreme Court declared the law unconstitutional, some four thousand euphoric same-sex couples had again rushed to the courthouse for marriage licenses, only to have their dreams shattered five months later when marriage was redefined in the state constitution by Prop 8.

Perry v. Schwarzenegger landed in 2009 on the docket of Chief Judge Vaughn R. Walker of the U.S. District Court for the Northern District of California. Walker, a smart, independent, and tough-minded jurist with libertarian leanings nominated by President George H. W. Bush, was determined to base his ruling on hard evidence achieved through rigorous cross-examination of allegations of fact by both sides. Quashing the injunction, he instructed both sides to prepare for trial. Lawyers were asked to present evidence on the purported justification for Prop 8, the effects of the initiative for same-sex couples and their families, and the effects for married heterosexual couples and their families. Judge Walker had also requested evidence on the nature of the "right to marry"—a fundamental constitutional right recognized in various Supreme Court decisions, such as *Loving*. In addition, he asked both sides to address the level of scrutiny that sexual orientation should receive under the equal protection clause.

. . .

AFTER THREE WEEKS of testimony and summary arguments, the trial ended on June 16—a brilliant twelve-day exercise in separating fact from belief. The Washington duo basked in the knowledge that their academic experts had proven far less vulnerable thanks to superb choices and to Boies's skill at cross-examining those assembled by opposing counsel. Over the course of the trial, they also relied on a telling sentence from Ginsburg in an earlier decision on a Christian student group in a state-funded institution that refused to admit homosexuals. It said, "Our decisions have declined to distinguish between status and conduct in this context." As Adam Liptak had pointed out at the time, context mattered. Ginsburg was talking about laws affecting lesbians and gays. Like Justice Brennan, she had inserted what Brennan's colleagues referred to as "time bombs"—seemingly innocuous casual statements that could be carried to their logical end in future cases. Calling sexual orientation a "status" suggests that homosexuality is not a choice, Liptak explained, noting that courts are better able to protect groups under equal protection whose characteristics are immutable.

On August 4, 2010, Judge Walker issued his decision. Finding for the plaintiffs, the district court struck down Prop 8 as a violation of their right to due process and equal protection based on sexual preference and gender. Paying due deference to the role of the initiative and the views of voters, Walker pointed out that, when challenged, voters' determinations—especially when they involved the classification of persons—cannot rest on "conjecture, speculation, or fears. Still less will the moral disapprobation of a group or class of citizens suffice, no matter how large the majority that shares that view. The evidence demonstrated beyond serious reckoning that Proposition 8 finds support only in such disapproval." As such, he concluded, "Proposition 8 is beyond the constitutional reach of the voters or their representatives." Equally impressive was the density of Walker's long decision, in which fifty-two pages were devoted exclusively to findings of fact.

Galvanized by the outcome, lesbians, gays, and their allies reveled throughout the state. Prop 8 supporters, reacting with equal intensity, denounced the ruling as a negation of the will of the people. Cooper appealed.

After two more years, in 2012, a panel of the liberal Ninth Circuit handed Prop 8 supporters yet another defeat. The narrow ruling, written by Judge Stephen R. Reinhardt, relied not on Walker's decision, as Olson and Boies had hoped, but on Kennedy's majority opinion in *Romer v. Evans,* which struck down a Colorado constitutional amendment banning laws passed to protect homosexuals. Compounding the legal duo's disappointment, Judge Reinhardt's ruling applied only to California and not to other states covered by the Ninth Circuit. It also skirted the question of whether Prop 8 targeted a suspect class or denied a fundamental right. Worse still, opposing counsel appealed for a rehearing before the entire Ninth Circuit. When the rehearing was denied, Cooper appealed to the Supreme Court in July 2012 just as two cases in the Second Circuit challenging DOMA were also being appealed. One of the two Second Circuit cases, *United States v. Windsor,* would earn equal billing with *Perry.*

· · ·

IN FEBRUARY 2009, Edith "Edie" Windsor had just returned from the hospital where she had been treated for a heart attack following the death of her partner, Thea Spyer. The two had been in a committed relationship, living together in a Greenwich Village apartment since the 1960s. In 1993, when New York City offered legal recognition of domestic partnerships, the two had registered and then purchased a beach house on Long Island. When Spyer's health further deteriorated, they had flown to Toronto for medical help, where they were legally married in 2007. But under DOMA, Windsor, as the sole heir, was not eligible for the unlimited marital deduction afforded a surviving spouse. Instead, she was obliged to pay estate tax bills—$363,053 to the federal government and $275,528 to the State of New York.

After exhausting much of her savings to pay the estate taxes, Windsor had turned to Lambda Legal and other gay rights organizations to explore the possibility of a suit against the U.S. government that would enable her to get her money back. Unable to find lawyers willing to take the case, she turned to Roberta Kaplan, a "powerhouse corporate litigator" who had served as co-counsel in an unsuccessful case for marriage equality in New York State.

Kaplan, aware that in 2008 New York courts had begun recognizing same-sex marriages that were legally conducted out of state, agreed to represent Windsor pro bono, convinced that her client indeed had a compelling story. She then forged a close working relationship with Mary Bonauto, who had devised the winning strategy for DOMA cases in Massachusetts and Vermont, and persuaded James Esseks, the director of the ACLU's LGBT and AIDS Project, to serve as co-counsel.

The brief would make clear that the judges did not have to decide the larger constitutional question about marriage equality. Nor did her client challenge the provision of DOMA that gave states the power to decline recognition of same-sex marriages performed elsewhere. Rather, Windsor would demand on equal protection grounds that the government refund the estate taxes that she had paid. It was clear that DOMA treated same-sex married couples differently from their heterosexual counterparts. Kaplan would also ask for the application of either strict or intermediate scrutiny, but like Ginsburg in the *Reed* brief she would take what she could get.

Kaplan filed suit on November 9, 2010, knowing that it was the job of the Department of Justice to defend laws passed by Congress, even though the administration had recommended DOMA's repeal. Yet neither Attorney General Eric Holder nor his deputy Tony West relished continuing to defend DOMA. As African Americans, they saw too many similarities between their own race's historic struggle for equal rights and that of homosexuals. Holder had already established a working group within the DOJ to take a new look at DOMA without considering precedent. The group finally concluded that if heightened scrutiny applied—and gays and lesbians certainly met the legal criteria for equal protection—then DOMA could not be found constitutional. But could the DOJ refuse to defend Section 3 of DOMA, which specified that marriage be defined as an opposite-sex union, without jeopardizing institutional credibility? "No," argued some of its top lawyers, including Neal Kumar Katyal, the acting solicitor general. With DOMA challenges from Connecticut and New York looming in the Second Circuit, Holder knew that a decision could not be delayed for long.

It was Super Bowl Sunday, February 6, 2011. The Obamas had invited friends, including the Holders, to watch the game at the White House. Holder, who had figured out a way to proceed, needed to clear his strategy with the president. Glimpsing Obama standing alone in the hallway near a portrait of John F. Kennedy, he approached. Obama started talking first. He began by saying that he did not think the government's position on Section 3 was what it should be and that he had concluded that DOMA ought to be subject to heightened scrutiny. It was "the right thing to do," the two men agreed, returning to the game.

. . .

KAPLAN GOT A CALL from the Justice Department on February 23, 2011, informing her that while the administration would continue to enforce DOMA, it would no longer defend a federal law that treated gay married couples differently. If Kaplan and her client won in the district court (which they did four months later), she would eventually have to argue her case in the Second Circuit against a lawyer representing the Bipartisan Legal Advisory Group of the U.S. House of Representatives who would argue for the constitutionality of Section 3. With oral argument now scheduled before a three-judge panel on September 27, 2012, Windsor had only a short wait before Kaplan called with good news. Applying intermediate scrutiny, the Second Circuit had ruled 2–1 that Section 3 of DOMA violated equal protection. Windsor was jubilant. But she knew it would take a favorable decision by the high court to get her money back.

. . .

ON DECEMBER 7, 2012, the justices met to vote whether to hear *Perry* (the Prop 8 case) and *Windsor*. The four liberals and Kennedy apparently suggested that both marriage-equality cases be dismissed. The nation was still much too deeply divided on the issue. Only eight states, plus the District of Columbia, allowed, or were about to allow, same-sex partners to marry. More states needed to do so before the Court could act. But as Scalia later revealed, the four conservatives sensed that time was not on their side. Obama's reelection and the recent decision of five of those eight states, plus the District of Columbia, to allow gay marriage suggested that their best chance to put an end to the momentum behind marriage equality was now. Thomas, Alito, and either Roberts or possibly Kennedy voted to hear both cases.

Their votes sparked hope and anxiety on both sides of the issue. When granting review, the justices had clearly left themselves plenty of exit strategies. Lawyers were told to address whether the Prop 8 opponents had legal standing to defend the measure after California officials failed to appeal the Ninth Circuit ruling. The same question applied to House Republicans in their defense of DOMA. Both cases could conceivably be dismissed on procedural grounds.

Even if procedural hurdles were overcome, the majority could affirm the Ninth Circuit's ruling in *Perry*, leaving bans on same-sex marriage intact in states other than California. Indeed, given Ginsburg's much-publicized criticism of the Court's broad sweep in *Roe v. Wade*, a strong argument could be made that the case should be decided narrowly, giving states more time to act.

Windsor's outcome was considered by legal experts to be less problematic. Marriage had traditionally been defined by states, not the federal government. Kennedy's interest in states' rights might align with that of liberal justices who viewed DOMA as a violation of equal protection. No one doubted that the view of the justice who had drafted the majority opinions in *Romer* and *Lawrence* would be pivotal.

Reflecting the intense interest in the two cases, the sidewalk in front of the Court filled up four days in advance of oral arguments with people eager to gain a ticket guaranteeing entry. Willing to brave the cold, wet weather, they had slept in soggy sleeping bags or on plastic lounge chairs under tarps.

When the justices assembled on March 26, 2013, to hear *Perry*, five of them made it quite clear to Cooper that they doubted whether Prop 8 supporters had standing. Turning to the merits of the case, Kennedy seemed perturbed by a point that Cooper had hammered throughout: the future consequences of allowing same-sex marriage. But then he reflected on the plight of "some 40,000 children in California who live with same-sex parents, and . . . want their parents to have full recognition and full status. The voice of those children is important in this case."

When Cooper, returning to the merits of the case, argued that the

Attorneys for plaintiffs, David Boies, far left, and Theodore Olson, far right, walk out of the U.S. Supreme Court with plaintiffs, from left, Sandy Stier, Kris Perry, Jeff Zarrillo, and Paul Katami, after California's Proposition 8 was argued before the Court in Washington, D.C., Tuesday, March 26, 2013.

key to marriage is procreation, Breyer pointed out the obvious: many married couples do not have children. Kagan asked how extending marriage benefits to gay couples could possibly hurt heterosexual couples. Cooper parried, responding that she had not asked the correct question. Kennedy replied that he thought Kagan deserved an answer. "It is impossible for anyone to foresee the future accurately enough to know what those real-world consequences would be," Cooper admitted.

When Olson rose to present his equal protection argument in *Perry,* the more conservative justices zeroed in. As Olson tried to convey what marriage meant to these couples, Roberts likened the situation to telling a child that somebody has to be their friend. "You can force the child, to say, 'This is my friend.' But it changes the definition of what it means to be a friend."

Donald Verrilli used his ten minutes to argue that waiting to expand marriage imposed "real costs" on same-sex parents and their children. Roberts responded that the administration's position would carry more force if it were prepared to argue that same-sex marriage must be allowed nationwide. But neither the solicitor general nor the Court seemed prepared to go that far.

. . .

THE FOLLOWING DAY began with extensive questions on standing in *Windsor*—this time directed at Paul Clement, George W. Bush's former solicitor general, who defended the interests of House Republicans. Addressing the merits of DOMA, Clement stated that Congress had been responding to Hawaii's initial judicial decision by trying to reverse the changing definition of marriage. Engaging in revisionist history, he claimed that assuring uniformity in matters of taxation was also an objective.

Kennedy promptly observed, "You are at a real risk with running in conflict with what has always thought to be the essence" of state power, which was to regulate marriage, divorce, and custody. All four liberals immediately jumped in, pressing Clement not on federalism but on equal protection principles. It was the states that treated same-sex married couples differently, Clement insisted. The federal government was just "helping" the states by taking the term "marriage" when it appeared in federal law and enforcing DOMA. Alert to the inconsistency of Clement's statement for those states where same-sex marriage was permitted, Kennedy and Ginsburg followed up.

"It's not as though there's this little Federal sphere and it's only a tax question," Ginsburg interjected. "It's as Justice Kennedy said, 1,100 statutes [that] affect every area of life." DOMA, she charged, effectively creates "two kinds of marriage: the full marriage, and then this sort of skim milk marriage." Kagan, indicating that there was something else at work in 1996 when DOMA was passed, read aloud the following excerpt from a House report: "Congress decided to reflect and honor collective moral judgment and to express moral disapproval of homosexuality." There was an audible response from the audience.

Seeking to repair the damage, Clement replied, "Look, we are not going to strike down a statute just because a couple of legislators may have had an improper motive." The question is, "Is there any rational basis for the statute?" That indeed is the question, Kennedy agreed, reminding Clement that the power to regulate marriage belongs to the states, not the federal government. Breyer poked further at Clement's argument about uniformity. But it was time for Solicitor General Verrilli to present his compromise proposal—one that elicited little interest from the justices.

. . .

THE FOLLOWING DAY Edie Windsor's lawyer, Roberta Kaplan, began her argument. Roberts, Scalia, and Alito peppered her with questions. Breyer and Sotomayor briefly intervened, giving Kaplan a chance to return to her argument as to why DOMA was unconstitutional. But neither Roberts nor Scalia let up. Roberts asked Kaplan if she thought all eighty-four senators who voted for DOMA based their vote on moral disapproval. Some clearly did, Kaplan replied. Much of the explanation she attributed to the prevailing presumption in 1996 that gay couples and straight couples were fundamentally different. Over the next decade and a half, society's understanding had changed.

Scalia promptly asked how she reconciled this alleged "sea change" in public understanding with the fact that only eight states permitted gay marriage. When Kaplan held her ground, Roberts pointed to a different explanation—the power of gay lobbyists. "[P]olitical figures are falling all over themselves to endorse your side of the case," he stated. Kaplan countered, "The fact of the matter, Mr. Chief Justice, is that no other group in recent history has been subjected to popular referenda to take away rights that have already been given or to exclude those rights, the way gay people have."

Having confirmed her reputation as a powerhouse litigator, Kaplan escorted her client out of the Court where they were surrounded by reporters. Windsor, now a frail eighty-three, had difficulty hearing and walking, although her spirits were as irrepressible as ever. Barely visible over the microphones, she discarded remarks prepared for her and proudly announced, "I'm Edie Windsor. . . . I am today an out lesbian . . . who just sued the United States of America, which is kind of overwhelming for me." Explaining her case, she added that although she and Spyer had been married only two of their forty years together, something "intangible but unmistakable changed" after they married. "For anybody who doesn't understand why we want it or why we need it, it is magic."

"Justices Cast Doubt on U.S. Law Defining Marriage" read the bold headline on the front page of *The New York Times*. Next to Ginsburg's photograph was her remark likening domestic partnerships to "skim milk marriage." The Los Angeles reporter for *The New York Times* marveled at the seismic shift in public opinion occurring in California and elsewhere. Yet veteran advocates cautioned against too much optimism prior to the ruling.

· · ·

AFTER AN AGONIZING THREE-MONTH WAIT, the day of the announcement arrived on a warm Wednesday morning in late June. When the Court convened, Justice Kennedy announced the majority decision. "The federal statute is invalid," he wrote, "for no legitimate purpose overcomes the purpose and effect to disparage and injure those whom the state, by its marriage laws, seeks to protect in personhood and dignity. By seeking to displace this protection and treating those persons as living in marriages less respected than others, the federal statute is in violation of the Fifth Amendment." Motivated by a desire to demean "the moral and sexual choices" of gay and lesbian couples, it humiliated "tens of thousands of children now being raised by same-sex couples."

When Kennedy finished, he stared straight ahead as Scalia lashed out in a cutting dissent. "By formally declaring anyone opposed to same-sex marriage an enemy of human decency, the majority arms well every challenger to a state law restricting marriage to its traditional definition."

A different 5–4 majority consisting of Roberts, Scalia, Ginsburg, Breyer, and Kagan stated that in *Perry* it was powerless to reach a decision because proponents of Prop 8 lacked standing to appeal the district court's opinion when state officials declined to do so. With Judge Walker's decision now in place, the practical result in California was to enable same-sex couples to marry as soon as the Ninth Circuit confirmed that the stay was lifted.

Though the high court had sidestepped a broad ruling, gays and lesbians had much to celebrate. Taken together, Obama's words at his second inaugural and the two decisions constituted a powerful message at the highest level of government about what is considered just and permissible and what is not. Both of the Court's rulings were careful and incremental. Disparate treatment of same-sex unions would still

Edith "Edie" Windsor, center, celebrates with her friend Donna Aceto, right, as she arrives at a news conference at the Lesbian, Gay, Bisexual and Transgender Community Center in New York, June 26, 2013.

persist in thirty-seven states, barring action by courts or legislatures. Yet by defining as unconstitutional restrictive definitions of "marriage" and "spouse," *Windsor* served as a precedent for other cases, just as Scalia had predicted.

· · ·

OVER THE NEXT YEAR and a half, judges in state and federal courts, relying on *Windsor*'s logic, struck down state bans in more than forty decisions. To the surprise of some on both sides of the issue, the Court announced in October 2014 that it would not grant a hearing on appeals, leaving the rulings intact. As Ginsburg explained in an interview, there is no need for the Court to intervene when lower courts are in agreement. True enough, but seasoned Court observers began speculating. Leaving the decisions intact served everyone's interest, observed Linda Greenhouse, inasmuch as differences among the justices were irreconcilable. Adam Liptak suggested that denial of appeals might also have been part of the liberal strategy to get the number of states up to the tipping point at which justices are more comfortable handing down sweeping rulings.

. . .

IN THE MEANTIME, the Ohio residents James Obergefell and John Arthur had been together nearly twenty years when Arthur was diagnosed with ALS (amyotrophic lateral sclerosis), often known as Lou Gehrig's disease. In 2011, the couple took a medical jet to Maryland, where they were married as Arthur lay on a stretcher on the tarmac of the Baltimore-Washington International Airport. Their home state refused to recognize the legality of the Maryland union and, when Arthur died two months later, rejected their request to have Obergefell's name listed on Arthur's death certificate. Obergefell sued. When the case reached the Sixth Circuit, it was combined with three other same-sex marriage cases, one each from the four states that constituted the circuit (Ohio, Tennessee, Michigan, and Kentucky). Ruling against the plaintiffs in November 2014, the Sixth Circuit became the only circuit court to uphold the constitutionality of same-sex marriage bans in the wake of *Windsor*. Lawyers for the plaintiffs appealed.

The Court that had successfully ducked the issue only three months earlier now had no choice. It agreed on January 16, 2015, to hear *Obergefell v. Hodges* in April. Lawyers were asked to address two sweeping questions: Does the Fourteenth Amendment include a right to marry for same-sex couples, and must states recognize same-sex marriages that took place in other states? Indicative of the rapidly changing sentiment, 201 members of Congress argued for heightened scrutiny for sexual orientation while 57 members urged against a Court-imposed decision that would short-circuit the democratic process in the fourteen states where same-sex marriage bans persisted.

When oral arguments began on April 28, all eyes were on Kennedy, whose evolution on gay rights since his appointment to the Court had been remarkable. Like many moderate California Republicans of his era—Olson included—Kennedy had never been a social conservative. As his former clerk Michael Dorf pointed out, the justice had gay friends. Also, his three prior decisions on gay rights were in the tradition of another California Republican, the former governor and chief justice Earl Warren.

Kennedy initially expressed reluctance about changing a conception of marriage that had existed for millennia. He also voiced reservations about shutting off debate—a reservation strongly articulated by Scalia, Roberts, Alito, and to a lesser degree Breyer. When conservatives continued to dwell on the long history of traditional marriage compared with same-sex marriage, Ginsburg offered a boost to the plaintiffs' lawyer Mary Bonauto, making a critically important point: marriage had changed. When the Court struck down Louisiana's Head and Master Rule in 1981, marriage had become a relationship of equals, making the institution for the very first time a viable aspiration for committed gay couples.

Alito then asked Bonauto, if the definition of marriage is just a commitment joining a loving couple, on what basis could the state withhold a license from two siblings or two women and two men? Scalia seemed more worried about ministers being forced to marry same-sex couples contrary to their religious beliefs. Bonauto assured him of the clergy's First Amendment rights. Kagan also pointed out that rabbis were free to refuse to marry a Jew and a non-Jew. Roberts's strong objection came as a warning to Bonauto: "[I]f you prevail here, there will be no more debate. . . . Closing off debate can close minds and it will have a consequence on how this new institution is accepted. People will feel very differently about something if they have a chance to vote on it than if it is imposed on them by the courts."

Solicitor General Verrilli responded with a powerful argument on behalf of the plaintiffs' right to a swift ruling based on equal protection. Delaying reflected the assumption that the problem would take care of itself over time. Because no one could predict the future with absolute clarity, the probable outcome, Verrilli ventured, would be a house divided. Many gay couples and their children would be relegated to second-class citizenship in much the same way that African Americans had been treated until the Court finally forced the states to end de jure segregation.

John Bursch, a former Michigan solicitor general who represented the four states that refused to recognize same-sex marriage, followed.

But his argument that states had an interest in binding children to their biological parents was demolished by Sotomayor and Kagan. When Bursch declared that the bans did not discriminate on the basis of sexual orientation, Kagan replied, "If you prevent people from wearing yarmulkes, you know there's discrimination against Jews."

Because Kennedy had not tipped his hand, the outcome remained uncertain. There had also been no discussion of heightened scrutiny. Rather, what had emerged were sharp divisions over two basic issues: Is there any good reason for a state's refusal to recognize same-sex marriage? And who gets to decide—the Court or the people? The answer would likely come at the end of the term in June. But that did not stop legal reporters from sifting the justices' remarks for clues.

On Saturday, June 13, Ginsburg spoke at the American Constitution Society, where she talked at length about the progress of the LGBT movement once lesbians and gays had come out of the closet. "People looked around and it was my next-door neighbor of whom I was fond, my child's best friend, even my child. These are people we know and we love and we respect and they are part of us." As she talked about the changing climate of acceptance, she never mentioned *Obergefell*. Yet, as Adam Liptak surmised, these "were not the words of a woman whose court was about to deal the gay rights movement a devastating setback."

. . .

ON JUNE 26, 2015, Kennedy delivered a historic victory for gay couples nationwide. "The right to marry," he wrote, "is a fundamental right inherent in the liberty of the person, and under the Due Process and Equal Protection Clause of the Fourteenth Amendment couples of the same sex may not be deprived of that right and liberty. Without the recognition, stability and predictability marriage offers," he continued, "their children suffer the stigma of knowing their families are somehow lesser. They also suffer the significant material costs of being raised by unmarried parents, relegated through no fault of their own to a more difficult and uncertain family life." The marriage laws at issue here "thus harm and humiliate the children of same-sex couples."

He explained that the Constitution's power and endurance lie in its ability to evolve along with the nation's consciousness. The Court itself has recognized that "new insights and societal understanding can reveal unjustified inequality within our most fundamental institutions that once passed unnoticed and unchallenged."

Kennedy's words elicited tears in the courtroom and euphoria among those outside who managed to get word of his ruling. But they brought no cheer to his more conservative colleagues, who were firmly convinced that the judicial activism of five members of the Court had usurped the power that properly belonged to the people. Roberts was so upset that he read aloud a lengthy point-by-point attack on each element of the ruling. Less methodical, Scalia hit hard at Kennedy's style, calling it "as pretentious as its content is egotistical." The ruling, he mocked, was a "judicial Putsch" and a "threat to American democracy." Alito and Thomas were no less opposed.

Speaking in the White House Rose Garden, President Obama called the ruling a victory for America that "affirms what millions of Americans already believed in their hearts: When all Americans are truly treated as equal, we are more free." The plaintiff Jim Obergefell agreed, stating that "America has taken one more step toward the promise of equality enshrined in our Constitution, and I'm humbled to be part of that." Meanwhile, jubilant crowds waved signs and rainbow flags outside the Supreme Court Building. In New York City, thousands reveled in and around the Stonewall Inn, while in San Francisco celebrants streamed into Harvey Milk Plaza. That night, the White House was bathed in rainbow colors, as was the Empire State Building, Niagara Falls, AT&T's globe logo, and Sleeping Beauty's Castle at Disney World in Orlando, Florida.

Within hours of the decision, officials in several southern and midwestern states began contemplating strategies including a "conscience clause" that would protect individuals with moral or religious objections to same-sex marriage. Indiana and Arkansas rushed to pass religious freedom laws, only to meet with public and corporate backlash from critics who charged gay couples would suffer discrimination. Governors in both states backed off, seeking a middle ground. But not Texas's senator Ted Cruz, who charged, "The Fortune 500 [companies are] running shamelessly to endorse the radical gay marriage agenda over religious liberty." There was some basis to his assertion, though it was not religious liberty that major companies sought to quash. Rather, it was differential treatment of employees that erodes company morale and offends consumers, especially those endorsing gay marriage.

. . .

RESISTANCE WOULD CONTINUE on the part of social conservatives, as it has in the wake of other major civil rights decisions—this time under the guise of religious liberty. Congressional Republicans resurrected a First Amendment defense bill that would prohibit federal agencies from "taking discriminatory action against a person on the basis that such person believes or acts in accordance with a religious belief or moral conviction." A year later the bill had still not been taken up by either of the two committees to which it was referred. That other challenges would persist does not invalidate *Obergefell*'s standing as a milestone both in a long, painful, and ongoing gay rights struggle and in constitutional interpretation. Infused with the rationale of anti-subordination and equality, Kennedy's concept of equal dignity, located in the double helix of due process and equal protection, lay the groundwork for new legal doctrine.

. . .

GINSBURG KNEW THAT marriage equality could have been achieved by relying on equal protection. She toyed briefly with the idea of writing a concurring opinion but decided the majority ruling would have greater power if it stood alone—a position she has maintained as leader of the minority. It was enough to know her 1970s litigation on marriage equality for heterosexual couples had paved the way for *Obergefell*. That a young gay male couple celebrated the decision with a selfie that included a large cutout of Ginsburg illustrated that at some level those young men understood her role in making that historic day possible.

With the term finally over, she was now free to bask in the praise heaped upon her jurisprudence in a volume of the *Harvard Law Review* scheduled to appear in the fall. One of the many tributes she would undoubtedly treasure was Mark Tushnet's appraisal of the dissenting portion of her opinion in the first Obamacare decision, *National Federation of Independent Business v. Sebelius* (2012). The dissent shows us "a judge at the height of her powers," Tushnet wrote, noting that it provided a sterling example of which topics to pick for most direct analysis and which to leave unaddressed.

Joined by Breyer, Sotomayor, and Kagan in her dissent, Ginsburg had pointed out that by tradition a Supreme Court justice should not offer to decide a constitutional issue that does not need to be decided. Because Roberts had upheld the health-care mandate as a tax, his argument that the Affordable Care Act (ACA) rested on an unconstitutional exercise of the commerce clause was not only gratuitous but flawed. It "harks back to the era in which the Court routinely thwarted Congress' efforts to regulate the nation's economy in the interest of those who labor to sustain it," she wrote. In fact, "[i]t finds no home in the text of the Constitution or our decisions."

. . .

IN ANOTHER OF THE ESSAYS, Martha Minow, dean of Harvard Law School, underscored Tushnet's characterization with a little-known case that illustrated both Ginsburg's legal craftsmanship and her enduring concern for equal justice. *M.L.B. v. S.L.J.* (1996) involved a Mississippi mother, Melissa Lumpkin Brooks, known in the annals of the Court as M.L.B., who had been denied the right to appeal a decree terminating her parental rights to her two minor children. She could not afford $2,352.36—the fee for a transcript of the trial and other records required for the appeal. When the Supreme Court of Mississippi ruled against her, her lawyer appealed.

In Ginsburg's ruling, she did not challenge the precedents constraining M.L.B.'s appeal. Rather, she had searched for exceptions, carefully quoting precedents that related to family status (for example, the state had to pay for the blood test of an indigent against whom a paternity case had been filed). To these family status exceptions, Ginsburg added a procedural due process decision requiring a state to demonstrate a clear-and-convincing-proof standard before terminating parental rights. Connecting all these precedents to M.L.B.'s situation, the opinion, Minow noted, might have appeared at first glance to be a string of "cut-and-pasted quotations." A calculated move on Ginsburg's part, those quotations from precedents successfully preempted any charge of a bold expansion of constitutional guarantees.

Using her own words to convey the gravity of the situation, she had pointed out that a petty offender would have received aid for a transcript in a criminal case but not a woman about to lose her parental rights in a civil case. In addition, she subtly shifted the focus—first, from due process and equal protection to simply what the Fourteenth Amendment requires; second, from an appeal conditioned on a records preparation fee to an appeal available except for M.L.B.'s inability to pay the cost; and third, from termination of parental rights to permanent branding of a mother as unfit to associate with her children. "Each of these shifts," Minow observed, "is well supported by close reasoning in the paragraphs between the opening statement and later restatement. By the time the question is restated, the conclusion seems nearly assured."

M.L.B. v. S.L.J. was a limited ruling applying only to family matters, Minow acknowledged. Yet it attested not only to Ginsburg's legal skill but also to her larger vision of equality—one that takes into account not just race and gender but also class, addressing barriers to fundamental fairness imposed on needy litigants. In an era when the Roberts Court was making it even more difficult for those who lacked deep pockets and political clout, Ginsburg's vision of equal justice, Minow concluded, was indeed to be celebrated.

. . .

OTHER ESSAYS FOCUSED on the dissents that would become part of the justice's legacy. Laurence Tribe praised Ginsburg's ability to unmask appearance-based defenses that judges find "difficult to corroborate and uniquely tempting to accept." Too often, he observed, such defenses fail to be subjected to the kind of scrutiny that unmasks clever rationalizations that serve to conceal serious constitutional violations. Commending Ginsburg's dissents in two life-and-death cases, Tribe focused first on *Baze v. Rees* (2008), which involved a case about Kentucky's use of drugs in lethal injections. The plaintiffs had argued that the particular "cocktail" did not provide adequate safeguards against excruciating pain, although it did include a drug that suppressed involuntary movement so as to promote the appearance of dignity in death. The second case was *Carhart,* in which the majority voted to ban a late-term abortion procedure resembling infanticide. Ginsburg's meticulous dissents in both cases, Tribe concluded, provided "gripping and precise" refutation of appearance-based defenses that undermine sound judicial methodology.

Lani Guinier took a different approach, noting the careful editing that enabled Ginsburg to condense a long dissent in *Ledbetter* into a short, colloquially worded oral version designed to send a clear warning that something had gone wrong. Intended to rally the press, legal advocacy groups, and politicians to press for a legislative remedy, Ginsburg had used her forceful, passionate voice to secure her objective. (Her dissent had also clarified Lilly Ledbetter's own statement when the Alabama grandmother subsequently testified before Congress.)

Shelby, Guinier observed, was not a dissent inviting immediate legislative remedy, which the justice correctly deemed unlikely without a Democratic majority in Congress. Yet it was no less an attempt to influence public dialogue about what kind of country we want this to be. Ginsburg, Guinier emphasized, never missed a chance in her indignant *Shelby* dissent to drive home examples of voter discrimination in ways that both undercut the majority argument and exposed the human consequences of the decision.

An example was Ginsburg's discussion of the problems of *Shelby*'s facial challenge. Given Alabama's long history of voter discrimination, Ginsburg chose an example not from 2006, when the VRA was reauthorized, but rather from as recently as 2010. In an FBI wiretap, two Alabama state senators referred to African Americans as "aborigines" as they plotted to suppress a referendum that would increase voter turnout. In choosing the example, the justice spoke not only to the problems of Alabama's facial challenge; she also did so in a shocking way that revealed the impact of the decision on African American communities. In addition, the wiretap quotation served to refute Roberts's "rosy" scenario of racial progress in which voter discrimination against minorities was portrayed as a relic of the past, unrelated to the issue before the Court.

The *Shelby* dissent is also noted for containing one of the justice's more memorable lines. Taking the majority to task for failing to engage with Congress's legislative record, which clearly demonstrated why Section 5 remained necessary, Ginsburg wrote, "Throwing out preclearance is like throwing away your umbrella in a rainstorm because you are not getting wet." Though "the umbrella metaphor" was surprisingly omitted from the justice's highly effective oral distillation, she used it later in interviews and speeches. The metaphor, noted Guinier, not only served to simplify complex ramifications of the Court's ruling in a way that

MIT students and community members celebrate the school's Women's and Gender Studies program by posing as Ginsburg, 2015.

ordinary people could remember but also provided the public with a language to participate in conversations about voting rights.

What the *Ledbetter* and *Shelby* dissents reveal, concluded Guinier, is the justice's firm conviction that the Court does not have the final word in democratic debate about the meaning of rights and law. Rather, "We, the People" play a key role in a dialogue with formal institutions about the core conflicts in our society.

. . .

THERE WOULD BE OTHER dissents and more tributes—the latter not just from distinguished legal scholars at elite universities but also from the millennials who took out phrases like "throwing away your umbrella in a rainstorm" and "skim milk marriage" and made them go viral across the internet. Ginsburg's indignation at the *Shelby* ruling inspired Shana Knizhnik, a young first-year law student at NYU, to start a Tumblr blog with the tongue-in-cheek name "Notorious R.B.G." (a reference to the late rapper Biggie Smalls, who had been known as the Notorious B.I.G.). One of Ginsburg's clerks told the eighty-one-year-old justice about the blog's existence and explained the parody. Ginsburg then learned that there was a cottage industry associated with the blog—T-shirts, coffee mugs, shoulder tattoos, homemade Halloween costumes for toddlers, small busts, cartoons, and more, all bearing her new moniker and slogans like "The Ruth Will Set You Free."

Amazed by her new pop culture status, she concluded that she and the murdered rapper indeed had something in common: they both hailed from Brooklyn. Exploring the blog that so delighted her granddaughters, she ordered T-shirts adorned with her photograph to give to friends. When she traveled in 2013 to the University of California's Boalt Hall at Berkeley to lecture, law students showed up wearing "Notorious R.B.G." T-shirts. Clearly enjoying evidence of her popularity among millennials, she asked of her young admirers that they fight for the things they care about, do it in a way that will lead others to join them, and maintain a sense of humor. Progress, she knew, is seldom linear. There are always new battles to fight and old ones to be refought.

CHAPTER 22

A Hobbled Court

In recent years, Ginsburg's legendary tenacity has been on full display. In 2014, Erwin Chemerinsky, dean of the University of California Law School at Irvine, first suggested that as the oldest member of the Court, Ginsburg should retire so that Obama could pick a replacement. Other liberal law professors, such as Randall Kennedy of Harvard, agreed, even urging Breyer to join her. But Ginsburg soon quashed the idea. She was keenly aware of the consequences of O'Connor's resignation, which, in retrospect, had been premature. As an octogenarian weighing less than a hundred pounds, the justice knew she was being watched for any sign of physical or mental decline and that health crises are often unpredictable. Indeed, as it turned out, she would need to have a stent inserted into her right coronary artery in November 2014, although she was back on the bench for oral argument five days later.

Always adept in her relations with the press, she let it be known that her work ethic was intact—a reality to which former clerks readily attest, recalling messages left on their voice mail at 2:00 or 3:00 in the morning. She was also the Court's "speed demon," taking an average of only sixty days from oral argument to issue her opinions—nearly a month faster than any of her colleagues. She did acknowledge that age had required minor adjustments. She had given up waterskiing, horseback riding, and parasailing—the latter an adventure she had enjoyed one summer when she and Marty together with Scalia and his wife, Maureen, were in France. (The apprehensive Scalia had admired her courage but fretted that his featherweight friend might never return to terra firma, which, of course, she did.) She also reminded journalists that she still worked out twice a week with her personal trainer, doing push-ups and bench presses as part of her exercise routine. Equally important, she pointed

Obama and Ginsburg hug before the State of the Union address, January 28, 2014.

In a 2014 interview, the retired justice John Paul Stevens stated that Ginsburg would not need his advice on retirement. He told her she would be fully capable of handling everything that comes along.

out that it would be impossible for President Obama to gain approval of a nominee as liberal as herself, especially after Republicans gained control of the Senate in the 2014 election. Determined to take it year to year, she let it be known that she intended to stay put as long as she could do the job at "full steam."

. . .

THAT GINSBURG WAS indeed operating at peak performance was apparent in yet another dissent—this one in 2014 involving women's reproductive health. A provision of the ACA requires employers' insurance coverage to include various means of contraception. Fought by antiabortion forces in Congress when the ACA was being drafted, the provision had subsequently become the focus of lawsuits initiated by irate business owners who objected that they were being forced to violate their religious beliefs or suffer potentially devastating economic penalties. The provision, they claimed, superseded the First Amendment's right to religious freedom and the stipulation in the 1993 Religious Freedom Restoration Act (RFRA) that the government not impose a "substantial burden" on believers. This was also the position taken by Judge Neil Gorsuch, federal appellate judge on the U.S. Court of Appeals for the Tenth Circuit, who viewed *Hobby Lobby* not as a case regarding women's access to contraception but as an issue of the store owners' religious freedom.

The ACLU and various women's groups countered that private businesses, such as the evangelical-owned chain of craft stores Hobby Lobby, should not be allowed to use the religious beliefs of their owners as an excuse for denying insurance coverage for emergency contraception (popularly known as the morning-after pill) or for an intrauterine device. The Constitution's establishment clause enforcing separation of church and state takes precedent over the RFRA.

The Supreme Court's ruling in *Burwell v. Hobby Lobby*, delivered on June 30, 2014, the last day of the spring term, proved to be highly controversial. Alito, writing for the majority, stated that "a corporation is simply a form of organization used by human beings to achieve desired ends" and that constitutional or statutory rights—in this case, religious freedom protections—are extended to these businesses for the purpose of protecting the rights of the individuals. The RFRA protects the religious liberties of the owners of "closely held" corporations such as Hobby Lobby, Alito continued, because the government had not proved that the contraception mandate was the least burdensome threat to religious liberty that could have been provided.

Ginsburg's strong dissent, joined by Sotomayor and Kagan, began with the Women's Health Amendment, which enhanced the initial ACA's minimum coverage requirements. This adjustment created a new category of preventive services specific to women's health in order to offset the fact that women paid significantly more than men for preventive care. Citing data from the Guttmacher Institute, a private research organization, Ginsburg pointed out that unless women were covered by insurance for an intrauterine device, cost barriers could operate to block many women from obtaining needed contraceptive care at all. Further, the Senate had voted down a "conscience amendment" that would have enabled employers or insurance providers to deny coverage based on asserted religious beliefs or moral convictions. In requiring that employers provide health-care insurance for employees, Congress had left health-care decisions—"including the choice among contraceptive methods—in the hands of women." Individual workers in consultation with their physicians should decide which methods to choose, not their employers.

She also emphasized the lack of precedent for recognizing a for-profit corporation's qualification for religious exemptions. This absence, she insisted, is "just what one would expect, for the exercise of religion is characteristic of natural persons, not artificial entities." No employer, she insisted, should be able to transfer that employer's religious beliefs onto people who do not share those beliefs.

Mindful of Roberts's and his fellow conservatives' penchant for creating precedents that could be used to undermine established protections, Ginsburg feared what *Hobby Lobby* might portend. In extending the recognition of religious freedom formerly reserved for religious nonprofits to for-profit companies, the Court, she warned, was venturing "into a minefield." What would prevent the majority from extending religious freedom from "closely held" corporations to all corporations, given its "immoderate" reading of RFRA?

. . .

DURING SUMMER RECESS, Ginsburg talked with the journalist Katie Couric about the controversial *Hobby Lobby* decision, effectively distilling the public message of her thirty-five-page dissent. Asked by Couric why she found the decision so disturbing, the justice replied, "I have never seen the free exercise of religion clause interpreted in such a way. . . . I certainly respect the belief of Hobby Lobby owners. On the other hand, they have no right to force that belief on hundreds and hundreds of women who work for them who don't hold that belief."

Women who gathered in New York for the thirtieth anniversary of the International Women's Health Coalition received a slightly different message from the justice. With respect to *Hobby Lobby,* she again stressed how essential it was to retain employer-provided insurance coverage for a full range of reproductive choices, especially for lower-income women. The Court, she declared, "didn't really get it either" in its 1980 decision (*Harris v. McRae*) upholding congressional denial of Medicaid funds for medically *necessary* abortions for indigent women. Recalling what the feminist classic *Our Bodies, Ourselves* had meant to her daughter and the passion that Jane's generation had felt about protecting their sexual and reproductive rights, she observed that many young women today take those rights for granted. Reminding her audience how easily rights can be eroded, she pointed out that *Roe v. Wade* now works only if a woman has the money for a plane, train, or bus ticket to the nearest abortion clinic in a state that still permits clinics to operate.

At Duke University Law School, she also shifted from *Hobby Lobby* to the state of reproductive freedom in the United States, reiterating that choice had become an empty concept for poor women. This "sorry situation" constitutes "a remaining barrier to gender parity," she concluded. Ginsburg's comment, her audience quickly recognized, referred also to the regression that had taken place on women's rights issues during the Republican Party's long "war on women." The Republican National Committee chair, Reince Priebus, claimed that the alleged GOP war was as fictitious as a "war on caterpillars." Maine's Republican senator Susan Collins knew better, chiding her party for throwing Congress back into debates on issues such as birth control and defunding Planned Parenthood "that most everyday people think were settled years ago." If Ginsburg seemed focused on women's health-care needs, it was because the pushback against abortion had come to include not only new restrictions that ranged from "petty to profound" but, for many Republican politicians, access to contraception as well.

. . .

THE SUMMER OF 2015 also offered more occasions for tributes. Harvard Law School had displayed a handsome photograph of Ginsburg in its 2014 exhibit of women lawyers and policy makers from around the globe who both promote change and inspire women. And at the end of the spring term in 2014, she found herself back in Cambridge again, where the Radcliffe Institute for Advanced Study at Harvard presented her with the Radcliffe Medal for her "transformative impact on society." Gathered under a tent in Harvard Yard, an appreciative audience of thirteen hundred offered several standing ovations. But the event that she most anticipated was the upcoming premiere of a new comic opera in which she and Scalia were the principals.

The two justices had previously been approached by Derrick Wang, a young composer, librettist, and pianist who wrote for Hasty Pudding Theatricals while an undergraduate at Harvard. Wang told them that while he was studying at the University of Maryland Law School, it occurred to him that he could portray their different perspectives on constitutional interpretation in song. The opera would conclude with a duet, "We Are Different, We Are One"—one in their shared reverence for the Constitution, the U.S. judiciary, and the Court on which they served. Would the two listen to some excerpts, Wang asked, and tell him whether his idea was worth pursuing? He left them with the libretto, including many footnotes indicating his sources. When the opera was completed, the two justices both prepared short prefaces.

Ginsburg, who revealed that her grade school teacher had told her to mouth the words of songs, not sing them, confided that if she could have chosen her talent, she would have chosen a glorious voice. What a thrill it would have been to become a great diva like Renata Tebaldi, Beverly Sills, or, in the mezzo range, Marilyn Horne. Hearing her own words sung in Wang's opera—other than in the shower or her dreams—was a fantasy come true. Scalia, less enthusiastic, noted in his preface that his father had a good tenor voice and had studied at the Eastman School of Music in Rochester, New York. His own finest musical moment had occurred at an evening after the Opera Ball at the British ambassador's residence when he joined two tenors from the Washington Opera. Together at the piano they replicated a performance of the famous Three Tenors (Luciano Pavarotti, José Carreras, and Plácido Domingo). Tongue in cheek, he professed to want to perform his own role in the opera, lamenting that his co-star refused to perform hers.

The June 13 premiere of *Scalia/Ginsburg* at the Castleton Festival took place on the Virginia estate of the celebrated conductor Lorin Maazel. Ginsburg had a front-row seat for the sold-out premiere, but Scalia was in Europe at the time. Other prominent Washingtonians attended, among them Solicitor General Donald Verrilli. For Court veterans like Verrilli, part of the enjoyment was identifying the context of quotations in the fast-paced repartee that had been updated to include barbs from Scalia dissents in the term just ended. Ginsburg, who was portrayed by a young Canadian soprano, shed tears as she saw Marty's favorite dessert, a frozen lime soufflé, being served onstage.

The cultural critic for *The Washington Post* offered a tempered assessment of the production while acknowledging that "there is much that is charming, clever, and amusing in the score." For Ginsburg, the unmistakable heroine of *Scalia/Ginsburg,* praise for the performance came easily. When the Scalia character (who in real-life called her his "best buddy" on the bench) is imprisoned for "excessive dissenting," her character bursts from the other side of a glass ceiling to rescue him. What Ginsburg would never have imagined that warm June evening was that these two best buddies were to have so little remaining time together on the bench.

· · ·

ON FEBRUARY 13, 2016, Scalia, the longest-serving member of the current Court, was found dead at a hunting lodge in West Texas after he failed to appear for breakfast. The immediate impact was an outpouring of tributes to a towering figure in conservative jurisprudence. A member of the Court noted for his brilliance, erudition, and wit, Scalia's stylistic genius and theory on interpretation had changed the way that many lawyers and judges thought about the law. As Kagan had acknowledged in her Scalia Lecture at Harvard Law School only months before—and as Justice Stevens had demonstrated in his *Heller* dissent—"We're all textualists now." All the justices paid tribute to their departed colleague, knowing that their time on the bench would now be duller without his outsize personality and wit.

Ginsburg's staunch friendship with Scalia, which went back to their years together on the U.S. Court of Appeals for the D.C. Circuit, had always seemed improbable to many. Neither of them expected to convert the other on matters of legal interpretation or political affiliation. Yet each understood the other's position and delighted in intellectual debate. Each was devoted to the craft of legal writing, taking pains to choose precisely the right word. Even when they voted on opposite sides of a case, when draft opinions circulated, the two would often call each other and say, "Wouldn't this be a better word" than what you had? Indeed, Ginsburg recalled in her tribute to Scalia how he had walked into her chambers and handed her a draft of his dissent in the VMI case. He had ruined her plans for the weekend, but his critique of her draft opinion had allowed her to strengthen the final version considerably.

The two justices, in fact, had much in common: formative years spent in Manhattan's outer boroughs, ethnic investment in family, love

Scalia and Ginsburg in India, 1994. They were seated according to weight, Scalia obviously being the heavier of the two.

Ginsburg and Scalia as supernumeraries in the Washington Opera production of Richard Strauss's Ariadne auf Naxos, *January 1994.*

of opera, fondness for traveling abroad for summer teaching, a shared sense of humor, and a real zest for life. While Ginsburg had always taken a dim view of her colleague's personalized dissents, she had always found Nino, if sometimes outrageous, also utterly charming and amusing. He had an "uncanny ability to make me smile, and often laugh," she would recall. He had also become a consummate shopping companion on long trips abroad, her partner on an elephant ride in India, and her fellow supernumerary when the two had appeared together in a Washington Opera production of Richard Strauss's *Ariadne auf Naxos*.

For years, the Ginsburgs and Scalias had dined together on New Year's Eve, when Marty and Maureen Scalia would prepare a gourmet dinner for families and friends using fowl or game that Scalia had shot. Scalia had also been the colleague who called her chambers after the intensely polarizing vote on *Bush v. Gore* and told her to go home and take a hot bath to relax. He even sent her roses every year on her birthday, attesting to their shared love of roses. Not only had she lost a dear friend, but the Court, she knew, would be "a paler place" without Scalia's wonderful stories and irrepressible wit.

Unfortunately, the death of the conservative icon on the Court also had a much larger impact, unleashing an ugly political spectacle. Mitch McConnell, the Republican majority leader of the Senate, announced within less than an hour after learning of Scalia's death that the Senate would refuse to hold hearings on a replacement prior to the election of a new president—still some nine months away. The framers of the Constitution had never intended the electorate to have a say in determining who should be a Supreme Court justice. But there was nothing in the document that compelled the Senate to fulfill its obligation to consider the president's nominee within a specified time frame.

Unprecedented, the preemptive blockade infuriated Democrats, who pointed out that Justice Kennedy had been nominated and confirmed in an election year. But lacking a majority, there was no way they could confirm Judge Merrick B. Garland, Obama's impeccably credentialed nominee.

At the heart of the obstruction was common recognition that Scalia's replacement could shift the ideological direction of the Court—the most consequential appointment in that respect since Thurgood Marshall retired and was replaced by Clarence Thomas. Confirming a justice to the Court who shared Ginsburg's and Sotomayor's perspective would have called into question a number of contentious precedents from *Citizens United,* to *Heller, Shelby, Hobby Lobby,* and *Glossip v. Gross,* which had prompted Breyer's and Ginsburg's objections to the death penalty. That the stakes were so high made the obstruction all the more vexing for Obama, underscoring the imperative of electing a forward-looking successor.

In the meantime, the 2016 spring term awaited with critical decisions to be made by the remaining eight justices. They now had to deal with fifty cases, knowing that an even 4–4 split between conservatives and liberals would leave the lower court decision intact, without setting a nationwide precedent and without offering any sense of the Court's reasoning. An early 4–4 deadlock in *Friedrichs v. California Teachers Association* temporarily saved public union dues from defeat, leaving intact a favorable ruling by the U.S. Court of Appeals for the Ninth Circuit. The case involved an effort by conservative activists and foundations to cripple public unions by prohibiting them from charging fees to nonmembers that supported collective bargaining. The premise was that the

Vice President Joe Biden (left) and President Barack Obama (right) applaud the Supreme Court nominee Merrick Garland in the Rose Garden at the White House in Washington, D.C., on March 16, 2016.

fees violated nonmembers' First Amendment rights. The litigant's goal in initiating the case was to overcome a string of precedents set by the Court dating back to 1977 that unions could assess agency fees from nonmembers in order to recover bargaining costs, provided the fees did not go toward political purposes. Because the 4–4 decision lacked the affirmation of those precedents, the issue would be left open to other anti-union challenges moving through the courts.

. . .

A SECOND DEADLOCK HAD more immediate consequences for young people who were brought to the United States as small children by unauthorized immigrant parents who had then grown up here. Their hope was to gain permanent residency or citizenship so they could pursue their educations and careers. When House Republicans failed to respond to an immigration reform bill passed by the Senate, Obama had used his presidential power to defer deportation for these young adults and their mixed-status families. (Younger members of such families, having been born here, were U.S. citizens.)

Questioning the president's authority to act without congressional authority, Texas and twenty-five other states had sued. Texas claimed that issuing these noncitizens driver's licenses imposed an additional financial burden on the state. Whether this kind of injury actually gave them standing to sue would be a question for the Court to decide along with the larger question of whether the president had exceeded his authority in *United States v. Texas.*

A ruling denying standing would have allowed Obama's initiative, Deferred Action for Parents of Americans and Lawful Permanent Residents (DAPA), to remain intact. Issues about presidential authority would be sidestepped. Instead, the Court split 4–4, which meant that the lower court injunction against DAPA would prevail. The president thus suffered the biggest legal defeat of his eight-year tenure in the White House. For the four million immigrants living in mixed-status households who had applied for the DAPA program, uncertainty loomed ahead.

Roberts and other members of the bench worked hard to avoid deadlock, as was evident when the two sides faced off over yet more cases pitting religious beliefs against federally mandated health-care requirements. Six cases had been consolidated into *Zubik v. Burwell,* one involving a Catholic group in Baltimore known as the Little Sisters of the Poor. The Sisters argued that merely by signing the form that would allow their institution to opt out because of religious objections, they would be complicit in facilitating a health-care system that provided contraception. Enabling was a sin for which the nuns did not wish to have to atone.

As Roberts searched for some balance that might be reached between the groups' theological beliefs and what the government could require of employers to fulfill health-care directives, he insisted there had to be some accommodation. Ginsburg pointed out that is precisely what the government tried to do by allowing these religious organizations to opt out by filing Form 700. Might the government provide free contraception to those women whose employers resisted for religious reasons? Alito suggested that would mean that "she'll have two insurance cards instead of one." Sotomayor objected, insisting that coverage should be seamless so as to dramatically reduce the number of unwanted pregnancies and abortions.

With the justices again divided, the Court less than a week later issued an unusual directive instructing the parties to file supplemental briefs examining possible alternative means of providing contraceptive coverage through their respective organizations' insurance companies "but in a way that does not require any involvement of petitioners beyond their own decision to provide health insurance without contraceptive coverage to employees." The insurance companies, the Court suggested, could subsequently notify the organizations' employees that they would supply cost-free contraceptive coverage. When all the parties agreed, the Court issued a per curiam decision on May 16, 2016, vacating the previous decisions of the circuit courts because the new option was feasible for the parties involved.

The larger question remained: how to reach some balance between religious freedom and the government's compelling interest in seeing that its citizens receive health care. Sotomayor and Ginsburg issued a concurrence stating that the resolution of *Zubik v. Burwell* should not be construed as a signal of where the Court stood on the issue. It could reach the same conclusion or a different one on each of the questions presented in the case. In other words, *Zubik v. Burwell* could not be regarded as a precedent.

· · ·

ON THE TWO most closely watched cases of the term, Ginsburg was delighted to see that the votes were not ties, thanks to Justice Kennedy, who seemed to be full of surprises.

Fisher v. University of Texas had been remanded to the federal appeals court in Texas in 2013 with the stipulation that it complete a more searching analysis of the university's rationale for using consideration of race as a means to improve its campus diversity. The case, *Fisher II*, was now back at the Supreme Court for oral arguments, thanks to Edward Blum and his Project on Fair Representation. At issue was whether the university could apply a "holistic" review of its applicants for its remaining openings after it had fulfilled its initial obligation of accepting the top 10 percent of graduating seniors in the state.

The Top Ten Percent Rule itself still galled Ginsburg, who had exposed its race-conscious origins in her previous dissent in *Fisher I*. This time, she pointed out that while the plan was designed to promote admissions of minority students, "it is totally dependent upon racially segregated neighborhoods [and] racially segregated schools" to achieve those numbers. "It [therefore] operates as a disincentive for a minority student to step out of that segregated community and attempt to get an integrated education." The Top Ten Percent Rule, she reiterated once again, had been "created because of race," making it—prima facie—a factor in admissions.

What the university sought to do in its holistic review of additional applicants was to add a small number of minority students whose economic and social class would bring a greater element of diversity to those automatically admitted under the Top Ten Percent Rule. Kennedy and other justices were frustrated at the perceived lack of facts provided to the Court since the previous hearings—"It's as if nothing had happened"—and suggested that a trial might be appropriate. As in *Fisher I,* the conservative justices expressed continuing skepticism about the benefit—and necessity—of the university's program.

When oral arguments concluded, observers expected the justices to strike down the University of Texas affirmative-action program, convinced that the university had still not provided a clear standard as to how it would measure "diversity" or its results. Although the university continued to argue that racial preferences were necessary to ensure that a "critical mass" of African Americans and Hispanics could be enrolled, it provided no explanation as to why ethnic preferences were confined to these two groups. Further, Justice Kennedy, as was well known, had yet to uphold a race-conscious plan in any form.

But to the surprise of many, the justice delivered the swing vote, writing an opinion that Ginsburg's former law clerk Richard Primus stated "might as well have been written by Justice Ruth Bader Ginsburg." Kennedy maintained that the use of race-conscious admissions programs at the University of Texas was lawful under the equal protection clause. Referring to the Top Ten Percent Rule, he agreed with the university that class rank alone does not allow a school to capture all the benefits of diversity. Although race consciousness played a role in a small number of admissions decisions, the justice wrote, it did not constitute evidence that the university was acting unconstitutionally, because it had "met its burden" of demonstrating that its admissions policy was narrowly tailored.

A frustrated Alito countered with a fifty-one-page dissent, insisting that UT had failed to do what the Court's previous decision demanded. It had failed to satisfy strict scrutiny because it did not identify "with any degree of specificity the interest that its use of race and ethnicity is supposed to serve." Nor had it presented evidence from admissions officers that the minorities admitted under this plan were likely to enroll in classes in which they were underrepresented, or even provide a definition of what the school meant by "critical mass." This, Alito charged, represented "affirmative action gone wild."

. . .

NEXT ON THE DOCKET was *Whole Woman's Health v. Hellerstedt.* In the rush to impose new restrictions on abortion in the wake of *Carhart,* Texas had passed a measure (H.B. 2) that required physicians performing abortions to have admitting privileges at nearby hospitals. In addition, abortion clinics in the state had to meet standards for "ambulatory surgical centers." Supporters of the new requirement insisted that its purpose was the protection of women's health. But in singling out abortion rather than other medical procedures involving comparable or greater risk, the new requirements, opponents countered, interfered with a woman's constitutional right to end her pregnancy. Whole Woman's Health challenged the law as it related to two of its Texas clinics, one in El Paso and another in McAllen. A federal district court upheld the challenge, determining the law to be unconstitutional. But the decision was overturned by a three-judge panel in the conservative Fifth Circuit.

Kennedy's vote would prove decisive. He had defended a woman's right to terminate her pregnancy only once before in *Planned Parenthood v. Casey* (1992). Working with Souter and O'Connor, he had arrived at a compromise that kept *Roe* intact while allowing some state restrictions on abortions that did not constitute an "undue burden" on pregnant women. In the interim, however, the Court had seldom applied the "undue burden" test. Nor had Kennedy done so in *Carhart,* when he voted to uphold restrictions that protected neither maternal health nor the potential life of the fetus. But as Ginsburg had told Katie Couric, "Justices continue to think and change."

When oral arguments began on March 2, 2016, Ginsburg went on the offensive. Stephanie Toti, a lawyer for the abortion clinics, had barely begun to speak when the justice interrupted to ask whether the petitioners had the right to challenge the law. Ginsburg believed the plaintiff had standing; she simply wanted to get that issue out of the way in order to deal with others that went to the merits of the case. In much the same way, she repeatedly interrupted Texas's solicitor general, Scott A. Keller, when he attempted to counter the U.S. solicitor general Donald B. Verrilli Jr., who had asserted that the Texas law would close most of the abortion facilities in the state while "exponentially" increasing "the obstacles women would have to face when seeking an abortion." Keller maintained that even with closures, less than 25 percent of Texas women would be more than a hundred miles away from a clinic. That number would be even less if the Santa Teresa, New Mexico, facility was used by those in the greater El Paso area. Ginsburg immediately threw the solicitor general off balance, pointing out that New Mexico had none of the requirements of H.B. 2. "If that's all right for the women in the El Paso area," she asked, "why isn't it right for the rest of the women in Texas?"

For the remainder of Keller's time, Ginsburg maintained the pressure, peppering him with questions. What was the benefit of requiring an ambulatory surgical center when the patient is only taking two abortion-inducing pills? Was it not more likely that any complications from the pill would occur near home, negating the necessity of a hospital near a clinic? What was the specific problem that the Texas legislature was responding to? What part of existing law was not sufficiently protective of women's health? Returning to *Casey,* she reminded Keller that the core issue remained a woman's "fundamental right to make this choice for herself. . . . The focus," she emphasized, "is on the woman and it has to be on the segment of women who are affected" by the intent and purposes of new laws.

On the last day of the spring term, Kennedy, who had been expected to ally with his conservative brethren, surprised his colleagues for the second time in less than a week. Providing the swing vote to strike down the new Texas requirements for imposing an "undue burden" on women's right to choose, he agreed that they did little to advance women's health and created substantial obstacles to abortion.

Specifically addressing the two principal requirements of H.B. 2, Breyer, whom Kennedy had chosen to write the majority opinion, concluded that "neither of these provisions offers medical benefits sufficient to justify the burdens upon access that each imposes." While conceding that increased driving distances do not necessarily constitute an undue burden, Breyer maintained that the multiple clinic closings, the substantial obstacles placed in the path of women seeking a pre-viability abortion, and "virtual absence of any health benefit" constituted an undue burden that made the Texas law invalid.

. . .

A CRIPPLED BENCH HAD weathered a difficult term. Although Roberts maintained silence about consequences for the Court and the nation, Ginsburg lamented the absence of a ninth justice to members of the press, observing that tie votes sowed legal confusion. Often those cases that had been decided were the product of compromises, taking critical issues off the table for the time being, as the liberal quartet had done in a Texas voting-rights decision, *Evenwel v. Abbott,* for which she had written the majority decision. Further, the number of new cases thus far designated for the October term was only a dozen—a marked slowdown from previous years.

Yet limitations notwithstanding, Ginsburg rejoiced in the unanticipated victories that Kennedy's vote had made possible. *Whole Woman's Health* had literally transformed the environment for women's reproductive rights in the state of Texas. The ripple effect would unquestionably generate waves of legal challenges in other Republican-controlled states where efforts to eviscerate *Roe* were continuing unabated. What the term—and Garland's nomination—had provided was a heady glimpse of what a Court no longer dominated by conservatives might accomplish. In what *The Wall Street Journal* caustically dubbed Ginsburg's end-of-term "victory lap," the justice not only praised Kennedy but provided a list of decisions she would like to see overturned. While the list contained no surprises for anyone familiar with Ginsburg's judicial record, her remarks confirmed her reputation as the most outspoken member of the high court now that Scalia was no longer present.

Appalled as she was by McConnell's partisan foot-dragging, Ginsburg was even more upset with Donald Trump, the real-estate mogul and reality television star who had become the front-runner for the GOP presidential nomination. Trump's inflammatory remarks about reviving the practice of torture, banning Muslim immigration, and deporting undocumented immigrants without a fair hearing raised fundamental questions about whether he had the knowledge and temperament to serve in the nation's highest office. Breaking sharply with judicial decorum, Ginsburg warned that a Trump presidency would be "a disaster for the country and the Court."

Her explicitly political remarks, made in interviews with the Associated Press, *The New York Times,* and CNN, unleashed a firestorm. Trump called her "a disgrace to the Court," subsequently tweeting, "Her mind is shot—resign!" Although there is no specific code of ethics that governs the behavior of members of the high court, justices are expected to be self-disciplined and circumspect. Legal ethics experts and editorialists on both sides of the political spectrum took Ginsburg to task. Her remarks injected further partisanship into the one branch of government that tries to maintain an image of impartiality in order to buttress its moral authority.

Privately, good friends fully shared her negative appraisal of Trump. But they wondered if she would have been so quick to break with tradition if Marty had been present to offer prior feedback. Had she become too outspoken with her increasing celebrity? She quickly apologized.

. . .

NO DOUBT HOPING to leave the furor inspired by her comments behind, Ginsburg departed for Barcelona to attend a July conference sponsored by New York University on Great Britain's vote to leave the European Union (popularly known as Brexit). She looked forward to spending time with the retired justice Stevens, who had also been invited along with Justice Alito. In addition, the cosmopolitan capital of the Catalonian region of Spain provided an art and architectural mecca. Later in July, she traveled to Venice for the five hundredth anniversary of the establishment of its old Jewish ghetto. It was an anniversary that hardly invited celebration but certainly deserved marking. An exhibition was scheduled for the Doge's Palace. More provocatively, Shakespeare's *Merchant of Venice* would be staged in the square of the old ghetto on June 25. On the second day of the play's run, a mock court hearing on Shylock's guilt would be held with real lawyers. Ginsburg would head the panel of judges determining the Jewish merchant's fate.

This was not the first time that she had taken part in a mock appeal. But never before had she heard an appeal staged in the monumental sixteenth-century Scuola Grande di San Rocco beneath the dramatic Renaissance murals adorning the ceiling and walls created by Venice's own Jacopo Tintoretto. The hearing began where the play ended. Shylock, the conniving moneylender, insists on collecting a pound of flesh from Antonio, who has defaulted on his loan. But the judge, who is really Portia disguised as a man, finds Shylock guilty of conspiring against Antonio and rules that half of his property must be handed over to Antonio and the other half to the state. Antonio agrees to forgo his half on the condition that Shylock convert to Christianity and will his estate to Jessica, Shylock's wicked and rebellious daughter who had run off with Lorenzo, played by Ginsburg's grandson, Paul Spera.

After two hours of argument and twenty minutes of deliberation in stifling heat that left the lawyers' shirts wet underneath their robes, Ginsburg announced the judges' findings. No court, they held, would grant Shylock his literal pound of flesh, nor could Antonio, as a defendant, decree Shylock's punishment. However, after four centuries of delay in seeking payment, Shylock had run out of time in asking for interest. On what to do with Portia, the "impostor" and "trickster," the jury was divided, but agreed that requiring her to attend law school at the University of Padua would be a start.

A reception followed at Venice's iconic Harry's Bar. Ginsburg's entrance prompted a round of applause. Paul Spera noted that his ever-alert grandmother, whom he accompanied, had been "disappointed" that two lines had been cut from a famous scene in the play. Former law students and clerks would instantly recognize in Spera's comment Ginsburg's legendary attention to detail. Then she was off to dinner, her elegant black fan in hand as the evening's events continued. Adding to the celebration, Paul's birthday had coincided with the rehearsal of *The Merchant of Venice,* and Jane Ginsburg had flown in from France to cook a late-night birthday dinner of assorted pastas for the cast.

· · ·

BACK IN WASHINGTON, Ginsburg enjoyed a brief visit with Paul's sister, Clara, who was working as a summer associate in New York for a large international law firm—Davis Polk & Wardwell—and for the smaller firm of Susman Godfrey. Acquiring the kind of corporate law experience that her grandmother had lacked when she applied for a judgeship in the Second Circuit, Clara planned to end the summer doing a short stint at Hillary Clinton's campaign headquarters in Brooklyn. Upon graduation from Harvard Law in May 2017, she had two clerkships lined up, one on the Second Circuit with Chief Judge Robert Katzmann. This was the same Robert Katzmann whom Senator Moynihan had chosen to introduce the nominee Ginsburg to members of the Senate prior to her confirmation. Because members of the Supreme Court were responsible for various judicial districts and Ginsburg had been assigned the Second, she and Katzmann had stayed in touch.

There were other ways that Clara appeared to be closing the circle begun by her grandmother. Though her father's family are Roman Catholics, Clara had chosen some years earlier to embrace her Jewish heritage. Staying with her grandmother during the summer of 2013 while interning at the Brookings Institution, Clara had insisted that they both attend services during the high holy days. Ginsburg, who had not done so for years, was in for a surprise. "The cantor," she recalled, "was a lovely soprano. Then there were all these women going up on the bimah and reading from the Torah." The prohibition on female participation among Orthodox Jews when her mother died had long alienated her from the formal rituals of the Jewish religion. Had women been included when she was seventeen, she mused, her own feelings might have been quite different.

August brought Ginsburg and some of her family back to Santa Fe for opera. James's two daughters would be off to school in the fall— Abby back to NYU and Mimi to board at the venerable Emma Willard School in Troy, New York. Patrice's son Sat Nam would be coming to Washington to study at the Georgetown University School of Foreign Service, providing Ginsburg a welcome escort for concerts.

· · ·

RETURNING HOME to prepare for the fall term, Ginsburg had a busy schedule ahead. In September, she would be off to Chicago when James and Patrice held the Soirée Cedille and then on to Notre Dame University Law School for a discussion with students.

October marked the publication of *My Own Words,* a superbly edited collection of some of Ginsburg's writings and speeches that touched on a range of topics. Selections included portions of the *Frontiero* brief as well

as bench announcements of important dissents. Included, too, were tributes to women "waypavers," among them the wives of earlier Supreme
Court justices such as Malvina Harlan, the wife of Justice John Marshall
Harlan. There were also lectures on the "workways" of the Court, its
lighter side, and on the importance of judicial independence.

Later in the month Jane and George would celebrate their thirty-fifth
anniversary. The couple had previously hosted joint fiftieth anniversary
celebrations in New York for both sets of parents, complete with musi-
cians. Ginsburg was eager to reciprocate. She had also agreed to explore
justice at the opera at the Washington National Opera with Francesca
Zambello prior to a performance of Mozart's *Marriage of Figaro*.

In November, when the Washington National Opera performed *The
Daughter of the Regiment,* she would make her one-night debut as the
Duchess of Krakenthorp, a cameo speaking role in which she had to
find out whether the title character, Marie, was worthy of marrying her
nephew. Her lines (which she helped to write) included "The best of the
house of Krakenthorp have open but not empty minds. The best are willing to listen and learn. No surprise, then, that the most valorous Krak-
enthorpians have been women." There was also "Applicants seeking a

Ginsburg's one-night debut as the Duchess of Krakenthorp in The Daughter of
the Regiment *at the Washington National Opera.*

station so exalted must have the fortitude to undergo strict scrutiny." But the biggest laugh would come later. In a reference to the bogus "birther" rumor fueled by Trump that Obama was not a U.S. citizen, the duchess asked whether Marie could produce a birth certificate, adding, "We must take precautions against fraudulent pretenders."

None of this, of course, involved the justice's "day job," which included cases on immigration and deportation, racial bias in the criminal justice system, and the death penalty. If the Court, still a member short, suffered a slowdown, Ginsburg's pace had not. Yet the election and the nomination of a crucial ninth justice had never been far from her mind. Like so many Democrats, she had assumed that Hillary Clinton would become the next president. But the symmetry of having one Clinton nominate her and the other choose her liberal-leaning replacement when she eventually chose to retire was not to be.

CHAPTER 23

An Election and a Presidency
Like No Other

In the presidential primaries, the leadership in both parties faced challenges from "outsiders." The general election was hard fought and rancorous, with the Republican candidate running one of the most explicitly racialized campaigns in recent American history. The final outcome was totally unexpected—the election of Donald Trump as the forty-fifth president of the United States. Ginsburg's worst fears had become reality.

. . .

ON THE DEMOCRATIC SIDE, Senator Bernie Sanders, an independent, proved to be a skillful candidate with immense appeal to younger voters and to those concerned about economic inequality. Thirty-five years of virtual wage stagnation for most workers, huge gains for the top 1 percent, lax regulatory and enforcement regimes, especially for Wall Street, and a slow recovery from the Great Recession—all provided the white-haired Vermonter with abundant targets. To the surprise of many centrist Democrats, Sanders's call to fight economic inequality and to reorient trade policy generated fervent grassroots enthusiasm, enabling him to carry twenty-two states in the primaries.

Republicans, eager to recapture the White House, pinned their hopes on the former Florida governor Jeb Bush, then on Florida's senator Marco Rubio, Ohio's governor John Kasich, even the ultraright Texas senator Ted Cruz—*anyone* but the bellicose Trump, whose "political spitballs" and insults dominated media coverage. But Trump, with his "Make America Great Again" baseball cap perched atop his head and his exaggerated look of knowing authority, kept winning over working-class whites.

Displaced in a globalized, high-tech economy since the 1970s, blue-collar workers correctly believed that a political establishment committed to the gains from free trade agreements had failed for decades to address the problems of those left behind. Years of economic hardship and the browning of "their" America had been followed by eight years of an elegant, highly educated president whose race symbolized other ethnic groups and recent arrivals who threatened the social status of downwardly mobile whites. Feeling "invisible" in the country that their ancestors had helped to build, they gravitated to Trump, who at least paid attention to their hollowed-out industry and cultural and demographic anxieties.

In declining Rust Belt towns, coal-mining Appalachia, and rural America, the pain and suffering of voters was real. Middle-aged white men and women with only a high school education at best, self-medicating with opioids and alcohol, died in record numbers between 1999 and 2013, pushing up their mortality rate some 11 percent—in sharp contrast with other groups in the United States, including minorities. But it remained to be seen whether the systemic economic and cultural problems contributing to their plight could be effectively remedied by a self-interested, fact-averse demagogue hawking nostalgia laced with racism, bigotry, and fear.

The highly qualified Hillary Clinton succeeded in repositioning herself to the left during the primaries with proposals for economic reform, paid family and medical leave, and sweeping criminal justice reform. Yet for all her past accomplishments and progressive proposals, she seemed lackluster and out of touch. The Clintons' considerable private wealth, acquired since Bill's presidency, plus Hillary's lavish speaking fees from Wall Street and nonstop fund-raising, created a disconnect with her claim to champion those left behind by globalism and a sluggish recovery. Despite her long effort to become the nation's first female president, Clinton failed to craft a concise, coherent reason why people should vote for her in 2016. "Stronger Together" did not suffice for a candidate following a two-term president of the same party at a time when Democrats needed a charismatic economic messenger.

Equally damaging was Clinton's failure to put to rest her use of a

Candidates Hillary Clinton and Donald Trump at the second presidential debate, 2016.

private email server for official communications during her tenure as Obama's secretary of state—a matter overblown by the press. Her obsession with her personal privacy harked back to the Whitewater scandal in the early 1990s. Voters were reminded of her refusal to turn over documents from her days at the Rose Law Firm in Little Rock that could potentially reveal her own ethical shortcomings. Even if there had been no violations of the law in her use of a private server, the allegations put her in the position of constantly having to defend her integrity. An FBI investigation, in which Director James Comey excoriated Clinton in July 2016 for her handling of classified emails, created serious doubts among voters about her honesty and trustworthiness, especially after the case was reopened in late October when a new batch of emails came to light. Although no damaging information ever emerged, Comey's unexpected announcement eroded Clinton's lead in the election.

In fact, the trust deficit preceded the FBI's investigation. Conservative talk-radio hosts, right-wing websites, and especially Fox News had resurrected old accusations against Clinton from Whitewater to Benghazi, providing social affirmation by constantly repeating what had never been verified. Seeds of suspicion had blossomed into certainty and finally into full-blown frenzy with Trump's incessant denunciations of "Crooked

Hillary" and the roar of his supporters shouting, "Lock her up!" directed at Clinton throughout the Republican Convention in Philadelphia. But the level of misogyny and malice set off alarm bells. The fragility of democracy in an unstable world where trust in established institutions and the informal norms that underpin them had already eroded among the disengaged and alienated created ample reason for worry.

· · ·

SUBSTANTIVE DEBATES by the two candidates offering real political solutions proved impossible. Facts, hard thinking, and careful formulation of policy positions in terms of realistic costs and benefits impact were alien to Trump, who was renowned for diverting journalists from substance. The media, suffused with entertainment values, did little to help. Commentators emphasizing the negative traits of both candidates left a pervasive sense of false equivalence between the two.

To the dismay of those who fervently hoped that the antiestablishment populism that swept Britain and overshadowed Europe could be stopped on this side of the Atlantic, the race substantially tightened at the end of October.

But reproducing the coalition that twice carried Obama to victory proved harder than anticipated. The coalition itself was inherently fragile. Some white and Hispanic supporters were upset by cultural changes that had occurred over the previous eight years—gay marriage, more Muslim immigrants, more violence against police officers, Black Lives Matter demonstrations. For many of those voters, Trump's nostalgia and certainty offered "a return to the mother's womb." Nor could sexism be discounted.

Worse still, the Clinton campaign found itself entrapped in a "web of leaks and propaganda" that U.S. intelligence agencies traced back to Moscow. Meddling in foreign elections, aiming to undermine faith in the democratic process, was a familiar ploy by the Kremlin. But targeting Hillary Clinton's electability and potential presidency by hacking Democrats' emails, publicizing the stolen content through WikiLeaks, and manipulating social media to spread "fake news" and pro-Trump messages to 126 million Americans on Facebook represented a new low in the downward spiral of U.S.-Russian relations. Three years in the planning, details of the Russian operation and how it reached twenty-one states would be revealed in a thirty-seven-page indictment by Trump's Justice Department in February 2018, findings that Trump would continue to resist.

. . .

CLINTON STILL MANAGED to win the popular vote by nearly three million, running strong in coastal citadels and scattered urban areas across the country. However, she lost the Electoral College when she failed to win over less educated white voters in Pennsylvania, Wisconsin, and Michigan who had previously voted for Obama—states she had been urged to revisit but declined.

How many minority votes Clinton lost in Rust Belt areas and elsewhere because of restrictions on voting rights remains "the biggest under-covered scandal of the 2016 campaign," wrote the investigative journalist and author Ari Berman. In 2012, one year prior to the *Shelby* decision, the Department of Justice received 18,146 submissions of voting changes for preclearance review as part of the Voting Rights Act Section 5 requirements. But by the time voters went to the polls in 2016, fourteen states had imposed new voting restrictions, including strict photo-ID requirements, early voting cutbacks, and registration restrictions.

The UC Berkeley students Josey Garcia and Gustavo Navarez comforting each other at a protest of Trump's election.

Removal of Section 5 oversight also allowed states to change their voting laws without public notice. Included were North Carolina and Florida, which Clinton had hoped to carry with help from minority voters. The number of polling places in the heavily gerrymandered Tar Heel State had been significantly reduced—a total of 158 eliminated in forty heavily black counties. Reductions in early voting options in North Carolina contributed to a decrease in African American participation by as much as 16 percent. In Florida, a state Clinton lost by only 119,770 votes, the GOP's refusal to restore voting rights to felons left one in four black residents disenfranchised.

In Wisconsin, which along with Mississippi and Virginia had enacted strict voter-ID laws, 300,000 voters lacked the proper forms of ID. How many of those disenfranchised would have voted for Clinton, erasing Trump's 22,738-vote lead, is impossible to determine. What is known is that Wisconsin experienced its lowest voter turnout in twenty years—an estimated reduction of approximately 400,000 primarily African American and Democratic-leaning citizens. Milwaukee alone—home to 70 percent of the state's African Americans—suffered a 13 percent reduction in turnout. By contrast, states where no new restrictions had been added between the 2012 and the 2016 elections saw an increase in turnout of 1.3 percent.

. . .

AS THE REALITY of a Trump presidency began to sink in, the chasm dividing the nation loomed larger than ever. Protesters carrying signs that read, "He's Not My President," poured into the streets. Drawn together in defense of liberal immigration and refugee policies, civil liberties, reproductive freedom, and Obama's legacy, they rallied not only in liberal bastions like New York, Washington, and Los Angeles but also in urban areas from Grand Rapids, Michigan, to Sarasota, Florida. Topping them all was the Women's March on Washington the day after the inauguration, which drew nearly 500,000 to the capital in a show of opposition. Replicated in hundreds of other cities across the United States, carefully planned protests simultaneously took place in eighty-one other countries.

Thanks to Trump's xenophobic rhetoric and the anonymity of the Internet, far-right extremism, long part of the river of darkness that runs

Half a million people at the Women's March on Washington, January 2017.
An additional 500,000 marched in cities throughout the world.

through American history, jumped the levees. Nationwide, hate crimes against Muslims shot up 62 percent in the first six months of 2016. Desecration of Jewish cemeteries occurred in Philadelphia and St. Louis, while Jewish community centers across the country endured bomb threats. Hangman's nooses, long a symbol of hate against African Americans, began showing up in alarming numbers: at a workstation in the U.S. Mint in Philadelphia, at the Hirshhorn Museum on the National Mall, on the campus of American University, and at schools in North Carolina and Florida. Lower-school teachers reported an increase in bullying: young boys arriving at class with swastikas drawn on their hands, Hispanic and black children told by white classmates to pack their bags because they were going to be deported. As the former FBI undercover agent and counterterrorism expert Michael German lamented, "Trump put away the dog whistle and picked up a bullhorn"—with predictable results for Muslims, Jews, blacks, immigrants, and gays.

A flurry of executive orders, vigorously applauded by Trump supporters, further compounded the alarm of his critics. Included were a ban on aid to international programs that provide abortion services (even though not paid for with U.S. funds) or counseling on abortion; reduced regulations on manufacturing; advancement of the controversial Dakota

Access and Keystone XL pipelines; and a rollback of Obama's policies to curb planet-warming carbon dioxide emissions, including the closing of coal-fired power plants. Consistent with his campaign rhetoric, Trump also issued orders for an aggressive crackdown on undocumented immigrants, the end of federal funding for "sanctuary cities" (municipalities that limit cooperation with federal authorities in detaining persons suspected of immigration law violations), and advancement of his promised border wall between the United States and Mexico. Most disruptive was the president's January 27 order for a three-month entry ban on immigration from seven predominantly Muslim countries: Iran, Iraq, Syria, Sudan, Libya, Somalia, and Yemen.

Ostensibly an effort to protect the United States from the arrival of foreign terrorists—although there had never been a terrorist attack by an immigrant from any of the targeted countries—the order imposed a flat ban on Syrian refugees. A three-judge panel of the Ninth Circuit issued a temporary restraining order, prompting the president to issue a revised ban.

More limited, it omitted Iraq after imposing new vetting procedures, deleted any reference to religion, and removed the ban on Syrian refugees. Superficially neutral, this second version raised critical questions for judges hearing a new round of challenges: Did the ban violate due process and the equal protection clause of the Fourteenth Amendment or the First Amendment's prohibitions with respect to religion? How much weight should be assigned to context and background, especially to Trump's campaign calls for "a total and complete shutdown of Muslims entering the United States"?

On March 15, 2017, district courts in Hawaii and Maryland blocked Trump's revised ban, as did the appeals courts. The Fourth Circuit, by a 10–3 margin, found that the travel ban "drips with religious intolerance, animus and discrimination." Shortly thereafter, a three-judge Ninth Circuit panel ruled that the president had "exceeded the scope of his authority." On June 1, the Trump administration appealed to the Supreme Court to set aside the Fourth Circuit ruling, accept the case for oral arguments, and affirm the president's authority. Then before the cases could reach the Court, Trump issued a new order with each country given its own set of restrictions, opening this latest ban to challenges by attorneys who challenged previous bans. In December, the Supreme

Court agreed to allow Trump's latest ban to go into effect pending a hearing in the spring. Oral arguments in April 2018, however, left Court watchers agreed that the conservative majority appeared unwilling to hem in the president, claiming national security grounds for deciding who could enter the United States.

. . .

APPALLED BY THE PRESIDENT'S EARLY ACTIONS, including his war against science and the mainstream press, liberals awaited the prospect of Trump judicial nominees with a sense of impending doom. The judicial Left will "be banished to the wilderness for perhaps decades," lamented the New York University Law School professor Barry Friedman. Ginsburg, about to turn eighty-four in March 2017, would face second-guessing for her refusal to retire when Obama might still have been able to get her replacement confirmed by a Democratic Senate, Friedman predicted. How long her health—and Breyer's—would hold up was anyone's guess. Both exercised regularly with a tough trainer, whom Ginsburg now called the "most important person" in her life. That Kennedy, now the longest-serving justice, was known to be considering retirement made it difficult to dismiss Friedman's worst-case scenario: a future Court in which only Sotomayor and Kagan would be left to stand against seven conservatives—including relatively young Trump nominees determined to push the balance even further to the right.

Prospects for the appellate bench were also equally dire. Republicans had blocked a number of Obama nominees, leaving 117 vacancies. And almost half of the 150 appellate judges were within retirement age. Trump's freedom to get his nominees confirmed could change the ideological makeup of the federal court system, eroding whatever ground remained between the elected branches of government and the judiciary. Within a few days after Trump's election, McConnell, in fact, had contacted White House counsel Don McGahn, encouraging him to streamline the nomination process with the help of conservative lawyers, notably Leonard Leo, executive vice president of the Federalist Society.

The immediate concern was Scalia's replacement. The eight-member Court had contented itself through 2016 with a "meat and potatoes" diet, assiduously avoiding spicy issues that might create a deadlock. But the hot issues could not be postponed indefinitely: gun rights, religious freedom, freedom of speech, immigration and deportation, restrictions on voting rights, and the rule-making authority of federal agencies. Democrats still believed passionately that the empty seat on the Court should have gone to the impeccably credentialed judge Merrick Garland, whose fans ran across the ideological spectrum. But McConnell had prepared the way for the Trump–Leo alliance to prevail. On January 31, the president promptly introduced his choice, Judge Neil M. Gorsuch of the Tenth Circuit Court of Appeals in Denver.

· · ·

AS A FOURTH-GENERATION COLORADOAN, Gorsuch offered geographic diversity. Yet he hardly fit the description of the "outsider" for whom Trump had expressed a preference. The son and grandson of Denver lawyers, young Gorsuch had moved to Washington as a teenager, attending private school and working as a Republican Senate page following Ronald Reagan's nomination of his mother, Anne Gorsuch Burford, to head the new Environmental Protection Agency. Moving on to Columbia College, young Gorsuch wrote a weekly column, first in the student newspaper *The Spectator* and then in *The Federalist Paper*, an alternative paper that he co-founded. At both publications, he displayed traits for which he would later become renowned: lucid writing, intellectual rigor, and staunchly conservative values.

Studying next at Harvard Law School and then at Oxford University, where he received his doctorate in law, Gorsuch returned to Washington in 1991 accompanied by his English bride, Marie Louise Burleston, an accomplished equestrian. Beginning a clerkship on the D.C. Circuit, he later moved over to the Supreme Court, where he clerked for Byron White until the justice retired and then for Kennedy. After ten years at the elite Washington litigation firm of Kellogg, Huber, Hansen, Todd, Evans & Figel, Gorsuch spent a brief stint as the third-ranking member of the Justice Department, where he was at the center of controversy over Bush administration policies for treatment of detainees at Guantánamo Bay. In 2006, George W. Bush nominated him to the Tenth Circuit Court of Appeals in Denver, confident that a conservative with an impressive résumé, a first-rate mind, and the backing of the Federalist Society would be easily confirmed.

Gorsuch quickly established a judicial reputation as an originalist,

Trump announces the nomination of Judge Neil Gorsuch to the Supreme Court as Marie Louise Gorsuch looks on, January 31, 2016.

subscribing to the judicial philosophy of interpreting the Constitution from the perspective of its original authors. Also a textualist, he was committed to considering only the words of the law being reviewed, ignoring legislative history or the consequences that might come with implementation. Precedent, of course, had to be considered but, in his view, could be discarded if it was determined to violate text—a position closely mirroring Scalia's. As Gorsuch once told law students at Case Western Reserve University, judges should seek "to apply the law as it is, focusing backward, not forward, and looking to text, structure, and history to decide what a reasonable reader at the time of the events in question would have understood the law to be—not to decide cases based on their own moral conviction or the policy consequences they believe might serve society best."

Gorsuch also shared Scalia's gift for writing in a way that makes his explanations understandable to people untrained in the law. Relying on a style that can at times be breezy and jocular, his manner was more courteous than that of the often-caustic Scalia. Ginsburg, who met Gorsuch during a trip to the U.K., attested not only to his writing skills but also to his sociability, describing him as "very easy to get along with."

Reaction to the nomination varied. In separate published letters to the Senate Judiciary Committee, 57 Harvard classmates and 154 Columbia alumni claiming to represent a wide range of political, religious, and socioeconomic backgrounds offered staunch support. Gorsuch's Harvard Law classmates considered him someone who would respect judicial modesty and provide impartial consideration on the merits of each case. Conservative and business groups also hailed the nomination, counting on Gorsuch to reinforce the Court's pro-business majority.

Far less sanguine, liberals worried about Gorsuch's views on a number of issues ranging from the future of administrative agencies, public sector unions, and campaign finance reform, to voting rights, abortion rights, and the rights of LGBTQ persons. Those familiar with his ruling in *Hobby Lobby* were acutely aware of his capacious view of religious freedom and corporate personhood as well as his limited concern for working women's access to contraceptives. Organized labor worried about his dissent in a case involving a truck driver who was fired for abandoning his trailer when its brakes froze in subzero temperatures. Gorsuch stuck to the letter of the law irrespective of the health of the driver, whose legs had become numb from the hypothermic cold. Those concerned about the fate of other regulations that protect the public's health and safety were also apprehensive because of the nominee's concurring opinion in *Gutierrez-Brizuela v. Lynch.* How, Gorsuch had asked, can the *Chevron* ruling "evade the chopping block"?

Democratic members of the Judiciary Committee faced a dilemma. They could honor the process, confirming a nominee who promised to be one of the most conservative justices in the history of the modern Court. Or they might employ the same obstructionist path that Republicans had taken when they refused even to meet with Judge Garland. But the fact remained that McConnell would have the necessary votes when the full Senate met. Democrats could choose to filibuster. Yet a filibuster would inevitably prompt Republicans to invoke the "nuclear option"—changing the required number of votes for ending debate to a simple majority. Either way Gorsuch would end up as the 113th justice.

· · ·

WITH NO GROUNDS for questioning the nominee's qualifications and temperament, Democrats on the Judiciary Committee chose to use the hearings to try to gain a better sense of where Gorsuch stood on the conservative spectrum. Would he stand up to Trump? But ever since Ginsburg had adopted her strategy of giving "no hints, no forecasts, no previews" of how she might rule on any specific issues, subsequent nominees had followed suit.

When the hearing began on March 20, 2017, Gorsuch presented himself to the Senate Judiciary Committee as a humble westerner and a mainstream judge who sought consensus. Emphasizing that his judgments were based only on the law and the facts of the case, he took pains to position himself above politics. Republican members of the committee outdid themselves with softball questions and comments on everything from rodeos to Colorado's best fly-fishing streams to the late justice White's jump shot, leaving the grilling to Democrats.

Responding to the Democrats' perception that he favored "the big guy," Gorsuch listed several cases that ran counter to their expectations, including a woman raped by college football players, a suit by Colorado residents against environmental damage caused by a nuclear plant, and a jurisdictional dispute in favor of the Ute Indian tribe over a Utah town. The *Chicago Tribune* underscored the nominee's defense, noting that the Democrats' case examples were just a small sample from the twenty-seven hundred the judge had decided, with 97 percent being unanimous and Gorsuch ruling with the majority 99 percent of the time.

The nominee quickly demonstrated that he could take care of himself. Senator Dianne Feinstein asked Gorsuch why, as a Justice Department official in 2005, he scribbled "yes" on a document next to a question about whether the CIA torture of terrorists had yielded valuable intelligence? Gorsuch admitted that he had no personal information that it did. He was merely acting as a lawyer defending a client. Senator Michael Bennet then pushed hard on whether a president has constitutional powers to override torture and wiretap statutes.

Asked whether he had any interest in international law and the rulings of judges in other democracies, Gorsuch allied himself firmly with Scalia and Roberts. "As a general matter, I'd say it's improper to look abroad when interpreting our constitution," he replied. Never departing from script, Gorsuch left Democrats on the committee with few answers when testimony concluded on March 22. He had, however, acknowledged that *Roe v. Wade* was a precedent that "should not be overturned lightly."

In fact, Gorsuch's calm, disarming manner made the hearings seem anticlimactic, observed a former staffer. As Neal Kumar Katyal, an acting solicitor general in the Obama administration, noted in his introductory remarks to the committee, the nomination of this "first-rate intellect and a fair and decent man . . . would sail through, close to 100–0," in a less partisan climate.

. . .

HOWEVER, AS KATYAL KNEW—and as Ginsburg had long lamented—judicial nominations had become increasingly partisan. Since Reagan's election in 1980, the GOP had borne a greater share of the blame. Republicans had more aggressively blocked Democratic nominees to federal trial and appeals courts and shown less inclination than Democrats to nominate centrists to the Supreme Court. After the Garland obstructionism and McConnell's promise to apply the "nuclear option" to seat Gorsuch, Democrats now had to decide how to proceed in a full Senate vote without ignoring their base. As Nan Aron, president of the liberal Alliance for Justice, pointed out, voters who were convinced that Gorsuch was too right leaning "would be very unforgiving to Democrats who prevented a filibuster from taking place." Messages and petitions flooded Minority Leader Charles Schumer's office demanding that campaign funds be withheld from Democratic senators supporting Gorsuch, underscoring Aron's point. Schumer concluded that there was greater political risk in compromising with Republicans over the nomination than in attempting to block it. But first he appealed to McConnell to "change the nominee," not the rules, should Gorsuch fail to receive the necessary sixty votes. McConnell shot back, "Few outside of New York and San Francisco believe that Ruth Bader Ginsburg is in the mainstream and Neil Gorsuch is not."

On April 7, 2017, after more than a year of bitter political rancor over the filling of Scalia's seat, only three Democrats crossed over to vote with Republican senators 55–45 to confirm the nominee.

The change in rules initiated by the GOP meant that presidents would now be able to confirm or be denied a nominee to the high court

Demonstrators protest the nomination of Neil Gorsuch outside the Supreme Court.

depending solely on whether their party could muster a simple majority in the Senate. Trump's rejection of the American Bar Association's ranking of future judicial nominees compounded the despair. This was not what the founding fathers, intent on checks and balances, had intended with respect to governance. Further, it did nothing to embellish the image of the Supreme Court as an impartial arbiter of the law.

Three days later, Gorsuch was sworn in at two separate ceremonies. A private session at the Court presided over by the chief justice was followed by a public ceremony in the White House Rose Garden with Justice Kennedy administering the oath as Trump watched. Seated with the other justices, Ginsburg recalled her high hopes only a little over a year earlier at Judge Garland's nomination. The epic 419-day struggle over Scalia's replacement had left the federal judiciary more politicized and the Court, as an institution, more vulnerable than at any time during her tenure.

. . .

WHEN THE COURT ASSEMBLED for the last two-week sitting of the term on April 17, nine chairs were once again occupied, with Gorsuch seated on the far right of the bench—the spot reserved for the Court's most junior member. While he could not rule on cases he had not heard, he came fully prepared for the thirteen remaining cases. An "exceptionally active" and persistent questioner, Gorsuch emphasized the language of the statutes as the key to finding the "right" result in even the most complicated cases. Solidifying the conservative bloc, he clearly intended to make his mark quickly, even at the risk of antagonizing his senior colleagues with the condescending tone of some of his dissents.

His first day on the job included oral arguments on a Missouri case challenging separation of church and state. In prior cases, the Court had permitted secular services such as fire and police protection as well as vouchers to private citizens that could then be used at religious schools. But it had drawn the line at states providing direct financial aid to churches.

Trinity Lutheran Church in Columbia, Missouri, wanted to resurface the playground used by its preschoolers. Applying to a state program that used recycled tires for resurfacing, the church was rejected. A provision in the Missouri Constitution bars money from the "public treasury" from going "directly or indirectly, in aid of any church, sect, or denomination of religion." Trinity Lutheran sued, claiming its First Amendment rights had been violated. On appeal, four justices agreed to hear the case, fully aware that it involved much more than just protecting the knees of preschoolers.

The Alliance Defending Freedom, the Christian-rights advocacy organization that had supplied the church with legal representation, had as its top priority more government aid to religious institutions. A priority shared by the conservative movement, it ran counter to the traditional view that religious schools must shoulder their financial burden without taxpayer subsidies if they want to provide religious instruction. In an age of limited resources when state budgets were already strained, public schools stood to lose if scarce state resources were extended to religious institutions through subsidies.

The question the justices had to decide thus lay at the intersection of two clauses of the First Amendment: one that bars government establishment of religion and the other that guarantees religion's free exercise. Kagan acknowledged in oral argument that she and her colleagues were confronted with a "fraught issue," one on which "nobody is completely sure they have it right." Ginsburg and Sotomayor posed tough questions to the plaintiff's lawyer, while others, including Kagan and Breyer, offered expressions of sympathy for Trinity Lutheran. Gorsuch left no doubt about which side he favored. As arguments ended, legal journalists had become convinced that the majority seemed prepared "to chip away at the wall between church and state."

In a 7–2 ruling, Roberts wrote that Missouri, in its efforts to separate church and state, had gone too far in denying religious institutions government grants intended for secular purposes. Ginsburg joined Sotomayor in a passionate dissent. The ruling, wrote Sotomayor, "weakens this country's longstanding commitment to church and state beneficial to both. If this separation means anything, it means that the government cannot, or at the very least need not, tax its citizens and turn that money over to houses of worship. The Court today blinds itself to the outcome this history requires and leads us instead to a place where separation of church and state is a constitutional slogan, not a constitutional commitment."

Breyer, who had not joined their dissent, also worried that the Roberts opinion decided too much. Gorsuch entertained no such doubts, objecting only to a footnote in which Roberts stipulated, "We do not address religious uses of funding or other forms of discrimination." Protesting the chief's disclaimer, Gorsuch wrote, "The general principles here do not permit discrimination against religious exercise—whether on the playground or anywhere else."

· · ·

THE COURT ALSO HAD to wrestle with an unprecedented number of immigration-enforcement cases. *Ziglar v. Abbasi* was unusual in several respects. Harking back to policies that were put in place after the 9/11 attacks, it was a class-action suit against high-level officials in the Bush administration. The suit had been filed by mostly Muslim immigrants, over seven hundred of whom had been swept up in Brooklyn and held in detention centers. Subjected to beatings, humiliating daily strip searches, and solitary confinement for as long as eight months, they were given only sporadic access to lawyers or family until the FBI determined that they were not terrorists. Their only crime, it turned out, was a lack of proper immigration status.

In 2009, the government had reached an out-of-court settlement with five of the original plaintiffs in the case. But Ahmer Iqbal Abbasi, a young Brooklyn cabdriver at the time of his arrest, complained that the individuals responsible for the policy that had set his ordeal in motion had never been held accountable.

With an eye on a possible Trump administration as well as that of George W. Bush, Rachel Meeropol, the lawyer representing Abbasi and five other plaintiffs, told the Court that if the government were to succeed in this case, "any Muslim or Arab noncitizen present in this country could be placed in solitary confinement for violating the immigration law." The Court, she said, "has a historic role to play in ensuring that race and religion do not take the place of legitimate grounds for suspicion and in deterring future federal officials from creating government policy to do the same."

Speaking on behalf of the government, the acting solicitor general, Ian Gershengorn, countered that only two weeks after 9/11, when the arrests took place, "you couldn't tell who was and was not" a possible terrorist. It would be a troubling expansion of the law if the Court decided that top government officials can be held personally liable for their policy decisions.

Ginsburg and Breyer were the only two liberals hearing the case because Sotomayor and Kagan had recused themselves. Addressing Gershengorn, Ginsburg said of the detainees, "You knew from Day 1, that many of them have nothing to do with terrorists, and yet you allow that system that might have been justified in October to persist for months and months when these people are being held in the worst possible conditions of confinement." Roberts's concerns lay elsewhere. "We don't want people forming policy to have to worry" that they will be required to pay personal damages if that policy is found to be in error. As the justices discussed other legal alternatives that might have been available to the detainees at the time, Breyer injected a healthy dose of skepticism. Lawyers representing wardens at federal detention centers assured the justices that lawsuits had already been filed against the guards inflicting the worst abuses and that "discipline" had been "meted out."

The case of Julius and Ethel Rosenberg received no mention in Breyer's long list of incidents in which national-security fears (and political calculation) contributed to miscarriages of justice in which government officials were complicit. But the connection was visible in the presence of Rachel Meeropol, the attorney for Abbasi and his fellow plaintiffs. Meeropol was the granddaughter of Ethel and Julius Rosenberg. In June 1953, at the height of McCarthyism, both Rosenbergs had been executed as Soviet spies. Subsequent research in U.S. and Soviet archives confirmed Julius's espionage but Ethel's minimal involvement. Yet J. Edgar Hoover had deliberately exaggerated Ethel's role in order to increase the FBI's leverage on Julius. He also insisted that federal prosecutors seek the death penalty for both, convincing President Eisenhower that Ethel was the ringleader, even though the FBI still remained uncertain as to whether she had even been aware of her husband's espionage activities.

Kennedy, writing for a 4–2 majority, acknowledged that the treatment of detainees was "tragic" and that there is "a proper balance to be struck, in situations like this one, between deterring constitutional violations and freeing high officials to make the lawful decisions necessary to the nation in times of great peril." Striking that proper balance, however, was the responsibility of Congress, not the judiciary.

Ginsburg joined Breyer's dissent, which he read from the bench. His gravest concern was the majority's view that "post 9/11 circumstance—the national security emergency—does or might well constitute a 'special factor' precluding lawsuits." Covering a long history of instances where the executive or legislative branch had taken action in time of war that "on later examination turned out unnecessarily and unreasonably to have deprived American citizens of their constitutional rights," he argued that later suits for monetary damages were a good way to check executive misconduct. "In such circumstances," he wrote, "courts have more time to exercise such judicial virtues as calm reflection and dispassionate application of the law to the fact. We have applied the Constitution to actions taken during periods of war and national-security emergency" before, he reminded his colleagues. "When protection of fundamental constitutional rights conflict with security needs, the court has a role to play."

. . .

THE COURT'S ROLE BECAME even more critical as Immigration and Customs Enforcement (ICE) issued detention orders at the rate of approximately eleven thousand per month, a 78 percent increase over the previous year. The Obama administration had also vigorously deported criminals as well as new arrivals crossing the border illegally. But Obama had tacitly recognized that 60 percent of undocumented immigrants in the United States had been here for a decade or more. Law-abiding and hardworking, they raised children, some of whom were U.S. citizens by birth. Mass deportations would wreak havoc not only on families but also on a significant portion of the economy dependent on undocu-mented labor—agriculture, construction, meatpacking, and hospital-ity in particular. Unable to get immigration reform through Congress that would provide undocumented immigrants already in the country a path to citizenship, the Obama administration simply flagged these non-citizens as a low priority for deportation. Trump, by contrast, pledged to deport millions of unauthorized immigrants, no matter their family ties or prior contributions.

Lawful permanent residents who had run afoul of law enforcement authorities at some point in the past were also vulnerable. The 1996 Immigration and Nationality Act (INA) mandated their deportation for "aggravated felonies," listing eighty crimes that qualified. Juan Esquivel-Quintana had been arrested for having sex with his legally underage sixteen-year-old girlfriend. Fighting deportation, he got his day at the Supreme Court in 2017. The justices unanimously agreed that his actions did not qualify as an aggravated felony meriting deportation. The Court declined, however, to be more specific about a residual clause of the Act, Section (16b), which calls for automatic deportation for "any other offense that is a felony and that, by its nature, involves a substantial risk that physical force against the person or property of another may be used in the course of committing that offense." The problem inherent in the justices' delay became apparent in the other cases, one of them that of James Dimaya.

Dimaya, a lawful permanent resident, had arrived in the United States from the Philippines at the age of thirteen. In his youthful years in California, he was arrested and convicted of burglary twice. After serving his second two-year term, he was slated for deportation as an aggravated felon under section 16(b). Dimaya's lawyer appealed the ruling of the immigration judge. Under the terms of section 16(b), the judge's determination did not allow for consideration of the particular facts relating to Dimaya's offenses. Rather judgment had to be based on an "ordinary" case. Yet a burglary conviction in California covers everyone from an armed home intruder to salesmen peddling shady products. His lawyer argued that there was an unconstitutional vagueness in a statute that required immigration judges to decide what kind of conduct the "ordinary case" of burglary involved and how much risk is required for it to qualify as a violent felony. Decision making would invariably be more speculative and arbitrary than is tolerated under the due process clause.

While his appeal was pending in the Ninth Circuit, the Supreme Court rejected a similar residual clause in the Armed Career Act that defined a "violent felony" as any felony that "otherwise involves conduct that constitutes a serious potential risk of physical injury to another" (*Johnson v. United States*, 2015). Relying on the Johnson case, the Ninth Circuit Court found for Dimaya, ruling that section 16(b) of the INA was also unconstitutionally vague. The Justice Department appealed. With conflicting rulings on this issue at the circuit level, the Supreme Court agreed to hear the case. But the result was an even split between liberals and conservatives.

Held over for argument on October 2, 2017, Deputy Solicitor General Edwin S. Kneedler would once again argue that immigration law is distinctive and that the Ninth Circuit had erred in relying on Johnson. Ginsburg led off the interrogation of Kneedler with Sotomayor and Kagan joining in followed by Gorsuch. "How am I supposed to know what ordinary is [with respect to burglary in California]?" Gorsuch asked. Kneedler, defending section 16(b), replied that Congress couldn't be expected to identify every crime by category. Really? Gorsuch asked. "Even when it's going to put people in prison and deprive them of liberty and result in deportation, we shouldn't expect Congress to be able to specify those who are captured by its laws?" Otherwise, the vagueness of 16(b) simply invites speculation as to whether there was "substantial risk of physical force." As he wrote in his opinion: "The truth is no one knows." With Gorsuch joining the liberals, Ginsburg assigned the majority opinion to Kagan.

The 5–4 ruling was promptly denounced by Trump and top officials, who demanded Congress close loopholes to deportation. Joshua Rosencranz, Dimaya's lawyer, replied that the decision did not interfere with the removal of those the president referred to as "bad hombres." Rather, "it's the hombres who live generally law-abiding lives but for what is often a youthful lapse that are protected by this decision." Immigration lawyers added other examples. A Salvadoran man who grabbed a baseball bat to defend himself from a gang of white men hurling racial slurs and then was convicted of a crime; a Cambodian immigrant who pleaded guilty to participating in a bar fight but had actually hidden in the bathroom.

. . .

INDEFINITE DETENTION POSED another threat for noncitizens caught in the ICE dragnet. Some were able to obtain court-appointed counsel and a bond hearing. But many more fell through the cracks. Illustrative was the case of Alejandro Rodriguez. A lawful permanent resident, he had been brought to the United States as an infant. After a youthful offense where he was caught riding in a stolen car, Rodriguez had become a dental technician but then was arrested again on a simple possession of drugs. Slated for deportation, he was kept in detention for more than three years without receiving a bond hearing. His legal team finally prevailed when the case bearing his name, which had been filed against the Department of Homeland Security, made its way from the U.S. District Court for the Central District of California to the Ninth Circuit Court of Appeals.

The Ninth Circuit Court reversed the district court's denial of petition for a class-action suit for Rodriguez and fellow plaintiffs to pursue their case for a bond hearing. It further stipulated that all noncitizens subject to mandatory detention must be brought before an immigration judge for a bond hearing at six-month intervals throughout their detention. And they are entitled to a release, the court said, unless the government can demonstrate that they pose a flight risk or a danger to the community. Predictably, the government appealed.

When *Jennings v. Rodriguez* reached the eight-member Court in November shortly after Trump's election, forty-one thousand individuals were already being held in immigration detention facilities. The solicitor general's office acknowledged that the average detention time was more than a year. Given Trump's stance on detention and deportation, the justices were keenly aware of the impact of their decision.

At issue was whether detainees like Rodriguez, who were lawful permanent residents, could be held indefinitely along with new arrivals, as the government claimed. Alternatively, must they be granted a judicial hearing as mandated by the Ninth Circuit?

In oral arguments, Acting Solicitor General Gershengorn told the justices that the Ninth Circuit's "one size fits all" six-month detention limit was at odds with the federal statute that says the government "shall detain" immigrants facing deportation. Liberals on the bench pressed Gershengorn hard on the fact that the Immigration and Nationality Act made no allowance for the length of time detainees were held before being granted a bond hearing. The chief justice pointed out that the Ninth Circuit had the option of striking down the statute as unconstitutional. Because it had not, "we can't just write a different statute because we think it would be more administrable." Kennedy agreed that the Court did not have a constitutional issue before it.

Kagan responded that she did not think that was enough to keep the Court from rendering a decision. "It seems to me that it's quite obvious what the court below thinks as to the constitutional question," or else it would not have ordered the six-month review. Rodriguez's ACLU lawyer Ahilan Arulanantham shared Kagan's premise, as did the American Bar Association and the National Association of Criminal Defense Lawyers, both of which had submitted amici briefs.

With a 4–4 tie in the making, *Jennings v. Rodriguez* was held over for rearguing. For the second reargument, the Court asked for additional briefs on the constitutional question of whether people held in the United States have a right to be free of unjustified indefinite detention. At issue was how to read the statutory language. Should the immigration laws be read narrowly to mean that asylum seekers and those fighting deportation are *not* entitled to periodic hearings to decide whether they might be released on bail while pursuing their appeal? Or should the law be read more broadly in light of the nation's founding documents and principles? Revealing the sharp disagreement among the justices, Breyer dissented from the bench to the majority narrow reading. He said, "We need only recall the words of the Declaration of Independence, its insistence that all men and women have 'certain unalienable rights.' We need merely recall that among them is the right to 'liberty.' It is not difficult to read the words of the statute as consistent with this basic right. I would find it more difficult, indeed I would find it alarming, to believe that Congress wrote these statutory words in order to put thousands of individuals at risk of lengthy confinement all within the United States but all without hope of bail," he concluded.

. . .

IN THE MEANTIME, Ginsburg had delivered a critical victory for gender equality in yet another deportation case, *Sessions v. Morales-Santana.* At issue was the constitutionality of the portion of the Immigration and Nationality Act that grants citizenship to a child born abroad to an unmarried U.S. citizen mother but imposes different requirements for transmission of citizenship to a child of an unwed citizen father. The sex-based differential was one to which Ginsburg had long objected.

When a 1998 Court majority in *Miller v. Albright* justified differential treatment based on a mother's biological relationship with the child, Ginsburg dissented, arguing that government policy was being shaped "to fit and reinforce the stereotype or historical pattern." Three years later, the majority made a similar justification in *Nguyen v. INS,* leading Ginsburg to join O'Connor's dissenting opinion that the government had not shown "exceedingly persuasive justification" for the different classifications. The Court issued a per curiam decision in the 2011 case of *Flores-Villar v. United States,* upholding the use of *Nguyen* in the appeals court. Although she did not provide a dissenting view to the decision, her line of questioning during oral arguments pressed the government to defend its ongoing use of differential treatment, going so far as to refer to the Court's previous decisions in *Frontiero* and *Wiesenfeld.*

The case was brought by Luis Ramón Morales-Santana, who was born in the then-U.S. occupied Dominican Republic to a father who was an American citizen and who wed his mother shortly thereafter, listing his name on his son's birth certificate. The family had moved back to the United States when Morales-Santana was thirteen, and he had become a lawful permanent resident. Subsequent convictions for various felonies led federal authorities to slate him for deportation. Fighting the order, he claimed American citizenship derived from his father. When his application to vacate the order was denied by an immigration judge, he filed a motion to reopen his application. At issue was the differential between section 1401(a)(7)'s requirement for unwed citizen fathers to transmit U.S. citizenship to a child and that of section 1409(c) applying to unwed citizen mothers. Morales-Santana claimed that the differential discriminated against his father's right to confer citizenship upon him. Hence the statute violated the equal protection clause of the Fifth Amendment.

Morales-Santana's father, José, had left the United States to take a job with an American firm in the Dominican Republic just twenty days shy of his nineteenth birthday. He therefore failed to meet the requirement that he live in the United States for a total of ten years, five of them after the age of fourteen, in order to transmit American citizenship to his son Luis Ramón, who was born before his parents married. Unwed citizen mothers, by contrast, required only a year's residence in the United States. The U.S. Court of Appeals for the Second Circuit observed in its review of the case that a man needs no more time than a woman "in order to have assimilated citizenship-related values to transmit to [his] child." Ruling that José Morales had been unconstitutionally penalized, the Second Circuit determined that Morales-Santana was entitled to U.S. citizenship. The government promptly appealed. Oral arguments in *Lynch v. Morales-Santana* were set for November 9, 2016.

The Court had to decide two questions. First, did the gender-based differential in requirements for the physical presence in the United States of an unwed citizen parent constitute a violation of equal protection? Second, did the Second Circuit decision constitute a conferral of U.S. citizenship on Morales-Santana in the absence of statutory authority to do so?

Arguing for the government, Deputy Solicitor General Edwin S. Kneedler made familiar points. The goal of Congress in creating the statute was to ensure that persons deriving citizenship "have a demonstrated and sufficient connection to the United States either in themselves or through their parents to warrant the conferral of citizenship." Differential gender requirements were also intended to ensure that a child of a citizen mother did not end up stateless. In previous decisions, Kneedler pointed out, the Court had "made clear that mothers and fathers are not typically similarly situated with respect to their legal status at the moment of birth."

Ginsburg immediately took issue with Kneedler's position that the mother is often the only legally recognized parent at the moment of birth. In many cases in the past, she pointed out, an unwed couple would receive a birth certificate "sometime after the child was born" with the name of both parents recorded. When Sotomayor further probed the justification for gender-based requirements, Kneedler responded that when a U.S. citizen father legitimizes a child, there are "competing ties" (created by the foreign-born mother) and that Congress wanted to ensure that the father's ties to his country were sufficiently strong. Ginsburg weighed in again, observing that the statutes in question had been written in 1940 and 1952—well before the Court recognized in "a whole series of cases" that gender-based distinctions in the law are suspect. She did not need to note her own role in many of those cases.

Morales-Santana's attorney Stephen Broome argued that disparate rules for unwed citizen mothers and fathers served neither of the government's professed interests—reducing statelessness and ensuring that citizenship is derived only by children who had absorbed American values from a citizen parent. His client's father's rights to transmit citizenship on equal terms with a similarly situated citizen mother had been violated.

Turning to remedies if the Court agreed, Breyer inquired whether "leveling up" the requirement for establishing eligibility or "leveling down" would make it more difficult for unmarried parents to confer citizenship on a child. Kennedy wondered if "leveling up" would create a problem if a significant number of people suddenly qualified for citizenship. Alito worried rather that "leveling up" would create new equal protection challenges based on illegitimacy. Roberts expressed his uncertainty as well.

Kagan then proposed an alternative remedy if a majority found that the statute's gender distinctions constituted an equal protection violation. The Court could stay its judgment for a period of time, giving Congress the opportunity to find a legislative solution. Ginsburg's repeated interventions indicated profound doubt that the gender distinctions could be justified under post-1970s equal protection doctrine, especially in an age of DNA testing when so many fathers raised their children.

Yet the question of an appropriate remedy remained. The justices were well aware that a 4–4 split would leave the Second Circuit's decision intact and conflicting rulings at the circuit court level unresolved. A compromise seemed in order.

In a 7–1 majority opinion, Ginsburg, informed by the scholarship of Kristin Collins, wrote that the statute was built on a faulty assumption "that unwed fathers care little about, indeed are strangers, to their children. Lump characterization of that kind, however, no longer passes equal protection inspection." The scheme, she pointed out, "permits the transmission of citizenship to children who have no tie to the United States so long as their mother was a U.S. citizen continuously present in the United States for one year at any point in her life prior to the child's birth. The transmission holds even if the mother marries the child's alien father immediately after the child's birth and never returns with the child to the United States." At the same time, she continued, "the legislation precludes citizenship by a U.S.-citizen father who falls a few days short of meeting the longer physical-presence requirements, even if the father acknowledges paternity on the day of the child's birth and raises the child in the United States."

Finally, Ginsburg argued, stipulating one rule for mothers and another for fathers puts Section 1409 in "the same genre as classification the Court had already declared unconstitutional in *Reed, Frontiero, Wiesenfeld, Goldfarb,* and *Westcott.*" Quoting her VMI opinion, she reiterated that successful defense of legislation that differentiates by gender requires "an exceedingly persuasive justification." The government's argument that the statute was intended to protect the child of a citizen father from statelessness by providing that the child would take the mother's citizenship was "an assumption without foundation." Recounting the gender-saturated history behind this particular statute, including the latest legal scholarship, she proceeded to demolish the government's rationale. She also pointed to findings of a ten-year study conducted by the UN's High Commissioner for Refugees (UNHCR), which concluded that discrimination against either mothers or fathers is a major cause for statelessness. A key component of the UNHCR's Campaign to End Statelessness had been elimination of gender discrimination in nationality laws. "In this light," she concluded, "we cannot countenance risk of statelessness as reason to uphold, rather than strike out, differential treatment of unmarried women and men with regard to transmission of citizenship to their children."

Then she turned to the remedy, which likely reflected the price of getting Roberts's vote, and probably Kennedy's as well. Instead of extending the lenient requirement for unwed citizen mothers to fathers, the majority applied the longer residence required of fathers to all parents. Inviting

Congress to address the issue and "settle on a uniform prescription that neither favors nor disadvantages any person," the Court thus affirmed the judgment of the Second Circuit in part and reversed it in part, leaving Morales-Santana out in the cold.

Thomas, joined by Alito, dissented, finding the equal protection ruling "unnecessary," given the remedial holding.

· · ·

LOOKING BACK at the 2016–17 session, it's clear that the justices had sought consensus by avoiding significant disputes. For example, they dismissed an appeal in a Virginia case on transgender rights after the Trump administration shifted the government's position. They turned down appeals in cases contesting restrictive voting laws in North Carolina and Texas. Yet racial discrimination had not gone unaddressed, with Roberts and Kennedy showing greater willingness to acknowledge systemic racism. Even Thomas joined the liberals in a 5–3 vote against North Carolina's Republican-controlled legislature, which had relied on racial gerrymandering when drawing the state's voting districts. Nor did the justices shy away from the death penalty. In a majority opinion authored by Ginsburg, the Court ruled that Texas must meet certain standards before executing mentally disabled prisoners.

Yet the impact of the election was patently evident in both the nomination of Gorsuch and the dramatic increase of immigration cases. It also made the outcome of *Ziglar v. Abbasi* all the more disappointing for those who valued civil liberties and lamented the disdain that the current president exhibited for the judicial process. By immunizing high-level officials from after-the-fact judicial review of their actions during times of crisis, the *Ziglar* decision threatened to free up officials in the executive branch to act without regard to constitutional restraints precisely when the pressure to overreach is greatest.

As Ginsburg looked ahead to the October term, she anticipated it would be far more contentious. Upcoming cases involved clashes over immigration, gay rights and religious freedom, the ability of employees to band together to address workplace issues, cellphone privacy, human rights violations by corporations, and partisan gerrymandering.

As it turned out, the Court would choose to punt on the case of the

Colorado baker, Jack Phillips, owner of the Masterpiece Cakeshop, who refused to bake a wedding cake for a same-sex couple, claiming doing so violated his religious beliefs and freedom of speech. Declining to rule on how far states can go in requiring fair treatment of LGBT people in the marketplace, the 7–2 decision turned on the lack of neutrality on religious freedom exhibited by the Colorado Civil Rights Commission in its determination that Phillips had violated Colorado's antidiscrimination law. "The outcome of cases like this in other circumstances must await further elaboration in the courts," Justice Kennedy would write, "all in the context of recognizing that these disputes must be resolved with tolerance, without undue disrespect to sincere religious beliefs, and without subjecting gay persons to indignities when they seek goods and services in the open market." Ginsburg, joined by Sotomayor, agreed in part but dissented in part. The bias of some Commission members toward Phillips's religiosity, she argued, did not negate the baker's violation of Colorado's antidiscrimination statute. "When a couple contacts a bakery for a wedding cake, the product they are seeking is a cake celebrating *their* wedding—not a cake celebrating heterosexual weddings or same-sex weddings—and that is what [the couple] were denied."

Her great concern, however, was how the Court would rule on political gerrymandering. While the justices had previously rejected redistricting maps designed to disenfranchise racial and ethnic minorities, they had never overruled a redistricting plan on the grounds that it disenfranchised voters by political party. Such cases were considered non-justiciable because there seemed to be no workable standard for adjudicating claims of hyper-partisanship, although Kennedy had left the door open should one emerge—which it did in 2017.

The district court had struck down a Republican-drawn map in Wisconsin on grounds of political discrimination, using a standard devised by two scholars. With ongoing suits over partisan gerrymandering in North Carolina, Maryland, and Pennsylvania, the Court had agreed to review *Gill v. Whitford*. Ginsburg believed that the Court's decision to hear the case was "perhaps the most important grant so far." Whatever the decision, it would be a landmark, affecting future elections.

. . .

Ginsburg in her chambers, 2013.

IN THE MEANTIME, the summer awaited. Ginsburg looked forward to a trip to Malta, where she would participate at a summer session for law students in the capital city of Valletta. The timing also coincided with a visit home to Valletta by the internationally renowned tenor Joseph Calleja, who had offered to act as her host, arranging for visits to historic palazzi, churches, and museums as the city celebrated its 450th birthday. After taking in the cultural and culinary richness of the island, she would move on to the Netherlands. The World Justice Forum was meeting at The Hague, and she had been invited to give a keynote address at the opening event.

Her summer agenda was packed: talks assessing the previous term; opera at Glimmerglass in Cooperstown, New York, where one of the four performances would be *Scalia/Ginsburg,* an address to the Utah Bar Association at the invitation of Senator Orrin Hatch; and then on to Aspen, where she had been asked to speak at the Aspen Institute about her rare "off the bench" friendship with Scalia, and finally to Santa Fe for a week of opera, friends, and family. James and Patrice would arrive with her son Sat Nam, who was en route to Stanford Law School, and Derrell Acon. Labor Day weekend, Ginsburg had agreed to officiate at the Brooklyn wedding of Shana Knizhnik, the creator of *Notorious R.B.G.*

If she walked carefully, often taking an arm offered to assure she did not trip, her confidence in her own judgment remained undiminished, as did her vision of justice. Never had her presence on the Court seemed more essential.

Epilogue

Legacy

The date was now August 24, 2017. The setting was the Santa Fe Opera, where Justice Ginsburg religiously returns every year for the summer's final week of performances. Opera lovers were gathered at tables set on the terrace for a preview dinner and a lecture on Donizetti's melodic masterpiece *Lucia di Lammermoor*. Shortly before the lecture was to begin, the Ginsburg party was shown to its table. Cameras flashed amid applause. The justice, always carefully put together, was elegantly attired. Without acknowledging the attention she attracted, she settled into her seat at the head of the table with her guests on either side. James Ginsburg anchored the opposite end of the table, flanked by his wife, Patrice, her son Sat Nam, and protégée Derrell.

Later, as audience members found their seats in the arc-shaped Crosby Theatre, the justice and her family were escorted in by the opera's general director, Charles MacKay, again triggering a round of applause. Under a roof supported by cables, with sides open to the elements, the justice had a clear view of the stage. Beyond was the view westward— blue sky and billowy white clouds with the Jemez and Sangre de Cristo Mountains in the distance. Panels patterned to resemble ceilings lined the back of the stage. On the panels would be projected background scenes for the glorious bel canto singing of Brenda Rae and her consummate performance as Lucia.

The following day it was Ginsburg's turn to take the stage. At the Lensic Performing Arts Center in downtown Santa Fe, she hosted apprentice vocalists in *Justice at the Opera*. Her appearance onstage brought the audience instantly to its feet for yet more hearty applause. Introduced by MacKay, who hailed her as opera's foremost ambassador, she introduced selections from eight operas and a Gilbert and Sullivan operetta. Her deft interweaving of opera history and the law delighted everyone, as did her dry wit. There were somber moments, too—especially when she introduced one of the most painful scenes in Philip Glass's moving Civil War opera *Appomattox,* which he had reworked to incorporate the civil rights era. The aria selected for performance represented the voice of a survivor of the 1873 Colfax massacre in Louisiana, when the Ku Klux Klan and the White League wantonly slaughtered some hundred black militiamen protecting the courthouse on Easter Sunday. The aim of the Klan and the White League was reassertion of white supremacy and black disenfranchisement. Appropriately, Ginsburg's commentary worked in voting rights and *Shelby,* leaving no doubt where she stood.

The standing applause at the conclusion of the performance rewarded the vocalists, but it was meant, too, for the elderly justice, who joined the young women and men taking a bow. Santa Fe could, of course, be considered "friendly" territory for Ginsburg. Applause from an opera audience was only to be expected. But these were by no means her only admirers. Her fans are to be found across the country and well beyond its borders, including the many web-surfing millennials who order T-shirts online emblazoned with "I ♥ Ruth Bader Ginsburg," "RBG Y'ALL," "Ruth Is Truth," or "Ruth Bader Ginsburg Is My Homegirl" or snap up coffee mugs, pennants, and removable tattoos and even Christmas tree decorations emblazoned with her image. A humorous *BuzzFeed* article, "19 Reasons Why Ruth Bader Ginsburg Is Your Favorite Supreme Court Justice," delights young adults with its photo captions, whimsy, and appreciative blogs. Many parents happily read to their children, especially very young daughters, the beautifully illustrated book *I Dissent: Ruth Bader Ginsburg Makes Her Mark,* while their older sisters delight in *Ruth Bader Ginsburg: The Case of R.B.G. vs. Inequality.*

The standing ovations, the lovely hand-tatted lace collar gifted to her by a student, the Notorious RBG Tumblr, the T-shirts and coffee mugs bearing her likeness, the children's books, the *R.B.G.* documentary, the forthcoming film starring Felicity Jones and Arnie Hammer as a young Ruth and Marty with the justice providing a cameo appearance, even the spoof on *Saturday Night Live*—all are evidence that Ginsburg has made her mark not only on the jurisprudence of the United States but also on American society and popular culture more broadly. Thoroughly enjoying her unexpected celebrity, she uses her many appearances to talk about issues and values important to her.

Nowhere was this more evident than in her request to preside over a naturalization ceremony at the New-York Historical Society, the oldest museum in the city. Presumably the first justice ever to do so, Ginsburg arrived clad in her Supreme Court robe and a multicolored collar symbolic of the diversity of those seated before her—201 new citizens from fifty-nine countries. Immediately identifying with her audience, she explained that her father had arrived in New York from Odessa, Russia, at thirteen with no money and no ability to speak English. "We are a nation made strong by people like you," she stated. Then in a powerful civics lesson, she presented the United States as a nation in the process of self-improvement. Referring to Alexis de Tocqueville's statement that the greatness of America lies not in being more enlightened than other nations, but rather in her ability to repair her faults, the justice described the new nation as "an imperfect union," beset by poverty, by the low number of citizens permitted to vote, and by the "struggle to achieve greater understanding of each other across racial, religious, and socioeconomic lines." Concluding that the country had made "huge progress" in representation and inclusiveness, she noted that "the work of perfection is scarcely done." She urged the newest citizens to vote, foster unity, and make America better.

· · ·

GINSBURG'S REPUTATION in comparative civil procedure forged in the 1960s is part of her legacy. But the portion for which she is most remembered began with her efforts to make her chosen profession more welcoming to women at a time when it was overwhelmingly white and male. She started with the Association of American Law Schools, helping to formulate the statement that became the AALS nondiscrimination policy with respect to women. Creating one of the first courses on "women and the law," she jointly authored the first casebook on sex-based discrimination. A law professor who blended scholarship, effective teaching, and inspired mentoring with pioneering advocacy throughout the 1970s, she contested gender hierarchy, linking it to the founding fathers' rebellion "against the patriarchal power of kings and the idea that political authority may rest on birth status." Offering a guiding hand in over sixty cases dealing with sex-based discrimination, including a dozen that reached the Court, she showed Americans with intellectual rigor and precision that women's rights are human rights and that gender bias in law and practice should not go unexamined. Her perceptive leadership and persuasive arguments led to prohibitions on statutes that reflect conventional stereotypes about men's and women's sex and family roles unless they can be supported by exceedingly persuasive justification of important governmental objectives. That phase of her career alone would earn her a place on *Time*'s list of one hundred most influential women.

Adding to her legacy was her record as a centrist judge on the U.S. Court of Appeals for the D.C. Circuit. During her thirteen-year tenure, Ginsburg became known for her fairness, close attention to the facts of each case, and decision making devoid of ideology. Her opinions, carefully crafted and thoroughly documented, were also notable for their restraint. Described as a judge's judge, she established a reputation for collegiality on what became in the Reagan-Bush years a politically fractious bench. Nor did she allow different approaches to the law to prevent her from forging lasting friendships with conservative notables, most especially Antonin Scalia and Robert Bork.

Not least, she never lost sight of the human beings behind each case. Clerks and staff were treated as members of an extended family whose birthdays were remembered as well as those of their children. Clerks especially were often beneficiaries of Marty's culinary treats and wit along with Ruth's sage advice on law and work-family balance.

Winning a seat on the Supreme Court, Ginsburg—like Thurgood Marshall before her—was fated to serve as a member of the minority among ever further right-leaning colleagues. In Ginsburg's case, this would last for over two decades (and counting). Yet as justice she was able to top off her years as a strategically savvy advocate with the ruling in *United States v. Virginia* that required an "exceedingly persuasive justification" for treating men and women differently. Her opinion for the majority made clear that the problem was not a single-sex educational institution as such. Rather, it was VMI's admissions policy, along with the state's hastily contrived women's leadership institute. Believing that history cannot be ignored in discrimination cases, she called attention to Virginia's long tradition of denying women equal education and professional access to the public sphere on the basis of stereotypes about their maternal and domestic roles. Perhaps the most significant of her contributions in *United States v. Virginia* was her clarification of how the state may regulate "inherent differences" between men and women. It may do so in ways that are designed to include groups long denied full citizenship status on equal terms in the life of the nation, but it may not do so in ways that perpetuate stereotyping and discrimination.

That same premise had been at the core of her stance on reproductive rights from her early *Struck* brief all the way to her forceful dissent in *Gonzales v. Carhart,* in which she sought to ground *Roe* in equal protection. The state may *not* deny a woman the right to decide whether to carry a pregnancy to term. Nor, if health problems dictate a late-term abortion, should the state substitute its judgment of the proper method for removal of the fetus for that of the physician, whose first obligation is to protect a pregnant woman's health.

Ginsburg's vision of gender equality has never been about simply gaining for women access to male preserves such as VMI so they could be "the same" as men. As an admirer of Olof Palme's Sweden, she knew that men's roles also had to change. Enabling men to assume caregiving responsibilities would allow women to escape some of the costs of child rearing so that both partners could utilize their talents and contribute financially. To support flexible gender roles, changes in public policy are essential. Education at all levels, she insisted, must ensure that in every field women are as welcome as men, and that extends to the job market as well. In 1975, she had called for "comprehensive income protection and medical benefits for pregnancy and childcare, financed through compulsory social insurance," parental leave that could be taken by either men or women, and comprehensive, non-means-tested child care.

With respect to family-care leave, her greatest Supreme Court accomplishment was *Nevada Department of Human Resources v. Hibbs* (2003), which upheld the Family and Medical Leave Act as applied to state governments. Chief Justice Rehnquist, limiting the new federalism doctrine that he had so forcefully championed, not only defended the FMLA but characterized the thirty years after *Frontiero* (1973) as a "period of ongoing and institutionalized constitutional violations" reflecting stereotypical judgments about "mothers-to-be and mothers" as members of the workforce. Ginsburg's fingerprints were all over the ruling, as was evident in her broad smile when asked if she had written it. Her denial does not negate her persuasive powers or the fact that the ruling embodied a message that she had long championed.

In her vision of feminism, men and women receive the same treatment only after gender norms have been reconstructed and social supports have been put in place. That process remains ongoing in a culture that still allows little deviation from the notion that manhood is closely identified with breadwinning. Ironically, Silicon Valley, which has done the most to transform how life is lived in the twenty-first century, is notorious for a work culture that valorizes long workdays and expects technological genius to take the male form. Ginsburg would obviously have preferred that gender reconstruction occur with less delay and that *Roe v. Wade* withstand unscathed the thousand cuts inflicted by opponents. But she is too familiar with history to assume that progress is linear. Like liberty, equality, she believes, is never really won, but has to be fought for by each generation.

Her pursuit of equality has been capacious, encompassing not only women but also men, African Americans, Hispanics, gays, immigrants, the poor, and the disabled. Her grasp of both structural and cultural factors that contribute to discrimination is sound, her proposal for affirmative action in the late 1970s was creative, and her contempt for continued obfuscation on race by some of her more conservative colleagues on the high court is undisguised.

Ginsburg has been equally insistent that neither faulty procedure nor lack of financial resources should hamper people's access to equal justice—what she often refers to as their "equal citizenship stature." The plight of the Mississippi mother Melissa Lumpkin Brooks, who could not afford the fees necessary to appeal loss of her parental rights to her two children, is one the justice does not forget. In other cases, she has repeatedly called attention to systematic failures across the country to provide defense counsel services for the indigent.

It is not just her empathy for "the less well off, the outsider in our society"—as Clinton noted at Ginsburg's nomination—that has caused the justice to be labeled "the conscience of the Roberts Court." Rather, as in her dissent in *Connick v. Thompson* (2011), it is empathy buttressed with hard research that established a larger "pattern of [prosecutorial] indifference" and violation of defendants' right to a fair trial for John Thompson, among others. Facts speak for themselves, calling into question all the more the majority's decision.

Ginsburg also possesses a keen eye for hypocrisy. Throughout her tenure on the high court, the conservative majority has boldly curtailed Congress's power under the commerce clause and the Tenth Amendment. Those decisions, as Christy Brzonkala's attorney discovered in *Morrison* (2000), were accompanied by others that sought to limit federal judicial power in a series of Fourteenth Amendment cases restricting federal authority in Section 5 cases. Yet the same majority that stripped the civil rights provision from the VAWA in the name of states' sovereignty voted a few months later in *Bush v. Gore* to reject a key element of state autonomy—Florida's right to administer its own election process. The "federalism five's" hypocrisy in choosing the latter case to reject states' rights and the principles of federalism that conservatives had long championed elicited from Ginsburg a brief but powerful rebuke.

Another example of judicial overreach that breached both judicial precedent and constitutional design was the majority ruling in *Shelby v. Holder* (2013), which voided a key provision of the 1965 Voting Rights Act. Strongly chastising the Court for scorning a long-standing precedent regarding Congress's power to enforce the Fourteenth and Fifteenth Amendments "without even acknowledging that it was doing so," Ginsburg expressed indignation at the majority's invocation of "equal sovereignty." In the past, the Court had held, "in no uncertain terms, that the principle 'applies only to the terms upon which States are admitted to the Union and not to remedies that have subsequently appeared.'" Ratcheting up "pure dictum" to produce a decision that appeared to rely on an earlier case (*Northwest Austin Municipal Utility District v. Holder*), she acidly observed, "One would expect more from an opinion striking at the heart of the Nation's signal piece of Civil Rights legislation."

The heart of Ginsburg's dissent in *Shelby* was the Court's failure to defer to congressional authority. Describing the lengthy, deliberate process that Congress had undertaken before reauthorizing the Voting Rights Act in 2006, she admonished the Court for its failure "to attempt to engage with the massive legislative record that Congress assembled." Instead, the Court substituted the majority's view for the conclusions that Congress had reached. Ginsburg wrote passionately about the stated purpose of the Reconstruction Amendments and how they shifted the relationship between Congress and the states, giving Congress special powers to override state sovereignty in order to implement the amendments. In failing to leave the fate of the act to the political process, she concluded, the Court had "err[ed] egregiously by overriding Congress' decision." "Hubris," she wrote, best describes the majority's willful "demolition of the VRA."

. . .

VALUING PRECEDENT, along with judicial constraint, fidelity to constitutional design, and attention to history and context, Ginsburg has fashioned a distinctive approach to jurisprudence that is hard to label. She is certainly not an originalist in the Scalia-Thomas-Gorsuch mode. Yet her treatment of the Reconstruction Amendments in her *Shelby* dissent demonstrated that she can adopt the originalism approach of close textual analysis, seeking the original meaning of specific constitutional provisions. Nor can she be described as a liberal activist in the Brennan mode, although her equal protection jurisprudence thrust her into the liberal category. As President Clinton said upon her nomination, Ginsburg "cannot be called a liberal or a conservative. She has proved herself too thoughtful for such labels." The justice, too, has generally avoided them.

She is an optimist, though not a naive one. She genuinely believes that law can help to rectify wrongs and that lawmaking institutions as well as the public can—and should—engage in dialogue about repairing our fragile and perilous world. She is also keenly aware of the constraints of the law as well as the reality of downstream resistance. Yet even in times of great personal duress, she has consistently used her considerable skills and experience to shape the law so that the arc might bend toward justice. And she does it with an advocate's canniness, a legal scholar's rigor and careful articulation, and a humanitarian's sensitivity to real-world impact. The law and the constitutional rights and liberties of the American people are the better for her ongoing efforts.

Yet as Ginsburg moved toward her eighty-sixth birthday, following an exceptionally bruising term, she had reason to worry about the fate of issues that she had long championed. The Roberts Court, which had dealt such brutal blows to democracy in *Citizens United* and *Shelby*, delivered more in the dismal 2017–18 term. Kennedy, who had previously voted with liberals to uphold abortion rights and affirmative action, sided with the conservatives throughout the term in every 5-to-4 divide. In a preview of what a solidly conservative majority could now accomplish, the Court allowed partisan gerrymandering to persist and sanctioned purges of infrequent voters from voting rolls. Businesses were freed to use arbitration clauses to keep workers from banding together to take legal action on workplace issues, and religiously oriented "crisis pregnancy" centers in California were no longer required to provide pregnant women with information about abortion.

That the majority overturned the California "crisis center" information requirement, as well as a forty-one-year-old precedent protecting the financial health of public-sector unions, provided additional examples of how the First Amendment, once a defense of the powerless, had under the Roberts Court become a weapon of powerful conservative interests. Also unmistakable was the majority's willingness to accept as "plausible" the unsubstantiated national security crisis claimed in defense of President Trump's travel ban. Kennedy had objected strongly to the Colorado civil rights commissions' lack of proper solicitude for the religious beliefs of the Masterpiece Cake baker. That he then failed in *Trump v. Hawaii* to hold the president fully accountable for his prior prejudicial statement about Muslim immigrants did not go unnoticed. Merely reminding government officials about the importance of free exercise of religion and the protection of the Establishment Clause was, in the words of one astute observer, "in fact an abdication." Sotomayor and Ginsburg jointly issued a blistering dissent, scolding the majority for failing to hold the executive branch to account as the Constitution demands. Breyer and Kagan also dissented on narrower grounds. But the conservative majority prevailed. The term as a whole underscored once again how a Court dominated by right-leaning judges can hurt ordinary Americans economically and politically, leaving the future of democracy in the United States more wobbly than ever.

Then on June 27, 2018, the last day of the spring term, Kennedy, who had been the swing vote since O'Connor left in 2006, announced that he would retire at the end of July. His departure would leave Roberts and possibly Gorsuch at the Court's ideological center.

In retrospect, Kennedy's decision seemed less shocking than first thought. It was widely known that he was thinking about retiring when Trump was elected. The new president, by no means the first to smooth the way for a replacement bearing his stamp, went to great lengths to praise Kennedy at Gorsuch's oath taking in April 2017, calling the senior justice "a great man of outstanding accomplishment." The White House also singled out Appeals Court judges Brett M. Kavanaugh and Raymond M. Kethledge as likely candidates for the next Supreme Court vacancy—both had clerked for Kennedy. Others nudged more directly. A month before the Court adjourned, Senator Charles E. Grassley, the Republican chair of the Senate Judiciary Committee, urged any justice thinking about retirement: "Do it yesterday." Pointing to midterm elections in November, the Iowa senator warned listeners that "you're never going to get the kind of people that are strict constructionists" if the Democrats win in November.

Once Kennedy announced his departure, Trump and McConnell had already pushed through the appointment of twenty-one new Republicans judges to the circuit courts—mostly white men under fifty—with more to come. They vowed to fill the empty seat on the Court before the election. The promise of another conservative stalwart from the ranks of the Federalist Society heralded an epic battle in the making. For Democrats, still seething over the difference the appointment of Judge Garland would have made in the Court's decisions, the stakes were immense. Landmark rulings on social issues could be imperiled, including Justice Kennedy's opinion in *Obergefell*. *Roe* could soon be gone. Even the age-old one-person-one-vote doctrine was vulnerable. Not only could individual and privacy rights could be reinterpreted, but so could the law on health care, employment, national security, and the environment. Further, there would likely be scant checks on the actions of the executive and legislative branches of government, given the politicization of the Court and Trump's success in discrediting the mainstream media.

For Republicans, traditionally more alert to the importance of the Court's composition than Democrats and liberals, confirmation of a second Trump nomination promised to further undermine the regulatory state to which economic conservatives have objected ever since the New Deal. Social conservatives, who willingly overlooked porn stars, trade wars, and Trump's shocking denouncement of his own intelligence agencies in Helsinki and refusal to confront Vladimir Putin on Russian meddling in U.S. elections—all in the hope that he would fulfill his campaign promise to transform the Court—had other issues on their agenda. If overturning *Roe v. Wade* topped the list, further shrinking of the church-state divide was a close second.

With a razor-thin majority in the Senate, Republicans had already begun pressuring red-state Democrats up for reelection for their votes. Fully aware that Senate Democrats lacked the filibuster, McConnell also knew that he could rely on a broken confirmation process in which candidates would avoid fair questions. Add to that a costly and extensive campaign on behalf of the president's pick, backed by more than a hundred conservative interest groups including the Judicial Crisis Network and the Koch-backed Americans for Prosperity.

The president chose Brett Kavanaugh, an impeccably credentialed fifty-three-year-old judge from the Court of Appeals of the D.C. Circuit. An originalist with a sharp legal mind, a conservative record, and political experience honed in the George W. Bush White House, Kavanaugh had long expressed strong support for executive power, hostility to regulatory agencies, support for gun rights and religious freedom, and skepticism of habeas corpus even when evidence of ties to terrorism was weak. Once confirmed, he would be in a position to change fundamentally the balance of power on the Court well into the twenty-first century. Yet a crucial question remained: Could a Supreme Court that has become rigidly divided by both ideology and party retain public confidence? A fierce confirmation battle would inevitably reinforce the public's current perception of partisanship on the one institution that is supposed to be the neutral arbiter of America's political and policy disputes. By 2019, it was predicted, Trump judges would be participating in more than 15,000 decisions a year, and almost all of those decisions would become the law of the land. For those who genuinely value judicial integrity, the question of public confidence continues to hover.

· · ·

MEANWHILE, GINSBURG KEPT an eye on events from a distant perch in Israel. She was in Tel Aviv on July 4 to receive a lifetime achievement award from the Genesis Prize Foundation at the Rabin Center, a left-leaning think tank. Praise from Israel's judicial elite provided a balm for the stinging losses of the spring term. "Law is about justice, and the experience of injustice gives one profound insight as to what justice should look like," said Israeli Supreme Court president Esther Hayut. "Through her decisions, Justice Ginsburg upholds the values without which democracy would be an empty vessel." Similarly, former Supreme Court president Aharon Barak called Ginsburg "one of the great legal minds of our time: an outstanding Jewish jurist whose relentless pursuit of human rights, equality, and justice for all stems from her Jewish values."

Initially, when offered the Genesis Foundation's annual prize, which comes with a cash award, Ginsburg had demurred. The presence of Israeli politicians on the selection committee, she feared, would run afoul of the Constitution's emoluments clause prohibiting government officials from receiving gifts from foreign powers. Only after the foundation agreed to create an apolitical selection committee for a lifetime achievement award had she relented, accepting a handsome dark blue glass sculpture of a shofar (ram's horn).

In Jerusalem the following day for a screening of *RBG,* the documentary about her life, and a conversation with Israeli filmmaker Benjamin Freidenburg, Ginsburg talked about the concept of *tikkun olam* that had been such a vital part of her heritage. Avoiding any mention of the looming nomination battle in Washington, she issued two pleas. The first was a call for bipartisanship in confirming federal judges; the second reiterated her longtime support for an equal rights amendment to the Constitution. Pulling out her pocket copy of America's foundational legal text, she spoke of her great-granddaughter, saying that she would like to tell her that "your equality is a fundamental tenet of the United States." Both pleas made clear the continuity of Ginsburg's commitment to equal justice. The struggle to repair the world never ceases.

Acknowledgments

An author of a book this long in the making is the beneficiary of the assistance of numerous individuals, organizations, and institutions. No words can fully express my gratitude for their contributions in helping me to bring this project to completion.

Although this is an unauthorized biography, I start with the most obvious—Ruth Bader Ginsburg—who made her personal files from her ACLU years available to the Library of Congress. Many of my endnotes in these chapters still retain her initial cataloging rather than the designations subsequently assigned by the Manuscript Division. I remain enduringly grateful not only to the justice but also to the archivist Janice Ruth for her help, then and more recently.

Subsequent interviews with the justice and initial ones with family members, friends, and associates provided stories and insight into the private/public interface in the making of a Supreme Court justice and the origins of her enduring commitment to civil liberties and equal rights. Listed by name in my "Note on Sources," these individuals provided contributions that were indispensable.

I am deeply indebted to the National Endowment for the Humanities for research support as well as to the University of California, Santa Barbara's Academic Senate Research Council and to its Interdisciplinary Humanities Center. The American Society for Legal History also contributed to this project by providing space for daylong meetings of the Feminist Legal Biography Workshop, which Constance Backhouse and I organized. Backhouse, Pnina Lahav, Tomiko Brown-Nagin, Barbara Babcock, Marlene Trestman, and more recently Felice Batlan and Serena Mayeri have provided invaluable questions, insights, inspiration, and encouragement. Members of the Legal History Workshop at Harvard Law School provided especially helpful comments on chapter 15, as did the commentators Nancy Cott and Judge Margaret Marshall. The Huntington Library Roundtable on Women Justices of the U.S. Supreme Court, and especially Rachel Moran, provided a useful comparative perspective on the nomination process. I am also grateful to Mary Beth Norton for inviting me to present a lecture on Ginsburg's undergraduate years at Cornell drawn from chapter 2 and to Cynthia Grant Bowman and the Dorothea S. Clarke Program on Feminist Jurisprudence at Cornell Law School for honing my thinking on the challenges of writing a biography of a sitting Supreme Court justice.

Nancy Dean, Elaine Engst, and Laura Miriam Linke were most helpful at the Carl A. Kroch Library, Cornell University, as were Diana Carey at the Schlesinger Library, Harvard University; Bruce Ragsdale, director of the Federal Judicial Center's History Office, Washington, D.C.; and Ben Primer at the Seeley G. Mudd Manuscript Library, Princeton University. Archivists also skillfully guided me through the William J. McGill Papers at Columbia University, the Dorothy Kenyon Papers at Smith College, and the Phineas Indritz Papers at Howard University. I am especially appreciative of Bevin Maloney's and Jason Kaplan's efforts on my behalf at the William J. Clinton Presidential Library and those of Jeff Flannery and Jennifer Brathovde in securing access to the Daniel P. Moynihan Papers, also at the Library of Congress Manuscript Division.

Assistance in locating photographs has been graciously provided by Clare Cushman, Supreme Court Historical Society; Andrea Hackman, curatorial assistant to the Supreme Court of the United States; Rebekah-Anne Gebler, intern in photography, Office of the Curator, the Supreme Court of the United States; Susan Barker, Smith College; Rosemary Morrow, *The New York Times;* Polly Nodine, Jimmy Carter Presidential Library; Lauren Morrell, Fred Schilling, Supreme Court Office of the Curator; Andrea Pereira, United Press International; Tricia Gessner, Associated Press; and Jill Birschbach, Getty Images.

Research assistance from undergraduate students at the University of California, Santa Barbara has been essential in gathering and organizing voluminous non-archival sources. Anthony Radosh, Tori Praul, Chelsea Owen, Susan Stoddard, Juan Carlos Ibarra, Anne Russell, and Evan Sherwood got me off to a good start. After a fire completely destroyed my home and all of my research in 2009, Cathy Kwon, Linda Han, Heidi Lu, Molly Nugent, Eden Slone, Dana Hoffenberg, and Francesca Nagle worked valiantly to get the project back on track, earning my lasting gratitude. Reina Sultan, Zac Smith, and Jordin Peurrang helped more recently. Graduate students in political science and history from Heather Arnold, Nicole Filler, and Rhoanne Esteban to Masha Fedorova-Warden, and Sasha Coles have pitched in admirably. Masha Fedorova-Warden's knowledge of Swedish was an additional asset. My own former graduate students Matthew Sutton and Leandra Zarnow, now published scholars themselves, as is Rachel Winslow, not only provided superb assistance during their graduate careers but continued to offer good counsel and enduring friendship throughout. For the daunting task of helping me prepare the manuscript for publication, I am deeply indebted to the indispensable efforts of Eric Fenrich. My thanks also extend to my colleague Ann Plane, who identified some of the talented people listed above after I was no longer an active member of the history faculty.

One of the great joys of the academic enterprise is the generosity of other scholars in one's own institution and beyond. My colleague and good friend Laura Kalman offered characteristically sage advice and good questions from the outset. Thomas Hilbink, Reva Siegel, Serena Mayeri, Mary Anne Case, and Mary Clark offered guidance and encouragement at an early stage. The late Stanley I. Kutler provided me with the best possible agent, Sandra Dijkstra, whose staunch support has never wavered. He also offered welcome comments on early chapters, as did William E. Leuchtenburg, Melvin Urofsky, and Barbara Sicherman. The late Gerda Lerner, in her inimitable fashion, wanted more social history and less law, but I concluded there are limits to readers' endurance. Pnina Lahav, Laura Kalman, Alice Kessler-Harris, Barbara Babcock, and especially Serena Mayeri read large portions of the manuscript. Juan Carlos Ibarra provided welcome expertise to the chapter on voting rights, among others. Nancy Cott read the chapter on same-sex marriage, offering sage advice. William Chafe and Benjamin J. "Jerry" Cohen read all twenty-three chapters to my great benefit. For Bill, unlike Jerry, no spousal obligation was involved, making his generosity all the more deeply appreciated. Many of these readers, who are far more expert in the law than I will ever be, might not have averted all errors in the manuscript, but they certainly made them fewer. I cannot express sufficiently my enduring gratitude for their efforts.

My editor, Victoria Wilson, has demonstrated endless patience, recognizing that the manuscript she initially contracted had morphed into something quite different. Pressing me constantly to cover the Court's latest term, she wanted to see the full arc of Ginsburg's remarkable life and career. I deeply appreciate her commitment, vision, and judgment throughout. My thanks also to Ingrid Sterner, copy editor extraordinaire, and Katie Schoder for her very effective work on book promotion.

Others have contributed to this book in different ways. The hospitality of Dorothy and Stanley Ross and Cynthia Harrison helped defray the costs of my earliest visits to Washington. Laura Kalman, Linda Kerber, Eileen Boris, Matthew Sutton, and Leandra Zarnow spearheaded an effort to help rebuild my professional library after the fire. The books sent by friends and publishers with whom I had been involved represented a new start, as did computer funds generously provided by my dean, now the executive vice-chancellor, David Marshall. In the wake of the fire, our dear friend Leatrice Luria not only offered us a roof over our heads. She also offered me a special gift: "We will love you no less if you choose not to go on with the book." Her words conferred a kind of release at that moment I longed for. Vicki Riskin and I have become "supporting sisters" in the process of meeting the high expectations of our editor, Victoria Wilson, at Knopf. I also wish to thank my many other Santa Barbara friends and those elsewhere who have provided encouragement and warm friendship over the years.

Finally, my greatest debt is to my husband, Jerry Cohen. He commented patiently on my drafts, shopped for and cooked our meals, went without my company on his frequent trips abroad, and made me laugh with his irrepressible sense of humor. Most of all, he sustained my confidence (more or less) that I would eventually finish. It is to him this book is dedicated. It is also dedicated to the memory of four very special friends who did not live to see the project's completion: L. Neil Williams Jr. of Atlanta, and Mercedes Eichholz, Léni Fé Bland, and Marsha Wayne of Santa Barbara.

Notes

PREFACE · An American Icon

ix **"People will find":** "The Supreme Court: Transcript of President's Announcement and Judge Ginsburg's Remarks," *New York Times,* June 15, 1993, A24.

x **"dual constitutional strategy":** Serena Mayeri, "Constitutional Choices: Legal Feminism and the Historical Dynamics of Change," *California Law Review* 92 (2004): 758.

xiii **"always everywhere and just":** Jeffrey Rosen, "The New Look of Liberalism on the Court," *New York Times Magazine,* Oct. 5, 1997.

xv **"a more capacious vision":** Serena Mayeri, "Reconstructing the Race-Sex Analogy," *William and Mary Law Review* 49 (2008): 1789–817.

xvi **originalism in theory:** Robert Post and Reva Siegel, "Originalism as a Political Practice: The Right's Living Constitution," *Fordham Law Review* 75, no. 2 (2006): 545–74.

xvi **"tiger justice":** The quotation is by Justice Souter as reported in Colleen Walsh, "Honoring Ruth Bader Ginsburg," *Harvard Gazette,* May 29, 2015.

ONE · Celia's Daughter

3 **By the end of summer:** Throughout this chapter, I have relied overwhelmingly on information from the following interviews: RBG, interviews by author, Washington, D.C., July 7, 2000, Sept. 3, 2001, Aug. 28, 2002, July 1, 2001, Sept. 24, 2004, and Sept. 1, 2006. Interviews were supplemented by notes relaying additional information. The justice has also made available two other transcripts of oral interviews: RBG, interviews by Maeva Marcus (Supreme Court historian), Washington, D.C., April 10, 1995, and Aug. 15, 1995; and RBG, interviews by Ronald J. Grele, Columbia University Oral History Project, Washington, D.C., Aug. 17–19, 2004. The fullest press accounts containing biographical information appeared at the time of RBG's nomination to the Court. See, for example, Neil A. Lewis, "Rejected as a Clerk, Chosen as a Justice," *New York Times,* June 15, 1993, A1; David Margolick, "Trial by Adversity Shapes Jurist's Outlook," *New York Times,* June 25, 1993, A1; Guy Gugliotta and Eleanor Randolph, "A Mentor, Role Model, and Heroine of Feminist Lawyers," *Washington Post,* June 15, 1993, A14; David Von Drehle, "Conventional Roles Hid a Revolutionary Intellect," *Washington Post,* July 18, 1993, A1; and David Von Drehle, "Redefining Fair with Simple, Careful Assault," *Washington Post,* July 19, 1993, A1. See also "Ruth Bader Ginsburg," in *Current Biography Yearbook, 1994* (New York: H. W. Wilson, 1994), 213–17. Unless otherwise indicated, all material in subsequent paragraphs is based on author's interviews and notes. Where I have relied on interviews by either Marcus or Grele, or upon RBG, *My Own Words,* I have so indicated.

4 **The name stuck:** Von Drehle, "Conventional Roles."

4   **In the Red Hook:** Leuchtenburg, *Franklin D. Roosevelt and the New Deal*, 1–3.

6   **If not quite the suburbs:** For information about Flatbush in the following paragraphs, see Sutton, *Magic Carpet;* Weld, *Brooklyn Is America;* Miller, *Brooklyn USA;* and Manbeck, *Neighborhoods of Brooklyn.*

7   **"amalgam of Jewish aunts":** Aviva Kempner, writer, producer, director, *Yoo-Hoo, Mrs. Goldberg* (Ciesla Foundation, 2009). Although most of the "golden age" of Yiddish radio is lost, recordings from the examples offered in the text can be found at the Yiddish Radio Project website.

7   **Other children on the street:** RBG, *My Own Words*, 6. RBG, interview by Grele, Aug. 17, 2004. I am grateful to the justice for giving me early access to these interviews conducted for the Columbia University Oral History Project. This particular superstition, RBG recalled, was entertained by two elderly women living on her block.

8   **Weathering the strains:** Kenneth Jackson's list of Brooklyn's notables in the arts alone also includes Joseph Heller, Zero Mostel, Joseph Papp, S. J. Perelman, and, more recently, Spike Lee and Wynton and Branford Marsalis. See Jackson's introduction to Manbeck, *Neighborhoods of Brooklyn*, xvii.

8   **"love learning, care about people":** Quoted in Bayer, *Women of Achievement*, 16.

10 **The sounds intrigued:** RBG, *My Own Words*, 4–5.

10 **Jo's quest for autonomy:** On the resonance of Jo March for girls, see Barbara Sicherman, "Reading *Little Women:* The Many Lives of a Text," in Kerber, Kessler-Harris, and Sklar, *U.S. History as Women's History*, 245–56.

10 **"smarter than her boyfriend":** Bayer, *Women of Achievement*, 19; and Carolyn G. Heilbrun, "Nancy Drew: A Moment in Feminist History," in Dyer and Romalov, *Rediscovering Nancy Drew*, 11–21.

10 **"envisioning of their own destiny":** Simone de Beauvoir quoted in Sicherman, "Reading *Little Women*," 259.

11 **"One of the many questions":** RBG, *My Own Words*, 87.

12 **These were all women:** RBG, interviews by author. I am indebted to the justice for also giving me a copy of her "Remarks for International Lion of Judah Conference," Washington Hilton Hotel, Oct. 18, 2004, in which she elaborates on the contributions of her list of past Jewish women of achievement. For an introduction to these individuals and their achievements, see Antler, *Journey Home;* and Reinharz and Raider, *American Jewish Women and the Zionist Enterprise.*

13 **"No Dogs or Jews Allowed":** RBG, *My Own Words*, 6. On camps, see Paris, *Children's Nature*, 86–95, 199–210.

13 **Camp Che-Na-Wah:** Paris, *Children's Nature*, 109, 128, 141–42, 147, 160; and Leslie Paris, "A Home Though Away from Home: Brooklyn Jews and Interwar Children's Summer Camps," in Abramovitch and Galvin, *Jews of Brooklyn*, 242–49.

13 **What she did know:** Paris, "A Home Though Away from Home," 242–49. RBG is dubious of Paris's description of Che-Na-Wah as "prestigious"; however, both Paris and Joan Jacobs Brumberg agree that summer camps in the Adirondacks had "significant cache" by virtue of their location. See Bond, Brumberg, and Paris, *"Paradise for Boys and Girls,"* 4. Sol Amster purchased the Lake Balfour property in 1922, and he and his new wife, Cornelia Schwartz Amster, opened Che-Na-Wah in 1923. The camp offered horseback riding and sailing, as well as a high ratio of staff to campers.

14 **Sharing with less fortunate:** Bayer, *Women of Achievement*, 24.

14 **"studiously avoid all war talk":** On camp policy regarding the war in Europe, see Bond, Brumberg, and Paris, *"Paradise for Boys and Girls,"* chap. 3; quoted on 89. On knowledge of the Holocaust, see Wyman, *Abandonment of the Jews.*

15 **"[T]he boy was out there":** Katie Couric, "Ruth Ginsburg on Trump, Kaepernick, and Her Lifelong Love of the Law," *The Katie Couric Interview*, Oct. 10, 2016.

15 **For school assembly:** RBG, *My Own Words*, 4.

16 **Moreover, early training:** On children's opera production and high school piano lessons in Manhattan, see RBG, interview by Grele, Aug. 17, 2004. RBG's old copy of Bach's *Well-Tempered Clavier* is now used by her son-in-law. See George T. Spera Jr. to RBG, March 15, 1983. Spera's letter and many others were written on the occasion of RBG's fiftieth birthday at the instigation of three of her clerks when she was serving as judge on the U.S. Court of Appeals for the D.C. Circuit. Friends and family were instructed to write, "When I think of RBG, I think of . . ." I am indebted to Jane Ginsburg for suggesting the Birthday Book (cited hereafter as RBG Birthday Book) as a source of relevant anecdotes and recollections, to Martin Ginsburg for making me a copy, and to RBG for giving me permission to quote from the letters.

18 **"the whole house went into mourning":** Quoted in Cook, *Alfred Kazin,* 13n21.

19 **War came when Kiki:** "The President's Message," *New York Times,* Dec. 9, 1941.

19 **Like other youngsters:** RBG, *My Own Words,* 7.

20 **"Since the beginning of time":** Ibid., 13.

21 **Endorsing the formation:** Ibid., 9. I am indebted to the late Richard Salzman, a former D.C. Superior Court judge, for providing me with an original copy of the essay and the June 24, 1946, graduation program, which recognizes RBG for outstanding achievement and service to her elementary school. Salzman and RBG were classmates, and his mother's collection of artifacts came into his possession upon her death. See Salzman, interview by author, Washington, D.C., Nov. 13, 2003.

22 **"Americans suddenly seemed":** Leandra Zarnow's work on Bella Abzug alerted me to the ideas and presence of Soshuk at East Midwood Jewish Center. Joan Bruder, who attended the same class as her friend Kiki, recalled their graduation and the award Kiki received. Joan Bruder Danoff, interview by author, July 27, 2004. RBG made no mention in our interviews of the Zionist sentiments that were becoming increasingly prominent among mainstream American Jews in her formative years.

24 **"all the right groups":** Margolick, "Trial by Adversity Shapes Jurist's Outlook"; Von Drehle, "Conventional Roles"; and Salzman, interview by author, Nov. 13, 2003. I have followed Von Drehle's wording regarding classmates' negative reactions to RBG.

26 **"convictions and self-respect":** Heilbrun, "Nancy Drew," 15. For an elaboration of what Celia meant by "be a lady," see RBG, interview by author, Sept. 24, 2004, and RBG's "International Women's Forum Lunch Remarks," Oct. 15, 1999.

26 **Her teachers later delivered:** RBG, *My Own Words,* 19.

26 **Yet no amount:** Davidman, *Motherloss.*

27 **"It is impossible":** The trauma of the minyan incident was called to my attention first by Jane Ginsburg and later confirmed by RBG, who provided me with a recent speech in which she quoted Szold's letter. It is that speech from which I have drawn the passage below. See RBG, "Remarks for International Lion of Judah Conference." On women saying the Kaddish, see Wieseltier, *Kaddish,* chap. 6. The unidentified lawyer and judge whom the author informs about his research on the issue (ibid., 189) I suspected was RBG, which she subsequently confirmed. Wieseltier bears correcting on one point: it was the funeral of her mother, not her father, that was critical. For the full version of the letter, see Henrietta Szold to Haym Peretz, Sept. 16, 1916, in Umansky and Ashton, *Four Centuries of Jewish Women's Spirituality,* 164–65. Seeing this minyan incident as a turning point in her relationship with religious institutions, RBG now believes she might have made a different decision as a young adult had Reform congregations been available and women been permitted to become rabbis.

27 **"She was the strongest":** Von Drehle, "Conventional Roles."

28 **"Kiki asked me to be her roommate":** Joan Bruder Danoff, interview by author, July 27, 2004.

29 **"She would have been proud of me":** Quoted in Edelman, *Motherless Daughters,* 306.

TWO · Cornell and Marty

30 **The prospect of being:** On the history of postwar Cornell, see Kammen, *Cornell,* chap. 7.

30 **Yet the seventeen-year-old:** All information and quotations are based on RBG interviews, cited in chap. 1, n1, as well as subsequent communications with the justice, unless otherwise indicated.

30 **Nearby Balch Hall:** Map of Ithaca from *Cornell Desk Book* for the class of 1954. On possible routes she might have taken, information on sites she would have passed in 1950, and the route she took, see author to RBG, April 21, 2004, facsimile; RBG to author, April 22, 2004, facsimile.

31 **"so that we wouldn't contaminate":** For a brief survey, see Engst, *Jewish Life at Cornell;* Levin, *Diary of David S. Kogan,* 120–220. Jews at Cornell were not a token minority. As RBG noted, there were enough Jewish coeds to fill two sororities plus those who never joined; however, there is no mistaking the "otherness" that Jewish students felt in the 1950s.

31 **The social distance between:** As of 1952, many fraternities and sororities had national restrictions on race, religion, and nationality that governed policies of local chapters. The Tri-Delt story was relayed in RBG, interview by author, Sept. 3, 2001. "Rigid" is RBG's characterization in the interview by Grele, Aug. 17, 2004.

31 **Even at the student union's:** Jon Greenleaf, interview by author, July 5, 2003. The degree of social distancing between Jews and non-Jews at Cornell is a matter on which memories of alumni interviewed diverge markedly. I have tried to take that divergence into account by attributing varying perceptions on a sensitive issue to that of specific individuals by name in the text, based on both initial interviews and subsequent correspondence.

31 **"easy to live with":** Joan Bruder Danoff, interview by author, July 27, 2004; and Irma Hilton, interview by author, July 22, 2004.

32 **Finally, Cornell coeds:** On dress code, see the *Cornell Desk Book* for the class of 1954; also, Von Drehle, "Conventional Roles."

32 **"drawing the line":** Sexual adventurism among unmarried Jewish women was considered *not* "good for the Jews," as is evident in the reception in 1955 of the best-selling Herman Wouk novel *Marjorie Morningstar,* although the Jewish press also faulted Wouk's characters for other offenses. See Barbara Sicherman, "Reading *Marjorie Morningstar,*" in Diner, Kohn, and Kranson, *Jewish Feminine Mystique?,* chap. 11. It took over four hundred pages in the novel before Marjorie loses her virginity. For a much fuller discussion of sexual containment, see Jane Sherron De Hart, "Containment at Home: Gender, Sexuality, and National Identity in Cold War America," in Kuznick and Gilbert, *Rethinking Cold War Culture;* and the classic work of Elaine Tyler May, *Homeward Bound,* chaps. 4–5. Though the rate of premarital pregnancy remained stable between 1920 and the 1960s, the nation's preoccupation with "sex" exploded, as evidenced by mass media coverage of the Kinsey Reports (1948 and 1953), Christine Jorgensen's "sex change" surgery, and congressional investigations of homosexuals in government.

33 **By contrast, Ruth's lack:** Bayer, *Women of Achievement,* 27.

33 **"I knew some pretty obscure libraries":** Within many Jewish families, girls were taught to "be smart enough to appreciate the man's brilliance but not 'too' smart to challenge it ('Why win the argument and lose the man?')." See Cantor, *Jewish Women/ Jewish Men,* 223. At Barnard College, as much as 40 percent of the student body confessed to playing "dumb" in mixed company lest they scare off a date from calling again. Friends confirm that bright Bryn Mawr women did the same well into the 1960s, and I certainly did as a Duke undergraduate in the mid-1950s. While in retrospect such behavior may be seen as calculating or hypocritical, we knew that we had to "play the

game," selectively suppressing more intellectual, competitive aspects of our identities. On Barnard, see Chafe, *Unfinished Journey,* 125; and, for fuller treatment, Chafe, *Paradox of Change.* The importance of class, race, and ethnicity with regard to the mystique is explored respectively in Meyerowitz, *Not June Cleaver;* and Sicherman, "Reading *Marjorie Morningstar.*"

33   **"A dedicated student?":** Irma Hilton, interview by author, July 22, 2004.

33   **"marvelously amusing":** All quotations in this and the following paragraphs from RBG, interviews by author.

35   **"Scary smart":** Margolick, "Trial by Adversity Shapes Jurist's Outlook"; and Hilton, interview by author, July 22, 2004.

35   **"If you want to win a case":** Quoted in Frost-Knappman and Shrager, *Quotable Lawyer,* 18.

36   **Alan Barth's columns:** Bagley, *Joe McCarthy and the Press,* 148–52.

36   **In doing so:** Cushman was editor of the Cornell University Press series on civil liberty. On research tasks assigned, see Elaine Bucklo, "From Women's Rights Advocate to Supreme Justice: Ruth Bader Ginsburg Speaks," *Litigation* 37 (2011): 8–9.

37   **Expanding the scope:** On Konvitz, see Douglas Martin, "M. Konvitz, Scholar of Law and Idealism, Is Dead at 95," *New York Times,* Sept. 11, 2003, A23. Also, Danelski, *Rights, Liberties, and Ideals.*

37   **Yet he clearly accomplished:** Danelski, *Rights, Liberties, and Ideals,* 2.

38   **"a lawyer could do something":** Quoted in Gilbert and Moore, *Particular Passions,* 156.

38   **"integrity, sense of responsibility and tact":** Carroll Arnold to the Harvard Law School Admissions Office, March 3, 1954, box 17, Arnold Correspondence, 1954–72, RBG Papers.

39   **Yet with the exception:** On the Cornell ethos in the 1950s, see Stephanie B. Goldberg, "The Second Woman Justice: Ruth Bader Ginsburg Talks Candidly About a Changing Society," *ABA Journal* 79 (Oct. 1993): 40–43. The epigraph, written by the anonymous Wellesley student, is quoted by RBG in the speech "Sex and Unequal Protection: Men and Women as Victims," Duke University Law School, Oct. 1971, RBG Papers.

39   **Others in the close-knit:** For gender roles and women's options, see Cantor, *Jewish Women/Jewish Men,* 169–75.

39   **But not Anita Zicht:** On Zicht and Rubenberg, see Irma Hilton to author, email, Nov. 15, 2013.

39   **At the time, neither Ruth:** On gender, sexuality, and policy, see Kessler-Harris, *Woman's Wage;* Kessler-Harris, *In Pursuit of Equity;* Canaday, *Straight State.*

40   **Marrying a young man:** Breines, *Young, White, and Miserable,* 193; Weiss, *To Have and to Hold;* and, of course, Friedan, *Feminine Mystique.*

40   **For those who secured:** There is extensive documentation by historians of discrimination against women, Jews, and other ethnic and racial groups in elite institutions and "male" professions. See, for example, Mary Roth Walsh, *"Doctors Wanted: No Women Need Apply."* For a personal account of prejudice against Jews at Yale, where he attended law school, and Harvard, where he taught, see Dershowitz, *Chutzpah,* chaps. 2–3.

40   **On many occasions:** RBG, interview by author, July 1, 2003. According to Irma Hilton, the girls even engaged in a barhopping episode that ended with RBG summoning male friends to escort them home safely. See Hilton, interview by author, July 22, 2004, and RBG, communication with author. Marty Ginsburg claims he offered to swipe one of the handsome copper mugs in which Moscow Mules were served, but his future wife declined his offer. See "Ruth Bader Ginsburg: A Second Circuit Tribute," a video in honor of RBG's seventieth birthday. (Cited hereafter as RBG Seventieth Birthday Video.) I am grateful to James Ginsburg for lending me a copy. I am also grateful to Elaine Ernst at the Kroch Library for helping document various activities in which RBG was engaged.

42   **"Ruth was a wonderful student":** Von Drehle, "Conventional Roles." For recollections of Marty's pursuit, according to M. Carr Ferguson, a Cornell classmate, see Claudia MacLachlan, "Mr. Ginsburg's Campaign for Nominee," *National Law Journal,* June 1993.

42   **"intellectual luminosity":** For reference to the blue plaid coat, see Martin D. Ginsburg to RBG, March 15, 1983, RBG Birthday Book.

42   **Though he failed:** Martin Ginsburg, interview by author, July 1, 2003; and RBG, interview by Grele, Aug. 17, 2004.

43   **"an intense intellectual":** RBG, interview by author, Aug. 17, 2004.

43   **"with the current communist peace offensive":** U.S. House of Representatives, Committee on Un-American Activities, *Report on the Communist "Peace" Offensive: A Campaign to Disarm and Defeat the United States,* 82nd Cong., 1st sess. (Washington, D.C., 1951), 87–90.

43   **Among the first American:** Glenn Altschuler and Isaac Kramnick, "The Morrison Case," *Cornell Alumni Magazine,* July/Aug. 2010. On Philip Morrison and his work with J. Robert Oppenheimer, see Bird and Sherwin, *American Prometheus,* 171–73, 298, 316, 320–21.

44   **Calls for the physicist's:** On Morrison's problems at Cornell, see Schrecker, *No Ivory Tower,* 150–60; also, Michael Ullmann, "Caught in a Crossfire: Deane Malott and Cornell During the McCarthy Era" (history honors thesis, Cornell University, 1980), chap. 3.

44   **For a university:** Ullmann, "Caught in a Crossfire," chap. 4; and "Marcus Singer of Cornell Appears at Velde Session," *Cornell Daily Sun,* May 27, 1953.

44   **"My loyalties always were":** U.S. House of Representatives, Committee on Un-American Activities, *Hearings on Communist Methods of Infiltration (Education) Part 5,* 83rd Cong., 1st sess., May 27, 1953, 1541, 1544, 1552–53.

44   **Marty and Ruth lamented:** Cornell's president, the business-oriented Deane Waldo Malott, who described himself as "an extremely conservative person politically and socially," publicly defended and probably saved the jobs of Morrison and Singer. However, he had little sympathy for either and kept Singer out of the classroom far longer than was necessary, further alienating Singer's colleagues in the Zoology Department. See Ullmann, "Caught in a Crossfire"; also "Singer Convicted for Contempt of Velde Committee," *Harvard Crimson,* March 17, 1956; "House Charges Singer with Contempt," *Cornell Daily Sun,* May 12, 1954; "University Relieves Prof. Singer After Indictment by Grand Jury," *Cornell Daily Sun,* Nov. 23, 1954, 1–2; "Cornell Relieves Marcus Singer of Teaching Duties," *Harvard Crimson,* Nov. 24, 1954, 1–2. For articles on students in support of Singer's trial, see "Council Urges Support of Singer for Honor, Conscience Ground," *Cornell Daily Sun,* May 5, 1954, 1; "A Moral Issue . . . Council Takes Wise Action," *Cornell Daily Sun,* May 6, 1954, 4; "The Great Awakening Fund for Dr. Singer," *Cornell Daily Sun,* May 21, 1954; "Fund for Singer," *Cornell Daily Sun,* May 26, 1954.

44   **"He was the only guy":** RBG, interviews by author, Aug. 28, 2002, and Aug. 17, 2004; also, Bayer, *Women of Achievement,* 29.

45   **Marty followed her lead:** RBG's reaction to the inequitable resources offered by Harvard Business School and Radcliffe's Management Training Program is particularly significant in light of her later position in the *Vorchheimer v. School District of Philadelphia,* 430 U.S. 703 (1977), and *United States v. Virginia,* 518 U.S. 515 (1996) cases. In none of the three pairs of institutions—Harvard Business School and Radcliffe's Management Training Program, Philadelphia's Central High School and the High School for Girls, Virginia Military Institute and Virginia Women's Institute for Leadership—did separate educational facilities offer equal educational opportunities.

45   **"that serious, blonde woman":** Joan B. Danoff and Stanley J. Landay to RBG, March 15, 1983, RBG Birthday Book.

46 **He was prepared to follow:** RBG, interview by Marcus, Aug. 10, 1995.
47 **She would move out:** On Rubenberg and Zicht, see Irma Hilton to author, email, Nov. 15, 2013.
47 **Marty's father, Ruth soon concluded:** RBG, interview by author, Sept. 1, 2006.
48 **By limiting attendance:** Evelyn Ginsburg to RBG, March 15, 2003. See RBG Birthday Book for the way the senior Ginsburgs found out about the engagement.
48 **"life partner":** "Life's partner" is RBG's term.
48 **Sealing her membership:** On golf clubs, see RBG, interview by Grele, Aug. 17, 2004. The problem, RBG explained, is that she is left-handed and the clubs were intended for right-handed players. I am informed by my husband, also a lefty, that clubs for left-handed players were then extremely difficult to find.
49 **"We had nearly":** Martin Ginsburg, interview by Nina Totenberg, in "Martin Ginsburg's Legacy: Love of Justice (Ginsburg)," *Weekend Edition Saturday,* NPR, July 3, 2010. See transcript at www.npr.org.
49 **"He would look at the target":** RBG, interview by Marcus, Aug. 15, 1995, is especially good on the details of life at Fort Sill and is the source for this and the following paragraph, unless otherwise noted. I have followed the language of the interview closely.
50 **A catch-22:** Unaccustomed to racial segregation, RBG initially misread a sign for a café restricted to whites as Joe White's Café rather than Joe's White Café. RBG, interview by Grele, Aug. 17, 2004.
50 **So she quietly certified:** Ibid. According to Marty, this discriminatory treatment of Indians in the local Social Security office was the only work-related frustration that so upset Ruth that she brought it home with her. Martin Ginsburg, interview by author, July 1, 2003.
50 **What he did know:** For an appreciative comment on Marty's cuisine, see Peter Huber, "Tribute to Justice Ruth Bader Ginsburg: 'Dining Chez Ginsburg,'" *Annual Survey of American Law* (1997): 19–21. Also see Alito and Supreme Court Spouses, *Chef Supreme.*
51 **She had visited Marty's Saturday:** On dinner guests and legal discussions, see Anthony I. Van Wye to RBG, March 15, 1983, RBG Birthday Book.
52 **When Marty got up:** On events relating to Jane's birth, see Evelyn Ginsburg to RBG, March 15, 1983, RBG Birthday Book; Martin Ginsburg, interview by author, July 1, 2003; and RBG, interviews by author.
53 **But could she do it with a child:** RBG related the decision-making process, but it was her son who described the nightmare. James Ginsburg (president of Cedille Records), interview by author, Chicago, July 30, 2003.
53 **Evelyn "was just there":** RBG, interview by author, Sept. 1, 2006.
53 **"If a male student":** RBG to author, Jan. 9, 2007.
54 **"A remarkable man":** RBG, interview by author, Sept. 1, 2006.
54 **"Harvard Law School has no glee club":** Quoted in Hope, *Pinstripes and Pearls,* 84.

THREE · Learning the Law on Male Turf

55 **"the legal equivalent":** Hope, *Pinstripes and Pearls,* 29.
55 **"think like lawyers":** Harry A. Blackmun, "In Memoriam: Erwin Nathaniel Griswold," *Harvard Law Review* 108 (1995): 979–1002. For more on "thinking like a lawyer," see Mertz, *Language of Law School.*
55 **Soia Mentschikoff:** Herma Hill Kay, "Ruth Bader Ginsburg, Professor of Law," *Columbia Law Review* 104 (2004): 1–20. Soia Mentschikoff was also the first woman on the faculty at the University of Chicago Law School, the first female to attain the status of partner in a major Wall Street law firm, and the first woman elected president of the Association of American Law Schools in 1974. See "Twenty-Two Portraits of Women at Columbia Law School," *Columbia Law School Report* (Fall 2002), 24; Bradley, *50 Most Influential Women in American Law,* 177–82; Robert Whitman, Soia Mentschikoff, and

Karl Llewellyn, "Moving Together to the University of Chicago Law School," *Connecticut Law Review* 24 (1992): 1119; Warren E. Burger, "Tribute to Dean Soia Mentschikoff," *University of Miami Law Review* 37 (1983): ix; and Smigel, *Wall Street Lawyer, Professional Organization Man?*, 46.

56 **"Why are you at Harvard Law School":** RBG, interview by author, June 27, 2000. RBG's account of the occasion in this and the following paragraphs varies slightly from that of Judith Richards Hope, *Pinstripes and Pearls: The Women of the Harvard Law Class of '64 Who Forged an Old Girl Network and Paved the Way for Future Generations* (New York: Scribner, 2008), 104–7. RBG's quotation is in the film *Paving the Way*, directed by Emma Joan Morris (CINE Golden Eagle, 1995), DVD.

57 **"lowly first year student":** RBG, "In Memory of Herbert Wechsler," *Columbia Law Review* 100 (Oct. 2000): 1359–61. See in that same issue, Harold Edgar, "In Memoriam—Herbert Wechsler and the Criminal Law: A Brief Tribute," 1347–58. Mitchel Ostrer, "A Profile of Ruth Bader Ginsburg," *Juris Doctor* 7 (1977): 34–38.

57 **"I watched in horror":** RBG, interviews by author.

57 **"that would not be considered":** Griswold, *Ould Fields, New Corne*, 173–74.

57 **"Dean Griswold, there are nine of us":** RBG, "Remarks," March 10, 2005.

58 **In the end, she:** RBG, interviews by author. For this and other recollections of Harvard, see also RBG, interview by Grele, Aug. 17, 2004; and Gilbert and Moore, *Particular Passions*, 157–58.

58 **derogatory nicknames:** Hope, *Pinstripes and Pearls*, 99. The designation "Bitch" was recalled by a male classmate in the context of formal remarks made at a Rotary Club meeting at the time of RBG's nomination to the Supreme Court. See Jorie Roberts, "Ginsburg Talk Highlights Celebration 25 Activities," *Harvard Law Record* 66 (1978): 9; also, Jeffrey Rosen, "The Book of Ruth: Judge Ginsburg's Feminist Challenge," *New Republic*, Aug. 2, 1993, 19.

58 **In an era when sexual:** The charitable explanation for what would now be defined as sexual harassment is put forth by Hope, *Pinstripes and Pearls*, 93.

58 **"tremendously engaging":** RBG, interview by Grele, Aug. 17, 2004.

59 **After frantically running:** The justice now marvels that she and her women classmates never complained about the lack of a bathroom in Langdell or the state of the one in Austin. See RBG, "Remarks," March 10, 2005, 9. Recalling other instances of blatant discrimination, she noted, "When I attended the Harvard Law School, there was no space in the dormitories for women. Women were not admitted to the Harvard Faculty Club dining tables. One could invite one's father but not one's wife or mother to the *Law Review* banquet." Bayer, *Women of Achievement*, 38.

60 **Astute lawyers, Hart proposed:** On the evolution of the course and course materials discussed in this and the following paragraphs, see Hart and Sacks, *Legal Process*, containing an introductory essay by William N. Eskridge Jr. and Philip P. Frickey. The book was published posthumously.

60 **"the most carefully worked-out":** Quoted in William N. Eskridge Jr. and Philip P. Frickey, "Commentary: The Making of the Legal Process," *Harvard Law Review* 107 (1994): 2031–55, 2039.

62 **How, they asked, can law:** On the political leanings of law professors, see Friedman, *American Law in the 20th Century*, 493. On the extent to which Hart, Wechsler, Sacks, and Bickel praised *Brown*, although it did not meet their test, see Kalman, *Strange Career of Legal Liberalism*, 27–32. For Hart's and especially Sacks's strength of commitment to racial integration, see the abridged version of the introduction of Eskridge and Frickey, "Commentary: The Making of the Legal Process," n114.

62 **The words "problem" and "anger":** RBG, interview by Grele, Aug. 17, 2004.

62 **"If that's what they're all like":** RBG, interview by Marcus, Aug. 15, 1995.

63 **"A wonderful New England grandmother":** RBG, interview by Grele, Aug. 17, 2004.

63   **a "wise, witty" wordsmith:** RBG, "In Memoriam: Benjamin Kaplan," *Harvard Law Review* 124 (April 2011): 1349. The editors of the *Harvard Law Review* dedicated this issue to Kaplan.

64   **Weekends provided a break:** RBG, interview by Grele, Aug. 17, 2004.

64   **"long, hypothetical fact-situations":** Ibid. For moot court experiences, see Herb Lobl to RBG, March 9, 1983; and Ronald M. Loeb to RBG, March 15, 1983, both in RBG Birthday Book. For more on Calvert Magruder, see Magruder Papers.

65   **"believed in me more":** Berry et al., "Ruth Bader Ginsburg: Women's Rights Advocate, Professor, Counsel, American Civil Liberties Union," in *Women Lawyers at Work*, 54. See Laura Jones, "Columbia's Leader in Legal Battle Against Sex-Based Discrimination," *Columbia Today* 1 (April 1975): 13–15.

65   **"For centuries":** RBG, introduction to Lowe, *Jewish Justices of the Supreme Court Revisited*, 3–4.

66   **"think like a lawyer":** What I am *not* suggesting is that rationalism is distinctively Jewish. To make such an assertion would be to ignore both the extent to which rationalism is also found in gentile worldviews and the long-standing difficulty of defining "Jewish." Nonetheless, rationalism as a mode of analysis is often highlighted by students of Jewish studies, whose primary enterprise involves teasing out whatever it means to be Jewish. See, for example, Heinze, *Jews and the American Soul*. See also Telushkin, *Jewish Humor*, 18.

66   **"Through the quiet force":** Thomas Ehrlich (counsel to the Carnegie Foundation), interview by author, July 12, 2004.

66   **Then, once the next issue:** RBG, interview by Grele, Aug. 17, 2004.

67   **"all . . . one could want":** Ibid.

67   **"in and out of the library stacks":** On Griswold and the *Harvard Law Review*, see Harry A. Blackmun, "In Memoriam: Erwin Nathaniel Griswold," 979. On RBG's proofreading skills and the pleasure of "reading against" her galley and page proof of the forthcoming *Harvard Law Review*, see respectively Susan Deller Ross to RBG, March 15, 1983, and Wilton S. Sogg to RBG, Jan. 31, 1983, RBG Birthday Book.

68   **"the nature, uses, limits":** Howard Raiffa, "In Memoriam: Albert M. Sacks," *Harvard Law Review* 105 (1991): 16–17; and RBG, interview by Grele, Aug. 17, 2004.

69   **"T'aint Whatcha Do":** Howard Raiffa, "In Memoriam." For the Fats Waller story told by Hart and retold by the Harvard Law alumnus and Yale president Kingman Brewster, see Kalman, *Yale Law School and the Sixties*, 60.

69   **"My emphasis is on process":** Quoted in Kalman, *Legal Realism at Yale*, 51.

70   **Leadership of the free:** Key consensus school scholarship includes Hofstadter, *American Political Tradition*, though Hofstadter also explored the dark side of that tradition. Schlesinger, *Vital Center;* and Boorstin, *Genius of American Politics*. See also Wall, *Inventing the "American Way."*

70   **"the affluent society":** See, for example, John Higham, "Changing Paradigms: The Collapse of Consensus History," *Journal of American History* 76 (1989): 460–66; Lears, *Culture of Consumption;* and Elaine Tyler May, *Homeward Bound*. More recently, see Schrecker, *Many Are the Crimes;* Sugrue, *Origins of the Urban Crisis;* and Corber, *Homosexuality in Cold War America*. The phrase "the affluent society" comes from John Kenneth Galbraith's book *Affluent Society*.

70   **Legal scholars on both:** Critiques on the Right came from the law and economics movement. How, asked Richard Posner and others, could Hart, Sacks, and other process scholars consider the law rational and purposive? Legislators, dependent on the support of special-interest groups, are in no position to act in a fair and impartial manner. Judges, Posner argues, cannot be relied on to supply a corrective. Unable to disrupt the political system through judicial activism, they often have to validate statutes that may be unfair, even unjust. Critiques from the Left came from the critical legal studies movement. Emphasizing injustice itself and noting structural bias, critical legal stud-

ies scholars pointed out that citizens simply do not have equal access to the legal process. For example, the poor and less educated are far less likely to vote and lack access to legislators and expert legal counsel. For a concise, evenhanded account of critiques, which I have oversimplified for purposes of brevity, see Eskridge, "Legislation and Pedagogy in the Post–Legal Process Era," *University of Pittsburgh Law Review* 48 (1987): 691–731.

70 **"how it ought to be":** Duxbury, *Patterns of American Jurisprudence,* 299.

70 **"optimistic view of citizens":** Eskridge and Frickey, "Commentary: The Making of the Legal Process," 2052–55.

71 **The disease that had:** Details of illness in the following paragraphs were from author's interviews and were supplemented in letters, notably RBG to author, Jan. 9, 2007.

71 **"While she was always":** Ronald M. Loeb, interview by author, July 27, 2004; and Loeb to RBG, March 15, 1983, RBG Birthday Book, in this and the following paragraph. Asked whether all students felt so positively toward RBG, Loeb responded that so far as he knew, they did—sentiments voiced by every classmate interviewed at Harvard or Columbia. RBG's helpfulness, friendliness, and modesty—traits universally mentioned—apparently disarmed critics at the very least and, at most, generated among friends powerful feelings of admiration and affection.

72 **"What I do recall vividly":** Ronald M. Loeb, interview by author, July 27, 2004; Loeb to RBG, March 15, 1983; RBG, interview by Grele, Aug. 17, 2004.

72 **Beyond her many admonitions:** For RBG's statement on working because she had a child to support, see RBG, interview by Marcus, Aug. 15, 1995.

73 **"what I had come to expect":** Martin D. Ginsburg, interview by author, July 1, 2003.

73 **"creative, deeply intelligent":** MacLachlan, "Mr. Ginsburg's Campaign for Nominee." Martin Ginsburg played a major role in the 1984 buyout of Ross Perot's EDS Corporation by General Motors. He is credited with creating the special Class E stock issue to buy EDS.

74 **"not made out an adequate":** Griswold's reply is reported in Gerald Gunther, "Ruth Bader Ginsburg: A Personal, Very Fond Tribute," *University of Hawaii Law Review* 20 (1998): 583.

74 **"We heard that the smartest":** Ibid. On Appel's initial reaction, see Margolick, "Trial by Adversity Shapes Jurist's Outlook." For quotation on lunches, see Nina Appel (dean emeritus of Loyola Law School), interview by author, July 14, 2004.

74 **"quiet, serious, conscientious":** Appel, interview by author, July 14, 2004; Von Drehle, "Conventional Roles."

75 **"Then, like a coda":** Von Drehle, "Conventional Roles," for Salzman quotations.

75 **The course she described as "extraordinary":** Richard Salzman, interview by author, Washington, D.C., Nov. 13, 2003. Salzman, who lived a block from RBG during their school years in Flatbush, was much less impressed with Wechsler than was RBG. For lecture, see Herbert Wechsler, "Toward Neutral Principles of Constitutional Law," *Harvard Law Review* 73 (1959): 360–61, esp. n10. For RBG's reaction, her observation that Wechsler's position "disquieted law students of my generation," and her account of the course and textbook, see "In Memory of Herbert Wechsler," 1359; also, Fallon, Meltzer, and Shapiro, *Hart and Wechsler's "The Federal Courts and the Federal System."* RBG attests that she keeps the volume "within arm's reach," available as an "aid or stimulant," as she deals with the Court's heavy workload. See "In Memory," 1359.

75 **"sensitive young student":** Wechsler to RBG, March 15, 1983, and Gunther to RBG, March 15, 1983, both in RBG Birthday Book; and "Professor Gerald Gunther Speaks at Investiture of Judge Ruth Ginsburg in Washington, D.C.," *Columbia Law Alumni Observer* 31 (Dec. 1980): 8–9.

76 **"professional courtesy":** Edmund M. Kaufman, interview by author, July 30, 2004.

76 **Happily situated in Greenhouse:** RBG, interview by author, July 1, 2003; and RBG, interview by Grele, Aug. 17, 2004.

76 **"Jane stood up in the middle":** Claire Stiepleman to RBG, March 15, 1983, RBG Birthday Book. Jane's operatic "debut" appears in Carol Saline and Sharon J. Wohlmuth, "Ruth Bader Ginsburg and Her Daughter, Jane Ginsburg," in *Mothers and Daughters*, 48.

77 **"That's my Mommy":** Berry et al., *Women Lawyers at Work*, 55. RBG's ability to captivate the youngest members of her family spans generations. When I was in Chicago interviewing her son, James Ginsburg, his younger daughter, who must have been around three, wandered in intent on conversing with her father. While James went into the kitchen to ask his former wife to retrieve the talkative little girl, I explained to her that I was asking her daddy questions about her grandmother. Her twinkling eyes widened noticeably. "You know my bubbe?" she asked, her voice filled with obvious delight.

FOUR · Sailing in "Uncharted Waters"

78 **White-shoe firms:** White-shoe refers to those white Anglo-Saxon Protestant firms made up of partners and associates whose summer dress traditionally entailed white shoes. While these firms might have a highly assimilated Jew for tax or real estate matters, they did not hire Jews. "Mixed" or "balanced" firms, which tried to maintain a fifty-fifty ratio, were next in the pecking order, followed by Jewish firms. Irish, Italians, Hispanics, and African Americans were even less desired by elite law schools and by major firms. Not until the 1980s did the Jewish "quota" fall. Data, collected in 1995, indicates that Jewish lawyers, while now earning as much as their Protestant counterparts, still faced greater difficulty making partnership in large non-Jewish firms. See Heinzet et al., *Urban Lawyers;* and Ronit Dinovetzer, "Social Capital and Constraints on Legal Careers," *Law and Society Review* 40 (2006): 445–79.

My explanation for RBG's rejection accords with her own. See RBG, interview by Grele, Aug. 18, 2004. Murray was well aware that at Paul, Weiss, Rifkind, Wharton & Garrison she counted as a "twofer."

79 **How could she:** RBG, interviews by author; RBG, interview by Marcus, Aug. 15, 1995; and RBG, interview by Grele, Aug. 18, 2004. See also Gilbert and Moore, *Particular Passions*, 158. When Myra Bradwell Day was held at Columbia Law School in 1980, other alumnae recounted similar stories, noting that they had viewed themselves as lawyers, not "women lawyers," and were surprised by the discrimination. As Sylvia Law, now a professor of law at New York University, recalled, "I had two alternate explanations. . . . One was that I really wasn't as good as I thought I was, and that depressed me. And the other was that my superiors didn't like me, and that depressed me. But it never occurred to me that the explanation was that I was a woman. In retrospect, this was precisely the reason." Quoted in "Myra Bradwell Day Forum Held at Law School," *Columbia Law Alumni Observer*, May 14, 1980, 8.

79 **"What were women lawyers":** RBG, "The Progression of Women in the Law," *Valparaiso University Law Review* 28 (1994): 1161–82, esp. 1173. Another of RBG's colleagues, she reported, placed women attorneys into two categories: "First, there are the social workers, the ones that devote themselves to the poor and the oppressed, the truly needy. That type was not cause for concern. The social workers do not figure at all in the real world of legal business, the professor said. Second, there are the backstagers, women who would find congenial work in drafting wills and contracts, and research and brief writing." Neither really counted.

79 **"rather diffident, modest and shy":** Quoted in Kay, "Ruth Bader Ginsburg, Professor of Law," 20.

79 **"To be a woman":** Gilbert and Moore, *Particular Passions,* 158. Asked subsequently by a law student at the University of Kansas about "the lowest point" of her career,

RBG responded with two stories, the first involving her job rejection and the second detailing the Drano crisis subsequently related. For press accounts containing this and other biographical information, see Lewis, "Rejected as a Clerk, Chosen as a Justice"; Margolick, "Trial by Adversity Shapes Jurist's Outlook"; Gugliotta and Randolph, "Mentor, Role Model, and Heroine of Feminist Lawyers"; Von Drehle, "Conventional Roles"; and Von Drehle, "Redefining Fair with Simple, Careful Assault."

80 **"awesome responsibility, and complete"**: Gunther, "Ruth Bader Ginsburg: A Personal, Very Fond Tribute," 586.

80 **"that small group of very good"**: Quotations are respectively from Peppers, *Courtiers of the Marble Palace;* and Gunther, "Ruth Bader Ginsburg: A Personal, Very Fond Tribute," 586. Information in this and the following paragraph is also based on Gunther to RBG, March 15, 1983, RBG Birthday Book.

80 **What would his wife**: RBG, interview by Grele, Aug. 18, 2004.

81 **The job was hers**: Judge Leonard Moore also granted an interview. RBG's immediate predecessor, Alvin Schulman, later professed his doubts about this account, recalling that he had narrowly beaten out a woman from Harvard. Alvin K. Hellerstein, another Palmieri clerk, was equally skeptical. See Schulman to RBG, May 2, 2001; Hellerstein to RBG, June 1, 2001; and RBG to Hellerstein and Schulman, June 22, 2001. RBG contacted Gunther, who stuck by his original account. Copies of these letters were made available to me by the justice. RBG later remarked that she was glad she hadn't known about the Gunther-Palmieri arrangement at the time because of the additional pressure it would have placed on her. RBG, interview by author, July 7, 2001.

82 **She learned just as quickly**: For this and the following paragraph, see RBG, interview by Marcus, Aug. 15, 1995. On deciphering the judge's handwriting, see Palmieri to RBG, March 15, 1983, RBG Birthday Book.

82 **"This is what I want"**: RBG, interview by Marcus, Aug. 15, 1995; and Gilbert and Moore, *Particular Passions,* 158.

83 **With over fifty**: RBG, interview by Marcus, Aug. 15, 1995; and Gunther, *Learned Hand,* 653.

83 **"Young lady, here I am"**: RBG, interview by Marcus, Aug. 15, 1995.

83 **Gender discrimination aside**: Palmieri to RBG, March 15, 1983, RBG Birthday Book.

84 **"She even show[ed] up"**: Ibid. and "Ruth Bader Ginsburg," in *Current Biography Yearbook, 1994,* 214.

84 **The justice, Sacks believed**: Michael E. Parrish, "Justice Frankfurter and the Supreme Court," in Lowe, *Jewish Justices of the Supreme Court Revisited,* 61–80.

85 **The odds, Ginsburg**: On Lucile Lomen, Douglas's clerk in 1944, see Clare Cushman, *Supreme Court Decisions and Women's Rights,* 235–41. For numbers on female clerks subsequently hired and by whom, see Peppers, *Courtiers of the Marble Palace,* chap. 2. As the author notes, minorities continued to fare quite poorly. Overall, graduates of elite law schools, especially Harvard, dominated in the number of Supreme Court clerks produced through the year 2000. Although there was a somewhat greater diversity in the Rehnquist Court, a handful of elite law schools remain the locus for recruitment.

85 **"a person of paradox"**: Parrish, "Justice Frankfurter and the Supreme Court," 64. Also see RBG, "The Supreme Court: A Place for Women," Wilson Lecture, Wellesley College, Wellesley, Mass., Nov. 13, 1998. For the quotation, see Parrish, "Frankfurter, Felix," anb.org.

85 **Palmieri swung into action**: On Palmieri's actions, see RBG, interview by Grele, Aug. 18, 2004. Strasser Spiegelberg is known today as the Fried Frank firm.

85 **"How would you like"**: RBG, interviews by author.

86 **Intrigued, Ginsburg promised**: Hans Smit (Stanley H. Fuld Professor of Law, Columbia University) to author, email, April 19, 2001.

86 **The opportunity proved "irresistible"**: RBG, interview by Grele, Aug. 18, 2004.

86 **Their almost daily lessons:** Ibid.

86 **"Ruth is basically a reserved":** RBG, "Introduction to Hans Smit," in Kay, "Ruth Bader Ginsburg, Professor of Law," n38. Smit, interview by author, March 31, 2008.

87 **By the late spring of 1962:** A mother as well as a member of the bar, Toni Chayes had clinched her argument by telling RBG, "If you have the chance to send your child to the best school in all of Manhattan, the Brearley School, and you send her, instead, to another place, you are doing your child a disservice." RBG, interview by Grele, Aug. 17, 2006. (The alternative was Hunter Elementary School, a public school for gifted children.)

88 **"good minds abroad":** RBG, interview by Grele, Aug. 18, 2004.

88 **Sweden's health-care and child-care policies:** An account of the impression left by the Finkbine incident is related in RBG, "Remarks for Panel Discussion on Current Topics in International Women's Rights," Association of the Bar of the City of New York, Dec. 13, 2001, supplied by RBG to the author. For a fuller discussion of Finkbine and the thalidomide problem, see Reagan, *Dangerous Pregnancies,* chap. 2.

89 **"We ought to stop":** Moberg is quoted in Rita Liljestrom, "Sweden," in Kamerman and Kahn, *Family Policy,* 33. See also Moberg, *Kvinnor och människor.*

89 **Predicting that the day:** Rita Liljestrom, "Sweden."

89 **"every cocktail party":** RBG is quoted in Von Drehle, "Conventional Roles."

89 **Based on a new:** Dahlström, *Changing Roles of Men and Women.*

89 **"the right to be human":** Hilda Scott, *Sweden's "Right to Be Human" Sex-Role Equality,* chap. 1.

90 **Hanks lived in the city:** RBG, interviews by author and supplemental notes of Jan. 19, 2007. Eva Hanks (professor of law, Cardozo School of Law, New York City), interview by author, March 28, 2008. On Gellhorn's admission that Columbia would have hired her much sooner had she been male, see Gellhorn to RBG, March 15, 1983, RBG Birthday Book.

91 **Knowing women held:** Hanks, interview by author, 2008; also, RBG, interview by Grele, March 18, 2004. For a brief account of women law faculty holding tenure or tenure-track positions at the Association of American Law Schools approved by the American Bar Association, see Kay, "Ruth Bader Ginsburg," 1–6.

91 **Offered the position:** RBG, interviews by author; also RBG, interview by Grele, Aug. 18, 2004.

91 **In the meantime, she was grateful:** RBG, interviews by author; also RBG, interview by Grele, Aug. 18, 2004; also, introductory note to RBG, "The Equal Rights Amendment Is the Way," *Harvard Law Journal* 1 (1978): 19.

92 **Ginsburg, seeing merit:** On schedule, see "In Memory of Dean Heckel: Comments of Ruth Bader Ginsburg," *Rutgers Law Review* 41 (1989): 477–78. On reception by male colleagues, see Lesley Oelsner, "Columbia Law Snares a Prize in the Quest for Women Professors," *New York Times,* Jan. 26, 1972. On fissions among faculty, see RBG, interview by Grele, Aug. 18, 2004. RBG likens Hanks's friendship and "tips" to those later received from Sandra Day O'Connor when RBG first joined the Court. See RBG, "Remarks for Rutgers," April 11, 1995 (in possession of the author).

92 **The trip was grueling:** On commuting, see Berry et al., *Women Lawyers at Work,* 64. In her franker moments, RBG would describe the commute with all its stops and changes as the commute from hell. It literally produced nightmares, she told me in our interview of Sept. 1, 2006.

93 **Nonetheless, the memory rankled:** Ibid., 63; "Ruth Bader Ginsburg," in *Current Biography Yearbook,* 214; and Ostrer, "Profile of Ruth Bader Ginsburg," 34.

93 **In just a few months:** Hanks, interview by author, March 28, 2008.

93 **"You were the very essence":** Joan B. Danoff to RBG, March 15, 1983, RBG Birthday Book; Ruth Watson Lubic, interview by author, July 27, 2004; and RBG, notes to author, Jan. 19, 2007, supplementing interviews.

93 **On September 8, 1965:** Von Drehle, "Conventional Roles." RBG's sentiments were based not just on having given birth but on the fact that the birth marked survival and regeneration, which is congruent with what the birth of a son must have meant to Marty. See Nina Totenberg, "A Look at Judge Ruth Bader Ginsburg's Life and Career," National Public Radio, July 6, 1993. I am grateful to Totenberg for making a transcript of the broadcast available to me.

94 **Moreover, it had to be:** The most comprehensive treatment of RBG's career at Rutgers is in Kay, "Ruth Bader Ginsburg," 2–20.

94 **Though fully aware:** RBG, interview by author, Sept. 1, 2006. Account of the months following birth based on my previous RBG interviews in this and following paragraphs.

95 **"Leave them undisturbed":** Patterson, *Grand Expectations.* Among the Court's many decisions generating controversy were *Baker v. Carr,* 369 U.S. 186 (1962); *Reynolds v. Sims,* 377 U.S. 533 (1964) (voting redistricting); *Engel v. Vitale,* 370 U.S. 421 (1962); *Abington School District v. Schempp,* 374 U.S. 203 (1963) (school prayer); *Gideon v. Wainright,* 372 U.S. 335 (1963); *Escobedo v. Illinois,* 378 U.S. 478 (1964) (criminal rights); *Jacobellis v. Ohio,* 378 U.S. 184 (1964) (obscenity and pornography); *Griswold v. Connecticut,* 381 U.S. 479 (1965) (privacy); *New York Times v. Sullivan,* 376 U.S. 254 (1964) (libel); *Garner v. Louisiana,* 368 U.S. 157 (1961); *Edwards v. South Carolina,* 372 U.S. 229 (1963); *Shuttlesworth v. City of Birmingham,* 373 U.S. 262 (1963); *Heart of Atlanta Motel v. United States,* 379 U.S. 241 (1964); and *Griffin v. County Board of Prince Edward County,* 377 U.S. 218 (1964) (racial discrimination). Brennan's quotation is in RBG, "In Memoriam: William J. Brennan," *Harvard Law Review* 111 (1997): 3.

95 **Just thinking about the man:** RBG, "In Memoriam: William J. Brennan." RBG might have been alluding in her remarks to a later period when she felt she had taken on too much, but this period after the birth of James she insists was the most difficult in terms of meeting dual commitments to family and career.

95 **"I schlepped Jane":** RBG to author, Jan. 19, 2007; see also RBG, "Remarks," March 10, 2005.

95 **"overcompensated on weekends":** Stephanie Francis Ward, "Family Ties: The Private and Public Lives of Justice Ruth Bader Ginsburg," *ABA Journal* 96 (2010): 36–43.

96 **Unable to return:** RBG, interview by Grele, Aug. 18, 2004.

96 **"What is his name?":** Jane Ginsburg, interview by author, May 6, 2003. RBG has no memory of the exchange after the dance, but agrees I should rely on Jane's account. What she does remember vividly is that the application for dance class was wait-listed, which she took to mean "no Jews wanted," so after Jane's "adamant" refusal to take part in the class, there was no second application. RBG to author, Jan. 19, 2007.

97 **Ruth responded reassuringly:** Jane Ginsburg, interview by author, May 6, 2003, and RBG to author, Jan. 19, 2007.

97 **"I was a resentful child":** For quotations on Jane's resentful nature, her mother's quiet disappointment, and RBG's searches and seizures of childhood debris, see Saline and Wohlmuth, *Mothers and Daughters,* 50; and for others see Berry et al., *Women Lawyers at Work,* 61–62.

97 **Their daughter's ingenuity:** For the camp letter story, I am indebted to James Ginsburg, interview by author, July 30, 2003. That RBG "giggles" when sufficiently amused is also attested to by her clerks. See Deborah Jones Merritt, "Tribute to Ruth Bader Ginsburg," *Annual Survey of American Law* (1997), xxxiii.

97 **"Mommy Laughed":** "Mommy Laughed" was so much a part of family history that Jane was not even sure at the time of our interview that it had appeared as a booklet; both parents confirmed that it did.

98 **Fortunately, the housekeeper:** RBG, interviews by author.

98 **"Deep burns distorted":** Berry et al., *Women Lawyers at Work,* 58–59.

98 **"She absolutely doesn't forgive":** Ibid. Also, RBG, "Remarks," March 10, 2005, 29. Jane Ginsburg, interview by author, May 6, 2003. Jane's quotation is in Saline and Wohlmuth, *Mothers and Daughters,* 50.

100 **But there were times:** RBG, interviews by author.

100 **"For the good students":** Linda P. Campbell and Linda M. Harrington, "Judge Ruth Bader Ginsburg: Portrait of a 'Steel Butterfly,'" *Chicago Herald Tribune,* June 27, 1993.

100 **"she clung to the lectern":** Hanks, interview by author, March 28, 2008.

100 **Colleagues and students roared:** Ibid. RBG described the incident when asked to identify photographs. She describes Hanks as a "great and good friend." See RBG, "Remarks," March 10, 2005.

100 **"We never sat together":** Hanks, interview by author, March 28, 2008. On playing by male rules that were not clearly disclosed, see Aisenberg and Harrington, *Women of Academe,* esp. chap. 3.

101 **"World Wars, Court calendars":** RBG, interview by author; Martin Ginsburg, interview by author, July 1, 2003; and Jane Ginsburg, interview by author, May 6, 2004. Also see Bernard and Joyce West to RBG, March 15, 1983, RBG Birthday Book.

101 **Another part was not:** RBG, interview by author.

101 **"They spoke another language":** RBG, interviews by author. Jane Ginsburg first alerted me to her summers in France.

102 **For that generation:** Svonkin, *Jews Against Prejudice.* For a history of legal liberalism and its relationship to New Dealers, see Kalman, *Strange Career of Legal Liberalism,* prologue and chap. 1.

103 **Protests were erupting:** Patterson, *Grand Expectations,* 694–97.

FIVE · The Making of a Feminist Advocate

104 **"one of the great turning points":** RBG quotation is from *Paving the Way,* directed by Morris.

104 **Spurred by advocates:** Skrentny, *Minority Rights Revolution,* 7. By the late 1960s, 70 percent of the high court's decisions involved individual rights in contrast with no more than 10 percent in the 1930s, when the property-rights claims of business and the wealthy consumed most of the justices' attention.

105 **Funding, organizational backing:** Epp, *Rights Revolution,* 3. Canada and Great Britain were simultaneously undergoing a rights revolution. See ibid., chaps. 3–4, on the United States.

105 **Though Ginsburg, who:** Daniel Horowitz, "Rethinking Betty Friedan and *The Feminine Mystique:* Labor Union Radicalism and Feminism in Cold War America," *American Quarterly* 48 (1998): 1–42, quotation is on 1. For fuller treatment, see Horowitz, *Betty Friedan and the Making of "The Feminine Mystique."* RBG's disappointment upon reading *The Feminine Mystique* was shared by others who, as Horowitz notes, found little new or exciting in Friedan's revelations and her approach limited.

106 **"full participation of women":** National Organization for Women, 1966 Statement of Purpose, reprinted in Kraditor, *Up from the Pedestal,* 363–64.

107 **An "ice woman":** Riegelman's quotation is in Strebeigh, *Equal,* 20.

107 **But handle it she did:** See, for example, RBG to L. Howard Bennet, July 29, 1970; RBG to Melvin Laird, Stanley Resor, Clark Case, and Major Gloria Olson, Sept. 17, 1970; RBG to Stephen Nagler, Dec. 7, 1970, RBG Papers.

107 **If the implicitly sexist:** On New Jersey ACLU work, see "Justice Ruth Bader Ginsburg Remembers," *Rutgers Tradition* (1995): 10–11; RBG, "Remarks on Women's Progress in the Legal Profession in the United States," *Tulsa Law Journal* 33 (1997): 13–21; RBG, "Introduction to Women and the Law: Facing the Millennium," *Indiana Law Review* 32 (1999): 1161–65. See also, RBG to Stephen Nagler, Sept. 20, 1971, RBG Papers.

107 **For the former Cornell:** RBG to Professor Jameson Doig, April 6, 1971, RBG Papers.

107 **But female employees:** "Justice Ruth Bader Ginsburg Remembers," 10–11; also, RBG comments in "Women on the Bench," *Columbia Journal of Gender and Law* 10 (2000–2001): 25–28.

108 **Such discrimination hurt:** As late as 1970, only 1.6 percent of women were employed as engineers. See www.nap.edu.

108 **Women had their own concerns:** Kalman, *Yale Law School and the Sixties,* esp. 218. See also Edward J. Bloustein, "In Remembrance of Dean Heckel," *Rutgers Law Review* 41 (1989): 475–77.

108 **At Yale, these young feminists:** Kalman, *Yale Law School and the Sixties,* 3.

109 **Ginsburg could not resist:** Strebeigh, *Equal,* 14.

109 **She discovered that she:** "Justice Ruth," Duke University Law School, www.law.duke.edu.

109 **What few exemptions:** There is now extensive literature on the early legal status of women. A good place to start is Dayton, *Women Before the Bar;* Hartog, *Man and Wife in America;* Basch, *In the Eyes of the Law;* Kerber, *No Constitutional Right to Be Ladies;* Edwards, *People and Their Peace;* and Pascoe, *What Comes Naturally.*

110 **"Whatever changes may have taken":** Italics mine. Drew's quotation is in Kerber, *No Constitutional Right to Be Ladies,* 163. According to Kerber, when the case first came to trial in Tampa in 1957, of the more than 46,000 women registered to vote in Hillsborough County, only 218 had registered for jury duty. Of the 218, the jury commissioner placed only 10 names in a pool of 1,000 names.

110 **"Despite the enlightened emancipation":** Kerber, *No Constitutional Right to Be Ladies,* 173–84; *Hoyt v. Florida,* 368 U.S. 57 (1961).

110 **"They can't help being influenced":** Kerber, *No Constitutional Right to Be Ladies,* 173–84; for RBG's quotation, see Jones, "Columbia's Leader in Legal Battle Against Sex-Based Discrimination," 13–15.

111 **It was that simple:** *Ballard v. United States,* 329 U.S. 187 (1946).

111 **"judicial paternalism":** On terms, see Judith Baer, *Chains of Protection;* and Grossberg, *Governing the Hearth.* The classic case involving "protective legislation" that limited working hours for women was *Muller v. Oregon,* 208 U.S. 412 (1908). See also Dalrymple, *Sexual Distinctions in the Law.*

111 **"Differentiated by these matters":** *Muller,* 208 U.S. 412.

112 **"The Constitution does not require":** *Goesaert v. Cleary,* 335 U.S. 464 (1948). Davidson, RBG, and Kay, *Text, Cases, and Materials on Sex-Based Discrimination,* 15–17.

112 **Gender discrimination—differentiation:** For an excellent survey on the variability of American gender definitions from 1500 to the present, see Ryan, *Mysteries of Sex.*

112 **Equality, as a principle:** An excellent introduction to race formation and theory and the historical trajectory of racial politics is Omi and Winant, *Racial Formation in the United States,* chap. 4. On the legal struggle, see Klarman, *From Jim Crow to Civil Rights.*

113 **So deeply ingrained were divisions:** On the interchangeability principle, see Pole, *Pursuit of Equality in American History,* 293–94; and Judith A. Baer, "How Is the Law Male? A Feminist Perspective on Constitutional Interpretation," in Goldstein, *Feminist Jurisprudence,* 147.

113 **In fundamental ways:** On the narrow interpretation of the Nineteenth Amendment and its consequences, see Reva Siegel, "She the People: The Nineteenth Amendment, Sex Equality, Federalism, and the Family," *Harvard Law Review* 115 (2002): 947–1046.

113 **Nor was the record:** John D. Johnson Jr. and Charles Knapp conclude that the performance of America's judges in this area could be "succinctly described as ranging from poor to abominable" in Johnson and Knapp, "Sex Discrimination by Law: A Study in Judicial Perspective," *New York University Law Review* 46 (1971): 676. See also

Reva Siegel, "The Modernization of Marital Status Law: Adjudicating Wives' Rights to Earnings, 1860–1930," *Georgetown Law Journal* 82 (1994): 2127. For the struggle to change women's legal status, see Van Burkleo, *Belonging to the World.*

113 **"How," she wondered, "have people":** RBG quoted in Gilbert and Moore, *Particular Passions,* 153. RBG, "Sex and Unequal Protection: Men and Women as Victims," *Journal of Family Law* 11 (1971): 347–49 (delivered as a lecture with the same title at Duke University Law School, Oct. 1971, RBG Papers). RBG publicized the results of her reading in numerous speeches and articles. See, for example, remarks for the New Jersey ACLU's Annual Awards Dinner, "Civil Liberties Union Efforts to Combat Sex Discrimination," 1971; also, RBG, "Men, Women, and the Constitution," *Columbia Journal of Law and Social Problems* 10 (1973): 77–112.

114 **Members of the President's:** Harrison, *On Account of Sex,* 110–42, 169.

114 **When Ginsburg proposed:** Strebeigh, *Equal,* 19.

115 **Heckel could be confident:** RBG describes her colleagues as "supportive or at least indulgent" in "Justice Ruth Bader Ginsburg Remembers," 11. Few scholars who tried to introduce courses on women into the university curriculum in those years escaped the objections that they were "too ideological" to be standard offerings. Rather, such highly political courses, they were told, should be offered as a voluntary, noncredit "add-on" in the manner of a "teach-in" on Vietnam.

115 **Women at Berkeley's:** On these pioneers, see Linda K. Kerber, "Writing Our Own Rare Books," *Yale Journal of Law and Feminism* 14 (2002): 429–31.

116 **Questions vastly outnumbered answers:** For RBG's attachment to Mill, see her use of the quotation from *The Subjection of Women* in "Introduction to Women and the Law—a Symposium," *Rutgers Law Review* 25 (1970); on the larger enterprise of course creation, see Kerber, "Writing Our Own Rare Books," 431–34.

116 **Examples were plentiful:** RBG to Barbara Schiller, May 21, 1971, RBG Papers, Miscellany Files, 1969–1972, box 19.

116 **Not only would participants:** Ibid.

117 **Why not add a symposium:** RBG, "Introduction to Women and the Law—a Symposium," 1–11.

117 **In 1971, the *Women's Rights Law Reporter:*** Ibid., 3.

118 **For now, it was exhilarating:** Ibid.; and Kerber, "Writing Our Own Rare Books," 429. On fatigue, see Bernard West to RBG, Feb. 16, 1983; and Gunilla Asp to RBG, March 15, 1983, both in RBG Birthday Book.

118 **"Given Vietnam, there was certainly":** For recollections of women at Boalt in the 1960s, see Rose Bird, "3d Year Girls Lament (Fondly Dedicated to Dean Hill)," *Writ* (1965): 2. Ruth Abrams is quoted in "Celebrating the Women of HLS," *Harvard Law Bulletin* 30 (1999). Alumnae at the University of Pennsylvania Law School whose recollections, though later in time, were just as negative are reported by Lani Guinier, Michelle Fine, and Jane Balin, "Becoming Gentlemen: Women's Experiences at One Ivy League Law School," *University of Pennsylvania Law Review* 143 (1994): 1–110. Quotation in Kalman, *Yale Law School and the Sixties,* 143.

119 **That would have to change:** On women in the profession, see Epstein, *Woman's Place,* and *Women in Law;* Doris L. Sassower, "Women in the Law," in Professional Women's Caucus, *Sixteen Reports on the Status of Women in the Professions* (New York, 1970); also Doris L. Sassower, "Women in the Law: The Second Hundred Years," *American Bar Association Journal* 57 (1971): 329–32. On specific women, see, for example, Biskupic, *Sandra Day O'Connor,* chap. 2.

119 **"overwhelming," just "staggering":** RBG does not recall the precise year in which she read *The Second Sex,* saying that it was "in the 1960s," in my interviews on Aug. 28, 2000, and Sept. 2, 2005. The year 1969 has been specified by Klebanow and Jonas; however, she questions how they would have known. See Diana Klebanow and Franklin L. Jonas, "Ruth Bader Ginsburg," in *People's Lawyers,* 361.

119 **"There was a passion":** Hanks, interview by author, March 28, 2008; and Tracy Schroth, "At Rutgers, Ginsburg Changed," *New Jersey Law Journal* 134 (1993): 32.

119 **"hippy-yippy-campy":** Carol Hanisch, "A Critique of the Miss America Protest," condensed and reprinted in Kerber and De Hart, *Women's America,* 577.

119 **"dangled from her wrist":** Ellen Goodman, "The Transformation of Justice Ginsburg," *Boston Globe,* June 29, 2007.

120 **"full participation in the mainstream":** National Organization for Women, 1966 Statement of Purpose.

121 **"land, like woman":** Quotation in Von Drehle, "Conventional Roles." For more on bias against women lawyers, see Phyllis D. Coontz, "Gender Bias in the Legal Profession: Women 'See' It, Men Don't," *Women and Politics* 15 (1995): 1–22.

121 **In this personal evolution:** Examples provided by RBG, interviews by author, July 27, 2000, Sept. 3, 2001, Aug. 28, 2002, and July 1, 2003.

121 **"I ask no favor for my sex":** Grimké, *Letters on the Equality of the Sexes and the Condition of Woman,* 10. An example of RBG's frequent use of this quotation is in Joint Reply Brief of Appellants and American Civil Liberties Union Amicus Curiae of Ginsburg et al. at 2–14, *Frontiero v. Laird,* 341 F. Supp. 201, 1123 (1972).

122 **In Switzerland, women:** RBG, "The Status of Women," *American Journal of Comparative Law* 20 (1972): 585–91; and RBG, "Introduction to Women and the Law—a Symposium," 1–11. See also Offen, *Globalizing Feminisms.*

SIX · Seizing the Moment

123 **"it was all a matter":** For RBG's statement "I was in the right place at the right time," see, for example, RBG, "On Taking Equal Rights Lightly," speech delivered upon receipt of the Society of American Law Teachers Award, Dec. 14, 1979, RBG Papers.

123 **"Chance," aptly observed:** Charles Nicolle in Fitzhenry, *Harper Book of Quotations,* 488.

123 **As a sixteen-year-old former:** Melvin Wulf (attorney), interview by author, New York City, Nov. 2, 2000; also, RBG, interview by author, Sept. 2, 2005.

123 **One could almost see:** Melvin Wulf (attorney), interview by author, New York City, Nov. 2, 2000; Sara Fritz, "Without Great Expectations Ginsburg Found Her Way to the Top," *Los Angeles Times,* July 21, 1983, 5.

124 **Even more effectively:** Eva Hanks, interview by author, New York City, March 28, 2008; Joan Bruder Danoff, interview by author, July 27, 2004; Irma Hilton, interview by author, July 22, 2004; and Nina Appel, interview by author, July 14, 2004.

124 **For Neier's plans:** RBG, interview by author, Sept. 2, 2005. Neier's quotation is in Walker, *In Defense of American Liberties,* 299–300; also, Neier, *Taking Liberties,* xxvi–xxvii.

125 **"Let's take it":** Martin D. Ginsburg, interview by author, July 1, 2003.

125 **Sex-discrimination cases:** Hoff, *Law, Gender, and Injustice.*

126 **First, they needed:** *Bolling v. Sharpe,* 347 U.S. 497 (1954).

126 **Because even appearing:** Martin D. Ginsburg, interview by author, July 1, 2003.

126 **"We will take the case":** RBG to Wulf, Nov. 17, 1970, RBG Papers.

127 **It took a series:** Martin D. Ginsburg, interview by author, Sept. 2, 2005.

127 **Moritz declined, holding:** Wulf to RBG, Feb. 2, 1971, quoted in Strebeigh, *Equal,* 26.

127 **Ruth now set:** The two became acquainted at Gannett House at Harvard when Dorsen, also a Harvard Law graduate, would stop by the *Harvard Law Review* office to pick up his date Nancy Boxley, who was also on the staff.

127 **In turning to Dorsen:** Dorsen also had among his credits supervision of the ACLU's amicus brief in the landmark 1963 case *Gideon v. Wainwright,* 372 U.S. 335 (1963).

127 **"one of the very best presentations":** For praise of Dorsen's strategic ability and wise counsel, see Neier, *Taking Liberties,* 14. Dorsen to RBG, April 12, 1971, RBG Papers.

128 **"the constitutional guarantees":** Points drawn from Brief for Petitioner-Appellant, Charles E. Moritz, at 20, *Moritz v. Commissioner of Internal Revenue,* 469 F.2d 466, RBG Papers.

129 **Nor was she personally:** Had Pauli Murray not been denied an appointment at Cornell in 1952 because the people who supplied her references—Eleanor Roosevelt, Thurgood Marshall, and A. Philip Randolph—were considered too radical, the paths of the two women might have crossed earlier. Similarly, when RBG had a summer job at Paul, Weiss, Rifkind, Wharton & Garrison, where Murray was employed, they did not become acquainted. Nor did she get to know Pilpel until the two later attended the same conference in Israel. For homage, see RBG, "Constitutional Adjudication in the United States as Means of Advancing the Equal Status of Men and Women Under the Law," *Hofstra Law Review* 26 (1997): 267; also see RBG quotation in Anne Firor Scott, *Pauli Murray and Caroline Ware,* 138–39.

129 **None had been more:** Kenyon was appointed to the League of Nations Committee on the Status of Women from 1938 to 1940 and served as the first U.S. delegate to the UN Commission on the Status of Women from 1947 to 1950.

130 **"a Cassandra crying out":** On the relative inactivity of the Women's Committee in the 1950s, see Alan Reitman to Pat Malin, Aug. 20, 1951, box 1948, Malin Papers. Archival material indicates that the low priority attached to women's issues was not for any lack of support on the part of the ACLU's president, Patrick Malin, but rather a reflection of national inactivity and the ACLU's—and Kenyon's own—preoccupation with McCarthyism. Women's rights activity revived with the introduction of equal pay bills in 1961 for which Kenyon testified before the House Committee on Education and Labor. See Testimony of Dorothy Kenyon on Equal Pay Bills H.R. 8898 and H.R. 10226 on April 27, 1962, box 210, Kenyon Papers. On abortion rights, see draft of speech, "The Legal Concept of Equality," April 2, 1959, 6–7, folder 227, box 23, Kenyon Papers. On her years as the lone feminist, see Kenyon to Fellow Board Members, Feb. 21, 1967, folder 2042, box 114, Murray Papers. For a superb analysis of Kenyon's contribution, see Samantha Barbas, "Dorothy Kenyon and the Making of Modern Legal Feminism," *Stanford Journal of Civil Rights and Civil Liberties* 5 (Oct. 2009): 423–46.

130 **She and Kenyon led:** See "Twenty-Two Portraits of Women at Columbia Law School," 25.

130 **"Now," she asked her:** Gilmore, *Defying Dixie,* 324–26; Murray, *Pauli Murray,* 311–15. Murray was not only a black woman but also a closeted lesbian. For her concerns about her sexuality, which surfaced during adolescence, see Anne Firor Scott's editorial comments in *Pauli Murray and Caroline Ware,* esp. 38. On her denial of admission to the University of North Carolina at Chapel Hill because of race and to Harvard Law School because of gender, see respectively Glenda Elizabeth Gilmore, "Admitting Pauli Murray," *Journal of Women's History* 14, no. 2 (2002): 62–67; and Rosalind Rosenberg, "The Conjunction of Race and Gender," *Journal of Women's History* 14, no. 2 (2002): 68–73. See Murray's own account of her family and her life in *Proud Shoes* and *Song in a Weary Throat. Song in a Weary Throat* was later republished as *Pauli Murray.* For a full biography, see Rosalind Rosenberg, *Jane Crow: The Life of Pauli Murray* (New York: Oxford University Press, 2017).

130 **By the time she:** Murray, *States' Laws on Race and Color.*

131 **In it, she and Mary:** On Kenyon's prior arguments against jury exemptions, see Kerber, *No Constitutional Right to Be Ladies,* chap. 4. Pauli Murray and Mary O. Eastwood, "Jane Crow and the Law: Sex Discrimination and Title VII," *George Washington Law Review* 34 (1965): 232–56.

132 **Similar myths and mechanisms:** Sources included Gunnar Myrdal, the Swedish sociologist, who made the same analogy in his classic 1944 study of U.S. race relations, *An American Dilemma: The Negro Problem and Modern Democracy;* as did Helen Hacker in her influential 1951 article "Women as a Minority Group," *Social Forces* 31

(Oct. 1951): 60–69. Simone de Beauvoir's comparison between women and African Americans in *The Second Sex* provided additional fodder.

132 **The willingness of the Supreme:** For an excellent discussion of sources as well as the power (and limitations) of the race-sex analogy in "Jane Crow," see Serena Mayeri, "'A Common Fate of Discrimination': Race-Gender Analogies in Legal and Historical Perspective," *Yale Law Journal* 110 (2001): 1045–87.

132 **As a member of President:** For Murray's earlier efforts to persuade feminists to use equal protection litigation in areas other than those affected by protective labor legislation, see Harrison, *On Account of Sex,* 126–36; Murray, *Pauli Murray,* chap. 29; and Murray to Mary Eastwood, Jan. 25, 1968, folder 957, box 51, Murray Papers.

132 **The "troika," as Kenyon:** Murray and Kenyon to the ACLU Board of Directors, telegram, Sept. 23, 1970. On delegate demands at the 1970 Biennial Conference, see "Resolution Proposed by the Ad Hoc Committee on Women's Rights," April 1970 draft and June 4, 1970, draft; Murray and Kenyon to Board, memo, Sept. 24, 1970; Harriet F. Pilpel Conference paper, "The Civil Liberties Aspects of Human Reproduction," June 3–7, 1970, all in folders 956–57, box 55, Murray Papers. The term "dual strategy" is Serena Mayeri's.

133 **In September 1970:** For vote count, see Murray's handwritten notation on Murray and Kenyon to the Board of Directors, telegram, Sept. 23, 1970; and Alan Reitman to Murray, Sept. 30, 1970, both in folder 956, box 55, Murray Papers.

133 **"Where there are several persons":** Idaho statute quoted in RBG, "Introduction to Women and the Law—a Symposium," 9; RBG to Wulf, April 6, 1971, RBG Papers.

134 **"*We* will write":** Wulf's reply to RBG's request is quoted in RBG Rutgers remarks. For these remarks, she apparently condensed history, indicating that Wulf agreed in the course of their visit in Newark.

134 **Rather, the justices should:** Wulf, interview by author, Nov. 2, 2000. The West German Constitutional Court had declared unconstitutional provisions in the civil code authorizing fathers to determine the education of a child when the parents disagreed and specifying that agrarian estates be inherited whole by the eldest son even when there were older daughters.

134 **"At the time, Ruth":** Wulf, interview by author, Nov. 2, 2000; Dorsen, interview by author, May 1, 2003; and Neier, *Taking Liberties,* 13. RBG agrees that the initiative came from Neier and Wulf and dates the official offer to an ACLU board meeting to which she was invited to discuss litigation possibilities following the November (1971) *Reed* decision. RBG, interview by Grele, Washington, D.C., Aug. 18, 2004. Unless otherwise indicated, all material in subsequent paragraphs is based on author's interviews and notes. Where I have relied on interviews by either Marcus or Grele, I have so indicated.

134 **"Civil liberties," she explained:** Quoted in Women's Rights Project, *With Liberty and Justice for Women: The ACLU's Contribution to Ten Years of Struggle for Equal Rights* (New York: American Civil Liberties Union, 1982), 5. RBG and Barbara Flagg, "Some Reflections on the Feminist Legal Thought of the 1970s," *University of Chicago Legal Forum* 9 (1989): 8–21, esp. 11.

135 **With access to relevant cases:** As an ACLU board member said of the money, "How much is hand wash and how much is real, I don't know . . . but I'll put up with it." On the Playboy Foundation's support for feminist causes—and the attacks it inspired in some feminist circles, though not on the ACLU's part—see Pitzulo, *Bachelors and Bunnies,* 150–67, esp. 165n100 and 166n10. For the financial resources of the ACLU compared with other women's rights groups involved in litigation, see Karen O'Connor and Lee Epstein, "Beyond Legislative Lobbying: Women's Groups and the Supreme Court," *Judicature* 67 (1983): 133–43; and Ruth B. Cowan, "Women's Rights Through Litigation: An Examination of the American Civil Liberties Union Women's Rights Project, 1971–1976," *Columbia Human Rights Law Review* 8 (1976): 377, 386–89.

135   **Unencumbered by the constraints:** For this and the following paragraphs, see Sarat and Scheingold, *Cause Lawyering;* and Scheingold and Sarat, *Something to Believe In.* See also Teles, *Rise of the Conservative Legal Movement,* esp. chap. 2. On public-interest law, see the entire issue of *The Yale Law Journal* 79 (1970).

135   **As anyone following the Swedish:** RBG's continued awareness of Palme and his efforts is evident both in her inclusion of Palme's speech titled "The Emancipation of Man" in her teaching materials and in her adoption of concepts and language in her briefs. See Olof Palme, "The Emancipation of Man: Address Before the Women's National Democratic Club," June 8, 1970, in Davidson, RBG, and Kay, *Text, Cases, and Materials on Sex-Based Discriminations,* ix. See also *Reed v. Reed,* 404 U.S. 71 (1971).

135   **"speak truth to power":** The quotation, almost a cliché, is Quaker in origin, going back to the eighteenth century.

136   **Though she had spent:** RBG, interviews with author.

136   **With the "old boy":** Graham, *Civil Rights Era.*

137   **Sacks might now:** Keller and Keller, *Making Harvard Modern,* esp. chaps. 14 and 18.

137   **"Crits [CLS] and their enemies":** Ibid., 438.

137   **She had learned her lesson:** Hanks, interview by author, March 28, 2008.

137   **"It really wasn't sexism":** Hans Smit (professor of law, Columbia University), interview by author, March 31, 2008.

137   **Nor did it mean:** "Women at Columbia," Columbia University Archives. Also see McCaughey, *Stand, Columbia,* 518.

137   **According to *The New York:*** "Women's Rights Study Begun at Universities," *New York Times,* April 5, 1970, 43; Phyllis Kaniss, "HEW Cracks Down on Universities for Discrimination Against Women," *Pennsylvanian,* Nov. 9, 1970, 1; Nancy Hicks, "Women on College Faculties Are Pressing for Equal Pay and Better Positions in Academic Hierarchy," *New York Times,* Nov. 21, 1971, 41.

138   **"Don't try to make her":** Hans Smit, interview by author, March 31, 2008. Smit apparently did not attend the meeting, because his colleagues were aware of his long-time support of RBG's appointment.

138   **"We're not going":** RBG, interview by Grele, Aug. 18, 2004.

138   **If she could reach:** Michael Sovern, an extraordinarily talented son of working-class Jews in the Bronx and a full professor at Columbia Law School at the age of twenty-eight, would become president of Columbia in 1980. His delighted predecessor, in introducing Sovern, said, "What can I say [except that] Columbia kvells." McCaughey, *Stand, Columbia,* 518. Sovern's evident pleasure in RBG's appointment and the fact that as Law School dean he was one of "the barons" (the term used to refer to the powerful semiautonomous heads of prestigious professional schools) augured well for her future.

138   **Now he could afford:** RBG, interviews with author.

139   **"This child has two parents":** Nina Totenberg, "No, Ruth Bader Ginsburg Does Not Intend to Retire Anytime Soon," NPR, Oct. 3, 2016.

139   **Also, she felt she no longer:** Brenda Feigen sensed a special protectiveness on RBG's part toward James, which I attribute to the Drano accident in chap. 4. Brenda Feigen (attorney), interview by author, Los Angeles, Aug. 13, 2003. On Dalton School phone calls, see James Ginsburg, interview by author, July 30, 2003; also, RBG and Martin Ginsburg, interviews by author. On observation that she "over compensated tremendously" with Jane and "was much more relaxed" with James, especially in exposing them to music, see RBG, "Remarks," March 10, 2005, 29–30.

139   **"a far richer theory":** Cary Franklin, "The Anti-stereotyping Principle in Constitutional Sex Discrimination Law," *New York University Law Review* 85 (2010): 83–173.

139   **In addition, she had secured:** RBG, *My Own Words,* 115.

139   **"If you want something":** RBG, interviews by author.

139   **a "major coup" for the university:** Oelsner, "Columbia Law Snares a Prize in the Quest for Women Professors," A39.

139 **Congratulatory letters:** Richard S. Salzman to RBG, Jan. 26, 1972; Joyce and Bernard West and Gerry Arnson Lavner to RBG, Jan. 26, 1972; Weinstein to RBG, Jan. 26, 1972; Palmieri to RBG, Jan. 26, 1972; William J. McGill to RBG, Feb. 4 and April 12, 1972; and RBG to McGill, April 21, 1972, all in box 17, RBG Papers.

140 **"A number of lawyers":** McGill to RBG, Feb. 4, 1972, box 17, RBG Papers.

141 **But sensibilities on both:** RBG to McGill, Feb. 10, 1972, RBG Papers.

141 **With no admission of guilt:** The fullest account is Rosenberg, *Changing the Subject,* chap. 6. See also McCaughey, *Stand, Columbia,* chap. 18. The situation was complicated by the fact that record keeping at Columbia was much more haphazard than at Harvard or Chicago, making it difficult to compile the data Pottinger requested. Also, according to one of his associates, McGill "didn't give a damn about affirmative action," though he clearly cared about Columbia's financial situation. Quotation is in Rosenberg, *Changing the Subject,* 250. McCaughey notes that because of severe budgetary restraints only three women had been hired by 1993. Not until the more prosperous later 1990s would the proportion of women grow to 28 percent. Also see RBG, interview by Grele. RBG to McGill, March 1, 1972, box RG 1971–1972, McGill Papers.

141 **Some saw affirmative:** Anderson, *Pursuit of Fairness,* 143.

141 **Even Ruth's old friend:** Rosenberg, *Changing the Subject,* 254. On women as teachers of law, see Walter Gellhorn and Louis Henkin, who noted how effectively RBG had dispelled the myth. Gellhorn to RBG, March 15, 1983; and Henkin to RBG, March 15, 1983, both in RBG Birthday Book.

142 **When asked what:** Sovern, *Improbable Life,* chap. 6.

142 **"accessibility with demanding standards":** Raiffa, "In Memoriam: Albert M. Sacks," 16; and Rabb in Pam Lambert, "Ginsburg and Rabb: Setting Precedents," *Columbia* (Summer 1980): 11. On other professors whom RBG sought to emulate, see RBG, interview by Marcus, July 14, 1997, 13.

143 **Both young lawyers:** Accounts of the maids' firings are contained in undated, unidentified newspaper clippings in Subject Files, Columbia University Archives. See especially clipping with Joel Dreyfuss byline.

143 **Hoping that a resolution:** For more on Janice Goodman as attorney for maids, see Veteran Feminists of America Salutes Feminist Lawyers, 1963–75, www.vfa.us.

143 **"Now, dear":** RBG, interview by Grele.

144 **The university, on the other:** Ibid.; also, RBG, interviews by author.

144 **McGill responded positively:** RBG to McGill, Jan. 17, March 1 and 6, April 4, 1972; and McGill to RBG, March 14, 1972, box RG 1971–1972, McGill Papers.

144 **In the end:** RBG to Elizabeth Langer, April 12, 1972, RBG Papers; also, RBG, interviews by author.

SEVEN · A First Breakthrough

147 **The wound proved fatal:** Unless otherwise noted, this and the following paragraphs are based on Clare Cushman, *Supreme Court Decisions and Women's Rights,* chap. 6; also, Memorandum Decision and Order, *Reed v. Reed* (1968); *Reed v. Reed,* 94 Idaho 542 (1969); and Jurisdictional Statement by Melvin L. Wulf and Allen R. Derr (July 21, 1970), in *Reed v. Reed,* RBG Papers.

147 **"of several persons claiming":** Quoted in Linda K. Kerber, "November 22, 1971: Sally Reed Demands Equal Treatment," in Rubel, *Days of Destiny,* 442. *Reed v. Reed,* 404 U.S. 71 (1971), 92 S. Ct. 251, 30 L.Ed. 2d, 225.

148 **He agreed to appeal:** The Derr quotation is in Kerber, "November 22, 1971," 443. I am grateful to Kerber for sharing with me her telephone interview with Derr, which provided the basis for this information.

148 **"rationally related to a permissible":** *Reed v. Reed,* 404 U.S. 71, 92 S. Ct. 251, 30 L.Ed. 2d 225.

148 **But at the very least:** RBG, interviews by author.

149 **"for want of a substantial federal question":** This term is used when there is no federal law related to the issue of the case.

149 **Working with them:** On the ACLU's initial involvement in *Reed* and the division of labor, see Derr to Wulf, March 24, 1970; Wulf to Derr, April 2, 1970; and Wulf to Margaret [*sic*] W. Griffiths, Sept. 16, 1971, all in box 1645, ACLU Papers. The Jurisdictional Statement and Reply Brief are contained in the *Reed v. Reed* case file, RBG Papers. Wulf was assisted by the NYU Law School student Eve Cary.

150 **Ginsburg had translated:** Strebeigh, *Equal,* 34–35.

150 **"It should be noted":** *Korematsu v. United States,* 323 U.S. 214 (1944), 216.

151 **As a fallback position:** RBG, interview by author.

151 **Having taken over the writing of the brief:** On RBG's use of Murray's race-sex analogy, see Serena Mayeri's carefully calibrated contextualization of Murray's approach in the 1960s versus RBG's approach in the early 1970s, when ERA was viable and offered an opportunity for fine-tuning permissible sex-based classification. Mayeri, "'Common Fate of Discrimination,'" 1045–87.

151 **To clinch the argument:** This and the following paragraphs are based on Brief for the Appellant, Wulf et al., at 5, 51, 59, *Reed v. Reed,* 404 U.S. 71 (1971). RBG also made much of the California Supreme Court's use of the race-sex analogy in *Sail'er Inn Inc. v. Kirby,* 485 P.2d 529 (1971), quoting from the decision.

152 **Assuming that the Court:** Deborah L. Markowitz, "In Pursuit of Equality: One Woman's Work to Change the Law," *Women's Rights Law Reporter* 11 (1989): 79n72.

152 **"must be reasonable":** The 1920 case was *F. S. Royster Guano v. Virginia,* 253 U.S. 412 (1920). Italics mine. See also Strebeigh, *Equal,* 41.

152 **Ginsburg then wove:** On RBG's effort to deal with what would appear counterintuitive, see Linda Greenhouse, "Introduction: Learning to Listen to Ruth Bader Ginsburg," *New York City Law Review* 7 (2004): 213.

152 **"creates a 'suspect classification'":** Brief for the Appellant, Wulf et al., *Reed v. Reed,* 404 U.S. 71 (1971).

153 **"My generation owed them":** Strebeigh, *Equal.*

153 **"I thought it fitting to inform":** Wulf claimed that adding the two women's names was his idea. On the debt owed Kenyon and Murray, see RBG, "Constitutional Adjudication in the United States as a Means of Advancing the Equal Stature of Men and Women Under the Law," 267; and "Justice Ruth Bader Ginsburg Remembers," 11. The three law students who worked on the brief were Janice Goodman, Mary Kelly, and Ann E. Freedman. See Wulf to Goodman, Kelly, and Freedman, June 29, 1971, box 1645, ACLU Papers.

153 **When the four research:** RBG, "Remarks," March 10, 2005, 6; and RBG, Remarks for Panel Discussion on Current Topics in International Women's Rights, Association of the Bar of the City of New York, Dec. 13, 2003, 1, in possession of the author.

154 **"Such favors I don't need":** Birch Bayh to Wulf, Aug. 25, 1971; Wulf to RBG, July 15, 1971; and Wulf to Norman Redlich, July 1, 1971, all in box 1645, ACLU Papers. Redlich had reversed the first and second points of the ACLU brief on standard of scrutiny. See Brief of the City of New York, Amicus Curiae, *Reed v. Reed,* 404 U.S. 71.

154 **"the locker-room humor":** RBG to Wulf, March 2, 1971; and RBG to Leo Kanowitz, April 13, 1971, both in box 1645, ACLU Papers.

154 **"There is . . . the very important":** Wulf to Allen R. Derr, June 4, 1971, box 1645, Wulf Papers.

154 **A successful defense:** On Norton, see Gill, *African American Women in Congress,* 100–13.

154 **Highly regarded as a principled:** Norton's feminist consciousness had been carefully nurtured by Kenyon and Murray following her employment as a member of the ACLU legal staff in 1965, though, as Norton noted, her experience with racial discrimina-

tion made sex-based discrimination readily apparent. Hartmann, *Other Feminists,* esp. 182–85.

155   **"You . . . know that I so sincerely":** Derr to Sally Reed, Oct. 9, 1971, box 1645, ACLU Papers.

155   **Wulf was correct:** Myron H. Bright, "The Power of the Spoken Word: In Defense of Oral Argument," *Iowa Law Review* 72 (1986): 35–46; David C. Savage, "Saying the Right Thing," in Choper, *Supreme Court and Its Justices,* 469–70; Andrea McAtee and Kevin T. McGuire, "Lawyers, Justices, and Issue Salience: When and How Do Legal Arguments Affect the U.S. Supreme Court?," *Law and Society Review* 41 (2007): 259–78; and John Szmer, Susan W. Johnson, and Tammy A. Sarver, "Does *the* Lawyer Matter? Influencing Outcomes on the Supreme Court of Canada," *Law and Society Review* 41 (2007): 279–304. Wulf's views reflect the classic advice offered by Justice Robert H. Jackson in his "Advocacy Before the United States Supreme Court," *Cornell Law Quarterly* 37 (1951): 1–16.

155   **It demonstrated "total ignorance":** Wulf to RBG, July 15, 1971; Wulf to Martha W. Griffith, July 6 and Sept. 16, 1971; and Wulf to Derr, Oct. 21, 1971; all in box 1645, ACLU Papers.

155   **"Study the brief":** Wulf to Derr, Oct. 8, 1971, box 1645, ACLU Papers.

156   **The Idaho lawyer:** For the transcript of the oral arguments that occurred on October 19, 1971, see Records of the Supreme Court of the United States, "Transcripts of Oral Arguments, 1968–1978, 1980–1992," Oct. Term 1971, box 1, entry 17, *Reed v. Reed,* esp. 1–22, Record Group 267, National Archives.

156   **"the worst oral argument":** Goodman to Wulf, Oct. 20, 1971; Wulf to Derr, Oct. 21, 1971; both in box 1645, ACLU Papers. RBG to Gerald Gunther, Dec. 26, 1972, RBG Papers. Blackmun graded the argument a D and added that *Reed* was "the worst argued case I have heard up to here." He was only marginally more favorable to Cecil Reed's attorney, to whom the justice gave a D plus. Interestingly, however, Blackmun's initial reaction to the brief—no doubt influenced by some recent cases involving equal protection and national origin—was that the appellant's argument for strict scrutiny was a "compelling one." See Bench Memo, No. 70-4-ASX, *Reed v. Reed,* Blackmun Papers. See also Greenhouse, "Introduction," 213.

156   **Wulf had remained confident:** Wulf to RBG, July 19, 1971; and Martha W. Griffith to Wulf, both in box 1645, ACLU Papers.

156   **"simply superb pieces":** Aryeh Neier, "Reflections on Ruth Bader Ginsburg's Leadership of the ACLU Women's Rights Project," American Civil Liberties Union, www.aclu.org.

156   **"If Mrs. Reed does not win":** Griffiths to Wulf, July 6, 1971, box 1645, ACLU Papers.

157   **"My first reaction":** RBG to author, Oct. 10, 2000.

157   **A unanimous Court:** In reversing the decision, the Court sent the case back to Idaho to decide on the basis of merit which of the Reeds should serve as administrator. Ultimately, the Reeds agreed to serve as co-administrators.

157   **"To give a mandatory preference":** *Reed v. Reed,* 404 U.S. 71 (1971), 76.

157   **The narrowness of the decision:** Wulf, interview by author, Nov. 2, 2000.

157   **To move faster:** On the cultural, racial, and political cleavage of the 1970s, as well as division over the Vietnam War, there is extensive literature. See, for example, Chafe, *Unfinished Journey;* Matusow, *Unraveling of America;* Rieder, *Canarsie;* Hunter, *Culture Wars;* Edsall and Edsall, *Chain Reaction;* and Himmelstein, *To the Right.* Controversial Supreme Court decisions include *Griggs v. Duke Power Co.,* 401 U.S. 424 (1971); *Swann v. Charlotte-Mecklenburg County Board of Education,* 402 U.S. 1 (1971); and *New York Times v. United States, United States v. Washington Post,* 403 U.S. 713 (1971); *Roe v. Wade,* 410 U.S. 113 (1973), and *Doe v. Bolton,* 410 U.S. 179 (1973), were pending.

158   **No longer would the Court:** *Reed,* 404 U.S. at 76.

158 **The press, quick to report:** Fred P. Graham, "Court, for First Time, Overrules a State Law That Favors Men," *New York Times,* Nov. 23, 1971, A1; Nick Kotz, "High Court Voids State Law as Biased Against Women," *Washington Post,* Nov. 23, 1971, A1; Ronald J. Ostrow, "High Court Extends Rights of Women: Voids Laws Giving Men an Arbitrary Preference," *Los Angeles Times,* Nov. 23, 1971, A1; Associated Press, *Arizona Republic,* Nov. 23, 1971; "Top Court Voids Probate Sex Bias Law," *Chicago Tribune,* Nov. 23, 1971, A6; S. J. Micciche, "High Court Advances Women's Rights," *Boston Globe,* Nov. 23, 1971; "High Court Spurs Women's Rights," *Detroit Free Press,* Nov. 23, 1971; "Women Won with Legal Fight," *Kansas City Times,* Nov. 24, 1971; "Women and the Fourteenth," *New York Times,* Nov. 23, 1971, A40; and "Victory for Women and for Justices," *Los Angeles Times,* Nov. 24, 1971, B6.

158 **"a smidgen of equality":** "A Smidgen of Equality," *Boston Globe,* Nov. 24, 1971.

158 **"a small, guarded step":** For more of RBG's public comments, see manuscript draft of "Comment on *Reed v. Reed,*" *Women's Rights Law Reporter* (1972), RBG Papers; and RBG, "The Burger Court's Grapplings with Sex Discrimination," in Blasi, *Burger Court,* 135.

158 **Legal scholars concurred:** For a sampling of law review coverage, see Laurie Bier, "Constitutional Law—Equal Protection—Sex Based Classification—*Reed v. Reed,* 404 U.S. 71 (1971)," *Wisconsin Law Review* (1972): 626–33; Judith A. De Boisblanc, "Constitutional Law: The Equal Protection Clause and Women's Rights," *Loyola Law Review* 19 (1973): 542–51; John P. Murphy Jr., "The *Reed* Case: The Seed for Equal Protection from Sex-Based Discrimination, or Polite Judicial Hedging?," *Akron Law Review* 5 (1972): 251–63; and "Recent Cases: Constitutional Law—Equal Protection—State Probate Code Discriminating in Favor of Males Violate Equal Protection Clause," *Vanderbilt Law Review* 25 (1972): 412–18. For the most astute assessment of the direction of the Court on equal protection following *Reed,* see Gerald Gunther, "The Supreme Court, 1971 Term—Foreword: In Search of Evolving Doctrine on a Changing Court: A Model for a Newer Equal Protection," *Harvard Law Review* 86 (1972). 1–306.

158 **However, to ignore:** RBG to Elizabeth Langer, April 12, 1972, RBG Papers.

159 **Others applied *Reed* narrowly:** Compare *Moritz v. Commissioner of Internal Revenue,* 469 F.2d 466 (10th Cir. 1972), with *Schattman v. Texas Employment Commission,* 459 F.2d 32 (5th Cir. 1972).

159 **"What *Reed* has wrought!":** See Gunther, "Foreword: In Search of Evolving Doctrine on a Changing Court," 17–48. A lower federal court relied on the ruling to invalidate, on constitutional grounds, guidelines issued under a federal job-training program that gave top priority to unemployed men while relegating women with preschool children to the bottom of the list. An Idaho law declaring the husband to be head of the family, with the right to determine where it lives, soon toppled. Several months later, a state court in Washington used the case for an even broader decision. Justice Marshall signaled his interpretation of *Reed* in his dissent in *San Antonio Independent School District et al. v. Rodriguez,* 411 U.S. 1 (1973), esp. 107. In *Reed,* the justices had "resorted to a more stringent standard of equal protection review." The Court, Marshall noted, was "unwilling to consider a theoretical and unsubstantiated basis for distinction—however reasonable it might appear—sufficient to sustain a statute discriminating on the basis of sex." In *Eisenstadt v. Baird,* 405 U.S. 438 (1972), a case involving a Massachusetts law restricting sales of contraceptives, Brennan explained why the Court had used the rational relationship test in *Reed*—not because it rejected sex as a suspect classification, but because the Idaho statute in question was so clearly invalid even under the more lenient standard of review. Other cases cited in RBG, "Comment on *Reed v. Reed,*" *Women's Rights Law Reporter* (1972), RBG Papers. RBG to Wulf, Feb. 7, 1973, RBG Papers.

EIGHT · Setting Up Shop and Strategy

160 **"no files, no staff"**: RBG, interviews by author.

160 **"the premier philanthropy"**: Neier, *Taking Liberties,* xxviii–xxix. Quotation in Hartmann, *Other Feminists,* 143.

161 **According to foundation policy:** Neier, *Taking Liberties,* xxviii–xxix; and RBG, interviews by author.

161 **Nor did Ginsburg:** Neier, *Taking Liberties,* 84; and RBG, interviews by author. RBG had included reproductive rights as one of six targeted areas in her initial memo outlining the project's objectives. For a classic statement that "the basic element of the rights of women is reproductive freedom of choice," see Pilpel's comments in her keynote speech for Myra Bradwell Day at Columbia Law School, April 8, 1980, at which both Pilpel and RBG spoke. See "Myra Bradwell Day Forum Held at Law School," Columbia University Law School, 1980, clipping in box 46, Biographical Files, RBG Papers.

161 **He was one of the most:** RBG, interviews by author. RBG regarded the criticism directed at the project for having taken money from the Playboy Foundation as the least of her worries. For her response, see RBG, "Equality for Women," *Playboy,* Sept. 1973, 52; and Harriet F. Pilpel, "Contraception and Freedom," *Playboy,* Jan. 1969, 51, and Harriet F. Pilpel, "Abortion Laws Challenged," *Playboy,* April 1970, 60. I thank Leigh Ann Wheeler for calling this correspondence to my attention.

161 **In ideology, style:** Feigen, *Not One of the Boys,* 1–71; and Wulf, interview by author, Nov. 2, 2000.

162 **Young feminist attorneys:** Brenda Feigen, interview by author, Aug. 13, 2003; M. E. Freeman and Lynn Hecht Schafran (attorneys), interviews by author, March 2, 2007; and Kathleen Peratis (attorney), interview by author, Nov. 3, 2003. Peratis, "Address of Kathleen Peratis on the Occasion of a Celebration of Twenty Years on the Bench of Hon. Ruth Bader Ginsburg and Unveiling of Her Portrait, November 3, 2000." (Cited hereafter as Peratis, "Address on RBG Portrait Dedication.") I am grateful to Peratis for giving me a copy of her remarks.

163 **"WOMEN WORKING":** "Tribute: The Legacy of Ruth Bader Ginsburg and WRP Staff," American Civil Liberties Council, March 7, 2006.

163 **What she had not expected:** RBG, interview by author. The children of Peratis and Susan Deller Ross were the first so-called ACLU babies. RBG and Sandra Day O'Connor would later attempt to make the Supreme Court a bit more family friendly for clerks, male and female.

163 **And it did, though:** Peratis, "Address on RBG Portrait Dedication."

163 **female *"sanctum sanctorum"*:** "Tribute: The Legacy of Ruth Bader Ginsburg and WRP Staff."

164 **"head is in the law":** Peratis, "Address on RBG Portrait Dedication"; see also Feigen's recollection in David Von Drehle, "Ruth Bader Ginsburg: Her Life and Law," *Washington Post,* July 19, 1993, 1, 3, 4–5. RBG's clerks also noted the extraordinary work environment she created. Indeed, Peratis voices similar sentiments expressed by Susan H. Williams and David Williams, "Sense and Sensibility: Justice Ruth Bader Ginsburg's Mentoring Style as a Blend of Rigor and Compassion," *University of Hawaii Law Review* 20 (Winter 1998): 589–93.

164 **"We whom she mentored":** Peratis, "Address on RBG Portrait Dedication."

164 **"[She] spoke to us":** M. E. Freeman, interview by author, March 2, 2007. For comments in a similar vein from RBG students and co-workers—all attorneys—see author's interviews with Lynn Hecht Schafran, March 2, 2007; Jane Booth, March 1, 2007; Kathleen Peratis, Nov. 3, 2003; Susan Reiger, March 1, 2007; and Brenda Feigen, Aug. 13, 2003. See also "Tribute: The Legacy of Ruth Bader Ginsburg and WRP Staff" for comments by Jill Goodman and Margaret Moses.

164 **"rare, radiant smile"**: "Professor Gerald Gunther Speaks at Investiture of Judge Ruth Ginsburg in Washington, D.C.," 8–9.

165 **When Ginsburg put down:** Author interviews with Freeman, March 2, 2007; Schafran, March 2, 2007; Booth, March 1, 2007; Peratis, Nov. 3, 2003; Reiger, March 1, 2007; and Feigen, Aug. 13, 2003.

165 **"I don't know if I fully":** Freeman, interview by author, March 2, 2007.

165 **"I just wanted to do":** Sandra Pullman, "Tribute: The Legacy of Ruth Bader Ginsburg at WRP Staff," ACLU.org.

165 **"We were all in awe":** Feigen, *Not One of the Boys*, 73; Feigen, interview by author; and RBG, interviews by author.

166 **More important, where:** Quotation in Jeffries, *Justice Lewis F. Powell Jr.*, 503. According to Jeffries, Sandra Day O'Connor was the first professional woman Powell came to know as a peer. Their friendship became quite close, although Powell apparently never really understood the extent or impact of the sex-based discrimination she had experienced because things had come so easily to him. See ibid., 502–11.

166 **"has all but recaptured":** Abraham, *Justices, Presidents, and the Supreme Court*, chap. 11.

166 **Specifically, this meant limiting:** William H. Rehnquist (assistant attorney general) to Leonard Garment (special counsel to the president), memo, reprinted in "Rehnquist: ERA Would Threaten Family Unit," *Legal Times*, Sept. 15, 1986. I am indebted to Reva Siegel for calling the memo to my attention. For evidence of Rehnquist's conservative views on *Brown* and other matters, see Tushnet, *Court Divided*, 13–31; also, Perry, *"Supremes,"* chap. 1.

166 **"I cannot help but think":** Abraham, *Justices, Presidents, and Senators*, 15–16.

167 **The ACLU had made:** Ibid., 204–7; and Urofsky, *Continuity of Change*, chap. 1.

167 **And he had been a vote for** *Reed:* "Profiles of the Justices," in Blasi, *Burger Court*, 239–55; Robert Henry, "The Players and the Play," in Schwartz, *Burger Court*; and Urofsky, *Continuity of Change*, chap. 1. Also, Hutchinson, *Man Who Once Was Whizzer White*.

168 **"A constitutional right":** House Committee on Armed Services, *Registration of Women: Hearings on H.R. 6569*, CIS-NO: 81-H201-15, 1980, 131. On traditionalist women's apprehensions about gender equality, see my co-authored book with Mathews, *Sex, Gender, and the Politics of ERA*, chap. 6. On "gendered imagination," see Kessler-Harris, *In Pursuit of Equity*, 5–6.

168 **Teague's certainty:** Quotation in Mathews and De Hart, *Sex, Gender, and the Politics of ERA*, 40.

168 **"Sam did not":** Ibid., chap. 2, on Ervin's testimony. RBG would have been familiar with his views inasmuch as the hearing occurred in 1970.

168 **"The response I got":** On the response that women have it better, see, among others, RBG, "Foreword to the Symposium: Women, Justice, and Authority," *Yale Journal of Law and Feminism* 14 (2002): 214–15. I have followed her wording closely. Jones, "Columbia's Leader in Legal Battle Against Sex-Based Discrimination," 14.

169 **"reconsider attitudes and values":** For excellent discussions of RBG's reliance on race-based constitutional law versus Title VII cases, see Kathleen M. Sullivan, "Constitutionalizing Women's Equality," *University of California Law Review* 90 (2000): 735–65; and Mary Anne Case, " 'The Very Stereotype the Law Condemns': Constitutional Sex Discrimination Law as the Search for Perfect Proxies," *Cornell Law Review* 85 (2000): 1447. RBG was certainly familiar with the Title VII case *Phillips v. Martin Marietta Corp.*, 400 U.S. 542 (1971), because, at the time, she was working on *Reed*. See RBG to Wulf, March 2, 1971, box 1645, ACLU Papers. See also Michael C. Dorf, "The Paths to Legal Equality: A Reply to Dean Sullivan," *University of California Law Review* 90 (May 2002): 791–813.

169 **But with only one EEOC case:** *Phillips,* 400 U.S. 542; and Mary Becker, "The Sixties Shift to Formal Equality and the Courts: An Argument for Pragmatism and Politics," *William and Mary Law Review* 40 (1998): 209–77.

170 **"constant dialogue":** Quoted in Jones, "Columbia's Leader in Legal Battle Against Sex-Based Discrimination," 14; and Stephanie B. Goldberg, "The Second Woman Justice: Ruth Bader Ginsburg," *ABA Journal* (Oct. 1993): 40–43.

170 **Here she would rely:** RBG, "Brown v. Board of Education in International Context," *Columbia Human Rights Law Review* 36 (2005): 500.

170 **Precedents already established:** Ibid.; and RBG, "Burger Court's Grapplings with Sex Discrimination," 135. For other sources that deal with initial decisions on litigation strategy, case selection, and her role as litigator/educator, see RBG, ACLU Women's Rights Project Prospectus, RBG Papers; Jones, "Columbia's Leader in Legal Battle Against Sex-Based Discrimination," 13–15.

171 **"Mr. Civil Rights":** Sandra Day O'Connor, "Thurgood Marshall: The Influence of a Raconteur," *Stanford Law Review* 44 (1992): 1220. Tushnet, *Making Constitutional Law;* Glen M. Darbyshire, "Clerking for Justice Marshall," *ABA Journal* (Sept. 1991): 48–51; and Klebanow and Jonas, *People's Lawyers.*

171 **That could promote the personal:** Neier, "Reflections on Ruth Bader Ginsburg's Leadership of the ACLU Women's Rights Project."

171 **In the absence of "original intent":** Feigen, *Not One of the Boys,* 75.

172 **"Justice," as Justice Benjamin:** Philip Marshall Brown, "The Codification of International Law," *American Journal of International Law* 29 (Jan. 1935): 32.

172 **"nudges" rather than "earthquakes":** In a hastily prepared prospectus for the project, which RBG compiled so that Neier would have something on paper at the time of her appointment, she listed six categories for litigation, although she knew at the time that choices would be informed by what was in the pipeline. See RBG, interview by author.

172 **The only way the solicitor:** On Griswold, see RBG, interview by Marcus, Aug. 8, 1996, 32, 26.

172 **In fact, he had previously:** Griswold to Murray, Jan. 31, 1963, box 49, folder 878, Murray Papers. Murray and Griswold both had strong ties to the NAACP, for which he served as an expert witness in *Brown v. Board of Education.*

172 **Surely he had to know:** RBG, "Remarks for Woodrow Wilson International Center for Scholars," May 21, 2002, RBG Papers. On Griswold's intentions, see RBG, interview by author, July 1, 2003; and Martin D. Ginsburg, interview by author, July 1, 2003.

173 **Either way, the appeals process:** RBG, interview by author; and Neier, "Reflections on Ruth Bader Ginsburg's Leadership of the ACLU Women's Rights Project," 1.

174 **Less than a third:** On changing public opinion, see Klein, *Gender Politics,* 90–93.

174 **the "New Nixon" emerged:** Neither the Equal Pay Act nor the Civil Rights Act was passed because of egalitarian feelings toward women. With respect to the former, male unionists backed legislation providing equal pay for the same work on the assumption that if employers had to pay women the same wages for the same work, the jobs would go to men. For background on the Civil Rights Act, see chap. 5 and Kessler-Harris, *Woman's Wage.* The settlement with AT&T in January 1973 prompted RBG to predict that "most companies will take [EEOC] guidelines a little more seriously now." See "Ma Bell Agrees to Pay Reparations," *Newsweek,* Jan. 20, 1973, 53–54. The term "New Nixon" refers to Nixon policies that echoed the more statesmanlike side of his contradictory personality.

174 **"radicals in robes":** I use "radicals in robes" to refer to the feminist Left, not to the fundamentalist Right, about whom Cass Sunstein writes in his *Radicals in Robes.*

174 **There were now more feminist:** Numbers remained small in all categories. Although Douglas hired his first female clerk in 1944–45, clerkships began to open when Black hired a woman in 1961, with Fortas and Marshall following. White and Rehnquist

hired their first female clerks in 1972. See RBG, "The First Female Law Clerks," in Clare Cushman, *Supreme Court Decisions and Women's Rights*, 236–37.

175 **Five journals devoted:** Fannie J. Klein, "Review Urged of Law Curriculum for Women," *New York Law Journal* 26 (1972): S9; Kerber, "Writing Our Own Rare Books," 429–51; also, RBG's remarks at the AALS, "Treatment of Women by the Law: Awakening Consciousness in the Law Schools," *Valparaiso University Law Review* 5 (1971): 480–88. Cowan, "Women's Rights Through Litigation," 373–412, esp. 377n17.

175 **In December 1970:** The only holdout was Virginia's Washington and Lee University.

175 **For those enrolling in the 1970s:** Sassower, "Women in the Law," 4; Roger M. Williams, "Law Schools: The Big Women Boom," *Saturday Review*, Sept. 21, 1974, 51–54; and RBG, "Introduction to Women and the Law—a Symposium," 1–11, esp. 7.

175 **Yet she was convinced:** RBG, interviews by author.

175 **"clearly planned" litigation:** Neier, "Reflections on Ruth Bader Ginsburg's Leadership of the ACLU Women's Rights Project," 1.

176 **"Ruth rode freely":** Feigen, *Not One of the Boys*, 75.

176 **"was making it up":** Jones, "Columbia's Leader in Legal Battle Against Sex-Based Discrimination," 14.

176 **"began as 'The World's Greatest' ":** Allen Axelrod to RBG, March 15, 1983, RBG Birthday Book.

<h2 style="text-align:center">NINE · "The Case That Got Away"</h2>

179 **Air force regulations:** Brief for Petitioner at 4–5, *Susan R. Struck v. Secretary of Defense*, 409 U.S. 1071 (1972).

179 **"The commission of any woman":** Quoted in Clare Cushman, *Supreme Court Decisions and Women's Rights*, 180.

180 **She had only one recourse:** Brief for Petitioner at 1–2, *Struck*, 409 U.S. 1071.

180 **Ginsburg thought "long and hard":** Quotation in *Hearings on Ruth Bader Ginsburg to Be Associate Justice of the Supreme Court of the United States*, Senate Judiciary Committee, 103rd Cong., 1st sess. (1993), 206.

180 ***Struck*, Ginsburg concluded:** Brief for Petitioner at 55, *Struck*, 409 U.S. 1071.

180 **unique physical characteristics:** Murray and Eastwood, "Jane Crow and the Law," 240n49.

180 **Worries that the ERA:** ERA strategists no doubt had in mind the objections of Senator Samuel J. Ervin, who believed that special treatment was a corollary of what he called "physiological and functional" differences between the sexes and who used every tactic at his command to preserve the traditional gender order. See Mathews and De Hart, *Sex, Gender, and the Politics of ERA*, chap. 2, n18. For an excellent treatment of this issue, see Reva B. Siegel, "Constitutional Culture, Social Movement Conflict, and Constitutional Change: The Case of the De Facto ERA," *University of California Law Review* 94 (2006): esp. 1360–65.

181 **Otherwise, the "unique physical characteristics":** Barbara A. Brown et al., "The Equal Rights Amendment: A Constitutional Basis for Equal Rights for Women," *Yale Law Journal* 5 (1971): 893–96; RBG, "Status of Women," 585, 589.

182 **Or they may seek:** See Brief for Planned Parenthood Federation of America, Aug. 11, 1971, esp. at 10–11, 30, 32, 34, *Roe v. Wade*, 410 U.S. 113 (1973), and *Doe v. Bolton*, 410 U.S. 179 (1973). Also, Brief Amicus Curiae on Behalf of New Women Lawyers et al., Aug. 2, 1971, at 7, *Roe*, 410 U.S. 113, and *Doe*, 410 U.S. 179.

182 **To do so, Ginsburg maintained:** Brief for Petitioner at 55, *Struck*, 409 U.S. 1071.

182 **In New York City:** Reagan, *When Abortion Was a Crime*. Also, Solinger, *The Abortionist*.

182 **Though motivated differently:** Environmentalists, worried about the effects of "population explosion" and the limitations of birth control, also viewed abortion bans as too

restrictive. Joffe, *Doctors of Conscience;* and Staggenborg, *Pro-choice Movement,* 13–28. On public opinion, see Judith Blake, "Abortion and Public Opinion: The 1960–1970 Decade," *Science,* Feb. 12, 1971, 540–49. Liberalization of abortion laws was occurring simultaneously in Europe. On why European abortion policy has been less divisive than in the United States, see Helene Silverberg, "State Building, Health Policy, and the Persistence of the American Abortion Debate," *Journal of Policy History* 9 (1997): 311–38.

183 **With legislative reform stalled:** Garrow, *Liberty and Sexuality,* 277, 341–42.

183 **"There is only one voice":** Betty Friedan, "Abortion: A Woman's Civil Right," reprinted in Greenhouse and Siegel, *Before Roe v. Wade,* 38–40.

183 **Initial lawsuits focused:** *People v. Belous,* 71 Cal.2d 954 (1969), and *United States v. Vuitch,* 402 U.S. 62 (1971).

183 **Although the New York:** Reva Siegel, "*Roe's* Roots: The Women's Rights Claims That Engendered *Roe,*" *Boston University Law Review* 90 (2010): 1875–907.

184 **the Supreme Court agreed in 1971:** Garrow, *Liberty and Sexuality,* esp. chap. 8; Weddington, *Question of Choice.*

184 **Margie Hames, a member:** *Doe v. Bolton,* 319 F. Supp. 1048 (1970). On Hames joining *Doe,* see Garrow, *Liberty and Sexuality,* 424–25.

184 **The argument for the right:** RBG to Wulf.

184 **What troubled Ginsburg:** Building on Justice Douglas's privacy rationale in a 1965 Connecticut birth control case (*Griswold v. Connecticut,* 381 U.S. 535 [1965]) and coupling it with Justice Harlan's dissent in a prior birth control case reclaiming substantive due process (*Poe v. Ullman,* 367 U.S. 497 [1961]), Roy Lucas, a young New York University graduate, had developed a model abortion brief supported by the ACLU among others. See Roy Lucas, "Federal Constitutional Limitations on the Enforcement and Administration of State Abortion Statutes," *North Carolina Law Review* 46 (1968): 730–78. On the model brief, see Garrow, *Liberty and Sexuality,* 352–53.

184 **As the controversy over Brown:** That Douglas's privacy rationale in *Griswold* had been combined with revived substantive due process in abortion arguments might also have made the privacy argument seem more vulnerable to RBG. It is hard to imagine that she would not have also known that other young feminist lawyers—among them New York's Nancy Stearns—were already making equality claims in abortion cases, tying them to a range of provisions in the Constitution, including equal protection. See also Greenhouse and Siegel, *Before Roe v. Wade,* esp. 140–47. See Brief of Amici Curiae Human Rights for Women Inc. at 11–12, *United States v. Vuitch,* 402 U.S. 62 (1971); Brief of Amici Curiae Joint Washington Office for Social Concerns et al. at 10–11, *Vuitch* 402 U.S. 62; and Brief of Amici Curiae New Women Lawyers et al. at 24–32, *Roe v. Wade,* 410 U.S. 113 (1973).

185 **When Justice Blackmun's initial draft:** See Yarbrough, *Harry A. Blackmun,* chap. 7.

185 **"Until very recent years":** Brief for Petitioner at 9, *Captain Susan R. Struck v. Secretary of Defense,* 409 U.S. 1071 (1972).

186 **"legitimate and compelling interest":** Opposition to Memorandum for the Respondents Suggesting Mootness at 1, *Struck,* 409 U.S. 1071.

186 **As applied, the regulations:** Brief for Petitioner, *Struck,* 409 U.S. 1071, for arguments in this and the following paragraphs.

186 **"opportunity for training":** Ibid., 35, 36. See also 52. RBG, "Speaking in a Judicial Voice," *New York University Law Review* 67, no. 6 (1992): 1205, 1208.

187 **Regulations that disregarded:** Brief for Petitioner at 11, 36, *Struck,* 409 U.S. 1071.

187 **It dispelled later criticism:** Judith Baer, "Advocate on the Court: Ruth Bader Ginsburg and the Limits of Formal Equality," in Maltz, *Rehnquist Justice,* 216–40.

188 **And it would be another seven:** Owen Fiss, "Groups and the Equal Protection Clause," *Philosophy and Public Affairs* 5 (1976): 107–77. MacKinnon, *Sexual Harassment of Working Women.* On additional merits of the *Struck* brief, see Neil S. Siegel and Reva

B. Siegel, "Struck by Stereotype: Ruth Bader Ginsburg on Pregnancy Discrimination as Sex Discrimination," *Duke Law Journal* 59 (2010): 771–98.

188 **What she did not anticipate:** RBG, interview by author.

189 **Trying to accommodate:** Exchanges went back and forth from the offices of Marshall and Brennan to Blackmun over the point at which state regulation should begin. See box 281, Brennan Papers; and box 150, Powell Papers.

189 **That right is broad enough:** *Roe v. Wade,* 410 U.S. 113 (1973), 162.

189 **Further, abortion could not:** *Doe v. Bolton,* 410 U.S. 179 (1973).

190 **"sweeping invalidation of any restriction":** *Roe,* 410 U.S. esp. at 221 for White and 171 for Rehnquist dissents.

190 **"It scaled the whole mountain":** Quotations in Garrow, *Liberty and Sexuality,* 603. On criticism from the legal academy, the most scathing attack came from John Hart Ely, "The Wages of Crying Wolf: A Comment on *Roe v. Wade,*" *Yale Law Journal* 82 (1973): 920–49.

190 **"abortion should not be a matter":** Quoted in Blake, "Abortion and Public Opinion," 540–49.

190 **But apart from circumstances:** Surveys by National Opinion Research Center, in Ladd and Bowman, *Public Opinion About Abortion,* 25. At the time *Roe* was decided, only fourteen states had adopted "reform" laws, and only four had passed "repeal" statutes, legalizing abortion. See Rachel Benson Gold, "Lessons from Before Roe: Will Past Be Prologue?," *Guttmacher Report on Public Policy* 6 (2003): 9.

190 **Catholic bishops had led:** On the Roman Catholic Church's position, see, for example, John T. Noonan Jr., "Abortion and the Catholic Church," *Natural Law Forum* 12 (1967): 85–131.

191 **Right-wing organizers:** "The family" for social conservatives meant the patriarchal, heterosexual, nuclear family defined by the formal relationship of marriage and a gendered division of labor. There is a huge body of literature, both academic and popular, on the contemporary family "crisis" and substantial scholarship on social conservatives' definition of family. See, for example, Judith Stacey, "The Right Family Values," in Lo and Schwartz, *Social Policy and the Conservative Agenda.* It should be noted, however, that not all "pro-lifers" were "family values" conservatives. The National Right to Life coalition also contained a socially "progressive" contingent that included Feminists for Life.

191 **Anticipating a barrage of cases:** The justice no longer recalls the incident. Considering how passionately she believed in a women's equality approach to reproductive rights, as indeed Aryeh Neier did, the request seems entirely plausible. See his *Taking Liberties,* 81–85. He resolved the problem by creating the Reproductive Freedom Project headed by Janet Benshoof. He notes, however, that subsequently the Ford Foundation would mistakenly claim proudly that both were directed by RBG. See ibid., xxviii, n4.

191 **Given her decidedly mixed:** Ibid., 80–83; and Judith Mears, "Taking Liberties," *Civil Liberties Review* 1 (1974): 136.

191 **"the single most important":** RBG to Pinzler et al., memo, May 21, 1979, 3, RBG-ACLU.

192 **"placed the woman alone":** RBG, "Some Thoughts on Autonomy and Equality in Relation to *Roe v. Wade,*" *North Carolina Law Review* 63 (1985): 373–86, quotation at 382, 383; and RBG, "Speaking in a Judicial Voice," 1185–209.

192 **"her full life's course":** RBG, "Some Thoughts on Autonomy and Equality in Relation to *Roe v. Wade,*" 383.

192 **Ginsburg also questioned Blackmun's:** Ibid., 381–82.

192 **Anchoring the abortion:** Ibid., 375.

192 **As written, she feared:** RBG, "Speaking in a Judicial Voice," 1205, 1208.

193 **"The rhetoric of privacy":** Sylvia Law, "Rethinking Sex and the Constitution," *University of Pennsylvania Law Review* 132 (1984): 1020. See, among others, Rhonda

Copelon, "Beyond the Liberal Idea of Privacy: Toward a Positive Right of Autonomy," in McCann and Houseman, *Judging the Constitution,* 287–314, esp. 304–5; Catharine A. MacKinnon, "Reflections on Sex Equality Under the Law," *Yale Law Journal* 100 (1991): 1281–328, esp. 1292; Catharine A. MacKinnon, "Roe v. Wade: A Study in Male Ideology," in Garfield and Hennessey, *Abortion,* 45–54; Reva Siegel, "Reasoning from the Body: A Historical Perspective on Abortion Regulation and Questions of Equal Protection," *Stanford Law Review* 44 (1992): 261–381; Kenneth L. Karst, "Equal Citizenship Under the Fourteenth Amendment," *Harvard Law Review* 91 (1977): 1–68, esp. 59; Sunstein, *Partial Constitution,* 258–61, esp. 270–85; and West, *Progressive Constitutionalism,* 199–200, 268–73.

193 **To do so, they feared:** "E.R.A. Means Abortion and Population Shrinkage," *Phyllis Schlafly Report,* Dec. 1974, clipping in carton 4, NARAL Papers.

193 **Beginning with *Maher:*** *Maher v. Roe,* 432 U.S. 464 (1977); *Beal v. Doe,* 432 U.S. 438 (1977); and *Poelker v. Doe,* 432 U.S. 519 (1977). Connecticut, Pennsylvania, and Missouri had stringent antiabortion laws prior to *Roe.* Justices Blackmun, Marshall, and Brennan vigorously dissented, viewing the bans as blatant efforts to undermine *Roe.*

193 **The Court considered the ban:** *Harris v. McRae,* 448 U.S. 297 (1980), and RBG, note to author, Aug. 18, 2008.

194 **She also knew that the concern:** *Maher,* 432 U.S. 464; *Beal,* 432 U.S. 438; and *Poelker,* 432 U.S. 519. .

194 **By 1982, Catholics:** Jacoby, *Souls, Bodies, Spirits;* Blanchard, *Anti-abortion Movement and the Rise of the Religious Right;* Cook, Jelan, and Wilcon, *Between Two Absolutes;* and Hunter, *Before the Shooting Begins,* chaps. 2–3.

194 **Ginsburg's "criticisms of *Roe*":** Kate Michelman quotation on tapes for the *Evening News,* ABC and NBC, June 14, 1993, Vanderbilt University Television News Archives, Nashville. These sentiments were so widely shared in feminist and pro-choice circles that President Clinton decided to read RBG's two law journal articles critiquing *Roe* himself before deciding to nominate her to the Court, rather than relying on staff. Once he read them, it was clear to the president, as to other careful readers, that RBG's criticism was directed at Blackmun's majority decision, not at the right to an abortion. See Toobin, *Nine,* 71.

194 **Ginsburg's alternative scenario:** See, for example, Rosemary Nossiff, "Why Justice Ginsburg Is Wrong About States Expanding Abortion Rights," *P.S.: Political Science and Politics* 27 (1994): 227–31; also, Nossiff, *Before Roe.* The point is also made by Helen Neuborne, executive director of the NOW Legal Defense and Educational Fund, and Marcy Wilder, senior staff lawyer for NARAL, among others. See Linda Greenhouse, "Judge Ginsburg Still Voices Strong Doubts on Rationale Behind Roe v. Wade Ruling," *New York Times,* June 16, 1993, A1; David J. Garrow, "History Lesson for the Judge: What Clinton's Supreme Court Nominee Doesn't Know About Roe," *Washington Post,* June 20, 1993, C3; and David J. Garrow, "Abortion Before and After *Roe v. Wade:* An Historical Perspective," *Albany Law Review* 62 (1999): 833–52. See also Kathleen M. Sullivan, "Law's Labor," *New Republic,* March 23, 1994, 42, 44; and Devins, *Shaping Constitutional Values.*

195 **"Justice Douglas":** Justice Harry A. Blackmun, interviewed by Justice Harry A. Blackmun Oral History Project, July 6, 1994–Dec. 13, 1999, 202, 505, JHBOHP; and Roe v. Wade Miscellany, folder 2, box 152, Blackmun Papers.

195 **"would have been regarded":** Quoted in Balkin, *What Roe v. Wade Should Have Said,* 252, 254.

195 **"virtual absence of judicial protection":** Neier, *Taking Liberties,* 84.

195 **Stearns, in fact, had advanced:** See excerpts from Plaintiffs Brief, *Abramovicz v. Lefkowitz,* in Greenhouse and Siegel, *Before Roe v. Wade,* esp. 140–47.

195 **NOW also provided:** Brief Amicus Curiae for the AAUW et al., Aug. 10, 1971, at 37, *Roe v. Wade* and *Doe v. Bolton.*

195 **Most significantly, Judge:** See Memorandum of Decision, *Abele v. Markle,* in Greenhouse and Siegel, *Before Roe v. Wade,* 177–82.

195 **"There was a disconnect":** Linda Greenhouse, "How the Supreme Court Talks About Abortion: The Implications of a Shifting Discourse," *Suffolk University Law Review* 42 (2008): 42, 45–46.

195 **But it is difficult:** Balkin, *What Roe v. Wade Should Have Said.*

196 **Ginsburg, however, clung:** RBG maintained her belief that had *Struck* been heard, it "would have proved extraordinarily educational for the Court and had large potential for advancing public understanding." See RBG, "Speaking in a Judicial Voice," 1200, 1202.

196 **Wishful thinking was a possibility:** Ibid., 1200.

196 **More apparent, too, might:** *Planned Parenthood of Southeastern Pennsylvania v. Casey,* 505 U.S. 833 (1992), a rare joint opinion put together by Justices Sandra Day O'Connor, David Souter, and Anthony Kennedy, affirms the right of abortion choice as a right of personhood and self-definition. Yet the opinion also upholds the right of the states to place restrictions on abortion so long as the requirements do not place an "undue burden" on women seeking an abortion before the fetus attains viability. Siegel and Siegel note several cases that would have come out differently in "Struck by Stereotype," 792–94n44.

196 **"*Roe* rage" was about:** The term is drawn from Robert Post and Reva Siegel, "*Roe* Rage: Democratic Constitutionalism and Backlash," *Harvard Civil Rights–Civil Liberties Law Review* (2007): 373–433.

196 **"as though they had been disowned":** Quoted in William N. Eskridge Jr., "Pluralism and Distrust: How Courts Can Support Democracy by Lowering the Stakes of Politics," *Yale Law Journal* 14 (2005): 1312.

196 **"I have nightmare visions":** Phyllis Zatlin Boring to RBG, n.d., RBG Papers.

TEN · A "Near Great Leap Forward"

197 **"Our idea," she explained:** For quotation and information on the Frontieros, see Clare Cushman, *Supreme Court Decisions and Women's Rights,* chap. 3.

198 **Described by Dees:** Dees, *Season for Justice,* 129–32.

198 **Specializing in what:** "Joseph Levin, Southern Poverty Law Center," Spoke, www.spoke.com.

198 **It was Johnson and Rives:** See Bass, *Unlikely Heroes;* Bass, *Taming the Story.*

198 **But this time the two men:** Johnson and McFadden were district court judges. Rives, a circuit judge on the U.S. Court of Appeals for the Fifth Circuit, sat on the panel by designation.

199 **This was not the end:** On the deliberations of the panel, see Serena Mayeri, "'When the Trouble Started': The Story of *Frontiero v. Richardson,*" in Schneider and Wildman, *Women and the Law Stories.*

199 **"a fair and substantial relation":** *F. S. Royster Guano v. Virginia,* 253 U.S. 412 (1920), 415.

199 **They would have to make:** RBG, interviews by author. On Morgan, see Walker, *In Defense of American Liberties,* 262–93.

200 **Then, with her usual dispatch:** RBG to Abernathy and Levin, Oct. 16, 1972, RBG Papers.

200 **"Nixonian low profile":** Levin to Wulf, Oct. 17, 1972, RBG Papers.

200 **"It was not a good strategy":** Abernathy to Brenda Feigen Fasteau, Oct. 19, 1972, RBG Papers.

201 **"Some things don't change":** RBG, notes to author, July 18, 2000.

201 **"It's our first opportunity":** Levin to Wulf, Oct. 17, 1971, RBG Papers.

201 **"I am not very good":** RBG to Levin, Oct. 24, 1972, RBG Papers.

201 **"I find myself trying"**: Levin to RBG, Oct. 27, 1972, RBG Papers.

201 **If all he wanted were**: RBG to Levin, Oct. 31, 1972, RBG Papers.

201 **"Frustrated"**: RBG used "frustrated" to characterize her response in an interview with author.

202 **"a question that need not"**: Appellant's Brief at 29n21, 36, *Frontiero v. Richardson,* 411 U.S. 677 (1973).

202 **She began her brief**: For this and the following paragraphs, see Brief Amicus Curiae of American Civil Liberties Union for the Appellants, *Frontiero v. Laird,* 409 U.S. 1123 (1973), in Kurland and Casper, *Landmark Briefs and Arguments of the Supreme Court of the United States,* 76:739–845, esp. 761–64.

202 **Like *Reed* and *Stanley***: *Stanley v. Illinois,* 405 U.S. 645 (1972), overturned an Illinois statute discriminating against unwed fathers in the custody and care of their children.

202 **But cutting off benefits**: Brief Amicus Curiae of American Civil Liberties Union for the Appellants, in Kurland and Casper, *Landmark Briefs and Arguments of the Supreme Court of the United States,* 76:821–25.

203 **Clear, concise, and tightly**: Levin to RBG, Oct. 27, 1972; and RBG to Levin, Oct. 31, 1972, both in RBG Papers.

203 **"I have never had an experience"**: Feigen, *Not One of the Boys,* 82.

203 **"I had written briefs before"**: Kathleen Peratis (attorney), interview by author, Oct. 2, 1998. Norman Dorsen, interview by author, May 8, 2003. RBG's insistence that briefs should be of high quality because they matter—as do other variables—was reinforced by the impact of her *Frontiero* brief. Her attention to detail is evident in a later letter to Mark Pulliam in which she wrote, "I attach considerable importance to the way I say things and do not permit editors, student or professional, to tamper with my style." See RBG to Pulliam, April 10, 1979, RBG Papers.

203 **Sending him a copy**: RBG to Levin, Dec. 5, 1972, RBG Papers.

203 **"In sum," Ginsburg concluded**: For this and the following paragraphs, see Joint Reply Brief of Appellants and American Civil Liberties Union Amicus Curiae at 2–14, *Frontiero v. Laird,* 409 U.S. 1123 (1973).

204 **Next came preparation**: The preparation for oral arguments for *Frontiero* became RBG's style in future cases. She wrote out only short outlines, believing that oral arguments should be "a conversation between the Court and the lawyers." See RBG, interview by Marcus, Washington, D.C., Aug. 8, 1996, 36–37.

204 **Despite the evident tension**: RBG, interviews by author.

204 **After finishing her usual exercise**: "Ruth Bader Ginsburg," in Berry et al., *Women Lawyers at Work,* 52, 55–56.

206 **On this particular Wednesday**: The Supreme Court Database, Washington University Law. Available at scdb.wustl.edu. Roland B. Colgrove argued that this Local Rule 13(d)(1) of the Revised Rules of Procedure of the U.S. District Court for the District of Montana, which stipulated the trial of civil cases will proceed with juries of six persons, violated the Seventh Amendment, and he sought a ruling to impanel a twelve-member jury. The Court disagreed, stating that the rule was compliant. *Colgrove v. Battin,* 413 U.S. 149 (1973).

In *Morris v. Weinberger,* 410 U.S. 422 (1973), the petitioner had been denied Social Security benefits for his adopted daughter because her court-approved adoption had not been supervised by a child-placement agency. However, Congress amended the relevant statutory provisions of the Social Security Act in the plaintiff's favor twenty days after the Court granted a writ of certiorari, which was dismissed as "improvidently granted."

The petitioners in *Hurtado v. United States,* 410 U.S. 578 (1973), argued that despite being incarcerated to assure their presence as material witnesses, they were entitled to the same $20 per diem compensation afforded to those who were not held. The

Court ruled for the plaintiffs and remanded the case to the district court for further proceedings based on the ruling that a material witness is entitled to the $20 per diem compensation, regardless of his incarceration status.

206 **He tried to stick:** Transcript of Oral Argument at esp. 848–56, *Frontiero v. Laird,* 409 U.S. 1123 (1973). An audio recording of the arguments is available at www.oyez.org.

206 **"the many butterflies":** Jessica Weisberg, "Supreme Court Justice Ruth Bader Ginsburg: I'm Not Going Anywhere," *Elle,* Sept. 23, 2014 (online excerpt from Oct. print issue).

206 **Her Brooklyn-inflected accent:** Ibid.; *Frontiero v. Laird;* Berry et al., *Women Lawyers at Work,* 52; Hirshman, *Sisters in Law,* 73–74. Nina Totenberg observed this as the moment "when Ruth starts to perform." See "No, Ruth Bader Ginsburg Does Not Intend to Retire Anytime Soon."

206 **"The newcomer to our shores":** Transcript of Oral Argument, *Frontiero v. Laird,* 855.

207 **"notion of what constitutes":** Ibid., 856.

207 **"I ask no favor for my sex":** Joint Reply Brief of Appellants and American Civil Liberties Union Amicus Curiae at 2–14, *Frontiero v. Laird,* 409 U.S. 1123 (1973); RBG, interview by Marcus, Aug. 8, 1996, 36–37; RBG, interview by author; and Norgren, *Belva Lockwood,* ix.

207 **"Ruth spoke eloquently":** Feigen, interview by author, Aug. 13, 2003.

207 **Were the justices politely:** Martin D. Ginsburg, interview by author, July 1, 2003.

207 **Ruth attributed the silence:** RBG, interviews by author.

207 **"very precise" but too "emotional":** H.A.B. Notes on 71-1694: *Frontiero v. Laird,* Jan. 17, 1973, folder 9, box 163, Supreme Court Case Files, Blackmun Papers.

207 **He disliked "emotion":** H.A.B. Notes on 70-4: *Reed v. Reed,* Oct. 18, 1970, folder 10, box 135, Supreme Court Case Files, Blackmun Papers.

208 **"Poor Joshua!":** *DeShaney v. Winnebago County,* 499 U.S. 189 (1989), esp. Blackmun's dissent. For popularization of this quotation, see "Law: Poor Joshua!," *Time,* March 6, 1989.

208 **"wary and a little grumpy":** Greenhouse, *Becoming Justice Blackmun,* 207–12, quotation on 209.

208 **As he had made clear:** H.A.B. Notes on No. 70-4: *Reed v. Reed,* Oct. 18, 1970, folder 10, box 135, Blackmun Papers.

208 **Next to Ginsburg's name:** H.A.B. Notes on 71-1694: *Frontiero v. Laird,* Jan. 17, 1973, folder 9, box 163, Blackmun Papers.

208 **Not only should:** Transcript of Oral Argument, *Frontiero v. Laird,* 409 U.S. 1123 (1973).

209 **And more to the point:** Listening to the audio version of the oral arguments attests to the level of discussion on the bench.

209 **Although she could not recall:** RBG, interview by author, Aug. 28, 2002; and Hope, *Pinstripes and Pearls,* 84.

209 **"a member of the club":** RBG, interview by author.

210 **He also knew that:** Initially, even Martin Ginsburg had no idea that RBG would become so effective in oral arguments. Martin D. Ginsburg, interview by author, July 1, 2003.

210 **"CJ keeps yapping":** Greenhouse, *Becoming Justice Blackmun,* 125.

211 **But with the exception:** Douglas notes, esp. note 18, box 1577, Douglas Papers. Brennan thought Warren was remarkable for his ability at conference to lead a thorough discussion of "every case on the agenda, with a knowledge of each case at his fingertips." Schwartz, *History of the Supreme Court,* 266. On the lack of discussion under Burger, see Rehnquist, *Supreme Court,* 290.

211 **Brennan directed one of his clerks:** On Stone's role, see Stern and Wermiel, *Justice Brennan,* 395. Brennan to the Conference, memo, Feb. 28, 1973, box 1577, William J. Brennan Papers.

212   **"In any event"**: "Whether it follows from the existence of a suspect classification that 'compelling interest' is the equal protection standard is another matter. I agree with Thurgood that we actually have a spectrum of standards. Rather than talking of a compelling interest," he continued, "it would be more accurate to say that there will be times—when there is a suspect classification or when the classification impinges on a constitutional right—that we will balance or weigh competing interests. Of course, the more of this we do on the basis of suspect classifications not rooted in the Constitution, the more we approximate the old substantive due process approach." White to Brennan, Feb. 15, 1973, box 1577, Douglas Papers. See also Woodward and Armstrong, *Brethren,* 301–3.

212   **"Perhaps we can avoid"**: Powell to Brennan, Feb. 15 and March 2, 1973; and Blackmun to Brennan, and Stewart to Brennan, Feb. 16 and March 5, 1973, both in box 1577, Douglas Papers. See also Douglas to Brennan, March 3, 1973, box 298, Brennan Papers.

212   **But when Powell**: H.A.B. Notes on 70-74: *Reed v. Reed,* Oct. 18, 1970, folder 10, box 135, Blackmun Papers.

212   **He was loath to become:**. Also see Abraham, *Justices, Presidents, and Senators,* 242–43.

213   **"I therefore don't see"**: Brennan to Powell, March 6, 1973, box 1577, Douglas Papers.

213   **But Powell, who was being wooed:** Powell's objection to Brennan's language as feminist is noted in Woodward and Armstrong, *Brethren,* 254–55.

213   **" 'shuttlecock' memos"**: Burger to Brennan, March 7, 1973; and Burger to Powell, March 8, 1973, both in box 1577, Douglas Papers.

214   **Urging his colleague not:** Stewart to Brennan, March 5, 1973, box 1577, Douglas Papers. Douglas had already joined Brennan. See Douglas to Brennan, March 3, 1973, Douglas Papers.

214   **"the right result"**: Woodward and Armstrong, *Brethren,* 303. Quotation in Abraham, *Justices, Presidents, and Senators,* 195.

214   **"Statutory distinctions"**: *Frontiero v. Richardson,* 411 U.S. 677 (1973), 1770.

215   **"classifications based upon sex"**: Ibid. at 1768, 1769, and 1771. The Court later backtracked on alienage.

215   **"The law came in"**: Chris Carmody, "Judge Ginsburg's Ex-clients Reflect upon Their Cases," *National Law Journal,* June 1993, 34.

215   **"by judicial action a major"**: *Frontiero,* 411 U.S. at 1773.

216   **The press showered him:** S. J. Micciche, "Supreme Court Rules Women in Uniform Equal in Spouses' Dependency Benefits," *Boston Globe,* May 15, 1973. For letters to Brennan, see Fran Harris to Brennan, May 15, 1973; Margaret de Lima Norgaard to Brennan, May 15, 1973; and Marna Becker to Brennan, May 15, 1973, all in box 298, Brennan Papers. Also Warren Weaver Jr., "Air Force Woman Wins Benefit Suit," *New York Times,* May 15, 1973, A10; "Summary of Actions Taken by the Supreme Court," *New York Times,* May 15, 1973, A10; "A 'Flaming Feminist' Lauds Court," *New York Times,* May 22, 1973, A36; John P. MacKenzie, "Military Sex Bias Is Barred," *Washington Post,* May 15, 1973, A1; Linda Mathews, "High Court Takes Major Step Toward Equality of the Sexes," *Los Angeles Times,* May 15, 1973, A1; and Tribune Wire Service, "Woman Air Force Officer Wins Fight for Benefits for Husband," *Chicago Tribune,* May 15, 1973, A6.

216   **Her sentiments were also:** Micciche, "Supreme Court Rules Women."

216   **"the old 'minimal' scrutiny"**: Jeffrey R. Sliz, "Constitutional Law—Sex Discrimination—Is It Finally Labeled 'Suspect'?," *Georgia State Bar Journal* 10 (1974): 493–99; Jeffrey R. Sliz, "Constitutional Law—Equal Protection—Fifth Amendment, Due Process—Plurality of Court Decides That Sex-Based Classifications Are 'Suspect.' *Frontiero v. Richardson,* 411 U.S. 677 (1973)," *Rutgers Camden Law Journal* 5 (1974): 348–64; Laurence H. Tribe, "The Supreme Court, 1972 Term," *Harvard Law Review* 87 (1973): 256–62; Kathleen L. Bogas, "Constitutional Law—Fourteenth Amendment—Classification Based on Sex Is Inherently Suspect," *Journal of Urban Law* 51 (1974):

535–45; Joseph M. Sartin Jr. and Kerry P. Camarata, "Constitutional Law—Sex Discrimination—Supreme Court Plurality Declares Sex a Suspect Classification," *Tulane Law Review* 48 (1974): 710–20; Susan Vitullo Walters, "Constitutional Law— *Frontiero v. Richardson,* Uniform Services Fringe Benefit Statute Which Presumes Spouses of Male Members to Be Dependent, but Requires Spouses of Female Members to Be Dependent in Fact, Is Violative of Due Process," *Loyola University Law Journal* 5 (1974): 295–313; and Betsy B. McKenny, "*Frontiero v. Richardson:* Characterization of Sex-Based Classification," *Columbia Human Rights Law Review* 6 (1974): 239–47. See also Gunther, "Supreme Court, 1971 Term—Foreword." More recent scholars, notably Reva Siegel and Serena Mayeri, have shifted their focus to Brennan's use of the race-sex analogy that RBG had presented in her amicus brief. See Reva B. Siegel, "Collective Memory and the Nineteenth Amendment: Reasoning About 'the Woman Question' in the Discourse of Sex Discrimination," in Sarat and Kearns, *History, Memory, and the Law,* 131–66; and Mayeri, "'Common Fate of Discrimination,'" 1045–87. The analogy, Siegel notes, effectively denied women's separate struggle in the American legal system. Mayeri objects to the comparative stance, as though women and blacks were mutually exclusive categories. She also notes that Brennan made the history of women's legal status relevant only insofar as it resembled antebellum racial subordination. In so doing, Brennan passed up the opportunity to provide "a meaningful account of the socio-historical interrelationship between race and sex inequality." Indeed, Brennan's opinion "could be read to imply that sex discrimination violated the equal protection guarantee *if and only if* it resembled discrimination based on race." See Mayeri, "'Common Fate of Discrimination,'" 1075.

216 **"near great leap forward":** RBG, "Burger Court's Grapplings with Sex Discrimination," 135. See also RBG, "Comment on *Frontiero v. Richardson,*" *Women's Rights Law Reporter* 1 (1973): 2–4. On efforts to keep the press informed, see RBG to Lesley Oelsner, Oct. 13, 1972, RBG Papers. Oelsner wrote for *The New York Times.*

216 **"Five" was the most important:** See Tushnet, *Court Divided,* 35.

216 **In his assessment:** Gunther, "Supreme Court, 1971 Term—Foreword," 1–306.

217 **The Burger Court, for the most part:** Ibid., 12. On the widespread scrutiny of inexact proxies, see Case, "'Very Stereotype the Law Condemns,'" 1447–91.

217 **"If and when it becomes":** Powell to Brennan, March 2, 1973, Brennan Papers.

217 **She had a new Social:** RBG to Phineas Indritz, Jan. 10, 1973, Indritz Papers.

ELEVEN · Coping with a Setback

218 **"There are no anecdotes":** Lambert, "Ginsburg and Rabb," 11.

218 **"marvelously wise":** RBG, interview by Marcus, Aug. 8, 1996, 24; and Neier, *Taking Liberties,* 13–14.

219 **"every nut from Waukegan":** Rabb, quoted in Lambert, "Ginsburg and Rabb." On Feigen's role on compulsory sterilization, see Wheeler, *How Sex Became a Civil Liberty,* 139–41. RBG to Elizabeth Langer, *Women's Rights Law Reporter,* April 14, 1972, RBG Papers; RBG to Phineas Indritz, Jan. 9 and 10, 1973, Indritz Papers. Indritz, a civil rights lawyer who had worked closely with Thurgood Marshall, was a founding member of NOW and worked with Representative Martha Griffiths on speeches and legislation.

219 **But with a full teaching:** Peratis, "Address on RBG Portrait Dedication"; and quotation from RBG to author, note, Aug. 2008. See also the excellent comparison of Marshall and RBG and their roles outside the courtroom by Michael J. Klarman, "Social Reform Litigation and Its Challenges: An Essay in Honor of Justice Ruth Bader Ginsburg," *Harvard Journal of Law and Gender* 32 (2009): 251.

219 **Ginsburg created the Equal Rights Advocacy Project:** Equal Rights Advocacy Project at Columbia University School of Law-Grant No. 730-0379, Report of Activi-

ties, Sept. 1973–March 1974, 3–4, 6, RBG Papers. The project also engaged in non-litigation efforts.

219 **For students like Lynn:** Jones, "Columbia's Leader in Legal Battle Against Sex-Based Discrimination," 15; Schafran, interview by author, March 2, 2007; and Freeman, interview by author, March 2, 2007. In a note to the author, RBG mentioned that Freeman was one of her "all-time favorite students."

220 **"rare display of good judgment":** Recounted in Neier to RBG, March 15, 1983, RBG Birthday Book.

220 **Reading in *Law Week:*** *Shevin v. Kahn,* 273 So. 2d 72 (1973); Brief for Appellants, *Kahn v. Shevin,* 416 U.S. 351 (1974); and RBG to John H. Fleming, Robert L. Deitz, and Allan B. Taylor, Dec. 18, 1974, RBG Papers. See also Strebeigh, *Equal,* 61–64.

220 ***Kahn v. Shevin* disrupted:** RBG, interview by author, Aug. 28, 2002.

221 ***Kahn* was "big trouble":** RBG, interview by Marcus, Aug. 13, 1996; Brief for Appellees, *Kahn,* 416 U.S. 351; and Reply Brief for Appellants, *Kahn,* 416 U.S. 351.

221 **"I'll give you a gold medal":** RBG to Mary McGowan Davis, Jan. 30, 1974, RBG Papers.

221 **Avoiding the analogy:** RBG to Marc Fasteau, Brenda Feigen Fasteau, and Christine Cassady Curtis, Nov. 13, 1973, RBG Papers.

221 **In 1973, wives earned:** Pew Research Center, *Breadwinner Moms: Mothers Are the Sole or Primary Provider in Four-in-Ten Households with Children—Public Conflicted About the Growing Trend* (Washington, D.C.: Pew Research Center, 2013).

221 **"Although discrimination against women":** Brief for Appellants at 4, *Kahn,* 416 U.S. 351; and Reply Brief for Appellants, *Kahn,* 416 U.S. 351. See also RBG to *Spokeswoman,* June 21, 1974, RBG Papers.

221 **Florida's tax exemption:** RBG to Marc Fasteau et al., memo, Nov. 1973, RBG Papers. See also Brief for Appellants, *Kahn,* 416 U.S. 351.

222 **Only then would she:** RBG to Gerald Gunther, Jan. 21, 1974, RBG Papers.

222 **"a fine job—strong throughout":** RBG to Gunther, Jan. 15, 1974; Gunther to RBG, Jan. 18, 1974, RBG Papers.

222 **"just a little boost":** RBG to William Hoppe, March 8, 1974, RBG Papers.

222 **Oral argument would require:** On *DeFunis,* see Deslippe, *Protesting Affirmative Action,* esp. chap. 4. RBG developed the distinction between race-based and sex-based preferences more fully in RBG, "Women, Equality, and the *Bakke* Case," *Civil Liberties Review* 4 (1977): 8–9; and esp. in RBG, "Realizing the Equality Principle," in Blackstone and Heslep, *Social Justice and Preferential Treatment,* 135–53.

223 **Bombarded by questions:** RBG to Hoppe, March 8, 1974, RBG Papers. RBG seemed to reject any notion that her own interrogation during oral arguments was as vigorous and testy as that of McKenzie when directly questioned, saying simply that *Kahn* was the wrong case at the wrong time, which of course it was. RBG, interview by author, July 1, 2003. With *DeFunis,* challenges to strict scrutiny of race no longer focused on elimination of racial barriers because of past racial subordination, but rather demands that the law itself be color-blind. This effectively rules out many substantive measures in law and policy designed to achieve racial justice, as affirmative-action cases from *Regents of the University of California v. Bakke,* 438 U.S. 265 (1978), to *Adarand Constructors v. Peña,* 515 U.S. 200 (1995), demonstrate. This increasingly conservative interpretation of strict scrutiny with regard to race affected, in turn, RBG's own thinking about strict scrutiny in relation to gender, as I indicate in a subsequent chapter.

223 **Not until the rebuttal:** Transcript of the Oral Arguments, *Kahn.*

224 **Surely she had made:** RBG to Hoppe, March 8, 1974; and RBG to *Kahn v. Shevin* (*Harvard Law Review*), Nov. 27, 1974, both in RBG Papers.

224 **"too smart":** Blackmun notes on 73–78: *Kahn v. Shevin,* Blackmun Papers. Blackmun gave RBG a B plus on her oral argument in all likelihood because of her effective

handling of his question on *Kahn* and *DeFunis*. What makes Blackmun's notes on *Kahn* of interest is his wish that the Court move to a middle-tier standard on sex discrimination.

224 **"women as widows are largely"**: Ibid. See also Douglas, Notes on Conference on 73–78, *Kahn v. Shevin*, March 1, 1974, Douglas Papers. On the nearly half a century when government policies were deliberately designed to exclude African Americans from benefits, see Katznelson, *When Affirmative Action Was White;* and Yuill, *Richard Nixon and the Rise of Affirmative Action.*

225 **"He didn't want to endanger"**: Ellman quoted at length in Marshall L. Small, "William O. Douglas Remembered: A Collective Memory by WOD's Law Clerks," *Journal of Supreme Court History* 32 (2007): 333–34n21.

225 **The draft "was short"**: *Kahn v. Shevin*, 416 U.S. 351 (1974), 356 (Douglas's majority).

225 **Having written an opinion:** Douglas, for all his talents, had grown increasingly more unpredictable in his behavior during the 1970s, his attention wandered for long stretches during oral arguments, and his opinions became shoddy in the view of his fellow justices. Though he had suffered from several strokes, he refused to resign. See Rosen, *Supreme Court,* chap. 3.

225 **"all those widowers"**: Ibid.; *Kahn,* 416 U.S. at 357–60 (Brennan and Marshall dissenting) and at 360–62 (White dissenting).

226 **His opinion, she lamented:** RBG to Robert A. Sedler, April 30, 1974; and RBG to Sara-Ann Determan, April 26 and 30, 1974, both in RBG Papers. See also RBG to Norman Dorsen, April 30, 1974; E. Sanford Read to RBG, Sept. 16, 1974; RBG to E. S. Read, May 2, 1975; and RBG to Hoppe, June 16, 1975, all in RBG Papers.

226 **Clearly the experience:** When Douglas announced his retirement, RBG confessed to being "deeply affected" and referred to it as a "dismal" day. See RBG to Shirley Bysiewicz, Nov. 13, 1975, RBG Papers. Allen Murphy in his debunking biography *Wild Bill* finds the justice's autobiographical account of his childhood poverty to be greatly exaggerated. Yet so long as Douglas genuinely believed his widowed mother was impoverished, that "fact" shaped his perception of *Kahn*. See also Douglas, *Go East, Young Man.*

226 **"be left with the blind"**: RBG, "Some Thoughts on Benign Classification in the Context of Sex," *Connecticut Law Review* 10 (1978): 817–18.

226 **Nor was she comforted:** *Schlesinger v. Ballard,* 419 U.S. 498 (1975); *Cleveland Board of Education v. La Fleur,* 414 U.S. 632 (1974); and *Geduldig v. Aiello,* 417 U.S. 484 (1974).

227 **a "Panglossian" rationale:** RBG to John H. Fleming, Robert L. Dietz, and Allan B. Taylor, Dec. 16, 1974, RBG Papers; and RBG, "Some Thoughts on Benign Classification in the Context of Sex," 817. RBG noted that the exemption was never extended to a female head of household who never married or whose marriage ended in divorce. See also RBG, "Burger Court's Grapplings with Sex Discrimination," 136–37.

227 **In her forthcoming lecture tour:** The Phi Beta Kappa Visiting Scholar was an honor bestowed on distinguished professors and entailed brief visits to selected campuses to speak to faculty and students.

227 **Women in the first-year law:** Whitney S. Bangall, "A Brief History of Women at CLS: Part 3," Columbia Law School.

227 **"male impersonators"**: "Ruth Bader Ginsburg: Women and the Law," Columbia Law School Report, 1994, 16–17; Dianne Zimmerman, professor, New York University School of Law, interview by author, March 1, 2007.

227 **her femininity and family:** "Myra Bradwell Day Forum Held at Law School," Columbia University Law School, 1980, RBG Papers; and "Ruth Bader Ginsburg: Women and the Law," 16–17.

227 **"I think I took every course"**: Jane Booth (associate general counsel, Columbia University), interview by author, Feb. 28, 2008.

228 **"someone [who], while being"**: Lynch, quoted in "Women Call Ginsburg Mentor, Role Model: A Pioneer, She Inspired 'A Whole Generation,'" *St. Louis Post-Dispatch,* June 16, 1993.

228 **"our hands are tied"**: RBG, interview by author, July 1, 2003.

228 **Turning to her female colleagues:** Rosenberg, *Changing the Subject,* 194–95.

228 **"a diminutive woman"**: Carol H. Meyer, "The First Activist Feminist I Ever Met," *Affilia* 9, no. 1 (1994): 85.

229 **While some called:** RBG, interview by Grele, Aug. 19, 2004. Both Sovern and George Cooper, a professor at the Law School who, with Harriet Rabb, ran the Employment Discrimination Clinic, strongly supported RBG's efforts.

229 **"could accomplish more"**: On RBG's late-night work habits, see "Ruth Bader Ginsburg," in Berry et al., *Women Lawyers at Work,* 64; on James Ginsburg's response, see the documentary film *Paving the Way,* directed by Morris; for RBG's late-night diet, see Jane Ginsburg, interview by author, May 6, 2003; and Liz Porter, "Former Clerks for Justice Ginsburg Reminisce," Columbia Law School.

229 **"Ruth, while never heavy-handedly"**: Kathleen Peratis, interview by author, May 7, 2003, and conversation with author, Nov. 3, 2000.

230 **"I could say a word"**: RBG to Philip B. Kurland, April 4, 1975, RBG Papers.

230 **"back on track"**: Quoted in Chafe, *Unfinished Journey,* 427.

TWELVE · Getting Back on Track

233 **Edna Stubblefield, a nineteen:** Marvin P. Morton Jr., "Statement of Case for Criminal Appellee," *Stubblefield v. Tennessee* (1973); Marvin P. Morton to Women's Rights Project, Jan. 24, 1974; RBG to Morton, Jan. 31, 1974; William R. Neese to RBG, Feb. 1 and 21, 1974; and RBG to Neese, Feb. 27, 1974, all in box 9, RBG Papers. Also see Erika Ballou, "Ruth Bader Ginsburg: A Brief Encounter with Justice," *Dicta: The Voice of Tulane Law School* 17 (April 2003): 2. In Henry County from July 1961 to January 1972, a total of 2,306 jurors had been selected by the jury commissioners and listed for jury duty. Of these, only 21 (0.9 percent) were women, although 1970 census figures indicated that women constituted 53.2 percent of the total adult population. Only 47 blacks had been listed, 2 percent of the total jurors selected in a county where blacks made up 15.3 percent of the population, according to Morton et al., Jurisdictional Statement by Appellant esp. at 10, *Stubblefield v. Tennessee,* 420 U.S. 903 (1974). The decision as to whether to hear *Stubblefield* had not been made at the time RBG argued *Healy.* See RBG to William R. Neese and Marvin P. Morton Jr., April 1 and 12, 1974; and RBG to Neese, Oct. 17, 1974, both in RBG Papers.

233 **"as the center of home"**: *Hoyt v. Florida,* 368 U.S. 57 (1961).

234 **Male plaintiffs contended:** *Healy v. Edwards,* 363 F. Supp. 1110 (1973). See also *Edwards v. Healy,* 421 U.S. 772 (1975).

234 **"deprives a jury"**: *Healy v. Edwards,* 363 F. Supp. 1110 (1973).

234 **"The thought is that the factors"**: *Ballard v. United States,* 329 U.S. 187 (1946), esp. 193.

235 **Hence there were compelling:** Memorandum in Opposition to Defendants' Motion to Dismiss and in Support of Plaintiffs' Cross-motion for Summary Judgment, *Healy v. Edwards,* 363 F. Supp. 1110 (1973).

235 **There was the *Stubblefield*:** See Schneider, *Battered Women and Feminist Lawmaking.*

235 **"would not constitute a disruption"**: Brief for Amicus Curiae of Rhonda Copelon et al., *Edwards v. Healy,* 421 U.S. 772 (1974). For a fuller version of these arguments, see Brief for Appellees, ibid. at 14, 16, 20–22.

236 **"appallingly overbroad"**: For full argument, see Brief for Appellees, Ginsburg et al., *Edwards v. Healy.* The U.S. District Court for the Eastern District of Louisiana included New Orleans and was in the Fifth Circuit.

236 **"jury service is not only a right"**: Ibid.

236 **Yet New Orleans–born jurists:** RBG, "Four Louisiana Giants in the Law," Judge Robert A. Ainsworth Jr. Memorial Lecture, Feb. 4, 2002, *Loyola Law Review* 48 (2002): 253–66.

237 **"Females, as individuals":** *Healy v. Edwards,* 363 F. Supp. 1110 (1973), esp. 1115. Also see RBG's use of this quotation in her speech "Four Louisiana Giants in the Law."

237 **"yesterday's sterile precedent":** *Healy v. Edwards,* 363 F. Supp. 1110 (1973), 1117.

237 **Because the two cases:** For RBG's criticism of the revised jury exemption, see Reply to Memorandum of Appellants Suggesting Mootness, *Healy v. Edwards,* 363 F. Supp. 1110 (1973). Also see *Taylor v. Louisiana,* 419 U.S. 522 (1975).

238 **"equal protection matter":** Transcript of Oral Argument at 3–12, esp. 8, *Edwards v. Healy,* 421 U.S. 772 (1974).

238 **"the new theory was that":** Ibid., 17, 20–32, 37.

238 **"that the two sexes are not fungible":** Ibid.

239 **Fifty-nine percent of Louisiana's:** Ibid.

239 **"The focus on women jurors":** Ibid.

240 **It was a compliment of sorts:** Nixon considered nominating two women—Sylvia Bacon and Mildred Lillie—to the Supreme Court mainly to "make a little political [hay]" and gain "every half a percentage point" he could, according to John Dean. For more on the process of Nixon's nomination of a replacement for Justice John Marshall Harlan II, see Dean, *Rehnquist Choice.*

240 **"We think it is no longer":** *Taylor v. Louisiana,* 419 U.S. 522 (1975), 537 (White majority).

240 **"smacks more of mysticism":** Ibid., 542 (Rehnquist dissenting).

241 **To all but die-hard:** For media coverage, see Warren Weaver Jr., "High Court Backs Women's Jury Rights," *New York Times,* Jan. 22, 1975, A1; Linda Mathews, "Exclusion of Women as Jurors Overruled," *Los Angeles Times,* Jan. 22, 1975, A7; John P. MacKenzie, "Court Upsets Bar to Women on Juries," *Washington Post,* Jan. 22, 1975, A1; UPI, "Jury Ban on Women Illegal," *Detroit Free Press,* Jan. 22, 1975; S. J. Micciche, "Court Rules States Can't Bar Women from Jury Duty," *Boston Globe,* Jan. 22, 1975; and W. Dale Nelson, "Court Backs Right of Women Jurors," *Oregonian,* Jan. 22, 1975. For legal scholars' reactions, see Kathleen M. Butler, "The Representative Cross Section Standard: Another Sixth Amendment Fundamental Right," *Loyola Law Review* 21 (1975): 995–1003; "The Supreme Court, 1974 Term," *Harvard Law Review* 89 (1975): 95–103; Carla A. Neely, "Constitutional Law: Jury Selection—Exclusion of Women from Jury Venire Violates Fundamental Sixth Amendment Right to a Representative Jury," *University of Florida Law Review* 28 (1975): 281–88; Kenneth J. Mulvey Jr., "Constitutional Law—Sixth Amendment—Systematic Exclusion of Women from Jury Service Violates the Sixth and Fourteenth Amendments," *Fordham Urban Law Journal* 3 (1975): 733–48; Martha Craig Daughtrey, "Cross Sectionalism in Jury-Selection Procedures After *Taylor v. Louisiana,*" *Tennessee Law Review* 43 (1975): 1–107; Richard H. Faught, "*Taylor v. Louisiana*: Constitutional Implications for Missouri's Jury Exemption Provisions," *Saint Louis University Law Journal* 20 (1975): 159–80; Kathryn Marie Krause, "Jury Selection—Sixth Amendment Right to a Fair Cross Section of the Community—a Change in Emphasis," *Missouri Law Review* 41 (1976): 446–56; and Elizabeth B. Leete, "*Taylor v. Louisiana*: The Jury Cross Section Crosses the State Line," *Connecticut Law Review* 7 (1975): 508–28.

241 ***Duren v. Missouri* (1979):** *Duren v. Missouri,* 439 U.S. 357 (1979).

241 **"weightier reasons":** *Taylor v. Louisiana,* 419 U.S. at 534 (White majority).

241 **But anticipation turned to grief:** For the cause of Paula's death, see RBG, interview by Marcus, Aug. 13, 1996.

242 **"mothers' benefits":** For case facts, see Brief for Appellee, *Weinberger v. Wiesenfeld,* 420 U.S. 636 (1975), in Kurland and Casper, *Landmark Briefs and Arguments of the Supreme Court of the United States,* 82:353–416.

242 **"TELL THAT TO GLORIA":** RBG to Phyllis Zatlin Boring, Dec. 27, 1972, RBG Papers; and RBG, interview by Marcus, July 14, 1997.

242 **"It's a great case":** RBG to Phyllis Zatlin Boring.

242 **"as soon as I get":** RBG to Jane Lifset, Jan. 9, 1973, RBG Papers.

242 **Because the ACLU would be:** Ibid.; RBG to Wiesenfeld, Jan. 10, 1973, RBG Papers.

243 **"Do you think you can arrange":** RBG to Oelsner, Feb. 8, 1973, RBG Papers.

243 **"very conservative":** RBG to Judith Mears, Aug. 30, 1973, RBG Papers. To refer to the district court as "very conservative" was diplomatic wording.

244 **"Hallelujah!" she exulted:** RBG to Lifset, June 1, 1973; RBG to the *Equal Rights Monitor,* April 28, 1975, both in RBG Papers. On the friendship, see Wiesenfeld to RBG, May 4, 1975, Oct. 20, 1978, and May 23, 1979; RBG to Wiesenfeld, Nov. 8, 1978; and Wiesenfeld to RBG, June 3, 1980, all in RBG Papers.

244 **"small, frail, and absolutely":** Wiesenfeld, telephone interview by author, Nov. 14, 2000.

244 **Because opposing counsel:** RBG to James V. Rowan, Jan. 18, 1974; and RBG to Jack Blumenfeld, Oct. 24, 1974, both in RBG Papers.

244 **Whether such responses:** Wiesenfeld, telephone interview by author, Nov. 14, 2000. Transcript of Oral Argument, *Wiesenfeld v. Secretary of HEW,* 367 F. Supp. 981 (1973). The price of equalization was also much emphasized when the case reached the Supreme Court, the solicitor general arguing that if other very closely analogous provisions were extended, the cost would rise to over $350 million annually.

245 **Though the core issues:** Strebeigh, *Equal,* 68–70.

245 **"A weird opinion":** *Wiesenfeld,* 367 F. Supp. 981. RBG to Judith Mears, Aug. 20, 1973; RBG to Lifset, June 1 and Dec. 17, 1973; Lifset to RBG, Jan. 9, 1974; and RBG to James V. Rowan, Jan. 18, 1974, all in RBG Papers.

245 **Bork could be counted:** Pacelle, *Between Law and Politics,* 124–29.

245 **"Mothers' benefits," like "widows' tax exemptions":** Transcript of Oral Argument at 3–19, *Weinberger v. Wiesenfeld,* 420 U.S. 636 (1975), 1233 (Brennan majority).

245 **To counter the argument:** "The fly in the ointment is *Kahn v. Shevin,*" RBG noted. See RBG to Jack Blumenfeld, Oct. 24, 1974, RBG Papers.

245 **"We will simply have":** RBG to Wiesenfeld, May 3, 1974, RBG Papers.

246 **Working from an eleven-page:** For this and subsequent paragraphs, see Brief for Appellee, *Weinberger v. Wiesenfeld,* 420 U.S. 636 (1975), in *Landmark Briefs and Arguments of the Supreme Court of the United States: Constitutional Law,* 353–416. See also Outline of Wiesenfeld brief, *Wiesenfeld* Supreme Court Case, RBG Papers.

246 **"while special deference":** Transcript of Oral Argument, *Wiesenfeld,* 420 U.S. 636.

247 **With a little help from Gerry:** Gunther advised RBG to take a look at a 1970 decision, *Welsh v. United States,* and especially Justice Harlan's concurring opinion. Welsh, she discovered, had claimed conscientious objector status—not because of "religious training and belief," as the military service exemption statute dictated, but because of strong moral and ethical beliefs that he characterized as "nonreligious." The Supreme Court, reversing the lower court decision upholding Welsh's conviction, had interpreted "religious" broadly to include Welsh's beliefs. Justice Harlan disagreed. He recognized that Congress said and meant religious conscientious objectors. But that limitation, Harlan concluded, violated the First Amendment's guarantee of free speech. The choice facing the Court, he suggested, was either enlargement—adding a class (nontheistic objectors)—or abrogation of the exemption altogether. The larger legislative intent behind the original statute was clearly to exempt conscientious objectors; the Court was therefore justified in extending the exemption. Other justices, while ruling in favor of Welsh, had not embraced Harlan's analysis, but RBG had decided to try it nonetheless. *Welsh v. United States,* 398 U.S. 333 (1970), esp. 344–67; and RBG, "Some Thoughts on Judicial Authority to Repair Unconstitutional Legislation," *Cleveland*

State Law Review 28 (1979): 301–24. Gunther's role was revealed in RBG, interview by author, Aug. 28, 2002.

247 **That could cost more:** RBG notes, *Wiesenfeld* case files and correspondence, RBG Papers.

247 **Upon leaving, she passed a woman:** RBG, interview by author, Aug. 28, 2002.

247 **In this "awesome" setting:** Wiesenfeld, telephone interview by author, Nov. 14, 2000.

247 **"As soon as Ruth uttered":** Williams, interview by author, March 4, 2000.

248 **the restriction to "widows only":** Transcript of Oral Argument at 3–19, esp. 7–9, *Wiesenfeld,* 420 U.S. 636.

248 **The question, Ruth assumed:** *Stanton v. Stanton,* 421 U.S. 7 (1975), for which Justice Blackmun wrote the majority opinion striking down the Utah law as a violation of equal protection.

248 **Ginsburg used much of her:** Transcript of Oral Argument at 3–19, esp. 7–9, *Wiesenfeld,* 420 U.S. 636. The cutoff amount for earnings was actually $2,980 and not the older figure of $2,400, which RBG cited on page 15.

249 **Berzon researched the history:** Judge Marsha S. Berzon (U.S. Court of Appeals for the Ninth Circuit), telephone interview by author, Aug. 24, 2010.

249 **"Justices Back Widowers' Equal Rights":** "I cried too!" RBG wrote to Milicent Tryon, March 24, 1975, RBG Papers. See Warren Weaver Jr., "Justices Back Widowers' Equal Rights," *New York Times,* March 20, 1975, A1.

249 **"forbids the gender-based":** *Wiesenfeld,* 420 U.S. at 645 (Brennan majority).

250 **Now, however, the provision:** Ibid. Although the Court was unanimous in its judgment, Brennan, who wrote the opinion, was joined by Justices Stewart, White, Marshall, and Blackman. Justice Powell filed a concurring opinion in which Chief Justice Burger joined. Justice Rehnquist filed an opinion concurring in the result. Douglas was ill and took no part in the decision.

250 **Those cases "made the law":** RBG, "Some Thoughts on Judicial Authority to Repair Unconstitutional Legislation"; RBG to author, Jan. 12, 2000.

250 **"back on track":** RBG, "The Supreme Court Back on Track: *Weinberger v. Wiesenfeld,*" n.d., RBG Papers.

250 **"compelling state interest":** *Stanton v. Stanton,* 421 U.S. 7 (1975), 17 (Blackmun majority).

251 **The Ginsburgs held a victory party:** The reaction of some of the ACLU lawyers, which was noted by Sylvia Law, a New York University Law School professor and feminist legal scholar, was reported in David Von Drehle, "Redefining Fair with a Simple Careful Assault—Step-by-Step Strategy Produced Strides for Equal Protection," *Washington Post,* July 19, 1993, A1. Information on the wedding ceremony and a photograph were provided by RBG, interview by author, Aug. 28, 2002.

THIRTEEN · Moving Forward on Shifting Political Ground

252 **After the turbulent 1960s:** On the bicentennial, see Zaretsky, *No Direction Home,* esp. chap. 4.

252 **Public intellectuals fueled:** Daniel P. Moynihan, "The American Experiment," *Public Interest* 41 (1975): 7; "America Now? A Failure of Nerve," *Commentary,* July 16, 1975; Lasch, *Culture of Narcissism; Lasch, Haven in a Heartless World; Zaretsky, No Direction Home,* esp. chap. 5; Harris Poll, Jan. 5, 1976.

252 **At the 1976 Republican convention:** "Republican Feminists Prepare to Fight for Convention Delegates, Rights Amendment, and Abortion," *New York Times,* Feb. 19, 1976, A25; Eileen Shanahan, "G.O.P. Feminists Angry at Party," *New York Times,* July 28, 1976, A9; Spencer Rich, "GOP Platform Panel Refuses to Support ERA," *Washington Post,* Aug. 12, 1976, A3; Joseph Lelyveld, "Normally Proper G.O.P. Women

Come Out Fighting over E.R.A.," *New York Times,* Aug. 17, 1976, A40. On the division of the GOP and especially Republican women over feminist issues, see Rymph, *Republican Women,* chap. 8, conclusion. For an excellent discussion of how a Republican convention with a majority of pro-choice delegates and an adamantly pro-choice First Lady came to adopt its abortion platform, see Daniel K. Williams, "The GOP's Abortion Strategy: Why Pro-choice Republicans Became Pro-life in the 1970s," *Journal of Policy History* 23 (2011): 512–39.

252 **"I don't think we will":** RBG to East, March 31, 1975, East Papers.

253 **The Court's attentiveness:** Critchlow, *Conservative Ascendancy.* For a superb recent study linking battles over gender and sexuality to this rightward tilt, see Self, *All in the Family.*

253 **Before the three-judge panel:** For contextualization of Oklahoma City politics in the case, see R. Darcy and Jenny Sanbrano, "Oklahoma in the Development of Equal Rights: The ERA, 3.2% Beer, Juvenile Justice, and *Craig v. Boren," Oklahoma City University Law Review* 22 (1997): 1009–49.

253 **"Fed-up with the whole":** Appellee Brief, *Walker v. Hall,* 399 F. Supp. 1304 (1975). The case, when submitted to the Supreme Court, was renamed because Craig had supplanted Walker and Boren had taken Hall's place as governor. For quotation, see Gilbert to RBG, May 27, 1977, RBG Papers.

254 **"something in between":** *Stanton v. Stanton,* 421 U.S. 7 (1975), 17 (Blackmun majority); Amy Leigh Campbell, "Raising the Bar: Ruth Bader Ginsburg and the ACLU Women's Rights Project," *Texas Journal of Women and the Law* 11 (2002): 237.

254 **"in view of your long":** RBG to Gilbert, Jan. 15, 1976, RBG Papers.

254 **"implore[d]" Ginsburg's presence:** Gilbert to RBG, Jan. 21, 1976, RBG Papers.

254 **"We don't have 5 votes":** *Stanton* was a decision in which the Court held unconstitutional a Utah statute requiring parental support for males until age twenty-one but for females only until age eighteen.

254 **"stay away from conclusive":** *Weinberger v. Salfi,* 422 U.S. 749 (1975).

254 **Further, Ginsburg encouraged:** RBG to Gilbert, Jan. 26 and Feb. 4, 1976, RBG Papers. See *Sail'er Inn Inc. v. Kirby,* 5 Cal. 3d 1, 485 P. 2d 529 (1971).

254 **She also volunteered:** Gilbert to RBG, Feb. 5, 1976; RBG to Gilbert, Feb. 16 and May 27, 1976; RBG to Richard Haitch, May 17, 1976; and Haitch to RBG, May 19, 1976, all in RBG Papers.

254 **"beginning to feel like":** Gilbert to RBG, Feb. 5, 1976, RBG Papers.

254 **"I think I succeeded":** Gilbert to RBG, Feb. 27, 1976, RBG Papers.

254 **"Your brief makes many strong":** RBG to Gilbert, March 4, 1976, RBG Papers.

255 **The amendment did not:** Brief Amicus Curiae of the American Civil Liberties Union esp. at 13, 15, 19–22, 25, 33, *Craig v. Boren,* 429 U.S. 190 (1976), in Kurland and Casper, *Landmark Briefs and Arguments of the Supreme Court of the United States: Constitutional Law, 1976 Term Supplement,* vol. 91 (Frederick, Md.: University Publications of America, 1978).

255 **"the concept of 'compensatory' ":** Ibid.

255 **"utterly failed to demonstrate":** Ibid.

255 **"But whatever support":** Ibid.

256 **And do submit:** RBG to Gilbert, June 23 and 7, 1976; Gilbert to RBG, June 29, 1976; RBG to Gilbert, July 2 and Sept. 8, 1976, all in RBG Papers.

256 **Her second case, scheduled:** *Coffin v. Secretary of Health, Education, and Welfare,* 400 F. Supp. 953 (1975); *Jablon v. Secretary of Health, Education, and Welfare,* 399 F. Supp. 118 (Md.1975); *Califano v. Goldfarb,* 396 F. Supp. 308 (1975); *Califano v. Hau,* 430 U.S. 960 (1977).

256 **"sometimes the best laid plans":** *Coffin,* 400 F. Supp. 953. For the quotation, see RBG, "Keynote Address at Hawaii ACLU Conference on Women's Legal Rights," March 16–17, 1978, RBG Papers, as quoted in Campbell, "Raising the Bar," 196.

256 **Three weeks before the judges:** Campbell, "Raising the Bar," 226–27; *Califano v. Goldfarb,* 430 U.S. 199 (1977); and RBG, interview by author, July 1, 2003.
257 **"We earned that money":** Anna Quindlen, "Leon Goldfarb Doubly Happy with Decision," *New York Times,* March 3, 1977, 19. Also see Leslie Maitland, "Indictment Says Lefkowitz Aide Accepted Bribe," *New York Times,* March 3, 1977, A1.
257 **Personalizing the injustice:** *Goldfarb v. Secretary of Health, Education, and Welfare,* 396 F. Supp. 308 (1975).
257 **"on the straight and narrow":** RBG to Jill Hoffman, Aug. 13, 1976 (the note to Hoffman is in the form of a postscript on the carbon of a letter to Gilbert). See RBG to Gilbert, Aug. 13, 1976, RBG Papers.
257 **"Dearest Amica," he later wrote:** Gilbert to RBG, May 27, 1977, RBG Papers.
257 **"Dear [Ranger] Fred," she replied:** RBG to Gilbert, May 27, 1976, RBG Papers. See also July 2, 1976, RBG Papers.
257 **Ginsburg, as well as court reporters:** On the changed tone, see *Washington Star* and *Boston Globe,* Oct. 6, 1976, RBG Papers.
258 **In other words, the rational:** For the next several paragraphs, see Transcripts of Oral Argument at 8–9, *Califano v. Goldfarb,* 430 U.S. 199 (1977). *Mathews v. Goldfarb* (No. 75-699) was redesignated *Califano v. Goldfarb* when Joseph A. Califano Jr. replaced F. David Mathews as the Secretary of Health, Education, and Welfare at the onset of the Jimmy Carter administration, which occurred approximately six weeks prior to the Court's decision.
258 **Unlike the Florida widows':** Brief for Appellee, *Mathews v. Goldfarb* (1976); Transcript of Oral Argument, *Califano v. Goldfarb.* For RBG's opening statement, see 20–22.
259 **If she answered directly:** RBG to Richard Larson, Oct. 14, 1976, RBG Papers; and Nina Totenberg (NPR legal correspondent), interview by author, Nov. 13, 2003. RBG, "Gender and the Constitution," *University of Cincinnati Law Review* 44 (1975): 1–41.
259 **"deeply entrenched discriminatory problems":** RBG, "Gender and the Constitution," 28–29.
259 **"invidious impact against women":** Transcript of Oral Argument, 22–26, *Califano v. Goldfarb.*
259 **"It is impossible to rationalize":** Ibid., 31–35.
260 **"merely a color-blind remedy":** RBG to Larson, Oct. 14, 1976, RBG Papers.
260 **Faced with the prospect:** *Webster v. HEW,* 430 U.S. 313 (1976).
261 **But that did not alleviate:** RBG to Gerard Lynch, March 28, 1977, RBG Papers.
261 **If, however, his colleagues:** Burger to Brennan, Nov. 15, 1976, Blackmun Papers.
261 **"some level of scrutiny":** Blackmun Conference Notes on *Craig v. Boren,* Oct. 8, 1976; and Powell to Burger, Blackmun, and Brennan, Oct. 14, 1976, both in Blackmun Papers. Also see Rehnquist to Brennan, Nov. 2, 1976; and Burger to Brennan, Oct. 18, 1976, both in Powell Papers.
262 **After several drafts:** RBG first introduced the idea of a middle tier in the *Frontiero* amicus brief.
262 **Brennan's discussion of why:** For an analysis of brokered judicial decision making that uses *Craig* as illustrative, see Epstein and Knight, *Choices Justices Make,* esp. 1–13, 57–58.
262 **"classifications by gender":** *Craig v. Boren,* 429 U.S. 190 (1976), 210, 217, 218.
262 **When the conference then turned:** Stewart to Burger, Oct. 18, 1976; Burger Memorandum to Conference, Oct. 20, 1976; and Stevens to Brennan, Oct. 21, 1976, all in Marshall Papers.
263 **"a remarkably fine job":** Stewart to Brennan, Dec. 14, 1976, Blackmun Papers.
263 **"considerable backing and filling":** Powell to Brennan, Dec. 6, 1976; Stewart to Brennan, Dec. 14, 1976; Burger, Memorandum to Conference, Jan. 3, 1977; Burger to Rehnquist, Jan. 4, 1977; Stevens to Rehnquist, Jan. 4, 1977; Stewart to Rehnquist, Jan. 4, 1977; all in Marshall Papers. See also *Califano v. Goldfarb,* 430 U.S. 199 (1977).

263 **"the accidental by-product":** RBG to Gerard Lynch, March 16 and 28, 1977, RBG Papers.

263 **Further, the automatic qualification:** *Califano,* 430 U.S. at 199–242.

264 **The remedial end matched:** Five justices joined in the per curiam decision. See *Califano v. Webster,* 430 U.S. 313 (1977).

264 **"After North Carolina's nay":** RBG to Barrett, March 16, 1977, RBG Papers.

264 **"Save at least a handshake":** Lynch to RBG, March 23, 1977, RBG Papers.

264 **"I was wondering what you'd think":** Ibid. Italics mine.

264 **"The *Webster* opinion":** RBG to Lynch, March 28, 1977, RBG Papers.

265 **Expounding to ACLU:** RBG, "The Supreme Court Clarifies the Distinction Between Invidious Discrimination and Genuine Compensation (*Califano v. Goldfarb* and *Califano v. Webster*)," RBG Papers. This statement was apparently prepared for Lesley Oelsner, the legal reporter for *The New York Times*. See RBG to Oelsner, April 5, 1977, RBG Papers.

265 **"also familiar" with the cases:** RBG to Jeffrey S. Saltz, Aug. 15, 1977, RBG Papers. As it turned out, Jane would make the *Law Review,* of which the future chief justice Roberts was editor.

265 **Yet legal analysts agreed:** Lesley Oelsner, "Sex Discrepancy in Old-Age Funds Is Unanimously Upheld by Justices," *New York Times,* March 22, 1977, 28.

265 **"important government interest":** See R. Broh Landsman, "Fifth Amendment Protection Against Gender-Based Discrimination in the Distribution of Survivors' Benefits: *Califano v. Goldfarb,*" *Southwestern Law Journal* 31 (1977): 1156–63; John V. Nordlund, "Constitutional Law: Equal Protection—Gender Discrimination—*Califano v. Goldfarb,*" *New York Law School Law Review* 23 (1977): 503–17; David M. Douglas, "Social Security: Sex Discrimination and Equal Protection," *Baylor Law Review* 30 (1978): 199–205; and Gregory Kaapuni, "*Califano v. Goldfarb*: An Equal Protection Standard for Gender-Based Discrimination," *University of West Los Angeles Law Review* 10 (1978): 67–85.

265 **"will remain a mask":** Kenneth L. Karst, "The Supreme Court, 1976 Term," *Harvard Law Review* 91 (1977): 1–301, esp. 188.

265 **Nor was the dramatic:** For RBG's testimony on extension of the ERA ratification deadline, see *Hearings on H.J. Res. 638: Equal Rights Extension, Before the Subcommittee on Civil and Constitution Rights of the House Committee on the Judiciary,* 95th Cong., 1st–2nd sess. (1977 and 1978).

266 **The brethren's "ostrich-like":** RBG, "Some Thoughts on the Benign Classification of Sex," *Connecticut Law Review* 10 (1978): 812–27.

266 **General Electric v. Gilbert:** For more on the story behind the *Gilbert* litigation, see Strebeigh, *Equal,* chap. 7.

266 **Only Brennan and Marshall:** *General Electric v. Gilbert,* 429 U.S. 125 (1976).

266 **Dismay did not begin:** RBG to Herma Hill Kay, Dec. 7, 1976, RBG Papers.

266 **"Women's Rights Movement":** Lesley Oelsner, "Supreme Court Rules Employers May Refuse Pregnancy Sick Pay: Women's Rights Movement Is Dealt Major Blow by 6–3 Ruling Rejecting Appeals Courts' View," *New York Times,* Dec. 8, 1976, A1.

266 **an "invented tradition":** Cary Franklin, "Inventing the 'Traditional Concept' of Sex Discrimination," *Harvard Law Review* 125 (2012): 1307. Rehnquist's intention was to use *Gilbert* to limit disparate impact in Title VII. See Mayeri, *Reasoning from Race,* 106–22.

267 **"places no obstacles":** *Maher v. Roe,* 432 U.S. 464 (1977), 464–90, esp. 482; RBG to Isabele Katz Pinzler, Phyllis Segel, Susan Berrensford, Margaret Berger, Jane Picker, and Chuck Guerrier, memo, May 21, 1979, RBG Papers.

267 **Both were expressions:** Mayeri, "'Common Fate of Discrimination,'" 1045–87.

267 **Hence Stewart's clever crafting:** *Geduldig v. Aiello,* 417 U.S. 484 (1974).

268   "eliminating institutional practices": RBG, "Gender and the Constitution," 1–41.

268   With affirmative action her best: Laura Kalman, "At the Border of Law and Politics: Bakke and Affirmative Action" (paper, the American Historical Association, San Diego, Jan. 10, 2010).

269   "a more capacious vision": See Mayeri, "Reconstructing the Race-Sex Analogy," 1789–854. For a more extensive discussion, see Mayeri, *Reasoning from Race;* RBG, "Some Thoughts on Benign Classification in the Context of Sex," 813–27; RBG, letter to the editor, *New Republic,* April 1977, 9.

270   But Powell, whom Brennan: On Brennan's efforts to persuade Powell, see Stern and Wermiel, *Justice Brennan,* 447–49.

270   "[T]he perception of racial": *Regents of the University of California v. Bakke,* 438 U.S. 265 (1978), 303 (Powell majority).

271   "robust exchange of ideas": Ibid., 312–13.

271   Yet Powell's decision: See "The Landmark Bakke Ruling," *Newsweek,* July 10, 1978, 19.

271   Ginsburg was not the only: Of the numerous articles by legal scholars on the meaning of *Bakke,* see, for example, Vincent Blasi, "*Bakke* as Precedent: Does Mr. Justice Powell Have a Theory?," *University of California Law Review* 67 (1979): 21–68.

271   "Did Justice Powell mean": RBG, Constitutional Law Lecture, Feb. 29, 1980, RBG Papers.

271   Other feminist legal scholars: RBG to Isabel Pinzler, Phyllis Segel, Susan Berresford, Margaret Berger, Jane Picker, Chuck Gerrier, memo, May 21, 1979, RBG Papers. For extensive critiques from other feminist legal scholars, see, for example, Nancy Gertner, "*Bakke* on Affirmative Action for Women: Pedestal or Cage?," *Harvard Civil Rights–Civil Liberties Law Review* 14 (1979): 209–14.

271   "alive and well": Mayeri, "Reconstructing the Race-Sex Analogy," 1831. For a definitive study, see Mayeri, *Reasoning from Race.*

272   Then, in a 1976 case: *Washington v. Davis,* 426 U.S. 229 (1976).

272   For nonveterans like Helen Feeney: For a fuller discussion of the Feeney case and of veterans' preferences, see Kerber, *No Constitutional Right to Be Ladies,* chap. 5.

272   The Court's newfound: RBG's reading of the likely disposition of Feeney proved accurate, as did her initial decision not to challenge veterans' preferences in the waning years of the Vietnam War. Traditional veterans' groups, Kerber notes, lobbied intensely against Feeney's challenge as a way of helping young Vietnam vets who they believed had gotten a raw deal—a response congruent with the larger enterprise of postwar remasculinization explored in Jeffords, *Remasculinization of America.* When the Court handed down its decision on June 5, 1979, *Personnel Administrator of Massachusetts v. Feeney,* 442 U.S. 256 (1979), joined prior civil rights rulings to create a framework that made it much more difficult for plaintiffs to successfully challenge facially neutral policies that have a discriminatory impact on women and minorities.

272   Furthermore, Justice Brennan: Brennan, who suffered from a sore throat and depleted energy since 1977, would begin cancer treatments in December 1978, according to his biographers. See Stern and Wermiel, *Justice Brennan,* 449–50.

273   The dual impact of unfavorable: See Reva Siegel, "Why Equal Protection No Longer Protects: The Evolving Form of Status-Enforcing State Action," *Stanford Law Review* 49 (1997): 1111–48.

273   "social and economic pressures": RBG to Isabelle Pinzler, Phyllis Segal, Susan Beresford, Margaret Berger, Jane Picker, and Chuck Guerrier, memo, May 21, 1979, RBG Papers.

273   "battle for control of the law": Teles, *Rise of the Conservative Legal Movement.*

FOURTEEN · An Unexpected Cliff-Hanger

277 **A little more than a year:** Cover of *Ms.*, Jan. 1978.
277 **Passage of the Omnibus:** On feminist involvement in judicial nominations in the Carter era, see Mary Clark, "Changing the Face of the Law: How Women's Advocacy Groups Put Women on the Federal Judicial Appointments Agenda," *Yale Journal of Law and Feminism* 14 (2002): 243–54.
277 **Most important, the bill:** On Carter's reform of judicial selections, see Goldman, *Picking Federal Judges,* chap. 7.
277 **At the White House signing ceremony:** On presidential leadership in the 1970s, see Kalman, *Right Star Rising,* esp. chaps. 6–10.
277 **"more than token":** President's Signing Statement Accompanying Executive Order No. 12059, Oct. 20, 1978, Carter Papers; "President Establishes Circuit Judge Nominating Commission by Executive Order," *American Bar Association Journal* 63 (April 1977): 554; Phyllis N. Segal, "Choosing Women Judges," *National NOW Times,* Aug. 1979. For more on the Omnibus Judgeship Act of 1978, see Jack J. Coe Jr., "Recruitment and Appointment of Federal Judges," *Loyola Los Angeles Law Review* 12 (1979): 1033–42.
278 **But as she waited:** RBG, interview by Sarah Wilson, July 5, 1995, 69, Federal Judicial Center.
278 **But such firms had never:** Ibid.; Griffin B. Bell, "What Went Wrong," in *Taking Care of the Law,* 40. On Bell's strong preference, see also Carter, *White House Diary,* 350.
278 **Ginsburg had her heart:** See copy of "Questionnaire for Prospective Nominees for United States Circuit Judgeship," Jan. 15, 1979, box 22, RBG Papers. As a result of the Omnibus Judgeship Bill, applying for the federal judgeship was something new. In fact, the idea of applying was odious to some people who believed that this crowning accomplishment of a career should come as an anointment. See Gerhardt, *Federal Appointment Process,* 118–20.
279 **"femocrats":** Kenney, *Gender and Justice,* chap. 4.
280 **"thwarting the ambition":** Babcock, *Fish Raincoats,* 160.
280 *Roe v. Wade* **advocate:** On the location of Weddington's office, which would prove critical, see Sarah Weddington, exit interview by Emily Soapes, Jan. 2, 1981, Carter Papers.
280 **"Insider" strategic knowledge:** Kenney, *Gender and Justice,* chap. 4.
281 **Norman Dorsen, then president:** Dorsen to Don Blinken, Dec. 22, 1978, RBG Papers (Second Circuit Judicial Selection).
281 **But when she arrived:** RBG, interview by Wilson, July 5, 1995.
281 **"You were as close":** Nina Totenberg, "Tribute to Justice Ruth Bader Ginsburg," *New York University Annual Survey of American Law* (April 1997): 33–37.
281 **"there was an unholy":** RBG, interview by Wilson, July 5, 1995.
281 **"Mrs. Ginsburg [has] been":** Carter, *White House Diary,* 397.
281 **described as "a natural":** RBG, interview by Wilson, July 5, 1995.
282 **Fortuitously, her old dean:** Gunther to RBG, March 20, 1979, RBG Papers.
282 **NOW's Legal Defense Fund:** Margaret Moses to Carter, telegram, Dec. 6, 1979.
282 **Columbia's executive vice president:** Sovern to Lawrence E. Walsh, Jan. 9, 1979; Rosenthal to Walsh, Jan. 18, 1979, both in RBG Papers.
282 **Distinguished members:** Smith to Joseph D. Tydings, Jan. 22, 1979, Smith to Benjamin R. Civiletti, Dec. 3, 1979, Spann to Benjamin R. Civiletti, Dec. 7, 1979, box 22 D.C. Circuit, Judiciary Appointment—General (1979), RBG Papers.
282 **So, too, did Abner Mikva:** Mikva, interview by Harry Krisler, April 12, 1999, University of California Television.
283 **"There are going to be":** RBG, interview by Wilson, July 5, 1995, 67.
283 **"I'm elated about *Westcott*":** *Orr v. Orr,* 440 U.S. 268 (1979); *Califano v. Westcott,* 443 U.S. 76 (1979). See RBG to Henry Freedman, Feb. 12 and March 16, 1979;

RBG to Diana Steele, March 1, 1979; RBG to Gunther, June 27, 1979, box 2, RBG Papers.

283 **"Mike Sovern's [letter] notes"**: RBG, interview by Barbara Babcock, June 4, 1979, RBG Papers.

284 **Attorney General Griffin Bell**: Bell's preferences were reflected in the merit selection committees as well as by other members of the Justice Department. See Kenney, *Gender and Justice,* chap. 4; Phyllis N. Segal to RBG, March 3, 1980, box 42, RBG Papers; Susan Ness, "A Sexist Selection Process Keeps Qualified Women off the Bench," *Washington Post,* March 26, 1978, C8.

284 **As *The New York Times:*** "The Uppity House and Federal Judges," *New York Times,* Feb. 18, 1978, 22; "Trials of Judicial Selection," *New York Times,* Nov. 26, 1978, E20; "That White Male Federal Bench," *New York Times,* Jan. 29, 1979, A16.

284 **"sanitize[d] my prior liberal"**: Patricia M. Wald, "Women of the Courts Symposium: Six Not-So-Easy Pieces: One Woman Judge's Journey to the Bench and Beyond," *University of Toledo Law Review* 36 (2005): 986.

284 **A man who radiated**: Mikva, interview by Harry Krisler, April 12, 1999.

284 **Longing for "some time"**: RBG, interview by Gunther, June 27, 1979.

285 **The previous summer Ruth**: RBG, "American Bar Association Visits the People's Republic of China," *American Bar Association Journal* 64 (Oct. 1978): 1516–25.

285 **"Far from being 'a leftist'"**: RBG, "A Study Tour of Taiwan's Legal System," *American Bar Association Journal* 66 (Feb. 1980): 165–70; RBG, interview by Yao Chia-wen, July 20, 1979; RBG, interview by Norman Dorsen, Dec. 17, 1979; RBG to Norman Dorsen, Dec. 17, 1979.

285 **Upon learning of his arrest**: See folder 6, box 21, RBG Papers.

285 **Nine members of the Congressional**: Congress members Elizabeth Holtzman, Margaret M. Heckler, Patricia Schroeder, Mary Rose Oakar, Barbara Mikulski, Gladys Noon Spellman, Millicent Fenwick, Lindy Boggs, and Geraldine Ferraro to President Jimmy Carter, July 10, 1979, Ginsburg WH Name File, Carter Papers.

285 **"She's brilliantly qualified"**: Babcock to the Attorney General and Associate Attorney General, March 12, 1979, Ginsburg WH Name File, Carter Papers.

286 **But there was little supporters**: RBG, interview by Wilson, July 5, 1995, 69.

286 **Once Bazelon's decision created**: National Women's Political Caucus with co-signers American Association of University Women, California Women Lawyers, Equal Rights Advocates, Federation of Organizations for Professional Women, NAACP Legal Defense Fund, National Conference of Puerto Rican Woman, Women's Equity Action League, Women's Legal Defense Fund, Women's Rights Project Center for Law and Social Policy, B'nai B'rith Women, Washington Chapter of Women's Division/National Bar Association to President Carter, telegram, Jan. 16, 1980, Ginsburg WH Name File, Carter Papers.

286 **But the numbers on the bench**: Kenney, *Gender and Justice,* chap. 4.

286 **But after a lengthy**: Weddington to author, email, May 9, 2011.

286 **Then she rushed downstairs**: Ibid.

286 **Just as she anticipated**: Laura A. Kiernan, "Feminist Picked for U.S. Court of Appeals Here," *Washington Post,* Dec. 16, 1979, A1.

287 **"Bravo! Bravo! Bravo!"**: Pauli Murray to RBG, Dec. 17, 1979, folder 8, box 21, RBG Papers.

287 **"What a splendid Christmas"**: Frank to RBG, Dec. 18, 1979, folder 8, box 21, RBG Papers.

287 **"We'll all be the better"**: Tribe to RBG, Dec. 17, 1979, folder 8, box 21, RBG Papers.

288 **"Time is of the essence"**: Telegram by National Women's Political Caucus, Carter Papers.

288 **"no big thing"**: "The Complaints of the Women's Lobby: When NOW Was Too Soon," *New York Times,* Dec. 19, 1979, A30.

288 **Her broadside angered:** See Carter, *White House Diary,* 378. Contrast Smeal's response with that of NOW's legal director, Phyllis Segal, and the NWPC's Susan Ness, both of whom displayed far greater understanding of the difficulties involved while simultaneously calling for more nominations of women to the judiciary. See Segal to RBG, March 3, 1980; Susan Ness and Fredrica Wechsler, "Women Judges—Why So Few?," *Graduate Women* 73 (Nov./Dec. 1979): 10–12; Kenney, *Gender and Justice,* chap. 4.

288 **Alarmed that Ginsburg's nomination:** Weddington to Fran Voorde, memorandum, Jan. 28, 1980, box 15, Ginsburg WH Name File, Carter Papers.

288 **Civiletti, annoyed with:** Ibid.

288 **Then, on February 2:** Lyle Denniston and Allan Frank, "Appellate Court Seat for Feminist Stalled," *Washington Star,* Feb. 2, 1980.

289 **"one-issue woman":** Douglas Lavine, "Court Prospect's Feminism Irks Senate Conservatives," *National Law Journal,* Dec. 1979, 8.

289 **"militant feminist":** "Ashbrook 01/22/80 and Crane 02/6/90," box 42, RBG Papers.

289 **"could bring about a vast revolution":** Ibid.

289 **The National Rifle Association:** Laura Kiernan, "Law Professor in Line for Bazelon's Seat," *Washington Post,* Sept. 25, 1979, B1.

289 **"Pro-family" forces:** Wald, "Women of the Courts Symposium," 986–87.

289 **Letters on Ginsburg's behalf:** See, for example, Chesterfield Smith to Joseph D. Tydings, Jan. 22, 1979, Smith to Civiletti, Dec. 3, 1979, Spann to Civiletti, Dec. 7, 1979, box 22 D.C. Circuit, Judiciary Appointments—General (1979), RBG Papers.

289 **To be described as a "militant feminist":** RBG to Herbert Wechsler, Jan. 28, 1980, box 22, D.C. Circuit Judicial Appointment—Opposition (1980), RBG Papers.

289 **Thinking more letters:** Ibid.; see also Segal to RBG, Feb. 25, 1980, March 3, 1980, box 22, D.C. Circuit Judicial Appointment—Opposition (1980), RBG Papers.

289 **When the ten new women:** RBG to Alice Heyman, June 18, 1973, box 42, RBG Papers; RBG, interview by Marcus, Sept. 3, 1997.

290 **Ted Kennedy, who:** RBG, interview by Wilson, July 5, 1995, 70–71.

290 **Once hearings were finally:** See, for example, Nina Totenberg, "Ginsburg: Will 'She' Sail As Smoothly as 'He' Would?," *Legal Times of Washington,* May 26, 1980, RBG Papers.

291 **When Hatch left the table:** For Millstein's recollection, see Ira M. Millstein, "Testimony Before the Senate Judiciary Committee Hearing on the Confirmation of Ruth Bader Ginsburg to Be an Associate Justice of the Supreme Court," July 23, 1993, folder no. 029738, OA/ID 21853, WHORM: Subject File, General, Clinton Presidential Records, William Clinton Presidential Library.

291 **For Marty, later one:** On Marty's teaching skills, see the numerous tributes on "Remembrances of Professor Ginsburg," *Georgetown Law,* www.law.georgetown.edu. On the rapid expansion of Fried, Frank, Harris, Shriver & Jacobson LLP between 1981 and 1987, see "Fried, Frank, Harris, Shriver & Jacobson LLP," www.top-law-schools .com.

291 **"Appellate judging has much in common":** *Hearings Before the Committee on the Judiciary United States Senate,* 96th Cong., 89/2, Serial No. 96-21, Part 7: 349 (statement of Ruth Bader Ginsburg, Nominee, Judge of Court of Appeals, District of Columbia).

291 **"That style of work and thought":** Ibid., 350.

291 **a more "balanced" candidate:** "United Families of America Testimony on Ginsburg Nomination," June 4, 1980, box 42, RBG Papers.

291 **"After many anxious weeks":** RBG to Alice Heyman, June 18, 1980, box 42, RBG Papers.

292 **the "dazzling smile":** "Professor Gerald Gunther Speaks at Investiture of Judge Ruth Ginsburg in Washington, D.C.," 8–9.

292 **Sonnet for Judge:** James Ginsburg to RBG, March 15, 1983, RBG Birthday Book.

293   **But soon other hallmarks:** Williams and Williams, "Sense and Sensibility," 589.

293   **"A meticulous writer":** Klarman to author, email, Nov. 19, 2013.

293   **Striving to meet Ginsburg's:** Williams and Williams, "Sense and Sensibility," 589.

294   **"He was the funniest person":** Klarman to author, email, Nov. 19, 2013.

294   **"I believe you're supposed":** James Ginsburg, "Thoughts on Dad," in Alito and Supreme Court Spouses, *Chef Supreme.*

295   **"I asked for a day off":** Klarman to author, email, Nov. 19, 2013.

295   **"Her rigorous interrogations":** Morrison, interview by author, April 10, 2010.

295   **"a tiger on the bench":** Williams and Williams, "Sense and Sensibility," 590.

295   **Not surprisingly, she generally:** For the next few paragraphs concerning RBG's time on the D.C. Circuit, I rely on Joel Klein's letter to Bernard Nussbaum, June 11, 1993, folder "Ginsburg, Ruth Bader," OA/Box Number CF 33, Clinton Presidential Records, Counsel's Office, Bernard Nussbaum, Clinton Presidential Library. For cases on civil rights, see *Wright v. Regan,* 656 F.2d 820 (1981), *Loe v. Heckler,* 768 F.2d 409 (1985), *McElvoy v. Turner,* 792 F.2d 194 (1986), *Spann v. Colonial Village,* 899 F.2d 24 (1990), and *O'Donnell Construction v. District of Columbia,* 963 F.2d 420 (1992). For cases on worker safety and labor rights, see *Wilson v. Johns-Manville Sales Corp.,* 684 F.2d 111 (1982), *Amalgamated Transit Union Int'l v. Donovan,* 767 F.2d 939 (1985), *Simpson v. Federal Mine Safety and Health Review Comm'n,* 842 F.2d 453 (1988), *West Coast Sheet Metal Inc. v. NLRB,* 938 F.2d 1356 (1991), and *United States Department of the Air Force v. FLRA,* 949 F.2d 475 (1991).

295   **but "indecent" speech:** See *New York Times v. Sullivan,* 376 U.S. 254 (1964). For RBG's application of the "actual malice" standard, see *Tavoulareas v. Piro,* 817 F.2d 762 (1987), 806–9 (RBG concurring). For the opinion on "indecent" speech, see *Action for Children's Television v. Federal Communications Commission,* 852 F.2d 1332 (1988) (RBG majority).

295   **She dissented in a First:** *Dkt Memorial Fund Ltd. v. Agency for Int'l Dev.,* 887 F.2d 275 (1989).

295   **And she sided with protesters:** *Community for Creative Non-violence v. Watt,* 703 F.2d 586 (1983), 605–8 (RBG concurring); reversed by the Supreme Court, *Clark v. Community for Creative Non-violence,* 468 U.S. 288 (1984).

295   **She also wrote a strong:** *Abourezk v. Reagan,* 785 F.2d 1043 (1986) (RBG majority).

296   **"the genius of our Constitution":** *In re Sealed Case,* 838 F.2d 476 (1988).

296   **Her dissent was later upheld:** *Morrison v. Olson,* 487 U.S. 654 (1988).

296   **The hearing was rejected:** *Goldman v. Secretary of Defense,* 739 F.2d 657 (1984).

296   **Carl E. Olsen argued:** *Olsen v. Drug Enforcement Administration,* 878 F.2d 1458 (1989).

296   **In her opinions on health:** See *Natural Resources Defense Council v. Gorsuch,* 685 F.2d 718 (1982); *NRDC v. Hodel,* 865 F.2d 288 (1988); and *National Coal Association v. Lujan,* 979 F.2d 1548 (1992).

296   **And in her opinions on searches:** Richard L. Lesher to William Clinton, July 21, 1993, "Ruth Bader Ginsburg," Folder no. 029738, OA/ID 21853, WHORM: Subject File, General, Clinton Presidential Records, Clinton Presidential Library.

296   **Overall, she distinguished:** See *United States v. Jackson,* 824 F.2d 21 (1987); *United States v. Gandy,* 868 F.2d 458 (1989); *United States v. Dockery,* 965 F.2d 1112 (1992); and *United States v. Chin,* 981 F.2d 1275 (1992).

297   **Ruth and Marty had, in fact:** Harry T. Edwards, "A Tribute to My Friend, the Honorable Ruth Bader Ginsburg," *New York University Annual Survey of American Law* 54 (1997): xv–xvii.

297   **In the 1984 *Dronenburg*:** Quotation from Jeffrey Rosen, "The Book of Ruth," *New Republic,* Aug. 2, 1993. For the case, see *Dronenburg v. Zech,* 741 F.2d 1388 (1984). Robert Bork, Antonin Scalia, and Stephen F. Williams presided.

297   **Other commentators also:** Nat Hentoff, "One Cheer for Judge Ginsburg," *Washington Post,* July 3, 1993, A23; Shilts, *Conduct Unbecoming,* 452.

298 **"she voted 94 percent"**: Klein to Nussbaum, June 11, 1993, Clinton Presidential Library.

298 **"a judicial prophet"**: Here, I am paraphrasing Rosen's statement in "Book of Ruth": "But even those who know [RBG] best cannot confidently predict whether the change in role will liberate her to act more as a judicial prophet and less as a priest."

298 **"the sole unifying force"**: Klein to Nussbaum, June 11, 1993, Clinton Presidential Library.

298 **Appealing for a temperate**: See RBG, "Speaking in a Judicial Voice," 1185, and "Styles of Collegial Judging: One Judge's Perspective," *Federal Bureau News and Journal* 39 (1992): 199.

298 **a survey of "leading centrists"**: Klein to Nussbaum, June 11, 1993, Clinton Presidential Library.

299 **George's flexibility and willingness**: For RBG's appreciative remarks about her son-in-law, see "Forty Years Later: Supreme Court Justice Ginsburg's Reflections, Four Decades After Her First Interview with AWIS National," *AWIS Magazine,* Oct. 3, 2013.

299 **When Paul and Clara**: Jane Ginsburg, "Daddy," in Alito and Supreme Court Spouses, *Chef Supreme,* 124. For the grandchildren's chocolate chip oatmeal cookie recipe, see 106.

299 **Remembering their son's**: Nathan J. Silverman, "Local Label Is a Chicago Classic, North Side's Cedille Records Up for First Grammy Award," *Inside* (Illinois).

299 **"its construction, nuance"**: Carr Ferguson, "Marty," in Alito and Supreme Court Spouses, *Chef Supreme,* 109–10.

300 **His work so pleased**: Pamala F. Olson, "ABA Section of Taxation 2006 Distinguished Service Award Recipient, Professor Martin D. Ginsburg," *ABA Section of Taxation News Quarterly* 25 (2006): 6.

300 **Marty and Ruth had deliberated**: Stephen Labaton, "The Man Behind the High Court Nominee," *New York Times,* June 17, 1993, A1.

301 **"ghastly number"**: MacLachlan, "Mr. Ginsburg's Campaign for Nominee," 33.

301 **"diligent academic to enormously"**: Martin D. Ginsburg, "Distinguished Service Award Presentation—May 5, 2006," *ABA Section of Taxation News Quarterly* 25 (2006): 7–8. MDG's speech, which was given when he accepted the award in 2006.

301 **Now "sanitized" after fourteen years**: Wald, "Women of the Courts Symposium," 986–87.

FIFTEEN · The 107th Justice

302 **Given the opportunity**: Ruth Marcus, "President Asks Wider Court Hunt," *Washington Post,* May 6, 1993, A1.

302 **"one of our nation's best"**: "Transcript of President's Announcement and Judge Ginsburg's Remarks."

302 **"Rose Garden Rubbish"**: Background Briefing by Senior Administration Officials, Office of the Press Secretary, White House, June 14, 1993, Part II: Box 1946, Daniel P. Moynihan Papers, Manuscript Division, Library of Congress, Washington, D.C.

302 **"You were terrific"**: Clinton to RBG, June 14, 1993, OA/ID 21853, FG051, Scan ID 033475, WHORM: Subject File, Clinton Presidential Records, Clinton Presidential Library.

303 **"certain zigzag quality"**: "Transcript of President's Announcement and Judge Ginsburg's Remarks."

303 **"Brit just didn't know"**: Hume and Clinton quotations in "The Supreme Court," *New York Times,* June 15, 1993, A1; Stephanopoulos, *All Too Human,* 166–75.

303 **"Clinton deserves unstinting"**: "Wise Choice: Justice Ruth Bader Ginsburg," *New Republic,* July 5, 1993, 7.

303 **Under the direction of:** Background Briefing by Senior Administration Officials, Office of the Press Secretary, White House, June 14, 1993, Part II: Box 1946, Moynihan Papers.

304 **Knowing that any political:** Thomas L. Friedman, "The Supreme Court: The 11th-Hour Scramble; After Hoping for a 'Home Run' in Choosing a Justice, Clinton May Be Just Home Free," *New York Times*, July 15, 1993; Toobin, *Nine*, chap. 5; Neil A. Lewis, "As Political Terrain Shifts, Breyer Lands on His Feet," *New York Times*, May 15, 1994, 10. For an excellent discussion on how the changing politics of judicial nominations circumscribed Clinton's choices, see Mark Silverstein and William Halton, "You Can't Always Get What You Want: Reflections on the Ginsburg and Breyer Nominations," *Journal of Law and Politics* 12 (1996): 459–79.

304 **Rather, Clinton wanted to get:** Background Briefing by Senior Administration Officials, Office of the Press Secretary, White House, June 14, 1993, Part II: Box 1946, Moynihan Papers.

305 **The White House conveyed:** Ibid.

305 **"not on the same":** See "Breyer and Ginsburg" note; also RBG, interview by Wilson, Sept. 25, 1995, 5.

305 **"remote and bookish":** Hirshman, *Sisters in Law*, 201.

305 **"appears to be an unusual synthesis":** Klein to Bernard Nussbaum, June 1, 1993, folder "Ginsburg, Ruth Bader," OA/Box Number CF 33, Clinton Presidential Records, Counsel's Office, Bernard Nussbaum, Clinton Presidential Library.

305 **"an accomplished advocate":** Ibid.

306 **"needed religious and gender":** Ibid.

306 **"Pat, She's the real thing":** Background Briefing by Senior Administration Officials, Office of the Press Secretary, White House, June 14, 1993, Part II: Box 1946, Moynihan Papers.

306 **"Judge Ginsburg's work":** Quoted in Robert Barnes, "Clinton Library Release of Papers on Ginsburg, Breyer Nominations Offer Insight, Some Fun," *Washington Post*, June 8, 2014, A13.

306 **Returning from Vermont:** Hirshman, *Sisters in Law*, 206, and RBG, *My Own Words*, 169.

307 **"I just wanted to":** Joan Biskupic, "Quick Confirmation of Ginsburg Sought," *Washington Post*, June 16, 1993, A1. Clinton had also done his homework, reading articles written by Ginsburg during her tenure on the D.C. Circuit, which no doubt helped him to reach conclusions about her jurisprudence. See, for example, RBG, "Remarks on Writing Separately," *Washington Law Review* 65 (1990): 133–50; RBG, "Styles of Collegial Judging," 199–201; RBG, "Interpretations of the Equal Protection Clause," *Harvard Journal of Law and Public Policy* 9 (1986): 41–45.

307 **What struck him:** Background Briefing by Senior Administration Officials, Office of the Press Secretary, White House, June 14, 1993, Part II: Box 1946, Moynihan Papers.

307 **"Tremendously impressed":** Clinton, *My Life*, 524. See also Harris, *Survivor*, chap. 5.

307 **In November 1991:** "First-Rate Centrists," *American Lawyer* 13 (Nov. 1991): 76.

307 **Indeed, her record on regulatory:** Marcia Coyle, "In Search of an Identity," *National Law Journal* 16 (1994): C1–C3.

307 **"a paragon of judicial restraint":** Jeffrey Rosen, "Ruth Bader Ginsburg: The New Look of Liberalism on the Court," *New York Times Magazine*, Oct. 5, 1997, SM60.

308 **As a graduate of:** On the conservative legal movement, see Teles, *Rise of the Conservative Legal Movement*.

308 **Ginsburg's reputation as:** Clinton had run as a New Democrat. On the shift of the Democratic Party to the center, see Kenneth S. Baer, *Reinventing Democrats*, esp. chaps. 6–8.

308 **"stand up to them":** See RBG, "Speaking in a Judicial Voice," 1185–209; RBG, "Styles of Collegial Judging," 199–201.

308 **"If I'm going to propose":** Background Briefing by Senior Administration Officials, Office of the Press Secretary, White House, June 14, 1993, Part II: Box 1946, Moynihan Papers.

309 **Downstairs in the living room:** Joan Biskupic, "Judge Ruth Bader Ginsburg Named to High Court; Nominee's Philosophy Seen Strengthening the Center," *Washington Post,* June 15, 1993, A1.

309 **"Marty had everything":** RBG, *My Own Words,* 168.

309 **"surprise selection":** Richard L. Berke, "Clinton Names Ruth Bader Ginsburg, Advocate for Women, to Court," *New York Times,* June 15, 1993, A1.

309 **"Pat Was Key":** "Pat Was Key to Top-Court Pick," *New York Post,* June 15, 1993; Marilyn Rauber, "Prez: Ruth Is 'Clearly Pro-choice,'" *New York Post,* June 16, 1993, 5.

309 **Marty attributed the palpable:** *Women's Equity Action League v. Cavazos,* 906 F.2d 742 (1990). RBG wrote an opinion holding that the courts had no authority to oversee "the procedures that government agencies use to enforce civil rights prescriptions controlling educational institutions that receive federal funds," at 744.

310 **But the problem involved:** *Dronenburg v. Zech,* 741 F.2d 1388 (1984). The judges concluded that they could not create a "constitutional right to engage in homosexual conduct" (1398). RBG's vote to not have the entire circuit rehear *Dronenburg* had been based on *Doe v. Commonwealth's Attorney for Richmond,* 425 U.S. 901 (1976).

310 **"measured motions":** RBG, "Speaking in a Judicial Voice," 1198.

310 **The legal historian David Garrow:** David J. Garrow, "Abortion Before and After *Roe v. Wade*: An Historical Perspective," Albany Law Review 62.3 (1999): 833–52. On pro-choice objection, see Greenhouse, "Judge Ginsburg Still Voices Strong Doubts on Rationale Behind Roe v. Wade Ruling." At the time of RBG's nomination, Kate Michelman of NARAL was quoted on *NBC Nightly News* as saying, "Her criticism of *Roe* raises concerns about whether she believes that the . . . right to choose is a fundamental right or a lesser right." On RBG's objection to the sweep of *Roe* and lack of legislative dialogue, see Garrow, "History Lesson for the Judge."

310 **Moreover, the influx:** For example, southern Baptists, the largest Protestant denomination, did not become firmly in the pro-life camp until eighteen years after *Roe v. Wade*. Laura Foxworth, "Southern Baptists for Life and the Challenge of Delivering the Southern Baptist Convention to the Pro-life Movement" (paper presented at the Annual Meeting of the OAH, Atlanta, April 11, 2014).

310 **Even President Clinton:** See, for example, Rauber, "Prez: Ruth Is 'Clearly Pro-choice.'" Also see Background Briefing by Senior Administration Officials, Office of the Press Secretary, White House, June 14, 1993, Part II: Box 1946, Moynihan Papers.

311 **But by 1987:** *California Federal Savings and Loan Association v. Guerra,* 479 U.S. 272 (1987). On the division over same versus equal treatment, especially as it related to pregnancy, see Wendy W. Williams, "Equality's Riddle: Pregnancy and the Equal Treatment/Special Treatment Debate," *New York University Review of Law and Social Change* 13 (1984–85): 325–80. Williams played a prominent role in drafting the bill that became the Pregnancy Discrimination Act. On *California Federal Savings and Loan Association v. Guerra,* see Stephanie M. Wildman, "Pregnant and Working: The Story of *California Federal Savings & Loan Ass'n. v. Guerra,*" in Schneider and Wildman, *Women and the Law Stories,* 253–76.

311 **In the legal academy:** For the mother-daughter analogy, see Chamallas, *Introduction to Feminist Legal Theory,* 17.

311 **They also faulted:** See, for example, David Cole, "Strategies of Difference: Litigating for Women's Rights in a Man's World," *Journal of Law and Inequality* 2 (1984): 33–96; Lucinda M. Finley, "Transcending Equality Theory: A Way Out of the Maternity and the Workplace Debate," *Columbia Law Review* 86 (Oct. 1986): 1118–82; Mary Becker, "Prince Charming: Abstract Equality," *Supreme Court Review* (1987): 203, 212–13, 218–24; and Mason, *Equality Trap.*

311 **In her influential study:** Gilligan, *In a Different Voice.*

311 **Accordingly, cultural feminists scrutinized:** On cultural or relational feminism in the legal academy, see, for example, Leslie Bender, "A Lawyer's Primer on Feminist Theory and Tort," *Journal of Legal Education* 1/2 (1988): 33–36; Judith Resnik, "On the Bias: Feminist Reconsiderations of the Aspirations for Our Judges," *Southern California Law Review* 61 (1988): 1878–944; and Carrie Menkel-Meadow, "Exploring a Research Agenda of the Feminization of the Legal Profession: Theories of Gender and Social Change," *Law and Social Inquiry* 14 (Spring 1989): 289–319.

311 **"essentially and irretrievably":** Robin West, "Jurisprudence and Gender," *University of Chicago Law Review* 55 (Winter 1988): 1–72, esp. 2.

311 **But while cultural:** Joan C. Williams, "Deconstructing Gender," *Michigan Law Review* 87 (1989): 797–845.

312 **Rather, it should be:** MacKinnon, *Sexual Harassment of Working Women.*

312 **That is, multiple forms:** See "Beyond Racism and Misogyny: Black Feminism and 2 Live Crew," in Cohen, Jones, and Tronto, *Women Transforming Politics,* 552–53; Kimberlé Crenshaw, "Demarginalizing the Intersection of Race and Sex: A Black Feminist Critique of Antidiscrimination Doctrine, Feminist Theory, and Antiracist Politics," *University of Chicago Legal Forum* (1989): 139–67. See also Regina Austin, "Sapphire Bound!," *Wisconsin Law Review* (May/June 1989): 539–78.

312 **None of these developments:** Marcia Greenberger, interview by author, Washington, D.C., Sept. 24, 2001.

312 **Yet collectively these new:** On the influence of poststructuralism, see Marie Ashe, "Mind's Opportunity: Birthing a Poststructuralist Feminist Jurisprudence," *Syracuse University Law Review* 38 (1987–88): 1129–73. On the application of multiple perspectives, see Martha Minow, "Foreword: Justice Engendered," *Harvard Law Review* 101 (1987): 10–95. The only public response from RBG is her co-authored article in which she put her own litigation in historical perspective, applauded the diversity of feminist jurisprudence, and urged against personal attacks as well as the assumption that one's particular feminist legal perspective is the only theoretically correct one. See RBG and Flagg, "Some Reflections on the Feminist Legal Thought of the 1970s," 9–21.

313 **When she read Katha:** Ibid.

313 **"the Constitution remained":** RBG and Flagg, "Some Reflections on the Feminist Legal Thought of the 1970s," esp. 13.

313 **"Such comment seems":** Ibid., 17.

313 **"the [current] tendency to":** Ibid., 21 (italics mine).

313 **Other administration-inspired reverses:** On the GOP and the Right, see Critchlow, *Phyllis Schlafly and Grassroots Conservatism,* esp. chaps. 10–11; and Melich, *Republican War Against Women,* esp. chaps. 9–17. On CEDAW and the continuing importance to the United States of its ratification, see Janet Benshoof, "U.S. Ratification of CEDAW: An Opportunity to Radically Reframe the Right to Equality Accorded Women Under the U.S. Constitution," *New York University Review of Law and Social Change* 35 (2011): 104–30. On other reverses, see Evans, *Tidal Wave,* chap. 6. For the impact on feminist organizations, see Ferree and Martin, *Feminist Organizations.*

314 **The destructive rhetoric:** Faludi, *Backlash,* esp. introduction.

314 **"by 1990 abortion clinics":** Evans, *Tidal Wave,* 182n21 for data.

314 **Or perhaps not:** Jeffrey Toobin, "Heavyweight: How Ruth Bader Ginsburg Has Moved the Supreme Court," *New Yorker,* March 11, 2013, 38–47. In nonunanimous cases, RBG voted with Bork 85 percent of the time and Wald 38 percent of the time. See Neil A. Lewis, "Judge Ginsburg's Opinions: At Center, Yet Hard to Label," *New York Times,* June 16, 1993, A1.

314 **"Nothing is so admirable":** On the continuing identification of RBG with "formal" equality, see Judith Baer, "Advocate on the Court: Ruth Bader Ginsburg and the Limits

of Formal Equality," in Maltz, *Rehnquist Justice,* chap. 8. Galbraith's quotation is in Kumar, *Dictionary of Quotations,* 189.

315 **Josephson, a retired partner:** See Stephanie Strom, "For Expert on Electoral College, Calls Never Stop," *New York Times,* Nov. 2, 2004, B1.

315 **The White House, Eizenstat:** Richard Davis, "The Ginsburg Nomination and the Press," *Journal of International Press and Politics* 1, no. 2 (March 1996): 85.

315 **Wasting no time:** For letters of support in favor of RBG's nomination, see Dorsen to Bernard Nussbaum, April 30, 1993; Sovern to William Clinton, April 16, 1993; Robert W. Meserve to Clinton, April 20, 1993, OA/ID 21853, FG051 WHORM: Subject File, Clinton Presidential Records, Clinton Presidential Library.

315 **Other familiar names:** For letters in support of RBG's nomination, see Berger to Bernard Nussbaum, April 27, 1993; Kay to William Clinton, April 24, 1993; Babcock to Nussbaum, May 20, 1993; Law to Clinton, April 12, 1993; Williams to Clinton, May 11, 1993; Susan Deller Ross to Clinton, May 18, 1993; Taub to Clinton, April 30, 1992; Peratis to Clinton, May 5, 1993; Benshoof to Clinton, May 13, 1993, OA/ID 21853, FG051 WHORM: Subject File, Clinton Presidential Records, Clinton Presidential Library.

315 **"distress that her remarks":** Ann W. Richards to Bruce Lindsey, May 31, 1993, OA/ID 21853, FG051, WHORM: Subject File, Clinton Presidential Records, Clinton Presidential Library; Davis, "Ginsburg Nomination and the Press," 85. The *Legal Times* published the Madison Lecture so that readers in the legal community might read it for themselves. See "Ginsburg Laments *Roe*'s Lack of Restraint," *Legal Times,* April 5, 1993. Also see Background Briefing by Senior Administration Officials, Office of the Press Secretary, White House, June 14, 2014, Part II: Box 1946, Moynihan Papers.

316 **"'The women are against her'":** Moynihan, *Portrait in Letters of an American Visionary,* 606; Martin D. Ginsburg, "Some Reflections on Imperfection," *Arizona State Law Journal* 39 (Fall 2007): 955.

316 **An old acquaintance:** Because of the delay in her nomination following the ill-fated nominations of Baird and Wood, Clinton apparently sought Reno's advice only at the last minute. Toobin, *Nine,* chap. 5.

316 **Nussbaum affirmed that:** Martin D. Ginsburg, "Some Reflections on Imperfection," 956. The letter is not among the Nussbaum Papers in the Clinton Library thus far released to the public.

316 **"a number of superbly qualified":** Davis, "Ginsburg Nomination and the Press," 86.

316 **"Washington is a sieve":** Martin D. Ginsburg, "Some Reflections on Imperfection," 956.

316 **Hess circulated the information:** Davis, "Ginsburg Nomination and the Press," 86–87.

316 **That he found "depressing":** Anthony Lewis, "Abroad at Home: How Not to Choose," *New York Times,* May 10, 1993, A19. Lewis's preferred nominee had been Breyer, according to his widow, Margaret H. Marshall, who retired in 2010 as chief justice of the Massachusetts Supreme Judicial Court.

317 **Next came Jeffrey Rosen's:** Jeffrey Rosen, "The List," *New Republic,* May 10, 1993, 12–15.

317 **"I've heard expressed":** Quoted in Murdoch and Price, *Courting Justice,* 421.

317 **As letters supporting:** Davis, "Ginsburg Nomination and the Press," 86, 97n13. See also MacLachlan, "Mr. Ginsburg's Campaign for Nominee," 33–34.

317 **But in the critical:** Alan Emory, "Sources Say Moynihan Key to Ginsburg's Nomination," *Watertown Daily Times,* June 18, 1993, 3, in Part II: Box 1946, Moynihan Papers.

317 **Among the many articles:** Labaton, "Man Behind the High Court Nominee."

317 **"It's a great love story":** Quoted in Eleanor Randolph, "Husband Triggered Letters Supporting Ginsburg for Court," *Washington Post,* June 17, 1993, A25. RBG read Flagg's letter to Woods according to Murdoch and Price in *Courting Justice,* 421.

318   **With Ginsburg's having the highest:** David Von Drehle, "ABA Panel Calls Ginsburg 'Well-Qualified' for Court," *Washington Post,* July 14, 1993, A12; Joan Biskupic, "With Revamped Panel, Confirmation Hearings May Lack Drama," *Washington Post,* July 20, 1993, A6.

318   **Still more sensational:** Davis, "Ginsburg Nomination and the Press," 78.

318   **"Make sure she is always allowed":** Robert A. Katzmann, "Reflections on the Confirmation Journey of Ruth Bader Ginsburg, Summer 1993," in Dodson, *Legacy of Ruth Bader Ginsburg,* 8.

318   **"Ruth . . . is always the same":** Edwards, "Tribute to My Friend, the Honorable Ruth Bader Ginsburg," xvi.

318   **The nominee made clear:** Katzmann, "Reflections on the Confirmation Journey of Ruth Bader Ginsburg, Summer 1993," 10.

319   **"keen sense of the big picture":** Ibid., 9.

319   **Meanwhile, Klain, Klein, and Katzmann:** Ibid., 9–10.

319   **"Flatbush Strategy":** Neil A. Lewis, "Ginsburg Promises Judicial Restraint If She Joins Court," *New York Times,* July 21, 1993, A1.

319   **"to be judged as a judge":** Statement of RBG, *Nomination of Ruth Bader Ginsburg to Be Associate Justice of the Supreme Court of the United States: Hearings Before the Committee on the Judiciary United States Senate,* 103rd Cong. 52 (1993), esp. 46, 52–53.

320   **central to her "life, to her well-being":** Ibid., 207.

320   **"It is her body":** Ibid.

320   **On gender equality:** Ibid., 243–44.

320   **Anticipating future cases:** Ibid., 140–41, 146, 322–33, 341, 359.

320   **"I am not going":** Ibid., 265, 192.

321   **"preternaturally controlled":** Elena Kagan, "Confirmation Messes, Old and New," *University of Chicago Law Review* 62 (Spring 1995): 919–42, esp. 926, 928.

321   **"There is some suspicion":** Lyle Denniston, "Which Judge Ginsburg Will Show Up Tuesday?," *Baltimore Sun,* Aug. 8, 1993.

321   **Yet for all the grousing:** Joan Biskupic, "Senate Panel Approves Ginsburg for Supreme Court Unanimously," *Washington Post,* July 10, 1993, A4.

321   **"official lovefest":** Kagan, "Confirmation Messes, Old and New," 920. Senators Jesse Helms (R-N.C.), Don Nickles (R-Okla.), and Robert C. Smith (R-N.H.) opposed, Helms objecting to RBG's positions on abortion and homosexuality. See Linda Greenhouse, "Senate, 96–3, Easily Affirms Judge Ginsburg as a Justice," *New York Times,* Aug. 4, 1993, B8. On the real vetting, see Silverstein and Halton, "You Can't Always Get What You Want," 459–79.

321   **It was a tribute:** U.S. Senate, "Nomination of Ruth Bader Ginsburg," "Judge Ruth Bader Ginsburg," and "Nomination of Ruth Bader Ginsburg, of New York, to Be an Associate Justice of the Supreme Court," 103rd Congress, 1st sess., Aug. 2, 1993, S10076–S10079, S10097, and S10109; U.S. Senate, "Statement on the Confirmation of Ruth Bader Ginsburg," "Nomination of Ruth Bader Ginsburg," "Votes on S. 919 and Ginsburg Nomination," 103rd Cong., 1st sess., Aug. 3, 1993, S10225 and S10111.

321   **On August 10:** For Clinton's remarks, see "President William Jefferson Clinton Swearing In of Ruth Bader Ginsburg, 10 Aug. 1993," OA/ID 21853, FG051, WHORM: Subject File, Clinton Presidential Records, Clinton Presidential Library.

321   **A small cohort of colleagues:** Hirshman, *Sisters in Law,* 214.

321   **Of the men before whom:** Greenhouse, *Becoming Justice Blackmun;* Barnhart and Schlickman, *John Paul Stevens,* esp. 206–7; and Stevens, *Five Chiefs,* chap. 5.

322   **Sandra Day O'Connor:** For a perceptive biography of O'Connor, see Biskupic, *Sandra Day O'Connor,* xix. Despite the inflated claim of the title, Linda Hirshman also provides an excellent account of O'Connor's route to the Court, her accomplishments, her "tightfisted votes for equality," and the extent to which she paved the way for RBG in *Sisters in Law,* 168.

323 **To treat the founding:** See Thurgood Marshall, "At the Annual Seminar of the San Francisco Patent and Trademark Association," Maui, Hawaii, May 6, 1987.

323 **"fainthearted originalist":** Scalia quoted in Jeffrey Toobin, "Partners," *New Yorker,* Aug. 29, 2011, 42. On Scalia's originalism, see Biskupic, *American Original;* also, Murphy, *Scalia.*

323 **Thomas, unyielding:** As it turned out, Thomas volunteered his help with certiorari tabulations. See RBG, "Remarks for American Law Institute Annual Dinner, 19 May 1994," *Saint Louis University Law Journal* 38 (1994): 883–84.

323 **"to repudiate . . . common sense":** *Citizens United v. Federal Election Commission,* 130 S. Ct. 876 (2010), 979 (Stevens concurring and dissenting).

324 **She would also discover:** RBG with Linda Greenhouse, "A Conversation with Justice Ginsburg," *Yale Law Journal Online* 122 (2013): 299.

324 **A Republican nominee to Brennan's:** See Biskupic, *Sandra Day O'Connor;* Biskupic, *American Original,* 88–89; Tushnet, *Court Divided;* Colucci, *Justice Kennedy's Jurisprudence.*

324 **"I am a judge born":** RBG, quoted in her "Address to the Annual Meeting of the American Jewish Committee," May 1995, reprinted in "See What Being Jewish Means to Me," Advertisement by the American Jewish Committee, *New York Times,* Jan. 14, 1996, A13. RBG also expressed her Jewish identity through organizational affiliations. Prior to her nomination to the Court, she was a member of the American Jewish Committee and the National Commission on Law and Social Action of the American Jewish Congress and served on the board of the American branch of the International Association of Jewish Lawyers and Jurists. See Malvina Halberstam, "Ruth Bader Ginsburg: The First Jewish Woman on the Supreme Court," *Cardozo Law Review* 19 (1998): 1442. Upon becoming a justice, she felt it appropriate for the first time in her adulthood to observe the holiest day in the Jewish calendar, Yom Kippur, by not coming to work.

325 **Visitors to Ginsburg's:** Author's recollections. For additional impressions, see also Rosen, "Ruth Bader Ginsburg: The New Look of Liberalism on the Court," SM60. See also RBG, interview by Brian Lamb, July 1, 2009.

325 **In addition, some 1,619 appeals:** Greenhouse, "Senate, 96–3, Easily Affirms Judge Ginsburg as a Justice," A1.

326 **But each memo still had:** Justice Stevens did not use the certiorari pool. See Barnhart and Schlickman, *John Paul Stevens,* 200.

326 **The two women bonded:** Ibid., 260–61.

326 **Neither hesitated to confront:** Hirshman, *Sisters in Law,* 210; Kempner, *Yoo-Hoo, Mrs. Goldberg.* RBG's comment on O'Connor appears in the Bonus Features.

326 **"I'm Sandra, Not Ruth":** Anita Blumstein Brody et al., "Women on the Bench," *Columbia Journal of Gender and Law* 12 (2003): 361.

326 **Judge Patricia Wald:** RBG with Greenhouse, "Conversation with Justice Ginsburg," 299.

326 **Despite O'Connor's presence:** RBG, *My Own Words,* 75.

SIXTEEN · Mother of the Regiment

327 **"Just do it":** O'Connor quotations in RBG, "A Tribute to Justice Sandra Day O'Connor," 119 *Harvard Law Review* (2006): 1240. RBG had been assigned the case *John Hancock Mutual Life Insurance Co. v. Harris Trust & Savings Bank,* 510 U.S. 86 (1993). Moved by O'Connor's gesture, RBG would later send similar notes to Sotomayor and Kagan when they announced their first opinions for the Court. See RBG, *My Own Words,* 90–91.

327 **"the most helpful":** Hirshman, *Sisters in Law,* 222–23.

327　**It was no surprise:** Ibid., 154–55 and 222–23. For more on the clerks, see 175 and 211–12.

327　**Ginsburg would undertake:** Tushnet, *Court Divided,* 67.

328　**Justices O'Connor, Kennedy, and especially Souter:** Colucci, *Justice Kennedy's Jurisprudence;* Maveety, *Justice Sandra Day O'Connor;* Tushnet, *Court Divided,* chap. 2. See also Sunstein, *Radicals in Robes.*

329　**Always willing to give:** *Planned Parenthood v. Casey,* 505 U.S. 833 (1992), 980 (Scalia dissenting); see Greenhouse, *Becoming Justice Blackmun,* chap. 8.

330　**On cases involving gender:** Joyce Ann Baugh et al., "Justice Ruth Bader Ginsburg: A Preliminary Assessment," *University of Toledo Law Review* 26 (1994): 1–34. On civil rights/civil liberties cases, Souter voted with the liberal bloc 60 percent of the time in contrast with RBG's 52 percent. See ibid., table 2, 32. See also Christopher E. Smith et al., "The First-Term Performance of Justice Ruth Bader Ginsburg," *Judicature* 78 (1994): 74–80.

330　**"an exceedingly persuasive justification":** *Kirchberg v. Feenstra,* 450 U.S. 455 (1981), 461, and *Mississippi University for Women v. Hogan,* 458 U.S. 718 (1982), 724 and n9, quoted in *Harris v. Forklift,* 510 U.S. 17 (1993), 26.

331　**In the Reagan-Bush years:** See Howard Winant, "Difference and Inequality: Post-modern Racial Politics in the United States," in Cross and Keith, *Racism, the City, and the State,* 108–28.

331　**Redistricting plans designed:** On voting rights and congressional districting, see *Shaw v. Reno,* 509 U.S. 630 (1993), and *Bush v. Vera,* 517 U.S. 952 (1996).

331　**The pragmatic O'Connor:** *Adarand Constructors v. Peña,* 515 U.S. 200 (1995), esp. 239–40 for Scalia and Thomas dissents.

332　**"strict in theory":** Ibid. at 237.

332　**"Properly," Ginsburg wrote:** *Fullilove v. Klutznick,* 448 U.S. 448 (1980), 519, quoted in *Adarand Constructors,* 515 U.S. at 237, 218, 275.

332　**If all went well:** See Cornelia T. L. Pillard, "*United States v. Virginia:* The Virginia Military Institute, Where the Men Are Men (and So Are the Women)," in Gilles and Goluboff, *Civil Rights Stories,* 265–92; and Katharine T. Bartlett, "Unconstitutionally Male? The Story of *United States v. Virginia,*" in Schneider and Wildman, *Women and the Law Stories,* 133–78. A longer, exemplary account on which I rely is Strum, *Women in the Barracks.*

332　**Most American colleges:** On the rush to coeducation from 1969 to 1974, see Malkiel, *"Keep the Damned Women Out."*

333　**The rather forbidding:** Jackson had been a professor at VMI before the outbreak of the war in which he gained renown as a brilliant military strategist. Accidentally shot by one of his own troops, he was buried in Lexington off the post. Cadets are required to salute his "marbled embodiment" each time they pass.

333　**No ordinary college:** Strum, *Women in the Barracks,* chap. 1.

333　**The purpose of the system:** For a skeptical view of whether the system produces its intended goals as opposed to far less desirable traits, see Mary Anne Case, "Two Cheers for Cheerleading: The Noisy Integration of VMI and the Quiet Success of Virginia Women's Institute for Leadership," *University of Chicago Legal Forum* (1999): 368–79.

334　**"We think the things":** Strum, *Women in the Barracks,* 39; on the "rat" system, see ibid., chap. 3.

334　**In 1972, black cadets:** The significance of the New Market charge is reinforced by a twenty-three-foot arch-shaped painting of the battle that covers part of the ceiling in Jackson Memorial Hall, where Sunday church services are held. Flanking the painting of the charge are two floor-length paintings, one of General Stonewall Jackson and the other of General Robert E. Lee. See Brodie, *Breaking Out,* chap. 1.

334　**By the mid-1970s:** Strum, *Women in the Barracks,* 29–31.

334 **That is, the degrading:** For examples of the seamy underside, see Pillard, *"United States v. Virginia,"* 265–92, esp. 270–71.

335 **A "network of connections":** Ibid., 271. In 1989, VMI alumni in Virginia included two congressmen, two state senators, the former Speaker of the House of Delegates, the managing partners of the two largest law firms, and many very prominent businessmen and industrialists.

335 **That some young women:** On ranking, see Bartlett, "Unconstitutionally Male?," 139n30. On gender integration of the service academies, which had occurred only after litigation and an order of Congress, see Stiehm, *Bring Me Men and Women.* On women and the military, see Francke, *Ground Zero;* also, Katzenstein and Reppy, *Beyond Zero Tolerance.*

335 **Keith had had her eye:** Strum, *Women in the Barracks,* 84–86.

335 **"Better Dead than Coed":** Ibid., chap. 6; Brodie, *Breaking Out,* 11; Neil Henderson and Peter Baker, "For VMI Cadets, It's Still 'Better Dead than Coed,'" *Washington Post,* Feb. 20, 1990, B1.

336 **With the dispute:** Patterson was ably assisted by Anne Marie Whittemore, a graduate (summa cum laude) of Vassar when it was still a women's college and of Yale Law School. Convinced that Vassar's move to coeducation had been a mistake and that its reputation had deteriorated, she considered her position on single-sex education to be at the "cutting edge of feminist theory." Hired over Patterson's objections by his Richmond law firm, she had rapidly become a partner and achieved a distinguished career. Like everyone else on the VMI legal team, she was adamant that the institute not be a victim of coeducation, especially its African American cadets, who had a high graduation rate. See Strum, *Women in the Barracks,* 97–98.

336 **"to prevent federal encroachment":** Quoted in Bartlett, "Unconstitutionally Male?," 145n66; Complaint at 1, *VMI v. Thornburgh,* No. 90-083 (W.D. Va. Filed Feb. 5, 1990); Complaint at 1, *VMI Foundation v. United States,* No. 90-084 (W.D. Va. Filed Feb. 5, 1990).

336 **Presented with VMI's suit:** When the Justice Department sued, it named Virginia in its suit along with VMI. See Motion of the United States for Summary Judgment, May 25, 1990, *United States v. Virginia.* With Wilder and his attorney general having declined to participate and Judge Jackson L. Kiser insisting that the commonwealth required representation, VMI's legal team led by Patterson took on the job at no cost to taxpayers.

336 **"exceedingly persuasive justification":** Strum, *Women in the Barracks,* chap. 7. Joe Hogan challenged his exclusion from the nursing school at the state-funded Mississippi University for Women. In a narrow opinion that applied only to the nursing school, the Court held that the school could not discriminate based on sex in its admissions policies. See *Mississippi University for Women v. Hogan,* 458 U.S. 718 (1982).

336 **They had an ally:** Bartlett, "Unconstitutionally Male?," 145.

337 **"distract male students":** Strum, *Women in the Barracks,* chap. 12; *United States v. Virginia,* 766 F. Supp. (W.D. Va. 1992), 1415.

337 **Judge Niemeyer had offered:** Niemeyer had been nominated to the district court by Reagan and then to the court of appeals by George H. W. Bush. For Niemeyer's opinion, see *United States v. Virginia,* 976 F.2nd 890 (4th Cir., 1992), 891–900.

337 **But that was to be the subject:** Strum, *Women in the Barracks,* chap. 14.

338 **"If VMI marches":** *United States v. Virginia,* 852 F. Supp. 471 (April 29, 1994), aff'd, remanded, 44 F.3d 1229 (4th Cir. 1995), 481, 478, 484.

338 **Solicitor General Drew Days:** Strum, *Women in the Barracks,* 253. See Brief for the United States in Opposition, *United States v. Virginia,* 518 U.S. 515 (1995).

338 **"tantamount to admission":** Strum, *Women in the Barracks,* 254n54.

338 **Women's legal advocacy organizations:** Brief for National Women's Law Center et al., *United States v. Virginia,* 116 S. Ct. 2264 (1995) (No. 94-1941); Amicus Curiae Brief

of 26 Private Women's Colleges, *United States v. Virginia*, 116 S. Ct. 2264 (1996) (No. 94-1941).

339 **Mary Baldwin College:** Amicus Curiae Brief of Mary Baldwin College, *Virginia*, 116 S. Ct. 2264 (No. 94-2107); Amicus Curiae Brief of Wells College, *Virginia*, 116 S. Ct. 2264 (No. 94-2107). See Scott Jaschik, "7 Women's Colleges Back All-Male Institute: They Tell Supreme Court They're Threatened; Others Call Them Dupes," *Chronicle of Higher Education*, April 7, 1993.

339 **A brief by seven:** Amicus Curiae Brief of the American Association of University Professors et al., *Virginia*, 116 S. Ct. 2264 (No. 94-2107).

339 **Resurrecting charges against the ERA:** Amicus Curiae Brief of Independent Women's Forum et al., *Virginia*, 116 S. Ct. 2264 (Nos. 94-1941, 94-2107).

339 **With palpable anger:** Amicus Curiae Brief of Women Active in Our Nation's Defense, Their Advocates and Supporters, *Virginia*, 116 S. Ct. 2264 (No. 94-2107); Strum, *Women in the Barracks,* chap. 18.

339 **Theodore B. Olson:** Jeffrey Toobin, "Money Unlimited," *New Yorker*, May 21, 2012, 39.

339 **"We have to decide":** Linda Greenhouse, "Justices Appear Skeptical of V.M.I.'s Proposal for Women," *New York Times*, Jan. 18, 1996, A18; Strum, *Women in the Barracks*, chaps. 18–19; Transcript of Oral Argument, *United States v. Virginia*, 518 U.S. 515 (1996).

340 **"[W]hat if a State":** Transcript of Oral Argument at 22–24, *Virginia*, 518 U.S. 515.

341 **This should be Ruth's:** Strum, *Women in the Barracks*, 282–83. Linda Hirshman indicates that Rehnquist rather than Stevens originally assigned the opinion to O'Connor. See Hirshman, *Sisters in Law*, 241.

341 **"a strong presumption":** *J.E.B. v. Alabama*, 511 U.S. 127 (1994), 152.

341 **She would call instead for "skeptical":** Strum, *Women in the Barracks*, 283.

341 **In her efforts:** Ibid., 284.

342 **Several "had an ending":** RBG quoted in ibid.

342 **"one of the Court's most important":** Linda Greenhouse, "Military College Can't Bar Women, High Court Rules," *New York Times*, June 27, 1996, A1.

342 **"Generalizations about":** *United States v. Virginia*, 518 U.S. 515 (1996), 550 (RBG majority).

342 **"Women seeking and fit":** Ibid. at 557.

342 **"However 'liberally' this plan":** Ibid. at 540.

342 **"More important than the tangible":** Ibid. at 553–54, citing *Sweatt v. Painter*, 339 U.S. 629 (1950).

343 **"a 'pale shadow' " of VMI:** Ibid. at 553, 555.

343 **"ancient and familiar fear":** Ibid. at 555n20.

343 **"may not be solidly grounded":** Ibid. at 545.

343 **Ginsburg traced the development:** In *J.E.B. v. Alabama*, 511 U.S. 127 (1994), 140n11, Blackmun's majority opinion stated that the equal protection clause does not allow states to discriminate on the basis of sex-based stereotypical generalizations "even when some statistical support can be conjured up for the generalizations." As Linda Hirshman points out, RBG had resented the assignment of the majority opinion in *J.E.B. v. Alabama* to Blackmun, given her earlier ACLU cases on exclusion of women jurors and her consistent argument that arrangements that appeared to benefit women actually harmed them. In her disciplined fashion, she treated Blackmun's drafts much as she had done the Oklahoma lawyer Fred Gilbert's efforts in *Craig v. Boren*, pressing Blackmun to include Alabama's sorry treatment of women jurors and improving the opinion in the process, though not without effort. See Hirshman, *Sisters in Law*, 226–28.

343 **"today's skeptical scrutiny":** *United States v. Virginia*, 518 U.S. 515 (1996), 559, 531, 533, 529 (RBG majority).

343 **"inherent differences":** Ibid. at 533.

344 **"functionally dead":** Ibid. at 558 (Rehnquist concurring); ibid. at 596 (Scalia dissenting).

344 **"Single-sex education":** Ibid. at 535 (RBG majority). At the time, single-sex public high schools were coming to be increasingly favored as a way of enhancing educational opportunities for low-income young women of color in urban areas on a voluntary basis. The Young Women's Leadership School of East Harlem served as a model. For the complex issues surrounding such schools, see Martha Minow's nuanced follow-up of *Vorchheimer,* "Single-Sex Public Schools," in Schneider and Wildman, *Women and the Law Stories,* esp. 122–32.

344 **"Sex classifications," she wrote:** *Virginia,* 518 U.S. at 533–34 (RBG majority).

344 **Hailed by advocates:** Eva M. Rodriguez, "Confusion from the High Court," *Connecticut Law Tribune* 9 (July 1996); Greenhouse, "Military College Can't Bar Women"; Joan Biskupic, "Supreme Court Invalidates Exclusion of Women by VMI," *Washington Post,* June 27, 1996. For additional press coverage, see Strum, *Women in the Barracks,* 295–96n70, 73–80, 83–84.

344 **Legal scholars parsed:** Even a cursory search in legal journals turns up at least fifty articles. Typical of varying views, see Karen Lazarus Kupetz, "Equal Benefits, Equal Burdens: 'Skeptical Scrutiny' for Gender Classification After *United States v. Virginia,*" *Loyola of Los Angeles Law Review* 30 (April 1997): 1333–77, a doctrinal shift to a new, more stringent standard; Mayeri, "Constitutional Choices," 755–830, more muscular standard; Amy Walsh, "Ruth Bader Ginsburg: Extending the Constitution," *John Marshall Law Review* 32 (Fall 1998): 197–225, raises the bar; Scott Smailer, "Justice Ruth Bader Ginsburg and the Virginia Military Institute: A Culmination of Strategic Success," *Cardozo Women's Law Journal* 4 (1998): 541–84, stricter tone to intermediate scrutiny; Elizabeth M. Schneider, "A Postscript on VMI," *American University Journal of Gender and the Law* 6 (Fall 1997): 59–64, important case and a victory for RBG but critical language is elusive and the standard of review ambiguous; regardless of what the opinion says, what the Court will do is another matter. On lower courts, see, for example, *Nabozny v. Podlesny,* 92 F.3d (7th Cir.) (1996), 446–61. Regarding VMI as a heightened standard, see 456n6, "We express no opinion on whether the Court's ruling heightens the level of scrutiny applied to gender discrimination in this circuit."

344 **What changes must:** To the institute's credit, administrators turned their full energies to preparing how to deal with everything from installation of tampon machines to pregnancy without altering the essentials of VMI. As at the service academies where students of the opposite sex exercise considerable power over one another, the transition was not easy. On VMI, see Brodie, *Breaking Out,* chaps. 4–9; also, Barkalow, *In the Men's House.*

344 **Framed, it hung outside:** Tushnet, *Court Divided,* 128.

345 **"marked Justice Ginsburg's apotheosis":** Minow, *In Brown's Wake,* 56.

345 **The Court's ruling:** Strum, *Women in the Barracks,* 287n27.

345 **"To me, it was winning":** Ibid., 285. On the Vorchheimer case, see *Vorchheimer v. School District,* affirmed per curiam, 430 U.S. 703 (1977). For the ACLU's efforts to salvage the case and keep Susan Vorcheimer's original lawyer Sharon K. Willis on board, and for RBG's evident displeasure at Willis's inadequacies, see the case files including RBG's handwritten comment in RBG MSS. Martha Minow puts the *Vorchheimer* case in the much broader perspective in "Single-Sex Public Schools: The Story of *Vorchheimer v. School District of Philadelphia,*" in *Women and the Law Stories,* chap. 3. She also updates Susan's story, adding that she became not a rabbi but an anthropologist and also married an anthropologist. Serena Mayeri argues that *Vorchheimer* was not representative of most sex-segregation litigation of the 1960s and 1970s and showed that drawing the comparison between sex segregation and race segregation could be a "pitfall" as a legal strategy in "The Strange Career of Jane Crow: Sex Segregation and

the Transformation of Anti-discrimination Discourse," *Yale Journal of Law and the Humanities* 18 (2006): 253–72.

345 **"I graduated from VMI":** Quoted in "Remarks by Justice Ruth Bader Ginsburg, Associate Justice, Supreme Court of the United States," *Annual Survey of American Law* (April 1997): xii.

346 **By the end of her third:** Strum, *Women in the Barracks,* 318–19.

346 **Nothing was said:** Bartlett, "Unconstitutionally Male?," 161.

347 **"Kept away from the pressures":** *United States v. Virginia,* 518 U.S. 515 (1996), 549.

347 **"This is still very much":** Strum, *Women in the Barracks,* 326.

347 **Many students and alumni:** Ibid., chap. 21.

347 **Yet they were never fully:** Bartlett, "Unconstitutionally Male?," 160–66.

347 **"the way that the litigation":** Pillard, *"United States v. Virginia,"* 289. Pillard, as assistant to the solicitor general, had drafted the government's brief. See also Bartlett, "Unconstitutionally Male?," and Case, "Two Cheers for Cheerleading."

348 **There is no doubt:** See RBG, "Gender and the Constitution."

SEVENTEEN · "I Cannot Agree"

349 **But the dread disease:** Linda Greenhouse, "Ruth Ginsburg Has Surgery for Cancer," *New York Times,* Sept. 18, 1999, A10; Sheryl Gay Stolberg, "Ginsburg Leaves Hospital, Prognosis on Cancer Is Good," *New York Times,* Sept. 29, 1999; Linda Greenhouse, "National Briefing Washington: Ginsburg Discusses Cancer," *New York Times,* May 9, 2001, A22.

350 **"She's never going to make":** Author's recollection.

350 **And Kathleen Peratis:** Peratis, "Address on RBG Portrait Dedication."

350 **"The result for women":** Catharine A. MacKinnon, "Disputing Male Sovereignty: On *United States v. Morrison,*" *Harvard Law Review* 114 (Nov. 2000): 149–50.

350 **Two new legislative:** The Family and Medical Leave Act of 1993 and the Violence Against Women Act of 1994.

351 **Mustering evidence that these:** This is not to deny that alcohol often played a part—as the nineteenth-century founders of the Woman's Christian Temperance Union knew.

351 **Even in 2014:** The problem of rape and other sexual assaults on college and university campuses has not diminished since 1994. Just under 12 percent of the assaults are currently reported and fewer still prosecuted because of inadequate action on the part of universities and police "biases." See Jackie Calmes, "Obama Seeks to Raise Awareness of Rape on Campus," *New York Times,* Jan. 23, 2014, A18.

351 **Similarly, the murder rate:** Russell, *Sexual Exploitation;* Russell, *Secret Trauma;* Gail Elizabeth Wyatt, "The Sexual Abuse of Afro-American and White-American Women in Childhood," *Child Abuse and Neglect* 9, no. 4 (1985): 507–19; Ronet Bachman and Raymond Paternoster, "A Contemporary Look at the Effects of Rape Law Reform: How Far Have We Really Come?," *Journal of Criminal Law and Criminology* 84 (1993): 554–57; *Women and Violence: Hearings Before the Committee on the Judiciary, U.S. Senate, June 20, August 29, and December 11, 1990,* 101st Cong. (1990); Committee on the Judiciary, *Violence Against Women: A Week in the Life of America,* S.Rep. 102–18, 102nd Cong. (1992).

351 **When he suggested:** Biden, *Promises to Keep,* 243.

351 **"a bunch of feminists":** "14 Women Are Slain by Montreal Gunman," *New York Times,* Dec. 7, 1989, A1.

352 **Thus, "if a woman":** This account follows Fred Strebeigh's account in "Ladies' Man," *New Republic,* Sept. 24, 2008; Lisa Heinzerling, "So Rape Isn't Hatred?," *Los Angeles Times,* May 4, 1990, B7.

352   **"rape charge if a woman":** Strebeigh, "Ladies' Man."

352   **"If Biden wants to do":** Quoted in Strebeigh, *Equal,* 344.

353   **She could target:** Ibid., chap. 22. For the full list of coalition organizations supporting the VAWA, see 346–47.

353   **The study, which had assumed:** Ibid.

354   **"critical to meeting":** Ibid.

354   **He urged the ABA:** "Chief Justice's 1991 Year-End Report," 3.

354   **"You cannot establish a cause":** "Statement of Hon. Joseph Biden, a Senator in Congress from the State of Delaware," in *Hearings, Before the Subcommittee on Crime and Criminal Justice,* 101st Cong., 2nd sess., Feb. 6, 1992, 10.

354   **Looking for a counterweight:** My account in this and the following paragraphs, unless otherwise indicated, follows the much more detailed description of events provided in Strebeigh, *Equal,* chap. 25.

354   **Its members, a moderate lot:** "National Association of Women Judges: History," National Association of Women Judges, www.nawj.org.

354   **Schafran knew just the woman:** Strebeigh, *Equal,* chap. 24.

354   **Brooksley Born:** On Born, see "Legends in the Law: A Conversation with Brooksley Born," *Washington Lawyer,* Oct. 2003.

355   **The ABA must not:** www.dcbar.org.

355   **"gender-based crime of violence":** Strebeigh, *Equal,* 411; *Griffin v. Breckenridge,* 403 U.S. 88 (1971), 102.

355   **Using "animus" (meaning extreme prejudice):** Strebeigh, *Equal,* chap. 24.

356   **Feeling as if "her soul":** Joan Biskupic, "Sex-Assault Law Under Scrutiny," *Washington Post,* Jan. 12, 2000, A11.

356   **"liked to get girls drunk":** Quoted in Strebeigh, *Equal,* 423. I have relied closely in this and the following paragraphs, unless otherwise noted, on Noonan, *Narrowing the Nation's Power,* chap. 6.

357   **She also sued Morrison:** *Brzonkala v. Virginia Polytechnic Institute and State University* and *Brzonkala v. Morrison,* 935 F. Supp. 772 (1996). Because institutions are rarely held accountable for upholding the requirements of Title IX, many colleges and universities have swept violence under the rug. In its entire history, the Department of Education's Office for Civil Rights (OCR) has never sanctioned a school for sexual-assault-related violations. The OCR's present threatened sanction—the full removal of federal funds from noncompliant schools—would penalize universities but also students generally. Senators Claire McCaskill, Kirsten Gillibrand, and Richard Blumenthal planned to introduce legislation in the fall of 2014 to provide the OCR with another tool at its disposal—the authority to levy fines against schools in violation of Title IX. In 2017, Trump's Department of Education announced a rollback of enforcement procedures and policies initiated by the Obama administration, leading advocates for accused students to claim a restoration of due process while advocates for victims warned that the changes would lead to devastating consequences in sexual harassment cases. See Alexandra Brodsky and Dana Bolger, "Want Colleges to Protect Students from Sexual Assault? Take Action to Give Title IX Teeth," *Nation,* July 8, 2014 and Sarah Brown, "What Does the End of Obama's Title IX Guidance Mean for Colleges?" *The Chronicle of Higher Education,* September 22, 2017.

357   **"might become hostile in the future":** *Brzonkala v. Virginia Polytechnic Institute and State University,* 132 F.3d 949, 959 (1997).

357   **He first cited *United States*:** Ibid., 953; *United States v. Lopez,* 514 U.S. 549 (1995).

358   **Her case dismissed:** *Brzonkala v. Virginia Polytechnic Institute and State University,* 169 F.3d 820 (1999).

358   **VAWA supporters submitting briefs:** Brief of Law Professors as Amici Curiae in Support of Petitioners, *United States v. Morrison,* 529 U.S. 598 (2000) (Nos. 99-5, 99-

29); Brief of the States of Arizona et al. in Support of Petitioners, *United States v. Morrison,* 529 U.S. 598 (2000) (Nos. 99-5, 99-29).

358 **But after a strong dissent:** *Brzonkala,* 132 F.3d at 953.

359 **"an attenuated and indirect relationship":** *Brzonkala,* 169 F.3d at 844.

359 **"family relationships":** Ibid.

359 **Despite a strong minority:** *United States v. Lopez,* 514 U.S. 549 (1995), 602.

359 **The Court's more right-leaning:** See, for example, *Seminole Tribe of Florida v. Florida,* 517 U.S. 44 (1996), which held that under the portion of the commerce clause involving Indian tribes, Congress did not have power to allow tribes to sue non-consenting states in federal court for breach of good-faith negotiations over gambling rights; *City of Boerne v. Flores,* 521 U.S. 507 (1997), which put new limits on congressional power to implement the Fourteenth Amendment with its "congruence and proportionality" test; *Printz v. United States,* 521 U.S. 898 (1997), which overturned a part of the Brady Handgun Violence Prevention Act, ordering local sheriffs to do background checks of would-be handgun purchasers; *Alden v. Maine,* 527 U.S. 706 (1999), which overturned parts of federal statutes that allowed individuals to sue a state for violating federal laws in labor disputes.

359 **With both constitutional:** On *Flores* and Section 5, see Robert C. Post and Reva B. Siegel, "Equal Protection by Law: Federal Antidiscrimination Legislation After *Morrison* and *Kimmel,*" *Yale Law Journal* 110 (Dec. 2000): 441–526.

359 **An ally on other:** Tushnet, *Court Divided,* 51.

359 **Meanwhile, members of the bar:** Strebeigh, *Equal,* 413.

360 **"one of the most persistent barriers":** Transcript of Oral Argument, *United States v. Morrison,* 529 U.S. 598 (2000).

360 **"Well, presumably Congress could":** Ibid.

361 **"I'm not sure that Congress":** Ibid.

361 **"When a woman is raped":** Quoted in Strebeigh, *Equal,* 437.

361 **The chief lobbied his longtime friend:** Ibid., 438.

361 **Not once were women mentioned:** *Morrison,* 529 U.S. at 628.

362 **Also ignored was:** Ibid.; *Heart of Atlanta Motel Inc. v. United States,* 379 U.S. 241 (1964).

363 **If state officials were failing:** *United States v. Morrison,* 120 S. Ct. 1740, 601–27 (2000).

363 **Given the Rehnquist majority's:** Much ink has been spilled over whether the Rehnquist Court's new federalism jurisprudence was pernicious or salutary, real or symbolic, ephemeral or lasting. For approaches that have tried to strike a middle ground, see, for example, Kathleen M. Sullivan, "From States' Rights Blues to Blue States' Rights: Federalism After the Rehnquist Court," *Fordham Journal of Law* 75 (2006): 799–813; Keck, *Most Activist Supreme Court in History,* chaps. 6–7. The most recent assessment is Banks and Blakeman, *U.S. Supreme Court and the New Federalism,* chap. 3.

363 **"Why," he asked:** *Morrison,* 529 U.S. at 600, 628, 615–31, 665 (Breyer dissenting).

363 **The white men who in 1886:** Freedman, *Redefining Rape,* esp. chap. 4, p. 76.

363 **However, as white citizens:** *United States v. Harris,* 106 U.S. 629 (1883); *Civil Rights Cases,* 109 U.S. 3 (1883). The Civil Rights Act of 1871 was also known as the Ku Klux Klan Act.

363 **By curtailing Section 5:** MacKinnon, "Disputing Male Sovereignty," 168.

364 **"The court applied":** Quoted in Linda Greenhouse, "Battle on Federalism," *New York Times,* May 17, 2000, A18.

364 **"This decision," Biden added:** Linda Greenhouse, "Women Lose Right to Sue Attackers in Federal Court," *New York Times,* May 16, 2000, A1.

364 **"At stake was nothing":** MacKinnon, "Disputing Male Sovereignty," 177.

364 **"Not one member of the Supreme Court":** Ibid., 176. MacKinnon acknowledges that Justice Breyer came closest, but she argues that RBG and Souter declined to join that part of Breyer's dissent. For a possible explanation, see Post and Siegel, "Equal Protection by Law," 441, who share MacKinnon's concern about the "ominous signals" sent by the Court about the future of federal antidiscrimination law.

365 **"Gush" and "Bore":** Patterson, *Restless Giant,* 409.

366 **Elsewhere ballots had "hanging chads":** In addition to voluminous press coverage of the postelection crisis, studies emerged immediately, among them Posner, *Breaking the Deadlock;* and Dershowitz, *Supreme Injustice.* Unless otherwise noted, I have relied in the following paragraphs on Gillman, *Votes That Counted,* and Toobin, *Too Close to Call.*

368 **That provision would end:** *Bush v. Palm Beach County Canvassing Board,* 531 U.S. 70 (2000), 71–78, esp. 76.

368 **"Only by examining":** *Gore v. Harris,* 772 So. 2d 1243 (2000), 1261.

368 **"the majority today departs from":** Application for Stay at 1–2, *Bush v. Gore,* 531 U.S. 98 (2000), (Stevens dissenting), American Presidency Project.

369 **threatened "irreparable harm" to Bush:** Ibid. (Scalia concurring). See also Biskupic, *American Original,* 238–39. Scalia had two sons working in the Florida campaign and Thomas's wife, Virginia, was deeply involved in the Bush campaign, but apparently neither of the two justices saw a conflict of interest.

370 **"shaken and demoralized":** Linda Greenhouse, *"Bush v. Gore:* A Special Report; Election Case a Test and Trauma for Justices," *New York Times,* Feb. 20, 2001, A1.

370 **"sullen hum":** Toobin, *Too Close to Call,* 256.

370 **"I thought your point":** Transcript of Oral Argument at 109, *Bush v. Gore,* 531 U.S. 98.

370 **"And there are different ballots":** Ibid.

371 **Faced with such polarized:** Toobin, *Too Close to Call,* 263–65.

371 **"Our consideration is limited":** *Bush v. Gore,* 531 U.S. at 109.

371 **The Court had never:** Indeed, Justices Rehnquist, Scalia, and Thomas only voted to uphold equal protection in 4 percent of non-affirmative-action cases over the prior ten-year period. In comparison, over the same period, the other justices voted to uphold equal protection in 74 percent of the cases. As the legal scholar Geoffrey Stone contends, the three justices "cast more votes (three, to be exact) to sustain the Equal Protection Clause claim in *Bush v. Gore* than they previously cast in all of the nonaffirmative action Equal Protection Clause cases that they considered in the previous decade." See Geoffrey R. Stone, "The Roberts Court, Stare Decisis, and the Future of Constitutional Law," *Tulane Law Review* 82 (2008): 1551.

371 **With early press accounts:** See Pamela S. Karlan, "Convictions and Doubts: Representation and the Debate over Felon Disenfranchisement," *Stanford Law Review* 56 (2004): 1157. Sociologists have estimated that if ex-offenders who had completed serving their sentences in Florida had been allowed to vote, and had voted only at the same rate as other people of the same socioeconomic background, age, and the like, Gore would have carried the state by more than thirty-one thousand votes. See Christopher Uggen and Jeff Manza, "Democratic Contraction? The Political Consequences of Felon Disenfranchisement in the United States," *American Sociological Review* (2002): 777, 793 table 4a.

371 **When Scalia saw the draft:** Toobin, *Too Close to Call,* 166–67.

371 **This might have been:** RBG told Scalia's biographer, "I love him. But sometimes I'd like to strangle him." See Biskupic, *American Original,* 277.

371 **But exercising her customary restraint:** RBG was later proven correct that the minority voters in Florida were penalized. While the turnout had been higher than in other elections, Florida was one of the nine states in 2000 that permanently disenfranchised felons, a third of whom were African American men. This prohibition, affecting an estimated 600,000 Florida felons who had done their time, presum-

ably affected Democrats adversely. Later estimates concluded that various state laws prevented approximately 3–9 million felons from voting in 2000, according to *The New York Times,* Oct. 24 and 27 and Nov. 9, 2004. Gore representatives alleged that thousands of Floridians, the majority African American, were inaccurately put on the felons list. Both Latinos and African Americans, according to Democrats, had also been prevented from registering in some areas. See Patterson, *Restless Giant,* 413n57.

371 **"Rarely has this Court":** *Bush v. Gore,* 531 U.S. 98 (2000), 8 (RBG dissenting).

372 **"disagreement with the Florida":** Ibid. at 1–2.

372 **"the recount adopted":** Ibid. at 9.

372 **"[O]rderly judicial review":** Ibid. at 10. For further discussion of RBG's federalism jurisprudence, see Deborah Jones Merritt, "The Once and Future Federalist," in Dodson, *Legacy of Ruth Bader Ginsburg.*

372 **"can only lend credence":** *Bush v. Gore,* 531 U.S. at 128–29 (Stevens dissenting).

373 **"looked like a survivor of Auschwitz":** Toobin, "Heavyweight," 47.

EIGHTEEN · Persevering in Hard Times

377 **Further, the administration's embrace:** Timothy Naftali, "George W. Bush and the 'War on Terror,'" and Fredrik Logevall, "Anatomy of an Unnecessary War: The Iraq Invasion," in Zelizer, *Presidency of George W. Bush,* chaps. 4 and 5.

377 **Conservative policies of deregulation:** Finlay, *George W. Bush and the War on Women;* "The War Against Women," *New York Times,* Jan. 12, 2003, 4; James T. Patterson, "Transformative Economic Policies: Tax Cutting, Stimuli, and Bailouts," Meg Jacobs, "Wreaking Havoc from Within: George W. Bush's Energy Policy in Historical Perspective," and Nelson Lichtenstein, "Ideology and Interest on the Social Policy Home Front," in Zelizer, *Presidency of George W. Bush,* chaps. 6–8; also, Gilens, *Affluence and Influence.*

378 **Yet her dissents:** Mary L. Dudziak, "A Sword and a Shield: The Uses of Law in the Bush Administration," in Zelizer, *Presidency of George W. Bush,* chap. 3.

378 **A foreign-born, nonmarital:** Compare U.S. Constitution, Amendment XIV, with 8 U.S.C., 1409 (2006).

378 **As a result of his conviction:** Nguyen was slated for deportation under the 1996 Illegal Immigration Reform and Immigrant Responsibility Act, passed after Republicans seized control of both the House and the Senate in 1994. Among its many provisions, the statute tightened grounds for deportation.

379 **Section 1409(a), she concluded:** Barnhart and Schlickman, *John Paul Stevens,* 256n5 (citing interview with RBG).

379 **Essentializing the mother-child bond:** *Nguyen v. INS,* 533 U.S. 53 (2001), 56–73; ibid. at 64 (Kennedy majority).

379 **The different rules were there:** Ibid. at 69–70.

379 **"real, everyday ties":** Ibid. at 65.

379 **The majority fostered:** Ibid. at 89.

379 **"depth and vitality":** Ibid. at 97. The ruling had a lasting impact. In *Flores-Villar v. United States* (2010), the Ninth Circuit Court applied the Supreme Court's holding in *Nguyen* that more onerous residency requirements in the Immigration and Nationality Act for fathers but not for mothers did not violate the equal protection clause. The provision at issue imposed a five-year residency requirement on U.S. citizen fathers but only a one-year requirement on mothers.

380 **Eight years in the making:** On the history and limitations of the FMLA, see Emily A. Hayes, "Bridging the Gap Between Work and Family: Accomplishing the Goals of the Family and Medical Leave Act of 1993," *William and Mary Law Review* 42 (2001): 1507–43. For a fuller discussion of RBG's prior actions in response to *Geduldig v. Aiello*

(1974) and *General Electric v. Gilbert* (1976), see chap. 8; also, chaps. 12 and 13 of this manuscript.

380 **In the eight cases:** For example, see *Laro v. New Hampshire,* 259 F.3d 1, 16 (1st Cir. 2001); *Hale v. Mann,* 219 F.3d 61, 68–69 (2nd Cir. 2000); *Chittister v. Department of Community and Economic Development,* 226 F.3d 223, 229 (3rd Cir. 2000); *Kazmier v. Widmann,* 225 F.3d 519, 529 (5th Cir. 2000); *Sims v. University of Cincinnati,* 219 F.3d 559, 566 (6th Cir. 2000); *Townsel v. Missouri,* 233 F.3d 1094, 1096 (8th Cir. 2000).

380 **Only in the Ninth:** *Hibbs v. Department of Human Resources,* 273 F.3rd 844 (9th Cir. 2001), 844–73.

380 **As a result, he faced:** Ibid.

380 **"would be a huge symbolic":** Quoted in Linda Greenhouse, "In Family Leave Case, Supreme Court Steps Back into Federalism Debate," *New York Times,* Jan. 12, 2003, L23.

380 **The solicitor general also:** Ibid. Forty-nine current and former members of Congress, many of whom had played leadership roles in the FMLA's development and passage, filed an amicus brief in support of Hibbs. But fourteen states agreed with Nevada that abrogation of their immunity amounted to a "constitutional insult." See ibid.

381 **Yet when the vote count:** Suzanna Sherry, "The Unmaking of a Precedent," *Supreme Court Review* (2003): 231–67.

381 **"narrowly targeted at the fault-line":** *Nevada Department of Human Resources v. Hibbs,* 538 U.S. 721 (2003), 724–40, 738 (italics mine).

381 **"congruent and proportional":** Ibid. at 724–40 (italics mine).

381 **"real sex differences":** Ibid. at 729–32.

381 **"Ruth, did you ghostwrite":** As Greenhouse observed of the RBG-Rehnquist relationship, "Obviously, you didn't see lots of things the same way, but you nurtured him and brought him along, for instance, in the Virginia Military Institute case. He didn't sign your opinion, but he joined your judgment. And he wrote *Hibbs.*" RBG with Greenhouse, "Conversation with Justice Ginsburg," 294. RBG appreciated his humor and fairness. She also discerned the humanity behind the "Nordic cool" of the man she always referred to as "My Chief." She especially appreciated the comfort and encouragement he provided during the months of chemotherapy and weeks of daily radiation during her yearlong bout with colorectal cancer, his suspension of weighty assignments, and his willingness to let her decide when she was strong enough to do more. See, for example, RBG, "In Memoriam: William H. Rehnquist," *Harvard Law Review* 119 (2005): 6–10, esp. 9. For an even more detailed description of his caring, see RBG with Greenhouse, "Conversation with Justice Ginsburg," 295–96. "My Chief" is not a designation she uses in referring to his successor.

382 **The summer of 2005:** Linda Greenhouse, "William H. Rehnquist, Chief Justice of Supreme Court, Is Dead at 80," *New York Times,* Sept. 4, 2005, 38; Richard W. Stevenson, "O'Connor to Retire, Touching Off Battle over Court," *New York Times,* July 1, 2005, A6.

382 **Although she and O'Connor:** For data, see Karen O'Connor and Alexandra B. Yanus, "Judging Alone: Reflections on the Importance of Women on the Court," *Critical Perspectives* 6 (Sept. 2010): 444.

383 **"a wise old man":** O'Connor, *Majesty of the Law,* 193. Other factors as well might have been at work. See, for example, Reva B. Siegel, "You've Come a Long Way, Baby: Rehnquist's New Approach to Pregnancy Discrimination in *Hibbs,*" *Stanford Law Review* 58, no. 6 (2006): 1883, and Adam Liptak, "Another Factor Said to Sway Judges to Rule for Women's Rights: A Daughter," *New York Times,* June 17, 2014, A14. The findings emerged from a study of twenty-five hundred votes by 224 federal appeals court judges.

383 **Four of her male counterparts:** For data, see O'Connor and Yanus, "Judging Alone," 443.

383 **After Ginsburg's arrival:** Barbara Palmer, "Justice Ruth Bader Ginsburg and the Supreme Court's Reaction to the Second Female Member," *Women and Politics* 24 (2008): 8.

384 **On a more personal level:** RBG, "Tribute to Justice Sandra Day O'Connor," 1239–45.

385 **Rehnquist, they agreed, would:** Greenhouse, "William H. Rehnquist, Chief Justice of the Supreme Court, Is Dead at 80," 38; Todd S. Purdum, "Eulogies for Rehnquist Recall a Man of Many Interests," *New York Times,* Sept. 8, 2005, A20; Charles Lane, "Chief Justice William Rehnquist Dies," *Washington Post,* Sept. 4, 2005, A1; Susan Levine and Charles Lane, "For Chief Justice, a Final Session with His Court," *Washington Post,* Sept. 7, 2005, A8.

385 **In his own terminal battle:** RBG, "In Memoriam: William H. Rehnquist," 9.

385 **Frequently referring to her fondness:** RBG, "A Conversation with Four Chief Justices," *Record of the Association of the Bar of the City of New York* 62 (2007): 257, 259.

385 **"the best Supreme Court advocate":** Roger Parloff, "On History's Stage, Chief Justice John Roberts Jr.," *Fortune,* Jan. 17, 2011, 64–75, quotation from 64.

386 **Journalists predicted he could:** Ibid.; see also Todd S. Purdum, Jodi Wilgoren, and Pam Belluck, "Court Nominee's Life Is Rooted in Faith and Respect for Law," *New York Times,* July 21, 2005, A1.

386 **Alito's refusal to consider:** For the full ACLU report, see *Report of the American Civil Liberties Union on the Nomination of Third Circuit Court Judge Samuel A. Alito Jr. to Be Associate Justice on the United States Supreme Court,* Dec. 9, 2005.

386 **Yet Democrats could not:** Carl Hulse and David D. Kirkpatrick, "After Memo, Democrats Are Taking Firmer Stance Against Alito Nomination," *New York Times,* Dec. 2, 2005, A24; "Judge Alito, in His Own Words," *New York Times,* Jan. 12, 2006, A30; Adam Nagourney, "From the Left, Calls to Press Alito Harder," *New York Times,* Jan. 12, 2006, A27; David D. Kirkpatrick, "Wider Fight Seen as Alito Victory Appears Secured," *New York Times,* Jan. 14, 2006, A1; David D. Kirkpatrick, "On Party Lines, Panel Approves Alito for Court," *New York Times,* Jan. 25, 2006, A1.

386 **Though the newest justice:** Her suspicions were later verified in a 2013 study which reported that one would have to go back to 1946 to find two justices as likely to vote in favor of business interests as Roberts and Alito. Lee Epstein, William M. Landes, and Richard A. Posner, "How Business Fares in the Supreme Court," *Minnesota Law Review* 97 (2013): 1449.

386 **Steeling herself for what:** Toobin, *Oath,* 58, 63.

386 **Baptized in a swimming:** Asked to comment about her troubled former client, Sarah Weddington wryly commented that in recent years Ms. McCorvey "thought she was not getting enough attention, and obviously Flip Benham was able to fill that need for her." See " 'Jane Roe' Joins Anti-abortion Group," *New York Times,* Aug. 11, 1995, A12; see also Joshua Prager, "The Accidental Activist," *Vanity Fair,* Feb. 2013, 108–67.

386 **In support of McCorvey's suit:** Reva Siegel and Sarah Blustain, "Mommy Dearest?," *American Prospect,* Oct. 2006, 22–27; on McCorvey's suit, see Jason A. Adkins, "Meet Me at the (West Coast) Hotel: The *Lochner* Era and the Demise of *Roe v. Wade,*" *Minnesota Law Review* 9, no. 500 (2005): 500–535. A similar suit was filed on behalf of Sandra Cano, plaintiff in the companion case, *Doe v. Bolton,* though neither McCorvey nor Cano had actually gotten abortions.

386 **McCorvey's suit failed:** See Jill Hasaday, "Protecting Them from Themselves: The Persistence of Mutual Benefits Arguments for Sex and Race Inequality," *New York University Law Review* 84, no. 6 (Dec. 2009), esp. 1478–82n68.

387 **"freedom of choice":** Reardon, *Making Abortions Rare,* ix–x.

387 **"the middle majority":** Ibid., 25–26.

387 **Late-term abortions:** Guttmacher Institute, "Fact Sheet: Induced Abortion in the United States," Feb. 2014.

388 **Antiabortion activists and legislators:** Siegel and Blustain, "Mommy Dearest?," 22. On use of this strategy in South Dakota, the first state to enact the ban, see Reva B. Seigel, "The New Politics of Abortion: An Equality Analysis of Woman-Protective Abortion Restrictions," *University of Illinois Law Review* 991 (2007): 1006–23; Reva B. Siegel, "The Right's Reasons: Constitutional Conflict and the Spread of Woman-Protective Antiabortion Argument," *Duke Law Journal* 57 (2008): 1641–92.

388 **In 2003, the Partial-Birth:** Indeed, respected physicians and representatives of medical organizations testified in congressional hearings that D&E had specific advantages. But their expertise had been rejected. See the *Partial-Birth Abortion Ban Act of 2003: Hearings Before the Subcommittee on the Constitution of the Committed on the Judiciary,* 108th Cong. (2003), 187–88.

388 **"the entire fetal head":** Partial-Birth Abortion Ban Act, Public Law 108-105, *United States Statutes at Large* (Nov. 5, 2003): 1201.

388 **The ban included:** *Stenberg v. Carhart,* 530 U.S. 914 (2000).

388 **He still had memories:** Linda Greenhouse, "Doctor Spurns Euphemism in Abortion Rights," *New York Times,* April 8, 2009, A7. As former chair of the surgery department at a Nebraska air force base, Carhart's resolve was no doubt stiffened by the fact that his home, horse farm, and most of his horses and household pets had been burned by antiabortion protesters.

388 **When the plaintiffs won:** Petition for a Writ of Certiorari, *Alberto R. Gonzales, Attorney General v. Leroy Carhart et al.,* No. 05-380 (U.S. July 8, 2005).

388 **"informed consent" regulation:** *Akron v. Akron Center for Reproductive Health,* 462 U.S. 416 (1983).

389 **"We also see no reason":** *Planned Parenthood v. Casey,* 505 U.S. 833 (1992).

389 **Thus the seeds:** Maya Manin, "Irrational Women: Informed Consent and Abortion Regret," in Thomas and Boisseau, *Feminist Legal History,* chap. 6; Reva B. Siegel, "Dignity and the Politics of Protection: Abortion Restriction Under *Casey/Carhart,*" *Yale Law Journal* 117 (2008): 1694–800. On the empirical effects of restrictions sanctioned by *Casey,* see Cahn and Carbone, *Red Families v. Blue Families,* chap. 6. On the changing conception of fetal "life," see also Khiara M. Bridges, "'Life' in the Balance: Judicial Review of Abortion Regulations," *U.C. Davis Law Review* 46 (2013): 1285–338.

389 **The Court had narrowly:** The majority had ruled that the ban was vague. *Stenberg v. Carhart,* 530 U.S. 914 (2000).

389 **Justice Kennedy, who had always:** On Kennedy's struggle with abortion, see Colucci, *Justice Kennedy's Jurisprudence,* chap. 2.

389 **Kennedy, the most reluctant member:** *Carhart,* 530 U.S. at 962 (Kennedy dissenting).

389 **The 5–4 vote in *Gonzales:*** Bridges, "'Life' in the Balance."

389 **Roberts, Alito, Kennedy:** The observation on religious affiliation, made initially by the legal scholar Geoffrey Stone, was picked up by the press. See Mark Sherman/Associated Press, "Kennedy May Be Key to Abortion Limits," *Washington Post,* April 19, 2007; Richard Allen Greene, "Court Abortion Verdict Raises Religion Question," *Politico,* April 18, 2007.

390 **It was a recourse:** *Gonzalez v. Carhart,* 550 U.S. 124 (2007), 1625–26 (Kennedy majority).

390 **"respect for the dignity of human":** Ibid. at 1633–34.

392 **"egregiously" wrong:** RBG quoted in Greg Moran, "No Retirement Plans for Justice Ginsburg," *San Diego Union-Tribune,* Feb. 8. 2013.

392 **"Today's decision is alarming":** *Carhart,* 550 U.S. at 1641 (RBG dissenting).

392 **"Today's opinion supplies":** Ibid. at 1644, 1646–47.

392 **"a *method* of abortion":** Ibid. at 1647.

393 **"Women who have abortions":** Ibid. at 1648–49. RBG compared *Mueller v. Oregon,* 208 U.S. 412 (1908), 422–23, and *Bradwell v. State,* 83 U.S. 130 (1873), with *United States v. Virginia,* 518 U.S. 515 (1996), n12, and *Califano v. Goldfarb,* 430 U.S. 199 (1977), 207.

393 "jeopardizes women's health": *Carhart,* 550 U.S. at 1652.

393 "In sum," she bluntly concluded: Ibid. at 1653.

393 Energized by their *Carhart:* Cahn and Carbone, *Red Families v. Blue Families.*

394 Parental notification, waiting periods: "Michigan's Attack on Women's Rights," *New York Times,* June 16, 2012, A22; Laura Bassett, "Virginia Ultrasound Bill Passes in House," *Huffington Post,* Feb. 23, 2012; Luisita Torregrosa, "In U.S., a Rekindled War over Abortion," *New York Times,* June 25, 2013; Ashley Woods, "Michigan's 'Rape Insurance' Abortion Rider Law Goes into Effect Today," *Huffington Post,* March 14, 2014; Grace Wyler, "Battles over Abortion Flare in 2014," *Time,* Feb. 6, 2014; Richard Fausset, "Law on Ultrasounds Reignites the Abortion Debate in a 2016 Battleground," *New York Times,* Jan. 11, 2016, A12.

394 In the years since: *Planned Parenthood Southeast Inc. v. Strange,* Civil Action No. 2:13cv405-MHT (2014).

394 In Texas, a state with 5.4 million: Manny Fernandez, "Both Sides Cite Urgency in Court Appeal of a Texas Law on Abortion Clinics," *New York Times,* Sept. 13, 2014, A14.

394 "The closing down of clinics": Kareem Abdul-Jabbar, "The Coming Race War Won't Be About Race," *Time,* Aug. 17, 2014. Some simply chose to walk to Mexico, despite warnings from staff in closing clinics of the dangers involved.

394 "hidden demand for self-induced": See graphs attached to article by Seth Stevens-Davidowitz, "The Return of the D.I.Y. Abortion," *New York Times,* March 6, 2016, SR2; also, Charles M. Blow, "The End of American Idealism," *New York Times,* March 7, 2016, 20.

394 "profoundly wrong": Linda Greenhouse, "Oral Dissents Give Ginsburg a New Voice," *New York Times,* May 31, 2007, A1.

394 Kennedy, whose thinking did not: For affirmative-action cases of the 2006–7 term, see *Parents Involved in Community Schools v. Seattle School District,* 551 U.S. 701 (2007), and *Meredith v. Jefferson County Board of Education,* 548 U.S. 938 (2006). On the death penalty, see *Uttecht v. Brown,* 551 U.S. 1 (2007). On faith-based programs, see *Hein v. Freedom from Religion Foundation Inc.,* 551 U.S. 587 (2007). On wage equity, see *Ledbetter v. Goodyear Tire & Rubber Co.,* 550 U.S. 618 (2007). On Kennedy, see Heather K. Gerken, "Justice Kennedy and the Domains of Equal Protection," *Harvard Law Review* 121 (2007): 104–29.

395 In November 1999, she filed: *Ledbetter,* 550 U.S. 618.

395 Other women at the Gadsden: Ibid. at 2187.

395 The U.S. Court of Appeals: *Ledbetter v. Goodyear Tire & Rubber Co.,* 421 F.3d 1169 (11th Cir. 2005), 1178.

395 The question now hinged: Linda Greenhouse, "Court Explores Complexities in Job Discrimination Case," *New York Times,* Nov. 28, 2006, A20.

396 Complicating the case further: Among them were *Nat'l RR Corp v. Morgan,* 536 U.S. 101 (2002); *Lorance v. AT&T Technologies Inc.,* 490 U.S. 900 (1989); *Bazemore v. Friday,* 478 U.S. 385 (1986); *Delaware State College v. Ricks,* 449 U.S. 250 (1980); *United Air Lines v. Evans,* 431 U.S. 533 (1977). See Michael Selmi, "The Supreme Court's 2006–2007 Term Employment Cases: A Quiet but Revealing Term," *Employee Rights and Employment Policy Journal* 11 (2007), n9.

396 "Mr. Russell, I thought your argument": Transcript of Oral Argument at 6, *Ledbetter,* 550 U.S. 618.

396 "I suppose all they'd": Ibid. at 6, 15, 16.

396 Then Kennedy raised: Ibid. at 11. See Robin Olinger Bell, "Justice Anthony M. Kennedy: Will His Appointment to the United States Supreme Court Have an Impact on Employment Discrimination?," *University of Cincinnati Law Review* 57 (1989): esp. 1045–50; also, David S. Cohen, "Justice Kennedy's Gendered World," *South Carolina Law Review* 59 (2008): 673–95.

396 **But what was equally:** Transcript of Oral Argument, *Ledbetter,* 550 U.S. 618.

397 **Such rulings reduce:** Toobin, *Oath,* 72–74.

397 **The "big guys":** Tushnet, *In the Balance,* 204.

397 **But Roberts and his:** *Dukes v. Wal-Mart Inc.,* 509 F.3d 1168 (2007). RBG wrote the dissent. On Walmart's employment culture, see Nelson Lichtenstein, "Why Working at Wal-Mart Is Different," *Connecticut Law Review* 39 (2007): 1649–84, and Featherstone, *Selling Women Short,* chap. 1.

397 **Hailed by business groups:** Nelson Lichtenstein, "Why Working at Wal-Mart Is Different," and Featherstone, *Selling Women Short,* chap. 1.

397 **"We apply the statute":** *Ledbetter,* 550 U.S. at 642, 987 (Alito majority).

397 **Justice Stevens, delighted:** Jeffrey Rosen, "The Dissenter, Justice John Paul Stevens," *New York Times Magazine,* Sept. 23, 2007, 50–57, 72, 76, 78–79, 81.

397 **"Title VII was meant":** Quoted in Robert Barnes, "Over Ginsburg's Dissent, Court Limits Bias Suits," *Washington Post,* May 30, 2007, A1.

398 **"Comparative pay information":** *Ledbetter,* 550 U.S. at 645 (RBG dissenting).

398 **Ginsburg turned next:** *Bazemore v. Friday,* 478 U.S. 385 (1986).

398 **"Congress never intended":** *Ledbetter,* 550 U.S. at 654 (RBG dissenting).

398 **"each paycheck less than":** Ibid. at 655.

398 **"The discrimination of which Ledbetter":** Ibid. at 657–61.

399 **The Labor Department:** For a fuller discussion, see, for example, Lichtenstein, "Ideology and Interest on the Social Policy Home Front"; also, Finlay, *George W. Bush and the War on Women.*

399 **And with the president's new nominees:** Selmi, "Supreme Court's 2006–2007 Term Employment Law Cases," 219.

399 **In less than two years:** Robert Pear, "Justices' Ruling in Discrimination Case May Draw Quick Action by Obama," *New York Times,* Jan. 4, 2009, A13.

399 **"I worked a lot":** Quoted in Barnes, "Over Ginsburg's Dissent, Court Limits Bias Suits."

399 **"setback for women":** Marcia Greenberger quoted in ibid.

399 **Workplace experts agreed:** Linda Greenhouse, "Justices' Ruling Limits Suits on Pay Disparity," *New York Times,* May 30, 2007, A1.

399 **"Rarely in the history":** Toobin, *Oath,* 81.

399 **Within hours of the decision's:** Barnes, "Over Ginsburg's Dissent, Court Limits Bias Suits." Senators Tom Harkin of Iowa, Barbara Mikulski of Maryland, and Barack Obama of Illinois jumped in behind Clinton to co-sponsor the bill. See Jacqueline Palank, "Democrats Will Try to Counter Ruling on Discrimination Suits," *New York Times,* July 13, 2007, A13.

399 **The media picked up:** See, for example, "As a Matter of Justice Congress Should Correct Ruling on Fair Pay," *Dallas Morning News,* June 5, 2007, A14; "Court Bias Deadline Too Tight," *Denver Post,* June 4, 2007, B7; "Injustice 5, Justice 4," *New York Times,* May 31, 2007, A18; "It Is Payback Time for New Court," *Cleveland Plain Dealer,* June 1, 2007, E1; Marcia Greenberger, "Paycheck Fairness Is Not a Burden," *Washington Post,* Aug. 20, 2007, A14; Nicole Gaouette, "House Bill to Lift Limits on Pay Suits," *Los Angeles Times,* July 31, 2007, A12.

400 **"We don't do that":** Ball, *Bush, the Detainees, and the Constitution,* 176. Lawyers in the administration interpreted a federal statute banning torture so as to allow the administration maximum latitude in the use of "enhanced" interrogation practices—a change that a bipartisan 9/11 commission would find not only excessive but in violation of the country's legal obligations to other nations. See Scott Shane, "U.S. Practiced Torture After 9/11, Nonpartisan Review Concludes," *New York Times,* April 16, 2013, A1. For full report, see Open Society Institute, *The Report of the Constitution Project's Task Force on Detainee Treatment,* April 2013.

401 "the political branches": *Boumediene v. Bush,* 553 U.S. 723 (2008), 755 (Kennedy majority). Roberts, Scalia, Thomas, and Alito dissented. In the preceding terror trials—*Rasul v. Bush,* 542 U.S. 466 (2004), *Hamdi v. Rumsfeld,* 542 U.S. 507 (2004), and *Hamdan v. Rumsfeld,* 548 U.S. 557 (2006)—the Court ruled in favor of detainees. Scalia and Thomas dissented in all three cases. Rehnquist joined them in *Rasul.* Stevens also dissented in *Hamdi.* In *Hamdan,* Alito dissented and Roberts did not participate. For a detailed discussion of these cases, see Ball, *Bush, the Detainees, and the Constitution;* on Scalia with the decisions of his colleagues in these cases, see Biskupic, *American Original,* chap. 15.

402 Not least was the squandering: Fisher, *Constitution and 9/11,* esp. chaps. 7, 9, 6, and 10.

402 Not least were the defeats: See *Arizona v. Gant,* 556 U.S. 332 (2009).

402 "What a joy": Quoted in Anthony Tommasini, "Justices Greet Diva: It's Ardor in the Court," *New York Times,* Nov. 1, 2008, C1.

402 "I'm not going to cry": Quoted in ibid.

402 "gloriously familiar voice": Ibid.

403 A brass band played: Monica Davey and John M. Broder, "Celebration and Sense of History at Chicago Park," *New York Times,* Nov. 5, 2008, P8.

403 "Something has changed": Ibid.

NINETEEN · Losing Marty and Leading the Minority

405 the symbolism inspired: See Sugrue, *Not Even Past,* esp. introduction, and David A. Hollinger, "Obama, the Instability of Color Lines, and the Promise of a Postethnic Future," *Callaloo* 31 (2008): 1033–37; Bonilla-Silva, *Racism Without Racists;* Alexander, *New Jim Crow;* Erin Aigner et al., "In a Decisive Victory, Obama Reshapes the Electoral Map," *New York Times,* Nov. 6, 2008, 10.

405 When the Court subsequently held: Toobin, "Heavyweight," 47.

405 As she got to know: Carmon and Knizhnik, *Notorious RBG,* 157.

405 Yet others, who during the campaign: Kenski, Hardy, and Jamieson, *Obama Victory;* Parker and Barreto, *Change They Can't Believe In,* chaps. 2, 5.

406 Something had to be done: On Greenspan and Bernanke's concern that the level of economic inequality had gone beyond what was healthy for the economy, see Frank, *Frank,* 350.

406 A disengaged but combat-weary: On perpetual war, see Dudziak, *War Time.* On white exhaustion and racial inequality, see Sugrue, *Not Even Past,* chap. 3, and Bonilla-Silva, *Racism Without Racists.*

406 But Republican opposition: On the first year of the new administration, see Alter, *Promise.* In a nation that is 40 percent moderate and 60 percent ideologically liberal or conservative, even a five- or ten-percentage-point shift in ideological preference had made a difference.

406 A few days after: Alec MacGillis, "Why Is Mitch McConnell Picking This Fight?," *New York Times,* Feb. 19, 2016, SR2.

406 manipulating the rules of Senate: Julian E. Zeltzer, "Tea Partied: President Obama's Encounters with the Conservative-Industrial Complex," in Zeltzer, *The Presidency of Barack Obama.*

406 Grassroots activists on the far right: Skocpol and Williamson, *Tea Party and the Remaking of Republican Conservatism,* 6; Vanessa Williamson, Theda Skocpol, and John Coggin, "The Tea Party and the Remaking of Republican Conservatism," *Perspectives on Politics* 9 (March 2011): 34.

During the 2010 general election, the GOP gained 64 House seats and 6 Senate seats. Of those backed by a Tea Party group or self-identified as a member of the movement, less than one-third won out of 130 House races, and 5 of 10 successfully gained a seat in the Senate, often in areas already strongly supportive of Republicans. The GOP made significant gains in the next two election cycles, but the Tea Party played a less prominent role, being labeled as "too extreme" by its opponents. By 2015, only 17 percent of Americans polled by Gallup identified themselves as Tea Party supporters, barely half the number from five years earlier. Christopher F. Karpowitz, "Tea Time in America? The Impact of the Tea Party Movement on the 2010 Midterm Elections," *PS: Political Science and Politics* 44 (April 2011): 303–9; Kate Zernike, "Tea Party Set to Win Enough Races for Wide Influence," *New York Times,* Oct. 15, 2010, A1; Alexandra Moe, "Just 32% of Tea Party Candidates Win," MSNBC, Nov. 3, 2010; Ian Gray, "Tea Party Election Results: Conservative Movement of 2010 Takes Pounding in 2012," *Huffington Post,* Nov. 7, 2012; Carl Hulse, "Republicans Face Struggle over Party's Direction," *New York Times,* Nov. 7, 2012, A1; Jim Norman, "In US, Support for Tea Party Drops to New Low," Gallup, Oct. 26, 2015.

406 **they also believed that minorities:** Skocpol and Williamson, *Tea Party and the Remaking of Republican Conservatism,* 10–11, 31, 65–71. See also Hochschild, *Strangers in Their Own Land.* Both books examine the Tea Party movement from the grassroots level, with Skocpol and Williamson focusing their fieldwork in Massachusetts, Virginia, and Arizona, while Hochschild focuses on the bayou region of Louisiana, an area considered a conservative hotbed.

406 **"take their country back":** The classic introduction to such movements is Richard Hofstadter, *Paranoid Style in American Politics.* On the Tea Party, see Skocpol and Williamson, *Tea Party and the Remaking of Republican Conservatism,* esp. 65–71.

407 **"change Tea Partiers could believe in":** Here I have slightly altered the title of Parker and Barreto's superb study of the Tea Party, *Change They Can't Believe In.* For a gendered perspective of the Tea Party, see Deckman, *Tea Party Women,* esp. 242–43.

407 **Aided by complicit right-wing media:** Skocpol and Williamson, *Tea Party and the Remaking of Republican Conservatism,* 9–13. For an excellent analysis of the Tea Party's rise and its ties to the Koch brothers, see Kevin Baker, "The Incredible True Story of the Tea Party's Rise to Power," *TakePart,* Oct. 30, 2015. See also Mayer, *Dark Money.* For the Koch brothers and their billionaire allies, the impetus is primarily economic. On the role of the media, see Hammer, *Messengers of the Right.*

407 **The election of 2008 produced:** See Tesler, *Post-Racial or Most-Racial?*

407 **It is to say that after 2008:** On racism in the Tea Party, see Parker and Barreto, *Change They Can't Believe In,* and Williamson, Skocpol, and Coggin, "Tea Party and the Remaking of Republican Conservatism," 34–35.

408 **Despite her friendships:** Hirshman, *Sisters in Law,* 267–70.

408 *Mad Men: Mad Men* was a television series on the AMC channel set in the 1960s. Acclaimed for its historical accuracy, the program retained all the sexism of the era.

408 **During oral arguments:** Transcript of Oral Argument at 22, 44–45, *Safford Unified School District v. Redding,* 557 U.S. 364 (2009).

409 **"shake [her] bra out":** Ibid. at 45–46.

409 **"not beyond human experience":** Ibid. at 58.

409 **"the Court's only female":** Nina Totenberg, "Court Hears School Strip Search Case," NPR, April 21, 2009; Joan Biskupic, "Ginsburg: Court Needs Another Woman," *USA Today,* May 5, 2009.

409 **Thanks to the press:** *Redding,* 557 U.S. at 2 (RBG concurring in part and dissenting in part).

409 **"eight rather well-fed men":** Adam Liptak, "Let Me Finish, Please: Conservative Men Dominate the Debate," *New York Times,* April 18, 2017, A13. Quotation in Charlie Rose, "Justice Ruth Bader Ginsburg Interview, Part 2," charlierose.com, Oct. 11, 2016. See also Jane Pauley, "Ruth Bader Ginsburg: Her View from the Bench," CBS News, Oct. 9, 2016; Joan Biskupic, *Breaking In,* 153.

410   **Even standing to cook:** On Marty's difficulty standing, see Jane Ginsburg's tribute to her father in Alito and Supreme Court Spouses, *Chef Supreme*, 123–26.

410   **"its disrespect for precedent":** The quotation is Jeffrey Toobin's description of Souter's perception of the Roberts Court. See Toobin, *Oath*, 168. See also Toobin, "Money Unlimited," 36–47.

410   **The chief justice's maneuvering:** Toobin, "Money Unlimited,"

410   **undermined the fundamental principle of democracy:** *Citizens United v. Federal Election Commission*, 558 U.S. 310 (2010), esp. Stevens's dissent on 393–96. Also see *McCutcheon v. Federal Election Commission*, 134 S. Ct. 1434 (2014), esp. Breyer's dissent, 1465. On the overruling, see Jeffrey Rosen, "RBG Presides," *New Republic*, Oct. 13, 2014, 18. Also see Ronald Dworkin, "The Decision That Threatens Democracy," *New York Review of Books*, May 13, 2010.

410   **She had joined Breyer's:** *Parents Involved v. Seattle School District, No. 1*, 551 U.S. 701 (2007), 803–7 (Breyer dissenting). The case dealt with a Seattle School District policy that allowed students to apply to any high school in the district. The district utilized a tiebreaker system to decide which students would be admitted to the most popular schools. Race was considered the second-most-important factor in the system. The Court found the district's racial tiebreaker plan unconstitutional. Breyer cited the precedent established by *Brown v. Board of Education*, 347 U.S. 483 (1954), and *Swann v. Charlotte-Mecklenburg County Board of Education*, 402 U.S. 1 (1971), 16. For the Louisville case, see *Meredith v. Jefferson County Board of Education*, 548 U.S. 938 (2006). Jefferson County Public Schools (JCPS) were integrated by a court order until 2000. After its release from the order, JCPS, with the idea of maintaining racial integration, implemented an enrollment plan that determined a student's placement based on place of residence and school capacity, as well as race. The Court found Jefferson County's enrollment plan unconstitutional.

410   **And then there was the *Heller*:** *District of Columbia v. Heller*, 554 U.S. 570 (2008). Legal precedent prior to *Heller* held that the Second Amendment protected only a state's right to maintain a militia and not an individual right to bear arms independent of the state's need for a militia. *Heller* was followed by *McDonald v. Chicago*, 557 U.S. 965 (2009), which furthered the majority's crusade against gun control. For a historian's perspective, see Winkler, *Gunfight*, Charles, *Armed in America*, Dunbar-Ortiz, *Loaded*, Pogue, *Chosen Country*, and Belew, *Bring the War Home*.

410   **Fortunately, the malignancy:** Radha Chitale, Joanna Schaffhausen, and Dan Child, "Ginsburg's Cancer May Have Been Caught Early Enough," ABC News, Feb. 5, 2009.

411   **Scheduling the surgery:** Adam Liptak, "Justice Ginsburg Undergoes Surgery for Pancreatic Cancer, Court Says," *New York Times*, Feb. 6, 2009, A12.

411   **Still, her delight at Jane's:** Jane Ginsburg had been elected a corresponding fellow of the British Academy for her contribution to the global community of intellectual property law. She had also been selected for the Phi Beta Kappa Society's Visiting Scholar Program, giving her the opportunity to deliver presentations in her area of expertise at U.S. universities. See Sara-Jane Adams and Jeff Wild, "The Cream of the Crop," *Intellectual Asset Management* (Jan/Feb. 2009): 57–58, and "Ginsburg Garners Honors in Britain, U.S.," *Columbia Law School Magazine* (Fall 2011): 7.

411   **"*I will live*":** RBG, interview by author.

412   **A copy of the bill:** Toobin, "Heavyweight," 38–47.

412   **"how the world works":** Transcript of Obama-Sotomayor Announcement, May 26, 2009.

412   **After working as an assistant:** Sotomayor, *My Beloved World*, 39; Keith B. Richburg, "Federal Judge Sonia Sotomayor Likely to Be on Obama's Supreme Court Shortlist; Backers Say She Meets Obama Requisites," *Washington Post*, May 7, 2009, A3; Sheryl Gay Stolberg, "Sotomayor, a Trailblazer and a Dreamer," *New York Times*, May 26, 2009.

412   **"a wise Latina woman":** For text of the lecture, see "Lecture: 'A Latina Judge's Voice,'" *New York Times,* May 15, 2009.

412   **Ultimately, Sotomayor's record:** Adam Liptak, "A Careful Pen with No Broad Strokes," *Washington Post,* May 27, 2009, A1; Jerry Markon, "Judge's Votes Show No Single Ideology," *Washington Post,* June 7, 2009, A4.

412   **"hold her own":** RBG quotations in this and previous sentence in Emily Bazelon, "The Place of Women on the Court," *New York Times,* July 7, 2009, MM22.

413   **Her mother, an elementary:** Lisa W. Foderaro and Christine Haughney, "Meet the Kagans," *New York Times,* June 20, 2010, MB1; Sheryl Gay Stolberg, Katharine Q. Seelye, and Lisa W. Foderaro, "Pragmatic New Yorker Chose a Careful Path to Washington," *New York Times,* May 11, 2010, A1.

413   **When Republicans blocked:** On Kagan's effective leadership, see Tushnet, *In the Balance,* 85–89.

413   **Obama had lured the first:** Peter Baker and Jeff Zeleny, "Obama Said to Pick Solicitor General for Court," *New York Times,* May 10, 2010, A1. See also Tushnet, *In the Balance,* 82–92.

414   **Nevertheless, in August:** Baker and Zeleny, "Obama Said to Pick Solicitor General for Court"; Stolberg, Seelye, and Foderaro, "Pragmatic New Yorker Chose a Careful Path to Washington"; Sheryl Gay Stolberg, "Confirmation Is Likely, but Not G.O.P. Support," *New York Times,* July 2, 2010, A16. The problem, however, was less Kagan's than Obama's lower approval rating at the time of her nomination and the opposition campaigns waged through social media as well as more traditional venues. See Nancy Maveety, "A Transformative Politics of Judicial Selection? President Obama and the Federal Judiciary," in Schier, *Transforming America,* chap. 8.

414   **Ginsburg found the two:** Mark Sherman, "Ruth Bader Ginsburg Considers Elena Kagan's Confirmation an 'Exhilarating' Development," *Huffington Post,* Aug. 4, 2010.

414   **"shrinking violet":** Adam Liptak, "A Most Inquisitive Court? No Argument There," *New York Times,* Oct. 8, 2013, A14; Robert Barnes, "Justices Crank Up the Volume," *Washington Post,* March 2, 2011, A3.

414   **Kagan's brilliance:** Tribe and Matz, *Uncertain Justice;* also "The Supreme Court: Draw Back the Curtain?," *Economist,* Jan. 10, 2015, 29.

414   **Someone who could:** Tushnet, *In the Balance,* ix–xi, vii, 94, 285.

414   **Asked by Obama:** Sotomayor related RBG's response to Obama. See Ian Frazier, "Sonia from the Bronx," *New Yorker,* Feb. 8, 2016.

415   **The five justices:** David Cole, "The Anti-Court Court," *New York Review of Books,* Aug. 14, 2014, 10–14.

415   **When he wrote for the minority:** On Stevens, I rely on Rosen, "Dissenter," 50–57, 72, 76, 78–79, 81, and Jeffrey Toobin, "After Stevens: What Will the Supreme Court Be Like Without Its Liberal Leader?," *New Yorker,* March 22, 2010, 38–47.

415   **reputation as a loner:** Jeffrey Toobin, "Without a Paddle: Can Stephen Breyer Save the Obama Agenda in the Supreme Court?," *New Yorker,* Sept. 27, 2010, 34–41.

415   **"flowery, discursive rhetorical":** Toobin, "Heavyweight."

415   **As her recent dissent:** See Lani Guinier, "Courting the People: Demosprudence and the Law/Politics Divide," *Harvard Law Review* 127 (2013): 437–44.

415   **"speak to a future age":** Maveety, "Transformative Politics of Judicial Selection?" See also Ruth Bader Ginsburg, "The Role of Dissenting Opinions," *Minnesota Law Review* 95.1 (2010): 1-8.

416   **She also resolved:** Toobin, "Heavyweight."

416   **When Ruth arrived:** RBG provided information on Marty's illness and a copy of his note to her to Jeffrey Toobin. See ibid., esp. 46.

417   **The next morning, the final:** *Christian Legal Society Chapter v. Martinez,* 561 U.S. 661 (2010); the quotation is in Totenberg, "Martin Ginsburg's Legacy."

417   **Marty, she believed:** Toobin, "Heavyweight," 46.

417 **"and each of your spouses"**: Adam Liptak, "Justices Bid Farewells on Last Day," *New York Times*, June 29, 2010, A18.

417 **"In their gestures"**: Hirshman, *Sisters in Law*, 278.

417 **Otherwise, she feared that Ruth**: Toobin, "Heavyweight."

418 **After graduating with honors**: RBG, interview by author, Aug. 31, 2014.

418 **"unbelievably wonderful"**: Ibid.

418 **Ruth would perform the wedding**: RBG to author, Aug. 16, 2010.

419 **With the house also available**: RBG, interview by author, Aug. 31, 2014. It is not clear whether the justice pays rent for the adobe or whether she and her family are houseguests.

419 **"discerning, intelligent operagoer"**: Anne Constable, "Santa Fe a Favorite Summer Getaway for Justice Ginsburg," *Santa Fe New Mexican*, Aug. 23, 2014.

419 **"fireside chat"**: Carlyn Rae Mitchell, "Supreme Court Justice Discusses Advances for Women," *Colorado Springs Gazette*, Aug. 28, 2010. The "fireside chat" was moderated by NPR's Nina Totenberg. Video of RBG's speech and the chat are available at www .c-span.org.

420 **"Happy Birthday"**: Ariane de Vogue, "Ruth Bader Ginsburg, Sonia Sotomayor Dish Out Supreme Court Lunchroom Secrets," CNN.com, June 2, 2016.

421 **Nina Totenberg, legal reporter**: Toobin, "Heavyweight."

421 **Ginsburg's genuine affection**: "Remarks by the President at Hanukkah Reception," White House, Dec. 8, 2011.

421 **One month later, during**: "Supreme Court Justice Ginsburg Expresses Admiration for Egyptian Revolution and Democratic Transition," press release, U.S. Embassy Cairo, Feb. 1, 2012.

421 **After Thompson was stripped**: *The New York Times* claimed that her argument was "more persuasive [than the ruling]." See *Connick v. Thompson*, 563 U.S. ___ (2011); "Failure of Empathy and Justice: The Court Refuses to See a Pattern of Abuse by Prosecutors Determined to Win at All Costs," *New York Times*, April 1, 2011, A26.

421 **That five of her colleagues**: Laurence Tribe and Joshua Matz argue that the Roberts Court displayed a "clear arc . . . conferring near-total immunity on prosecutors and police." See *Uncertain Justice*, 301–4, esp. 304. RBG's majority opinion in *Bullcoming v. New Mexico*, 564 U.S. ___ (2011), argued that a criminal defendant had the right "to be confronted with the witnesses against him," specifically, the person who had conducted the lab analysis of evidence rather than a surrogate. In *Leal Garcia v. Texas*, 564 U.S. ___ (2011), RBG, Sotomayor, and Kagan joined Breyer's dissent when the Court denied an application for a stay of execution of Humberto Leal Garcia Jr., a Mexican national convicted of kidnapping, rape, and murder who insisted that the police failed to inform him of his right to contact the Mexican consulate.

421 **Milestones earlier in her tenure**: "Symposium: The Jurisprudence of Justice Ruth Bader Ginsburg," *University of Hawaii Law Review* 20 (1998): 581–795; "Symposium: Celebration of the Tenth Anniversary of Justice Ruth Bader Ginsburg's Appointment to the Supreme Court of the United States," *Columbia Law Review* 104 (2004): 1–252; "Symposium: The Jurisprudence of Justice Ruth Bader Ginsburg: A Discussion of Fifteen Years on the U.S. Supreme Court," *Ohio State Law Journal* 70 (2009): 797–1126.

421 **Those familiar with**: Laura Krugman Ray, "Justice Ginsburg and the Middle Way," *Brooklyn Law Review* 68 (2003): 629–83, esp. 680. Ray characterizes RBG's middle way as "a remarkably precise reflection of her theories of appellate judging" in which she follows the path of moderation, judging each case on its merits, exercising judicial restraint, seeking resolutions that protect the institutional well-being of the court and its pronouncements, and writing in detached, impersonal language that suppresses individuality.

422 **"justice is not to be taken"**: Lecture at Yale Law School (1923) as quoted in Brown, "Codification of International Law," 32.

422 **"Measured motions":** RBG, "Speaking in a Judicial Voice," 1185–209.

423 **When approaching cases:** Ray, "Justice Ginsburg and the Middle Way," 629–82.

423 **Her dissents, like her opinions:** Ibid.

423 **Any hope of influencing:** *Parents Involved in Community Schools v. Seattle School District No. 1,* 551 U.S. 701 (2007). The Seattle case had been united with *Meredith, Custodial Parent and Next Friend of McDonald v. Jefferson County Bd. of Ed et al.,* No. 05–915, from Louisville, Kentucky. The respective cities sought to maintain diversity at their schools by using race as a means of limiting transfers or as a tiebreaker for admission to particular schools. Linda Greenhouse, "Justices, Voting 5–4, Limit the Use of Race in Integration Plans," *New York Times,* June 29, 2007, A1.

423 **"strained fury":** Tribe and Matz, *Uncertain Justice,* 20.

423 **The class-action suits:** *Wal-Mart v. Dukes,* 564 U.S. __ (2011).

424 **Lacking the resources:** Tribe and Matz, *Uncertain Justice,* chap. 8.

424 **"[J]udges must defer":** Ibid., 131.

424 **Breyer, Ginsburg, and Sotomayor:** *Holder v. Humanitarian Law Project,* 561 U.S. 1 (2010) (Breyer dissenting).

424 **In subsequent decisions:** See, respectively, *Beard v. Banks,* 548 U.S. 521 (2006); *Garcetti v. Ceballos,* 547 U.S. 410 (2006); and *Morse v. Frederick,* 551 U.S. 393 (2007).

424 **She was no longer willing:** The same observation is made by Hirshman in *Sisters in Law,* 292.

424 **"supplement[s] the dry reason":** Adam Liptak, "When Words on Paper Don't Convey Enough Ire," *New York Times,* March 9, 2010, A12.

424 **"nuclear option":** William D. Blake and Hans J. Hacker, " 'The Brooding Spirit of the Law': Supreme Court Justices Reading Dissents from the Bench," *Justice System Journal* 31, no. 1 (2010): 1–25; the term "nuclear option" appears on page 3. This study covers dissents read from the bench between the 1969 and the 2007 terms. Supplemental data through the 2013 term was graciously provided by Dr. Hacker through email correspondence. In *Miller v. Johnson,* RBG countered the majority opinion that attempted to eliminate any racial considerations, arguing, "Statutory mandates and political realities may require States to consider race when drawing district lines." *Miller v. Johnson,* 515 U.S. 900 (1995), 949 (RBG dissenting). Four years later, she maintained that when modern technology permits the near-instantaneous transfer of assets, the district courts should be permitted to preliminarily freeze those assets despite the lack of legal tradition. See *Grupo Mexicano de Desarrollo, S. A. v. Alliance Bond Fund Inc.,* 527 U.S. 308 (1999). In 2001, the Court was divided on the issue of "catalyst theory," with RBG insisting that the Buckhannon care facility, whose litigation caused a change in law, be considered the prevailing party, even though the case was dropped without conclusion after that change. See *Buckhannon Board & Care Home Inc. v. West Virginia Department of Health and Human Resources,* 532 U.S. 598 (2001). The First Amendment rights of Minnesota judicial candidates formed the basis of *Republican Party of Minnesota v. White,* 536 U.S. 765 (2002), with the 5–4 majority insisting that the state's "announce clause" that prohibited candidates from announcing their views on legal and political issues was unconstitutional. RBG maintained that the clause acted as a safeguard to judicial impartiality. The 2003 decision in *American Insurance Assn. v. Garamendi,* 539 U.S. 396 (2003), nullified a California law that required insurance companies to disclose information regarding policies held by people in Europe from 1920 to 1945 in an attempt to help Holocaust victims. RBG argued that the law only required the disclosure of information, but did not authorize litigation of Holocaust claims. Finally, the 7–2 majority sent *Cheney v. United States District Court for D.C.,* 542 U.S. 367 (2004), back to the district court, stating that it should have considered separation-of-powers claims and that in order to stop discovery, proceedings should be considered because of the potential interference with presidential activity. RBG disagreed, stating that the district court would keep discovery within appropriate limits.

425 **"black and grim"**: Blake and Hacker, "'Brooding Spirit of the Law'"; Hacker email. Quotation is in Pauley, "Ruth Bader Ginsburg: Her View from the Bench."

425 **At the end of the 2012**: On June 24, 2013, RBG read her dissent for *University of Texas Southwestern Medical Center v. Nassar*, 570 U.S. ___ (2013), *Comcast Corp. v. Behrend*, 569 U.S. ___ (2013), and *Vance v. Ball State University*, 570 U.S. ___ (2013). The following day, she did the same for *Shelby County v. Holder*, 570 U.S. ___ (2013).

425 **Dissents from the bench**: Blake and Hacker, "'Brooding Spirit of the Law,'" 7–8, and Liptak, "When Words on Paper Don't Convey Enough Ire," A12.

425 **In the process, a dissent**: See Christopher Schmidt's comments on dissents from the bench and the role of legal journalists and commentators, "Justice Sotomayor's First Oral Dissent," *ISCOTUS* (blog), April 25, 2014.

425 **Her image became that**: Alisha Parlapiano, "When the Eight-Member Supreme Court Avoids Deadlocks, It Leans Left," *New York Times,* June 27, 2016; Adam Liptak, "Chief Justice John Roberts Amasses a Conservative Record, and Wrath from the Right," *New York Times,* Sept. 28, 2015, A16: Adam Liptak, "Right Divided, Disciplined Left Steered Justices," *New York Times,* July 1, 2015, A1. As of the 2015 term, Sotomayor is ranked as slightly more liberal than RBG. The charts that *The New York Times* uses to demonstrate the individual ideological drift of the Supreme Court justices are based on Martin-Quinn scores, which quantify the interests of each justice relative to his or her legal decisions. See Andrew D. Martin and Kevin M. Quinn, "Dynamic Ideal Point Estimation via Markov Chain Monte Carlo for the U.S. Supreme Court, 1953–1999," *Political Analysis* 10 (2002): 134–53.

425 **That he now wore**: Toobin, "After Stevens," 38–47.

425 **"I regard her as the founding"**: Kenji Yoshino, "Sex Equality's Inner Frontier: The Case of Same-Sex Marriage," *Yale Law Journal* 122 (2013): 275–81, quotation on 280.

426 **Ginsburg responded with**: Ibid. In April 2016, Yale announced that its two new residential colleges would be named after Pauli Murray and Benjamin Franklin. Despite decades of alumni and student protest, the university also announced that the residential college named after the pro-slavery vice president John C. Calhoun would retain its name. See Glenda Elizabeth Gilmore, "At Yale, a Right That Doesn't Outweigh a Wrong," *New York Times,* April 29, 2016.

426 **On May 26, 2011**: See listing for the 2011 honorary degrees at www.harvard.edu. The video of the birthday celebration is in the possession of James Ginsburg.

427 **"Being so close"**: Charlie Rose interview, "Justice Ruth Bader Ginsburg, Part 1," Oct. 10, 2016. Available at charlierose.com.

TWENTY · Race Matters

428 **They also raised the ire**: Perry, *Michigan Affirmative Action Cases,* 56, 59–60.

428 *Grutter v. Bollinger* **challenged**: On the intervening years, see Anthony S. Chen and Lisa M. Stulberg, "Racial Inequality and Race-Conscious Affirmative Action in College Admissions: A Historical Perspective on Contemporary Prospects and Future Possibilities," in Harris and Lieberman, *Beyond Discrimination,* 105–34. For a fuller account of the cases, see Perry, *Michigan Affirmative Action Cases.*

428 **The kind of forward-looking**: Brief for Amici Curiae 65 Leading American Businesses in Support of Respondents, on Writs of Certiorari to the United States Court of Appeals for the Sixth Circuit, *Grutter v. Bollinger,* 539 U.S. 306 (2003) (Nos. 02-241 and 02-516); Consolidated Brief of Lt. Gen. Julius W. Becton Jr. et al. as Amici Curiae in Support of Respondents, on Writs of Certiorari to the United States Court of Appeals for the Sixth Circuit, *Grutter v. Bollinger,* 539 U.S. 306 (2003), and *Gratz v. Bollinger,* 539 U.S. 244 (2003); *Grutter v. Bollinger,* 539 U.S. 306 (2003), 311–44, esp. 316 (O'Connor majority).

429 **"a compelling state interest":** *Grutter v. Bollinger,* 539 U.S. 306 (2003), 311–44, esp. 316 (O'Connor majority).

429 **Two students with identical:** Perry, *Michigan Affirmative Action Cases,* 56.

429 **Her application rejected:** Ibid., 64.

429 **In order to create:** Ibid., 56, 59–60.

429 **While the percentage:** Ibid.

429 **A nonminority candidate:** *Gratz v. Bollinger,* 539 U.S. 244 (2003), 303 (RBG dissenting).

430 **"a disguised quota":** Transcript of Oral Argument at 22, ibid.

430 **"the factor of race":** Ibid. at 270, 272 (Rehnquist majority).

430 **"This insistence on 'consistency'":** Ibid. at 298–301 (RBG dissenting). On 301, RBG is quoting Stephen L. Carter, "When Victims Happen to Be Black," *Yale Law Journal* 97 (1987–88): 434.

430 **"Actions designed to burden":** *Gratz,* 539 U.S. at 301 (RBG dissenting).

430 **"the mere assertion of a laudable":** Ibid. at 301–4 (RBG dissenting).

431 **Former "foot soldiers":** Coyle, *Roberts Court,* 88. On the GOP's conservative egalitarianism, see Chen, *Fifth Freedom,* esp. chap. 6. In *League of United Latin American Citizens v. Perry,* 548 U.S. 399 (2006), Kennedy, joined by Stevens, Souter, RBG, and Breyer, ruled that one Texas voting district, 23, violated the Voting Rights Act and needed to be redrawn. The Court did not throw out the entire Texas districting plan, however. Scalia, Roberts, and Alito dissented to the redrawing of District 23. Roberts cited a previous decision upholding the constitutionality of a Latino district. But Kennedy did not dissent. Kennedy stated that District 23 had been redrawn in a way that clearly prevented Latino voters from electing a candidate of their choosing. For the Louisville case, see *Meredith v. Jefferson County Board of Education,* 548 U.S. 938 (2006). For the Seattle case, see *Parents Involved v. Seattle School District No. 1,* 551 U.S. 701 (2007).

431 **"The whole point":** Transcript of Oral Argument at 35, *Schuette v. Coalition to Defend Affirmative Action,* 572 U.S. ___ (2014).

431 **Rigorous scrutiny, he insisted:** *Grutter v. Bollinger,* 539 U.S. 306 (2003), 387–90 (Kennedy dissenting). On Kennedy's evolving views on race-equality cases, especially affirmative action, see Gerken, "Justice Kennedy and the Domains of Equal Protection," 104–30; also, Reva B. Siegel, "From Colorblindness to Antibalkanization: An Emerging Ground of Decision in Race Equality Cases," *Yale Law Journal* 120 (2011): 1278–366.

431 **With possibly five justices:** Opposition to affirmative action at the state level had been building since the 1990s. A *Washington Post*–ABC poll conducted in 2013 found that 76 percent of the U.S. population believed it should be terminated. Although Democrats were more supportive than Republicans, nearly eight in ten whites and African Americans and almost seven in eleven Hispanics objected to race-based admissions. See Scott Clement, "Most in U.S. Oppose Race-Based Admissions," *Washington Post,* June 12, 2013, A3. There was some speculation in the press that the increased resentment of race-based admissions was related to Obama's reelection.

431 **None proved more:** On Blum and his one-man Project on Fair Representation, see Joan Biskupic, "Special Report: Behind U.S. Race Cases, a Little-Known Recruiter," Reuters, Dec. 4, 2012; Morgan Smith, "One Man Standing Against Race-Based Laws," *New York Times,* Feb. 23, 2012, A21; Krissah Thompson, "A Supreme Courter," *Washington Post,* Feb. 26, 2013, C1; Liz Halloran, "Force Behind Race-Law Rollback Efforts Talks Voting Rights Case," NPR, Feb. 26, 2013. On his use of websites to recruit possible plaintiffs for affirmative-action cases, see Adam Liptak, "Unofficial Enforcer of Ruling on Race in College Admissions," *New York Times,* April 7, 2014, A16.

431 **UT, like other universities:** *Sweatt v. Painter,* 339 U.S. 629 (1950).

431 **In response, the state:** For a more detailed history, see *Fisher v. Texas,* 556 F. Supp. 2d 603 (U.S. Dist. 2008).

432 **The underlying objective:** For an argument on behalf of UT by the U.S. solicitor general, Donald B. Verrilli, see Transcript of Oral Argument at 59–72, *Fisher v. Texas,* 570 U.S. 279 (2013); also see comments of UT's director of admission, Kedra Ishop, in Adam Liptak, "Race and College Admissions, Facing a New Test by the Justices," *New York Times,* Oct. 8, 2012, A1.

432 **"special circumstances":** These included socioeconomic status, race, whether English is spoken at home, and whether the student came from a single-parent family.

432 **The university also committed:** *Fisher,* 556 F. Supp. 2d 603.

432 **"[T]he only other difference":** Quoted in Nicole Hannah-Jones, "A Colorblind Constitution: What Abigail Fisher's Affirmative Action Case Is Really About," *ProPublica,* March 18, 2003.

433 **She was also offered:** Ibid.

433 **When Fisher lost:** *Fisher,* 556 F. Supp. 2d 603, and *Fisher v. Texas,* 169 F.3d 295 (5th Cir. 2012).

433 **To show such solicitude:** Julie Dressner and Edwin Martinez, "The Scars of Stop-and-Frisk," *New York Times,* June 12, 2012; Reva B. Siegel, "The Supreme Court 2012 Term, Foreword: Equality Divided," *Harvard Law Review* 127, no. 1 (2013): 1–94, n310.

433 **The importance of the case:** Robert Barnes, "Court Keeps Alive Affirmative Action," *Washington Post,* June 25, 2013, A1.

433 **"independent add on":** Transcript of Oral Argument at 23, *Fisher v. University of Texas,* 570 U.S. 279 (2013).

433 **"Should someone who is one-quarter":** Ibid. at 35.

434 **As drafts circulated:** Biskupic, *Breaking In,* chap. 11.

434 **Thomas, like Sotomayor:** Sotomayor was a proud beneficiary of affirmative action, while Thomas felt that his degrees from Yale were cheapened as a result. See Sotomayor, *My Beloved World;* and Thomas, *My Grandfather's Son.*

434 **Sidestepping the decisive:** Biskupic, *Breaking In,* chap. 11. In the wake of *Grutter,* opponents of affirmative action in Michigan had successfully passed a ballot measure amending the state's constitution to ban race-conscious considerations in any state institution. *Schuette v. Coalition to Defend Affirmative Action,* a test of the ban's constitutionality, would come before the Court in October 2013.

434 **"available, workable race-neutral":** Italics mine. *Fisher,* 570 U.S. at 10 (Kennedy majority).

434 **"Janus-faced logic":** Quoted in Tribe and Matz, *Uncertain Justice.*

435 **She also took a swipe:** *Fisher,* 570 U.S. at (RBG dissenting).

435 **"I have said before":** Ibid.

435 **The conservative justices put** *Fisher:* Adam Liptak, "With Subtle Signals, Justices Request the Cases They Want to Hear," *New York Times,* July 7, 2015, A14.

436 **They also turned a blind eye:** In *United States v. Cruickshank,* 92 U.S. 542 (1875), the Supreme Court prevented the prosecution of whites who murdered freed people in Louisiana in order to prevent them from holding a public meeting, thereby limiting freedmen's right to bear arms and freely assemble. In *Hall v. DeCuir,* 95 U.S. 485 (1877), the Court struck down a Louisiana law that required racial integration in public transportation. In 1883, the Supreme Court refused to apply the Fourteenth Amendment to protect blacks and whites who married each other, and not long after that the Court declared that federal prosecutors could not charge twenty whites who had broken into a jail, beaten three black prisoners, and murdered a fourth. See *Pace v. Alabama,* 106 U.S. 583 (1883), and *United States v. Harris,* 106 U.S. 629 (1883). In the same year, the Court struck down the Civil Rights Act of 1875, declaring that the federal government did not have the power to regulate private actors who chose to discriminate. See *Civil Rights Cases,* 109 U.S. 3 (1883); *Pope v. William,* 193 U.S. 621 (1904).

436   **By World War II:** Keyssar, *Right to Vote,* chaps. 4–5.

436   **Their methods included intimidation:** For more extensive accounts, see Foner and Mahoney, *America's Reconstruction;* Litwack, *Trouble in Mind;* and Keyssar, *Right to Vote.*

436   **In 1965, only 335:** On Selma and voting rights, see Gary May, *Bending Toward Justice,* 53–170.

437   **Once national television:** Keyssar, *Right to Vote,* chap. 4.

437   **To expand the vote:** Thurber, *Republicans and Race,* 226.

437   **"It is wrong":** Lyndon Baines Johnson, "Address to a Joint Session of Congress on Voting Legislation," March 15, 1965, Washington, D.C.

437   **Facing a powerful:** Gary May, *Bending Toward Justice.* Though most southern Democrats voted negatively, forty southern congressmen voted for the VRA. Keyssar, *Right to Vote,* 211.

437   **"active participants":** Quotation in Pamela S. Karlan, "Loss and Redemption: Voting Rights at the Turn of a Century," *Vanderbilt University Law Review* 50 (1997), 316n84.

437   **The right to vote:** The question of what precisely constitutes a fair chance for minorities to have their policy interests represented and what procedures might achieve that result has become a matter of much debate. For ideas on this complex question, see esp. Guinier, *Tyranny of the Majority.*

437   **The Voting Rights Act of 1965:** Voting Rights Act of 1965, Public Law 89–110, Jan. 4, 1965, 79 Stat. 437. The original act was amended in 1975 to include other minorities, including Hispanic, Asian, and Native American citizens, who congressional hearings had established suffered discrimination. See Voting Rights Act Amendments of 1975, Public Law 94–73, Aug. 6, 1975, 89 Stat. 400.

438   **Eager to build the GOP:** Berman, *Give Us the Ballot,* 68–95, 123–44.

438   **Republican-nominated justices:** *City of Mobile v. Bolden,* 446 U.S. 55 (1980), 66 (Stewart majority).

438   **Von Spakovsky, in turn:** Berman, *Give Us the Ballot,* 213–35 and esp. chaps. 5–8. See also Pamela S. Karlan, "Lessons Learned: Voting Rights and the Bush Administration," *Duke Journal of Constitutional Law and Public Policy* 4 (2009): 17–20. According to an exhaustive study done by Loyola University Law School, voter fraud—the impersonation of someone in order to vote more than once or at all—was found in only thirty-one of one billion vote samples. Election fraud—ballot stuffing, vote buying, and machine rigging—is less rare. See Jim Rutenberg, "Overcome," *New York Times Magazine,* Aug. 2, 2015, 36. George Derek Musgrove refers to voter-restricting efforts as "harassment ideology," a movement that arose as a white backlash to the large number of African American officials being elected to office following the passage of the VRA. See *Rumor, Repression, and Racial Politics.* His research builds off the pioneering work of Mary R. Sawyer that examined the harassment of black elected officials, first in *The Dilemma of Black Politics* and then in *The Harassment of Black Elected Officials.*

439   **Most states with a significant:** Richard H. Pildes, "Political Avoidance, Constitutional Theory, and the VRA," *Yale Law Journal* Pocket Part 117 (2007): 148–54.

439   **GOP ascendency in what had:** On concerns as to how the "congruence and proportionality" requirement introduced in *City of Boerne v. Flores,* 521 U.S. 507 (1997), and its progeny might impact any changes in a new reauthorization bill, see Nathaniel Persily, "The Promise and Pitfalls of the New Voting Rights Act," *Yale Law Journal* 117 (2007): 192–95.

439   **Most important, any attempt:** Expansion of the coverage formula to include recent bad actors such as Florida and Ohio would also "heap a new and costly administrative scheme" onto jurisdictions unaccustomed to needing federal permission for voting law changes. See Persily, "Promise and Pitfalls of the New Voting Rights Act," 210.

439   **Since 1982, the Court:** *Flores,* 521 U.S. at 519 (Kennedy majority).

439   **Adherence to federalism:** Persily, "Promise and Pitfalls of the New Voting Rights Act," 180.

439   **The House and Senate Judiciary:** U.S. House, Subcommittee on the Constitution of the Committee on the Judiciary, *To Examine the Impact and Effectiveness of the Voting Rights Act,* Hearing, Oct. 18, 2005 (Serial No. 109–70) (Washington, D.C.: Government Printing Office, 2006).

439   **What emerged was evidence:** Ibid. Supporters of renewal were also aware that the Court's conservatives had been complaining about the cost to federalism imposed by Section 5. See *Miller v. Johnson,* 515 U.S. 900 (1995), 926.

440   **Nevertheless, "second generation":** Fannie Lou Hamer, Rosa Parks, and Coretta Scott King Voting Rights Act Reauthorization and Amendments Act of 2006, Public Law 109-246, Section 2(b)(2)-(3), 120 Stat. 580, July 27, 2006.

440   **In what appeared:** Raymond Hernandez, "After Challenges, House Approves Renewal of Voting Rights Act," *New York Times,* July 14, 2006, A13.

440   **The Senate followed:** Carl Hulse, "By a Vote of 98–0, Senate Approves 25-Year Extension of Voting Rights Act," *New York Times,* July 21, 2006, A16; caption to photograph by Erik Jacobs, "Bush Signs Extension of Voting Rights Act," *New York Times,* July 28, 2006, A22. GOP congressmen from Georgia and Texas had been particularly active in stalling the House bill initially.

440   **"political avoidance":** I am indebted to Persily for many of these points.

440   **Constitutional scholars pointed:** Persily, "Promise and Pitfalls of the New Voting Rights Act," 191–92.

440   **New fiats from the Court:** See, for example, *Shaw v. Reno,* 509 U.S. 630 (1993); *Shaw v. Hunt,* 517 U.S. 899 (1996); *Miller v. Johnson,* 515 U.S. 900 (1995); *Bush v. Vera,* 517 U.S. 952 (1996); *United States v. Hayes,* 555 U.S. 415 (2009), 129 S. Ct. 1079; *Reno v. Bossier Parish School Board,* 528 U.S. 320 (2000). For contrasting views of *Shaw* and its progeny, see Kousser, *Colorblind Injustice,* and Thernstrom, *Voting Rights—and Wrongs.* For a superb analytical justification for race-based redistricting as a remedy, see Pamela S. Karlan and Daryl J. Levinson, "The Importance of Political Deliberation and Race-Conscious Redistricting: Why Voting Is Different," *University of California Law Review* 84 (1996): 1201–32.

440   **"If it weren't for the Voting":** Quoted in Adam Liptak, "Review of Voting Rights Presents Test of History v. Progress," *New York Times,* April 28, 2009, A16.

441   **His equally wary Latino:** Nina Perales, "*Shelby County v. Holder:* Latino Voters Need Section 5 Today More than Ever," *SCOTUSblog,* Feb. 12, 2013.

441   **politically "open market":** Blum, *Unintended Consequence of Section 5 of the Voting Rights Act,* 7.

441   **"perhaps the most important":** RBG, "Remarks for Second Circuit Judicial Conference," Bolton Landing, N.Y., June 12, 2009, www.supremecourt.gov.

441   **His aggressive questioning:** Berman, *Give Us the Ballot,* 149–52. For an example, see Transcript of Oral Argument at 27–29, 31–32, *Northwest Austin Municipal Utility District No. 1 v. Holder,* 557 U.S. 193 (2009).

441   **"insufficient and that conditions":** *Northwest Austin v. Holder,* 557 U.S. 193 (2009), 8 (Roberts majority).

441   **"The Act imposes":** Ibid., italics mine. The only dissent was that of Thomas, who would have declared Section 5 unconstitutional. Roberts, supporting his concerns about the impact of Section 5 on federalism, referred to a "tradition" of equal sovereignty and to *South Carolina v. Katzenbach* (1996), neither of which supports his dicta. See Zachary S. Price, "NAMUDNO's Non-existent Principle of State Equality," *New York University Law Review* 88 (2013): 24–40.

442   **"a departure from the fundamental":** *Northwest Austin,* 557 U.S. 193 (2009), 8 (Roberts majority).

442 **"the evil that Section 5"**: Ibid.

442 **"a canny strategist"**: Adam Liptak, "Roberts Court Shifts Right, Tipped by Kennedy," *New York Times,* July 1, 2009, A1.

442 **"anticipatory overruling"**: Richard L. Hasen, "Anticipatory Overrulings, Invitations, Time Bombs, and Inadvertence: How Supreme Court Justices Move the Law," *Emory University Law Journal* 61 (2012): 782–84.

442 **"Remember that line"**: Quoted in "The Battle, Not the War, on Voting Rights," *Room for Debate* (blog), *New York Times,* June 22, 2009.

442 **When Congress failed:** Blum had discovered the Calera conflict while surfing the Justice Department's website and cold-called a county official offering to finance a suit if the Court ruled narrowly in *Northwest Austin.* See Biskupic, "Special Report: Behind U.S. Race Cases, a Little-Known Recruiter."

442 **The Civil Rights Division had rejected:** Transcript of Oral Argument at 54, *Shelby County v. Holder,* 570 U.S. 2 (2013).

442 **Turned down in district court:** *Shelby County v. Holder,* 811 F. Supp. 2d 424 (U.S. Dist. 2011). The much-publicized case elicited the predictable lineup of amici briefs. Allied on the color-blind side were conservative advocacy groups such as the Cato Institute and the Pacific Legal Foundation along with the attorneys general of Texas, Arizona, and Alaska. Color-conscious policy adherents supporting Section 5 included minority legal defense groups, constitutional scholars and academics, the congressional leaders Senator Harry Reid and Representative John Lewis, who had been severely beaten on "Bloody Sunday" in Selma, and the attorneys general of four states covered by Section 5. See Briefs for *Shelby County v. Holder,* 679 F.3d 848 (D.C. Cir. 2012) (No. 12-96),

442 **Losing again in a split decision:** *Shelby County,* 679 F.3d 848.

442 **The question on which:** Grant of Certiorari at 12, *Shelby County,* 570 U.S. 2.

443 **At the Capitol, a ceremonial:** Nia-Malika Henderson, "Rosa Parks Honored with Capitol Statue," *Washington Post,* Feb. 27, 2013; Laura W. Murphy, "The State of Equality and Justice in America: The Pendulum Swings Between Joy and Despair," *Washington Post,* March 4, 2013.

443 **"Just think about this state"**: Transcript of Oral Argument at 5, *Shelby County,* 570 U.S. 2.

444 **the "equal footing" doctrine:** Ibid. at 21–26. RBG's reference was to *South Carolina v. Katzenbach,* 383 U.S. 301 (1966).

444 **"a bigger problem in Virginia"**: Transcript of Oral Argument at 40, *Shelby County,* 570 U.S. 2.

444 **"Is it the government's contention"**: Ibid. at 29–31, 41.

444 **"perpetuation of a racial"**: Ibid. at 47.

444 **Sotomayor and Kagan zeroed in:** Ibid. at 66.

444 **The sharp ideological:** Robert Barnes, "Justices Weigh Voting Rights," *Washington Post,* Feb. 28, 2013, A1.

445 **"Why the [White] South"**: William F. Buckley Jr., "Why the South Must Prevail," *National Review,* Aug. 24, 1957, 149.

445 **The civil rights movement advanced:** Nancy MacLean, "Neo-Confederacy Versus the New Deal: The Regional Utopia of the Modern American Right," in Lassiter and Crespino, *Myth of Southern Exceptionalism,* 311.

445 **Reagan, who had opposed:** Bob Herbert, "Righting Reagan's Wrongs," *New York Times,* Nov. 13, 2007, A29.

445 **"state sovereignty"**: *Northwest Austin* had stimulated legal scholarship on the majority's "reinvention" of state sovereignty or, as Franita Tolson would demonstrate, its confusion of state autonomy and congressional sovereignty. See Franita Tolson, "Reinventing Sovereignty? Federalism as Constraint on the Voting Rights Act," *Vanderbilt Law Review* 65 (2012): 1195–259. The constitutional law professor Joseph Fishkin called

"state sovereignty" a concept that "seems poised to rise, zombie-like, in clothes just new enough to avoid any obvious shades of the 'senatorial toga of [John C.] Calhoun.'" See "The Dignity of the South," *Yale Law Journal Online* 175 (2013), Forum, June 8, 2013.

The concept would receive more attention from legal scholars following its reemergence in *Shelby v. Holder*. Judge Richard A. Posner bluntly stated, "This is a principle of constitutional law of which I have never heard—for the excellent reason that . . . there is no such principle." See Richard A. Posner, "The Voting Rights Act Ruling Is About the Conservative Imagination," *Slate: Supreme Court 2013: The Year in Review,* June 26, 2013. After a lengthy investigation of the historical record, Abigail Molitor concluded that while the concept had not emerged out of the blue, it was not the fundamental principle that the majority claimed it to be in *Shelby*. See Abigail B. Molitor, "Understanding Equal Sovereignty," *University of Chicago Law Review* 81 (2014): 1839–82, see esp. 1877.

For the latest in a long line of books critiquing the turn taken in the Court's federalism jurisprudence under Rehnquist, see Barber, *Fallacies of States' Rights*.

446   **It was the most significant:** Samuel Issacharoff, "Beyond the Discrimination Model on Voting," *Harvard Law Review* 127 (2013): 102.

446   **"the Act imposes current burdens":** *Shelby County v. Holder,* 570 U.S. 2 (2013), 2, 9, 15–16 (Roberts majority).

446   **"Our decision in no way":** Ibid. at 28.

446   **Consistent with the post–Civil War amendments:** Ibid., 1 (RBG dissenting).

446   **"the grand aim of the act":** Ibid. at 35.

447   **Evident as well:** Ibid. at 7, 9–20.

447   **"whether Congress has rationally":** Ibid. at 10, 23, 30.

447   **"unprecedented extension of the equal":** Ibid. at 31, 36. For a devastatingly authoritative indictment of Roberts's decision, see Ackerman, *Civil Rights Revolution,* chap. 14.

448   **"That commitment has been disserved":** MLK and RBG quotations in Mark Walsh, "A 'View' from the Court," *SCOTUSblog,* June 25, 2013.

448   **This was the second time:** John Paul Stevens, "The Court and the Right to Vote: A Dissent," *New York Review of Books,* Aug. 15, 2013. For an equally critical and far more detailed analysis, see Reva B. Siegel, "Supreme Court 2012 Term, Foreword," esp. 9–74.

448   **Texas promptly announced:** On states other than Alabama, especially Texas with its growing Latino population, see Jim Rutenberg, "Block the Vote," *New York Times Magazine,* Dec. 20, 2015, 32–37, 57.

448   **In North Carolina, where Republicans:** Adam Liptak, "Justices Void Oversight of States, Issue at Heart of Voting Rights Act," *New York Times,* June 26, 2013, A1. See also Richard Fausset, "North Carolina Is a Battlefield for Voter Laws," *New York Times,* March 11, 2016, A1. For an authoritative account of how racial lines are being redrawn by the negative portrayal of the rapidly growing Latino population and the impact on politics, see Abrajano and Hajnal, *White Backlash*.

448   **"Disgusting," declared Rosanell Eaton:** Both quotations in Rutenberg, "Overcome," 30. Obama had carried the state in 2008.

448   **"The past is never dead":** Faulkner, *Requiem for a Nun,* act 1, scene 3. Legislatures in Georgia, Florida, South Carolina, Tennessee, West Virginia, Arkansas, North Carolina, and Virginia created new restrictions in the South. West Virginia was the only state that had a Democrat-controlled legislature and governor. Mississippi's changes were passed by a voter referendum. See "New Voting Restrictions in Place for 2016 Presidential Election," Brennan Center for Justice at NYU School of Law, Nov. 2, 2016.

449   **Spurred by specious claims:** Elizabeth Drew, "Big Dangers for the Next Election," *New York Review of Books,* May 21, 2015. By 2016, Democrats had total control of only seven states.

449   **By 2016, a total:** Those fourteen states are Alabama, Arizona, Indiana, Kansas, Mississippi, Nebraska, New Hampshire, Ohio, Rhode Island, South Carolina, Tennessee,

Texas, Virginia, and Wisconsin. Georgia, North Carolina, and North Dakota were removed following successful legal challenges. See "New Voting Restrictions in Place for 2016 Presidential Election."

TWENTY-ONE · The Right Thing to Do

450 **At a time when:** Robert Barnes, "Supreme Court Justice to Conduct Gay Nuptials," *Washington Post,* Aug. 31, 2013, A1.

450 **"apartheid of the closet":** William N. Eskridge Jr., "Privacy Jurisprudence and the Apartheid of the Closet, 1846–1961," *Florida State University Law Review* 24 (1997): 703–840.

450 **Years of slow, painful:** For a definitive new history of the struggle for same-sex marriage, see Nathaniel Frank, *Awakening: How Gays and Lesbians Brought Marriage Equality to America* (Cambridge: Harvard University Press, 2017).

450 **Leading the drumbeat:** By the 1970s, when open expressions of anti-Semitism and racism were no longer socially acceptable and anticommunism was subsiding, homosexuals and feminists became the new bête noire of the religious Right. The organizations within that coalition differ somewhat in the ways they challenge the LGBT movement but are united in the passion with which they fight. See Galligher and Bull, *Perfect Enemies.*

450 **For those convinced that:** Nussbaum, *From Disgust to Humanity,* esp. chap. 5.

451 **"perfectly capable of filling":** *Perry v. Schwarzenegger,* 704 F. Supp.2d 921 at 940 (N.D. Cal. 2010), 244 (Cott testimony).

451 **Political radicals found challenge:** See, for example, Johnston, *Lesbian Nation;* Martin Duberman writes of the emergence of a gay male "machismo" style in the wake of Stonewall, the national shift toward greater political conservatism in the 1970s, and Anita Bryant's antigay campaign in Florida, as well as other forms of backlash—none of which would have whetted the appetite for gay marriage. See Duberman, *Martin Duberman Reader.*

451 **Resistance would soften:** Shilts, *And the Band Played On.*

451 **Understandably, some in the gay community:** Klarman, *From the Closet to the Altar,* chap. 3.

452 **Parental responsibilities, in turn:** Mamo, *Queering Reproduction;* Rivers, *Radical Relations,* chap. 7. Same-sex couples were able to target sympathetic judges, making the institutional context in which they had to operate less vulnerable to opposition than has been the case with other items on the gay agenda. See Mucciaroni, *Same Sex, Different Politics.*

452 **These developments, characteristic:** For an excellent, brief account of the structural and cultural developments occurring from the mid-1960s onward that contributed to the change in the model and meaning of marriage, see Nancy F. Cott's groundbreaking, *Public Vows,* chap. 9, esp. 202–4. Pushback came from the family values movement, which was part of the social and religious Right.

452 **Yet in a social revolution:** Opposition was in part generational and in part political. For concerns that moving same-sex marriage to the top of the gay agenda represented mainstreaming the movement and diversion of focus from structural inequalities of greater importance to the lives of working-class LGBT people, see Cathy J. Cohen, "What Is This Movement Doing to My Politics?," *Social Text* 61 (Winter 1999): 111–18; Martin B. Duberman, "Class Is a Queer Issue," in *Martin Duberman Reader,* 354–61; and John D'Emilio, "The Campaign for Marriage Equality: A Dissenting View," in *In a New Century,* chap. 26.

452 **The justices had waited:** Such statutes still existed in only thirteen states and were rarely enforced. See Eskridge, *Dishonorable Passions,* chap. 9.

452 **"Liberty presumes an autonomy":** *Lawrence v. Texas,* 539 U.S. 558 (2003), 562 (Kennedy majority). See Richards, *Sodomy Cases.*

452 **Friends and foes alike:** In the dissent, Scalia wrote that state laws against same-sex marriage would not be sustained. See *Lawrence,* 539 U.S. at 590 (Scalia dissenting). For press on same-sex marriage after *Lawrence,* see Rick Santorum, "Gay Unions: A Matter of Rights or a Threat to Traditional Marriage?," *USA Today,* July 10, 2003, A13.

452 **But when a judge in Hawaii:** On May 5, 1993—and in a subsequent clarification on May 27—the Supreme Court of Hawaii remanded the case to trial court to determine whether the state could meet the standard of strict scrutiny in demonstrating that the denial of marriage licenses to same-sex couples compelled state interests and did not unnecessarily curb constitutional rights. In December 1996, Judge Kevin S. C. Chang ruled in favor of the plaintiffs, instructing the state to issue marriage licenses to qualified same-sex couples. *Baehr v. Lewin,* 74 Haw. 530, 852 P.2d 44 (1993), reconsideration and clarification granted in part, 74 Haw. 645, 852 P.2d 74 (1993); *Baehr v. Miike,* Circuit Court for the First Circuit, Hawaii No. 91-1394.

453 **"A dream issue":** Klarman, *From the Closet to the Altar,* 59.

453 **DOMA further stipulated:** Defense of Marriage Act, H.R. 3396, 104th Cong., 1st sess. (1996), sec. 7.

453 **"bedrock of civilization":** Klarman, *From the Closet to the Altar,* chap. 4. Senator Robert Byrd of West Virginia speaking for DOMA to the Senate floor, H.R. 3396, *Congressional Record,* 104th Cong., 2nd sess., 1996, 142, S10109. Representative Gerry Studds objected to such inflammatory and offensive language being used. Senator Phil Gramm from Texas stated, "I stand with the traditional family. I do not believe 5,000 years of recorded history have been in error. I believe the traditional family— the union of a man and a woman, upon which our entire civilization is based—is unique, and I believe it is the foundation of our prosperity, our freedom, and our happiness. I want to defend this and I am confident that we will do so on this very day" (S10105).

453 **Having vetoed the Partial-Birth:** Note the socially conservative language also in the Personal Responsibility and Work Opportunity Act of 1996, Pub. L. No. 104-193.

453 **"politically clobbered":** Becker, *Forcing the Spring,* 10. On actions of the Clinton administration with respect to the LGBT community, see Craig A. Zimmerman, "A 'Friend' in the White House? Reflections on the Clinton Presidency," in D'Emilio, Turner, and Vaid, *Creating Change,* chap. 5; also, Juliet Eilperin, "Raw Politics Explains Why DOMA Got Wide Support in 1996," *Washington Post,* March 28, 2013.

453 **On November 18:** *Goodridge v. Department of Public Health,* 798 N.E.2d 941 (Mass. 2003).

453 **Their aim was to put:** Only six states had defined marriage as the union of a man and a woman prior to 2004, although thirty-one states had statutes reflecting that definition. In the wake of *Lawrence* and *Goodridge,* Mississippi, Missouri, and Oregon passed ballot measures adhering to the traditional definition, while Arkansas, Georgia, Kentucky, Louisiana, Michigan, North Dakota, Ohio, Oklahoma, and Utah approved measures prohibiting recognition of same-sex civil unions. See Sue Connell, "The Money Behind the 2004 Marriage Amendments," Institute on Money in State Politics, Jan. 27, 2006, followthemoney.org. President George W. Bush backed a federal marriage amendment to the Constitution, which Democrats blocked.

453 **"Our journey is not complete":** Barack Obama, Inaugural Address, Jan. 21, 2013.

454 **As a state senator:** Jo Becker, " 'Mr. President, How Can We Help You Evolve More Quickly?,' " *New York Times Sunday Magazine,* April 20, 2014, MM20.

454 **"equal citizenship stature":** Neil S. Siegel, "Equal Citizenship Stature: Justice Ginsburg's Constitutional Vision," *New England Law Review* 43 (2009): 799–855. Suggesting the similarities in the basic constitutional outlooks of the justice and the president,

Siegel uses to great effect Senator Obama's 2008 speech on race relations, "Address at the National Constitution Center: A More Perfect Union," National Constitution Center, March 18, 2008.

454 **Fortuitously, the president's hand:** Amid the homophobic backlash surrounding DOMA, activists in what had become the LGBT movement used the media to full advantage. Forty-two million viewers watched as Ellen DeGeneres "came out" in a 1997 episode of the ABC sitcom *Ellen* that landed the lesbian comedian on the cover of *Time* magazine. Revealing her sexual orientation also earned her an attack from the Reverend Jerry Falwell, who labeled her Ellen "Degenerate." The sitcom *Will & Grace* brought gay characters and a gay milieu into homes across the country, becoming the most watched television program for young adults in the eighteen to forty-nine age bracket. See Bruce Handy, "He Called Me Ellen Degenerate?," *Time,* April 14, 1997, 86, and Jack Myers, "Will & Grace: The TV Series That Changed America," *HuffPost Gay Voices,* Aug. 30, 2014.

454 **By 2012, Log Cabin:** Nick Wing, "Laura Bush: Gay Marriage Should Be Legal, Abortion Should Remain Legal," *Huffington Post,* May 5, 2010; Dan Eggen, "Cheney Comes Out for Gay Marriage, State-by-State," *44: The Obama Presidency* (blog), *Washington Post,* June 1, 2009.

454 **Thirty states now had:** "Same-Sex Marriage Laws," National Council on State Legislatures, June 6, 2015, ncsl.org; Ross Toro, "States Where Gay Marriage Is Legal (Infographic)," *Live Science,* www.livescience.com, April 26, 2013.

454 **National polls consistently:** Klarman, *From the Closet to the Altar,* 218.

454 **Other nations led the way:** These nations included Canada, the Scandinavian countries, Belgium, the Netherlands, Portugal, Spain, and South Africa. Pierceson, *Same-Sex Marriage in the United States,* chap. 3.

454 **Five months before:** Becker, *Forcing the Spring,* chap. 30.

454 **Their bold move alarmed:** On prior strategy, see Yoshino, *Speak Now,* 43–48.

455 **"neither the time":** Ibid., 24. Though an unlikely champion of progressive causes, Olson was no stranger to gay rights. When serving in the Reagan Justice Department, he had insisted that a prosecutor could not be denied a promotion because of his sexual preference. And as solicitor general under George W. Bush, he had objected to the Federal Marriage Amendment, telling Bush that it was bad policy and had no place in the Constitution. Religious belief could not justify government restrictions on civil marriage either legally or morally. See Becker, *Forcing the Spring,* 13; Yoshino, *Speak Now,* 22–24.

455 **Because neither Governor:** See Becker, *Forcing the Spring,* and Yoshino, *Speak Now.*

455 **But Governor Schwarzenegger objected:** Ibid., 16–21. On California's prior history of conflict over marriage equality, see Yoshino, *Speak Now.*

455 **Then, in May 2008:** Jean-Paul Renaud, "Rush Expected for Marriage Licenses," *Los Angeles Times,* June 20, 2008, B5.

455 *Perry v. Schwarzenegger: Perry v. Schwarzenegger* was renamed *Perry v. Brown* when Jerry Brown became governor in 2011. When both governors refused to defend it, Dennis Hollingsworth—the official sponsor of Prop 8—stepped in, causing the case to be renamed *Hollingsworth v. Perry.*

455 **Quashing the injunction:** *Perry v. Schwarzenegger,* 704 F. Supp.2d 921 at 940 (N.D. Cal. 2010) (Motion for Preliminary Injunction).

456 **In addition, he asked both sides:** Ibid. (Summary Judgment Hearing).

456 **"Our decisions have declined":** *Christian Legal Society Chapter v. Martinez,* 561 U.S. 661 (2010), 23 (RBG majority).

456 **As Adam Liptak had pointed out:** Adam Liptak, "Looking for Time Bombs and Tea Leaves on Gay Marriage," *New York Times,* July 19, 2010, A11.

456 **"conjecture, speculation, or fears":** *Perry v. Schwarzenegger,* 704 F. Supp.2d at 940, 24–26 (Walker opinion).

457 **After two more years:** *Perry v. Brown,* 671 F.3d 1052 (9th Cir. 2012).

457 **It also skirted the question:** Kennedy had written the opinion not only in *Lawrence v. Texas* but also in *Romer v. Evans,* striking down a Colorado amendment barring local gay rights ordinances. Even during his earlier tenure on the Ninth Circuit, Kennedy, who was from Northern California, had authored an opinion in 1980 that was quite gay-friendly. See *Romer v. Evans,* 517 U.S. 620 (1996), 623–24; *Beller v. Middendor,* 632 F.2d 788 (9th Cir. 1980).

457 **One of the two:** The district court issued its decision on *Perry* in August 2010, with the circuit court ruling following in February 2012. Windsor won a summary judgment in June 2012, a decision that was upheld by the Second Circuit Court of Appeals four months later. *Perry v. Schwarzenegger,* 704 F. Supp.2d at 940; *Perry v. Brown,* 671 F.3d 1052; *Windsor v. United States,* 833 F. Supp.2d 394 (SDNY 2012); *Windsor v. United States,* F.3d 169 (2d Cir. 2012).

457 **In February 2009:** Unless otherwise indicated, this, and the following paragraphs, draw from Ariel Levy, "The Perfect Wife," *New Yorker,* Sept. 30, 2013, 54.

457 **"powerhouse corporate litigator":** See Kaplan's web page at Kaplan & Company, LLP, www.kaplanandcompany.com.

458 **Kaplan would also ask:** Brief for the Respondent at 15, *United States v. Windsor,* 570 U.S. ___ (2013).

458 **With DOMA challenges:** The criteria for a classification deserving intermediate scrutiny include illegitimacy, gender, race, national ancestry, and ethnic origin. The classification must be "substantially related to a legitimate state interest" to survive constitutional attack. See *Mills v. Habluetzel,* 456 U.S. 91 (1982). My account closely follows Becker, *Forcing the Spring,* 255–59.

459 **"the right thing to do":** Becker, *Forcing the Spring,* 248–49, with Holder's quotation on 249.

459 **Kaplan got a call:** Ibid., 259.

459 **If Kaplan and her client:** *Windsor v. United States,* 833 F. Supp.2d 394 (S.D.N.Y. 2012). The district court judge Barbara S. Jones based her ruling on rational scrutiny.

459 **Applying intermediate scrutiny:** Ibid.

459 **Only eight states:** Massachusetts, Maine, New Hampshire, Vermont, Connecticut, New York, Iowa, and Washington.

460 **Thomas, Alito, and either Roberts:** Adam Liptak, "Who Wanted to Take the Case on Gay Marriage? Ask Scalia," *New York Times,* March 3, 2015, A1.

460 **Both cases could conceivably:** Adam Liptak, "Justices to Hear Two Challenges on Gay Marriage," *New York Times,* Dec. 8, 2012, A1.

460 **No one doubted:** Adam Liptak, "Questions and Answers About a Potentially Decisive Moment for Gay Americans," *New York Times,* March 26, 2013, A14.

460 **Willing to brave the cold:** Jeremy W. Peters, "Cold, Wet Wait for Tickets to Supreme Court's Same-Sex Marriage Cases," *New York Times,* March 25, 2013, A14.

460 **"some 40,000 children":** Transcript of Oral Argument at 21, *Hollingsworth v. Perry,* 570 U.S. ___ (2013).

461 **"It is impossible":** Ibid. at 14–18. Quotations appear on 14 and 18.

461 **"You can force the child":** Ibid. at 44–45.

462 **But neither the solicitor:** Ibid. at 49–63. Quotation appears on 59.

462 **"You are at a real risk":** Transcript of Oral Argument at 59–70, *United States v. Windsor,* 570 U.S. ___ (2013). Quotations appear on 59 and 70.

462 **"It's not as though":** Ibid. at 70.

462 **"Congress decided to reflect":** Ibid. at 74.

462 **"Look, we are not going":** Ibid. at 74–80. Quotation appears on 74–75.

463 **"[P]olitical figures are falling":** Ibid. at 106–8.

463 **"I'm Edie Windsor":** Jeremy W. Peters, "Plaintiff, 83, Is Calm Center in a Legal and Political Storm," *New York Times,* March 28, 2013, A1. The quotations are from Wind-

sor except for "intangible but unmistakable changed," which is Peters's paraphrase of her words.

464 **"skim milk marriage"**: Adam Liptak and Peter Baker, "Justices Cast Doubt on U.S. Law Defining Marriage," *New York Times,* March 28, 2013, A1.

464 **The Los Angeles reporter:** Three more states—Rhode Island, Delaware, and Minnesota—were about to legalize same-sex marriage. Jennifer Medina, "Anticipation Turns to Acceptance as California Awaits Marriage Ruling," *New York Times,* June 24, 2013, A15.

464 **"The federal statute is invalid":** *Windsor,* 570 U.S. at 23–26 (Kennedy majority).

464 **"By formally declaring":** While rationales and predictions differed, Scalia, Roberts, Alito, and Thomas issued three separate dissents, with Thomas joining Alito's dissent on Parts II and III. Scalia's quotation is ibid. at 24 (Scalia dissenting).

464 **With Judge Walker's decision:** Kate Mather, "Kamala Harris Calls for Same-Sex Marriage to Resume 'Immediately,'" *Los Angeles Times,* June 26, 2013.

465 **Yet by defining as unconstitutional:** Yoshino, *Speak Now,* 262.

465 **Over the next year:** Adam Liptak, "Supreme Court Delivers Tacit Win to Gay Marriage," *New York Times,* Oct. 7, 2014, A1.

465 **As Ginsburg explained:** Robert Barnes, "Justices Agree to Hear Case on Gay Marriage," *Washington Post,* Jan. 17, 2015, A1.

465 **Leaving the decisions:** Linda Greenhouse, "Something Happening Here," *New York Times,* Oct. 15, 2014.

465 **Adam Liptak suggested:** Adam Liptak, "In Same-Sex Marriage Calculation, Justices May See Golden Ratio," *New York Times,* Nov. 24, 2014, A16. Liptak notes that neither Scalia nor Thomas appears to have been part of the decision.

466 **When the case reached:** *Obergefell v. Wymyslo,* No. 1:13-cv-501 (S.D. Ohio 2013); *Tanco v. Haslam,* No. 3:13-cv-01159 (M.D. Tenn. 2014); *DeBoer v. Snyder,* No. 12-CV-10285 (E.D. Mich. 2014); *Bourke v. Beshear,* No. 3:13-CV-750-H (W.D. Ky. 2014).

466 **Ruling against the plaintiffs:** *DeBoer v. Snyder,* 772 F.3d 388 (6th Cir. 2014).

466 **Does the Fourteenth Amendment:** David Savage, "High Court to Rule on Gay Unions," *Los Angeles Times,* Jan. 17, 2015, A1. In *DeBoer v. Snyder,* Michigan officials had requested an initial en banc hearing—a request for all Sixth Circuit judges to hear the appeal rather than just the three-judge panel—due to the importance of the case and increasing the likelihood of an expeditious consideration. DeBoer's attorneys countered that a panel hearing, rather than an en banc hearing, would most likely "expedite the court's consideration of the case." In addition, similar appeals in other circuits had been heard by three-judge panels, including *Hollingsworth v. Perry.* The request was denied. Neither party in *Hollingsworth* requested an initial en banc review at the district level. After the Sixth Circuit upheld the ban, all four plaintiffs opted to appeal directly to the Supreme Court, bypassing the option for an en banc hearing. See Plaintiffs' Appellees' Response to State Defendants-Appellants' Petition for Initial Hearing En Banc at 2–4, *DeBoer v. Snyder.*

466 **Indicative of the rapidly:** Not surprisingly, 148 amici briefs poured into the Court— double the number addressing both procedural issues and the merits of the cases. Brief of 167 Members of the U.S. House of Representatives and 44 U.S. Senators as Amici Curiae in Support of Petitioners and Brief of 57 Members of U.S. Congress as Amici Curiae in Support of Respondents, *Obergefell v. Hodges,* 576 U.S. ___ (2015).

466 **Also, his three prior decisions:** Adam Liptak, "Surprising Friend of Gay Rights Movement in the Highest of Places," *New York Times,* Sept. 2, 2013, A10.

467 **When the Court struck:** Transcript of Oral Argument on Question 1, *Obergefell v. Hodges,* 576 U.S. ___. RBG's comments regarding Louisiana appear on 70–72.

467 **Kagan also pointed:** Ibid. at 23–26.

467 **"[I]f you prevail here":** Ibid. at 22.

467 **Many gay couples:** Ibid. at 28–41, esp. 28–29.

468   **"If you prevent people"**: Ibid. at 82. Arguments the following day proved anticlimactic inasmuch as a nationwide ruling on marriage equality would render moot the question of states' recognition of same-sex marriages performed elsewhere in the United States. See Transcript of Oral Argument on Question 2, ibid.

468   **But that did not stop**: See Mello, *Courts, the Ballot Box, and Gay Rights*, 1–2. Mello, a political scientist, argues that the Supreme Court had yet to determine a consistent answer as to whether citizens can use ballot measures or referendums to vote directly on issues related to fundamental rights. *Obergefell* held the fate of twenty-eight separate ballot measures defining marriage as between one man and one woman. In addition to *Obergefell*, the Court issued a 6–2 plurality decision defending Michigan's right to determine affirmative-action policy through the ballot measure process (RBG concurred with Sotomayor's dissent; Kagan did not participate in the case). See *Schuette v. Coalition to Defend Affirmative Action*, 572 U.S. ___ (2014) (Kennedy majority). Shortly after the *Obergefell* decision, RBG delivered the 5–4 majority opinion in *Arizona State Legislature v. Arizona Independent Redistricting Commission*, 576 U.S. ___ (2015), upholding Arizona voters' right to alter their redistricting policy through popular referendum.

468   **"People looked around"**: Adam Liptak, "Justices' Words Are Combed for Clues as Major Decisions Loom at Court," *New York Times*, June 16, 2015, A16.

468   **"The right to marry"**: *Obergefell*, 576 U.S. at 3 (Kennedy majority).

469   **"new insights and societal"**: Ibid. at 4; RBG, Breyer, Sotomayor, and Kagan joined in the ruling.

469   **Kennedy's words elicited**: Mark Sherman, "Court Declares Nationwide Right to Same-Sex Marriage," *Washington Post*, June 26, 2015.

469   **Roberts was so upset**: *Obergefell*, 576 U.S. ___ (Roberts dissenting).

469   **"as pretentious as its content"**: Ibid. at 1, 6–8 (Scalia dissenting).

469   **Alito and Thomas**: Ibid. (Alito and Thomas dissenting). Legal scholars welcoming the ruling acknowledge that in landmark cases like *Brown, Griswold*, and *Obergefell* doctrine provides a set of arguments and justifications for positions and decisions that shape the surrounding legal, political, and cultural context in which the Court intervenes. Yet the justices who write them do not always produce models of legal reasoning as was the case in *Brown* and *Griswold*. See, for example, Michael Klarman, "Marriage Equality and Racial Equality," *Harvard Law Review* 127 (Nov. 2013): 127–60, and Douglas NeJaime's response, "Doctrine in Context," *Harvard Law Review Forum* 127 (Nov. 2013): 10–18.

469   **"affirms what millions"**: Robert Barnes, "Supreme Court Rules in Favor of Gay Marriage," *Washington Post*, June 27, 2015, A1.

469   **"America has taken one"**: Jim Obergefell, "My Husband," whitehouse.com, June 26, 2015.

469   **Meanwhile, jubilant crowds**: Barnes, "Supreme Court Rules in Favor of Gay Marriage"; "Crowds Celebrate Same-Sex Marriage Ruling at Historic Stonewall Inn," newyork.cbslocal.com, June 26, 2015; Janet O and Elissa Harrington, "Crowd Gathers in San Francisco to Celebrate Historic Same-Sex Marriage Ruling," abc7news.com, June 26, 2015; "A Rainbow Revolution," lgbtweekly.com, June 27, 2015.

469   **"conscience clause"**: Erik Eckholm, "Conservative Lawmakers and Religious Groups Seek Exemptions After Ruling," *New York Times*, June 27, 2015, A14; Sarah Pulliam Bailey and Michelle Borenstein, "Faith-Based Groups Fear Losing Their Tax-Exempt Status and Federal Funding," *Washington Post*, June 27, 2015, A10; Campbell Robertson and Richard Pérez-Peña, "Bills on 'Religious Freedom' Upset Capitols in Two States," *New York Times*, April 1, 2015, A1. According to the National Conference of State Legislatures, twenty-one separate states already have some form of religious freedom acts. An additional fifteen states debated religious freedom bills during 2015, including Mississippi, Georgia, and North Carolina. See www.ncsl.org. Public and corporate backlash forced the governors to either veto or consider modifying the bills. Efforts failed in

Montana, South Dakota, Utah, West Virginia, and Wyoming. In North Carolina, the debate has spilled over onto the issue of transgendered individuals being allowed to use the bathroom for whichever gender they identify with rather than the one designated for their birth sex.

469 **"The Fortune 500":** Jonathan Martin, "Parties Trade Places in Culture Wars in Skirmish over Religious Rights," *New York Times,* April 3, 2015; Jacob Bogage, "Marking Cultural Shift, Corporations Express Support for Landmark Decision," *New York Times,* June 26, 2015, A11.

470 **"taking discriminatory action":** H.R. 2802, 14th Cong. (2015).

470 **Infused with the rationale:** On this concept, see Kenji Yoshino, "A New Birth of Freedom? *Obergefell v. Hodges,*" *Harvard Law Review* 129 (Nov. 2015): 147–79, and Laurence H. Tribe, "Equal Dignity: Speaking Its Name," *Harvard Law Review Forum Online* 129 (Nov. 2015). For concerns that equal dignity has elicited among legal scholars who applaud the outcome of *Obergefell,* see, among others, Jack Balkin, "Obergefell and Equality," *Balkinization,* balkin.blogspot.com, June 28, 2015, and Jeffrey Rosen, "The Dangers of a Constitutional 'Right to Dignity,'" *Atlantic Online,* April 29, 2015. Somewhat different objections were raised by Yuvraj Joshi in "The Respectable Dignity of *Obergefell v. Hodges,*" *University of California Law Review Circuit* 6 (Nov. 2015): 117–25.

470 **She toyed briefly:** "Justice Ginsburg Discusses Historic Rulings and Groundbreaking Advocacy," *Duke Law Magazine* (2015): 6.

470 **"a judge at the height":** Mark Tushnet, "The Dissent in *National Federation of Independent Business v. Sebelius,*" *Harvard Law Review* 127 (Nov. 2013), 485.

471 **"harks back to the era":** *National Federation of Independent Business v. Sebelius,* 132 S. Ct. 2566 (2012), 2609, 2621 (RBG concurring in part, dissenting in part).

471 **She could not afford:** *M.L.B. v. S.L.J.,* 519 U.S. 102 (1996).

471 **"cut-and-pasted quotations":** Martha Minow, "*M.L.B. v. S.L.J.,* 519 U.S. 102 (1996)," *Harvard Law Review* 127 (Nov. 2013): 464.

472 **"Each of these shifts":** Ibid. Thomas dissented, claiming that precedents either did not support the conclusion or should be rejected and that the ruling would open the gates to a flood of demands for free assistance by civil appellants in other kinds of cases. Thomas was joined by Scalia, with Chief Justice Rehnquist also joining in all but Part II. Kennedy concurred, complimenting RBG's opinion for "its most careful and comprehensive recitation of precedents" but implying that the ruling should be limited to family matters. See *M.L.B.,* 519 U.S. at 128–44. Quotation appears on 128. On remand, the Mississippi Court of Appeals restored M.L.B.'s visitation rights.

472 **In an era when the Roberts:** See Judith Resnik, "Fairness in Numbers: A Comment on *AT&T v. Concepcion, Wal-Mart v. Dukes,* and *Turner v. Rogers,*" *Harvard Law Review* 125 (2011): 78–170.

It is worth noting that the effect of *Ashcroft v. Iqbal* (2009), which changed the requirements for bringing a lawsuit in federal courts from a lenient standard that presumed a claim to be true unless proven not to be beyond a doubt to a standard requiring that judicial discretion find a claim to be "plausible on its face," had been especially hard on African American complainants. Blacks had much greater difficulty convincing white judges than black judges that their claims of racial discrimination should be heard. See Jonathan Shaw, "The Roberts Court," *Harvard Magazine Online,* Sept. 29, 2015.

472 **"difficult to corroborate":** Laurence H. Tribe, "Respecting Dissent: Justice Ginsburg's Critique of the Troubling Invocation of Appearance," *Harvard Law Review* 127 (Nov. 2013): 479.

472 **"gripping and precise":** Ibid., 480. See *Baze v. Rees,* 553 U.S. 35 (2008), and *Gonzales v. Carhart,* 550 U.S. 124 (2007).

473 **Her dissent had also clarified:** Lani Guinier, "Courting the People," 437–44, esp. 440.

473 **In addition, the wiretap quotation:** I continue her tribute by combining it with another she wrote focusing on *Shelby* (2013). See Lani Guinier, "Justice Ginsburg: Demosprudence Through Dissent," in Dodson, *Legacy of Ruth Bader Ginsburg,* chap. 14. "Demosprudence," as Guinier explains, is a term that she and Professor Gerald Torres coined to describe the process of making and interpreting law from an external ("people driven"), not just an internal, perspective.

473 **"Throwing out preclearance":** *Shelby County v. Holder,* 570 U.S. ___ (2013), 33 (RBG dissenting).

473 **The metaphor, noted Guinier:** Guinier, "Justice Ginsburg: Demosprudence Through Dissent."

474 **Rather, "We, the People":** Ibid.

475 **"The Ruth Will Set You Free":** See notoriousrbg.tumblr.com.

475 **Exploring the blog:** Zeke J. Miller, "Ruth Bader Ginsburg Says She Has Quite a Large Supply of Notorious RBG Shirts," *Time,* time.com, Oct. 19, 2004; Katie Couric, "Exclusive: Ruth Bader Ginsburg on Hobby Lobby, Roe v. Wade, Retirement, and Notorious R.B.G.," Yahoo, www.yahoo.com, July 31, 2014.

475 **Clearly enjoying evidence:** Stephanie Garlock, "Ginsburg Discusses Justice and Advocacy at Radcliffe Day Celebration," *Harvard Magazine,* May 29, 2015.

TWENTY-TWO · A Hobbled Court

476 **In 2014, Erwin Chemerinsky:** Erwin Chemerinsky, "Much Depends on Ginsburg," *Los Angeles Times,* March 15, 2014.

476 **Other liberal law professors:** Randall Kennedy, "The Case for Early Retirement," *New Republic,* April 27, 2011.

476 **She was keenly aware:** Doctors had not predicted the extraordinary rapidity with which Alzheimer's would take over John O'Connor's mind, rendering his wife unrecognizable.

476 **Indeed, as it turned out:** Adam Liptak, "Justice Ginsburg Is Recovering After Heart Surgery to Place a Stent," *New York Times,* Nov. 27, 2014, A21.

476 **The apprehensive Scalia had admired:** Ariane de Vogue, "Scalia-Ginsburg Friendship Bridged Opposite Ideologies," www.cnn.com, Feb. 14, 2016.

478 **"full steam":** Richard Wolf, "Ginsburg's Dedication Undimmed After 20 Years on Court," *USA Today,* Aug. 1, 2013, 1A; Garrett Epps, "Don't Tell Ruth Ginsburg to Retire," *Atlantic,* March 18, 2014; quotation in Adam Liptak, "Court Is 'One of Most Activist,' Ginsburg Says, Vowing to Stay," *New York Times,* Aug. 25, 2013, A1.

478 **Fought by antiabortion forces:** Robert Barnes, "Health Law's Contraceptive Decree Spurs Court Battles," *Washington Post,* May 23, 2013, A1.

478 **This was also the position:** *Hobby Lobby v. Sebelius,* 723 F.3d 1114 (10th Cir. 2013) (Gorsuch, joined by Kelly and Tymkovich, Circuit Judges, concurring); Ephrat Livni, "What We Really Know About US Supreme Court Nominee Neil Gorsuch Based on His Controversial Hobby Lobby Decision," *Quartz,* Feb. 2, 2017. Eugene Volokh and Steve Vladeck state that Gorsuch's judicial history confirms strong commitment to religious freedom as both a constitutional and a statutory right. But he also depends on the text of the law as well as precedent when rendering a decision. Mark K. Matthews and John Frank, "Neil Gorsuch on Religion: Hobby Lobby, Euthanasia, and Other Cases," *Denver Post,* Feb. 13, 2017; Steve Vladeck, "Hobby Lobby and Executive Power: Neil Gorsuch's Key Rulings," *CNNPolitics,* Feb. 1, 2017.

478 **"a corporation is simply":** *Burwell v. Hobby Lobby,* 573 U.S. ___ (2014), 18 (Alito majority). *Burwell v. Hobby Lobby* and *Conestoga Wood Specialties v. Sebelius* had been consolidated in November 2013, when the Court agreed to hear the case. *Sebelius*

v. Hobby Lobby had been redesignated *Burwell v. Hobby Lobby* after Sylvia Burwell replaced the recently resigned Kathleen Sebelius as the secretary of health and human services. The Hobby Lobby chain of stores was owned by the evangelical Christians David Green, Barbara Green, and other relatives, while Mennonites owned Conestoga Wood Specialties.

479 **"including the choice among"**: *Burwell v. Hobby Lobby,* 573 U.S. at 3–4, 6 (RBG dissenting).

479 **"just what one would expect"**: Ibid. at 14.

479 **"into a minefield"**: Ibid. at 34–35.

480 **"I have never seen"**: Couric, "Exclusive: Ruth Bader Ginsburg on Hobby Lobby, Roe v. Wade, Retirement, and Notorious R.B.G."

480 **Reminding her audience:** Juhie Bhatia, "Ruth Bader Ginsburg Scrutinizes Court's Gender Rulings," womensenews.org, Sept. 12, 2014.

480 **This "sorry situation":** Samantha Lachman, "Ruth Bader Ginsburg Calls 'Choice' an Empty Concept for Poor Women," *Huffington Post,* July 30, 2015.

480 **"war on caterpillars":** Gail Collins, "Godfathers, Caterpillars, and Golf," *New York Times,* April 6, 2012, A17.

480 **"that most everyday people":** Kathleen Parker, "What the *#@% Is Wrong with Republicans?!," *Newsweek,* Aug. 27, 2012.

480 **If Ginsburg seemed focused:** Eric Eckholm, "Access to Abortion Falling as States Pass Restrictions," *New York Times,* Jan. 4, 2014, A1.

481 **"transformative impact on society":** Colleen Walsh, "Supreme Court Associate Justice Receives Radcliffe Medal for Her Career Battling for Individual Rights," *Harvard Gazette Online,* May 29, 2015; Adam Liptak, "Justices' Calendars Full, and Hard to Check," *New York Times,* June 2, 2015, A10.

481 **When the opera was completed:** RBG and Antonin Scalia, "Prefaces to Scalia/Ginsburg: A (Gentle) Parody of Operatic Proportions," *Columbia Journal of Law and the Arts* 38 (2015): 237.

482 **Tongue in cheek, he professed:** Ibid.

482 **Ginsburg, who was portrayed:** Jess Bravin, "Justice Ginsburg's Spin on a Supreme Opera, 'Scalia/Ginsburg,'" *Wall Street Journal,* July 13, 2015. Scalia was in Rome and unable to attend.

482 **"there is much that is charming":** Philip Kennicott, "'Scalia/Ginsburg': An Affectionate Comic Opera Look at the High Court," *Washington Post,* July 12, 2015.

482 **On February 13, 2016:** David G. Savage, "Supreme Court Justice Antonin Scalia Dies at 79," *Los Angeles Times,* Feb. 13, 2016.

482 **The immediate impact:** For a sampling, see Adam Liptak, "Justice Scalia, Who Led Court's Conservative Renaissance, Dies at 79," *New York Times,* Feb. 14, 2016, A1; "Antonin Scalia's Remarkable Legacy," *Washington Post,* Feb. 14, 2016; David B. Rifkin Jr. and Lee A. Casey, "Justice Scalia Kept Constitutional Originalism in the Conversation—No Small Legacy," *Los Angeles Times,* Feb. 15, 2016. For scholarly assessments, see Laurence H. Tribe, "The Scalia Myth," *NYR Daily,* March 10, 2016, and Robert Post, "Justice for Scalia," *New York Review of Books,* June 11, 1998. A distinctly more critical journalistic point of view comes from Linda Greenhouse, "Resetting the Post-Scalia Supreme Court," *New York Times,* Feb. 18, 2016.

482 **A member of the Court:** "Justice Ruth Bader Ginsburg Eulogy at Justice Scalia Memorial Service," C-SPAN, March 1, 2016.

482 **"We're all textualists now":** The quotation appears at 8:25 of the video "The Scalia Lecture | A Dialogue with Justice Elena Kagan on the Reading of Statutes," available at YouTube. See also *District of Columbia v. Heller,* 554 U.S. 570 (2008) (Stevens dissenting).

483 **"Wouldn't this be a better word":** Pauley, "Ruth Bader Ginsburg: Her View from the Bench."

483   **He had ruined:** "The Scalia Lecture | A Dialogue with Justice Elena Kagan on the Reading of Statutes."

484   **"uncanny ability to make":** Couric, "Exclusive: Ruth Bader Ginsburg on Hobby Lobby, Roe v. Wade, Retirement, and Notorious R.B.G."

484   **He had also become a consummate:** "Justice Ruth Bader Ginsburg Eulogy at Justice Scalia Memorial Service."

484   **"a paler place":** Rose, "Justice Ruth Bader Ginsburg Interview, Part 2."

485   **Mitch McConnell, the Republican:** MacGillis, "Why Is Mitch McConnell Picking This Fight?"

485   **The framers of the Constitution:** Garry Wills, "The Next Justice? It's Not Up to Us," *New York Review of Books,* Feb. 15, 2016.

485   **Unprecedented, the preemptive blockade:** Ronald Reagan nominated Kennedy from the Ninth Circuit to the Supreme Court on November 11, 1987, to replace the retiring Lewis F. Powell Jr. His nomination followed the failed nomination of Robert Bork, who was rejected by the Senate when Democrats objected to his outspoken conservative philosophy and positions. Reagan's second choice, Douglas Ginsburg, withdrew his name from consideration after admitting to marijuana use as a college student and Harvard Law School professor.

485   **But lacking a majority:** MacGillis, "Why Is Mitch McConnell Picking This Fight?" On Garland's nomination, see Michael D. Shear and Gardiner Harris, "Obama Pick Engages Supreme Court Battle," *New York Times,* March 17, 2016, A1; "Merrick Garland for the Supreme Court," *New York Times,* March 17, 2016, A24; Adam Liptak and Sheryl Gay Stolberg, "Deference, with Limits," *New York Times,* March 17, 2016, A1; Juliet Eilperin and Mike DeBonis, "President Obama Nominates Merrick Garland to the Supreme Court," *Washington Post,* March 16, 2016; Ed Rogers, "The Nomination of Merrick Garland Is a Futile Charade," *Washington Post,* March 16, 2016.

485   **That the stakes were so high:** Adam Liptak, "Supreme Court Nominee Could Reshape American Life," *New York Times,* Feb. 19, 2016, A1. For an examination of the ideological struggles over the Court during the "long" 1960s and how it "haunted and scarred" the modern nomination process, see Kalman, *Long Reach of the Sixties,* ix–xii and chap. 4.

486   **The litigant's goal:** *Abood v. Detroit Board of Education,* 431 U.S. 209 (1977).

486   **Because the 4–4 decision:** *Friedrichs v. California Teachers Association,* 578 U.S. ___ (2016). See also Adam Liptak, "Justices' 4–4 Tie Gives You Win in Labor Lawsuit," *New York Times,* March 29, 2016.

487   **Whether this kind of injury:** *United States v. Texas,* 579 U.S. ___ (2016).

487   **For the four million immigrants:** Adam Liptak and Michael D. Shear, "Justices Divided on Obama's Plan for Immigrants," *New York Times,* April 18, 2016, A1; Robert Barnes, "Supreme Court Won't Revive Obama Plan to Shield Illegal Immigrants from Deportation," *Washington Post,* June 23, 2016; Pratheepan Gulasekaram and Karthick Ramakrishnan, "How the Supreme Court's Deadlock Will Change Immigration Politics," *Washington Post,* June 24, 2016.

487   **Ginsburg pointed out:** Transcript of Oral Argument at 18, *Zubik v. Burwell,* 578 U.S. ___ (2016); Adam Liptak, "Justices Seem Divided on Requirements for Birth Control Coverage," *New York Times,* March 24, 2016, A14.

487   **"she'll have two insurance cards":** Transcript of Oral Argument at 51, *Zubik,* 578 U.S. ___.

487   **Sotomayor objected, insisting:** Ibid. at 32.

488   **"but in a way that does not":** "Zubik v. Burwell," *SCOTUSblog;* Adam Liptak, "Supreme Court Hints at Way to Avert Time on Birth Control Mandate," *New York Times,* March 29, 2016, A10.

488   **When all the parties agreed:** *Zubik,* 578 U.S. ___ (per curiam).

488   **Sotomayor and Ginsburg issued:** Ibid. (Sotomayor concurring).

488   **"it is totally dependent upon"**: Transcript of Oral Argument at 9–10, *Fisher v. University of Texas*, 579 U.S. ___ (2016).

489   **"It's as if nothing"**: Ibid. at 20, 64; "Race and College Admissions at the Supreme Court," *New York Times*, Dec. 9, 2015, A38; Ilya Somin, "On Today's Fisher II Supreme Court Oral Argument on Affirmative Action," *Washington Post*, Dec. 9, 2015.

489   **Although the university continued**: Somin, "On Today's Fisher II."

489   **Further, Justice Kennedy**: Adam Liptak, "Court Skeptical of Weighing Race in College Entry," *New York Times*, Dec. 9, 2015, A1; Robert Barnes, "Court Divided over University of Texas Race-Conscious Admissions," *Washington Post*, Dec. 9, 2015.

489   **"might as well have been written"**: Richard Primus, "Affirmative Action in College Admissions Here to Stay," *New York Times*, June 23, 2016, A27.

489   **Although race consciousness played**: *Fisher*, 579 U.S. at 15, 19 (Kennedy majority).

490   **"with any degree of specificity"**: Ibid. at 1–2, 32, 51 (Alito dissenting).

490   **"ambulatory surgical centers"**: Act of July 12, 2013, 83rd Leg., 2nd C.S., chap. 1, §§1-12, 2013 Tex. Sess. Law Serv. 4795–802.

490   **A federal district court**: *Whole Woman's Health v. Lakey*, 46 F. Supp. 3d 673, 676 (W.D. Tex. 2014).

490   **But the decision was overturned**: *Whole Woman's Health v. Cole*, 790 F.3d 563, 576 (5th Cir. 2015).

490   **"Justices continue to think"**: Couric, "Exclusive: Ruth Bader Ginsburg on Hobby Lobby, Roe v. Wade, Retirement, and Notorious R.B.G."

491   **Ginsburg believed the plaintiff**: Transcript of Oral Argument at 3–4, *Whole Woman's Health v. Hellerstedt* (15–274); Ariane de Vogue, "How Ruth Bader Ginsburg Steered the Court on Texas' Abortion Law," CNN.com, June 15, 2016.

491   **"the obstacles women would have"**: Transcript of Oral Argument at 24, *Whole Woman's Health* (15–274).

491   **"If that's all right"**: Ibid. at 37; Mark Joseph Stern, "The Most Important Exchange of Wednesday's SCOTUS Abortion Arguments," *Slate*, March 2, 2016.

491   **"fundamental right to make"**: Transcript of Oral Argument at 41–43, 53–54, 72, *Whole Woman's Health* (15–274). The full context of the exchange between Keller and the bench can be found on pages 36–73.

491   **"neither of these provisions"**: *Whole Woman's Health*, 579 U.S. at 2, 4 (Breyer majority).

492   **Often those cases that**: *Evenwel v. Abbott*, 578 U.S. ___ (2016).

492   **Further, the number of new cases**: Oliver Roeder, "The Supreme Court's Caseload Is on Track to Be the Lightest in 70 Years," *FiveThirtyEight*, May 17, 2016.

492   ***Whole Woman's Health* had**: Adam Liptak, "Supreme Court Strikes Down Texas Abortion Restrictions," *New York Times*, June 28, 2016; Manny Fernandez and Abby Goodnough, "Opinion Transforms Texas' Abortion Landscape," *New York Times*, June 28, 2016, A12; "Reactions to the Supreme Court Ruling on Texas' Abortion Law," *New York Times*, June 27, 2016.

492   **What the term**: Erwin Chemerinsky, "What if the Supreme Court Were Liberal?," *Atlantic*, April 6, 2016.

492   **"victory lap"**: "Ruth Ginsburg's Victory Lap," *Wall Street Journal*, July 11, 2016.

493   **"a disaster for the country"**: Adam Liptak, "Ginsburg Has a Few Words About Trump," *New York Times*, July 11, 2016, A1; Helena Andrews-Dyer, "Add Ruth Bader Ginsburg to the List of Celebrities Threatening to Ditch the U.S. if Trump Becomes President," *Washington Post*, July 11, 2016; Joan Biskupic, "Justice Ruth Bader Ginsburg Intensifies Criticism of Trump: 'He Is a Faker,'" CNN.com, July 13, 2016; Mark Joseph Stern, "RBG Just Risked Her Legacy to Insult Trump," *Slate*, July 12, 2016.

493   **"Her mind is shot—resign!"**: Mark Sherman, "AP Interview: Ginsburg Doesn't Want to Envision a Trump Win," AP, July 8, 2016; Liptak, "Ginsburg Has a Few

Words About Trump"; Joan Biskupic, "Justice Ruth Bader Ginsburg Calls Trump a 'Faker,' He Says She Should Resign," CNN, July 13, 2016; Michael D. Shear and Maggie Haberman, "Trump Calls Ginsburg 'a Disgrace to the Court,'" *New York Times,* July 13, 2016, A9; Brent Kendall, "Donald Trump's Response to Ruth Bader Ginsburg's Barbs: 'Resign!,'" *Wall Street Journal,* July 23, 2016; twitter.com/realdonaldtrump.

493 **Although there is no specific:** Canon 5 of the Code of Conduct for United States Judges provides that judges refrain from political activity, including endorsing or opposing candidates for public office. Although Supreme Court justices "consult the Code of Conduct," they are not considered strictly bound by that code like the lower court jurists. Instead, the justices are viewed as the sole judges of their own conduct, leaving the Court as the only part of our federal government without an enforceable ethics code. See *Guide to Judiciary Policy, Volume 2: Ethics in Judicial Conduct,* Part A: Codes of Conduct, Chapter 2: Code of Conduct for United States Judges. The quotation above is from Chief Justice John Roberts in a 2011 year-end report, cited in Stephen Gillers, "Can a Supreme Court Justice Denounce a Candidate? It's Clearly Not Right for Justices to Say Which Candidate They Support," *New York Times,* July 12, 2016. See also Jonathan Turley, "With Ginsburg Apology, Congress Should Look at the Real Problem," *Chicago Tribune,* July 15, 2016; Daniel W. Drezner, "Justice Ruth Bader Ginsburg Has Crossed Way, Way over the Line," *Washington Post,* July 12, 2016; "Mr. Trump Is Right About Justice Ginsburg," *New York Times,* July 13, 2016, A18; "Justice Ginsburg's Inappropriate Comments on Donald Trump," *Washington Post,* July 12, 2016.

493 **Her remarks injected further:** For a sampling of criticism and support for RBG's comments, see Erwin Chemerinsky, "Can a Supreme Court Justice Denounce a Candidate? Justices Have Free Speech Rights Too," *New York Times,* July 12, 2016; Aaron Blake and Robert Barnes, "In Her Remarks on the Presumptive GOP Nominee, Ruth Bader Ginsburg May Have Trumped Her Usual Outspokenness," *Washington Post,* July 11, 2016; Aaron Blake, "In Bashing Donald Trump, Some Say Ruth Bader Ginsburg Just Crossed a Very Important Line," *Washington Post,* July 11, 2016; Stern, "RBG Just Risked Her Legacy to Insult Trump"; Burgess Everett and Seung Min Kim, "Democrats Chide Ginsburg over Trump Barbs," *Politico,* July 12, 2016; Noah Feldman, "It's Fine for Supreme Court Justices to Speak Their Minds," *Bloomberg View,* July 12, 2016; Mark Tushnet, "The Flap over Justice Ginsburg's Interviews," *Balkinization,* July 12, 2016; Aaron Blake, "Here's How Unprecedented Ruth Bader Ginsburg's Anti-Trump Comments Were," *Washington Post,* July 13, 2016; Brent Kendall and Jacob Gershon, "Ginsburg's Trump Comments Draw Criticism," *Wall Street Journal,* July 13, 2016; William G. Ross, "Ginsburg's Remarks About Trump Are Part of a Trend Toward Inappropriate Extra-judicial Speech," *Jurist,* July 13, 2016; Jeffrey Toobin, "Ruth Bader Ginsburg's Slam of Trump," CNN, July 13, 2016.

493 **"good friends fully shared:** Michael Tomasky, "The Dangerous Election," *New York Review of Books,* March 24, 2016.

493 **Ginsburg would head the panel:** "The Venetian Ghetto: Hidden Secrets," *Economist,* June 18, 2016.

493 **This was not the first time:** The previous event took place on March 15, 2007, at the John F. Kennedy Center for the Performing Arts in Washington, D.C. Justice Anthony Kennedy presided, while RBG served on the jury. See Mark Sherman, "Kennedy Presides over Hamlet Trial," *USA Today,* March 9, 2007.

493 **But never before had she heard:** Rachel Donadio, "Ginsburg Weighs Fate of Shylock," *New York Times,* July 28, 2016, C1.

494 **Shylock's wicked and rebellious:** Ibid.

494 **After two hours of argument:** The seriousness of the arguments owed much to RBG, who had asked the lawyers to provide briefs. RBG, interview by author, Sept. 2, 2016.

494   **"impostor" and "trickster":** Donadio, "Ginsburg Weighs Fate of Shylock."

494   **Paul Spera noted that his ever-alert:** Ibid.

494   **Adding to the celebration:** RBG, interview by author, Sept. 2, 2016.

495   **"The cantor," she recalled:** RBG, interview by author, 2014.

496   **She had also agreed to explore:** Michael Cooper, "Terence Blanchard's Opera, 'Champion,' Is Among Kennedy Center's Season Highlights," *ArtsBeat* (blog), *New York Times*, March 8, 2016.

496   **"The best of the house":** I have relied heavily on the Associated Press account, "Standing Ovation Greets Justice Ruth Bader Ginsburg Cameo in DC Opera," *Los Angeles Times*, Nov. 13, 2016.

497   **None of this, of course:** Adam Liptak "Justices Returning to Bench to Face Volatile, Even if Not Blockbuster, Docket," *New York Times*, Oct. 2, 2016, A16. *Ziglar v. Abbasi*, No. 15-1358, is a consolidation of three cases asking whether noncitizens detained after 9/11 have the right to sue for damages against individual government officials. *Sessions v. Dimaya*, No. 15-1498 (originally *Lynch v. Dimaya*), examines whether immigration law is unconstitutionally vague in defining aggravated or violent felonies in deportation cases. Breyer dissented in *Sireci v. Florida*, 580 U.S. ___ (2016), when the Court declined to hear the case that argued prolonged delays in carrying out executions caused additional suffering.

TWENTY-THREE · An Election and a Presidency Like No Other

498   **On the Democratic side:** "Bernie Sanders Confirms Presidential Run and Damns America's Inequities," *Guardian*, April 30, 2015; "Sen. Bernie Sanders on Taxes, Trade Agreements, and Islamic State," *PBS NewsHour*, May 18, 2015; Bernie Sanders, "The TPP Must Be Defeated," *Huffington Post*, May 21, 2015; Bernie Sanders, "Prepared Remarks—Portsmouth Organizing Event with Bernie Sanders and Hillary Clinton," BernieSanders.com, July 12, 2016.

498   **But Trump, with his:** Michael Tomasky, "Can He Be Stopped?," *New York Review of Books*, April 21, 2016; Mark Danner, "The Magic of Donald Trump," *New York Review of Books*, May 26, 2016; Emily Nussbaum, "Guilty Pleasures," *New Yorker*, July 31, 2017, 22–26.

499   **Displaced in a globalized:** Susan Chira, "The Myth of Female Solidarity," *New York Times*, Nov. 13, 2016, SR7; Hochschild, *Strangers in Their Own Land*, 15–16, 227.

499   **Middle-aged white men:** Anne Case and Angus Deaton, "Rising Morbidity and Mortality in Midlife Among White Non-Hispanic Americans in the 21st Century," *Proceedings of the National Academy of Sciences* 112, no. 49 (2015): 15078–83; Carina Storrs, "Death Rate on the Rise for Middle-Aged White Americans," CNN, Nov. 4, 2015; Andrew J. Cherlin, "Why Are White Death Rates Rising?," *New York Times*, Feb. 22, 2016, A19.

499   **But it remained to be seen:** Danner, "Magic of Donald Trump"; Vance, *Hillbilly Elegy*.

499   **The highly qualified Clinton:** See Mark Leibovich, "Her Way," *New York Times Magazine*, Oct. 16, 2016, 4–45, 67, esp. 43.

499   **Equally damaging:** Elizabeth Drew, "How It Happened," *NYR Daily*, Nov. 12, 2016, Clinton initially denied any wrongdoing, insisting that the accusation was a partisan attack before later claiming that while it was a "mistake" to use the server, no classified material had been at risk.

500   **Her obsession with her personal:** For more on Whitewater and Clinton's quest to protect her image, see Chafe, *Bill and Hillary*, esp. 140–49 and 339–43.

500   **An FBI investigation:** For a very extensive behind-the-scenes account, see Matt Apuzzo et al., "In Trying to Avoid Politics, Comey Shaped an Election," *New York Times*, April 23, 2017, A1. See also Jeffrey Toobin, "James Comey's Letter and the

Problem of Leaks," *New Yorker,* Oct. 29, 2016; Jeffrey Toobin, "Clinton Investigation Mania, Part 2," *New Yorker,* Nov. 16, 2016; and Tim Weiner, "What Was James Comey Thinking? Inside the FBI's Story About Hillary Clinton's Emails," *Esquire,* Dec. 13, 2016.

500   **Conservative talk-radio hosts:** Drew, "How It Happened." The Whitewater scandal developed out of a 1978 real estate development—the Whitewater Development Corporation—that the Clintons took part in with James B. and Susan McDougal, who purchased a small savings and loan named Madison Guaranty. An investigation into its demise by the federal Resolution Trust Corporation named the Clintons as "potential beneficiaries" of illegal activities at the bank. After a highly politicized federal investigation during Bill Clinton's presidency, the couple was exonerated. See "Whitewater Timeline" at www.cnn.com.

    After a September 11, 2012, attack on the U.S. consulate in Benghazi, Libya, killed Ambassador Chris Stevens and three other Americans, Republicans charged that Secretary of State Hillary Clinton turned down requests for additional security, then attempted to blame the attacks on a spontaneous uprising in response to an anti-Muslim video when she knew they were planned terrorist operations. See Josh Voorhees, "Benghazi, Explained," *Slate,* Oct. 21, 2015. For a summary of other Clinton controversies, see David A. Graham, "From Whitewater to Benghazi: A Clinton-Scandal Primer," *Atlantic,* Nov. 6, 2016.

501   **"Lock her up!":** David A. Fahrenthold, Mary Jordan, and Louisa Loveluck, "The GOP's New Convention Theme: 'Lock Her Up!,'" *Washington Post,* July 20, 2016; Kristen East, "Clinton: I Was Saddened by 'Lock Her Up' Chants," *Politico,* July 24, 2016; Frank Bruni, "I'm O.K.—You're Pure Evil," *New York Times,* June 18, 2017, SR3. For evidence of how anti-Clinton attacks had been arranged well in advance of the campaign by Bannon and his allies, see Green, *Devil's Bargain.*

501   **the level of misogyny:** Thomas B. Edsall, "Democracy Can Plant the Seeds of Its Own Destruction," *New York Times,* Oct. 19, 2017. Edsall's concerns are not limited to the United States. See also Sasha Polokow-Suransky, *Go Back Where You Came From* and Levitsky and Ziblatt, *How Democracies Die.*

501   **Commentators emphasizing the negative:** Amy Chozick, "Clinton's Campaign of Hope and Missteps," *New York Times,* Nov. 10, 2016, P1.

501   **To the dismay of those:** Nicholas Kristof, "Lies in the Guise of News in the Trump Era," *New York Times,* Nov. 13, 2016, SR11; Sean McElwee and Jason McDaniel, "Economic Anxiety Didn't Make People Vote Trump, Racism Did," *Nation,* May 8, 2017. In 2017 elections, the anti-immigration and anti-euro Alternative for Germany party won seats in parliament for the first time, and the center-right People's Party and the far-right Freedom Party in Austria collected 58 percent of the vote. As a result, left and centrist politicians, including Austria's Sebastian Kurz and Germany's Angela Merkel had shifted their immigration positions closer to the populist stances in order to retain voters. Associated Press, "Populism Again Casts Shadow over Booming Eurozone Economy," *New York Times,* June 16, 2017; Associated Press, "Populist Parties Gain More Victories in European Politics," *New York Times,* Oct. 16, 2017; Matthew Goodwin, "European Populism Is Here to Stay," *New York Times,* Oct. 20, 2017.

501   **"a return to the mother's":** "This Land Is Trump's America," *New York Times Magazine,* Nov. 20, 2016, 37–45.

501   **Nor could sexism:** Nina McLozano-Reich, "Sexism, Alive and Well in 2016 Presidential Campaign," *HuffPost,* February 8, 2016.

501   **Three years in the planning:** See Evan Osnos, David Remnick, and Joshua Yaffa, "Active Measures: What Lay Behind Russia's Interference in the 2016 Election—and What Lies Ahead?," *New Yorker,* March 6, 2017, 40–55. Following the election, intelligence officials insisted that there was no indication that Russian hackers had altered the bottom-line vote count. But they gave no such assurances about the back-end vot-

ing systems, where the disruption could prevent voters from even casting ballots. In the twenty-one states that reported such problems, including the key swing states of Virginia, North Carolina, and Florida, there has been no official determination as to whether the problems were accidents, random incidents associated with computer systems, or the results of Russian hacking. See Nicole Perlroth, Michael Wines, and Matthew Rosenberg, "Little Effort to Investigate in States Targeted by Election Hacking," *New York Times,* Sept. 2, 2017, A1.

502 **Clinton still managed:** Clinton received 65,853,516 votes compared with 62,984,825 for Trump. Federal Election Commission, Official 2016 Presidential General Election Results, Jan. 30, 2017. Available at www.fec.gov.

502 **However, she lost the Electoral College:** Nate Cohn, "Turnout Was Not Driver of Clinton's Defeat," *New York Times,* March 29, 2017, A17. In the 1990s, white working-class voters split evenly between the two parties in presidential elections. By 2012, they favored Mitt Romney over Obama in every state but Iowa. In 2016, exit polls showed that 43 percent of union households voted for Trump. See Reid J. Epstein and Janet Hook, "In Their Coastal Citadels, Democrats Argue over What Went Wrong," *Wall Street Journal,* Nov. 18, 2016. See also Nate Cohn, "Why Trump Won: Working-Class Whites," *New York Times,* Nov. 9, 2017; Aaron Blake, "Who Likes President Obama and Voted for Donald Trump? Lots of People," *Washington Post,* Nov. 16, 2017.

502 **"the biggest under-covered":** Ari Berman, "The GOP's Attack on Voting Rights Was the Most Under-covered Story of 2016," *Nation,* Nov. 9, 2016.

502 **In 2012, one year prior:** Leadership Conference on Civil and Human Rights, *Warning Signs: The Potential Impact of Shelby County v. Holder on the 2016 General Election* (June 2016), 13. Available at www.civilrights.org.

502 **But by the time voters:** "New Voting Restrictions in Place for 2016 Presidential Election," Brennan Center for Justice at NYU School of Law, updated Nov. 2, 2016. Those fourteen states are Alabama, Arizona, Indiana, Kansas, Mississippi, Nebraska, New Hampshire, Ohio, Rhode Island, South Carolina, Tennessee, Texas, Virginia, and Wisconsin.

503 **Removal of Section 5:** Arizona, Georgia, and Virginia also were no longer under federal oversight. Combined, the five states represented eighty-four electoral votes in the presidential election. In addition, each was expecting tight races for the Senate and governorships. Leadership Conference on Civil and Human Rights, *Warning Signs,* 2.

503 **The number of polling places:** Leadership Conference on Civil and Human Rights, *The Great Poll Closure* (Nov. 2016). Available at www.civilrights.org. In addition to North Carolina, the other five states were Texas, Arizona, Louisiana, Mississippi, and Alabama. While Texas was Trump country, Republicans' use of gerrymandering and voter-ID laws to discriminate against minority voters effectively denied Democrats two Latino-majority congressional seats. See Ari Berman, "Texas's Redistricting Maps and Voter-ID Laws Intentionally Discriminated Against Minority Voters," *Nation,* March 13, 2017; *Perez v. Abbott,* SA-11-CV-360 (W.D. Tex. 2017).

503 **Reductions in early voting:** Berman, "GOP's Attack"; Jeremy W. Peters, Richard Fausset, and Michael Wines, "Black Turnout Drops, Boding Ill for Clinton," *New York Times,* Nov. 2, 2016, A1; Joan Walsh, "Will North Carolina Lead the Way to a New South," *Nation,* Nov. 9, 2016. For a more detailed analysis of the change in black voting from 2008 through 2016, see Ari Berman, "North Carolina's Voter ID Law Could Block 218,000 Registered Voters from the Polls," *Nation,* March 14, 2016.

503 **In Florida, a state Clinton:** Alice Miranda Ollstein, "Republicans Were Wildly Successful at Suppressing Voters in 2016," *ThinkProgress,* Nov. 15, 2016; "New Voting Restrictions in Place for 2016 Presidential Election."

503 **In Wisconsin, which along with:** "New Voting Restrictions in Place for 2016 Presidential Election," Michael Finnegan, "Final Wisconsin Recount Tally Strengthens Trump's Victory," *Los Angeles Times,* Dec. 12, 2016. The Dane County Clerk's office

and the University of Wisconsin Political Science Department are conducting a joint study of the November election to provide quantifiable data on the factors that may inhibit voting, including the Wisconsin voter-ID requirement. See Amos Mayberry, "UW Study Hopes to Find Effect of Wisconsin Voter ID Laws," *Badger Herald,* Oct. 4, 2017.

503   **By contrast, states:** Guy Cecil, "Voter Suppression Memo," *Priorities USA,* May 3, 2017; Ari Berman, "Wisconsin's Voter-ID Law Suppressed 200,000 Votes in 2016 (Trump Won by 22,748)," *Nation,* May 8, 2017. Alabama, New Hampshire, and Rhode Island changed to non-strict voter-ID laws and experienced an increased turnout, albeit by only 0.7 percent. A subsequent study by two University of Wisconsin political scientists estimated that nearly 17,000 registered Wisconsin voters were kept from the polls in November as a result of the state's strict voter-ID law. Professor Kenneth R. Mayer and the doctoral student Michael G. DeCrescenzo concluded that the law prevented voters with Democratic tendencies from going to the polls, either because they did not have an acceptable ID or because they believed that the one they did possess would not be accepted. See Michael Wines, "Wisconsin Law Deterred Voters, Study Finds," *New York Times,* Sept. 25, 2017, A15.

503   **"He's not my President":** Shira Tarlo, "'Not My President's Day': Thousands Protest at Anti-Trump Rallies Across U.S.," NBC News, Feb. 20, 2017. Other cities in the NBC report include Boston, Dallas, Chicago, Kansas City, Denver, Milwaukee, Salt Lake City, and Atlanta.

503   **Topping them all:** Tim Wallace, Karen Yourish, and Troy Griggs, "Trump's Inauguration vs. Obama's: Comparing the Crowds," *New York Times,* Jan. 20, 2017; Tim Wallace and Alicia Parlapiano, "Crowd Scientists Say Women's March in Washington Had 3 Times as Many People as Trump's Inauguration," *New York Times,* Jan. 20, 2017. This contrasted with an estimated 160,000 on the National Mall who attended the swearing in of the new president.

503   **Replicated in hundreds:** Kiersten Schmidt and Sarah Almukhtar, "Where Women's Marches Are Happening Around the World," *New York Times,* Jan. 20, 2017.

503   **Thanks to Trump's xenophobic:** The latest surge in potential members for the extreme Right has come largely from teenagers and individuals in their twenties—mostly men—who have been influenced by videos, blogs, and tweets from far-right internet personalities promoting extreme racial beliefs. The "alt-light" movement has successfully drawn young people by framing their efforts as defending Western culture rather than making explicit racist appeals. They also provide easy scapegoats to blame for what they perceive to be the nation's problems—liberals, feminists, migrants, and globalists. Collectively, the number of alt-right and alt-light online followers runs into the millions. Once adherents become involved, they have used social media as their primary means of further increasing their numbers and fighting back against the perceived oppressions of the Left. See Jesse Singal, "Undercover with the Alt-Right," *New York Times,* Sept. 20, 2017, A23.

504   **Nationwide, hate crimes:** Julia Preston, Katharine Q. Seelye, and Farah Stockman, "Donald Trump Win Has Blacks, Hispanics, and Muslims Bracing for a Long 4 Years," *New York Times,* Nov. 10, 2016, P8; Liam Stack, "Trump Win Seen as 'Devastating Loss' for Gay and Transgender People," *New York Times,* Nov. 11, 2016, P9; Yamiche Alcindor, "Minorities Worry What a 'Law and Order' Donald Trump Presidency Will Mean," *New York Times,* Nov. 12, 2016, A16; Eric Lichtblau, "Attacks Against Muslim Americans Fueled Rise in Hate Crime, F.B.I. Says," *New York Times,* Nov. 14, 2016, A14; Adeel Hassan, "Refugees Discover 2 Americas: One That Hates, One That Heals," *New York Times,* Nov. 15, 2016, A1; Julia Preston and Jennifer Medina, "Young Immigrants Fear Deportation by Trump," *New York Times,* Nov. 20, 2016, A18.

504   **Desecration of Jewish cemeteries:** Spurred by his daughter Ivanka, a convert to Judaism, and a tour of the National Museum of African American History and Cul-

648 · Notes to Pages 504–505

ture, Trump finally denounced the bomb threats and anti-Semitism. Julie Hirschfeld Davis, "After Weeks of Silence, Trump Condemns a Rise in Anti-Semitic Threats," *New York Times,* Feb. 22, 2017, A13.

504 **Hangman's nooses, long a symbol:** Sheryl Gay Stolberg and Caitlin Dickerson, "Nooses, Potent Symbols of Hate, Crop Up in Rash of Cases," *New York Times,* July 6, 2017, A11.

504 **Lower-school teachers:** Examples drawn from quotations of more than twenty-five thousand educators surveyed after the election. See "Teaching Tolerance Responds to Election's Negative Impact," *Southern Poverty Law Center Report* (Spring 2017): 4.

504 **"Trump put away the dog":** Clare Foran, "How the President, the Police, and the Media Embolden the Far-Right," *Atlantic,* Aug. 17, 2017. On August 12, 2017, a rally of neo-Nazis and white nationalists in support of a Confederate statue in Charlottesville, Virginia, turned violent when they were confronted by counterdemonstrators. German sees Trump's response to the deadly events as one of a long series of actions the president has taken to side with and endorse the viewpoint of far-right ideological movements and reinforce their sense of victimization. For a more detailed account of the events and the president's response, see Sheryl Gay Stolberg and Brian M. Rosenthal, "White Nationalist Protest Leads to Deadly Violence," *New York Times,* Aug. 13, 2017, A1; "The Hate He Dares Not Speak Of," *New York Times,* Aug. 14, 2017, A18; Glenn Thrush and Rebecca R. Ruiz, "A White House Statement on Virginia Is Also Found Wanting," *New York Times,* Aug. 14, 2017, A1; Michael D. Shear and Maggie Haberman, "Trump Again Says Two Sides at Fault in Rally Violence," *New York Times,* Aug. 16, 2017, A1.

504 **A flurry of executive orders:** Donald J. Trump, "Presidential Memorandum Regarding the Mexico City Policy," Jan. 23, 2016; Donald J. Trump, "Presidential Memorandum Streamlining Permitting and Reducing Regulatory Burdens for Domestic Manufacturing," Jan. 24, 2016; Donald J. Trump, "Presidential Memorandum Regarding Construction of the Dakota Access Pipeline," Jan. 24, 2016; Donald J. Trump, "Presidential Memorandum Regarding Construction of the Keystone XL Pipeline," Jan. 24, 2016; Donald J. Trump, "Presidential Executive Order on Promoting Energy Independence and Economic Growth," March 28, 2016; Donald J. Trump, "Executive Order: Enhancing Public Safety in the Interior of the United States," Jan. 25, 2016; Donald J. Trump, "Executive Order: Border Security and Immigration Enforcement Improvements," Jan. 25, 2016. See also Clifford Krauss and Diane Cardwell, "Policy's Promise for Coal Power Has Its Limits," *New York Times,* March 29, 2017, A1.

505 **Most disruptive was the president's:** Donald J. Trump, "Executive Order: Protecting the Nation from Foreign Terrorist Entry into the United States," Jan. 27, 2016.

505 **Ostensibly an effort:** Ibid. Federal officials disputed the necessity of the order. See Maria Sacchetti and Matt Zapotosky, "Trump's New Entry Ban to Be Challenged in Courts Hours Before It Takes Effect," *Washington Post,* March 14, 2016.

505 **A three-judge panel:** *Minnesota v. Trump,* No. 17-35105, D.C. No. 2:17-cv-00141 (9th Cir., Feb. 7, 2017). Revisions in the new ban include removing Iraq from the list, exempting legal permanent residents and green card holders, and lifting the indefinite ban on Syrians. See Donald J. Trump, "Executive Order: Protecting the Nation from Foreign Terrorist Entry into the United States," March 6, 2016.

505 **"a total and complete shutdown":** Adam Liptak, "Campaign Pledge of Muslim Ban Haunts the President in Court," *New York Times,* March 17, 2017, A1.

505 **On March 15, 2017, district courts:** *Hawaii and Ismail Elshikh v. Trump,* 1:17-00050 DKW-KSC (9th Cir. Ct., March 15, 2017) (Order Granting Motion for Temporary Restraining Order); *International Refugee Assistance Project v. Trump,* 8:17 CV-00361-TDC (4th Cir. Ct., March 15, 2017) (Memorandum Opinion). See also Elise Foley, Cristian Farias, and Willa Frej, "Donald Trump's New Travel Ban Challenged in

Courts Across the Country," *Huffington Post,* March 15, 2017; Josh Gerstein, "9th Circuit Will Hear Revised Trump Travel Ban in May," *Politico,* April 3, 2017. The Hawaii case moved up to the Ninth Circuit Court of Appeals, while the Maryland case would be heard in the Fourth Circuit.

505 **"drips with religious intolerance":** *International Refugee Assistance Project v. Trump,* No. 17-1351 (4th Cir. 2017), 12; *Hawaii v. Trump,* No. 17-15589 (9th Cir. June 12, 2017); Josh Gerstein, "Ninth Circuit Upholds Block on Trump's Travel Ban," *Politico,* June 12, 2017.

505 **On June 1, the Trump:** Ann E. Marimow and Robert Barnes, "Federal Appeals Court Maintains Freeze of Trump's Travel Ban. Attorney General Vows Supreme Court Appeal," *Washington Post,* May 25, 2017.

505 **Then before the cases:** *Trump v. International Refugee Assistance Project,* 582 U.S. ___ (2017), 12 (per curiam). It would not apply to those "who have a credible claim of a bona fide relationship"—for example, a family member of someone living in the country, a student admitted to a university, or an individual with an employment offer in hand. Excluded were refugees who had no prior connection to the United States and were dependent on refugee assistance projects willing to sponsor them. The September 24 order indefinitely banned almost all travel to the United States from seven countries: Iran, Libya, Syria, Yemen, Somalia, Chad, and North Korea. Citizens of Iraq and select individuals in Venezuela would face additional restrictions or heightened scrutiny. The ban, however, would not apply to legal permanent residents, current visitors with valid visas, or refugees. See Donald J. Trump, "Presidential Proclamation Enhancing Vetting Capabilities and Processes for Detecting Attempted Entry into the United States by Terrorists or Other Public-Safety Threats," whitehouse.gov, Sept. 24, 2017; Michael D. Shear, "Trump Imposes New Travel Ban on 7 Countries," *New York Times,* Sept. 25, 2017, A1; Amy Howe, "Justices End 4th Circuit Travel-Ban Challenge," *SCOTUSblog,* Oct. 10, 2017; Amy Davidson Sorkin, "What Does Trump's New Travel Ban Mean for the Supreme Court," *New Yorker,* Sept. 26, 2017.

505 **In December:** Miriam Jordan, "Ninth Circuit Judges Rule Against Latest Ban," *New York Times,* Dec. 23, 2017, A17; Adam Liptak, "President's Travel Ban, Already Headed to Supreme Court, Is Rejected Again," *New York Times,* Feb. 16, 2018, A14.

506 **Oral arguments in April:** Robert Barnes, Ann E. Marimow, and Matt Zapotosky, "Supreme Court's Conservative Justices Appear to Back Trump's Authority for Travel Ban," *Washington Post,* April 25, 2018; Adam Liptak and Michael D. Shear, "Supreme Court Signal Support for a Travel Ban," *New York Times,* April 26, 2018, A1.

506 **Appalled by the president's:** Michael M. Grynbaum, "Trump Calls the News Media the 'Enemy of the American People,'" *New York Times,* Feb. 17, 2017; Nolan D. McCaskill, "Trump Tweets: Press 'Is the Enemy of the American People,'" *Politico,* Feb. 17, 2017. Historically, the phrase "an enemy of the people" has referred to political dissenters, dating to Roman times and the emperor Nero. It gained prominence during the French Revolution, then in Nazi Germany when Propaganda Minister Joseph Goebbels referred to Jews as "a sworn enemy of the German people." Its widest use arose when Vladimir Lenin and Joseph Stalin used the term *vrag naroda* (enemy of the nation/people), a reference to those who disagreed with Bolshevik ideologies in the newly formed Soviet Union. Most recently, Venezuela's Hugo Chávez called political dissenters "enemies of the homeland." See Veronika Bondarenko, "Trump Keeps Saying 'Enemy of the People'—but the Phrase Has a Very Ugly History," *Business Insider,* Feb. 27, 2017; and Amanda Erickson, "Trump Called the News Media an 'Enemy of the American People.' Here's a History of the Term," *Washington Post,* Feb. 18, 2017.

506 **"be banished to the wilderness":** Adam Liptak, "Court Is Set to Tilt Right, but It May Play a Surprising Role: Impeding Trump," *New York Times,* Nov. 10, 2016, P7;

David G. Savage, "Trump's Victory Ensures a Conservative Majority on the Supreme Court," *Los Angeles Times,* Nov. 9, 2016.

506 **"most important person":** Ben Schreckinger, "I Did Ruth Bader Ginsburg's Workout," *Politico,* Feb. 27, 2017.

506 **That Kennedy, now the longest-serving:** Liptak, "Court Is Set to Tilt Right."

506 **Trump's freedom to get:** "Trumping the Law," *Economist,* Nov. 25, 2017, 30.

507 **But McConnell had prepared:** Ibid.

507 **On January 31:** "A Coloradan on the Highest Court in the Land," *Denver Post,* Feb. 1, 2017; Robert Barnes, "Trump Picks Colo. Appeals Court Judge Neil Gorsuch for Supreme Court," *Washington Post,* Jan. 31, 2017; Adam Liptak, "A Nominee Who Echoes Scalia's Style," *New York Times,* Feb. 1, 2017, A26.

507 **As a fourth-generation Coloradoan:** Matt Ford, "Trump Nominates Neil Gorsuch for the U.S. Supreme Court," *Atlantic,* Jan. 31, 2017; Sara Clarke, "10 Things You Didn't Know About Neil Gorsuch," *U.S. News & World Report,* Jan. 31, 2017; Josh Gerstein, "Neil Gorsuch: Who Is He? Bio, Facts, Background, and Political Views," *Politico,* Jan. 31, 2017; Charlie Savage, "Justice Dept. Job Put Gorsuch at the Center of Controversy on Bush Terror Policies," *New York Times,* March 16, 2017, A13. See also Tony Mauro, "Trump Chooses Neil Gorsuch, Ivy League Conservative, for Supreme Court," *National Law Journal,* Jan. 31, 2017; Tony Mauro, "Neil Gorsuch: In His Own Words," *National Law Journal,* Jan. 31, 2017.

507 **In 2006, George W. Bush:** Adam Liptak, "A Nominee Who Echoes Scalia's Style," *New York Times,* Feb. 1, 2017, A1; Robert Barnes, "Trump Picks Colorado Appeals Court Judge Neal Gorsuch for Supreme Court," *Washington Post,* Jan. 29, 2017. Now that he's been confirmed, it marks the first time a sitting justice sat on the bench with a former clerk.

508 **"to apply the law":** Mauro, "Neil Gorsuch: In His Own Words."

508 **Relying on a style:** Barnes, "Trump Picks Colo. Appeals Court Judge"; Liptak, "Nominee Who Echoes Scalia's Style"; Eugene Volokh, "Supreme Court Nominee Neil Gorsuch on Religious Freedom," *Washington Post,* Jan. 31, 2017; Mark Sherman, "High Court Nominee Praised for Breezy, Witty Writing Style," AP, March 8, 2017.

508 **"very easy to get along with":** Max Greenwood, "Ginsburg: Trump Supreme Court Nominee Neil Gorsuch Is 'Very Easy to Get Along With,'" *Hill,* Feb. 6, 2017.

509 **In separate published letters:** Harvard Law Classmates of Neil Gorsuch, "Why We Support Neil Gorsuch for the Supreme Court," *RealClearPolitics,* March 9, 2017; Larson Holt, "Over 150 Alumni Call for Gorsuch's Confirmation to Supreme Court," *Columbia Spectator,* March 8, 2017; 150 Columbia and Barnard Alumni to Senate Judiciary Committee Chairman Charles Grassley and Ranking Member Dianne Feinstein, Senate Majority Leader Mitch McConnell, and Senate Minority Leader Chuck Schumer, March 7, 2017. Available at www.confirmgorsuch.com.

509 **Conservative and business:** Callum Borchers, "Trump's Nomination of Neil Gorsuch Is a Promise Kept to Conservative Media," *Washington Post,* Jan. 31, 2017; Volokh, "Supreme Court Nominee Neil Gorsuch on Religious Freedom"; Julie Hirschfeld Davis and Mark Landler, "Trump's Court Pick Sets Up Political Clash," *New York Times,* Feb. 1, 2017, A1; Amy Davidson Sorkin, "Neil Gorsuch and Justices Past," *New Yorker,* Feb. 1, 2017; Kyle Peterson, "Trump's Supreme Court Whisperer," *Wall Street Journal,* Feb. 3, 2017. On the nominee's hostility to same-sex marriage, see Neil Gorsuch, "Liberals 'n' Lawsuits," *National Review Online,* Feb. 7, 2005.

509 **Far less sanguine, liberals:** Alliance for Justice, *The Gorsuch Record,* 1–2, 51. Available at www.afj.org. See also "Neil Gorsuch and the Supreme Court," *New York Times,* Feb. 1, 2017, A26; Christina Cauterucci, "What Neil Gorsuch, Trump's SCOTUS Pick, Means for American Women," *Slate,* Feb. 1, 2017; Dahlia Lithwick, "The Case Against Neil Gorsuch," *Slate,* March 20, 2017; Richard L. Hasen, "Why Gorsuch Could Lead Court in Wrong Direction," CNN, March 1, 2017.

509   **Those familiar with his ruling:** *Hobby Lobby v. Sebelius,* 723 F.3d 1114 (10th Cir. 2013). For the similarly themed *Little Sisters v. Burwell,* he was not part of the three-judge panel, but he joined a dissent when the case was denied an en banc review. See *Little Sisters v. Burwell* (10th Cir., July 14, 2015).

509   **Gorsuch stuck to the letter:** After being instructed to either remain with his vehicle until a repair team arrived or drive the truck while pulling the trailer with its failed brakes, Alphonse Maddin waited over three hours in freezing temperatures in an unheated truck for assistance. He then drove away without the trailer, claiming his feet and legs were going numb, and was subsequently fired for abandoning his trailer. When the Tenth Circuit Court of Appeals affirmed the lower court's ruling that the company violated whistle-blower protections of the Surface Transportation Assistance Act, Gorsuch dissented, arguing, "The trucker in this case wasn't fired for *refusing* to operate his vehicle." Instead, Maddin was fired "only after he declined the statutorily protected option (refuse to operate) and chose instead to *operate* his vehicle in a manner he thought wise but his employer did not." See Marcia Coyle, "Lawyers in Gorsuch 'Frozen Trucker' Case Surprised at Attention," *National Law Journal,* March 22, 2017, and *Transam Trucking Inc. v. Administrative Review Board,* No. 15-9504 (10th Cir. 2016), 19–20.

509   **"evade the chopping block":** *Gutierrez-Brizuela v. Lynch,* 834 F.3d 1142, 1143 (10th Cir. 2016), 14–15. According to *Chevron,* judges must defer to an agency's interpretation of ambiguous laws issued by Congress. Thomas, along with Gorsuch and others, has expressed concern that this predisposes judges to the government's position rather than allowing for independent judgment. See *Chevron U.S.A. Inc. v. Natural Resources Defense Council Inc.,* 467 U.S. 837 (1984). Conservative legal scholars raised the constitutional objection that Congress's power to make rules cannot be delegated to federal agencies. See, for example, Hamburger, *Is Administrative Law Unconstitutional?,* as well as his abbreviated version for the general reader *Administrative Threat.*

509   **Democratic members of the judiciary:** Neither Samuel A. Alito Jr. nor Clarence Thomas, two current Supreme Court justices, received sixty confirmation votes. See Linda Qiu, "Lessons and Interpretations on the Court Nomination Process," *New York Times,* April 4, 2017, A13.

510   **"no hints, no forecasts":** Adam Liptak, "Avert, Sidestep, Rethink: Justices' Advice on Hearings," *New York Times,* March 20, 2017, A16; Jeffrey Toobin, "Behind Neil Gorsuch's Non-answers," *New Yorker,* April 3, 2017.

510   **When the hearing began:** Matt Flegenheimer, "At Senate Hearing, Gorsuch Tries to Position Himself Above Politics," *New York Times,* March 21, 2017, A20.

510   **"the big guy":** Benjamin Wallace-Wells, "Neil Gorsuch Makes the Case for His Own Independence," *New Yorker,* March 22, 2017.

510   **The *Chicago Tribune*:** "Neil Gorsuch Earns His Supreme Court Seat," *Chicago Tribune,* March 23, 2017.

510   **The nominee quickly demonstrated:** Adam Liptak et al., "Highlights from Judge Gorsuch's Confirmation Hearing," *New York Times,* March 22, 2017.

510   **"As a general matter":** Ibid.

510   **Never departing from script:** Matt Flegenheimer, "Of Horse v. Duck, Mutton Busting, and Other Diversions," *New York Times,* March 23, 2017, A16.

511   **"should not be overturned lightly":** Adam Liptak and Matt Flegenheimer, "Gorsuch Asserts He Would Be Able to Buck Trump," *New York Times,* March 22, 2017, A1.

511   **In fact, Gorsuch's calm:** Liam Donovan, "Schumer's Folly," *Politico,* March 30, 2017.

511   **"first-rate intellect":** Wallace-Wells, "Neil Gorsuch Makes the Case for His Own Independence"; Matt Flegenheimer et al., "Six Highlights from the Gorsuch Confirmation Hearing," *New York Times,* March 20, 2017.

511   **Republicans had more aggressively:** Since 1981, Republicans had been more aggressive about blocking Democratic nominees to federal trial courts, resulting in a failure

rate of 14 percent for Democrats as opposed to just 7 percent for Republican nominees. Among appeals court nominees, there was a 23 to 19 percent gap. The difference would have been even greater had Democrats not invoked the "Reid rule" in 2013, which allowed the Senate to confirm a nominee with a simple majority rather than the mandated two-thirds margin. The rule change permitted the Democrats to counter the Republican attempts to block many highly qualified Obama nominees. See David Weigel, "Progressives Cheer Democratic Obstruction—and Aim at Supreme Court," *Washington Post,* Jan. 31, 2017; Hewitt, "Democrats Made Confirmation Easier for Trump Nominees. The GOP Should Fix That."

511   **After the Garland obstructionism:** Matt Flegenheimer, "Democrats' Quandary on Gorsuch: Appease the Base or Honor the Process," *New York Times,* Feb. 14, 2017.

511   **"would be very unforgiving":** "The Supreme Court as Partisan Tool," *New York Times,* April 5, 2017, A22; Ari Berman, "The Democratic Filibuster of Neil Gorsuch Is On," *Nation,* April 3, 2017; Robert Barnes, Ed O'Keefe, and Ann E. Marimow, "Schumer: Democrats Will Filibuster Gorsuch Nomination," *Washington Post,* March 23, 2017; Charlie Savage, "Is Filibuster Fight the Main Event, or Merely the Undercard?," *New York Times,* April 4, 2017, A1.

511   **Schumer concluded that:** Donovan, "Schumer's Folly."

511   **"change the nominee":** Matt Flegenheimer et al., "Senate Democrats Plan to Filibuster over Supreme Court Nominee," *New York Times,* March 24, 2017, A17.

511   **"Few outside of New York":** Amy Davidson Sorkin, "Gorsuch Wins, the Filibuster Loses," *New Yorker,* April 6, 2017.

511   **On April 7, 2017:** The vote to end debate ended 55–45, short of the necessary sixty with four Democrats voting with the Republicans. Mitch McConnell changed his vote from yes to no as a matter of procedure to begin the process of eliminating the three-fifths requirement. The vote to keep the sixty-vote threshold fell along party lines, 52–48. The second vote to end debate passed with a simple majority, 55–45, with McConnell now voting yes and Bennet voting no. The motion to reconsider had identical voting, and a final attempt to postpone the nomination also fell along party lines. Two independents voted with the Democrats. See Wilson Andrews et al., "How Senators Voted on the Gorsuch Filibuster and the Nuclear Option," *New York Times,* April 6, 2017.

511   **The change in rules:** Matt Flegenheimer, "At Root of Battle over the Court Nominee: 'They Started It,'" *New York Times,* April 1, 2017, A16.

512   **Trump's rejection of the American Bar:** Adam Liptak, "White House Cuts A.B.A. out of Judge Evaluations," *New York Times,* April 1, 2017, A16.

512   **A private session:** Adam Liptak and Matt Flegenheimer, "Court Nominee Is Confirmed After Bruising Year-Long Fight," *New York Times,* April 8, 2017, A1; Julie Hirschfeld Davis, "Neil Gorsuch Is Sworn In as Supreme Court Justice," *New York Times,* April 10, 2017; Robert Barnes and Ashley Parker, "Neil M. Gorsuch Sworn In as 113th Supreme Court Justice," *Washington Post,* April 10, 2017; Dan Merica, "Neil Gorsuch: Trump Celebrates Supreme Court Success," *CNNPolitics,* April 10, 2017.

513   **Solidifying the conservative:** Adam Liptak, "Confident and Assertive, a New Justice in a Hurry," *New York Times,* July 4, 2017, A13.

513   **But it had drawn:** David Cole, "How Far Will the Court Go?," *NYR Daily,* June 28, 2017.

513   **"directly or indirectly":** *Trinity Lutheran Church v. Comer,* 788 F.3d 779 (8th Cir. 2015).

513   **The Alliance Defending Freedom:** Linda Greenhouse, "The Roberts Court, 2017 Edition," *New York Times,* April 27, 2017.

513   **In an age of limited:** Jeffrey Toobin, "The Conservative Agenda for Gorsuch's First Week," *New Yorker,* April 18, 2017.

513 **confronted with a "fraught issue"**: Transcript of Oral Argument, *Trinity Lutheran Church v. Missouri*, 582 U.S. __ (2017).

514 **"to chip away at the wall"**: Robert Barnes, "Justices Express Sympathy with Missouri Church at Supreme Court Hearing," *Washington Post*, April 19, 2017; Adam Liptak, "Supreme Court Considers the Church-State Divide," *New York Times*, April 20, 2017, A16.

514 **In a 7–2 ruling**: *Trinity Lutheran Church*, 582 U.S. at esp. 11 (Roberts majority).

514 **"weakens this country's"**: Ibid. at 1–2 (Sotomayor dissenting).

514 **Breyer, who had not**: Ibid. at 1–2 (Breyer concurring).

514 **"We do not address religious"**: Ibid. at n3 on 14 (Roberts majority).

514 **"The general principles"**: Ibid. at 3 (Gorsuch concurring in part).

515 **But Ahmer Iqbal Abbasi**: Abigail Hauslohner and Ann E. Marimow, "Supreme Court Case Sets the Stage for Future Officials' Accountability," *Washington Post*, Jan. 17, 2017; Brief of Professors of Civil Procedure as *Amici Curiae* in Support of Respondents, and Questions Presented Report, *Ziglar v. Abbasi*, Nos. 15-1358, 15-1359, 15-1363.

515 **"any Muslim or Arab noncitizen"**: Transcript of Oral Argument at 28, *Ziglar v. Abbasi*, 582 U.S. __ (2017).

515 **"you couldn't tell who"**: Ibid. at 8.

515 **"discipline" had been "meted out"**: Ibid. at 27.

516 **He also insisted that federal**: See Ronald and Joyce Milton, *A Search for the Truth* (New York: Henry Holt & Co., 1983) and Alan M. Dershowitz, "Spies and Scapegoats," *New York Times*, Aug. 14, 1983, Section 7, page 1. Note that in the wake of the execution, the names of the Rosenbergs' two small sons was changed to Meeropol.

516 **"a proper balance"**: Ibid. at 28 (Kennedy majority).

516 **"post 9/11 circumstance"**: Robert Barnes, "High Court: U.S. Officials Can't Be Held Liable for Alleged Unconstitutional Treatment of Noncitizens," *Washington Post*, June 19, 2017.

516 **"on later examination"**: *Abbasi*, 582 U.S. at 20, 23–24 (Breyer dissenting). Rachel Meeropol, the attorney for Abbasi and his fellow plaintiffs, was the granddaughter of Ethel and Julius Rosenberg. In June 1953, at the height of McCarthyism, both Rosenbergs had been executed as Soviet spies. Subsequent research in U.S. and Soviet archives confirmed Julius's espionage but Ethel's minimal involvement.

516 **The Court's role became even more**: Caitlin Dickerson, "Expanding the Deportation Dragnet," *New York Times*, Aug. 22, 2017, 12.

517 **Trump, by contrast, pledged**: Kenneth Roth, "Trump's Cruel Deportation Policies," *New York Review of Books*, Aug. 11, 2017.

517 **"aggravated felonies"**: *Esquivel-Quintana v. Sessions*, 581 U.S. __ (2017). *Sessions v. Dimaya* addressed the same issue but was carried over to the fall. See *Sessions v. Dimaya*, No. 15-1498.

518 **Decision making would invariably**: Brief for Respondent, *Lynch v. Dimaya*, 15-1498 and Transcript of Oral Arguments, 2nd Hearing, *Sessions v. Dimaya*, 584 U.S. __ (2018).

518 **Relying on the Johnson**: *Johnson v. United States*, 576 U.S. __ (2015); *Dimaya v. Lynch*, 803 F. 3d 1110 (9th Cir. 2015).

518 **The Justice Department appealed**: Robert Barnes, "Supreme Court Begins New Term with Case on Whether Workers Can Be Forced into Individual Arbitration," *Washington Post*, Oct. 2, 2017.

518 **"How am I supposed to know"**: Transcript of Oral Arguments, 2nd Hearing, *Sessions v. Dimaya*, 584 U.S. __ (2018), esp. 21 and 30.

518 **"The truth is no one knows"**: *Sessions v. Dimaya*, 584 U.S. __ (2018), 1 (Gorsuch concurring).

518 **With Gorsuch joining the liberals**: *Sessions v. Dimaya*, 584 U.S. __ (2018) (Kagan majority). Roberts and Thomas filed dissenting opinions.

518 **"it's the hombres who live":** Quote in Marcia Sacchetti, "Thousands of Immigrants Could Benefit from Supreme Court Ruling, Lawyers Say," *Washington Post,* April 18, 2018.

518 **Immigration lawyers added:** Ibid.

519 **His legal team finally:** *Rodriguez v. Robbins,* Nos. 13-56706, 13-56755 (9th Cir. Oct. 28, 2015), 56–57.

519 **And they are entitled:** Ibid.

519 **When *Jennings v. Rodriguez:*** Lauren Etter, "Record Number of Undocumented Immigrants Being Detained in U.S.," Bloomberg, Nov. 10, 2016.

519 **Given Trump's stance:** Breyer noted, "We're dealing with tens of thousands, hundreds of thousands or millions of people, possibly." Transcript of Oral Argument at 56, *Jennings v. Rodriguez,* No. 15-01204.

520 **"one size fits all":** Ibid. at 4.

520 **"we can't just write":** Ibid. at 62.

520 **"It seems to me":** Ibid. at 59.

520 **Rodriguez's ACLU lawyer:** Respondents' Brief; Amicus Brief of the American Bar Association; Amicus Brief of National Association of Criminal Defense Lawyers et al., ibid.

520 **"We need only recall":** *Jennings v. Rodriguez,* 583 U.S. ___ (2018), 32 (Breyer dissenting).

521 **Although she did not provide:** *Miller v. Albright,* 523 U.S. 420 (1998) at 460 (RBG dissenting); *Nguyen v. INS,* 533 U.S. 53 (2001), 74 (O'Connor dissenting); Transcript of Oral Argument, *Flores-Villar v. United States,* 564 U.S. ___ (2011).

521 **Hence the statute violated:** *Sessions v. Morales-Santana,* 582 U.S. ___ (2017), 4–6 (RBG majority).

522 **He therefore failed:** Ibid.

522 **"in order to have assimilated":** *Morales-Santana v. Lynch,* No. 11-1252 (2d Cir. July 8, 2015), 24.

522 **Ruling that José Morales:** Ibid. at 41.

522 **"have a demonstrated and sufficient":** Transcript of Oral Argument at 3–4, *Morales-Santana,* 582 U.S. ___.

522 **"sometime after the child":** Ibid. at 7–17.

523 **His client's father's rights:** Ibid. at 27.

523 **Turning to remedies:** Ibid., 33–47.

523 **Ginsburg's repeated interventions:** Ibid., 40–48.

523 **"that unwed fathers care":** Ibid. at 18–19 (RBG majority).

524 **"the same genre":** Ibid. at 9, 21–22.

525 **"settle on a uniform":** Ibid. at 28.

525 **"unnecessary," given the remedial:** Ibid. at 1 (Thomas dissenting).

525 **They turned down appeals:** Adam Liptak, "A Cautious Supreme Court Sets a Modern Record for Consensus," *New York Times,* June 27, 2017.

525 **Yet racial discrimination:** See *Buck v. Davis,* 580 U.S. ___ (2017), and *Peña Rodriguez v. Colorado,* 580 U.S. ___ (2017).

525 **Even Thomas joined:** *Cooper v. Harris,* 581 U.S. ___ (2017).

525 **In a majority opinion:** *Moore v. Texas,* 581 U.S. ___ (2017).

525 **It also made the outcome:** See, for example, Abby Phillip, Thomas Gibbons-Neff, and Dan Lamothe, "Trump Announces Ban on Transgender People in U.S. Military," *Washington Post,* July 26, 2017; Julie Hirschfeld Davis and Maggie Haberman, "Trump Pardons Exsheriff Seen as Migrant Foe," *New York Times,* Aug. 26, 2017, A1; and Michael D. Shear and Julie Hirschfeld Davis, "Trump Moves to End DACA and Calls on Congress to Act," *New York Times,* Sept. 5, 2017.

525 **By immunizing high-level:** See Cole, "How Far Will the Court Go?" I have followed Cole's wording closely.

525 **Upcoming cases involved clashes:** Amy Howe, "Argument Analysis: Six-Justice Court Sympathetic to Government in Detainee Case," *SCOTUSblog*, Jan. 18, 2017.

526 **"The outcome of cases":** *Masterpiece Cakeshop, Ltd. v. Colorado Civil Rights Comm'n,* 584 U.S. ___ (2018), 18 (Kennedy majority).

526 **"When a couple contacts":** *Masterpiece Cakeshop, Ltd. v. Colorado Civil Rights Comm'n,* 584 U.S. ___ (2018), 5 (Ginsburg dissenting).

526 **Such cases were considered:** *Vieth v. Jubelirer,* 541 U.S. 267 (2004).

526 **The district court had struck:** Nicholas O. Stephanopoulos and Eric McGhee applied a mathematical model to the Republican plan by calculating the difference in "wasted" votes between the two parties, then dividing that result by the total number of votes cast to obtain an "efficiency gap." Votes were deemed wasted as the result of "packing" and "cracking." For example, packing occurs when a significant number of one party's voters are consolidated into a single district, thereby wasting each vote beyond the bare minimum required to select that party's candidate. In contrast, cracking spreads those same voters over several districts that have small majorities of the opposing party, which waste each vote cast by the minority party. According to the study, there would be no gap in the nonpartisan environment. In 2012 and 2014, Wisconsin realized gaps of 13.3 percent and 9.6 percent. Wisconsin voters challenging the redistricting argue that any gap that exceeds 7 percent violates the Constitution, while critics of the suit argue that that number is arbitrary. There is no indication, however, that the Supreme Court would accept the formula or its interpretations. See Adam Liptak, "When Does Gerrymandering Cross a Line?," *New York Times,* May 16, 2017, A18.

526 **"perhaps the most important":** The case deals with "extreme political gerrymandering" where the party in control receives lopsided advantages by drawing voting districts that heavily favor their own candidates. See Vann R. Newkirk II, "The Supreme Court Takes on Partisan Gerrymandering," *Atlantic,* June 19, 2017, and Adam Liptak, "Sweeping Docket Awaits a Full-Strength Court," *New York Times,* Oct. 2, 2017, A1.

527 **The World Justice Forum:** RBG, interview by author, Santa Fe, New Mexico, Aug. 25, 2017.

527 **Her summer agenda was packed:** Ibid.

EPILOGUE · Legacy

530 **"Ruth Bader Ginsburg Is My Homegirl":** See, for example, "I ♥ Ruth Bader Ginsburg" T-shirts, www.zazzle.com, and Shana Knizhnik, Notorious R.B.G., notorious rbg.tumblr.com.

530 **"19 Reasons Why Ruth":** Jamison Doran, "19 Reasons Why Ruth Bader Ginsburg Is Your Favorite Supreme Court Justice," *BuzzFeed,* July 30, 2013.

530 **Many parents happily read:** Levy and Baddeley, *I Dissent,* and Winter and Innerst, *Ruth Bader Ginsburg.*

530 **The standing ovations:** Paige Lavender, "This Student's Contribution to Ruth Bader Ginsburg's Collar Collection Did Not Go Unnoticed," *HuffPost,* Dec. 6, 2017; Melena Ryzik, "The Supreme Court's Ninja Warrior," *New York Times,* May 12, 2018, AR26.

531 **"We are a nation made strong":** Liz Robbins, "Ignoring Contentiousness, Justice Ginsburg Celebrates New Citizens," *New York Times,* April 20, 2018, A23.

531 **Creating one of the first:** Davidson, RBG, and Kay, *Text, Cases, and Materials on Sex-Based Discrimination.*

532 **"against the patriarchal power":** RBG, "Speaking in a Judicial Voice," *New York University Law Review* 67 (1992): 1188.

532 **That phase of her career:** Charlotte Alter, "Here Are 11 Influential Women You Should Know," *Time,* April 16, 2015.

532 **"exceedingly persuasive justification":** *United States v. Virginia,* 518 U.S. 515 (1996), 1 (RBG majority).

533　**"inherent differences":** Ibid. at 533 (RBG majority).

533　**That same premise had been:** *Gonzales v. Carhart,* 550 U.S. 124 (2007).

533　**"comprehensive income protection":** RBG, "Gender and the Constitution."

533　**"period of ongoing":** Reva B. Siegel, "You've Come a Long Way, Baby," 1871–989.

534　**That process remains ongoing:** Some distressing current studies indicate not only the persistence of the breadwinning male norm but that men who deviate from it by taking family leave incur backlash from women as well as other men. See Joan C. Williams, "Beyond the Tough Guise: Ruth Bader Ginsburg's Reconstruction Feminism," in Dodson, *Legacy of Ruth Bader Ginsburg,* esp. 67–70.

534　**Ironically, Silicon Valley:** Liz Mundy, "Why Is Silicon Valley So Awful to Women?," *Atlantic,* April 2017.

534　**Her pursuit of equality:** The only group not mentioned in various cases previously discussed are the disabled. See Samuel R. Bagenstos, "Justice Ginsburg and the Judicial Role in Expanding 'We the People': The Disability Rights Cases," *Columbia Law Review* 104 (Jan. 2004): 49–59.

534　**"equal citizenship stature":** Neil S. Siegel, "Equal Citizenship Stature," 799–855.

534　**The plight of the Mississippi mother:** *M.L.B. v. S.L.J.,* 519 U.S. 102 (1996).

534　**In other cases, she:** *Kowalski v. Tesmer,* 543 U.S. 125 (2004) (RBG dissenting).

534　**"the less well off":** "Transcript of President's Announcement and Judge Ginsburg's Remarks."

534　**Rather, as in her dissent:** *Connick v. Thompson,* 563 U.S. ___ (2011) (RBG dissenting).

535　**"federalism five's":** John Q. Barrett, "The 'Federalism Five' as Supreme Court Nominees, 1971–1991," *St. John's Journal of Legal Commentary* 21 (2007): 485–96.

535　**"without even acknowledging":** *Shelby County v. Holder,* 570 U.S. ___ (2013), 23–24 (RBG dissenting).

535　**"to attempt to engage":** Ibid.

536　**"err[ed] egregiously":** Ibid. at 37.

536　**"Hubris," she wrote:** Ibid. at 30.

536　**Yet her treatment:** See also her discussion of the commerce clause in *National Federation of Independent Business v. Sebelius* (2012), which upheld the Affordable Care Act.

536　**"cannot be called a liberal":** Berke, "Clinton Names Ruth Ginsburg, Advocate for Women, to Court."

536　**She is an optimist:** Here I fully agreed with Scott Dodson. See his "Coda: Ginsburg, Optimism, and Conflict Management," in Dodson, *Legacy of Ruth Bader Ginsburg,* 233–36.

537　**partisan gerrymandering:** *Abbott v. Perez,* 585 U. S. ____ (2018); *Benisek v. Lamone,* 585 U. S. ____ (2018); *Gill v. Whitford,* 585 U.S. ___ (2018); *North Carolina v. Covington,* 585 U.S. ___ (2018).

537　**"crisis pregnancy" centers:** *Epic Systems Corp. v. Lewis,* 584 U.S. ___ (2018) and *National Institute of Family and Life Advocates v. Becerra,* 585 U.S. ___ (2018).

537　**"crisis center":** *Janus v. State, County, and Municipal Employees,* 585 U.S. ___ (2018), 26 (Kagan dissenting). In her dissent to the Janus decision, Justice Kagan insisted that the majority was "weaponizing the First Amendment" by justifying conservative interpretations of the law. This ruling, she argues, ends healthy, democratic debates among state and local governments regarding fair-share arrangements currently in place. Instead, the majority has declared its winner, "turning the First Amendment into a sword" to use against "workaday economic and regulatory policy." See also Adam Liptak, "How Free Speech Was Weaponized by Conservatives," *New York Times,* June 29, 2018, A1. On the frequency which the Roberts Court rules for conservative speech rather than free speech, see Lee Epstein, Andrew D. Martin, and Kevin Quinn, "6+ Decades of Freedom of Expression in the U.S. Supreme Court," June 30, 2018. Available at http://

epstein.wustl.edu/. On efforts of the National Right to Work Committee and like-minded organizations to move from the political fringes to the law of the land, see Moshe Z. Marvit, "For 60 Years, This Powerful Conservative Group Has Worked to Crush Labor," *Nation,* July 5, 2018.

537 **accept as "plausible":** *Trump v. Hawaii,* 585 U.S. ___ (2018).

537 **"in fact an abdication":** David Cole, "The Supreme Court Looks Away," *New York Review of Books Daily,* July 2, 2018.

537 **Sotomayer and Ginsburg jointly issued:** *Trump v. Hawaii,* 585 U.S. ___ (2018) (Sotomayor dissenting). RBG joined the dissent.

537 **The term as a whole:** For further development of this point, see Stephen E. Gottlieb, *Unfit for Democracy: The Roberts Court and the Breakdown of American Democracy* (New York: New York University Press, 2018).

537 **Then on June 27, 2018:** Michael D. Shear, "Trump Set to Tilt Court as Kennedy Retires," *New York Times,* June 27, 2018, A1; Robert Barnes, Justice Kennedy, the pivotal swing vote on the Supreme Court, announces retirement," *Washington Post,* June 27, 2018.

538 **"a great man of outstanding":** Adam Liptak and Maggie Haberman, "Behind Scenes, Urging Justice to Move Aside," *New York Times,* June 27, 2018, A1.

538 **The White House also singled:** Michael D. Shear and Maggie Habberman, "Trump Meets Four Finalists for Court Seat," *New York Times,* July 2, 2018, A1.

538 **"Do it yesterday":** Grassley quotes in ibid.; see also Michael D. Shear, "Trump Set to Tilt Court as Kennedy Retires," *New York Times,* June 27, 2018, A1.

538 **For Democrats, still seething:** On how Garland would likely have voted, see the remarks of those interviewed by Liptak and Parlapiano, "Foundation Was in Place." On the political implications of a Court vacancy, see also Carl Hulse, "Confirmation Fight Adds to a Volatile Year," *New York Times,* June 27, 2018, A15; Jonathan Martin, Jeremy W. Peters, and Elizabeth Dias, "Confirmation Quickly Becomes Fresh Inflammatory Issue for Midterm," *New York Times,* June 27, 2018, A17; Michael D. Shear and Thomas Kaplan, "Court Vacancy in Election Year Jolts the Parties," *New York Times,* June 28, 2018, A1.

538 **Not only could individual:** Noah Feldman, "Tipping the Scales," *New York Review of Books,* July 19, 2018.

538 **For Republicans, traditionally:** Peter Baker, "A Three-Decade Dream for Conservatives Is in Reach," *New York Times,* July 10, 2018, A1. On the impact of the Kennedy's resignation from the perspective of liberals and conservatives respectively, see, for example, Jeffrey Toobin, "How Trump's Supreme Court Pick Could Undo Kennedy's Legacy, *The New Yorker,* July 9/16, 2018, and David French, "Justice Kennedy Retires, and the Legal and Political Ramifications Are Immense," *National Review,* June 27, 2018.

539 **An originalist with a sharp:** Adam Liptak, "Moderating Force as Lawyer, a Conservative Stalwart as Judge," *New York Times,* July 10, 2018, A1; Brett Kavanaugh's Pro-Democracy, Let-the-People-Govern-Themselves Vision," *Washington Post,* July 10, 2018; Philip Bump, "How Brett Kavanaugh Would Shift the Supreme Court to the Right," *Washington Post,* July 10, 2018; Jacob Gershman, "Brett Kavanaugh Has Shown Deep Skepticism of Regulatory State," *Wall Street Journal,* July 9, 1018.

539 **By 2019, it was predicted:** Hugh Hewitt, "Trump's Massive Impact on the Federal Bench," *Washington Post,* May 22, 2018.

540 **"Law is about justice":** Sam Sokol, "In Jerusalem, Ruth Bader Ginsburg celebrates her commitments to *tikkun olam*," *Cleveland Jewish News,* July 5, 2018. Available at www.clevelandjewishnews.com.

540 **Only after the foundation:** Ibid.

540 **"your equality is a fundamental":** Ibid.

Bibliography

A Note on Sources

The archival materials needed to complete this project were obtained from a wide variety of sources, beginning with the ACLU File, 1967–80, the Speeches and Writings File, which documents Ginsburg's endeavors to promote women's rights. The Miscellany File constitutes Part I of the Ruth Bader Ginsburg Papers located in the Manuscript Division of the Library of Congress, from which the case files especially proved indispensable. Ginsburg's personal papers have subsequently been added to the collection, though they are not yet open to the public. Neither is material pertaining to the years 1979–92, when she served as judge on the U.S. Court of Appeals for the D.C. Circuit. Papers from her tenure as associate justice of the Supreme Court (1993–) will not be available to researchers until a hundred years after the last justice with whom she has served is no longer alive.

Justice Ginsburg graciously provided me with access to transcripts of three extensive interviews not yet accessible to the public. The first, conducted by Maeva Marcus (Supreme Court historian), was recorded for the Court in 1995; the second, done by Ronald J. Grele for the Columbia University Oral History Project, was completed in 2004; the third, conducted for Sarah Wilson in 1995, resides at the Federal Judicial Center. Although there is some overlap, these three interviews cover different aspects of Ginsburg's life and work prior to her move to the Supreme Court. Wilson's interview for the Federal Judicial Center concentrates primarily on Ginsburg's nomination to and early service on the U.S. Court of Appeals for the D.C. Circuit.

These interviews, plus my own with the justice, as well as members of her immediate family, her law school classmates, her former colleagues at Rutgers Law School in Newark, her ACLU associates, her former law students at Columbia, and her clerks at the U.S. Court of Appeals for the D.C. Circuit helped provide key material for the earlier sections of this book, along with the ACLU case files and related material. So, too, did "The Birthday Book," a collection of letters solicited by her clerks from friends for her fiftieth birthday celebration. Each letter begins, "When I think of Ruth Bader Ginsburg . . ." Collectively, they provided choice bits of information that I would not otherwise have obtained.

The late judge Richard Salzman offered recollections of his schoolmate Kiki Bader, including her early writing in their elementary school newspaper that his mother had saved. My account of Ginsburg's college experience was enriched by interviews and correspondence with friends from her freshman year at Cornell and by material at the Cornell University Library. Her intense interest in the impact of McCarthyism on civil liberties was fostered by research she undertook for one of her professors and also by the experience of two faculty members who were targeted by anti-Communists. The ordeal of those two scientists was closely followed in *The Cornell Daily Sun*, the student newspaper. An undergraduate thesis written under the direction of the late historian Michael Kammen by Michael Ullmann—titled "Caught in a Crossfire: Deane Malott and Cornell During the McCarthy Era"—provided superb insight into the pressures brought to bear on Cornell's president Malott. It also highlighted how Malott's own conservative leanings affected his handling of the crisis. Ellen Schrecker's finely researched history of the age of McCarthyism *Many Are the Crimes* superbly contextualizes events at Cornell.

In writing about Ginsburg's legal education, I found the work of Neil Duxbury, William N. Eskridge Jr., Philip Frickey, and Laura Kalman especially helpful. Collectively, the work of these legal scholars substantially informed my understanding of jurisprudence, especially legal realism and, more important, process theory, which reigned during Ginsburg's years in law school.

Interviews with the late Hans Smit of Columbia Law School provided a wonderful portrait of the justice as a young lawyer at work on the Columbia Law School's Project on International Procedure. Eva Hanks offered a highly perceptive account of their experience together as faculty members at Rutgers Law School in Newark, New Jersey. The William J. McGill Papers at Columbia University's Presidential Archive reveals interesting correspondence between McGill and Ginsburg as she offered McGill astute but unsought advice on how to respond to the gender wars then raging on the Columbia campus.

That Ginsburg had already become part of legal feminists' efforts to reshape federal statutes and constitutional jurisprudence, and the legal profession itself, is evident from the papers of Dorothy Kenyon at Smith College as well as the papers of Catherine East, Mary Eastwood, and most especially Pauli Murray at the Schlesinger Library at Harvard University. Studies fleshing out this effort include Fred Strebeigh's compelling account *Equal.* Serena Mayeri's prizewinning *Reasoning from Race,* Linda Greenhouse and Reva B. Siegel's *Before Roe v. Wade,* and David Garrow's voluminously detailed *Liberty and Sexuality: The Right to Privacy and the Making of Roe v. Wade* all proved essential. Rosalind Rosenberg's newly published biography of Pauli Murray, *Jane Crow,* belongs on this list.

In writing about the ACLU years, I found useful Austin Sarat and Stuart Scheingold's articulation of "cause lawyering as a protean and heterogeneous enterprise that continues to reinvent itself in confrontation with a vast array of challenges." Steven M. Teles and Ann Southworth also enhanced my familiarity with the conservative legal movement's counterthrust.

Of varying usefulness are the papers of justices before whom Ginsburg argued her cases. Justices William Brennan, William O. Douglas, Thurgood Marshall, and Harry A. Blackmun deposited their papers in the Manuscript Division of the Library of Congress. Those of Justice Lewis F. Powell reside at the Law School of Washington and Lee University. Biographies of each of the justices help understand how they responded to Ginsburg's litigation, most notably Linda Greenhouse's *Becoming Justice Blackmun.*

Ginsburg's transition from advocate to judge and justice draws on interviews with Barbara Babcock, Sarah Weddington, and Patricia Wald, all of whom served in the Carter administration. Babcock and Weddington helped illuminate resistance within the Justice Department to Ginsburg's eventual nomination to the U.S. Court of Appeals for the D.C. Circuit. Judge Wald, Professors Michael Klarman and Deborah Jones Merritt (both former clerks), and the Washington attorney Alan B. Morrison provided useful perspectives on Ginsburg's years as a federal judge.

The Clinton Papers at the president's library in Little Rock proved invaluable for understanding the vetting of top candidates for Justice Byron White's seat on the Court as well as the advice that Clinton received. Included in the Clinton Papers are letters supporting and a few opposing Ginsburg's candidacy. The Daniel P. Moynihan Papers in the Library of Congress's Manuscript Division attest to the powerful New York senator's role in securing the nomination for Ginsburg. Both press accounts and my own interviews with the justice reveal the considerable efforts of Martin D. Ginsburg on his wife's behalf. So, too, does Robert Katzmann's essay "Reflections on the Confirmation Journey of Ruth Bader Ginsburg, Summer, 1993," in Scott Dodson's *Legacy of Ruth Bader Ginsburg.*

My understanding of the rights revolution, selection of federal judges, the Supreme Court nomination process, the influence of oral argument, the evolving role of clerks, judicial behavior, strategy and constraints, the interplay of social movements, politics, and constitutional change, and popular constitutionalism has been shaped by political scientists and legal scholars. Among the political scientists are Charles R. Epp, Lee Epstein, Lawrence Baum, Michael A. Bailey, Forrest Maltzman, James F. Spriggs II, Paul J. Wahlbeck, Sheldon Goldman, Saul Brenner, Sally Kenney, Nancy Maveety, Jeffrey A. Segal, Howard Gillman, and Richard Davis. A number of distinguished legal scholars whose work has furthered my education include Lucas Powe, Laurence Tribe, Mark Tushnet, Robert Post, Kenneth Karst, Cass Sunstein, Richard Posner, Jack Balkin, Barry Friedman, Michael Klarman, and Kenji Yoshino.

The work of feminist legal scholars has been absolutely indispensable, especially that of Reva Siegel. It was Siegel who first alerted me to how rights, seemingly achieved, have been repeatedly undercut and transformed. Herma Hill Kay, Catharine A. MacKinnon, Sylvia Law, Elizabeth M. Schneider, the late Rhonda Copelon, Kimberlé Crenshaw, Katharine Bartlett, Mary Anne Case, Lani Guinier, Martha Minow, Nina Pillard (now judge Cornelia T. L. Pillard), Neil S. Siegel, Joan C. Williams, Martha Chamallas, Deborah L. Rhode, Cynthia Grant Bowman, Serena Mayeri, Kristin Collins, Cary Franklin, and Linda Kerber all contributed to my understanding of aspects of Ginsburg's work as law professor, advocate, judge, and justice.

I have also benefited greatly from the work of legal journalists, specifically the books, columns, and reports of Linda Greenhouse, Jeffrey Toobin, Adam Liptak, David Cole, Jeffrey Rosen, Joan Biskupic, Marcia Coyle, Jan Crawford Greenburg, Robert Barnes, David Savage, Nina Totenberg, Dahlia Lithwick, Tony Mauro, and Lyle Denniston. Among the many journalists upon whose work I relied are David Von Drehle, Lesley Oelsner, David Margolick, Jim Rutenberg, Michael Tomasky, Emily Bazelon, Ari Berman, Amy Davidson, Elizabeth Drew, and Matt Flegenheimer.

Ginsburg has written extensively about her ACLU cases, the ERA, affirmative action for women, and related matters in legal journals, especially during the 1970s. Her recently published collection of writings, *My Own Words,* ably introduced by the editors Mary Hartnett and Wendy Williams, includes selections that vary from school newspaper editorials to bench remarks on recent cases.

Other books with helpful portions on Ginsburg's early career include Janis M. Berry et al., *Women Lawyers at Work,* Lynn Gilbert and Gaylen Moore, *Particular Passions,* and Rosalind Rosenberg, *Changing the Subject.* Amy Leigh Campbell's *Raising the Bar* chronicles the ACLU years. Irin Carmon and Shana Knizhnik's *Notorious RBG: The Life and Times of Ruth Bader Ginsburg* is a lighthearted, wonderfully illustrated account of the justice and her emergence as a celebrity among millennials. Linda Hirshman's *Sisters in Law,* a dual biography of Sandra Day O'Connor and Ginsburg, offers a compelling account of how these very different women complemented each other in advancing gender equality on the Court. Scott Dodson's *Legacy of Ruth Bader Ginsburg* offers valuable and diverse perspectives from scholars and court watchers on various periods in Ginsburg's life and the array of doctrinal areas on which she exerted influence over the course of her long career.

In writing about cases in which Ginsburg participated as lawyer, advocate, judge, or justice, I have relied on the abundant literature produced by historians and social scientists for background material. Nowhere was this literature more valuable than in my chapters on race and on sexuality, as endnotes indicate. Cases figuring prominently in the book are listed below.

Case Summaries

Hoyt v. Florida, 368 U.S. 57 (1961). Florida automatically registered men for jury service, but women were excluded unless they volunteered. Gwendolyn Hoyt, believing that women should be obliged to serve on juries if she was to be fairly judged by a jury of her peers, appealed her conviction by an all-male jury and lost in the lower courts. The Supreme Court unanimously upheld the Florida law on the grounds that there was no evidence that the state had arbitrarily acted to exclude women from the jury pool. Ginsburg, also believing that women no less than men should be obliged to serve on juries, considered *Hoyt* a precedent in need of overturning, which occurred in 1975 in *Taylor v. Louisiana* (see below), when the Court held that a defendant has the right to a jury that is representative of the community.

Reed v. Reed, 404 U.S. 71 (1971). The Idaho Code specified a preference for male appointees to act as estate administrators. Sally Reed challenged the law, and the Supreme Court, for the first time in its history, struck down the statute as unconstitutional sex-based discrimination. Ginsburg wrote the appellant brief for Sally Reed in the summer of 1971, building on the brief for *Moritz* written just a few months earlier.

Moritz v. Commissioner of Internal Revenue, 469 F.2d 466 (10th Cir. 1972). The IRS granted a tax deduction to never-married, employed daughters for nursing expenses related to care of an elderly parent, but the agency rejected Charles E. Moritz's claim to a deduction for the care of his mother. When Moritz lost his challenge to the Tax Court's ruling, Ginsburg and her husband, Martin D. Ginsburg, took the case in order to test whether the federal court would consider discrimination based on sex as a violation of the Fourteenth Amendment's equal protection clause. The U.S. Court of Appeals for the Tenth Circuit ruled that Moritz was entitled to the deduction, endorsing the Ginsburgs' argument.

Struck v. Secretary of Defense, 409 U.S. 1071 (1972). A U.S. Air Force regulation mandated the dismissal of a pregnant woman unless she opted for an abortion, while her male partner could remain in the military and receive bonuses for reenlisting. Captain Susan Struck, an unmarried Roman Catholic, chose to carry her pregnancy to term and to surrender the baby for adoption while on leave. Having had the baby, she ran afoul of another regulation that denied readmission to the air force to a female service member who had given birth. Appealing the regulations to the Court with a powerful brief written by Ginsburg, Struck was granted a waiver allowing her to resume her career before the case was heard but assuring its dismissal and a change in air force regulations.

Roe v. Wade, 410 U.S. 113 (1973); *Doe v. Bolton,* 410 U.S. 179 (1973). A Texas ban on abortions except for the purpose of saving the woman's life and Georgia's unduly burdensome qualifications for obtaining an abortion were both challenged. In a landmark decision, the Court struck down the Texas and Georgia statutes as improperly interfering with the right of a woman to choose to terminate her pregnancy, violating her right to privacy and her personal liberty as guaranteed by the due process clause of the Fourteenth Amendment (the right to be left alone); however, it placed limits on the exercise of that right, particularly balancing the state's interest in protecting the health of pregnant women along with "the potentiality of human life."

Frontiero v. Richardson, 411 U.S. 677 (1973). A federal statute stipulated that male officers in the U.S. Air Force automatically received spousal benefits for their wives but that a female officer must demonstrate that she was contributing more than half of her husband's living expenses. Sharron Frontiero challenged the statute as a violation of the due process clause of the Fifth Amendment and the equal protection clause of the Fourteenth Amendment. The Court voided sex differentiation in the distribution of spousal benefits but differed as to whether sex ought to be treated as a suspect category as Ginsburg urged in her brief and oral argument.

DeFunis v. Odegaard, 416 U.S. 312 (1974). Admissions procedures for the University of Washington Law School provided that minority applicants be considered without regard to their individual grades or scores. Marco DeFunis sued, claiming that the school's affirmative-action policy gave preference to minority applicants over white candidates who were better qualified. It was a reverse discrimination case, which the Court determined to be moot because DeFunis had been provisionally admitted to the university as the case moved through the courts and he was scheduled to graduate within months of the time the decision was rendered.

Kahn v. Shevin, 416 U.S. 351 (1974). Florida law provided a property tax exemption of up to $500 for widows irrespective of need—but not for widowers. Mel Kahn challenged the law as an unfair sex-based distinction, but the Supreme Court upheld the distinction as valid because women were more likely to suffer economically after the loss of a spouse than men. Ginsburg, knowing that the justices were not yet ready to hear a reverse discrimination case, reluctantly agreed to represent Kahn, suffering her only loss as litigator for the ACLU Women's Rights Project.

Weinberger v. Wiesenfeld, 420 U.S. 636 (1975). The Social Security Administration (SSA) paid survivors' benefits only to widowed mothers entrusted with the care of a child but not to widowers. Stephen Wiesenfeld was denied Social Security survivors' benefits after his wife, Paula, died during childbirth and he assumed full care of his son. Wiesenfeld then challenged the SSA provision as a violation of equal protection. The Court ruled in his favor, requiring the survivors' benefits for the care of dependent children be sex neutral. Ginsburg argued the case for Wiesenfeld both in the lower courts and in the Supreme Court.

Taylor v. Louisiana, 419 U.S. 522 (1975); *Edwards v. Healy,* 421 U.S. 772 (1975). Both cases challenged the composition of all-male juries in Louisiana. While an amendment to the state's constitution rendered *Healy* moot (Ginsburg's case, which she had won in the lower court), the Court decided that Billy Taylor had been denied his right to a jury consistent with a cross section of his peers. The decision had taken Ginsburg's arguments in *Healy* into account, specifically that men and women experienced life differently. The presence of both sexes on the juries, therefore, was required in order to more accurately reflect these varying perceptions.

Craig v. Boren, 429 U.S. 190 (1976). An Oklahoma statute permitting women to drink "near beer" at the age of eighteen while men were required to wait until age twenty-one was challenged as discriminatory by the Oklahoma State student Curtis Craig and by Carolyn Whitener, co-owner of a convenience store. The Court ruled that Oklahoma's use of sex-based classifications for administrative purposes violated the equal protection clause in the Fourteenth Amendment. What made the case significant was the Court's creation of an intermediate standard of scrutiny that required supporters of the challenged statute to demonstrate that sex-based differentiation is *substantially* related to an important government objective. Ginsburg wrote an amicus brief and provided extensive aid and oversight to the plaintiff's lawyer in the writing of his brief.

Califano v. Goldfarb, 430 U.S. 199 (1977). The SSA required that widowers prove that a deceased wife had supplied three-fourths of the family income, while widows received benefits automatically. Seventy-year-old Leon Goldfarb challenged the requirement after the death of his wife, Hannah, who had been fully employed. The Court ruled that different treatment of widows and widowers constituted invidious discrimination against women who had earned more than their surviving male partners. Ginsburg represented Goldfarb on his appeal to the Court, emphasizing the significance of Hannah's earnings.

Califano v. Webster, 430 U.S. 313 (1977). When calculating retiree benefits, the Social Security Act allowed different formulas for calculating a retired male wage earner's average monthly wage compared with a similarly situated female wage earner as a means of rectifying women's unequal pay. William Webster challenged the provision upon his own retirement. The Court in a per curiam decision ruled that Social Security benefit calculations that were more favorable toward retired female workers constituted constitutionally permissible differential treatment in the interests of gender equality.

University of California Board of Regents v. Bakke, 438 U.S. 265 (1978). The University of California, Davis Medical School set aside 16 percent of its admissions slots for under-represented minority applicants. Allan Bakke, his application twice rejected, sued the university claiming reverse discrimination after outscoring all of the "disadvantaged" applicants. Nine justices issued six separate opinions for a deeply fractured Court, ruling that while universities may continue to use race as a criterion in admissions, they could not constitutionally use numerical quotas.

United States v. Virginia, 518 U.S. 515 (1996). Since its inception in 1839, the Virginia Military Institute had had an all-male student body. After a female high school graduate filed a complaint with the Office of Civil Rights at the Justice Department, the college filed suit to prevent the federally imposed admission of women. Upon appeal from the lower courts, the Court found the exclusion of women at a publicly funded institution to be unconstitutional. Ginsburg's opinion for the 7–1 majority stated that institutions seeking to continue differential treatment or denial of opportunity must provide "exceedingly persuasive" justification that would survive "skeptical scrutiny."

United States v. Morrison, 529 U.S. 598 (2000). The Violence Against Women Act of 1994 (VAWA) provided federal funds for investigating and prosecuting violent crimes against women and instituted mandatory restitution from those convicted of a crime of violence motivated by an "animus based on the victim's gender." It also allowed civil suits on the part of victims in cases that were left unprosecuted. Christy Brzonkala filed a civil suit against her assailants Antonio Morrison and James Crawford under the provisions of VAWA, having failed in the lower court to obtain a conviction. Upon appeal, the Court majority, ignoring data showing the adverse effects of sexual violence on interstate commerce, struck down Section 13981 of the VAWA, claiming that Congress had overstepped its powers under the commerce clause by creating a federal remedy for a problem that had traditionally been viewed as a state issue. Justice Souter was joined in his dissent by Stevens, Ginsburg, and Breyer.

Bush v. Gore, 531 U.S. 98 (2000). Poorly constructed ballots were the focal point of an exchange of lawsuits involving the presidential candidates George W. Bush and Al Gore in which the Florida vote would prove decisive. Gore asked for a manual recount in four counties instead of throughout Florida, while Bush wanted the current tallies certified. After the Florida Supreme Court authorized the recount and extended the state-mandated deadline, attorneys for Bush appealed to the Supreme Court. They argued, first, that the Florida Supreme Court had violated the federal Constitution by usurping the state legislature's role in the selection of electors. Second, the Bush coalition maintained that the manual recount violated the due process and equal protection clauses because it was an "arbitrary and disparate treatment" of a ballot already cast. The record suggested that inconsistent standards of counting ballots in the various precincts and counties violated Bush's right to equal protection, as well as the rights of the voters. The Court focused on the latter topic, issuing a per curiam decision stating that the decision of the Florida Supreme Court did "not satisfy the minimum requirements for nonarbitrary treatment of voters." Breyer, Ginsburg, Souter, and Stevens wrote separate dissents.

Stenberg v. Carhart, 530 U.S. 914 (2000). A partial-birth abortion is a surgical procedure that removes an intact fetus from the uterus in a late-term abortion because it is considered less likely to damage a woman's cervix than a dismembering of the fetus. A Nebraska law banned partial-birth abortions with no consideration for the health of the pregnant woman and subjected state physicians performing the procedure to revocation of their licenses. Dr. LeRoy Carhart challenged the ban's constitutionality, claiming that the law was vague and placed an undue burden on women seeking abortions as well as physicians such as himself. The Court struck down the ban because it placed an undue burden on a woman's right to make a decision to abort and did not allow an exception for her health.

Nguyen v. INS, 533 U.S. 53 (2001). U.S. immigration law automatically granted citizenship to a child born abroad out of wedlock to an American mother and an alien father, while a child born to an American father and an alien mother had to meet more complex requirements. The additional prerequisites were based on the premise that the birth mother is more likely than the father to establish the required relationship with the child needed to grant citizenship. The Immigration and Naturalization Service had begun deportation proceedings against Tuan Anh Nguyen after he pleaded guilty to two counts of sexual assault on a child. Nguyen, having been abandoned after birth by his Vietnamese mother and reared by his American father, had failed to apply for U.S. citizenship by age eighteen as required, but challenged the sex-based classifications as an equal protection violation nonetheless. The Court upheld the differentiation, stating that the discriminatory means employed aided the achievement of an important governmental objective—assuring the biological connection between the child and the citizen parent. Ginsburg, Breyer, and Souter joined O'Connor's dissent, which argued that the government had not shown "exceedingly persuasive justification" for the different classifications nor had it established how those classifications related to the achievement of important governmental objectives of parental bonding with the citizen parent.

Gratz v. Bollinger, 539 U.S. 244 (2003). For undergraduate admission to the College of Literature, Science, and the Arts, the University of Michigan used a set of scores based on a variety of measures with certain points assigned for underrepresented minority students. Jennifer Gratz and Patrick Hamacher filed suit, claiming reverse discrimination. Rehnquist's opinion for the 6–3 majority held that the admissions policy was not sufficiently narrowly tailored to meet the strict scrutiny standard. In her dissent, Ginsburg countered that equal protection required permitting government decision makers to distinguish between exclusionary and inclusionary policies—actions intended to deny participation and measures to counter the effects of past discrimination.

Grutter v. Bollinger, 539 U.S. 306 (2003). The University of Michigan Law School sought to ensure a "critical mass" of underrepresented minority students to contribute to a "diverse and academically outstanding" student body. Although it did not define diversity solely in terms of racial and ethnic status, the university did make specific reference to the inclusion of African American, Hispanic, and Native American students. Barbara Grutter filed suit, claiming that the Law School discriminated against her by using race as a "predominant" factor. In a 5–4 ruling, Ginsburg joined O'Connor's majority opinion, which stated that the university's Law School could maintain its narrowly tailored race-conscious policy because minority status was just one of several factors used in its individual review of each applicant for admission and that a diverse student body promoted "a compelling state interest."

Nevada Department of Human Resources v. Hibbs, 538 U.S. 721 (2003). The Family and Medical Leave Act of 1993 (FMLA) granted job protection and unpaid leave for covered family and medical issues. William Hibbs was fired from the Nevada Department of Human Resources after he refused to return to work on the date indicated, believing he still had time remaining on his FMLA leave to take care of his wife. He subsequently filed suit, claiming his dismissal was a violation of the FMLA. Upon appeal, Nevada—and fourteen other states—argued that the Eleventh Amendment prevented a state from being sued by its own citizens in federal court. Ginsburg sided with the 6–3 majority, ruling that Congress was acting within its power in rescinding immunity given to states against suits, thereby allowing state employees to recover monetary damages for violations of the FMLA.

Hamdi v. Rumsfeld, 542 U.S. 507 (2004). The writ of habeas corpus requires the person or entity detaining another individual to bring that person before a judge to determine whether the incarceration is legally justified. The father of the American-born Yaser Hamdi, who was held at Guantánamo after being accused of fighting with the Taliban, appealed to the Supreme Court for the right of habeas corpus. A four-justice plurality, written by O'Connor, recognized that Congress had expressly authorized the detention of enemy combatants when it had passed the Authorization for Use of Military Force (AUMF) shortly after the terror attacks on September 11, 2001. American citizens, however, still retain the rights of due process. Ginsburg joined Souter's dissent on the first point, insisting that the AUMF did not authorize the detention of Hamdi.

Gonzales v. Carhart, 550 U.S. 124 (2007). The Partial-Birth Abortion Ban Act of 2003 subjected any doctor who performed the procedure to a fine and imprisonment. Dr. LeRoy Carhart and other physicians who performed late-term abortions sued to stop the act from going into effect. By a 5–4 vote, the Court upheld the act, even though it lacked an exemption related to the mother's health, stating that it did not impose an undue burden on the rights of women to obtain an abortion. Ginsburg read her dissent aloud from the bench, calling the decision "alarming" in that it accepts federal attempts to ban an accepted medical procedure and "blesses a prohibition" that lacks an exception for a woman's health.

Ledbetter v. Goodyear Tire & Rubber Co., 550 U.S. 618 (2007). The policy of the Equal Employment Opportunity Commission is that each pay period of uncorrected discrimination is seen as a new incident of discrimination. In 1998, Lilly Ledbetter filed suit against her employer, Goodyear Tire, for sex discrimination related to pay. The majority used a procedural issue—she had not demonstrated Goodyear's discriminatory intent within 180 days of its occurrence—to rule that employers could not be sued for pay discrimination under Title VII of the Civil Rights Act of 1964. Ginsburg in a strong dissent from the bench suggested that legislative action might be necessary because the Court's interpretation had strayed from the act's core purpose. In 2009, Congress passed the Lilly Ledbetter Fair Pay Act allowing prior acts of discrimination to be part of a claim.

Northwest Austin Municipal Utility District No. 1 v. Holder, 557 U.S. 193 (2009). Section 5 of the Voting Rights Act of 1965 (VRA) provided a "preclearance requirement" under which targeted areas with historic patterns of voting discrimination were required to submit any alteration of voting practices to the U.S. attorney general for approval. The district sought an exemption from Section 5 while also arguing that the section was unconstitutional. The Court ruled that the district could apply for an exemption, but it made no ruling on the constitutionality of Section 5. However, Roberts warned in his majority opinion that "the Act imposes current burdens and must be justified under current needs," setting the stage for *Shelby County v. Holder.* All of the other justices, including Ginsburg, joined in the opinion. Clarence Thomas joined in part and dissented in part.

Citizens United v. Federal Election Commission, 558 U.S. 310 (2010). The Bipartisan Campaign Reform Act (BCRA) of 2002 expanded the scope of the Federal Election Campaign Act of 1971, limiting "electioneering communications"—a broadcast, cable, or satellite communication that is distributed for a fee and mentions a specific federal candidate—within thirty days of a primary election. Citizens United sought an injunction against the Federal Election Commission, claiming that the application of the BCRA to its film *Hillary: The Movie* violated the First Amendment. The Court held that corporations and unions have First Amendment rights as do individuals and that the government could not restrict their political expenditures on both electioneering communications and advocacy for or against a particular candidate. They may not, however, contribute directly to any candidate or political party. Ginsburg, Breyer, and Sotomayor joined Stevens in dissent.

Fisher v. University of Texas, 570 U.S. 279 (2013); *Fisher v. University of Texas,* 579 U.S. ___ (2016).* After the Court's 2003 ruling in *Grutter* allowed race to be a factor in admissions to the University of Michigan, the University of Texas modified its admissions process to include admitting African Americans from more privileged socioeconomic backgrounds

---

* Page numbers and Supreme Court citations are assigned only after U.S. Reports has created a printed bound volume. At the time that this manuscript was submitted for publication in May 2018, the most recent release by the Government Printing Office was volume 567, which included cases for the 2011 term. Cases from subsequent volumes typically use three underscores until an official page number has been assigned. Any case citations from these later volumes that include a page number are based upon unofficial reporting and are subject to change with the official volume publication.

to create a greater variety in experience among its black students. Abigail Fisher filed suit after she was denied admission, claiming that the use of race in admissions decisions violated the equal protection clause of the Fourteenth Amendment. Fisher appealed to the Supreme Court, which sent the case back to the lower courts to reconsider. Writing for the seven-member majority, Kennedy stipulated that colleges and universities must conduct "a careful judicial inquiry into whether a university could achieve sufficient diversity *without* using racial classifications." Ginsburg dissented, taking issue with the majority's claim to allow colleges and universities to value racial diversity while also tightening even further the requirements for taking race into account. The case made its way back to the Supreme Court in 2016. In *Fisher II*, a 4–3 majority ruled that while race consciousness played a role in a small number of admissions decisions, the university's policy was narrowly tailored and therefore constitutional.

Shelby County v. Holder, 570 U.S. 2 (2013). Shelby County, Alabama, sought a declaratory judgment that the 2006 renewal of Section 5 and Section 4(b) of the VRA was unconstitutional. It argued that by only applying to a limited number of states, Section 5 violated the equal sovereignty of the states. Section 4, which included a formula devised in 1972 to identify problem areas, imposed an undue burden on the covered states because it did not take "current needs" into consideration. After being denied in the lower courts, Shelby County appealed to the Supreme Court, where a 5–4 majority let Section 5 stand but ruled that Section 4, based on old data, was not constitutional. Ginsburg's powerful dissent took the majority to task for failing to engage with congressional findings on current forms of voting discrimination, for failing to defer to congressional authority in assessing the need for the VRA, and for equating the paucity of enforcement actions under Section 5 with evidence that the act was no longer needed in the designated areas where there was repeated evidence of voter discrimination.

Hollingsworth v. Perry, 570 U.S. ___ (2013). A California ballot initiative, Proposition 8, amended the state constitution to stipulate that "only marriage between a man and a woman is valid or recognized in California." Two same-sex couples filed suit, claiming the amendment violated their right to equal protection and due process based on sexual preference. When the State of California chose not to defend the Proposition 8 change, proponents of the ballot initiative stepped in as defendant-interveners. Losing in the lower courts, they appealed. The Supreme Court in a 5–4 vote ruled that supporters of Proposition 8 did not, in fact, have standing to appeal, effectively allowing same-sex marriages to continue in California.

United States v. Windsor, 570 U.S. ___ (2013). The Defense of Marriage Act (DOMA) defined marriage as a legal union between one man and one woman. Edie Windsor filed suit when the Internal Revenue Service denied her claim to the federal estate tax exemption for surviving spouses following the death of her partner, Thea Spyer. When the case reached the Supreme Court, Kennedy's opinion for the 5–4 majority ruled DOMA to be in violation of the Fifth Amendment because the statute prevented same-sex couples from sharing in the protections given by the federal recognition of marriage.

Burwell v. Hobby Lobby Stores, 573 U.S. ___ (2014). The 1993 Religious Freedom Restoration Act stipulated that the government not impose a "substantial burden" on believers, while a provision in the Affordable Care Act (ACA) required employers' insurance coverage to include various means of contraception. The evangelical owners of the Hobby Lobby craft stores filed suit, arguing that they should not be forced to provide emergency contraception (popularly known as the morning-after pill) or an intrauterine device, which they claimed violated their religious beliefs. The Court ruled that religious freedom protections should be extended to owners of "closely held" corporations. Ginsburg's dissent that for-profit corporations cannot be considered religious entities was joined by Breyer, Kagan, and Sotomayor.

Obergefell v. Hodges, 576 U.S. ___ (2015). Several states, including Ohio, had statutes that banned same-sex marriages and refused to recognize those marriages performed in other states. James Obergefell filed suit after Ohio failed to recognize his marriage to John Arthur, which had taken place in Maryland. Consolidating six cases on appeal, the Court, in a majority opinion written by Kennedy, ruled that the right to marry "is a fundamental right inherent in the liberty of the person. . . . Couples of the same sex may not be deprived of that right and liberty." The Kennedy opinion laid the groundwork for a shift in legal doctrine, rejecting past subordination in favor of "equal dignity" where all individuals share an equal measure of personal autonomy and freedom in defining themselves rather than having that identity defined by the state.

Zubik v. Burwell, 578 U.S. ___ (2016). Similar to *Hobby Lobby, Zubik,* a consolidation of six cases, including that of the Little Sisters of the Poor, pitted religious beliefs against federally mandated health-care requirements. Several religious organizations challenged lower court decisions that upheld the ACA mandate. The groups argued that although an exemption allowed their institutions to opt out, they would still be morally complicit in facilitating a health-care system that provided contraceptive coverage. The Court issued a per curiam decision vacating the lower courts' decisions when the opposing parties agreed to examine alternative solutions, but also stipulated that it had reached no decision on the merits of the case.

United States v. Texas, 579 U.S. ___ (2016). Obama announced an executive action, the Deferred Action for Parents of Americans and Lawful Permanent Residents (DAPA) initiative, to delay deportation of unauthorized immigrants who have children who were born in the United States. Several states, including Texas, obtained a temporary injunction, arguing that DAPA violated the Constitution because it was arbitrary and capricious and had not gone through the notice-and-comment process of the Administrative Procedure Act. Also, they argued that the president had exceeded his powers, violating the take-care clause of the Constitution ("The President . . . shall take care that the laws be faithfully executed"). The Obama Justice Department appealed, but the Court issued an unsigned per curiam decision stating "the judgment is affirmed by an equally divided court," allowing the lower court injunction against DAPA to stand.

Whole Woman's Health v. Hellerstedt, 579 U.S. ___ (2016). Texas Law H.B. 2 required physicians performing abortions to have admitting privileges at nearby hospitals and for abortion clinics to meet the standards set for ambulatory surgical centers in the state. The Whole Woman's Health clinic and other abortion providers challenged the law as unnecessary because it did little to advance women's health and, by forcing clinic closings, created substantial obstacles to women seeking abortions. A 5–3 majority determined that the law represented an "undue burden" to women seeking an abortion with Ginsburg writing a concurrence to Breyer's opinion in which she noted the relative safety of abortions compared with other medical procedures. Laws that limited access to abortions in the name of safety "cannot survive judicial inspection."

Sessions v. Morales-Santana, 582 U.S. ___ (2017). In a case similar to *Nguyen v. INS* (2001), *Sessions v. Morales-Santana* focused on gender-based differentials in the transmission of U.S. citizenship to a child born abroad to unwed parents. Luis Ramón Morales-Santana challenged Section 1409(c) of the Immigration and Nationality Act—the government's requirement that unwed fathers have a minimum of ten years of U.S. residency in order to pass American citizenship to their children in contrast with the one year stipulated for unwed mothers. Ginsburg's opinion, written for the 7–1 majority, held that the prerequisite was "incompatible" with "the equal protection of the laws."

Trinity Lutheran Church v. Comer, 582 U.S. ___ (2017). Trinity Lutheran Church in Columbia, Missouri, wanted to resurface the playground used by its preschoolers but claimed its First Amendment rights had been violated when its application to a state program using recycled tires for that purpose was denied. The State of Missouri maintained that its constitution barred any aid to religious groups, direct or indirect. The Court's majority held that the exclusion of churches from state programs open to other charitable groups violates the Constitution's protection of religious freedom. Roberts's opinion maintained that the exclusion of a religious organization from a public benefit for which it is qualified solely on the basis of it being a church is "odious to our Constitution." Sotomayor's dissent, which Ginsburg joined, argued that the ruling would lead the nation "to a place where separation of church and state is a constitutional slogan, not a constitutional commitment."

Ziglar v. Abbasi, 582 U.S. ___ (2017). *Ziglar v. Abbasi* consolidated three cases asking whether noncitizens detained after 9/11 have the right to sue for damages against individual government officials. The case focused on 762 men, primarily Muslims from Arab and South Asian countries, arrested for violations of immigration regulations, who claimed that they had been held as persons "of interest" in detention centers under unreasonably harsh conditions solely because of their race, religion, and ethnicity. Writing for the 4–2 majority (Justices Sotomayor and Kagan had recused themselves, and Gorsuch had not been on the Court to hear oral arguments), Justice Kennedy held that while they did not condone the alleged treatment, lawsuits seeking financial compensation were not the proper way to address misconduct related to a national security crisis, because they could lead officials to "second-guess difficult but necessary decisions." Qualified immunity was valid in instances where reasonable officials in a given situation could not have foreseen the potential illegalities of their policy decisions. Ginsburg joined Breyer's dissent, maintaining that lawsuits for damages were a valid means of checking executive misconduct.

Author's Interviews

Nina Appel
Janet Benshoof
Judge Marsha S. Berzon
Jane Booth
Joan Bruder Danoff
Norman Dorsen
Thomas Ehrlich
Brenda Feigen
Anita Fial
M. E. Freeman
James Ginsburg
Jane Ginsburg
Martin Ginsburg
Ruth Bader Ginsburg
Marcia Greenberger
Jon Greenleaf
Eva Hanks
Irma Hilton
Edmund Kaufman
Sylvia Law
Ronald Loeb
Ruth Watson Lubic
Alan Morrison
Kathleen Peratis
Susan Rieger
Richard Salzman
Lynn Hecht Schafran
Elizabeth Schneider
Hans Smit

Nina Totenberg
Laurence Tribe
Sarah Weddington
Stephen Wiesenfeld
Wendy Webster Williams
Melvin Wulf
Diane Zimmerman

Paper Collections/Archival Research

Columbia University Rare Book & Manuscript Library, New York
William J. McGill Papers, 1929–79

Howard University School of Law Archives, Washington, D.C.
Phineas Indritz Papers, 1932–97

Jimmy Carter Presidential Library and Museum, Atlanta
Jimmy Carter Presidential Papers

Library of Congress, Washington, D.C.
Ruth Bader Ginsburg Papers, 1897–2005

Library of Congress Manuscript Division, Washington, D.C.
Harry A. Blackmun Papers, 1913–2001
William J. Brennan Papers, 1945–98
William O. Douglas Papers, 1801–1980
Thurgood Marshall Papers, 1949–91
Daniel P. Moynihan Papers, 1955–2000

Schlesinger Library, Harvard University, Cambridge, Massachusetts
Catherine East Papers, 1916–96
Pauli Murray Papers, 1910–85

Seeley G. Mudd Manuscript Library, Princeton, New Jersey
American Civil Liberties Union Records: Subgroup 4, 1933–2000

Sophia Smith Collection, Smith College, Northampton, Massachusetts
Dorothy Kenyon Papers, 1850–1998

Washington and Lee University School of Law, Lexington, Virginia
Lewis F. Powell Jr. Collection, 1937–99

William J. Clinton Presidential Library, Little Rock, Arkansas
Ruth Bader Ginsburg and Stephen Gerald Breyer Nomination Records, 1993–94

Journal Articles

Adams, Sara-Jane, and Jeff Wild. "The Cream of the Crop." *Intellectual Asset Management* (Jan/Feb. 2009): 57–59.
Adkins, Jason A. "Meet Me at the (West Coast) Hotel: The *Lochner* Era and the Demise of *Roe v. Wade.*" *Minnesota Law Review* 9, no. 500 (2005): 500–535.

Ashe, Marie. "Mind's Opportunity: Birthing a Poststructuralist Feminist Jurisprudence." *Syracuse University Law Review* 38 (1987–88): 1129–73.

Austin, Regina. "Sapphire Bound!" *Wisconsin Law Review* (May/June 1989): 539–78.

Bachman, Ronet, and Raymond Paternoster. "A Contemporary Look at the Effects of Rape Law Reform: How Far Have We Really Come?" *Journal of Criminal Law and Criminology* 84 (1993): 554–74.

Bagenstos, Samuel R. "Justice Ginsburg and the Judicial Role in Expanding 'We the People': The Disability Rights Cases." *Columbia Law Review* 104 (Jan. 2004): 49–59.

Barbas, Samantha. "Dorothy Kenyon and the Making of Modern Legal Feminism." *Stanford Journal of Civil Rights and Civil Liberties* 5 (Oct. 2009): 423–46.

Barrett, John Q. "The 'Federalism Five' as Supreme Court Nominees, 1971–1991." *St. John's Journal of Legal Commentary* 21 (2007): 485–96.

Baugh, Joyce Ann, Christopher E. Smith, Thomas R. Hensley, and Scott Patrick Johnson. "Justice Ruth Bader Ginsburg: A Preliminary Assessment." *University of Toledo Law Review* 26 (1994): 1–34.

Becker, Mary. "Prince Charming: Abstract Equality." *Supreme Court Review* (1987): 201–47.

———. "The Sixties Shift to Formal Equality and the Courts: An Argument for Pragmatism and Politics." *William and Mary Law Review* 40 (1998): 209–77.

Bell, Robin Olinger. "Justice Anthony M. Kennedy: Will His Appointment to the United States Supreme Court Have an Impact on Employment Discrimination?" *University of Cincinnati Law Review* 57 (1989): 1037–71.

Bender, Leslie. "A Lawyer's Primer on Feminist Theory and Tort." *Journal of Legal Education* 1/2 (1988): 3–37.

Benshoof, Janet. "U.S. Ratification of CEDAW: An Opportunity to Radically Reframe the Right to Equality Accorded Women Under the U.S. Constitution." *New York University Review of Law and Social Change* 35 (2011): 104–30.

Bier, Laurie. "Constitutional Law—Equal Protection—Sex Based Classification—*Reed v. Reed*, 404 U.S. 71 (1971)." *Wisconsin Law Review* (1972): 626–33.

Blackmun, Harry A. "In Memoriam: Erwin Nathaniel Griswold." *Harvard Law Review* 108 (1995): 979–1002.

Blake, Judith. "Abortion and Public Opinion: The 1960–1970 Decade." *Science,* Feb. 12, 1971, 540–49.

Blake, William D., and Hans J. Hacker. "'The Brooding Spirit of the Law': Supreme Court Justices Reading Dissents from the Bench." *Justice System Journal* 31, no. 1 (2010): 1–25.

Blasi, Vincent. "*Bakke* as Precedent: Does Mr. Justice Powell Have a Theory?" *California Law Review* 67 (1979): 21–68.

Bloustein, Edward J. "In Remembrance of Dean Heckel." *Rutgers Law Review* 41 (1989): 475–77.

Bogas, Kathleen L. "Constitutional Law—Fourteenth Amendment—Classification Based on Sex Is Inherently Suspect." *Journal of Urban Law* 51 (1974): 535–45.

Bridges, Khiara M. "'Life' in the Balance: Judicial Review of Abortion Regulations." *U.C. Davis Law Review* 46 (2013): 1285–338.

Bright, Myron H. "The Power of the Spoken Word: In Defense of Oral Argument." *Iowa Law Review* 72 (1986): 35–46.

Brody, Anita Blumstein, Ruth Bader Ginsburg, L. Priscilla Hall, Lindsey Miller-Lerman, Felice K. Shea, and Rena Katz Uviller. "Women on the Bench." *Columbia Journal of Gender and Law* 12 (2003): 361–82.

Brown, Barbara A., Thomas I. Emerson, Gail Falk, and Ann E. Freedman. "The Equal Rights Amendment: A Constitutional Basis for Equal Rights for Women." *Yale Law Journal* 5 (1971): 872–985.

Brown, Philip Marshall. "The Codification of International Law." *American Journal of International Law* 29 (Jan. 1935): 25–39.

Bucklo, Elaine. "From Women's Rights Advocate to Supreme Justice: Ruth Bader Ginsburg Speaks." *Litigation* 37 (2011): 8–15.

Burger, Warren E. "Tribute to Dean Soia Mentschikoff." *University of Miami Law Review* 37 (1983): ix–xi.

Butler, Kathleen M. "The Representative Cross Section Standard: Another Sixth Amendment Fundamental Right." *Loyola Law Review* 21 (1975): 995–1003.

Campbell, Amy Leigh. "Raising the Bar: Ruth Bader Ginsburg and the ACLU Women's Rights Project." *Texas Journal of Women and the Law* 11 (2002): 157–243.

Carmody, Chris. "Judge Ginsburg's Ex-clients Reflect upon Their Cases." *National Law Journal,* June 1993, 34.

Carter, Stephen L. "When Victims Happen to Be Black." *Yale Law Journal* 97 (1987–88): 420–47.

Case, Anne, and Angus Deaton. "Rising Morbidity and Mortality in Midlife Among White Non-Hispanic Americans in the 21st Century." *Proceedings of the National Academy of Sciences* 112, no. 49 (Dec. 8, 2015): 15078–83.

Case, Mary Anne. "Two Cheers for Cheerleading: The Noisy Integration of VMI and the Quiet Success of Virginia Women's Institute for Leadership." *University of Chicago Legal Forum* (1999): 347–80.

———. "'The Very Stereotype the Law Condemns': Constitutional Sex Discrimination Law as the Search for Perfect Proxies." *Cornell Law Review* 85 (2000): 1447–91.

Clark, Mary. "Changing the Face of the Law: How Women's Advocacy Groups Put Women on the Federal Judicial Appointments Agenda." *Yale Journal of Law and Feminism* 14 (2002): 243–54.

Coe, Jack J., Jr. "Recruitment and Appointment of Federal Judges." *Loyola Los Angeles Law Review* 12 (1979): 1033–42.

Cohen, Cathy J. "What Is This Movement Doing to My Politics," *Social Text* 61 (Winter 1999): 111–18.

Cohen, David S. "Justice Kennedy's Gendered World." *South Carolina Law Review* 59 (2008): 673–95.

Cole, David. "Strategies of Difference: Litigating for Women's Rights in a Man's World." *Journal of Law and Inequality* 2 (1984): 33–96.

Coontz, Phyllis D. "Gender Bias in the Legal Profession: Women 'See' It, Men Don't." *Women and Politics* 15 (1995): 1–22.

Cowan, Ruth B. "Women's Rights Through Litigation: An Examination of the American Civil Liberties Union Women's Rights Project, 1971–1976." *Columbia Human Rights Law Review* 8 (1976): 373–411.

Crenshaw, Kimberlé. "Demarginalizing the Intersection of Race and Sex: A Black Feminist Critique of Antidiscrimination Doctrine, Feminist Theory, and Antiracist Politics." *University of Chicago Legal Forum* (1989): 139–67.

Darcy, R., and Jenny Sanbrano. "Oklahoma in the Development of Equal Rights: The ERA, 3.2% Beer, Juvenile Justice, and *Craig v. Boren.*" *Oklahoma City University Law Review* 22 (1997): 1009–49.

Daughtrey, Martha Craig. "Cross Sectionalism in Jury-Selection Procedures After *Taylor v. Louisiana.*" *Tennessee Law Review* 43 (1975): 1–107.

Davis, Richard. "The Ginsburg Nomination and the Press." *Journal of International Press and Politics* 1, no. 2 (March 1996): 78–99.

De Boisblanc, Judith A. "Constitutional Law: The Equal Protection Clause and Women's Rights." *Loyola Law Review* 19 (1973): 542–51.

Dinovetzer, Ronit. "Social Capital and Constraints on Legal Careers." *Law and Society Review* 40 (2006): 445–79.

Dorf, Michael C. "The Paths to Legal Equality: A Reply to Dean Sullivan." *California Law Review* 90 (May 2002): 791–813.

Douglas, David M. "Social Security: Sex Discrimination and Equal Protection." *Baylor Law Review* 30 (1978): 199–205.

Edgar, Harold. "In Memoriam—Herbert Wechsler and the Criminal Law: A Brief Tribute." *Columbia Law Review* 100 (Oct. 2000): 1347–58.

Edwards, Harry T. "A Tribute to My Friend, the Honorable Ruth Bader Ginsburg." *New York University Annual Survey of American Law* 54 (1997): xv–xvii.

Ely, John Hart. "The Wages of Crying Wolf: A Comment on *Roe v. Wade.*" *Yale Law Journal* 82 (1973): 920–49.

Epstein, Lee, William M. Landes, and Richard A. Posner. "How Business Fares in the Supreme Court." *Minnesota Law Review* 97 (2013): 1431–72.

Eskridge, William N., Jr. "Legislation and Pedagogy in the Post–Legal Process Era." *University of Pittsburgh Law Review* 48 (1987): 691–731.

———. "Pluralism and Distrust: How Courts Can Support Democracy by Lowering the Stakes of Politics." *Yale Law Journal* 14 (2005): 1281–328.

———. "Privacy Jurisprudence and the Apartheid of the Closet, 1846–1961." *Florida State University Law Review* 24 (1997): 703–840.

Eskridge, William N., Jr., and Philip P. Frickey. "Commentary: The Making of the Legal Process." *Harvard Law Review* 107 (1994): 2031–55.

Faught, Richard H. "Taylor v. Louisiana: Constitutional Implications for Missouri's Jury Exemption Provisions." *Saint Louis University Law Journal* 20 (1975): 159–80.

Finley, Lucinda M. "Transcending Equality Theory: A Way Out of the Maternity and the Workplace Debate." *Columbia Law Review* 86 (Oct. 1986): 1118–82.

Fishkin, Joseph. "The Dignity of the South." *Yale Law Journal Online* 175 (2013), Forum, June 8, 2013.

Fiss, Owen. "Groups and the Equal Protection Clause." *Philosophy and Public Affairs* 5 (1976): 107–77.

Franklin, Cary. "The Anti-stereotyping Principle in Constitutional Sex Discrimination Law." *New York University Law Review* 85 (2010): 83–173.

———. "Inventing the 'Traditional Concept' of Sex Discrimination." *Harvard Law Review* 125 (2012): 1307–80.

Garrow, David J. "Abortion Before and After *Roe v. Wade:* An Historical Perspective." *Albany Law Review* 62 (1999): 833–52.

Gerken, Heather K. "Justice Kennedy and the Domains of Equal Protection." *Harvard Law Review* 121 (2007): 104–30.

Gertner, Nancy. "*Bakke* on Affirmative Action for Women: Pedestal or Cage?" *Harvard Civil Rights–Civil Liberties Law Review* 14 (1979): 173–214.

Gilmore, Glenda Elizabeth. "Admitting Pauli Murray." *Journal of Women's History* 14 (Summer 2002): 62–67.

Ginsburg, Martin D. "Distinguished Service Award Presentation—May 5, 2006." *ABA Section of Taxation News Quarterly* 25 (2006): 7–8.

———. "Some Reflections on Imperfection." *Arizona State Law Journal* 39 (Fall 2007): 949–61.

Ginsburg, Ruth Bader. "American Bar Association Visits the People's Republic of China." *American Bar Association Journal* 64 (Oct. 1978): 1516–25.

———. "Brown v. Board of Education in International Context." *Columbia Human Rights Law Review* 36 (2005): 489–93.

———. "Comment on *Frontiero v. Richardson.*" *Women's Rights Law Reporter* 1 (1973): 2–4.

———. "Constitutional Adjudication in the United States as Means of Advancing the Equal Status of Men and Women Under the Law." *Hofstra Law Review* 26 (1997): 263–71.

———. "A Conversation with Four Chief Justices." *Record of the Association of the Bar of the City of New York* 62 (2007): 255–86.

———. "The Equal Rights Amendment Is the Way." *Harvard Law Journal* 1 (1978): 19–26.

——. "Foreword to the Symposium: Women, Justice, and Authority." *Yale Journal of Law and Feminism* 14 (2002): 214–15.

——. "Gender and the Constitution." *University of Cincinnati Law Review* 44 (1975): 1–41.

——. "In Memoriam: Benjamin Kaplan." *Harvard Law Review* 124 (April 2011): 1345–61.

——. "In Memoriam: William H. Rehnquist." *Harvard Law Review* 119 (2005): 6–10.

——. "In Memoriam: William J. Brennan." *Harvard Law Review* 111 (1997): 3–5.

——. "In Memory of Dean Heckel: Comments of Ruth Bader Ginsburg." *Rutgers Law Review* 41 (1989): 477–78.

——. "In Memory of Herbert Wechsler." *Columbia Law Review* 100 (Oct. 2000): 1359–61.

——. "Interpretations of the Equal Protection Clause." *Harvard Journal of Law and Public Policy* 9 (1986): 41–45.

——. "Introduction to Women and the Law—a Symposium." *Rutgers Law Review* 25 (1970).

——. "Introduction to Women and the Law: Facing the Millennium" *Indiana Law Review* 32 (1999): 1161–65.

——. "Men, Women, and the Constitution." *Columbia Journal of Law and Social Problems* 10 (1973): 77–112.

——. "The Progression of Women in the Law." *Valparaiso University Law Review* 28 (1994): 1161–82.

——. "The Role of Dissenting Opinions." *Minnesota Law Review* 95.1 (2010): 1–8.

——. "Remarks for American Law Institute Annual Dinner, May 19, 1994." *Saint Louis University Law Journal* 38 (1994): 883–84.

——. "Remarks on Women's Progress in the Legal Profession in the United States." *Tulsa Law Journal* 33 (1997): 13–21.

——. "Remarks on Writing Separately." *Washington Law Review* 65 (1990): 133–50.

——. "Sex and Unequal Protection: Men and Women as Victims." *Journal of Family Law* 11 (1971): 347–62.

——. "Some Thoughts on Autonomy and Equality in Relation to *Roe v. Wade*." *North Carolina Law Review* 63 (1985): 375–86.

——. "Some Thoughts on Benign Classification in the Context of Sex." *Connecticut Law Review* 10 (1978): 813–27.

——. "Some Thoughts on Judicial Authority to Repair Unconstitutional Legislation." *Cleveland State Law Review* 28 (1979): 301–24.

——. "Speaking in a Judicial Voice." *New York University Law Review* 67 (1992): 1185–210.

——. "Four Louisiana Giants in the Law." Judge Robert A. Ainsworth Jr. Memorial Lecture, Feb. 4, 2002. *Loyola Law Review* 48 (2002): 253–66.

——. "The Status of Women." *American Journal of Comparative Law* 20 (1972): 585–91.

——. "A Study Tour of Taiwan's Legal System." *American Bar Association Journal* 66 (Feb. 1980): 165–70.

——. "Styles of Collegial Judging: One Judge's Perspective." *Federal Bureau News and Journal* 39 (1992): 199–201.

——. "Treatment of Women by the Law: Awakening Consciousness in the Law Schools." *Valparaiso University Law Review* 5 (1971): 480–88.

——. "A Tribute to Justice Sandra Day O'Connor." *Harvard Law Review* 119 (2006): 1239–45.

——. "Women, Equality, and the *Bakke* Case." *Civil Liberties Review* 4 (1977): 8–9.

——. "Women on the Bench." *Columbia Journal of Gender and Law* 10 (2000–2001): 25–28.

Ginsburg, Ruth Bader, and Barbara Flagg. "Some Reflections on the Feminist Legal Thought of the 1970s." *University of Chicago Legal Forum* 9 (1989): 9–21.

Ginsburg, Ruth Bader, and Antonin Scalia. "Prefaces to Scalia/Ginsburg: A (Gentle) Parody of Operatic Proportions." *Columbia Journal of Law and the Arts* 38 (2015): 237.

Ginsburg, Ruth Bader, with Linda Greenhouse. "A Conversation with Justice Ginsburg." *Yale Law Journal Online* 122 (2013): 283–301.

Gold, Rachel Benson. "Lessons from Before Roe: Will Past Be Prologue?" *Guttmacher Report on Public Policy* 6 (2003): 9.

Goldberg, Stephanie B. "The Second Woman Justice: Ruth Bader Ginsburg Talks Candidly About a Changing Society." *ABA Journal* 79 (Oct. 1993): 40–43.

Greenhouse, Linda. "How the Supreme Court Talks About Abortion: The Implications of a Shifting Discourse." *Suffolk University Law Review* 42 (2008): 41–59.

———. "Introduction: Learning to Listen to Ruth Bader Ginsburg." *New York City Law Review* 7 (2004): 391–451.

Guinier, Lani. "Courting the People: Demosprudence and the Law/Politics Divide." *Harvard Law Review* 127 (Nov. 2013): 437–444.

Guinier, Lani, Michelle Fine, and Jane Balin. "Becoming Gentlemen: Women's Experiences at One Ivy League Law School." With Ann Bartow and Deborah Lee Stachel. *University of Pennsylvania Law Review* 143 (1994): 1–110.

Gunther, Gerald. "Ruth Bader Ginsburg: A Personal, Very Fond Tribute." *University of Hawaii Law Review* 20 (1998): 583–87.

———. "The Supreme Court, 1971 Term—Foreword: In Search of Evolving Doctrine on a Changing Court: A Model for a Newer Equal Protection." *Harvard Law Review* 86 (1972): 1–306.

Hacker, Helen. "Women as a Minority Group." *Social Forces* 31 (Oct. 1951): 60–69.

Halberstam, Malvina. "Ruth Bader Ginsburg: The First Jewish Woman on the Supreme Court." *Cardozo Law Review* 19 (1998): 1441–54.

Hasaday, Jill. "Protecting Them from Themselves: The Persistence of Mutual Benefits Arguments for Sex and Race Inequality." *New York University Law Review* 84 (Dec. 2009): 1464–539.

Hasen, Richard L. "Anticipatory Overrulings, Invitations, Time Bombs, and Inadvertence: How Supreme Court Justices Move the Law." *Emory University Law Journal* 61 (2012): 779–800.

Hayes, Emily A. "Bridging the Gap Between Work and Family: Accomplishing the Goals of the Family and Medical Leave Act of 1993." *William and Mary Law Review* 42 (2001): 1507–43.

Higham, John. "Changing Paradigms: The Collapse of Consensus History." *Journal of American History* 76 (1989): 460–66.

Hollinger, David A. "Obama, the Instability of Color Lines, and the Promise of a Postethnic Future." *Callaloo* 31 (2008): 1033–37.

Horowitz, Daniel. "Rethinking Betty Friedan and *The Feminine Mystique:* Labor Union Radicalism and Feminism in Cold War America." *American Quarterly* 48 (1998): 1–42.

Huber, Peter. "Tribute to Justice Ruth Bader Ginsburg: 'Dining Chez Ginsburg.'" *Annual Survey of American Law* (1997): 19–21.

Issacharoff, Samuel. "Beyond the Discrimination Model on Voting." *Harvard Law Review* 127 (2013): 95–126.

Jackson, Robert H. "Advocacy Before the United States Supreme Court." *Cornell Law Quarterly* 37 (1951): 1–16.

Johnson, John D., Jr., and Charles Knapp. "Sex Discrimination by Law: A Study in Judicial Perspective." *New York University Law Review* 46 (1971): 675–747.

Joshi, Yuvraj. "The Respectable Dignity of *Obergefell v. Hodges.*" *California Law Review Circuit* 6 (Nov. 2015): 117–25.

Kaapuni, Gregory. "Califano v. Goldfarb: An Equal Protection Standard for Gender-Based Discrimination." *University of West Los Angeles Law Review* 10 (1978): 67–85.

Kagan, Elena. "Confirmation Messes, Old and New." *University of Chicago Law Review* 62 (Spring 1995): 919–42.

Karlan, Pamela S. "Convictions and Doubts: Representation and the Debate over Felon Disenfranchisement." *Stanford Law Review* 56 (2004): 1147–70.

———. "Lessons Learned: Voting Rights and the Bush Administration." *Duke Journal of Constitutional Law and Public Policy* 4 (2009): 17–29.

Karlan, Pamela S., and Daryl J. Levinson. "The Importance of Political Deliberation and Race-Conscious Redistricting: Why Voting Is Different." *University of California Law Review* 84 (1996): 1201–32.

Karpowitz, Christopher F. "Tea Time in America? The Impact of the Tea Party Movement on the 2010 Midterm Elections." *PS: Political Science and Politics* 44 (April 2011): 303–9.

Karst, Kenneth L. "Equal Citizenship Under the Fourteenth Amendment." *Harvard Law Review* 91 (1977): 1–68.

———. "The Supreme Court, 1976 Term." *Harvard Law Review* 91 (1977): 1–301.

Kay, Herma Hill. "Ruth Bader Ginsburg, Professor of Law." *Columbia Law Review* 104 (2004): 1–20.

Kerber, Linda K. "Writing Our Own Rare Books." *Yale Journal of Law and Feminism* 14 (2002): 429–51.

Klarman, Michael J. "Marriage Equality and Racial Equality." *Harvard Law Review* 127 (Nov. 2013): 127–60.

———. "Social Reform Litigation and Its Challenges: An Essay in Honor of Justice Ruth Bader Ginsburg." *Harvard Journal of Law and Gender* 32 (2009): 251–302.

Klein, Fannie J. "Review Urged of Law Curriculum for Women." *New York Law Journal* 26 (1972): S9.

Krause, Kathryn Marie. "Jury Selection—Sixth Amendment Right to a Fair Cross Section of the Community—a Change in Emphasis." *Missouri Law Review* 41 (1976): 446–56.

Kupetz, Karen Lazarus. "Equal Benefits, Equal Burdens: 'Skeptical Scrutiny' for Gender Classification After *United States v. Virginia*." *Loyola of Los Angeles Law Review* 30 (April 1997): 1333–77.

Landsman, R. Broh. "Fifth Amendment Protection Against Gender-Based Discrimination in the Distribution of Survivors' Benefits: Califano v. Goldfarb." *Southwestern Law Journal* 31 (1977): 1156–62.

Lavine, Douglas. "Court Prospect's Feminism Irks Senate Conservatives." *National Law Journal,* Dec. 1979, 8.

Law, Sylvia. "Rethinking Sex and the Constitution." *University of Pennsylvania Law Review* 132 (1984): 955–1040.

Leete, Elizabeth B. "Taylor v. Louisiana: The Jury Cross Section Crosses the State Line." *Connecticut Law Review* 7 (1975): 508–28.

Lichtenstein, Nelson. "Why Working at Wal-Mart Is Different." *Connecticut Law Review* 39 (2007): 1649–84.

Lucas, Roy. "Federal Constitutional Limitations on the Enforcement and Administration of State Abortion Statutes." *North Carolina Law Review* 46 (1968): 730–78.

MacKinnon, Catharine A. "Disputing Male Sovereignty: On *United States v. Morrison*." *Harvard Law Review* 114 (Nov. 2000): 135–78.

———. "Reflections on Sex Equality Under the Law." *Yale Law Journal* 100 (1991): 1281–328.

Markowitz, Deborah L. "In Pursuit of Equality: One Woman's Work to Change the Law." *Women's Rights Law Reporter* 11 (1989): 73–97.

Martin, Andrew D., and Kevin M. Quinn. "Dynamic Ideal Point Estimation via Markov Chain Monte Carlo for the U.S. Supreme Court, 1953–1999." *Political Analysis* 10 (2002): 134–53.

Mayeri, Serena. "'A Common Fate of Discrimination': Race-Gender Analogies in Legal and Historical Perspective." *Yale Law Journal* 110 (1981): 1045–87.

———. "Constitutional Choices: Legal Feminism and the Historical Dynamics of Change." *California Law Review* 92 (2004): 755–840.

———. "Reconstructing the Race-Sex Analogy." *William and Mary Law Review* 49 (2008): 1789–854.

———. "The Strange Career of Jane Crow: Sex Segregation and the Transformation of Anti-discrimination Discourse." *Yale Journal of Law and the Humanities* 8 (2006): 187–272.

McAtee, Andrea, and Kevin T. McGuire. "Lawyers, Justices, and Issue Salience: When and How Do Legal Arguments Affect the U.S. Supreme Court?" *Law and Society Review* 41 (2007): 259–78.

McKenny, Betsy B. "Frontiero v. Richardson: Characterization of Sex-Based Classification." *Columbia Human Rights Law Review* 6 (1974): 239–47.

Mears, Judith. "Taking Liberties." *Civil Liberties Review* 1 (1974): 136.

Menkel-Meadow, Carrie. "Exploring a Research Agenda of the Feminization of the Legal Profession: Theories of Gender and Social Change." *Law and Social Inquiry* 14 (Spring 1989): 289–319.

Meyer, Carol H. "The First Activist Feminist I Ever Met." *Affilia* 9, no. 1 (1994): 85–87.

Minow, Martha. "Foreword: Justice Engendered." *Harvard Law Review* 101 (1987): 10–95.

———. "*M.L.B. v. S.L.J.*, 519 U.S. 102 (1996)." *Harvard Law Review* 127 (Nov. 2013): 461–67.

Molitor, Abigail B. "Understanding Equal Sovereignty." *University of Chicago Law Review* 81 (2014): 1839–82.

Mulvey, Kenneth J., Jr. "Constitutional Law—Sixth Amendment—Systematic Exclusion of Women from Jury Service Violates the Sixth and Fourteenth Amendments." *Fordham Urban Law Journal* 3 (1975): 733–48.

Murphy, John P., Jr. "Recent Cases: Constitutional Law—Equal Protection—State Probate Code Discriminating in Favor of Males Violate Equal Protection Clause." *Vanderbilt Law Review* 25 (1972): 412–18.

———. "The *Reed* Case: The Seed for Equal Protection from Sex-Based Discrimination, or Polite Judicial Hedging?" *Akron Law Review* 5 (1972): 251–63.

Murray, Pauli, and Mary O. Eastwood. "Jane Crow and the Law: Sex Discrimination and Title VII." *George Washington Law Review* 34 (1965): 232–56.

Neely, Carla A. "Constitutional Law: Jury Selection—Exclusion of Women from Jury Venire Violates Fundamental Sixth Amendment Right to a Representative Jury." *University of Florida Law Review* 28 (1975): 281–88.

NeJaime, Douglas. "Doctrine in Context." *Harvard Law Review Forum* 127 (Nov. 2013): 10–18.

Ness, Susan, and Fredrica Wechsler. "Women Judges—Why So Few?" *Graduate Women* 73 (Nov./Dec. 1979): 10–12.

Noonan, John T., Jr. "Abortion and the Catholic Church." *Natural Law Forum* 12 (1967): 85–131.

Nordlund, John V. "Constitutional Law: Equal Protection—Gender Discrimination—Califano v. Goldfarb." *New York Law School Law Review* 23 (1977): 503–17.

Nossiff, Rosemary. "Why Justice Ginsburg Is Wrong About States Expanding Abortion Rights." *P.S.: Political Science and Politics* 27 (1994): 227–31.

O'Connor, Karen, and Lee Epstein. "Beyond Legislative Lobbying: Women's Groups and the Supreme Court." *Judicature* 67 (1983): 133–43.

O'Connor, Karen, and Alexandra B. Yanus. "Judging Alone: Reflections on the Importance of Women on the Court." *Critical Perspectives* 6 (Sept. 2010): 441–52.

O'Connor, Sandra Day. "Thurgood Marshall: The Influence of a Raconteur." *Stanford Law Review* 44 (1992): 1217–20.

Olson, Pamala F. "ABA Section of Taxation 2006 Distinguished Service Award Recipient, Professor Martin D. Ginsburg." *ABA Section of Taxation News Quarterly* 25 (2006): 6.

Ostrer, Mitchel. "A Profile of Ruth Bader Ginsburg." *Juris Doctor* 7 (1977): 34–38.

Palmer, Barbara. "Justice Ruth Bader Ginsburg and the Supreme Court's Reaction to the Second Female Member." *Women and Politics* 24 (2008): 1–23.

Persily, Nathaniel. "The Promise and Pitfalls of the New Voting Rights Act." *Yale Law Journal* 117 (2007): 174–254.

Pildes, Richard H. "Political Avoidance, Constitutional Theory, and the VRA." *Yale Law Journal* Pocket Part 117 (2007): 148–54.

Post, Robert C., and Reva B. Siegel. "Equal Protection by Law: Federal Antidiscrimination Legislation after *Morrison* and *Kimmel*." *Yale Law Journal* 110 (Dec. 2000): 441–526.

———. "*Roe* Rage: Democratic Constitutionalism and Backlash." *Harvard Civil Rights–Civil Liberties Law Review* (2007): 373–433.

Price, Zachary S. "NAMUDNO's Non-existent Principle of State Equality." *New York University Law Review* 88 (2013): 24–40.

Raiffa, Howard. "In Memoriam: Albert M. Sacks." *Harvard Law Review* 105 (1991): 16–17.

Ray, Laura Krugman. "Justice Ginsburg and the Middle Way." *Brooklyn Law Review* 68 (2003): 629–83.

Resnik, Judith. "Fairness in Numbers: A Comment on *AT&T v. Concepcion, Wal-Mart v. Dukes,* and *Turner v. Rogers*." *Harvard Law Review* 125 (2011): 78–170.

———. "On the Bias: Feminist Reconsiderations of the Aspirations for Our Judges." *Southern California Law Review* 61 (1988): 1878–944.

Roberts, Jorie. "Ginsburg Talk Highlights Celebration 25 Activities." *Harvard Law Record* 66 (1978): 9.

Rodriguez, Eva M. "Confusion from the High Court." *Connecticut Law Tribune* 9 (July 1996).

Rosenberg, Rosalind. "The Conjunction of Race and Gender." *Journal of Women's History* 14 (Summer 2002): 68–73.

Sartin, Joseph M., Jr., and Kerry P. Camarata. "Constitutional Law—Sex Discrimination— Supreme Court Plurality Declares Sex a Suspect Classification." *Tulane Law Review* 48 (1974): 710–20.

Sassower, Doris L. "Women in the Law: The Second Hundred Years." *American Bar Association Journal* 57 (1971): 329–32.

Schneider, Elizabeth M. "A Postscript on VMI." *American University Journal of Gender and the Law* 6 (Fall 1997): 59–64.

Schroth, Tracy. "At Rutgers, Ginsburg Changed." *New Jersey Law Journal* 134 (1993): 32.

Selmi, Michael. "The Supreme Court's 2006–2007 Term Employment Cases: A Quiet but Revealing Term." *Employee Rights and Employment Policy Journal* 11 (2007): 219–54.

Sherry, Suzanna. "The Unmaking of a Precedent." *Supreme Court Review* (2003): 231–67.

Siegel, Neil S. "Equal Citizenship Stature: Justice Ginsburg's Constitutional Vision." *New England Law Review* 43 (2009): 799–855.

Siegel, Neil S., and Reva B. Siegel. "Struck by Stereotype: Ruth Bader Ginsburg on Pregnancy Discrimination as Sex Discrimination." *Duke Law Journal* 59 (2010): 771–98.

Siegel, Reva B. "Constitutional Culture, Social Movement Conflict, and Constitutional Change: The Case of the De Facto ERA." *California Law Review* 94 (2006): 1323–419.

———. "Dignity and the Politics of Protection: Abortion Restriction Under *Casey/Carhart*." *Yale Law Journal* 117 (2008): 1694–800.

———. "From Colorblindness to Antibalkanization: An Emerging Ground of Decision in Race Equality Cases." *Yale Law Journal* 120 (2011): 1278–366.

———. "The Modernization of Marital Status Law: Adjudicating Wives' Rights to Earnings, 1860–1930." *Georgetown Law Journal* 82 (1994): 2127–211.

———. "The New Politics of Abortion: An Equality Analysis of Woman-Protective Abortion Restrictions." *University of Illinois Law Review* 991 (2007): 1006–23.

———. "Reasoning from the Body: A Historical Perspective on Abortion Regulation and Questions of Equal Protection." *Stanford Law Review* 44 (1992): 261–381.

———. "The Right's Reasons: Constitutional Conflict and the Spread of Woman-Protective Antiabortion Argument." *Duke Law Journal* 57 (2008): 1641–92.

———. "*Roe*'s Roots: The Women's Rights Claims That Engendered *Roe*." *Boston University Law Review* 90 (2010): 1875–907.

———. "She the People: The Nineteenth Amendment, Sex Equality, Federalism, and the Family." *Harvard Law Review* 115 (2002): 947–1046.

———. "The Supreme Court 2012 Term, Foreword: Equality Divided." *Harvard Law Review* 127, no. 1 (2013): 1–94.

———. "Why Equal Protection No Longer Protects: The Evolving Form of Status-Enforcing State Action." *Stanford Law Review* 49 (1997): 1111–48.

———. "You've Come a Long Way, Baby: Rehnquist's New Approach to Pregnancy Discrimination in *Hibbs*." *Stanford Law Review* 58, no. 6 (2006): 1871–989.

Silverberg, Helene. "State Building, Health Policy, and the Persistence of the American Abortion Debate." *Journal of Policy History* 9 (1997): 311–38.

Silverstein, Mark, and William Halton. "You Can't Always Get What You Want: Reflections on the Ginsburg and Breyer Nominations." *Journal of Law and Politics* 12 (1996): 459–79.

Sliz, Jeffrey R. "Constitutional Law—Equal Protection—Fifth Amendment, Due Process—Plurality of Court Decides That Sex-Based Classifications Are 'Suspect.' *Frontiero v. Richardson*, 411 U.S. 677 (1973)." *Rutgers Camden Law Journal* 5 (1974): 348–64.

———. "Constitutional Law—Sex Discrimination—Is It Finally Labeled 'Suspect'?" *Georgia State Bar Journal* 10 (1974): 493–99.

Smailer, Scott. "Justice Ruth Bader Ginsburg and the Virginia Military Institute: A Culmination of Strategic Success." *Cardozo Women's Law Journal* 4 (1998): 541–84.

Small, Marshall L. "William O. Douglas Remembered: A Collective Memory by WOD's Law Clerks." *Journal of Supreme Court History* 32 (2007): 297–334.

Smith, Christopher E., Joyce Ann Baugh, Thomas R. Hensley, Scott Patrick Johnson. "The First-Term Performance of Justice Ruth Bader Ginsburg." *Judicature* 78 (1994): 74–80.

Stone, Geoffrey R. "The Roberts Court, Stare Decisis, and the Future of Constitutional Law." *Tulane Law Review* 82 (2008): 1533–59.

Sullivan, Kathleen M. "Constitutionalizing Women's Equality." *California Law Review* 90 (2000): 735–65.

———. "From States' Rights Blues to Blue States' Rights: Federalism After the Rehnquist Court." *Fordham Journal of Law* 75 (2006): 799–813.

Szmer, John, Susan W. Johnson, and Tammy A. Sarver. "Does *the* Lawyer Matter? Influencing Outcomes on the Supreme Court of Canada." *Law and Society Review* 41 (2007): 279–304.

Tolson, Franita. "Reinventing Sovereignty? Federalism as Constraint on the Voting Rights Act." *Vanderbilt Law Review* 65 (2012): 1195–259.

Totenberg, Nina. "Tribute to Justice Ruth Bader Ginsburg." *New York University Annual Survey of American Law* (April 1997): 33–37.

Tribe, Laurence H. "Equal Dignity: Speaking Its Name." *Harvard Law Review Forum Online* 129 (Nov. 2015).

———. "Respecting Dissent: Justice Ginsburg's Critique of the Troubling Invocation of Appearance." *Harvard Law Review* 127 (Nov. 2013): 479.

———. "The Supreme Court, 1972 Term." *Harvard Law Review* 87 (1973): 1–314.

Tushnet, Mark. "The Dissent in *National Federation of Independent Business v. Sebelius*." *Harvard Law Review* 127 (Nov. 2013): 481–85.

Uggen, Christopher, and Jeff Manza. "Democratic Contraction? The Political Consequences of Felon Disenfranchisement in the United States." *American Sociological Review* (2002): 777–803.

Wald, Patricia M. "Women of the Courts Symposium: Six Not-So-Easy Pieces: One Woman Judge's Journey to the Bench and Beyond." *University of Toledo Law Review* 36 (2005): 979–93.

Walsh, Amy. "Ruth Bader Ginsburg: Extending the Constitution." *John Marshall Law Review* 32 (Fall 1998): 197–225.

Walters, Susan Vitullo. "Constitutional Law—Frontiero v. Richardson, Uniform Services Fringe Benefit Statute Which Presumes Spouses of Male Members to Be Dependent, but Requires Spouses of Female Members to Be Dependent in Fact, Is Violative of Due Process." *Loyola University Law Journal* 5 (1974): 295–313.

Ward, Stephanie Francis. "Family Ties: The Private and Public Lives of Justice Ruth Bader Ginsburg." *ABA Journal* 96 (2010): 36–43.

Wechsler, Herbert. "Toward Neutral Principles of Constitutional Law." *Harvard Law Review* 73 (1959): 360–61.

West, Robin. "Jurisprudence and Gender." *University of Chicago Law Review* 55 (Winter 1988): 1–72.

Whitman, Robert, Soia Mentschikoff, and Karl Llewellyn. "Moving Together to the University of Chicago Law School." *Connecticut Law Review* 24 (1992): 1119–29.

Williams, Daniel K. "The GOP's Abortion Strategy: Why Pro-choice Republicans Became Pro-life in the 1970s." *Journal of Policy History* 23 (2011): 512–39.

Williams, Joan C. "Deconstructing Gender." *Michigan Law Review* 87 (1989): 797–845.

Williams, Susan H., and David C. Williams. "Sense and Sensibility: Justice Ruth Bader Ginsburg's Mentoring Style as a Blend of Rigor and Compassion." *University of Hawaii Law Review* 20 (Winter 1998): 589–93.

Williams, Wendy W. "Equality's Riddle: Pregnancy and the Equal Treatment/Special Treatment Debate." *New York University Review of Law and Social Change* 13 (1984–85): 325–80.

Williamson, Vanessa, Theda Skocpol, and John Coggin. "The Tea Party and the Remaking of Republican Conservatism." *Perspectives on Politics* 9 (March 2011): 25–43.

Wulf, Melvin. "Advocacy Before the United States Supreme Court." *Cornell Law Quarterly* 37 (1951): 1–16.

Wyatt, Gail Elizabeth. "The Sexual Abuse of Afro-American and White-American Women in Childhood." *Child Abuse and Neglect* 9, no. 4 (1985): 507–19.

Yoshino, Kenji. "A New Birth of Freedom? *Obergefell v. Hodges*." *Harvard Law Review* 129 (Nov. 2015): 147–79.

———. "Sex Equality's Inner Frontier: The Case of Same-Sex Marriage." *Yale Law Journal* 122 (2013): 275–81.

Books

Abraham, Henry J. *Justices, Presidents, and Senators: A History of U.S. Supreme Court Appointments from Washington to Clinton*. New York: Rowman & Littlefield, 1999.

Abrajano, Marisa, and Zolan L. Hajnal. *White Backlash: Immigration, Race, and American Politics*. Princeton, N.J.: Princeton University Press, 2015.

Abramovitch, Ilana, and Sean Galvin. *Jews of Brooklyn*. Hanover, N.H.: University Press of New England for Brandeis University Press, 2002.

Ackerman, Bruce. *The Civil Rights Revolution*. Vol. 3 of *We the People*. Cambridge, Mass.: Harvard University Press, 2014.

Aisenberg, Nadya, and Mona Harrington. *Women of Academe: Outsiders in the Sacred Grove*. Amherst: University of Massachusetts Press, 1988.

Alexander, Michelle. *The New Jim Crow: Mass Incarceration in the Age of Colorblindness*. New York: New Press, 2012.

Alito, Martha-Ann, and Supreme Court Spouses. *Chef Supreme: Martin Ginsburg*. Washington, D.C.: Supreme Court Historical Society, 2011.

Alter, Jonathan. *The Promise: President Obama, Year One*. New York: Simon & Schuster, 2011.

Anderson, Terry H. *The Pursuit of Fairness: A History of Affirmative Action*. New York: Oxford University Press, 2004.

Antler, Joyce. *The Journey Home: How Jewish Women Shaped Modern America*. New York: Schocken Books, 1997.

Babcock, Barbara. *Fish Raincoats: A Woman Lawyer's Life*. New Orleans: Quid Pro Books, 2016.

Baer, Judith. *The Chains of Protection: The Judicial Response to Women's Labor Legislation*. Westport, Conn.: Greenwood Press, 1978.

Baer, Kenneth S. *Reinventing Democrats: The Politics of Liberalism from Reagan to Clinton*. Lawrence: University Press of Kansas, 2000.

Bagley, Edwin R. *Joe McCarthy and the Press*. Madison: University of Wisconsin Press, 1991.

Balkin, Jack M., ed. *What Roe v. Wade Should Have Said: The Nation's Top Legal Experts Rewrite America's Most Controversial Opinion.* New York: New York University Press, 2005.

Ball, Howard. *Bush, the Detainees, and the Constitution: The Battle over Presidential Power in the War on Terror.* Lawrence: University Press of Kansas, 2007.

Banks, Christopher P., and John C. Blakeman. *The U.S. Supreme Court and the New Federalism: From the Rehnquist to the Roberts Court.* New York: Rowman & Littlefield, 2012.

Barber, Sotirios. *The Fallacies of States' Rights.* Cambridge, Mass.: Harvard University Press, 2013.

Barkalow, Carol. *In the Men's House: An Inside Account of Life in the Army by One of West Point's First Female Graduates.* With Andrea Rabb. New York: Poseidon Press, 1990.

Barnhart, Bill, and Gene Schlickman. *John Paul Stevens: An Independent Life.* DeKalb: Northern Illinois University Press, 2010.

Basch, Norma. *In the Eyes of the Law: Women, Marriage, and Property in Nineteenth-Century New York.* Ithaca, N.Y.: Cornell University Press, 1982.

Bass, Jack. *Taming the Story: The Life and Times of Judge Frank M. Johnson Jr. and the South's Fight over Civil Rights.* Athens: University of Georgia Press, 1993.

———. *Unlikely Heroes: The Dramatic Story of Southern Judges of the Fifth Circuit Who Translated the Supreme Court's Brown Decision into a Revolution for Equality.* New York: Simon & Schuster, 1981.

Bayer, Linda. *Women of Achievement: Ruth Bader Ginsburg.* Philadelphia: Chelsea House, 2000.

Becker, Jo. *Forcing the Spring: Inside the Fight for Marriage Equality.* New York: Penguin Books, 2014.

Belew, Kathleen. *Bring the War Home: The White Power Movement and Paramilitary America.* Cambridge: Harvard University Press, 2018.

Bell, Griffin B. *Taking Care of the Law.* New York: Mercer University Press, 1982.

Berman, Ari. *Give Us the Ballot: The Modern Struggle for Voting Rights in America.* New York: Farrar, Straus & Giroux, 2015.

Berry, Janis M., et al. *Women Lawyers at Work.* Boston: Massachusetts Continuing Legal Education, 1993.

Biden, Joe. *Promises to Keep: On Life and Politics.* New York: Random House, 2007.

Bird, Kai, and Martin J. Sherwin. *American Prometheus: The Triumph and Tragedy of J. Robert Oppenheimer.* New York: Knopf, 2006.

Biskupic, Joan. *American Original: The Life and Constitution of Supreme Court Justice Antonin Scalia.* New York: Sarah Crichton Books, 2009.

———. *Breaking In: The Rise of Sonia Sotomayor and the Politics of Justice.* New York: Sarah Crichton Books, 2014.

———. *Sandra Day O'Connor: How the First Woman on the Supreme Court Became Its Most Influential Justice.* New York: HarperCollins, 2005.

Blackstone, William F., and Robert D. Heslep, eds. *Social Justice and Preferential Treatment: Women and Racial Minorities in Education and Business.* Athens: University of Georgia Press, 1977.

Blanchard, Dallas A. *The Anti-abortion Movement and the Rise of the Religious Right: From Polite to Fiery Protest.* New York: Twayne, 1994.

Blasi, Vincent, ed. *The Burger Court: The Counter-revolution That Wasn't.* New Haven, Conn.: Yale University Press, 1986.

Blum, Edward. *The Unintended Consequences of the Voting Rights Act.* Washington, D.C.: AEI Press, 2007.

Bond, Hallie, Joan Jacobs Brumberg, and Leslie Paris. *"A Paradise for Boys and Girls": Children's Camps in the Adirondacks.* Blue Mountain Lake, N.Y.: Adirondack Museum/Syracuse University Press, 2006.

Bonilla-Silva, Eduardo. *Racism Without Racists: Color-Blind Racism and the Persistence of Inequality.* 4th ed. New York: Rowman & Littlefield, 2013.

Boorstin, Daniel. *Genius of American Politics*. Chicago: University of Chicago Press, 1953.

Bradley, Dawn Berry. *The 50 Most Influential Women in American Law*. Los Angeles: Lowell House, 1997.

Bravin, Jess. *The Terror Courts: Rough Justice at Guantanamo Bay*. New Haven, Conn.: Yale University Press, 2013.

Breines, Wini. *Young, White, and Miserable: Growing Up Female in the Fifties*. Boston: Beacon Press, 1992.

Brodie, Linda Fairchild. *Breaking Out: VMI and the Coming of Women*. New York: Vintage Books, 2001.

Cahn, Naomi, and June Carbone. *Red Families v. Blue Families: Legal Polarization and the Creation of Culture*. New York: Oxford University Press, 2010.

Canaday, Margot. *The Straight State: Sexuality and Citizenship in Twentieth-Century America*. Princeton, N.J.: Princeton University Press, 2009.

Cantor, Aviva. *Jewish Women/Jewish Men: The Legacy of Patriarchy in Jewish Life*. New York: Harper Collins, 1995.

Carmon, Irin, and Shana Knizhnik. *Notorious RBG: The Life and Times of Ruth Bader Ginsburg*. New York: Dey Street Books, 2015.

Carter, Jimmy. *White House Diary*. New York: Farrar, Straus & Giroux, 2010.

Chafe, William H. *Bill and Hillary: The Politics of the Personal*. New York: Farrar, Straus & Giroux, 2012.

———. *The Paradox of Change: American Women in the Twentieth Century*. New York: Oxford University Press, 1991.

———. *The Unfinished Journey: America Since World War II*. New York: Oxford University Press, 1995.

Chamallas, Martha. *Introduction to Feminist Legal Theory*. 3rd ed. New York: Wolters Kluwer, 2013.

Charles, Patrick J. *Armed in America: A History of Gun Rights from Colonial Militias to Concealed Carry*. Buffalo, N.Y.: Prometheus Books, 2018.

Chen, Anthony S. *The Fifth Freedom: Jobs, Politics, and Civil Rights in the United States, 1941–1972*. Princeton, N.J.: Princeton University Press, 2009.

Choper, Jesse, ed. *The Supreme Court and Its Justices*. Chicago: American Bar Association, 2001.

Clinton, Bill. *My Life*. New York: Random House, 2005.

Cohen, Cathy, Kathy Jones, and Joan C. Tronto, eds. *Women Transforming Politics: An Alternative Reader*. New York: New York University Press, 1997.

Colucci, Frank J. *Justice Kennedy's Jurisprudence: The Full and Necessary Meaning of Liberty*. Lawrence: University Press of Kansas, 2009.

Cook, Elizabeth Adell, Ted G. Jelan, and Clyde Wilcon. *Between Two Absolutes: Public Opinion and the Politics of Abortion*. Boulder, Colo.: Westview Press, 1992.

Cook, Richard M. *Alfred Kazin: A Biography*. New Haven, Conn.: Yale University Press, 2007.

Corber, Robert. *Homosexuality in Cold War America: Resistance and the Crisis of Masculinity*. Durham, N.C.: Duke University Press, 1997.

Cott, Nancy F. *Public Vows: A History of Marriage and the Nation*. Cambridge, Mass.: Harvard University Press, 2000.

Coyle, Marcia. *The Roberts Court: The Struggle for the Constitution*. New York: Simon & Schuster, 2013.

Critchlow, Donald. *The Conservative Ascendancy: How the GOP Right Made Political History*. Cambridge, Mass.: Harvard University Press, 2007.

———. *Phyllis Schlafly and Grassroots Conservatism: A Woman's Crusade*. Princeton, N.J.: Princeton University Press, 2005.

Cross, Malcolm, and Michael Keith, eds. *Racism, the City, and the State*. New York: Routledge, 1993.

Cushman, Clare, ed. *Supreme Court Decisions and Women's Rights*. Washington, D.C.: CQ Press, 2000.

Cushman, Robert. *The Independent Regulatory Commissions*. New York: Octagon Books, 1972.

Dahlström, Edmund, ed. *The Changing Roles of Men and Women*. Translated by Gunilla Anderman and Steven Anderman. London: Gerald Duckworth, 1967.

Dalrymple, Candice. *Sexual Distinctions in the Law: Early Maximum Hours Decisions in the United States Supreme Court, 1905–1917*. New York: Taylor & Francis, 1987.

Danelski, David J. *Rights, Liberties, and Ideals: The Contributions of Milton R. Knovitz*. Littleton, Colo.: Fred B. Rothman, 1983.

Davidman, Lynn. *Motherloss*. Berkeley: University of California Press, 2000.

Davidson, Kenneth M., Ruth Bader Ginsburg, and Herma Hill Kay. *Text, Cases, and Materials on Sex-Based Discrimination*. Minneapolis: West, 1974.

Dayton, Cornelia Hughes. *Women Before the Bar: Gender, Law, and Society in Connecticut, 1639–1789*. Chapel Hill: University of North Carolina Press, 1995.

Dean, John. *The Rehnquist Choice: The Untold Story of the Nixon Appointment That Redefined the Supreme Court*. New York: Free Press, 2001.

de Beauvoir, Simone. *The Second Sex*. New York: Knopf, 1953.

Deckman, Melissa. *Tea Party Women: Mama Grizzlies, Grassroots Leaders, and the Changing Face of the American Right*. New York: New York University Press, 2016.

Dees, Morris. *A Season for Justice: The Life and Times of Civil Rights Lawyer Morris Dees*. With Steve Fiffer. New York: Charles Scribner's Sons, 1991.

D'Emilio, John. *In a New Century: Essays on Queer History, Politics, and Community Life*. Madison: University of Wisconsin Press, 2014.

D'Emilio, John, William B. Turner, and Urvashi Vaid, eds. *Creating Change: Sexuality, Public Policy, and Civil Rights*. New York: St. Martin's Press, 2002.

Dershowitz, Alan M. *Chutzpah*. New York: Touchstone, 1991.

———. *Supreme Injustice: How the High Court Hijacked Election 2000*. New York: Oxford University Press, 2001.

Deslippe, Dennis. *Protesting Affirmative Action: The Struggle over Equality After the Civil Rights Revolution*. Baltimore: Johns Hopkins University Press, 2012.

Devins, Neal. *Shaping Constitutional Values: Elected Government, the Supreme Court, and the Abortion Debate*. Baltimore: Johns Hopkins University Press, 1996.

Diner, Hasia, Shira Kohn, and Rachel Kranson, eds. *A Jewish Feminine Mystique? Jewish Women in Postwar America*. New Brunswick, N.J.: Rutgers University Press, 2010.

Dionne, E. J., Jr., Norman J. Ornstein, and Thomas Mann. *One Nation After Trump: A Guide for the Perplexed, the Disillusioned, the Desperate, and the Not-Yet Deported*. New York: St. Martin's Press, 2018.

Dodson, Scott, ed. *The Legacy of Ruth Bader Ginsburg*. New York: Cambridge University Press, 2015.

Douglas, William O. *Go East, Young Man: The Early Years: The Autobiography of William O. Douglas*. New York: Random House, 1974.

Duberman, Martin B. *The Martin Duberman Reader: The Essential Historical, Biographical, and Autobiographical Writings*. New York: New Press, 2013.

Dudziak, Mary L. *War Time: An Idea, Its History, Its Consequences*. New York: Oxford University Press, 2012.

Dunbar-Ortiz, Roxanne. *Loaded: A Disarming History of the Second Amendment*. San Francisco: City Light Publishers, 2018.

Duxbury, Neil. *Patterns of American Jurisprudence*. Oxford: Clarendon Press, 1995.

Dyer, Carolyn Stewart, and Nancy Tillman Romalov, eds. *Rediscovering Nancy Drew*. Iowa City: University of Iowa Press, 1995.

Edelman, Hope. *Motherless Daughters: The Legacy of Loss*. Cambridge, Mass.: Da Capo Press, 2006.

Edsall, Thomas, and Mary Edsall. *Chain Reaction: The Impact of Race, Rights, and Taxes on American Politics*. New York: W. W. Norton, 1992.

Edwards, Laura F. *The People and Their Peace: Legal Culture and the Transformation of Inequality in the Post-revolutionary South*. Chapel Hill: University of North Carolina Press, 2009.

Engst, Elaine D. *Jewish Life at Cornell, 1865–2005*. Ithaca, N.Y.: Cornell University, 2006.

Epp, Charles R. *The Rights Revolution: Lawyers, Activists, and the Supreme Court in Comparative Perspective*. Chicago: University of Chicago Press, 1998.

Epstein, Cynthia Fuchs. *A Woman's Place: Options and Limitations in Professional Careers*. Berkeley: University of California Press, 1970.

———. *Women in Law*. Urbana: University of Illinois Press, 1993.

Epstein, Lee, and Jack Knight. *The Choices Justices Make*. Washington, D.C.: CQ Press, 1998.

Eskridge, William N., Jr. *Dishonorable Passions: Sodomy Laws in America, 1861–2003*. New York: Viking, 2008.

Evans, Sara M. *Tidal Wave: How Women Changed America at Century's End*. New York: Free Press, 2003.

Fallon, Richard H., Jr., Daniel J. Meltzer, and David L. Shapiro. *Hart and Weschler's "The Federal Courts and the Federal System."* 4th ed. Westbury, N.Y.: Foundation Press, 1996.

Faludi, Susan. *Backlash: The Undeclared War Against American Women*. New York: Crown, 1991.

Faulkner, William. *Requiem for a Nun*. New York: Random House, 1951.

Featherstone, Liza. *Selling Women Short: The Landmark Battle for Workers' Rights at Wal-Mart*. New York: Basic Books, 2004.

Feigen, Brenda. *Not One of the Boys: Living Life as a Feminist*. New York: Knopf, 2000.

Ferree, Myra Marx, and Patricia Yancey Martin, eds. *Feminist Organizations: Harvest of the New Women's Movement*. Philadelphia: Temple University Press, 1995.

Finlay, Barbara. *George W. Bush and the War on Women: Turning Back the Clock on Progress*. London: Zed Books, 2006.

Fisher, Louis. *The Constitution and 9/11: Recurring Threats to America's Freedoms*. Lawrence: University Press of Kansas, 2008.

Fitzhenry, Robert I., ed. *The Harper Book of Quotations*. New York: HarperCollins, 1993.

Foner, Eric, and Olivia Mahoney. *America's Reconstruction: People and Politics After the Civil War*. Baton Rouge: Louisiana State University Press, 1995.

Francke, Linda Bird. *Ground Zero: The Gender Wars in the Military*. New York: Simon & Schuster, 1997.

Frank, Barney. *Frank: A Life in Politics from the Great Society to Same-Sex Marriage*. New York: Farrar, Straus & Giroux, 2015.

Frank, Nathaniel. *Awakening: How Gays and Lesbians Brought Marriage Equality to America*. Cambridge: Harvard University Press, 2017.

Freedman, Estelle. *Redefining Rape: Sexual Violence in the Era of Suffrage and Segregation*. Cambridge, Mass.: Harvard University Press, 2013.

Friedan, Betty. *The Feminine Mystique*. New York: W. W. Norton, 1965.

Friedman, Lawrence M. *American Law in the 20th Century*. New Haven, Conn.: Yale University Press, 2002.

Frost-Knappman, Elizabeth, and David S. Shrager. *The Quotable Lawyer*. New York: New England Publishing Associates, 1986.

Galbraith, John Kenneth. *The Affluent Society*. New York: Houghton Mifflin, 1958.

Galligher, John, and Chris Bull. *Perfect Enemies: The Religious Right and the Politics of the 1990s*. New York: Crown, 1996.

Garfield, J., and Patrick Hennessey, eds. *Abortion: Moral and Legal Perspectives*. Amherst: University of Massachusetts Press, 1984.

Garrow, David J. *Liberty and Sexuality: The Right to Privacy and the Making of Roe v. Wade*. Rev. ed. Berkeley: University of California Press, 1998.

Gerhardt, Michael. *The Federal Appointment Process: A Constitutional and Historical Analysis.* Durham, N.C.: Duke University Press, 2000.

Gilbert, Lynn, and Gaylen Moore. *Particular Passions: Talks with Women Who Have Shaped Our Times.* New York: C. N. Potter, 1981.

Gilens, Martin. *Affluence and Influence: Economic Inequality and Political Power in America.* Princeton, N.J.: Princeton University Press, 2012.

Gill, LaVerne McCain. *African American Women in Congress: Forming and Transforming History.* New Brunswick, N.J.: Rutgers University Press, 1997.

Gilles, Myriam E., and Risa L. Goluboff, eds. *Civil Rights Stories.* New York: Foundation Press, 2008.

Gilligan, Carol. *In a Different Voice: Psychological Theory and Women's Development.* Cambridge, Mass.: Harvard University Press, 1993.

Gillman, Howard. *The Votes That Counted: How the Court Decided the 2000 Presidential Election.* Chicago: University of Chicago Press, 2001.

Gilmore, Glenda Elizabeth. *Defying Dixie: The Radical Roots of Civil Rights, 1919–1950.* New York: W. W. Norton, 2008.

Ginsburg, Ruth Bader. *My Own Words.* With Mary Hartnett and Wendy W. Williams. New York: Simon & Schuster, 2016.

Goldman, Sheldon. *Picking Federal Judges: Lower Court Selection from Roosevelt Through Reagan.* New Haven, Conn.: Yale University Press, 1997.

Goldstein, Leslie Friedman, ed. *Feminist Jurisprudence: The Difference Debate.* Boston: Rowman & Littlefield, 1992.

Graham, Hugh Davis. *The Civil Rights Era: Origins and Development of National Policy, 1960–1972.* New York: Oxford University Press, 1990.

Green, Joshua. *Devil's Bargain: Steve Bannon, Donald Trump, and the Storming of the Presidency.* New York: Penguin, 2017.

Greenhouse, Linda. *Becoming Justice Blackmun: Harry Blackmun's Supreme Court Journey.* New York: Henry Holt, 2005.

Greenhouse, Linda, and Reva B. Siegel, eds. *Before Roe v. Wade: Voices That Shaped the Abortion Debate Before the Supreme Court Ruling.* New York: Kaplan, 2010.

Grimké, Sarah. *Letters on the Equality of the Sexes and the Condition of Woman.* 1838. Reprint, New York: Reprint Services, 1970.

Griswold, Erwin N. *Ould Fields, New Corne: The Personal Memoirs of a Twentieth Century Lawyer.* St. Paul: West Group, 1992.

Grossberg, Michael. *Governing the Hearth: Law and Family in Nineteenth-Century America.* Chapel Hill: University of North Carolina Press, 1985.

Guinier, Lani. *The Tyranny of the Majority: Finding Fairness in Representation.* New York: Free Press, 1994.

Gunther, Gerald. *Learned Hand: The Man and the Judge.* Cambridge, Mass.: Harvard University Press, 1994.

Hamburger, Philip. *The Administrative Threat.* New York: Encounter Books, 2017.

———. *Is Administrative Law Unconstitutional?* Chicago: University of Chicago Press, 2015.

Hammer, Nicole. *Messengers of the Right: Conservative Media and the Transformation of American Politics.* Philadelphia: University of Pennsylvania Press, 2016.

Haney-López, Ian. *Dog Whistle Politics: How Coded Racial Appeals Have Reinvented Racism and Wrecked the Middle Class.* New York: Oxford University Press, 2014.

Harris, Frederick C., and Robert C. Lieberman, eds. *Beyond Discrimination: Racial Inequality in a Postracist Era.* New York: Russell Sage, 2013.

Harris, John F. *The Survivor: Bill Clinton in the White House.* New York: Random House, 2005.

Harrison, Cynthia. *On Account of Sex: The Politics of Women's Issues, 1945–1968.* Berkeley: University of California Press, 1989.

Hart, Henry M., Jr., and Albert M. Sacks. *The Legal Process: Basic Problems in the Making and Application of Law*. Westbury, N.Y.: Foundation Press, 1994.

Hartmann, Susan M. *The Other Feminists: Activists in the Liberal Establishment*. New Haven, Conn.: Yale University Press, 1998.

Hartog, Hendrik. *Man and Wife in America: A History*. Cambridge, Mass.: Harvard University Press, 2000.

Heinze, Andrew R. *Jews and the American Soul: Human Nature in the Twentieth Century*. Princeton, N.J.: Princeton University Press, 2004.

Heinzet, John P., et al. *Urban Lawyers: The New Social Structure of the Bar*. Chicago: University of Chicago Press, 2005.

Himmelstein, Jerome. *To the Right: The Transformation of American Conservatism*. Berkeley: University of California Press, 1990.

Hirsch, H. N. *The Enigma of Felix Frankfurter*. New York: Basic Books, 1981.

Hirshman, Linda. *Sisters in Law: How Sandra Day O'Connor and Ruth Bader Ginsburg Went to the Supreme Court and Changed the World*. New York: Harper, 2015.

Hochschild, Arlie Russell. *Strangers in Their Own Land: Anger and Mourning on the American Right*. New York: New Press, 2016.

Hoff, Joan. *Law, Gender, and Injustice: A Legal History of U.S. Women*. New York: New York University Press, 1994.

Hofstadter, Richard. *The American Political Tradition: The Men Who Made It*. New York: Knopf, 1948.

——— . *The Paranoid Style in American Politics, and Other Essays*. Cambridge, Mass.: Harvard University Press, 1964.

Hope, Judith Richards. *Pinstripes and Pearls: The Women of the Harvard Law Class of '64 Who Forged an Old-Girl Network and Paved the Way for Future Generations*. New York: Scribner, 2003.

Horowitz, Daniel. *Betty Friedan and the Making of "The Feminine Mystique": The American Left, the Cold War, and Modern Feminism*. Amherst: University of Massachusetts Press, 1998.

Hunter, James Davison. *Before the Shooting Begins: Searching for Democracy in America's Culture War*. New York: Free Press, 1994.

——— . *Culture Wars: The Struggle to Define America*. New York: Basic Books, 1991.

Hutchinson, Dennis. *The Man Who Once Was Whizzer White: A Portrait of Justice Byron White*. New York: Free Press, 1998.

Jacoby, Kerry N. *Souls, Bodies, Spirits: The Drive to Abolish Abortion Since 1973*. Westport, Conn.: Praeger, 1998.

Jeffords, Susan. *The Remasculinization of America: Gender and the Vietnam War*. Bloomington: Indiana University Press, 1989.

Jeffries, John. *Justice Lewis F. Powell Jr*. New York: Fordham University Press, 1994.

Joffe, Carole. *Doctors of Conscience: The Struggle to Provide Abortion Before and After Roe v. Wade*. Boston: Beacon, 1995.

Johnston, Jill. *Lesbian Nation: The Feminist Solution*. New York: Simon & Schuster, 1973.

Kalman, Laura. *Legal Realism at Yale, 1927–1960*. Chapel Hill: University of North Carolina Press, 1986.

——— . *The Long Reach of the Sixties: LBJ, Nixon, and the Making of the Contemporary Supreme Court*. New York: Oxford University Press, 2017.

——— . *Right Star Rising: A New Politics, 1974–1980*. New York: W. W. Norton, 2010.

——— . *The Strange Career of Legal Liberalism*. New Haven, Conn.: Yale University Press, 1998.

——— . *Yale Law School and the Sixties: Revolt and Reverberations*. Chapel Hill: University of North Carolina Press, 2005.

Kamerman, Sheila B., and Alfred J. Kahn, eds. *Family Policy: Government and Family Policies in Fourteen Countries*. New York: Columbia University Press, 1978.

Kammen, Carol. *Cornell: Glorious to View*. Ithaca, N.Y.: Cornell University Press, 2003.

Katzenstein, Mary Fainsod, and Judith Reppy, eds. *Beyond Zero Tolerance: Discrimination in Military Culture*. New York: Rowman & Littlefield, 1999.

Katznelson, Ira. *When Affirmative Action Was White: An Untold Story of Racial Inequality in Twentieth-Century America*. New York: W. W. Norton, 2005.

Keck, Thomas M. *The Most Activist Supreme Court in History: The Road to Modern Judicial Conservatism*. Chicago: University of Chicago Press, 2004.

Keller, Morton, and Phyllis Keller. *Making Harvard Modern: The Rise of the Modern University*. New York: Oxford University Press, 2001.

Kenney, Sally J. *Gender and Justice: Why Women in the Judiciary Really Matter*. New York: Routledge, 2013.

Kenski, Kate, Bruce W. Hardy, and Kathleen Hall Jamieson. *The Obama Victory: How Media, Money, and Message Shaped the 2008 Elections*. New York: Oxford University Press, 2010.

Kerber, Linda K. *No Constitutional Right to Be Ladies: Women and the Obligations of Citizenship*. New York: Hill and Wang, 1998.

Kerber, Linda K., and Jane Sherron De Hart, eds. *Women's America: Refocusing the Past*. 6th ed. New York: Oxford University Press, 2004.

Kerber, Linda K., Alice Kessler-Harris, and Kathryn Kish Sklar, eds. *U.S. History as Women's History: New Feminist Essays*. Chapel Hill: University of North Carolina Press, 1995.

Kessler-Harris, Alice. *In Pursuit of Equity: Women, Men, and the Quest for Economic Citizenship in Twentieth-Century America*. New York: Oxford University Press, 2003.

———. *A Woman's Wage: Historical Meanings and Social Consequences*. Lexington: University Press of Kentucky, 1990.

Keyssar, Alexander. *The Right to Vote: The Contested History of Democracy in the United States*. New York: Basic Books, 2000.

Klarman, Michael J. *From Jim Crow to Civil Rights: The Supreme Court and the Struggle for Racial Equality*. New York: Oxford University Press, 2004.

———. *From the Closet to the Altar: Courts, Backlash, and the Struggle for Same-Sex Marriage*. New York: Oxford University Press, 2013.

Klebanow, Diana, and Franklin L. Jonas. *People's Lawyers: Crusaders for Justice in American History*. Armonk, N.Y.: M. E. Sharpe, 2003.

Klein, Ethel. *Gender Politics*. Cambridge, Mass.: Harvard University Press, 1984.

Kousser, J. Morgan. *Colorblind Injustice: Minority Voting Rights and the Undoing of the Second Reconstruction*. Chapel Hill: University of North Carolina Press, 1999.

Kraditor, Aileen S., ed. *Up from the Pedestal*. Chicago: Quadrangle, 1968.

Kumar, Manoranjan. *Dictionary of Quotations*. New Delhi: APH, 2008.

Kurland, Philip B., and Gerhard Casper, eds. *Landmark Briefs and Arguments of the Supreme Court of the United States: Constitutional Law*. Frederick, Md.: University Publications of America, 1975–.

Kuznick, Peter J., and James Gilbert, eds. *Rethinking Cold War Culture*. Washington, D.C.: Smithsonian Institution Press, 2001.

Ladd, Everett Carll, and Karlyn H. Bowman. *Public Opinion About Abortion: Twenty-Five Years After Roe v. Wade*. Washington, D.C.: AEI Press, 1997.

Lasch, Christopher. *The Culture of Narcissism: American Life in an Age of Diminishing Expectations*. New York: W. W. Norton, 1978.

———. *Haven in a Heartless World: The Family Besieged*. New York: Basic Books, 1977.

Lassiter, Matthew, and Joseph Crespino, eds. *The Myth of Southern Exceptionalism*. New York: Oxford University Press, 2010.

Lears, T. Jackson. *The Culture of Consumption: Critical Essays in American History, 1880–1980*. New York: Pantheon Books, 1983.

Leuchtenburg, William E. *Franklin D. Roosevelt and the New Deal, 1932–40*. New York: Harper & Row, 1963.

Levin, Meyer, ed. *The Diary of David S. Kogan*. New York: Beechhurst Press, 1955.

Levy, Debbie, and Elizabeth Baddeley. *I Dissent: Ruth Bader Ginsburg Makes Her Mark.* New York: Simon & Schuster Books for Young Readers, 2016.

Litwack, Leon. *Trouble in Mind: Black Southerners in the Age of Jim Crow.* New York: Knopf, 1999.

Lo, Clarence Y. H., and Michael Schwartz, eds. *Social Policy and the Conservative Agenda.* Malden, Mass.: Blackwell, 1998.

Lowe, Jennifer M., ed. *The Jewish Justices of the Supreme Court Revisited: Brandeis to Fortas.* Washington, D.C.: Supreme Court Historical Society, 1994.

MacKinnon, Catharine A. *Sexual Harassment of Working Women: A Case of Sexual Discrimination.* New Haven, Conn.: Yale University Press, 1979.

Malkiel, Nancy Weiss. *"Keep the Damned Women Out": The Struggle for Coeducation.* Princeton, N.J.: Princeton University Press, 2016.

Maltz, Earl M., ed. *Rehnquist Justice: Understanding the Court Dynamic.* Lawrence: University Press of Kansas, 2003.

Mamo, Laura. *Queering Reproduction: Achieving Pregnancy in the Age of Technoscience.* Durham, N.C.: Duke University Press, 2007.

Manbeck, John B., ed. *The Neighborhoods of Brooklyn.* New Haven, Conn.: Yale University Press, 1998.

Mason, Mary Ann. *The Equality Trap.* New York: Simon & Schuster, 1988.

Mathews, Donald G., and Jane Sherron De Hart. *Sex, Gender, and the Politics of ERA: A State and the Nation.* New York: Oxford University Press, 1990.

Matusow, Allen. *The Unraveling of America: A History of Liberalism in the 1960s.* New York: Perennial, 1984.

Maveety, Nancy. *Justice Sandra Day O'Connor: Strategist on the Supreme Court.* New York: Rowman & Littlefield, 1996.

May, Elaine Tyler. *Homeward Bound: American Families in the Cold War Era.* New York: Basic Books, 1988.

May, Gary. *Bending Toward Justice: The Voting Rights Act and the Transformation of American Democracy.* New York: Basic Books, 2013.

Mayer, Jane. *Dark Money: The Hidden History of the Billionaires Behind the Rise of the Radical Right.* New York: Doubleday, 2016.

Mayeri, Serena. *Reasoning from Race: Feminism, Law, and the Civil Rights Revolution.* Cambridge, Mass.: Harvard University Press, 2011.

McCann, Michael W., and Gerald L. Houseman. *Judging the Constitution: Critical Essays on Judicial Lawmaking.* Boston: Scott, Foresman, 1989.

McCaughey, Robert A. *Stand, Columbia: A History of Columbia University in the City of New York.* New York: Columbia University Press, 2003.

McCoy, Alfred W. *Torture and Impunity: The U.S. Doctrine of Coercive Interrogation.* Madison: University of Wisconsin Press, 2012.

Melich, Tanya. *The Republican War Against Women: An Insider's Report from Behind the Lines.* New York: Bantam Books, 1998.

Mello, Joseph. *The Courts, the Ballot Box, and Gay Rights: How Our Governing Institutions Shape the Same-Sex Marriage Debate.* Lawrence: University Press of Kansas, 2016.

Mertz, Elizabeth. *The Language of Law School: Learning to "Think Like a Lawyer."* Oxford: Oxford University Press, 2007.

Meyerowitz, Joanne, ed. *Not June Cleaver: Women and Gender in Postwar America, 1945–1960.* Philadelphia: Temple University Press, 1994.

Miller, Rita Seiden, ed. *Brooklyn USA: The Fourth Largest City in America.* New York: Brooklyn College Press, 1979.

Minow, Martha. *In Brown's Wake: Legacies of America's Educational Landmark.* New York: Oxford University Press, 2010.

Moberg, Eva. *Kvinnor och människor* [Women and men]. Stockholm: Bonnier, 1962.

Moynihan, Daniel Patrick. *A Portrait in Letters of an American Visionary*. New York: PublicAffairs, 2010.

Mucciaroni, Gary. *Same Sex, Different Politics: Success and Failure in the Struggles over Gay Rights*. Chicago: University of Chicago Press, 2008.

Murdoch, Joyce, and Deb Price. *Courting Justice: Gay Men and Lesbians v. the Supreme Court*. New York: Basic Books, 2002.

Murphy, Bruce Allen. *Scalia: A Court of One*. New York: Simon & Schuster, 2014.

———. *Wild Bill: The Legend and Life of William O. Douglas*. New York: Random House, 2003.

Murray, Pauli. *Pauli Murray: The Autobiography of a Black Activist, Feminist, Lawyer, Priest, and Poet*. Knoxville: University of Tennessee Press, 1987.

———. *Proud Shoes: The Story of an American Family*. New York: Harper, 1956.

———. *Song in a Weary Throat: An American Pilgrimage*. New York: Harper & Row, 1987.

———. *States' Laws on Race and Color*. Athens: University of Georgia Press, 1977.

Musgrove, George Derek. *Rumor, Repression, and Racial Politics: How the Harassment of Black Elected Officials Shaped Post–Civil Rights America*. Athens: University of Georgia Press, 2012.

Myrdal, Gunnar. *An American Dilemma: The Negro Problem and Modern Democracy*. New York: McGraw-Hill, 1944.

Neier, Aryeh. *Taking Liberties: Four Decades in the Struggle for Rights*. New York: PublicAffairs, 2003.

Noonan, John T., Jr. *Narrowing the Nation's Power: The Supreme Court Sides with the States*. Berkeley: University of California Press, 2003.

Norgren, Jill. *Belva Lockwood: The Woman Who Would Be President*. New York: New York University Press, 2008.

Nossiff, Rosemary. *Before Roe: Abortion Policy in the States*. Philadelphia: Temple University Press, 2001.

Nussbaum, Martha C. *From Disgust to Humanity: Sexual Orientation and Constitutional Law*. New York: Oxford University Press, 2010.

O'Connor, Sandra Day. *The Majesty of the Law: Reflections of a Supreme Court Justice*. New York: Random House, 2003.

Offen, Karen, ed. *Globalizing Feminisms, 1799–1945*. New York: Routledge, 2010.

Omi, Michael, and Howard Winant. *Racial Formation in the United States: From the 1960s to the 1990s*. 2nd ed. New York: Routledge, 1994.

Pacelle, Richard L., Jr. *Between Law and Politics: The Solicitor General and the Structuring of Race, Gender, and Reproductive Rights Litigation*. College Station: Texas A&M University Press, 2003.

Paris, Leslie. *Children's Nature: The Rise of the American Summer Camp*. New York: New York University Press, 2008.

Parker, Christopher S., and Matt A. Barreto. *Change They Can't Believe In: The Tea Party and Reactionary Politics in America*. Princeton, N.J.: Princeton University Press, 2013.

Pascoe, Peggy. *What Comes Naturally: Miscegenation Law and the Making of Race in America*. New York: Oxford University Press, 2009.

Patterson, James T. *Grand Expectations: The United States, 1945–1974*. New York: Oxford University Press, 1996.

———. *Restless Giant: The United States from Watergate to Bush v. Gore*. New York: Oxford University Press, 2007.

Peppers, Todd C. *Courtiers of the Marble Palace: The Rise and Influence of the Supreme Court Law Clerk*. Stanford, Calif.: Stanford University Press, 2006.

Perry, Barbara A. *The Michigan Affirmative Action Cases*. Lawrence: University Press of Kansas, 2007.

———. *"The Supremes": Essays on the Current Justices of the Supreme Court of the United States*. New York: Peter Lang, 1999.

Pierceson, Jason. *Same-Sex Marriage in the United States: The Road to the Supreme Court.* Lanham, Md.: Rowman & Littlefield, 2013.

Pitzulo, Carrie. *Bachelors and Bunnies: The Sexual Politics of "Playboy."* Chicago: University of Chicago Press, 2000.

Pole, J. R. *The Pursuit of Equality in American History.* Berkeley: University of California Press, 1978.

Posner, Richard A. *Breaking the Deadlock: The 2000 Election, the Constitution, and the Courts.* Princeton, N.J.: Princeton University Press, 2001.

Reagan, Leslie J. *Dangerous Pregnancies: Mothers, Disabilities, and Abortion in Modern America.* Berkeley: University of California Press, 2010.

———. *When Abortion Was a Crime: Women, Medicine, and the Law in the United States, 1867–1973.* Berkeley: University of California Press, 1998.

Reardon, David C. *Making Abortions Rare: A Healing Strategy for a Divided Nation.* Dover, Del.: Acorn Books, 1996.

Rehnquist, William H. *The Supreme Court: How It Was, How It Is.* New York: William Morrow, 1987.

Reinharz, Shulamit, and Mark A. Raider, eds. *American Jewish Women and the Zionist Enterprise.* Waltham, Mass.: Brandeis University Press, 2005.

Richards, David A. J. *The Sodomy Cases: Bowers v. Hardwick and Lawrence v. Texas.* Lawrence: University Press of Kansas, 2009.

Rieder, Jonathan. *Canarsie: The Jews and Italians of Brooklyn Against Liberalism.* Cambridge, Mass.: Harvard University Press, 1985.

Rivers, Daniel Winunwe. *Radical Relations: Lesbian Mothers, Gay Fathers, and Their Children in the United States Since World War II.* Chapel Hill: University of North Carolina Press, 2013.

Rosen, Jeffrey. *The Supreme Court: The Personalities and Rivalries That Defined America.* New York: Henry Holt, 2006.

Rosenberg, Rosalind. *Changing the Subject: How the Women of Columbia Shaped the Way We Think About Sex and Politics.* New York: Columbia University Press, 2004.

Rubel, David, ed. *Days of Destiny: Crossroads in American History.* New York: DK Adult, 2001.

Russell, Diana E. H. *The Secret Trauma: Incest in the Lives of Girls and Women.* New York: Basic Books, 1986.

———. *Sexual Exploitation: Rape, Child Sexual Abuse, and Workplace Harassment.* New York: Sage, 1984.

Ryan, Mary P. *Mysteries of Sex: Tracing Women and Men Through American History.* Chapel Hill: University of North Carolina Press, 2006.

Rymph, Catherine E. *Republican Women: Feminism and Conservatism from Suffrage Through the Rise of the New Right.* Chapel Hill: University of North Carolina Press, 2006.

Saline, Carol, and Sharon J. Wohlmuth. *Mothers and Daughters.* New York: Doubleday, 1997.

Sarat, Austin, and Thomas R. Kearns, eds. *History, Memory, and the Law.* Ann Arbor: University of Michigan Press, 1999.

Sarat, Austin, and Stuart Scheingold, eds. *Cause Lawyering and the State in a Global Era.* New York: Oxford University Press, 2001.

Sawyer, Mary R. *The Harassment of Black Elected Officials: Ten Years Later.* Washington, D.C.: Voter Education and Registration Action, 1989.

Scheingold, Stuart A., and Austin Sarat. *Something to Believe In: Politics, Professionalism, and Cause Lawyering.* Stanford, Calif.: Stanford University Press, 2004.

Schier, Steven E., ed. *Transforming America: Barack Obama in the White House.* New York: Rowman & Littlefield, 2011.

Schlesinger, Arthur, Jr. *The Vital Center: The Politics of Freedom.* Boston: Houghton Mifflin, 1949.

Schneider, Elizabeth M. *Battered Women and Feminist Lawmaking.* New Haven, Conn.: Yale University Press, 2000.

Schneider, Elizabeth M., and Stephanie M. Wildman, eds. *Women and the Law Stories*. New York: Foundation Press | Thomson Reuters, 2011.

Schrecker, Ellen. *Many Are the Crimes: McCarthyism in America*. Princeton, N.J.: Princeton University Press, 1999.

———. *No Ivory Tower: McCarthyism and the Universities*. New York: Oxford University Press, 1986.

Schwartz, Bernard. *The Burger Court: Counter-revolution or Confirmation?* New York: Oxford University Press, 1998.

———. *The History of the Supreme Court*. New York: Oxford University Press, 1993.

Scott, Anne Firor, ed. *Pauli Murray and Caroline Ware: Forty Years of Letters in Black and White*. Chapel Hill: University of North Carolina Press, 2006.

Scott, Hilda. *Sweden's "Right to Be Human" Sex-Role Equality: The Goal and Reality*. Armonk, N.Y.: M. E. Sharpe, 1982.

Self, Robert O. *All in the Family: The Realignment of American Democracy Since the 1960s*. New York: Hill and Wang, 2012.

Shilts, Randy. *And the Band Played On: Politics, People, and the AIDS Epidemic*. New York: St. Martin's Press, 1987.

———. *Conduct Unbecoming: Gays and Lesbians in the U.S. Military*. New York: Macmillan, 1994.

Skocpol, Theda, and Vanessa Williamson. *The Tea Party and the Remaking of Republican Conservatism*. New York: Oxford University Press, 2012.

Skrentny, John D. *The Minority Rights Revolution*. Cambridge, Mass.: Harvard University Press, 2002.

Smigel, Erwin O. *The Wall Street Lawyer, Professional Organization Man?* Bloomington: Indiana University Press, 1964.

Solinger, Rickie. *The Abortionist: A Woman Against the Law*. New York: Free Press, 1995.

Sotomayor, Sonia. *My Beloved World*. New York: Knopf, 2013.

Sovern, Michael I. *An Improbable Life: My 60 Years at Columbia and Other Adventures*. New York: Columbia University Press, 2014.

Staggenborg, Suzanne. *The Pro-choice Movement: Organization and Activism in the Abortion Conflict*. New York: Oxford University Press, 1991.

Stephanopoulos, George. *All Too Human: A Political Education*. New York: Little, Brown, 1999.

Stern, Seth, and Stephen Wermiel. *Justice Brennan: Liberal Champion*. Boston: Houghton Mifflin Harcourt, 2010.

Stevens, John Paul. *Five Chiefs*. New York: Little, Brown, 2011.

Stiehm, Judith Hicks. *Bring Me Men and Women: Mandated Change in the U.S. Air Force Academy*. Berkeley: University of California Press, 1981.

Strebeigh, Fred. *Equal: Women Reshape American Law*. New York: W. W. Norton, 2009.

Strum, Philippa. *Women in the Barracks: The VMI Case and Equal Rights*. Lawrence: University Press of Kansas, 2002.

Sugrue, Thomas J. *Not Even Past: Barack Obama and the Burden of Race*. Princeton, N.J.: Princeton University Press, 2010.

———. *The Origins of the Urban Crisis: Race and Inequality in Postwar Detroit*. Princeton, N.J.: Princeton University Press, 1996.

Sunstein, Cass R. *The Partial Constitution*. Cambridge, Mass.: Harvard University Press, 1993.

———. *Radicals in Robes: Why Extreme Right-Wing Courts Are Wrong for America*. New York: Basic Books, 2005.

Sutton, Joseph A. D. *Magic Carpet: Aleppo-in-Flatbush*. New York: Thayer-Jacoby, 1979.

Svonkin, Stuart. *Jews Against Prejudice: American Jews and the Fight for Civil Liberties*. New York: Columbia University Press, 1997.

Teles, Steven M. *The Rise of the Conservative Legal Movement: The Battle for Control of the Law*. Princeton, N.J.: Princeton University Press, 2008.

Telushkin, Joseph. *Jewish Humor: What the Best Jewish Jokes Say About the Jews*. New York: HarperCollins, 1992.

Tesler, Michael. *Post-Racial or Most-Racial? Race and Politics in the Obama Era*. Chicago: University of Chicago Press, 2016.

Thernstrom, Abigail. *Voting Rights—and Wrongs: The Elusive Quest for Racially Fair Elections*. Washington, D.C.: AEI Press, 2009.

Thomas, Clarence. *My Grandfather's Son*. New York: HarperCollins, 2007.

Thomas, Tracy A., and Tracey Jean Boisseau, eds. *Feminist Legal History: Essays on Women and the Law*. New York: New York University Press, 2011.

Thurber, Timothy N. *Republicans and Race: The GOP's Frayed Relationship with African Americans, 1945–1974*. Lawrence: University Press of Kansas, 2013.

Toobin, Jeffrey. *The Nine: Inside the Secret World of the Supreme Court*. New York: Anchor Books, 2008.

———. *The Oath: The Obama White House and the Supreme Court*. New York: Doubleday, 2012.

———. *Too Close to Call: The Thirty-Six-Day Battle to Decide the 2000 Election*. New York: Random House, 2002.

Tribe, Laurence, and Joshua Matz. *Uncertain Justice: The Roberts Court and the Constitution*. New York: Henry Holt, 2014.

Tushnet, Mark. *A Court Divided: The Rehnquist Court and the Future of Constitutional Law*. New York: W. W. Norton, 2005.

———. *In the Balance: Law and Politics on the Roberts Court*. New York: W. W. Norton, 2013.

———. *Making Constitutional Law: Thurgood Marshall and the Supreme Court, 1961–1991*. New York: Oxford University Press, 1997.

Umansky, Ellen M., and Dianne Ashton, eds. *Four Centuries of Jewish Women's Spirituality: A Sourcebook*. Boston: Beacon Press, 1992.

Urofsky, Melvin I. *The Continuity of Change: The Supreme Court and Individual Liberties, 1953–1986*. Belmont, Calif.: Wadsworth, 1991.

Van Burkleo, Sandra F. *Belonging to the World: Women's Rights and American Constitutional Culture*. New York: Oxford University Press, 2001.

Vance, J. D. *Hillbilly Elegy: A Memoir of a Family and Culture in Crisis*. New York: HarperCollins, 2016.

Walker, Samuel. *In Defense of American Liberties: A History of the ACLU*. 2nd ed. Carbondale: Southern Illinois University Press, 1999.

Wall, Wendy L. *Inventing the "American Way."* New York: Oxford University Press, 2008.

Walsh, Mary Roth. *"Doctors Wanted: No Women Need Apply": Sexual Barriers in the Medical Profession, 1835–1975*. New Haven, Conn.: Yale University Press, 1977.

Warner, Mary R. *The Dilemma of Black Politics: A Report on Harassment of Black Elected Officials*. Sacramento, Calif.: M. R. Warner, 1977.

Weddington, Sarah. *A Question of Choice: By the Lawyer Who Won Roe v. Wade*. New York: Penguin Books, 1993.

Weiss, Jessica. *To Have and to Hold: Marriage, the Baby Boom, and Social Change*. Chicago: University of Chicago Press, 2000.

Weld, Ralph Foster. *Brooklyn Is America*. New York: Columbia University Press, 1950.

West, Robin. *Progressive Constitutionalism: Reconstructing the Fourteenth Amendment*. Durham, N.C.: Duke University Press, 1994.

Wheeler, Leigh Ann. *How Sex Became a Civil Liberty*. New York: Oxford University Press, 2013.

Wieseltier, Leon. *Kaddish*. New York: Knopf, 1998.

Winkler, Adam. *Gunfight: The Battle over the Right to Bear Arms in America*. New York: W. W. Norton, 2011.

Winter, Jonah, and Stacy Innerst. *Ruth Bader Ginsburg: The Case of R.B.G. vs. Inequality*. New York: Harry N. Abrams, 2017.

Woodward, Bob, and Scott Armstrong. *The Brethren: Inside the Supreme Court*. New York: Simon & Schuster, 2005.

Wouk, Herman. *Marjorie Morningstar*. New York: Doubleday, 1955.

Wyman, David S. *The Abandonment of the Jews: America and the Holocaust, 1941–1945*. New York: Pantheon Books, 1984.

Yarbrough, Tinsley E. *Harry A. Blackmun: The Outsider Justice*. New York: Oxford University Press, 2008.

Yoshino, Kenji. *Speak Now: Marriage Equality on Trial*. New York: Crown, 2015.

Yuill, Kevin L. *Richard Nixon and the Rise of Affirmative Action: The Pursuit of Racial Equality in an Era of Limits*. New York: Rowman & Littlefield, 2006.

Zaretsky, Natasha. *No Direction Home: The American Family and the Fear of National Decline, 1968–1980*. Chapel Hill: University of North Carolina Press, 2007.

Zelizer, Julian E., ed. *The Presidency of George W. Bush: A First Historical Assessment*. Princeton, N.J.: Princeton University Press, 2010.

Zeltzer, Julian E. ed. *The Presidency of Barack Obama: A First Historical Assessment*. Princeton: Princeton University Press, 2018.

Government Sources

U.S. Congress. House. Committee on Armed Services. *Registration of Women: Hearings on H.R. 6569*, 96th Cong., 2nd sess., 1980.

U.S. Congress. House. Committee on Un-American Activities. *Hearings on Communist Methods of Infiltration (Education) Part 5*. 83rd Cong., 1st sess., May 27, 1953.

U.S. Congress. House. Committee on Un-American Activities. *Report on the Communist "Peace" Offensive: A Campaign to Disarm and Defeat the United States*. 82nd Cong., 1st sess., 1951.

U.S. Congress. House. Subcommittee on Civil and Constitution Rights of the House Committee on the Judiciary. *Hearings on H.J. Res. 638: Equal Rights Extension*. 95th Cong., 1st–2nd sess., 1977 and 1978.

U.S. Congress. House. Subcommittee on the Constitution of the Committee on the Judiciary. *To Examine the Impact and Effectiveness of the Voting Rights Act*. 109th Cong., 1st sess., Oct. 18, 2005.

U.S. Congress. Senate. Committee on the Judiciary. *Hearings*. 96th Cong., 2nd sess., 1979.

U.S. Congress. Senate. Committee on the Judiciary. *Nomination of Ruth Bader Ginsburg to Be Associate Justice of the Supreme Court of the United States: Hearings*. 103rd Cong., 2nd sess., 1993.

U.S. Congress. Senate. Committee on the Judiciary. *Women and Violence*. 101st Cong., 2nd sess., June 20, Aug. 29, and Dec. 11, 1990.

U.S. Congress. Senate. Subcommittee on Crime and Criminal Justice. *Hearings*. 102nd Cong., 1st sess., Feb. 6, 1992.

Organization Sources

Connell, Sue. *The Money Behind the 2004 Marriage Amendments*. Institute on Money in State Politics, 2006. Available at followthemoney.org.

Leadership Conference on Civil and Human Rights. *Warning Signs: The Potential Impact of Shelby County v. Holder on the 2016 General Election*. June 2016.

Open Society Institute. *The Report of the Constitution Project's Task Force on Detainee Treatment*. April 2013.

Professional Women's Caucus. *Sixteen Reports on the Status of Women in the Professions*. New York, 1970.

Report of the American Civil Liberties Union on the Nomination of Third Circuit Court Judge Samuel A. Alito Jr. to Be Associate Justice on the United States Supreme Court. Dec. 9, 2005.

Women's Rights Project. *With Liberty and Justice for Women: The ACLU's Contribution to Ten Years of Struggle for Equal Right.* New York: American Civil Liberties Union, 1982.

Non-archival Short Interviews

Couric, Katie. "Exclusive: Ruth Bader Ginsburg on *Hobby Lobby, Roe v. Wade,* Retirement, and Notorious R.B.G.," Yahoo.com, July 31, 2014.

———. "Ruth Ginsburg on Trump, Kaepernick, and Her Lifelong Love of the Law." *The Katie Couric Interview,* Oct. 10, 2016.

Kempner, Aviva, writer, producer, director. *Yoo-Hoo, Mrs. Goldberg.* Ciesla Foundation, 2009.

Morris, Emma Joan, director. *Paving the Way.* CINE Golden Eagle, 1995.

Pauley, Jane. "Ruth Bader Ginsburg: Her View from the Bench." CBS News, Oct. 9, 2016.

Rose, Charlie. "Justice Ruth Bader Ginsburg Interview, Part 1." CharlieRose.com, Oct. 10, 2016.

———. "Justice Ruth Bader Ginsburg Interview, Part 2." CharlieRose.com, Oct. 11, 2016.

Totenberg, Nina. "A Look at Judge Ruth Bader Ginsburg's Life and Career," NPR, July 6, 1993. Transcript obtained from Ms. Totenberg.

———. "Martin Ginsburg's Legacy: Love of Justice (Ginsburg)." *Weekend Edition Saturday,* NPR, July 3, 2010.

———. "No, Ruth Bader Ginsburg Does Not Intend to Retire Anytime Soon." NPR, Oct. 3, 2016.

Index

Page numbers in *italics* refer to illustrations.

Michelman, Kate, 194
Michigan, 466
Michigan, University of (UM), xv
    affirmative action issues at, 428–36
Mikulski, Barbara, 285, 385
Mikva, Abner, 282–3, 284, 289, 291, 292,
    297, 413
military, U.S.
    ban on gays in, 453
    "don't ask, don't tell" policy of, 414
    sex-based housing allowances of,
        197–8
millennials, RBG embraced by, 474–5
Milne, A. A., 9, 10
minorities, affirmative action and, 220
minority women, 312
Minow, Martha, 471–2
Miranda rights, 320
Mississippi, 386, 394, 471
Mississippi University for Women v. Hogan,
    336, 341, 343, 383
Missouri, 241
MIT, Women's and Gender Studies
    Program, *474*
Mitchell, George, 304, 308
M.L.B. v. S.L.J., 472–3
Monaghan, Henry, 417
Montgomery, Ala., 197
    bus boycott in, 198
    voting-rights march to, 437
Montgomery bus boycott, 443
Montreal, Canada, 351, 352
Morgan, Charles "Chuck," 199, 204
Moritz, Charles E., 124–5, 128, 172, 301
Moritz case, 126–9, 133–4, 139, 152, 159, 175,
    247
    gender stereotyping in, 152
    Griswold and, 172
morning-after pill, 478
Morrison, Alan, 295
Morrison, Antonio, 356–7, 361
Morrison v. Olson, 296
Morse decision, 424
mortgage market, 377
motherhood
    gender stereotyping and, 181, 185, 186
    physical limitations imposed by, 181–2
Moynihan, Daniel Patrick, ix, 306, 308, 315,
    316, 318–19
Ms., 161, 277
Mubarak, Hosni, 421
Muller v. Oregon, 172, 180

Murray, Pauli, 148, 151, 153, 154, 172, 180, 181,
    198, 202, 206, 233, 267, 287, 426
"My Day" column, 12

NAACP Legal Defense and Educational
    Fund, 440
NAACP Legal Defense Fund, 150, 153, 168,
    170–1
Nabokov, Vladimir, xvii
Nagasaki, 20
Nancy Drew detective series, 10
NARAL, 316
Nathan Bader Inc., 28
Nation, 313
National Abortion Rights Action League
    (NARAL), 1904
National Advisory Committee for Women,
    288
National Association for the Advancement
    of Colored People (NAACP), and 2000
    election, 366
National Association of Criminal Defense
    Lawyers, 358
National Association of Women Judges,
    326, 354
National Conference on Women and Law,
    175
National Federation Business, 153
*National Federation of Independent Business
    v. Sebelius,* 470–1
National Law Journal, 315, 317
National Organization for Women (NOW),
    153, 161, 171, 195, 200
    Legal Defense Fund of, 282, 316, 359, 361
National Public Radio, 420
National Review, 445
National Rifle Association (NRA), 289, 410
National Women's Political Caucus
    (NWPC), 282, 317
    Judicial Selection Committee of, 288
    Legal Support Caucus of, 286
Nebraska, 389–90
Neier, Aryeh, 156, 171, 175, 191, 195, 219–20
    WRP and, 160–1
Neponsit, 15
Neshoba County Fair, Mississippi, 445
Ness, Susan, 286, 288
Nevada Department of Human Resources,
    380
*Nevada Department of Human Resources v.
    Hibbs,* 379–81
New Brunswick *Home News,* 242

Illustration Credits

140   Courtesy of Ruth Bader Ginsburg

149   Special Collections and Archives, Boise State University Library

162   Courtesy of Brenda Feigen

181   Bettmann / Getty Images

200   Bettmann / Getty Images

210   Photograph by Harris and Ewing, Collection of the Supreme Court
       of the United States

211   Photograph by Newark News Staff, Collection of the Supreme Court
       of the United States

230   Courtesy of Kathleen Peratis

249   AP Photo

269   Collection of the Supreme Court of the United States

270   Collection of the Supreme Court of the United States

279   Courtesy of Ruth Bader Ginsburg

280   Courtesy of Ruth Bader Ginsburg

287   Bettmann / Getty Images

290   Courtesy of Jimmy Carter Library

293   Collection of the Supreme Court of the United States

294   Photograph by Chase Studio, Collection of the Supreme Court
       of the United States

298   Collection of the Supreme Court of the United States

300   Courtesy of Ruth Bader Ginsburg

303   Clinton Presidential Materials Project

319   AP Photo / Marty Nighswander

322   Photograph by the White House Office of Photography. Courtesy
       of the Collection of the Supreme Court of the United States

324   AP Photo / Doug Mills

329   Photograph by Richard W. Strauss, Smithsonian Institution, Collection
       of the Supreme Court of the United States

330   Anders Overgaard / Trunk Archive

331   David Hume Kennerly / Getty Images

345   *Washington Post* / Getty Images

346   *Washington Post* / Getty Images

352   Mark Wilson / Getty Images

362   AP Photo

365   Courtesy of Catherine MacKinnon

369   Larry Downing / Reuters

382   AP Photo / Ed Bailey

383   AP Photo / J. Scott Applewhite

384   Win McNamee / Getty Images

387   Danita Delimont / Alamy

390   Reuters

391 George Bridges / Getty Images

400 U.S. Navy / Getty Images

401 U.S. Army / Criminal Investigation Command (CID). Seized by the U.S. Government

403 Michael G. Stewart

408 Ralf-Finn Hestoft / Corbis via Getty Images

409 Stuart Carlson / United Press Syndicate

411 Brooks Kraft LLC / Corbis via Getty Images

413 Steve Petteway, Collection of the Supreme Court of the United States

414 Photograph by Steven Petteway, Collection of the Supreme Court of the United States

420 *Washington Post* / Getty Images

422 James Ginsburg and Patrice Michaels

426 *Boston Globe* / Getty Images

435 AP Photo / Susan Walsh

443 Mandel Ngan / Getty Images

461 Ken Cedeno / Getty Images

465 Timothy Clary / Getty Images

474 Chantal Acacio and Marol Escajeda / MIT Technique

477 (top) AP Photo / J. Scott Applewhite

477 (bottom) AP Photo

483 Collection of the Supreme Court of the United States

484 AP Photo / Steven R. Brown

486 Nicholas Kamm / Getty Images

496 Photograph by Scott Suchman

500 Chip Somodevilla / Getty Images

502 Elijah Nouvelage / Reuters

504 Bryan Woolston / Reuters

508 The White House

512 Paul J. Richards / Getty Images

527 AP Photo / Charles Dharapak

ABOUT THE AUTHOR

JANE SHERRON DE HART is professor emerita of history at the University of California, Santa Barbara. She lives in Santa Barbara, California.

A NOTE ON THE TYPE

This book was set in Adobe Garamond. Designed for the Adobe Corporation by Robert Slimbach, the fonts are based on types first cut by Claude Garamond (ca. 1480–1561). Garamond was a pupil of Geoffroy Tory and is believed to have followed the Venetian models.

Composed by North Market Street Graphics,
Lancaster, Pennsylvania

Printed and bound by Berryville Graphics,
Berryville, Virginia

Designed by Cassandra J. Pappas